The

GOSPEL *of* CHRIST
CRUCIFIED

John P. H...

1 Peter 1:3

The

GOSPEL *of* CHRIST
CRUCIFIED

A THEOLOGY *of* SUFFERING BEFORE GLORY

JOHN P. HARRIGAN

PAROIKOS
PUBLISHING

To all those who love his appearing.

Come, Lord Jesus!

CONTENTS

LIST OF FIGURES

PREFACE

This book developed out of a class that I taught in various contexts over a fifteen-year period. Beyond that, it is simply the outgrowth of my conversion to Christ in college and my earnest desire to know and understand the God to whom I surrendered my life. May he receive all the honor and glory due his name.

Having been raised completely outside of the church, I hold little regard for denomination or tradition. Over the years, I have found this to be both a blessing and a curse. It is a blessing in that there is freedom to receive truth from various traditions without being obligated to adhere to the dogma of any one in particular. It is a curse in that most traditions demand a great loyalty to both their method and message, which can create a lonely road for the sojourning soul. As this age quickens to its end, however, I believe such sectarianism will become increasingly irrelevant (as it presently is in many areas of the world where the church commonly experiences persecution and martyrdom).

Written generally at a popular level, the body of this book is designed for students and pastors, and the endnotes are given for further study. Most in the academy will likely condemn it as naïvely conservative and overly reductionistic. The liberal will bewail its biblicism. The missiologist will complain of overtheologizing. Reformed believers might eschew its apocalyptic framework and its assertion of Jewish election. Dispensationalists may question its emphasis on the cross and the Holy Spirit. And charismatics will probably bemoan its copious quotations of Scripture. Be that as it may, I have striven to faithfully recapitulate the apostolic witness, and my ultimate desire is simply that "love may abound more and more, with knowledge and all discernment" (Phil. 1:9).

Throughout the years, many people have spurred me on "to contend for the faith that was once for all delivered to the saints" (Jude 3). In particular, I would like to thank Brandon McBride, Jeff Melton, Jim Greenwood, Mike Harrison, Daniel Rupp, Lance Luttrell, Jack Chaney, Lee Harper, Rich Stevenson, Tim Miller, Richee Parks, Chad Brewer, Andrew Steinke, Jonathan Fackler, Matt Quinn, Stephen Holmes, Jimmy Shyr, David Ladish, and Joel Richardson. These men, each in their own way, have challenged me, sharpened me, and shown me "sincere brotherly love" (1 Peter 1:22). Without them this work never would have come to pass.

I want to express my heartfelt gratitude to the many who have supported my family through prayers and finance during the five years it took to write this book. Their kindness, faithfulness, and love have been a well of strength to me that I am sure they will never know. A debt of gratitude is also due to Peter Hartgerink for his years of friendship, theological honing, and editorial work. Thanks to Katherine Lloyd for managing the publishing process and for interior design and typesetting. Thanks to Andy Sloan for his professional editorial services. He was truly a delight to work with. Appreciation is also due to Lisa Ham for proofing the final manuscript and to Donna Huisjen for providing a subject index and Scripture index.

Finally, my deepest gratitude goes to my wife Lydia, whose love, support, and encouragement have been a consistent means of God's grace to me—not only in this work, but in all of life.

INTRODUCTION

W hat is the gospel?"
Some years ago I witnessed a seasoned missionary fumble around in response to this question during a public presentation. The incident left quite an impression on me because it seemed to exemplify the struggles I had seen throughout the church, at both a popular and academic level.

The gospel is the very lifeblood of the church, for it informs its identity, purpose, and values. Unfortunately, it has been so chastened and generalized (e.g., "God loves you and has a wonderful plan for your life") that it has become largely irrelevant to the modern world, which suffers from a host of ailments including pluralism, relativism, and hedonism.

The intent of this book is to impart a concise yet holistic explanation of the gospel. I believe this explanation is not found in the minutiae of theological detail commonly found in so many biblical and systematic theologies, but rather in the outlining of redemptive history as a whole and in the emphasizing of its major redemptive events (creation, covenants, cross, consummation, etc.). Indeed, we will engage in theological arguments, but only for the sake of greater clarity and simplicity concerning the redemptive narrative, which I believe holistically forms the Bible's good news.

Chapter 1 is an abstract introduction to the nature of truth and the concept of worldview. How we interpret the Bible (i.e., hermeneutics), and how we understand life in general, is conditioned by our worldview—*and vice versa.* Our search for truth is caught up in the antiphonal hermeneutical voices of the Bible and our own worldview. Back and forth we continually reform and regenerate our minds in accordance with either the eternal word of God (cf. Rom. 12:2; Eph. 1:18) or the systems of thought produced by the world. Thus it is helpful (though some may find it a bit tedious) to examine the concept of worldview and its different components. All worldviews (i.e., belief systems) have the same basic elements, which give context and meaning to our lives as they answer the primal questions of existence—questions such as Who am I? Where did I come from? And where am I going?

As with most games, we seek to know the field of play, the players on the field, the rules of the game, the history of the game, and the goal of the game. Similarly, our worldview tells us the field of existence, the main players of existence, the laws of existence, the history of existence, and the future of existence.

Chapter 2 examines the framework of the Judeo-Christian worldview—its field of play, so to speak—which is summarized in the Bible's first verse: "In the beginning, God created the heavens and the earth" (Gen. 1:1). Throughout the Scriptures the heavens are understood as physical, plural, and continuous. That is, there are multiple heavens above the earth, which is below, and they are substantial and real, not immaterial and ethereal. Moreover, they are continuous, meaning there are no clear lines of delineation between the heavens. Thus movement between the heavens and the earth is relatively easy and smooth. Throughout the Scriptures both angels and humans ascend and descend through the heavens. This view of the universe stands in stark contrast to the common Western view of a singular "heaven," which is immaterial and discontinuous with the materiality of earth.

Within this unified framework of the heavens and the earth, God is presented as dwelling within creation (cf. 1 Kings 8:43; Ps. 102:19; Isa. 63:15; etc.). He stretches the heavens as a tent, so to speak (cf. Isa. 40:22; Ps. 104:2), dwelling at the height of the heavens within a paradisal temple (cf. Ps. 11:4; Mic. 1:2; Heb. 8:5; Rev. 11:19). Likewise, humanity is created in an earthly paradise, resembling the divine heavenly dwelling, with angels mediating between the two. In this way, the playing field of life with its initial players is set out in the opening chapters of Genesis. Such ideas may seem strange to the modern ear, but ancient readers would have had few qualms about them.

Chapter 3 outlines the biblical hope for a restored creation. There will be a *new* heavens and *new* earth (Isa. 65:17; Rev. 21:1). As it was in the beginning, so it will be in the end when "the time comes for God to restore everything" (Acts 3:21, NIV). This renewal of the heavens and the earth is the basic thrust of the Bible's vision for the future (cf. Matt. 19:28; 2 Peter 3:13). However, this rejuvenation cannot be accomplished by the strength or ingenuity of humankind. Rather, God alone will carry out this great vision.

The event whereby God creates a new heavens and earth is described throughout the Scriptures as the "day of the Lord" (Isa. 13:6; Zech. 14:1; Mal. 4:5; Acts 2:20; 1 Cor. 5:5; 1 Thess. 5:2; 2 Peter 3:10). God will come suddenly with his angels to purge the heavens and earth of ungodliness and unrighteousness. It will be a day that is cataclysmic and apocalyptic beyond all imagination or description. It will be a day of divine wrath, judgment, and recompense. The sins of humanity will finally be rectified, and God will finally be honored in his wise governance over creation.

The day of the Lord is the predominant theme of both the Old and New Testaments. Moreover, it is the event that ultimately unifies the Christian and

Jewish Scriptures, for all hold to the ultimate divine end that God "has *fixed a day* on which he will judge the world in righteousness" (Acts 17:31). Furthermore, the day of the Lord is so dynamic and extraordinary that it creates a fundamental delineation of time: "this age" before the day and "the age to come" after the day (cf. Matt. 12:32; Eph. 1:21; Heb. 6:5).

Human sin and depravity will progress until the end of this age when God judges humanity on the last day, rewarding the righteous with eternal life and punishing the wicked with eternal fire. Through the day of the Lord, God will initiate the age to come, which will go on in righteousness, peace, and joy for unending ages (i.e., "eternity").

Because the day of the Lord and the age to come are markedly punitive in nature, this age is broadly defined by divine mercy. Everything that happens before the last day must be understood as a restraint of divine wrath and judgment upon sin. This age *is* this age because the day of judgment has not yet arrived. Indeed, God is patient, not wanting any to perish but all to repent and be saved (2 Peter 3:9). As such, the event of the cross exemplifies all divine activity during this age. God has ultimately shown humanity his mercy and love by offering his Son, that we might be saved from the wrath to come (cf. John 3:16; Rom. 5:8–9; Titus 3:4–7).

This age, therefore, can be broadly described as "cruciform" (i.e., shaped like the cross), while the age to come is generally "apocalyptic" (i.e., established by the day of the Lord). If we seek to describe biblical theology as a whole, it is best summarized as *cruciform-apocalypticism*. Though there are indeed temporal blessings and judgments, these must be understood within the greater narrative of Scripture, pointing us to the eternal blessings and judgments to come.

Chapter 4 focuses on the role of God's Spirit in creation. The Spirit was the agent of life in the beginning (Gen. 2:7; Ps. 33:6), and the Spirit will be the agent of life in the end (Rom. 8:11; 2 Cor. 3:6). By means of the Holy Spirit, the dead will be raised to life on the last day and judged according to their deeds. Thus all activity of the Holy Spirit in this age is understood in light of the activity of the Spirit in both the beginning and the end. This is why the New Testament describes the Holy Spirit as a "firstfruits" or "guarantee" of the resurrection (Rom. 8:23; 2 Cor. 5:5; Eph. 1:14). What we have received in a small measure in this age is an assurance of what we will receive in the age to come.

Chapter 5 introduces the concept of Christ, or Messiah, and tracks the development of messianic expectation throughout the Scriptures. God could have chosen to restore creation through his Spirit without any external involvement or mediation. He has chosen, however, to execute the day of the Lord by means of someone else: a human being whom he will appoint. In this way, the Christ/Messiah is simply God's agent, "anointed" to act on his behalf. Thus the day of the Lord will be "the day of Christ" (Phil. 1:10; 2:16), when the Messiah comes and, by the Spirit of God, raises the dead, punishes the wicked, and creates the new heavens and new earth.

Though this messianic expectation could have been stated outright from the beginning, God chose to reveal it progressively. After the initial sin of Adam and Eve, God promised that an offspring of Eve would be born who would crush Satan's head (Gen. 3:15). This same promise of an anointed offspring is reiterated to both Abraham (Gen. 12:3; 17:7; 22:18) and David (2 Sam. 7:12; 1 Chron. 17:11). Hence God's agent would be born "the son of David, the son of Abraham" (Matt. 1:1). Such messianic expectation was commonly assumed when Jesus was "called Christ" (Matt. 1:16; John 4:25).

Thus the apostolic witness emphasized the messianic character of Jesus (Acts 2:36; 5:42; 8:5; 9:22; etc.), because "he is the one *appointed* by God to be *judge* of the living and the dead" (Acts 10:42). The event of the cross did not change any of the previously held messianic hopes. Those hopes, rather, were only intensified, as God "has fixed a day on which he will judge the world in righteousness *by a man* whom he has appointed; and of this he has *given assurance* to all by raising him from the dead" (Acts 17:31).

Chapter 6 details the kingdom that the Messiah will establish when he comes (i.e., "the kingdom of God"). The new earth will have a definite form and structure, as the resurrection and eternal life will be administrated by means of the messianic kingdom. The Messiah will rule from Jerusalem, over Israel, and to the ends of the earth. The messianic kingdom, therefore, will be fundamentally "Israelocentric," for Jesus will return to "redeem Israel" (Luke 24:21), "restore the kingdom to Israel" (Acts 1:6), and rule forever as "king of the Jews" (Matt. 2:2). In this way, eternal life will be administrated "to the Jew first, and also to the Gentile" (Rom. 2:10, KJV).

The New Testament clearly repudiates any idea that God no longer relates to humanity on the basis of ethnicity (though, of course, he does not show favoritism according to ethnicity). He is still the "God of Israel"; and he has not rejected the Jewish people—even in their unbelief (cf. Rom. 11:1,11)—for "the gifts and the calling of God are irrevocable" (Rom. 11:29). The idea that Jesus somehow changed, reinterpreted, or spiritually realized the hope of the Jewish messianic kingdom is a grave misunderstanding. Along with the day of the Lord, the resurrection of the dead, and Old Testament messianic expectations, the cross did not change the hope of the kingdom of God. Rather, it only *amplified* the Jewish apocalyptic expectations. Concerning our "entrance into the eternal kingdom of our Lord and Savior Jesus Christ" (2 Peter 1:11), "we have the prophetic word more fully confirmed" (v. 19).

Some may question why Jewish election (a topic so central to the Scriptures) is not addressed until chapter 6. My answer is that the choosing of the Jewish people is predicated on a number of eschatological concepts that are often overlooked in modern presentations of the gospel. Thus chapters 1 through 5 seek to lay a foundation, generally addressing Genesis 1–11 and extrapolating the main themes therein (i.e., worldview, human depravity, divine judgment, eternal life, messianic expectation, etc.) to their eschatological conclusions. Chapter 6 picks up in Genesis 12 and extends God's choice of the Jewish people in light of the apocalyptic framework previously laid out. In this way, biblical theology is more pointedly summarized as *Jewish cruciform-apocalypticism.*

In light of this Jewish eschatological hope, chapter 7 embarks on an explanation of the crucifixion and death of the Messiah. Why would God allow his "anointed one" to die? Moreover, how and where was this prophesied in the Old Testament? These questions are the substance of the Emmaus Road encounter (Luke 24:13–27), where Jesus explains his rhetorical question, "Was it not necessary that the Messiah should *suffer* these things and then enter into his *glory?*" (v. 26, NRSV). The redemption of Israel (v. 21) and the eschatological glory would indeed come. God deemed it necessary, however, that his Christ should suffer first.

Over the centuries, many have sought to identify the content of Jesus' exposition on the road to Emmaus. Assuming the New Testament is a faithful representation of what Jesus revealed to his apostles during his forty days of postresurrection teaching (Acts 1:3), we can identify four broad areas of explanation concerning a suffering Messiah. First, Jesus would have pointed to direct prophecies concerning the suffering of God's Servant (Isa. 53; Ps. 22; Dan. 9:26; etc.). Second, because of the fallen nature of this age, the wicked generally prosper and the righteous generally suffer. Moreover, the wicked have always persecuted the righteous (cf. Matt. 5:10–12; Acts 7:51–52). If God has allowed all of the righteous to suffer, why would he spare the Righteous One? Third, in light of his crucifixion during the Passover festival, Jesus undoubtedly would have interpreted the Jewish calendar typologically, pointing to redemptive history as a whole (cf. Luke 22:16; 1 Cor. 5:7). Fourth, and most importantly, Jesus would have interpreted the sacrificial system typologically, pointing to the necessity of a vicarious, sin-bearing sacrifice that holistically reconciles the enmity between God and humanity (cf. Eph. 5:2; Heb. 8–10).

Chapter 8 unpacks the sacrificial interpretation of the Messiah's death. The apostolic declaration of the "forgiveness of sins" (Acts 5:31; 10:43; 13:38; 26:18) assumes this sacrificial understanding, because "without the shedding of blood there is no forgiveness of sins" (Heb. 9:22). God accounts the Messiah's death as a "sin offering" (Rom. 8:3, NIV) by which depraved humans are "declared righteous" (Rom. 2:13; 3:20, NIV) in his sight. Such sacrificial shedding of the Messiah's "blood" is referenced throughout the New Testament (cf. 1 Cor. 10:16; Eph. 1:7; Heb. 9:14; 1 Peter 1:19), for by his blood propitiation is made (cf. Rom. 3:25; 1 John 4:10), justification is accomplished (cf. Rom. 5:9; Titus 3:7), and redemption is achieved (cf. Eph. 1:7; Heb. 9:15).

These reconciliatory realities (cf. 2 Cor. 5:19; Col. 1:20) do not negate or reinterpret the Jewish eschatological framework, but rather reinforce it. Thus the day of the Lord and the restoration of the kingdom to Israel are never questioned when speaking of the ways in which God relates to the death of his Messiah. God has simply provided propitiation in light of the day of wrath, justification in light of the day of judgment, and redemption in light of the day of recompense. In this way, God has worked reconciliation between himself and humanity, granting eternal life to those who repent and believe—both Jew and Gentile.

Though rather simple and straightforward, these divine workings create a great challenge of faith. Modern sensibilities militate against both the apocalyptic realities of Jewish eschatology and the substitutional realities of sacrificial atonement. Nevertheless, these must be received by faith, which is the means by which God has ordained our participation in both Christ crucified and Christ glorified. If we live this life by faith in his sacrifice (cf. Rom. 6:5; Gal. 2:20), then we will be found in him on the last day according to that faith, inheriting with him eternal glory (cf. Rom. 8:17; Phil. 3:9–11). Regrettably, those who lack faith—that is, those who put their faith in the ways of the world and the strength of the flesh (cf. Phil. 3:19; Col. 2:8; 1 Tim. 6:5)—will be destroyed. Thus we are called to persevere in the cruciform-apocalyptic faith handed down to us, which depends not on human strength but casts itself continually upon God's mercy in the cross unto the day of Christ Jesus.

Chapter 9 concludes the book with a summary of the characteristic elements of the apostolic witness. In light of the great eschatological courtroom where all of humanity will be charged with their sins (i.e., the day of judgment), Jesus commissioned the apostles to be his "witnesses" (Acts 1:8; Luke 24:48). The legal connotations were evident to all. The apostles sought to testify faithfully to the acts of God throughout redemptive history, particularly his workings in the Messiah being sent the first time as a sacrifice and the second time as a judge (cf. Acts 3:19-26; Heb. 9:28). So Peter summarized that Jesus "commanded us to preach to the people and to testify that he is the one appointed by God to be judge of the living and the dead. To him all the prophets bear witness that everyone who believes in him receives forgiveness of sins through his name" (Acts 10:42–43). For the sake of this testimony, God gave believers the gift of the Holy Spirit to embolden and empower the proclamation of the truth, both in word and deed, even unto death and martyrdom.

I believe that in the apostolic witness we find a faithful proclamation of the gospel in its fullness. When we consider the testimony of the apostles as a whole we see that it was rather unsophisticated (in contrast to much modern theological exposition). The apostles sought to communicate a simple, linear timeline of events (see figure 0.1), which begins with creation (cf. Rom. 5; 1 Cor. 15); incorporates faithfulness to the covenants, particularly those with Abraham, Moses, and David (cf. Acts 1:6; Rom. 9–11); highlights the implications of the cross (cf. Rom. 3:21–26; Col. 1:20–23); emphasizes the empowerment of the Spirit (cf. Rom. 8; 1 Cor. 2); and strives toward the day of the Lord (cf. Rom. 13:12; 1 Cor. 1:8; Phil. 1:6). In this way, the apostolic witness can be holistically described as creational, covenantal, cruciform, charismatic, and apocalyptic.

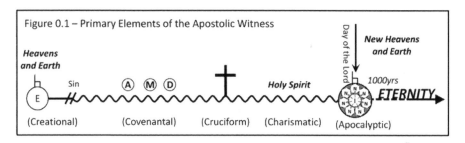

Figure 0.1 – Primary Elements of the Apostolic Witness

In stark contrast, much of the modern church's proclamation scoffs at the historicity of Genesis, flagrantly rejects God's covenantal dealings with the Jews, sets aside a substitutionary-sacrificial understanding of the cross, scorns the gift of the Spirit, and ignores the return of Jesus. Though various movements and traditions seek to emphasize one or two of these elements (often to the detriment of other elements), few of them seem to seek a proclamation that *holds them all together*. Yet it is the holistic proclamation of redemptive history, from beginning to end, that comprises the gospel and characterizes the faithful witness.

If we investigate the reasons why and how the apostolic witness has been distorted, the answers become quite complex. Much has happened in the last two thousand years, and millions of human beings have devoted incalculable time and energy to expounding the Bible. (Anyone who has been to seminary can testify to the mountains of literature.) For the sake of clarity, nevertheless, here are a few generalities concerning the primary perversions of the apostolic witness.

First, the earliest and most prominent distortion is Platonism. The common idea found throughout church history of an amorphous heavenly destiny, in which we float on a cloud forever playing a harp, is directly traceable to Platonic and Neoplatonic influences on the early church. Second, roughly from the time of Constantine, "realized eschatology" has sought to reinterpret the

Jewish messianic kingdom and actualize it spiritually in this age by setting up a utopian order through the strength of the flesh. Third, after the Enlightenment, evolutionism has relentlessly sought to invalidate the historical account of Genesis, without which there is no vision or direction for the restoration of all things.

These three ideologies (Platonism, realized eschatology, and evolutionism—and their myriad of theological derivatives) are broadly the source of most corruptions of the apostolic witness (see figure 0.2).

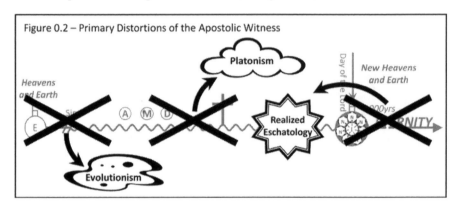

Figure 0.2 – Primary Distortions of the Apostolic Witness

Each of these aberrant ideologies produces its own effects. Though they can function independently, they are often combined (e.g., liberalism often incorporates both evolutionism and realized eschatology). Each is devastating in its own right, however, because any perversion of the timeline breaks the timeline as a whole. Like removing one piece of a mousetrap, deviation from the fundamental chronology of the Bible, or any of its major elements, ruins its functionality entirely.

Though each of these ideologies warps the biblical timeline in its own way, the combination of these ideologies (and the multitude of their theological offspring) results in exponential confusion and theological disarray. Therefore, in an effort to clarify issues and bring some relevance to modern thought, each chapter ends with a broad summary of the history and impact of these distortions upon biblical thought (though a sustained critique of evolutionism is beyond the scope of this work). The appendix focuses solely on realized eschatology and the Scripture passages commonly referenced for its support.

Chapter One

✦

HERMENEUTICS

W hat is truth? This was not only the question Pilate posed to Jesus in John 18:38, but it is the fundamental question of humanity. Dictionaries generally define *truth* as that which accords with and conforms to reality. The biblical terms (Heb. *'ĕmeth*, Gk. *alētheia*) express the same.[1] Truth conveys reality. Thus, the search for truth is humankind's primal quest. Who am I? Why do I exist? What is the meaning of life? Truth is that which explains and gives meaning to our existence, because truth is that which corresponds to how things actually are.

Truth tells us what does and does not exist. It tells us whether something is important or irrelevant. It conveys value, which in turn instills morality. It explains to us the meaning of history: its origin and its destiny. It tells us how things ought to be, while simultaneously condemning our falsehood. It informs hope and dashes delusion. Though universally attainable, it is strangely elusive. It transcends intellect and knowledge—the simpleton often submits to it while the intelligent person "conceives mischief and brings forth falsehood" (Ps. 7:14, NASB). Though we long to walk in truth, we all sense a universal bondage to deception.

Pilate's question about truth was in response to Jesus' declaration, "For this purpose I have come into the world—to bear witness to the truth" (John 18:37). As Christians, we believe that the Scriptures, canonized in the Old and New Testaments, contain the truth.[2] Jesus witnessed to the truth contained in the Old Testament, and those Scriptures witnessed to him (John 5:39). The life, death, and resurrection of Jesus verified that those Scriptures tell us what reality actually is. They tell us who God is and who we are—where we came from and where we are going. They tell us the purpose and meaning of life. They tell us the truth.

In our pluralistic world, however, there are many sacred writings that claim to speak the truth—Buddhist, Hindu, Islamic, naturalistic (in a practical sense), etc.[3] Whose account is actually correct? Whose perspective is reliable? Which sacred books are trustworthy? As fallen human beings we really have no way of knowing. Adherents of every religion claim their texts are divinely inspired. However, Judeo-Christianity asserts that it has proof that its Scriptures tell us the truth.[4] Its proof does not rest on its superior arguments or the accurate transmission of its holy documents (though we heartily affirm these), but rather on the claim that a man has actually overcome the prime existential ill: death.

Such an a posteriori argument was the primary approach used by the early church in its proclamation. Only one presentation of truth has produced a resurrected human being, and thus the Jewish Scriptures are true and "made more certain" (2 Peter 1:19, NIV). Paul demonstrates this clearly as he summarizes redemptive history to the Athenians: "The God who made the world and everything in it is the Lord of heaven and earth and does not live in temples built by hands. . . . From one man he made every nation of men, that they should inhabit the whole earth; and he determined the times set for them and the exact places where they should live. . . . He has set a day when he will judge the world with justice by the man he has appointed. He has *given proof* of this to all men *by raising him from the dead*" (Acts 17:24–31, NIV).

Paul explained the nature of the relationship between God and humankind, recounting their history from beginning to end, and then he justified God's right to judge with the assertion that Jesus was raised from the dead. The declaration of Jesus' resurrection was the primary means of convincing people that God had indeed inspired the prophets and their Scriptures, which communicate the coming day of judgment. If we deny the historical and bodily resurrection of Jesus, then we have no proof of the Judeo-Christian Scriptures—and their message of the day of the Lord, the new heavens and new earth, etc.—over and against any other holy texts (the reasons may be persuasive, but not certain).[5] As Paul said, "If Christ has not been raised, then our preaching is in vain and your faith is in vain" (1 Cor. 15:14).

Those who affirm that the Judeo-Christian Scriptures proclaim the truth *exclusively* are generally known as "evangelicals." This label roughly derives from Martin Luther's identification of the "evangelical church," which believed in *sola scriptura* (Latin for "by Scripture alone"), versus the Roman Catholic Church, which was viewed as tainted by its tradition.[6] Though historically difficult to define, evangelicalism is ultimately an approach to truth based upon the exclusivity of the Scriptures, for the evangelical "seeks to construct his theology on the teaching of the Bible, the whole Bible, and nothing but the Bible."[7] From the Reformers to the Puritans to the Pietists to the revivalists to the fundamentalists to the neo-evangelicals, common theological themes follow this "high view" of the Scriptures.[8]

Unlike Luther's singular struggle with Catholic tradition, modern evangelicals struggle with many challenges to their source of truth. Whether those challenges are represented by various forms of higher biblical criticism, naturalistic empiricism, pluralistic relativism, or neo-charismatic prophecy, the evangelical spirit seeks truth from the Scriptures alone. Based upon the resurrection of Jesus, we have assurance that this approach will prove true in the end.

HERMENEUTICS AND WORLDVIEW

Though evangelicals agree that the Bible is the sole source of truth, there is much disagreement about the content and meaning of that truth. What happens when two (or twenty or two hundred) people equally committed to the authority of the Scriptures read the same words and come away with different meanings? Whose interpretation is correct? Who actually understands the truth of the Bible?

These are the questions of hermeneutics—"the discipline that deals with principles of interpretation."[9] How we interpret the Bible dictates the outcome of our inheritance of truth. We may desire truth, and we may come to the Bible alone to find it, but our actual receiving of the truth is dependent upon our hermeneutics.

Unfortunately, hermeneutics and biblical interpretation have become exceedingly complicated in modern times. Those who venture into this boggy marsh seldom come back unscathed.[10] However, the ancient biblical writers (e.g., David, Amos, Peter), though often "uneducated, common men" (Acts 4:13), showed no signs of confusion or hesitancy in their proclamation of the truth. How do we approach the Scriptures so that we come out with the same interpretation and proclamation as those within them? How do we know, for example, what Paul meant by "my gospel" (Rom. 2:16; 16:25; 2 Tim. 2:8)? What did *he* intend for his hearers to understand? Likewise, what did David or Daniel or John desire their hearers to hear?

This issue of "authorial intent" is further complicated by the presence of the Holy Spirit.[11] As evangelicals, we believe the Scriptures are inspired by the Spirit of God, as Peter clearly declared: "No prophecy of Scripture comes from someone's own interpretation. For no prophecy was ever produced by the will of man, but men spoke from God as they were carried along by the Holy Spirit" (2 Peter 1:20–21). Here lies the great chasm between conservatives and liberals.[12] Generally, liberals view the authorial intent of the Scriptures primarily from the human side, while conservatives view it more from the divine perspective.

When we ask, *What does the book of Isaiah mean?* we must first ask, *What did the Spirit of God intend to say through Isaiah?* Then we can move on to how Isaiah might have understood the words uttered through him. Though the writers are fallen, the message spoken through them by the Holy Spirit remains infallible.[13] Thus we are left with something of a hermeneutical Great Commandment: seek first God and his intent for the text, and secondly seek the intent of the human author, a person like yourself.[14]

In the quest to understand divine and human authorial intent, scholarship since the time of Luther has developed the "grammatico-historical method," which asks the question, What do the *words themselves* mean in their *historical context*?[15] To understand what the Bible is actually saying, we must understand basic linguistic issues (English word meanings and syntax often do not correspond to the original Greek and Hebrew), and we must understand basic differences in literary genre (e.g., narrative, poetic, wisdom, prophetic, epistolary, and apocalyptic literature). Simply put, people say things in different ways.[16] Moreover, people say things in specific historical contexts, which involve cultural, geographical, and political issues. All of this helps us understand the occasion and purpose of the biblical writings. Though the Holy Spirit transcends the human condition, he has chosen to dwell within that condition, and thus these issues must be taken into account.

While engaging in grammatico-historical interpretation, a modern Westerner quickly realizes there are many assumptions and presuppositions held by the biblical writers that are totally foreign to us today. Furthermore, we often recognize that ancient peoples held fundamentally different pretheoretical intuitions—that is, what intuitively seemed normal, real, and right to them might seem the opposite to us.[17] Such differences of intuitions and presuppositions in turn lead to different methodologies of interpretation (i.e., hermeneutics) that likewise often seem strange and awkward to the modern reader.[18] Similarly, when we read someone from within a particular historical tradition—e.g., Francis of Assisi, Martin Luther, or John Wesley—we encounter yet another layer of intuitions and presuppositions, which in turn dictates other methodologies of interpretation. Weeding through the endless list of conflicting ideas, linguistics, and cultural phenomena can quickly become overwhelming.

What then lies behind and dictates the presuppositions of the biblical writers? The answer to this question unlocks many of the confusing aspects of biblical hermeneutics. That answer is *worldview*, which is generally defined as "an interpretive framework through which or by which one makes sense out of the data of life and the world."[19] The difference between our framework and that of the biblical writers creates much of the tension we encounter while reading the Scriptures.

One's worldview, as N. T. Wright aptly describes, "embraces all deep-level human perceptions of reality,"[20] and as such it *creates* our intuitions and presuppositions about life, which in turn *dictate* our broad methodologies of interpretation. The issues of worldview are further compounded when we read someone else with another worldview (e.g., the medieval worldview of Thomas Aquinas or Anselm of Canterbury) commenting on the already foreign worldview of the biblical writers. Again, overwhelming.

In addition, we must ask the greater question: *What is the worldview of the Holy Spirit?* Since God is a person, how does he view life? What intuitively seems true to him? What are his assumptions? How does he interpret existence? Surely, as it really is. And this is the purpose of the Scriptures he has given us: to tell us the truth concerning how life really is.[21] Thus, we ultimately seek to know 1) the mind of God, while taking into consideration 2) the mind and worldview of the biblical writers and 3) the mind and worldview of those within the various traditions of interpretation (see figure 1.1).

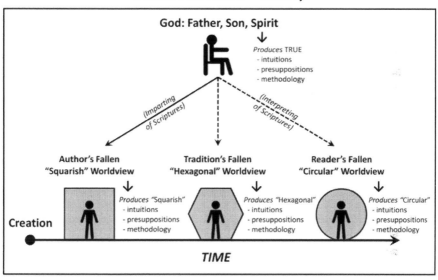

Divine Worldview = Reality

Figure 1.1 – The Historical Interaction between Worldview and Hermeneutics

The individual worldviews of the biblical authors may have indeed been flawed. Men such as Moses, David, and Paul were obviously fallen and broken—their sins are plain to see (e.g., Ex. 2:12; 2 Sam. 11; Acts 9:1). As believers, however, we fundamentally hold that *the oracles transcend the stewards,* even at a worldview level, and as such the Scriptures deliver to us the divine worldview itself.[22]

Isaiah, for example, may not have understood the ultimate nature of reality, yet the words he spoke, in and of themselves, convey it. This tension is clearly referenced in Peter's words that "the prophets who prophesied about the grace that was to be yours searched and inquired carefully" (1 Peter 1:10).[23] Though many find such an idea rather archaic and naïve, we must approach the oracle and the prophet on their own terms and in right relation. In this way, under the guidance of the Holy Spirit who leads us into all truth (John 16:13; 1 John 2:20), we seek to know God and life as they really are.

COMPONENTS OF WORLDVIEW

Since differing worldviews produce differing intuitions and presuppositions, which in turn create differing methods of interpretation, the task of biblical hermeneutics must begin by addressing the nature and function of worldview. Though the study of worldview is a relatively recent one, David Naugle points out that "conceiving of Christianity as a worldview has been one of the most significant developments in the recent history of the church."[24] Derived from the German *Weltanschauung*,[25] the term "worldview" has a complex history plagued by vague definitions.[26] Most simply default to a common dictionary definition, such as "a particular philosophy of life or conception of the world."[27]

In recent times, however, evangelicals have produced a wealth of literature studying various aspects of worldview and its wide usage.[28] The Christian faith has been elaborately articulated within a worldview framework, especially within the Reformed tradition of the twentieth century.[29] Though having been analyzed from a multitude of angles, it seems most helpful for the purposes of this study to break down the concept of worldview into its most basic components: ultimate reality (all that exists), protology (study of origins), eschatology (study of final things), and soteriology (study of salvation). Each of these will be explained and contrasted within the major worldviews modernly held (i.e., Hinduism, Buddhism, naturalism, Islam, and Judeo-Christianity). These basic components of worldview then provide human beings, within their various traditions, a conceptual framework for existence that answers the most basic questions of life concerning identity, purpose, origin, destiny, etc.[30]

Consider life as a game. Most games have rules, goals, players, and fields upon which to play. In the game of life, one's worldview assumes an ultimate reality, which is much like the *field of play*. It is often taken for granted, and in the larger scheme of the game it is usually considered of less import. Yet, playing soccer on a basketball court raises significant challenges. Often the field of play inherently shapes the understanding of the rules and purpose of the game itself. Our worldview is our playing field for life. Defining one's playing field can be difficult, however, since most people rarely think about it. They are simply on it.

Our playing field is our ultimate reality—that is, the sum total of that which we understand to exist.[31] It is our "macro-model," which includes "the *whole* of reality."[32] Whatever we know to comprise "everything" defines the parameters of our worldview,[33] the study of which is technically termed "metaphysics."[34]

For example, Hindus understand ultimate reality to be *Brahman*, an all-encompassing divine matrix of existence from which all things emerge and into which all things are reabsorbed, only to be reincarnated once more. *Brahman* is then structurally divided into various levels of heavens (*svargam*) above the earth and hells (*narakam*) beneath.[35] Buddhists generally assume the Brahmanic makeup of reality but divide it into "three realms" (*tri-dhatu*):[36] the highest realm of "formlessness" (*arupa-dhatu*), the middle realm of "pure form" (*rupa-dhatu*), and the lower realm of "sense" or "desire" (*kama-dhatu*).[37] Taoists see a basic progression from the *tao* (the flow of the universe), which differentiates into the *yin* and *yang* (cosmic principles of opposite), which in turn produce the *wanwu* (the "ten thousand things" of the manifest cosmos).[38] Naturalism simply believes that "nature is all there is, and all basic truths are truths of nature."[39] Islam and Christoplatonism[40] (the Christian derivative of Neo-Platonism, which will be discussed later at length) view reality dualistically: material versus immaterial, "natural" versus "supernatural." Conversely, Judeo-Christianity views the universe as an integrated and dynamic whole: "the heavens and the earth" (Gen. 1:1).[41] All of these are different articulations of what makes up the sum total of reality. They are different frameworks, or "metaphysical constructs," for understanding our existence (see figure 1.2).

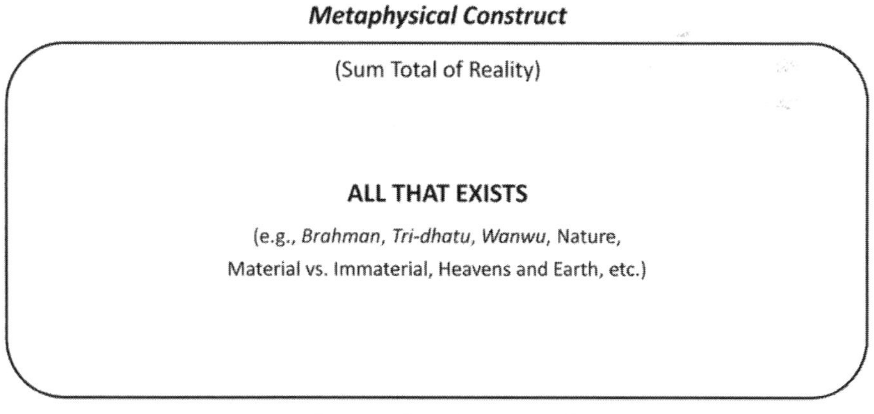

Metaphysical Construct

(Sum Total of Reality)

ALL THAT EXISTS

(e.g., *Brahman, Tri-dhatu, Wanwu,* Nature,
Material vs. Immaterial, Heavens and Earth, etc.)

Figure 1.2 – The Metaphysical Construct of Worldview

There are also various "players" on the playing field of worldview: for example, God, gods, avatars, spirits, ghosts, humans, animals, etc. Where the players are situated on their respective fields greatly determines their identity, their purpose, and how they interact with each other. Some fields are highly integrated and interactive, while others are sharply divided, creating distance and detachment—the Athenians' "unknown god" (Acts 17:23) comes to mind.

Though the field and the players on it are important, they do not constitute the substance of a game, the bulk of which is found in its *movement* played out in *time*. Because time dictates so many aspects of our existence, worldviews broadly facilitate an explanation of history. These histories generally involve three things: 1) when things began (protology); 2) where things are ultimately going (eschatology); and 3) how things became wrong and, conversely, how they will ultimately be made right (soteriology).[42] In other words, within the sum total of reality, worldviews attempt to explain the origin, remediation, and conclusion of existence (see figure 1.3).[43]

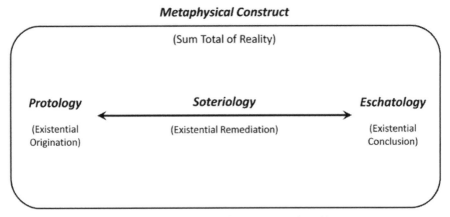

Metaphysical Construct

(Sum Total of Reality)

Protology — **Soteriology** → **Eschatology**

(Existential Origination) — (Existential Remediation) — (Existential Conclusion)

Figure 1.3 – Primary Universal Components of Worldview

In this way, worldviews are generally characterized by *stories*. These stories explain how things were, which gives context to how things are, which in turn tells us how things are going to play out.[44] By giving us an explanation of the past, present, and future, worldviews seek to answer the "basic questions" of life: "*Who* are we, *where* are we, what is *wrong*, and what is the *solution*?"[45] Our worldview provides answers for the multitude of existential questions concerning our identity, purpose, ethics, and so on (see figure 1.4).[46] As such, they become the "controlling stories" to which we unconsciously conform our own story.[47] David Naugle summarizes:

> Such stories are considered sacred, and they provide the adhesive that unites those who believe in them into a society characterized by shared per-

spectives and a common way of life. They also provide a tenacious grid by which competing narratives and alternate claims to truth are judged. Controlling stories, therefore, function in a regulatory fashion both positively and negatively, and are able to bind those who accept them into an intellectual or spiritual commonwealth. Thus the bulk of human praxis does seem to be under the jurisdiction of a worldview, including the significant activities of reasoning, interpreting, and knowing.[48]

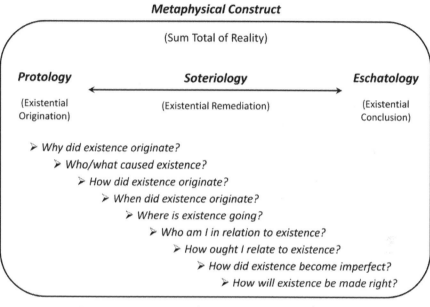

Metaphysical Construct

(Sum Total of Reality)

Protology   **Soteriology**   **Eschatology**

(Existential   (Existential Remediation)   (Existential
Origination)   Conclusion)

➢ Why did existence originate?
  ➢ Who/what caused existence?
    ➢ How did existence originate?
      ➢ When did existence originate?
        ➢ Where is existence going?
          ➢ Who am I in relation to existence?
            ➢ How ought I relate to existence?
              ➢ How did existence become imperfect?
                ➢ How will existence be made right?

Figure 1.4 – Basic Existential Questions Answered by Worldview

Thus worldview provides a generally coherent "system" of belief that enables a person to function in life and cope with its often harsh realities.[49] And it is the realities of life that drive people to *utter dependence* upon their worldview. Commitment to one's worldview is not optional.[50] There are no "existential relativists." People believe what they believe about their existence—nothing more, nothing less. One cannot hold to multiple and conflicting theories of existence. Those who reject allegiance to their own worldview convert to another one or become mentally unstable. Simply put, we all have a worldview, and we all live by it.

Though space prohibits a detailed exposition of all the major worldviews, let us look briefly at the basic stories of a few to get a feel for what these universal components look like within different belief systems. Within Hinduism (a worldview notoriously difficult to generalize and/or harmonize), there are three primary players/gods created protologically out of the existential matrix of *Brahman*—Brahma, Vishnu, and Shiva (the *Trimurti*)—who are responsible for creating, maintaining, and destroying the world, respectively. As these players and their functions are defined protologically, so a Hindu eschatology of perpetual cosmic birth, maintenance, destruction, and rebirth is easily deduced.[51] The fall of man destroyed the "Golden Age" (*Satya Yuga*) established by Brahma and ushered in the darkness of *samsara* (the cycle of birth and death within the cosmos) driven by *karma* (the deeds of the cosmos) based on *dharma* (the law of the cosmos). Vishnu (among other gods/*devas*) now maintains this cycle, and he has various *avatars* ("incarnations"): for example, Rama, Krishna, Narasimha, and Kalki. The goal is to escape the cycle of *samsara* and attain *moksha* ("freedom, liberation") by detachment of self unto the realization of ultimate nonexistence through oneness with *Brahman*. This was the original design of humanity by Brahma, and Shiva will eschatologically cleanse the universe so that Brahma can recreate it in perfect union with *Brahman*, ushering in a new Golden Age (see figure 1.5).[52]

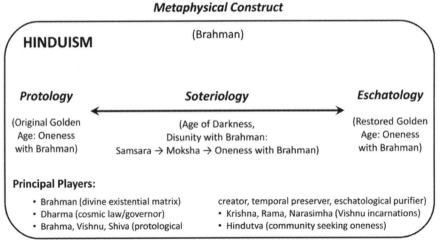

Figure 1.5 – Hindu Worldview with Its Primary Existential Components

Akin to Hinduism, naturalism holds to a broadly monistic construction of the universe, with nature functioning as its existential matrix (often personified as "Mother"). Its protology is found in the "big bang," and its players are strictly materialistic. Nature's existence holds intrinsic energy and patterns of functioning, which are generally articulated as "laws." As nature is materialistic and purely random, "survival" constitutes its highest purpose.[53] Though ultimately mediocre, the meaning of life boils down to fitness and reproduction, by any means. Naturalistic soteriology is simply "progress," which is accomplished by death and the weeding out of the unfit (i.e., "natural selection"). Naturalistic eschatology is thus assumed to be perpetual fitness and progress (see figure 1.6).

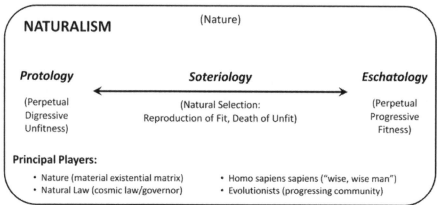

Figure 1.6 – Naturalistic Worldview with Its Primary Existential Components

The Judeo-Christian worldview frames reality within "the heavens and the earth" (Gen. 1:1), which are integrated, continuous, and dynamic (see chapter 2). The purpose of creation is to glorify its Creator, for "of Him and through Him and to Him are all things, to whom be glory forever" (Rom. 11:36, NKJV). The protology of this worldview involves a sinless creation without death and suffering, and its eschatology seeks the "restoration of all things" (Acts 3:21, NASB).[54] There will be "new heavens and a new earth" (Isa. 65:17; cf. Rev. 21:1), which will be inaugurated by the "day of the Lord" (Isa. 13:6; Mal. 4:5; 2 Peter 3:10).[55] This salvation is carried out by Jesus Christ, "judge of the living and the dead" (Acts 10:42; cf. 2 Tim. 4:1; 1 Peter 4:5), who also suffered as a substitutionary "sacrifice" for the forgiveness of sins (Eph. 5:2; Heb. 10:12). This messianic suffering before eschatological glory (cf. Luke 24:26; Heb. 9:28; 1 Peter 1:11) defines the essential story line of the Judeo-Christian worldview (see figure 1.7).[56]

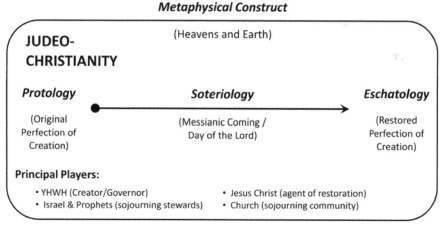

Figure 1.7 – Judeo-Christian Worldview with Its Primary Existential Components

"Christoplatonism" combines elements of Judeo-Christianity with Platonism. The worldview of Plato (c. 427-347 BC) involves a dualistic framework for reality: the immaterial "intelligible" world versus the material "perceptual" world. The former is eternal, consisting of ideal "forms," while the latter was created, comprised of corrupt "copies."[57] Platonic protology involves the eternal ideal state and a debased material creation, which sets up its eschatological return to immateriality.[58] Salvation is thus found in transcending materiality by enlightenment and/or death (see figure 1.8).[59] Those who have enlightenment of the greater metaphysical reality (i.e., the philosophers) should then rule over the earth so as to help liberate the unlearned.[60]

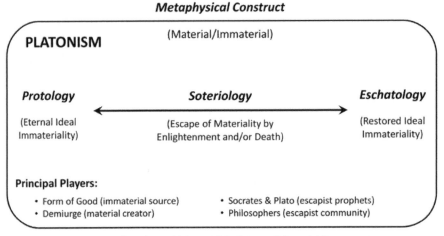

Figure 1.8 – Platonic Worldview with Its Primary Existential Components

Western thought, as Alfred Whitehead is known for saying, is "a series of footnotes to Plato."[61] This dualistic world of material versus immaterial (later termed "natural" versus "supernatural") slowly became the playing field upon which Judeo-Christianity was played.[62] Instead of a story line that ended in the restoration of all things and the resurrection of the body, the church began to look forward to the eternal existence of the soul in an immaterial heaven. J. Christiaan Beker described this shift as "a fall from the apocalyptic world of early Christianity to Platonic categories of thought."[63] By the fourth and fifth centuries such Christoplatonic thought became the standard.

The invention of Islam in the seventh century was another semi-Platonic derivative (though reviving something of a generic apocalypticism), seeking a heavenly destiny and roughly framing itself as the fulfillment of the Judeo-Christian tradition, which was prevalent at the time.[64] Throughout the

Middle Ages, the Hellenistic (i.e., Greek) worldview remained little changed, and though the Reformation restored to Christianity the centrality of the cross and substitutionary atonement (see chapter 8), it did little to restore a biblical playing field, so to speak.[65] The twentieth century, however, inaugurated a radical upheaval of Platonic thought.

BIBLICAL PROTOLOGY
AND ESCHATOLOGY

Modern biblical scholarship has been broadly characterized as grappling with the Bible's protology and eschatology. On the one hand, studies in ancient Near Eastern and Hebraic thought have provoked heated discussions concerning Genesis and the nature of the biblical worldview.[66] On the other hand, research concerning apocalypticism and Jewish eschatology has systematically dismantled Platonic notions of floating on a cloud forever playing a harp.[67] As N. T. Wright observes,

> As good creational monotheists, mainline Jews were not hoping to escape from the present universe into some Platonic realm of eternal bliss enjoyed by disembodied souls after the end of the space-time universe. If they died in the fight for the restoration of Israel, they hoped not to 'go to heaven', or at least not permanently, but to be raised to new bodies when the kingdom came, since they would of course need new bodies to enjoy the very much this-worldly *shalom*, peace and prosperity that was in store.[68]

In addition, the rise of Jewish scholarship in the twentieth century propelled studies concerning the "Jewish roots" of Christianity.[69] Unfortunately, many of these areas of study were dominated by those of liberal leanings who ultimately framed their conclusions within a naturalistic box—that is, the Bible and its human authors were simply the product of a primitive and obsolete worldview, which tells a generally irrelevant story to modern man.[70]

Because conservatives receive the Scriptures as the word of God concerning the truth of existence, their wrestling with the implications of Jewish eschatology and protology has been more difficult. The liberal can speak freely about the simple message of the Bible because in the end he/she is under no obligation to actually believe it.[71] The conservative, however, is forced to grapple with such things because of his/her personal convictions concerning the Bible's authority and potency. Thus, due to the stigma and "embarrassment"[72] of the biblical worldview, its Jewish leanings, and its apocalyptic conclusions—"like a renegade relative in attendance at a family reunion"[73]—many simply avoid the unambiguous message of the Scriptures.[74]

The Bible's protology and eschatology are quite simple and straightforward. The Scriptures as a whole speak of a literal creation and an apocalyptic restoration of creation centered around the day of the Lord. This is taken for granted by conservative orthodox Jews, but its acceptance by the Christian academy has been exceedingly slow and arduous. Unfortunately, the reckless approach of various popular movements—particularly the creationist movement[75] and the Bible prophecy movement[76]—have resulted in a common disdain for biblical protology and eschatology. Though these movements have manifold problems in both content and methodology, they do interpret the Scriptures at face value in a literalistic manner, as would a first-century Jew.[77]

Though popular distortions abound, biblical protology must be taken seriously. Naturalistic explanations for the infinite complexities of life are radically deficient.[78] Many of the building blocks of life are "irreducibly complex,"[79] and the probability of their evolution by chance is "essentially zero."[80] The "icons" of evolution have been shown to be heavily slanted in their presentation (e.g., Darwin's finches, the Miller-Urey experiment, and vertebrate homology), or outright fraudulent (e.g., peppered moths and Haeckel's embryos).[81] Even radiometric dating has been shown to have serious flaws.[82] No evolutionist can even begin to adequately explain gigantism in the fossil record,[83] especially concerning the sauropods (dwarfing the largest modern land animals by a factor of ten or more)—How *on this earth* did they ever exist?[84] And the handful of questionable transitional fossils will never cover up the glaring lack of *missing chains* in the fossil record.[85]

Moreover, the utter lack of any signs of erosion in the geologic column argues for the rapid deposition of sedimentary layers in a global deluge,[86] which is also a superior explanation for the earth's uniform stratification and fossilization.[87] The discovery of ancient unfossilized DNA, bacteria, and soft tissue—even *T. rex* blood[88]—also argues forcefully for recent fossilization.[89] Other age-limiting factors, such as the recession of the moon,[90] the "faint young sun paradox,"[91] and the earth's decaying magnetic field,[92] will not be resolved by evolutionists, because they cannot be resolved. Furthermore, the plate tectonic theory is hopelessly flawed—Where is *the rubble* in the trenches (among a host of other questions)?[93]

Though evolutionists may respond with vindictive condescension,[94] only a nonuniformitarian history of the earth (i.e., one with a radical geological catastrophe like the flood of Noah) can account for the earth's major features.[95] It seems that only scientists outside the Christian academy are bold enough to state the plain realities of evolutionism, while theologians are too afraid to question the naturalistic status quo.[96]

CONCLUSION

The historicity of biblical protology is important because it dictates the playing field, the players, and the subsequent story of our worldview, which in turn fundamentally informs our identity, our understanding of life, and our interpretation of the Bible. Many receive Genesis theologically or doctrinally, but when push comes to shove they reject it existentially. It is little more than an ancient myth, which bears little upon modern society and its dealings. This is not the case with the biblical writers, who clearly interpreted Genesis plainly and literally (cf. Ex. 20:11; 31:17; Ps. 8:3–8; Matt. 19:4; 1 Tim. 2:13–14).

Moreover, the historicity of biblical protology is the foundation upon which the Bible's eschatology is built, for creation will be restored to its original *historical* state (cf. Matt. 19:28; Acts 3:21; Rom. 8:21). Sin and death entered creation at a historical point in the past through Adam (cf. Rom. 5:12–19; 1 Cor. 15:21–22), and they will be judged and eradicated at a historical point in the future through Jesus Christ (Acts 17:31; 2 Cor. 5:1–10). To undermine the historicity of Genesis is to subvert the very heart of the biblical message.

Most liberal theologians simply dismiss the Bible's protology and eschatology as delusional concepts generated by a primitive and outdated worldview.[97] Many conservative theologians find these concepts to be such an embarrassment that they avoid talking about them altogether, or they neutralize them through various literary and typological techniques of reinterpretation.[98] However, the word of God does not need our mitigation. It simply calls for us to accept its incisive message at face value.

Furthermore, in light of its glorious protology we must *hold together* its apocalyptic eschatology with its cruciform center (as we will see in chapter 3). To break the cohesion of such a timeline is to break the biblical story as a whole. One cannot drive a car without wheels, nor one lacking an engine. All the parts must hold together. So it is with a biblical worldview. Within the framework of the heavens and the earth, all the parts, *from beginning to end*, must work together for it to work at all.

Chapter Two

❂

BIBLICAL
WORLDVIEW

Before looking at the Bible's theology in detail, we must establish the parameters of its worldview—its field of play, so to speak. The understanding of one's worldview is a difficult task because we are all confined within the world we are trying to comprehend. Because no one is able to transcend their existence, our worldview is inescapably an *internal*-view.

The human situation is thus something of a "fishbowl conundrum." Ask ten fish to define the fishbowl within which they live, and you will get ten different "fishbowl-views." Moreover, the task of understanding the fishbowl is complicated by the issues of mortality—the fish are mostly deaf, dumb, and blind, while the water is murky green, "subjected to frustration" (Rom. 8:20, NIV), awaiting a radical cleansing (cf. 2 Thess. 1:8; 2 Peter 3:7; Rev. 21:5).

Like fish trying to understand their fishbowl, humans throughout history have tried to understand the nature of their existence. Some set out on a quest to test the limits of their own half-deaf-dumb-and-blind sensibilities. Others sit around endlessly philosophizing and deconstructing the realities of their fishy existence. Others seek knowledge from sources that transcend their bowl. Unfortunately, various sources give conflicting accounts, since not all masters are truthful in their relations with fish. Strangely, the "sensible" fish often ridicule the "religious" fish because of their "superstitions" and "presuppositions." They argue that the fishbowl consists of only that which we can understand, observe, measure, and test—a very *ichthus*-centric approach indeed!

This parable of the fishbowl gives us a picture of the true condition of humanity. Like fish in a bowl, humans construct various worldviews in an attempt to explain the nature and function of their existence. Based on a belief in the inerrant inspiration of the Judeo-Christian Scriptures, we will seek to understand our existence by studying the worldview set forth in the Bible. This foundation will then sustain a biblical theology and, consequently, a biblical practice.

THE BIBLICAL WORLDVIEW: THE HEAVENS AND THE EARTH

The Bible describes the totality of existence in its first verse: "In the beginning, God created the heavens and the earth" (Gen. 1:1). The heavens and the earth, and all therein, are understood to make up "all things" (Isa. 44:24; John 1:3; Acts 3:21; 1 Cor. 15:28; Eph. 1:10; 3:9; Col. 1:16; Heb. 1:2; 2:10; 2 Peter 3:4; Rev. 4:11; 21:5), and they are referenced throughout the Scriptures as the basic playing field upon which God, humans, angels, demons, plants, and animals function. The delineation of the heavens and the earth, however, does not imply a metaphysical split between the two, but rather a functional and governmental categorization. As the psalmist summarizes, "The heavens are the LORD's heavens, but the earth he has given to the children of man" (Ps. 115:16).

The verses following Genesis 1:1 describe how the heavens and the earth were formed. On day one, the Spirit of God hovered over the "waters" (Heb. *mayim*), and light was created (vv. 2–5), presumably within the waters.[1] On day two, God created "an expanse in the midst of the waters" (v. 6). Despite the attempts of modernists to circumvent the text, this "expanse" (Heb. *rāqîaʿ*) is simply equated with the "heavens" (v. 8, AT).[2] In this way, the heavens (Heb. *šāmayim*) were created in the midst of the waters (Heb. *mayim*). Far from a solid "dome over the earth,"[3] the expanse/heavens are simply the cosmic "space amidst the waters"[4]—that is, the space between the eternal cosmic waters and the waters of the earth, commonly referred to as "the water planet."[5] Thus, not only is the earth "formed out of water and through water" (2 Peter 3:5), but also the entire cosmos is understood to be forged and encapsulated by water.[6]

The process of separating the waters above the "expanse" from the waters below and calling it "heavens" (Gen. 1:8, AT) is elsewhere described as "stretching out the heavens" (Ps. 104:2; cf. Job 9:8; Isa. 42:5; 44:24; 45:12; 51:13; Jer. 10:12; 51:15; Zech. 12:1). Consider the following verses:

> I made the earth
> and created man on it;
> it was my hands that *stretched out the heavens,*
> and I commanded all their host.
> (Isa. 45:12)

It is he who made the earth by his power,
>who established the world by his wisdom,
>and by his understanding *stretched out the heavens*.
(Jer. 10:12)

Thus declares the LORD, who *stretched out the heavens* and founded the earth and formed the spirit of man within him . . . (Zech. 12:1)

The intended meaning of the *rāqîaʿ* and *šāmayim* is the "stretched expanse" in the midst of the cosmic waters. Hence we see a basic model for interpreting the first three days of creation (see figure 2.1).[7]

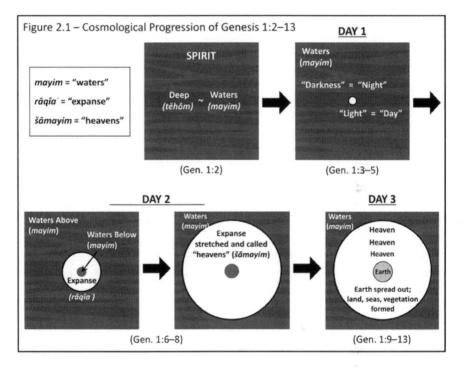

Figure 2.1 – Cosmological Progression of Genesis 1:2–13

DAY 1

mayim = "waters"
rāqîaʿ = "expanse"
šāmayim = "heavens"

SPIRIT

Deep (tĕhôm) ~ Waters (mayim)

(Gen. 1:2)

Waters (mayim)

"Darkness" = "Night"

"Light" = "Day"

(Gen. 1:3–5)

DAY 2

Waters Above (mayim)
Waters Below (mayim)
Expanse (rāqîaʿ)

Waters (mayim)
Expanse stretched and called "heavens" (šāmayim)

(Gen. 1:6–8)

DAY 3

Waters (mayim)
Heaven
Heaven
Heaven
Earth
Earth spread out; land, seas, vegetation formed

(Gen. 1:9–13)

As seen in this diagram, the heavens are described as *plural*. The Hebrew word for heavens (*šāmayim*) is used over four hundred times in the Old Testament, and it is always in the plural form. Moreover, the plural is sometimes used in tandem (*šāmeh hʾšāmayim*), "heavens of heavens" (Deut. 10:14; 1 Kings 8:27; 2 Chron. 2:6; 6:18; Neh. 9:6; Ps. 148:4), which is often translated "height of the heavens" or "highest heavens" (NASB, NIV, NLT), referring to the region(s) of God's dwelling. The translation of *šāmayim* into the singular by various English translations is generally arbitrary.[8] The biblical worldview clearly understands the heavens to be plural.[9]

Within this framework, the heavens are described in the Scriptures as *continuous*. They are the abode of birds (Gen. 1:20; 2:19; Dan. 2:38); of clouds, rain, and thunder (Gen. 8:2; Job 38:29; Isa. 55:10); of sun, moon, and stars (Gen. 1:14–18; Deut. 4:19; Ps. 8:3); of idols, spirits, and powers (Ex. 20:4; Deut. 3:24; Isa. 24:21); and of God himself (Deut. 26:15; 1 Kings 8:30; Ps. 2:4). All of these things function together in the heavens, and there are no clear lines of distinction between them. There are delineations between different areas of the heavens, as Paul distinguishes the "third heaven" (2 Cor. 12:2), but there is not a substantial change of existence between these regions.[10]

This continuity between the heavens allows for ease of movement within the heavens and between the heavens and the earth. Thus God often "came down" to meet with people or evaluate their affairs (Gen. 11:5; cf. Gen. 18:21; Ex. 19:11; etc.). Likewise, individuals such as Enoch (Heb. 11:5; cf. Gen. 5:24) and Elijah (2 Kings 2:11) were "taken up" into the heavens. Conversely, it was commonly understood that Elijah would come back down before the day of the Lord (Mal. 4:5), which Jesus affirmed on the Mount of Transfiguration (Matt. 17:11). Paul likewise was "caught up," whether in the body or out of the body (2 Cor. 12:2–3). And after Jesus was "taken up" before the disciples (Acts 1:2), two angels declared, "This Jesus, who was taken up from you into heaven, will come in the same way as you saw him go into heaven" (v. 11). This was not abnormal to the disciples, since movement between the heavens and the earth was both familiar and logical.[11]

The heavens are also assumed to be inherently *physical* in nature. In contrast to the later Platonic concept of a singular, ethereal heaven, the Scriptures describe the heavens as tangible, substantial, and concrete. There are audible sounds, voices, and songs (Isa. 6:3; 2 Cor. 12:4; Rev. 4–5). There are physical objects, such as thrones, altars, and thresholds (1 Kings 22:19–23; Isa. 6:1–7; Ezek. 1:25–28; Dan. 7:9–10). Furthermore, time exists in the various regions of the heavens (Rev. 8:1), and this time generally coincides with time on earth (cf. 1 Kings 22:19–23; Dan. 7:9–12; Rev. 11:18–19). The heavens are therefore clearly *dynamic* in nature, rather than static, as in Hellenistic thought. This perspective leads to the conclusion that the physicality seen in heaven is roughly analogous to the physicality known on earth.[12]

These plural, continuous, and physical heavens were universally understood as *real locations*, not "states of being."[13] In addition, their relationship to the earth was positional. The heavens are "above" and the earth is "below" (cf. Gen. 6:17; Deut. 4:39; 1 Kings 8:23; Ps. 50:4; etc.).[14] Accordingly, God "looks down" from the heavens upon his creation (Ps. 33:13; 53:2; cf. Deut. 26:15; Ps. 80:14; 102:19; Isa. 63:15)—"Look down from heaven and see, from your holy and beautiful habitation" (Isa. 63:15). God's habitation is understood to be at the height of the heavens (Job 25:2; Ps. 148:1; Isa. 14:13)—"Is not God in the heights of heaven?" (Job 22:12, NIV).[15]

The primary implication of God's governance of creation from the heights of the heavens is his *dwelling within creation*. Though relatively foreign to the modern mind, the Scriptures universally declare that God dwells within what he has made (e.g., 1 Kings 8:43; Ps. 102:19; Isa. 57:15; 63:15; etc.).[16] He does not dwell in the "great beyond" (as is common language in modern theological circles), nor does he dwell beyond the cosmic waters (as is common in reconstructions of ancient Near Eastern thought). He dwells within the heavens, as Isaiah described:

> Do you not know?
>> Have you not heard?
> Has it not been told you *from the beginning*?
>> Have you not understood since the earth was founded?
> He sits enthroned above the circle of the earth,
>> and its people are like grasshoppers.
> He stretches out the heavens like a canopy,
>> and spreads them out *like a tent to live in*.
> He brings princes to naught
>> and reduces the rulers of this world to nothing.
> (Isa. 40:21–23, NIV)

God dwells within creation as a human being dwells within a tent. But why does this matter? *Proximity evokes pathos.* What would my children think if I lived in a different house than them? How would they feel? What would they think of my heart and of my leadership? Would they trust me? Probably not. More than likely they would grow up with a deep sense of abandonment. So the modern church, under Hellenistic influence, suffers from a "cosmic loneliness," so to speak, which pervades much of its theology and practice. The Scriptures, however, reveal to us a God whose habitation is within creation, because he loves what he has made, and it is very good in his sight.

Some may question if this cohabitation compromises God's sovereignty. Does my living within a house mean my house limits me or rules over me? Of course not. God is completely separate from and transcendent over his creation, yet his greatness in sovereignty is only magnified by his nearness of presence. As Isaiah says, "For this is what the high and lofty One says—he who lives forever, whose name is holy: 'I live in a high and holy place, but also with him who is contrite and lowly in spirit, to revive the spirit of the lowly and to revive the heart of the contrite'" (Isa. 57:15, NIV).

In regard to his sovereignty, God also rules from a *real throne*. As the heavens are concrete and tangible, so also is the throne of God (cf. Isa. 6:1; Ezek. 1:26; Rev. 4:2–6). Biblical writers universally speak of the divine throne as they would the throne of an earthly king. The throne of God is not a metaphor, intended only to refer to a figurative "reign of God." Rather, it is a real seat in a real place in real time from which God rules over a real domain.

The Bible means quite literally that God is the "great King" (Ps. 47:2; 95:3; Jer. 10:10; Mal. 1:14) and the "everlasting King" (Jer. 10:10), for his dominion includes all of creation. Not only is he the "Most High" (Isa. 14:14; Dan. 7:18; Luke 6:35), but he is also God "Almighty" (Gk. *pantokratōr*, Rev. 4:8; 16:7)—that is, "the ruler over all things."[17] Hence the eternal declaration, "Around the throne, on each side of the throne, are four living creatures, full of eyes in front and behind. . . . Day and night they never cease to say, 'Holy, holy, holy, is the Lord God Almighty [Gk. *pantokratōr*], who was and is and is to come!'" (Rev. 4:6–8).

God's domain is the whole of creation—that is, the heavens and the earth (cf. Deut. 10:14; 1 Chron. 29:11; Ps. 24:1)—which is his "universal kingdom," so to speak (cf. Ps. 103:19; 145:13; Dan. 4:34).[18] As David said, "The LORD has established his throne in the heavens, and his kingdom rules over all" (Ps. 103:19). So also, at the end of his life, David said, "Yours, O LORD, is the greatness and the power and the glory and the victory and the majesty, for all that is in the heavens and in the earth is yours. Yours is the kingdom, O LORD, and you are exalted as head above all" (1 Chron. 29:11).

God's throne in the height of the heavens is also set within a *real temple* (cf. Ps. 11:4; 18:6; 29:9; 150:1; Isa. 6:1; Jonah 2:7; Mic. 1:2; Hab. 2:20; Rev. 11:19; 14:15–18; 15:5–8; 16:1). Like the divine throne, God's heavenly "sanctuary" (Ps. 28:2; 96:6; cf. Ps. 102:19; Heb. 8:2,5; 9:24) is not a metaphor for an ethereal holy nature. God is indeed holy, but he is holy within a real temple.[19] Consider the following texts:

> The LORD is in his holy *temple*;
>> the LORD is on his heavenly throne.
> He observes the sons of men;
>> his eyes examine them.
> (Ps. 11:4, NIV)

> Praise the LORD!
> Praise God in his *sanctuary*;
>> praise him in his mighty heavens!
> Praise him for his mighty deeds;
>> praise him according to his excellent greatness!
> (Ps. 150:1–2)

> Hear, you peoples, all of you;
>> pay attention, O earth, and all that is in it,
> and let the Lord GOD be a witness against you,
>> the Lord from his holy *temple.*
> For behold, the LORD is coming out of his place,
>> and will come down and tread upon the high places of the earth.
> (Mic. 1:2–3)

Thus we have a context for the opening of the heavenly temple in the book of Revelation: "Then God's temple in heaven was opened, and the ark of his covenant was seen within his temple. There were flashes of lightning, rumblings, peals of thunder, an earthquake, and heavy hail" (Rev. 11:19). It is from his heavenly dwelling that God rules over all of creation, administrating all things in the heavens and the earth. Thus, the heavenly temple is the *locus of creation.* It is the reference point for all divine, angelic, demonic, and human activity. It is the "command center," so to speak, of the universe. The earthly tabernacle was simply "patterned" after the heavenly one (cf. Ex. 25:40; Acts 7:44; Heb. 8:5; 9:24).[20] It was designed to inherently witness and testify to God's governance over all of creation.[21]

From protological creation (cf. Gen. 2:2–3; Isa. 40:21–23) to eschatological consummation (cf. Rev. 11:19; 14:15; 15:5; 16:1), the heavenly temple is the reference point for all divine redemptive activity. So when someone saw the "footstool" (1 Chron. 28:2; Ps. 99:5; 132:7; Lam. 2:1), it was meant to point them to the throne above, and subsequently to the judgment to come, which is based upon humanity's original sin. All of this would have been quite elementary to a believer living in the ancient world.[22]

The clearest demonstration of this belief in a real heavenly temple is found in Hebrews 8–10. The "throne of the Majesty" (8:1) is within the "true tabernacle set up by the Lord, not by man" (8:2, NIV). The "earthly tabernacle" (9:1, NIV) that Moses erected was simply "according to the pattern" (8:5) of the heavenly tabernacle (cf. Ex 25:9,40; 26:30; 27:8). It was a "man-made sanctuary that was only a copy of the true one" (9:24, NIV). Moreover, not only was the structure itself a "copy and shadow of what is in heaven" (8:5, NIV), but the ministry of the priests (8:3–5; 9:6–7,21–22; 10:1–2,11) was also a "shadow of the good things to come" (10:1) found in the ministry of Christ.

As the earthly sanctuary and its "copies of the heavenly things" were purified with the blood of sacrifices, so also "the heavenly things themselves" were purified by the blood of Christ (9:23). He entered the heavenly sanctuary "to offer himself" (9:25) and "to bear the sins of many" (9:28). And after he had "offered for all time a single sacrifice for sins, he sat down at the right hand of

God" (10:12), and since that time "he waits for his enemies to be made his footstool" (10:13, NIV) on the day of the Lord (cf. Ps. 110:1; Acts 2:35).[23]

Within a biblical worldview, this is all very straightforward. There is no "mystical" language or "spiritual" rhetoric. It is simply an interpretive narration of historical events that have taken place within the biblical cosmos. What is more, Christ's ascension into substantial heavens and into a real temple, offering his own blood on a literal altar on behalf of depraved humanity, is the actual *substitutionary mechanism* of atonement in the sight of God.[24] Without a definite event and a tangible sacrificial offering, the atonement breaks down into figurative abstraction—which, unfortunately, has been the norm throughout much of the history of atonement theory.[25]

Not only does God "build his upper chambers in the heavens" (Amos 9:6), but the chambers of his temple are also surrounded by gardens, or a "paradise" (note that the Greek *paradeisos* translates the "garden" of Eden in the Septuagint—that is, the "paradise" of Eden).[26] So Paul references the heavenly paradise: "I know a man in Christ who fourteen years ago was caught up to the third heaven—whether in the body or out of the body I do not know, God knows. And I know that this man was caught up *into paradise*—whether in the body or out of the body I do not know, God knows—and he heard things that cannot be told, which man may not utter" (2 Cor. 12:2–4).

Paul's third-heaven experience was not unfamiliar in his day, and by no means would anyone have questioned the reality of a "paradise" in the height of the heavens.[27] It was common knowledge, since deities were understood to dwell in "garden-temples."[28] Most of the ancient world believed the gods dwelled in some sort of idyllic paradise above.[29] The polytheism is obviously perverse, but the metaphysical construct is an aspect of truth that people today have foolishly cast aside as mythical.[30]

This basic framework of a plural, continuous, and physical heavens, within which God rules from a paradisal-temple, ultimately informs the context and meaning of the statement, "Let us make man in our image, in our likeness, and let them rule . . . over all the earth" (Gen. 1:26, NIV). As humanity was created in the image of God to rule, so also Eden was viewed as a garden-temple in the likeness of God's garden-temple in the height of the heavens (see figure 2.2).[31]

Though man's kingship is obvious in the Genesis creation account (1:26,28; cf. Ps. 8:4–8), his priesthood is less apparent. However, the priesthood of humanity and the Edenic garden-temple are clearly inferred from eschatological texts that describe the end as a restoration of the beginning (cf. Matt. 19:28; Acts 3:21; Rev. 21:3). Echoing the creation of humankind, the redeemed are declared to be "a kingdom and *priests* to our God, and they shall reign on the earth" (Rev. 5:10). This dual kingly and priestly function is the broad theme of the book of Revelation from beginning (1:6) to end (22:5). When Jesus returns and sets up his throne upon the earth, the redeemed "will be *priests* of God and of Christ, and they will *reign* with him" (Rev. 20:6). Thus the protological reality of humanity's kingly priesthood before God is easily deduced eschatologically. It is not a novel development or an unforeseen revelation; it is inherent to being human, because we were designed to be kings and priests in the garden.

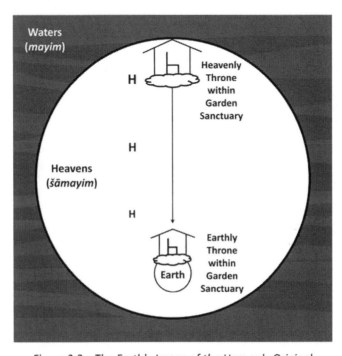

Figure 2.2 – The Earthly Image of the Heavenly Original

There are, however, explicit references to the protological priesthood of man in the Scriptures. Ezekiel 28 speaks of Eden as an idyllic "sanctuary" (v. 18),[32] which was then desecrated.[33] Psalm 36:7–9 also compares the temple to Eden, since the Hebrew word (*ʿēden*) means "luxury, delight, pleasure"—"The children of mankind [Heb. *ʾādām*] take refuge in the shadow of your wings. They feast on the abundance of your house [i.e., temple, cf. 1 Kings 6:1; Isa. 2:2; etc.], and you give them drink from the river of your delights [Heb. *ʿēden*]. For with you is the fountain of life [cf. tree of life]; in your light do we see light."

Furthermore, many scholars have listed the various similarities between the garden of Eden and the tabernacle and/or Jerusalem temple.[34] A partial list follows:

- God "walked" (Heb. *hālak*) in both, representing his unique presence (Gen. 3:8; Lev. 26:12; Deut. 23:14; 2 Sam. 7:6–7).

- Human beings are commanded to "serve/work" (Heb. *'ābad*) and "keep/guard" (Heb. *šāmar*) both, representing their priestly role and function (Gen. 2:15; Num. 3:7–8; 8:25–26; 18:5–6; 1 Chron. 23:32).

- The structure of both is threefold, with an entrance facing east (Gen. 2:8; 3:24; Ezek. 8:16; 40:6). See figure 2.3 for illustration.[35]

- Both are situated on a mountain (Gen. 2:10; 2 Chron. 3:1; Isa. 2:2; Ezek. 28:13–16), and both are guarded by cherubim (Gen. 3:24; Ex. 25:18–22; 26:31; 1 Kings 6:23–35; Ezek. 28:14).

- Rivers flow out of both Eden (Gen. 2:10) and the eschatological temple in Jerusalem (Ezek. 47:1–12; Rev. 22:1–2).

- Precious metals and stones are used in and adorn both (Gen. 2:11–12; Ex. 25:7–31; Ezek. 28:13).

- Trees filled the garden (Gen. 2:9), and arboreal decorations adorned the temple (1 Kings 6:18–35; 7:18–20). Moreover, the tree of life and the tree of knowledge (Gen. 2:9) seem to be symbolized in the sanctuary lampstand and law, respectively.[36]

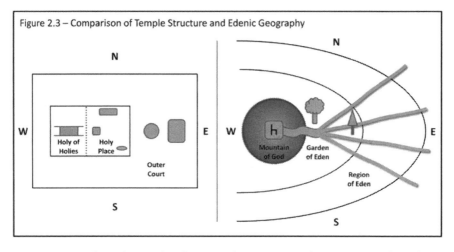

Figure 2.3 – Comparison of Temple Structure and Edenic Geography

Later Jewish tradition also depicts Adam as a priestly minister in the Edenic temple.[37] The combination of Genesis, Revelation, and the prophets all paint a picture that I believe was clear in the minds of the New Testament writers (cf. Luke 24:51; 2 Cor. 12:2; Heb. 8–10; Rev. 15; etc.)—that God ruled over creation from a paradisal-temple in the height of the heavens, and humans were created in his image as kingly priests to rule over the earth from the paradisal-temple of Eden. The heavens and the earth were created to enhance the glory of God as reflected in the creation of humankind, and consequently the two realities organically correspond to one another.[38]

Within this patterned arrangement there is also a *divine hierarchy* under the governance of God, by which he holds together all things with absolute power, authority, and dominion (cf. Eph. 1:20–21; Col. 1:16–17). There are "powers" (Rom. 8:38; Eph. 6:12), "rulers" (Eph. 3:10; Col. 1:16), and "authorities" (Col. 2:15; 1 Peter 3:22; cf. Isa. 24:21; 34:4) in the "midheaven" (Rev. 8:13; 14:6; 19:17, NRSV). Note Paul's descriptions of the heavenly hierarchy:

> For by Him [Christ] all things were created, both in the heavens and on earth, visible and invisible, whether *thrones or dominions or rulers or authorities*—all things have been created through Him and for Him. He is before all things, and in Him all things hold together. (Col. 1:16–17, NASB)

> Put on the whole armor of God, that you may be able to stand against the schemes of the devil. For we do not wrestle against flesh and blood, but against *the rulers*, against *the authorities*, against *the cosmic powers* over this present darkness, against *the spiritual forces* of evil in the heavenly places. (Eph. 6:11–12)

Such powers and rulers are clearly angelic and/or demonic entities, since they dwell in "heavenly places" (Eph. 3:10; 6:12; cf. 1 Peter 3:22). Some are "ministering spirits" (Heb. 1:14; cf. Ps. 104:4) who "do his bidding" (Ps. 103:20, NRSV) and "patrol the earth" (Zech. 1:10; 6:7). Others "did not stay within their own position of authority" (Jude 6), and now go "to and fro on the earth" (Job 1:7; 2:2) like a lion "seeking someone to devour" (1 Peter 5:8). In addition, there is often conflict between the two (cf. Dan. 10:20; Rev. 12:7), which presumably also takes place in the mid-heavens.[39] Such conflict, however, will come to an end in the future, as Isaiah describes: "In that day the LORD will punish the powers in the heavens above and the kings on the earth below. They will be herded together like prisoners bound in a dungeon; they will be shut up in prison and be punished after many days" (Isa. 24:21–22, NIV).

The powers in the heavens are described in the Scriptures as divine intermediaries between God and humans (cf. Ps. 91:11; Dan. 7:10; Acts 7:53; Gal. 3:19; Heb. 1:14; 2:2). These powers and principalities—that is, the "host of heaven" (1 Kings 22:19; Dan. 4:35; cf. Ps. 103:21; Luke 2:13), "sons of God" (Deut. 32:8; Job 1:6; 2:1; 38:7), or "heavenly beings" (Ps. 8:5; 29:1; 89:6)—were understood to be part of a *divine council*, which exists to "administer the affairs of the cosmos."[40] For "God has taken his place in the divine council; in the midst of the gods he holds judgment" (Ps. 82:1). This is how Micaiah would have understood "the LORD sitting on his throne with all the host of heaven standing around him on his right and on his left" (1 Kings 22:19, NIV). Likewise, the psalmist declares,

> Let the heavens praise your wonders, O LORD,
>   your faithfulness in *the assembly of the holy ones*!
> For who in the skies can be compared to the LORD?
>   Who among the heavenly beings is like the LORD,
> a God greatly to be feared in *the council of the holy ones*,
>   and awesome above all who are around him?
> (Ps. 89:5–7)

According to this arrangement, it is assumed that in the beginning angels ministered to God by ascending and descending (cf. Gen. 28:12; John 1:51) between the heavenly and Edenic temples, administrating the glory of God throughout creation.[41] And even though many powers and principalities have forsaken their positions of authority, God Most High still remains completely sovereign over his creation (cf. Jer. 27:5; Hab. 2:13; Zeph. 2:10; Rev. 4:8). The heavens and the earth still "belong" to the Lord (cf. Deut. 10:14; Ps. 24:1; 50:12). He still does "as he pleases with the powers of heaven and the peoples of the earth" (Dan. 4:35, NIV; cf. Ps. 115:3; 135:6). They are still "under authority" (Matt. 8:9), and even demons are subject to "begging" (cf. Matt. 8:31). Thus rebellious powers encounter a divine "hedge" (Job. 1:10; Isa. 5:5) and have no liberty to wreak havoc beyond their ordained limits (cf. Job 2:6; 1 Cor. 10:13; James 4:7). Moreover, demons are even used by God to execute divine wrath (cf. 1 Kings 22:22; Judg. 9:23; Rev. 17:17) and to test people's hearts (cf. 1 Sam. 16:14; Luke 22:31; 2 Thess. 2:11).

Like the powers in the heavens, all the treasonous kingdoms of men are like the "grass" that withers (Ps. 37:2; 90:5; 92:7; 103:15), like "flowers" that fade (Job 14:2; Isa. 40:7; James 1:10)—like "grasshoppers" (Isa. 40:22), "a worm" (Job 25:6), or "a drop from a bucket" (Isa. 40:15)—"they are nothing; together they are only a breath" (Ps. 62:9, NIV). The Lord simply "laughs" at them and "scoffs" at their games (cf. Ps. 2:4; 37:13; 59:8). And often, unbeknown to them, he orchestrates their rise and fall (cf. Ex. 9:16; Jer. 27:6; John 19:11; Acts 17:26). Effortlessly, "he removes kings and sets up kings" (Dan. 2:21). The idea that God is "at war" is myopic at best.[42]

Therefore, "for the Lord's sake" (1 Peter 2:13) we are commanded to be "submissive to rulers" (Tit. 3:1) and "subject to the governing authorities" (Rom. 13:1), since God is *ultimately* responsible for their positions. So Jesus said to Pilate, "You would have no authority over me at all unless it had been given you from above" (John 19:11). Likewise, Jesus was given all authority by the Father (cf. Matt. 28:18; John 5:22; Heb. 2:8), for "God placed all things under his feet and appointed him to be head over everything" (Eph. 1:22, NIV). By this divine delegation of authority, Christ is "the blessed and only Sovereign, the King of kings and Lord of lords. . . . To him be honor and eternal dominion" (1 Tim. 6:15–16). In this way, God is truly the Almighty (Gk. *pantokratōr*), for "from him and through him and to him are all things" (Rom. 11:36).

Our understanding of God's kingship and governance are dramatically affected by how we view the heavens and the earth. Divine sovereignty simply "fits" better within a biblical worldview.[43]

MODERN CONCEPTIONS OF THE BIBLICAL WORLDVIEW

The worldview of the Bible and the interpretation of "the heavens and the earth" have become quite contentious in modern times.[44] Since around the turn of the twentieth century, scholars have reconstructed the biblical world-view based upon the mythical worldviews of the ancient Near East.[45] At first it was primarily Babylonian and Persian mythologies that were accommodated, but then studies were generalized to include Assyrian, Hittite, Canaanite, and Egyptian myths also. Today it is widely assumed that the Israelites held to the same "cosmic geography" as their neighbors.[46]

Such an idea is not inherently problematic. Most scholars, though, take the next step and say *the Bible itself* teaches an ancient Near Eastern view of the cosmos, assuming the Scriptures arose out of human culture and understanding. For the evangelical, this is no small error. We believe the Bible is a recorded oracle, ultimately produced by the Holy Spirit (see 2 Peter 1:21; 2 Tim. 3:16), and thus transcending the human steward. Though an ancient Israelite—the prophet Isaiah, for example—may have held the same worldview as his cultural neighbors, we cannot say that the oracles delivered through him teach such things. The Holy Spirit would stand just as critical of Isaiah's ancient Near Eastern worldview as he does of our modern anthropocentric worldview, which dichotomizes between material and immaterial.

For this reason, I believe the Bible uses *equivocal language*, meaning God chose to minimize the use and definition of language concerning the nature of the cosmos so that it would be equally open to interpretation throughout time and across cultures.[47] This was a loving decision on the part of God, considering the reality of human mortality. How would you describe the creation and properties of glass to a mostly deaf, dumb, and blind fish when referencing his fishbowl? You would probably limit the use and definition of words so as to be universally understood and received by a variety of fish.

How then has modern scholarship reconstructed the worldview(s) of ancient Near Eastern peoples? The general consensus is summarized by the phrase "three-storied universe,"[48] which involves 1) the heavens, 2) the earth, and 3) the underworld. Such a view assumes the earth to be flat and surrounded by water, with a large metallic dome covering it. The sun, moon, and stars float across this dome like lily pads, and cosmic oceans surround everything. Finally, beneath the earth is Sheol/Hades; and beyond the oceans is the heavenly dwelling of God. Figure 2.4 shows two typical pictorial renditions.[49]

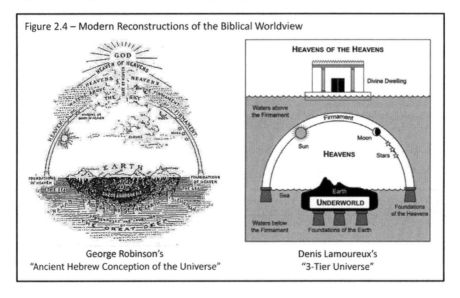

Figure 2.4 – Modern Reconstructions of the Biblical Worldview

George Robinson's
"Ancient Hebrew Conception of the Universe"

Denis Lamoureux's
"3-Tier Universe"

The initial problem with this common rendering is that *not all ancient Near Eastern peoples saw the world this way*—that is, there is no "uniform primitive view."[50] In fact, it is devilishly hard to find any sources that present this picture in a straightforward manner (most cosmologies have to be gleaned from far-fetched and fantastical mythology).[51] But the commonalities that do exist, particularly a manifold vertical universe,[52] ought to be interpreted as the remnants of true cosmology rather than as the imaginations of Stone Age peoples. Similar reasoning ought to be applied to the more than two hundred flood myths derived from the ancient world.[53] The commonalities between the stories do not mean the Bible coopted its flood narrative. Instead, the flood actually happened, and the hundreds of flood myths are simply corrupted accounts of the real event—so too concerning the parallels between the Bible and ancient cosmologies.

The second problem with the modern rendering of the biblical worldview is the portrayal of the *rāqîaʿ* (Gen. 1:6–8) as a metal dome, or "vault," over the earth. Many scholars and modern translations do translate *rāqîaʿ* generically as an "expanse," which provides room for interpretation.[54] Solid-dome advocates, however, prefer the antiquated "firmament," which is a transliteration of the Latin *firmamentum* used to translate the Greek *stereōma* (both of which imply a firm or solid structure).[55] But since the Hebrew noun *rāqîaʿ* has limited use in the Old Testament, its meaning is generally derived etymologically. Scholars typically argue that since *rāqîaʿ* is derived from the verb *rāqaʿ*, meaning to "flatten," "beat out," or "spread out," then the *rāqîaʿ* must be solid, akin to the object (e.g., a metal plate) being beaten out. However, *the emphasis carried over from the verb is the action of spreading or stretching, not the substance which is beaten out.*[56] This is clearly demonstrated by the many instances of prophetic commentary describing the Lord "stretching out" the heavens (cf. Job 9:8; Ps. 104:2; Isa. 42:5; 44:24; 45:12; 51:13; Jer. 10:12; 51:15; Zech. 12:1). The act of stretching out is clearly the point being made by Scripture's use of *rāqîaʿ*.

It seems reasonable that the substance of the *rāqîaʿ* is the "space-time fabric" within which creation functions.[57] Solid-domers would say this amounts to "concordism"—the mantric cry of modern critics of the Bible.[58] Nevertheless, a view of the *rāqîaʿ*/*šāmayim* as a stretched atmospheric expanse is the model that best corresponds to the Bible's own description of birds flying across it (Gen. 1:20; Deut. 4:17), powers and principalities dwelling in it (Duet. 3:24; Isa. 24:21), people ascending and descending through it (John 3:13; Rev. 11:12), and the Lord sitting enthroned at the height of it (Ps. 2:4; 103:19) and executing his judgments in the midst of it (Isa. 11:4; 34:5; Joel 2:30).

Ultimately, those who argue for a solid *rāqîaʿ* avoid the obvious: Genesis 1:8 equates the expanse with the heavens. So also do Psalm 19:1 and 150:1, which incorporate Hebrew parallelism, a poetic means of repetition designed to reinforce the same idea.[59] *Rāqîaʿ* equals *šāmayim*. All etymological arguments for a solid *rāqîaʿ* fail in light of this fact. Attempts by solid-domers to substantiate a difference between the *rāqîaʿ* and the *šāmayim* are groundless.[60]

The third major problem with the common reconstruction of the biblical worldview involves the divorce of the heavens (*šāmayim*) from the heavens of heavens (*šāmeh h'šāmayim*). With the intrusion of a solid *rāqîaʿ*, God's dwelling in the "upper heavens" above the dome must be separated from the "lower heavens" under the dome.[61] This, however, is another baseless assumption. Nowhere in the Scriptures is there a division between the heavens and the heavens of heavens, and nowhere are the heavens of heavens depicted as being beyond the cosmic waters.[62] The heavens and the highest heavens are always part and parcel with one another (cf. Deut. 10:14; 1 Kings 8:27; 2 Chron. 2:6; 6:18; Neh. 9:6; Ps. 148:4). Note their amalgamated relationship:

> You alone are the LORD. You have made *the heavens, the heaven of heavens* with all their host, the earth and all that is on it, the seas and all that is in them. (Neh. 9:6, NASB)

> To the LORD your God belong *the heavens, even the highest heavens,* the earth and everything in it. (Deut. 10:14, NIV)

> But will God indeed dwell on the earth? Behold, *heaven and the highest heaven* cannot contain you; how much less this house that I have built! (1 Kings 8:27)

Beginning with the pagan derivation of the Scriptures, critics project a reductionistic metal-dome interpretation upon the *rāqîaʿ*, which forces them to delineate between the *rāqîaʿ* and the *šāmayim*, which in turn forces them to divide the *šāmayim* from the *šāmeh hʾšāmayim*, thus placing God's dwelling beyond creation. Such a hermeneutical approach to the "primitive cosmology" of the "scientifically naïve" is obviously prejudiced by a naturalistic bias.[63] No wonder the Bible's worldview has become the very source of skepticism for many in the last century, requiring either disbelief or a *sacrificium intellectus.*[64]

THE CHRISTOPLATONIC WORLDVIEW

On the playing field of life, the average Westerner views reality in a simple, dualistic manner involving two worlds: one material, the other immaterial. Generally labeled "natural" versus "supernatural," this structure has a long and complicated history of development. Its general ancestry, though, traces back to Hellenism and Greek philosophy.[65]

Unfortunately, there is no single "Greek worldview," but rather a conglomeration of different beliefs that molded a common way of thinking. Akin to Darwin's relationship to modern evolutionism, the primary bellwether of ancient Greek thought was Plato (c. 427–347 BC), who was a self-proclaimed disciple and mouthpiece of Socrates (c. 470–399 BC). Plato established the Academy (c. 387 BC) on the north side of Athens and there schooled a young man named Aristotle (384–322 BC).[66] In turn, Aristotle mentored a number of young noblemen, including three future kings: Ptolemy, Cassander, and Alexander III of Macedon.

These three men, particularly Alexander, made it their life ambition to civilize and enlighten the entire known world of their time. And in a stunning display of zeal and ambition, Alexander conquered kingdoms from the

Ionian Sea to the Himalayas in only ten years (333–323 BC), creating the largest empire in the ancient world at his time. Founding nearly twenty cities that bore his own name, Alexander settled Greek colonists everywhere he went and ushered in what is known in history books as the "Hellenistic Age" (323–30

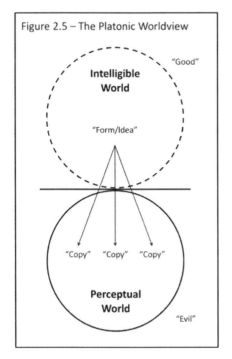

Figure 2.5 – The Platonic Worldview

BC).[67] From this point it was only a matter of time before the ardent zeal of Hellenism would consume the ancient world, laying the historical foundation for the development of Western society.

Such philosophical "good news" was ultimately derived from the worldview within which it was framed. Plato's understanding of the universe involved two basic parts: the "intelligible" world and the "perceptual" world. The intelligible world is comprised of perfect "forms," which then produce corrupt "copies" in the perceptual world (see figure 2.5). The form, or "idea," of something is its true essence, while the copy is its debased manifestation.[68]

Forms are universal realities, such as "chair-ness" or "red-ness." Copies are particular expressions of those forms that we are able to perceive or sense, such as the red rocking chair in the corner of the living room. Though immaterial, the intelligible world is actually more "real" than the material perceptual world because it is the eternal source of existence.[69] Those who seek reality in materiality by their senses are "barbarians" who live without divine inspiration.[70] Thus, those who seek to see with their eyes are actually blind.[71]

The Platonic worldview is technically termed "metaphysical dualism"— that is, reality is composed of two substantially and qualitatively different parts.[72] However, the qualities and their distinction from one another are ultimately determined by human perception. The perceptual, or "sensible," world refers to the perception and senses of humanity. Thus, anthropocentrism, or "human-centeredness," is the defining characteristic of the entire system of thought. The starting point of Hellenistic philosophy and all subsequent Western tradition is this: *The parameters of reality are defined by human perception.* Though no one in the modern world actually believes in forms and copies, this broad approach to interpreting reality was passed on to later generations.[73]

Such metaphysical wranglings may seem unimportant to many. Nevertheless, anthropocentrism lies at the very heart of original sin. Pride and moral autonomy are derived from the exaltation of self, which is based upon an orientation to self. To bind reality at a worldview level to human perception provides the ultimate greenhouse for humanism and every form of ungodliness—the floodgates of which broke during the Enlightenment and continue to inundate to this day. Though many regard Greek philosophy as benign (or even beneficial) to the Christian faith, it should be remembered that Socrates was widely believed in his day to be demonized, a fact greatly mitigated or completely ignored by modern historians.[74] Unfortunately, many early Christians also disregarded this testimony.

In the centuries following Alexander's conquests, one of the cities he named after himself—Alexandria, Egypt—became a hub of Hellenistic teaching and propagation, and the home of the largest library in the ancient world. It was here that a catechetical school was established which, under the leadership of Clement (c. 150–211) and Origen (c. 182–251), sought to assimilate Christianity and Greek philosophy.[75] The progeny was neither Platonism nor Christianity but "Christoplatonism," a mongrel child that continues to grow to this day both in size and stature.[76]

Akin to its heretical Gnostic cousins (note especially Basilides and Valentinus, both educated in Alexandria), Christoplatonism gained momentum throughout the third and fourth centuries with the rise of Egyptian monasticism and the Catechetical School of Alexandria, both of which found liberty under the Alexandrian Patriarchate.[77] The impact of the Alexandrian school of thought, especially through the spread of desert monasticism, cannot be overstated.[78] As Athanasius said, "The desert had become a city."[79] Darkened as it was, it did indeed become something of a "city on the hill" for the future not only of Western monasticism but also of the Western theological tradition in general.[80] However, such a trajectory must be wholeheartedly rejected from its inception. With Tertullian, we cry,

> These are "the doctrines" of men and "of demons" produced for itching ears of the spirit of this world's wisdom: this the Lord called "foolishness," and "chose the foolish things of the world" to confound even philosophy itself. . . . Indeed heresies are themselves instigated by philosophy. From this source came the Aeons, and I know not what infinite forms, and the trinity of man in the system of Valentinus, who was of Plato's school.

From the same source came Marcion's better god, with all his tranquility; he came of the Stoics. Then, again, the opinion that the soul dies is held by the Epicureans; while the denial of the restoration of the body is taken from the aggregate school of all the philosophers. . . . *What indeed has Athens to do with Jerusalem?* What concord is there between the Academy and the Church? What between heretics and Christians? Our instruction comes from "the porch of Solomon" [cf. Acts 3:11], who had himself taught that "the Lord should be sought in simplicity of heart." *Away with all attempts to produce a mottled Christianity of Stoic, Platonic, and dialectic composition!* We want no curious disputation after possessing Christ Jesus, no inquisition after enjoying the gospel! With our faith, we desire no further belief. For this is our palmary faith, that there is nothing which we ought to believe besides.[81]

Though it has become common today to downplay the differences between Greek and Hebrew thought, Tertullian clearly presents a chasm of thinking between Athens and Jerusalem.[82] It can be confidently asserted that the dominant source of heresy in the early church was Hellenistic philosophy and mythology, which are diametrically opposed to the Jewish faith. These are indeed two different ways of thinking, or "patterns" of thought.[83]

Moreover, beyond the symptomatic concerns of Greek versus Hebrew thought (e.g., abstract versus concrete, stoic versus emotive, secular versus sacred, individualistic versus communal)[84] lies the fountainhead of divergent worldviews—that is, the "Greek view" of the universe (material and immaterial) versus the "Hebrew view" of the universe (heavens and earth).[85] As the biblical heavens were consolidated and relegated to ideal immateriality (and the earth was conversely relegated to evil materiality), the prime eschatological doctrines of the apostolic church—that is, the day of the Lord, the resurrection of the dead, and the messianic kingdom (cf. 1 Cor. 15:19–26; 2 Tim. 4:1; 1 Peter 1:13; etc.)—were abandoned.[86] The biblical heavens were transformed into the distant, detached, and ethereal realm of "heaven" so common to Western tradition, and the hope of the return of Jesus and a new creation slowly became marginalized amidst the multitude of polemical Christoplatonist controversies during the fourth and fifth centuries.

The perversion of the first verse of the Bible is thus an ultimate source of perversion throughout the rest of the Scriptures. Instead of beginning with plural, continuous, physical, and dynamic heavens, we start with a *singular, discontinuous, nonphysical, and static* "heaven," which in turn becomes the field upon which the rest of redemptive history is played out (see figure 2.6).

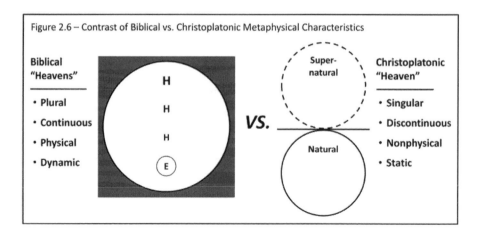

Figure 2.6 – Contrast of Biblical vs. Christoplatonic Metaphysical Characteristics

The whole "spiritual" hermeneutic of the School of Alexandria, which in turn ultimately determined the Western theological tradition, operated upon the basis of this distortion.[87] As Origen articulates,

> And again [Paul] says, "We shall be caught up in the clouds to meet Christ in the air, and so shall we ever be with the Lord." We are therefore to suppose that the saints will remain there [in their progress to ideal immateriality] until they recognize the twofold mode of government in those things which are performed in the air. . . . If anyone indeed be pure in heart, and holy in mind, and more practiced in perception, he will, by making more rapid progress, quickly ascend to a place in the air, and reach the kingdom of heaven, through those mansions, so to speak, in the various places *which the Greeks have termed spheres, i.e., globes, but which holy Scripture has called heavens*; in each of which he will first see clearly what is done there, and in the second place, will discover the reason why things are so done: and thus he will in order pass through all gradations, following Him who hath passed into the heavens, Jesus the Son of God, who said, "I will that where I am, these may be also."[88]

In like manner, most modern believers reinterpret what "holy Scripture has called heavens." Rather than opening their Bible and reading, "In the beginning God created the heavens and the earth," they intuit, *In the beginning God created the natural/material and the supernatural/immaterial.*[89] But the words natural and supernatural simply do not exist in the Bible.[90] The continued use of them is unhelpful and destructive—not to mention untruthful.[91] Biblical terminology (such as "divine," "miraculous," "heavenly," etc.) is much more appropriate and profitable. Nonbiblical terminology confounds the issues and makes the quest for true correspondence with the word of God all the more difficult.[92]

When trying to identify the lack of correspondence between the Scriptures and modern presentations of the gospel, we must begin with the issues of worldview. Otherwise we are doomed to perpetual theological dissonance, akin to placing a soccer team on a basketball court and exhorting them, "Score!" Once you change the field of play, all the rules and roles of the game get confounded. So it is when you try to place biblical entities in a Hellenistic worldview (see figure 2.7).

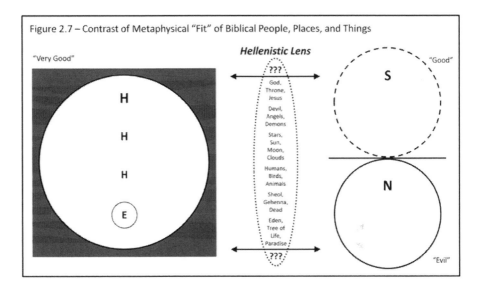

Figure 2.7 – Contrast of Metaphysical "Fit" of Biblical People, Places, and Things

As discussed previously, one's worldview is the ultimate determining factor of one's hermeneutics. Once the first verse is changed, then the interpretation of the rest of the Bible is changed. From Genesis to Revelation—the creation, the fall, the covenants, the prophets, the cross, the church, the day of the Lord, and the new heavens and new earth—everything takes on a different meaning. And it is this meaning, the theology and "good news" of the Bible, which is ultimately at stake in the enterprise of articulating and clarifying a biblical worldview.

Chapter Three

✸

BIBLICAL THEOLOGY

The worldview of the Bible sets the stage for the development of its theology. Within the framework of the heavens and the earth, humanity is created in an idyllic environment for the infinite growth of life, love, and general well-being (Gen. 1–2). However, this primal condition is tested by means of choice, and humanity is found wanting (Gen. 3). This cluster of protological events sets in motion the wheels of biblical theology, which works out the tension between divine holiness and human depravity—the remediation of the alienation between God and humankind.

The Scriptures present a clear and simple answer to the predicament raised by Adam and Eve. God will vindicate his own righteousness and judge the sins of humanity. He will fix what man has broken, and he will correct what man has perverted. The deep longing for life to be *made right* is the driving force behind the Scriptures. Old Testament and New, the Bible is essentially prophetic in nature, "declaring the end from the beginning" (Isa. 46:10), looking forward to the denouement of what went wrong in the garden.

OVERVIEW OF BIBLICAL THEOLOGY

This "end" of biblical revelation is encapsulated in a singular event referred to as "the day of the Lord" (Isa. 13:6,9; Ezek. 30:3; Joel 1:15; 2:1,11,31; 3:14; Amos 5:18; Obad. 15; Zeph. 1:7,14; Zech. 14:1; Mal. 4:5; Acts 2:20; 1 Cor. 5:5; 1 Thess. 5:2; 2 Thess. 2:2; 2 Peter 3:10). This future day will humble the pride, sin, and rebellion that began in the garden—that is, "The haughtiness of man shall be humbled, and the lofty pride of men shall be brought low, and the LORD alone will be exalted in that day" (Isa. 2:17; cf. Isa. 13:11; Mal. 4:1).

Our history books write endlessly about the glory of humankind—our progression, our knowledge, our civilization. We press blindly toward the exaltation of humanity, crying out for "the day of man," so to speak, with ever-increasing zeal and ambition. However, "a day is coming *for the Lord*" (Zech. 14:1), when God will be glorified and honored—for "all mankind will come to bow down before Me, says the LORD" (Isa. 66:23, NASB).

Because the effects of sin are both progressive and cumulative in nature, the day of the Lord is *essentially apocalyptic.*[1] Biblical history, from beginning to end, is a narrative in which anticipation steadily builds toward a final cataclysm with God.[2] Hence the emphatic cry of the prophets: "Alas for the day! For the day of the LORD is near, and it will come as destruction from the Almighty" (Joel 1:15, NASB; cf. Isa. 13:6).

Isaiah outlines the apocalyptic conclusion of biblical history:

See, the day of the LORD comes,
    cruel, with wrath and fierce anger,
to make the earth a desolation,
    and to destroy its sinners from it.
For the stars of the heavens and their constellations
    will not give their light;
the sun will be dark at its rising,
    and the moon will not shed its light.
I will punish the world for its evil,
    and the wicked for their iniquity;
I will put an end to the pride of the arrogant,
    and lay low the insolence of tyrants.
(Isa. 13:9–11, NRSV)

Blind to the horror of sin, deaf to the cry of the prophets, and ignorant of the impending judgment, people press on in their pride and arrogance toward "the coming of the great and terrible day of the LORD" (Mal. 4:5, NASB). It will be the ultimate calamity, catastrophic beyond all human imagination: "The earth shall reel to and fro like a drunkard, and shall totter like a hut; its transgression shall be heavy upon it, and it will fall, and not rise again" (Isa. 24:20, NKJV). Akin to the Noachian flood, it will consume the earth violently with fire: "Neither their silver nor their gold shall be able to deliver them on the day of the wrath of the LORD. In the fire of his jealousy, all the earth shall be consumed; for a full and sudden end he will make of all the inhabitants of the earth" (Zeph. 1:18).[3]

Therefore the totality of human and divine existence is moving toward this *single climactic moment* in history, which itself defines all prior moments and the interactions therein.[4] Ancient cultures—such as Canaanite, Mesopotamian,

Persian, Babylonian, Greek, and Roman—were apocalyptic simply because humanity is created in the image of God and history itself is apocalyptic.[5] Though often corrupted (akin to ancient corruptions of worldview, creation, and the flood), apocalypticism remains a driving force throughout history and across culture, because humanity intuitively knows the ultimate end of its unrighteousness.[6] Thus, since the sin of Adam and Eve, God has generally related in mercy; yet the Scriptures prophesy that human life is moving unidirectionally, like a giant arrow, toward the judgment of the day of the Lord (see figure 3.1).[7]

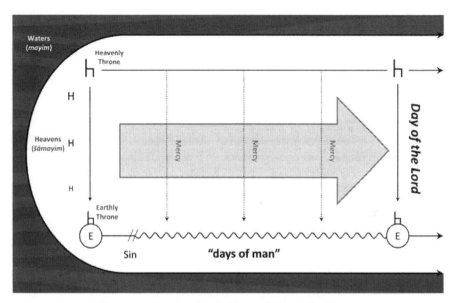

Figure 3.1 – The Cataclysmic Nature of Redemptive History

Though the day of the Lord will be "a day of distress and anguish, a day of ruin and devastation, a day of darkness and gloom" (Zeph. 1:15), it will finally overturn the order of sin and ungodliness established by Adam and Eve. A new order—an order of righteousness—will prevail, both in the heavens and on the earth: "In that day the LORD will punish the powers in the heavens above and the kings on the earth below" (Isa. 24:21, NIV).

In this way God will create "new heavens and a new earth, and the former things shall not be remembered or come into mind" (Isa. 65:17; cf. 66:22). The former corrupt order will be forgotten, for "The wicked shall be no more. . . . But the meek shall inherit the earth, and shall delight themselves in the abundance of peace" (Ps. 37:10–11, NKJV). Hence "We are looking forward to a new heaven and a new earth, the home of righteousness" (2 Peter 3:13, NIV). So the Scriptures conclude with the apostle John's summary vision:

Then I saw *a new heaven and a new earth*, for the first heaven and the first earth had passed away. . . . I heard a loud voice from the throne saying, "Now the dwelling of God is with men, and he will live with them. They will be his people, and God himself will be with them and be their God. He will wipe every tear from their eyes. There will be no more death or mourning or crying or pain, for *the old order of things has passed away*." (Rev. 21:1–4, NIV)

John continues in the next verse, "He who was seated on the throne said, "Behold, I am making all things new"" (Rev. 21:5). It is this "making all things new" that constitutes the ultimate purpose of the day of the Lord: *the restoration of original glory*—a new heavens and new earth without sin and death. The purpose of divine judgment is to correct the error of sin and make right that which went so grievously wrong. Consequently, Peter summarizes with the phrase "restoration of all things" the events of the return of Jesus and the day of the Lord: "Repent therefore . . . that He may send Jesus Christ, who was preached to you before, whom heaven must receive until the times of restoration of all things, which God has spoken by the mouth of all His holy prophets since the world began" (Acts 3:19–21, NKJV).

"All things" here references the heavens and the earth (cf. Eph. 1:10; Col. 1:16; Heb. 1:3), for in the end God will restore the heavens and the earth to their original state.[8] This restoration is the substantive message of all the prophets "since the world began." Likewise, Jesus speaks of "the renewal of all things":

Truly I tell you, at *the renewal of all things*, when the Son of Man is seated on the throne of his glory, you who have followed me will also sit on twelve thrones, judging the twelve tribes of Israel. And everyone who has left houses or brothers or sisters or father or mother or children or fields, for my name's sake, will receive a hundredfold, and will inherit *eternal life*. (Matt. 19:28–29, NRSV)

Again, "all things" here refers to the present heavens and earth which will be "renewed" or "regenerated" to something akin to their original state of perfection.[9] This approach to the Scriptures has thus been termed "the new creation model."[10] As such, biblical theology can safely be summarized as *eschatologically restored protology* (see figure 3.2).[11] In fact, "in the beginning" categorically anticipates "in the end."[12]

This renewal will also involve the restoration of *eternal life* to humanity. Death is antithetical to life. Human beings were not meant to die but rather to regenerate perpetually by means of the tree of life (cf. Gen. 3:22; Rev. 22:2). Death was instituted by God to humiliate sin and pride so as to bring repentance (cf. Gen. 3:19; Ps. 73:3–20; Rom. 8:20). Nevertheless, the order of death under which humanity now lives will be dramatically overturned in an event inaugurated by the day of the Lord called "the resurrection of the dead" (Matt. 22:31; Acts 23:6; 1 Cor. 15:21,42; Heb. 6:2).

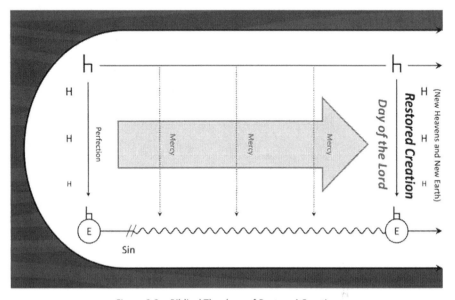

Figure 3.2 – Biblical Theology of Restored Creation

Paul gives us the clearest outline of the resurrection of the dead in 1 Corinthians 15. As death came by the sin of Adam—for "in Adam all die" (v. 22)—so life will come by the return of Jesus—for "in Christ shall all be made alive" (v. 22). At his coming he will destroy "every rule and every authority and power" (v. 24): "For he must reign until he has put all his enemies under his feet. The last enemy to be destroyed is death" (vv. 25–26). This destruction of the enemies of God—sin and its effects—constitutes the substance of the day of the Lord and a theology of new heavens and a new earth.

Paul goes on to describe the radical transformation of the resurrection:

We shall not all sleep, but we shall all be changed, in a moment, in the twinkling of an eye, at the last trumpet. For the trumpet will sound, and the dead will be raised imperishable, and we shall be changed. For this perishable body must put on the imperishable, and this mortal body must put on immortality. When the perishable puts on the imperishable, and the mortal puts on immortality, then shall come to pass the saying that is written: "Death is swallowed up in victory." (1 Cor. 15:51–54)

The biblical hope is the overcoming and "swallowing up" of even death itself. Death is neither normal nor natural.[13] We look forward to the new order of existence when death will be enveloped, consumed, and devoured by life. Just as everything in creation continually breaks down in this life—"moth and rust destroy" (Matt. 6.19)—so all things will continually rejuvenate after the day of the Lord. Creation itself will breathe *life*. The reason people long for perpetual progress (and delude themselves with an evolutionary perversion) is because we were actually made for perpetual and progressive regeneration: life, which gives birth to life, which gives birth to life, *ad infinitum*.[14]

Consequently, the new heavens and new earth will be a *restored paradise*. As Eden was paradisal in the beginning, so the earth will once again be paradisal (cf. Isa. 51:3; Rev. 2:7; 22:1–5).[15] From Jerusalem will flow "the river of the water of life" (Rev. 22:1), and "everything will live where the river goes" (Ezek. 47:9). It will be gloriously arboreal (cf. Ezek. 47:7,12), and the restored tree of life will bring "the healing of the nations" (Rev. 22:2; cf. Ezek. 47:12). A real tree of life on a real earth with real fruit will be one of the concrete mechanisms by which the old order of death will be overturned.

Moreover, the new earth will generate life holistically: morally, socially, and ecologically. It will have an atmosphere and culture in which everything is revitalized. Though the nature of this age is "predatory," so to speak, the age to come will be peaceable and nonaggressive, as Isaiah prophesies:

"Behold, I will create
  new heavens and a new earth.
The former things will not be remembered,
  nor will they come to mind. . . .
The wolf and the lamb will feed together,
  and the lion will eat straw like the ox,
  but dust will be the serpent's food.
They will neither harm nor destroy
  on all my holy mountain,"
    says the LORD.
(Isa. 65:17,25, NIV)

Because everything on the earth was put under the dominion of Adam (Gen. 1:26–28), the animals in this passage reflect the nature and character of humanity's righteous and peaceable government in the age to come.[16] Because of Adam's sin, fear and anxiety are normative for this age (see Gen. 3:7,10); but God will judge the earth, fill it with his glory, and restore it to its original shameless condition (see Gen. 2:25). Thus it will "feel" safe, protected, and secure, for "no longer will there be anything accursed" (Rev. 22:3).[17] This is the vision of the new heavens and the new earth set out in the Scriptures, as Isaiah describes:

> He shall strike the earth with the rod of his mouth,
>   and with the breath of his lips he shall kill the wicked.
> Righteousness shall be the belt of his waist,
>   and faithfulness the belt of his loins.
> The wolf shall dwell with the lamb,
>   and the leopard shall lie down with the young goat,
>   and the calf and the lion and the fattened calf together;
>   and a little child shall lead them.
> The cow and the bear shall graze;
>   their young shall lie down together;
>   and the lion shall eat straw like the ox.
> The nursing child shall play over the hole of the cobra,
>   and the weaned child shall put his hand on the adder's den.
> They shall not hurt or destroy
>   in all my holy mountain;
> for the earth shall be full of the knowledge of the LORD
>   as the waters cover the sea.
> (Isa. 11:4–9, NIV)

When God strikes the earth, the order of sin, death, and anxiety will be overturned, thus ushering in a universal "knowledge of the LORD." Such a hope for a new creation is succinctly articulated by Paul in Romans 8:18–24:

> For I consider that the sufferings of this present time are not worth comparing with *the glory that is to be revealed to us*. For the creation waits with eager longing for the revealing of the sons of God. For the creation was subjected to futility, not willingly, but because of him who subjected it, in hope that *the creation itself will be set free from its bondage to corruption* and obtain the freedom of the glory of the children of God. For we know that the whole creation has been groaning together in the pains of childbirth until now. And not only the creation, but we ourselves, who have the firstfruits of the Spirit, groan inwardly as we wait eagerly for adoption as sons, *the redemption of our bodies*. For in this hope we were saved.

The day of the Lord is the delineating event between "the sufferings of this present time" and "the glory that is to be revealed to us" (v. 18).[18] Though creation was subjected to death and futility because of the sin of Adam, it looks forward to being "set free from its bondage to corruption" (v. 21). Likewise, we look forward to the "redemption of our bodies" (v. 23) in the resurrection.

This is the biblical "hope" (v. 24) of salvation, which will come suddenly and dramatically—akin to "childbirth" (v. 22).

Based upon the character of God and the nature of redemptive history, the biblical writers naturally understood that God would restore what he made.[19] Because he is faithful, he will not give up on his creation. As my son often said when he was only three years old, "Jesus is coming back, and he will fix everything like it was in the beginning." Though exceedingly simplistic, this fundamental relationship between God and creation and redemptive history cannot be overstressed.[20] Its historical controversion has caused incalculable confusion, pain, and despair. Moreover, the incisive witness of the church has been blunted by a lack of emphasis on the severity of the day of the Lord concerning the punishment of all wickedness.

Biblical theology thus culminates in the day of the Lord, which exorcises sin from the heavens and from the earth, restoring to creation its original glory.[21] As such, the Bible is symmetrical—as it begins in Genesis, so it concludes in Revelation.[22] In the beginning there is the creation by the hand of God, the planting of the garden of Eden with the tree of life, the marriage of Adam and Eve, the victory of Satan through human sin, and the subsequent entrance of death and suffering. In the end, though, there is the new creation of God, the restoration of the garden of Eden with the tree of life, the marriage of Jesus (the "last Adam") and his bride (the redeemed), the overcoming of Satan through the final judgment upon human sin, and the subsequent eradication of death and suffering.[23]

In light of the biblical worldview of "the heavens and the earth" (Gen. 1:1), we look forward to God "making all things new" (Rev. 21:5) in hope of a "new heavens and a new earth" (2 Peter 3:13).[24] The Judeo-Christian faith is set within this broad structure. Protology and eschatology are not parts or aspects of biblical theology; they are, rather, the framework within which all theology is built.[25]

THE CENTRALITY OF THE DAY OF THE LORD

The day of the Lord is the principal event prophesied from Genesis to Revelation. Peter associates "the words spoken in the past by the holy prophets" (2 Peter 3:2, NRSV) with "the day of judgment" (v. 7)—that is, "the day of the Lord" (v. 10). It is ultimately concerning "the time for restoring all the things" that God "spoke by the mouth of his holy prophets long ago" (Acts 3:21). It is the day to which "all the prophets bear witness" (Acts 10:43), when Jesus will be appointed "judge of the living and the dead" (v. 42; cf. Acts 17:31).

To appreciate the centrality of the day of the Lord in the Scriptures, we must do a cursory survey of its appearance in both the Old and New Testaments.

The Day of the Lord in the Old Testament

The Old Testament goes into great detail concerning the day of the Lord. This day is described along royal, judicial, and economic lines, in accordance with the nature, character, and function of God's governance over the heavens and the earth.

The day of the Lord is characteristically *royal*, because God is "a great king over all the earth" (Ps. 47:2), "the living God and the everlasting King" (Jer. 10:10). He sits "enthroned as king forever" (Ps. 29:10), "a great King above all gods" (Ps. 95:3). The common usage of royal language throughout the Scriptures ("lord," "master," "throne," "dominion," "rule," etc.) is not metaphorical but literal. God really is a king, who truly sits enthroned over creation, with everything actually reporting to him. "For I am a great King, says the Lord of hosts, and my name will be feared among the nations" (Mal. 1:14). He rules, as does an earthly king (being created in his image), yet he rules in righteousness and integrity (cf. Ps. 89:14; 97:2; 145:17).

Because God is the great King, his day is ultimately concerned with "the glory due his name" (Ps. 29:2; 96:8). He is a real king who demands real honor and respect: "If I am a master, where is my fear?" (Mal. 1:6). Moreover, he seeks the absolute allegiance and loyalty of the nations: "To me every knee shall bow, every tongue shall swear allegiance" (Isa. 45:23). His name alone is to be exalted: "Be still, and know that I am God. I will be exalted among the nations, I will be exalted in the earth!" (Ps. 46:10). Service to other gods is considered utterly treasonous, and accordingly service to God Most High is the first commandment (Ex. 20:3; Deut. 5:7). To violate this order breaks down the very fabric of the cosmic hierarchy that ensures the well-being of creation.

The violation of God's royal honor is the ultimate source of divine anger and wrath. Being created in God's image, humans likewise get angry as a result of dishonor and disrespect. If someone, for example, rejects my authority in the workplace or curses me in front of others, I become angry because my dignity, honor, and value have been violated and disregarded. Similarly, God is quite displeased with the treachery of humanity's egotism and rebellion. We have broken his commands and "stirred him to jealousy with strange gods" (Deut. 32:16; cf. Ps. 78:58; Jer. 44:8). The "wrath," "fury," and "anger" of God pervade the entire corpus of the Old Testament.[26] For "the Lord is avenging and wrathful; the Lord takes vengeance on his adversaries and keeps wrath for his enemies" (Nah. 1:2). Thus God says, "I will satisfy my fury" (Ezek. 21:17); and "My anger will be spent and I will satisfy My wrath on them, and I will be appeased" (Ezek. 5:13, NASB).

Taken to its eschatological conclusion, the day of the Lord is therefore understood as the ultimate satisfaction of divine anger. It will be the "day of wrath" (Prov. 11:4; Zeph. 1:15), "the day of his wrath" (Ps. 110:5), and "the day of the wrath of the LORD" (Zeph. 1:18). "Behold, the day of the LORD comes, cruel, with wrath and fierce anger" (Isa. 13:9). It will be "the day of the anger of the Lord" (Zeph. 2:2; cf. Lam. 2:22)—"the day of his fierce anger" (Isa. 13:13; cf. Lam. 1:12). So the day of the Lord is understood in its royal context (see figure 3.3).

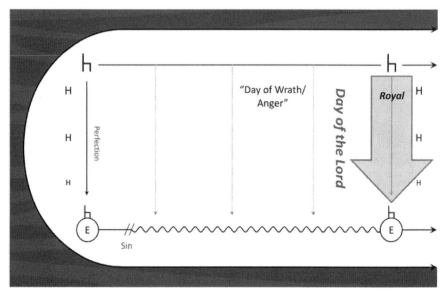

Figure 3.3 – The Royal Nature of the Day of the Lord

When the day of the Lord comes, God will "shatter kings on the day of his *wrath*" (Ps. 110:5). He will "speak to them in his *wrath*, and terrify them in his *fury*" (Ps. 2:5), for "the LORD is *enraged* against all the nations, and *furious* against all their host; he has devoted them to destruction, has given them over for slaughter" (Isa. 34:2). As the prophet Habakkuk foresaw, "You marched through the earth in *fury*; you threshed the nations in *anger*" (Hab. 3:12). So also Isaiah: "I have trodden down the peoples in my *anger*, made them drunk in my *fury*, and brought down their strength to the earth" (Isa. 63:6, NKJV). Jeremiah adds:

> Behold, the storm of the LORD!
> *Wrath* has gone forth,
>   a whirling tempest;
>   it will burst upon the head of the wicked.
> The *anger* of the LORD will not turn back

Until he has executed and accomplished
    the intents of his heart.
In the latter days you will understand it clearly.
(Jer. 23:19–20)

"According to what they have done, so will he repay *wrath* to his enemies and retribution to his foes" (Isa. 59:18, NIV). "For behold, the LORD will come in fire, and his chariots like the whirlwind, to render his *anger in fury*, and his rebuke with flames of fire" (Isa. 66:15). "And in *anger and wrath* I will execute vengeance on the nations that did not obey" (Mic. 5:15). So Isaiah describes:

Behold, the name of the LORD comes from afar,
    burning with his anger, and in thick rising smoke. . . .
to sift the nations with the sieve of destruction,
    and to place on the jaws of the peoples a bridle that leads astray. . . .
And the LORD will cause his majestic voice to be heard and the descending blow of his arm to be seen, in *furious anger* and a flame of devouring fire, with a cloudburst and storm and hailstones.
(Isa. 30:27–30)

Indeed the Lord holds "the cup of his *wrath*" (Isa. 51:17), and he will make all the nations drink "this cup of the wine of *wrath*" (Jer. 25:15). So the psalmist cries, "Pour out your *anger* on the nations that do not know you, and on the kingdoms that do not call upon your name!" (Ps. 79:6). And David: "On no account let them escape; in your *anger*, O God, bring down the nations" (Ps. 56:7, NIV). Likewise, "Your hand will find out all your enemies; your right hand will find out those who hate you. You will make them as a blazing oven when you appear. The LORD will swallow them up in his *wrath*, and fire will consume them" (Ps. 21:8–9). Though "the nations rage" (Ps. 2:1; 46:6), "The LORD laughs at the wicked, for he sees that their day is coming" (Ps. 37:13, NRSV).

When the day of the Lord comes, the proclamation will go out, "Say among the nations, 'The LORD reigns!'" (Ps. 96:10; cf. Ps. 93:1; 97:1; 99:1). And all the ends of the earth will "fear him" (Ps. 67:7), for righteous fear is the product of genuine honor. Thus, "Nations will *fear* the name of the LORD, and all the kings of the earth will *fear* your glory" (Ps. 102:15). The nations will finally declare, "It is the LORD your God you shall *fear*" (Deut. 6:13). In this way the kingship that God instituted at creation will be restored on the day of the Lord, and God will be rightly feared and honored.

The day of the Lord in the Old Testament is also characteristically *judicial*. Not only is God Most High a king, but "God is a righteous *judge*, and a God who feels indignation every day" (Ps. 7:11; cf. Ps. 50:6; 75:7). God is a real judge, not an ethereal principle or metaphor of justice. A real person rules over the heavens and the earth, and he really executes judgments. Moreover, he is really going to punish humanity's unrighteousness: "At the time I have planned, I will bring *justice* against the wicked" (Ps. 75:2, NLT).

Judgment is simply the means by which a standard of righteousness is set. So also the divine Judge will establish righteousness and justice upon the earth, as Isaiah says: "When your judgments come upon the earth, the people of the world learn righteousness" (Isa. 26:9, NIV). These judgments are in reference to Isaiah 24, when God punishes the powers in the heavens and the kings on the earth. Therefore the day of the Lord is understood as the ultimate day when God judges creation and sets right the sins of humankind (see figure 3.4).

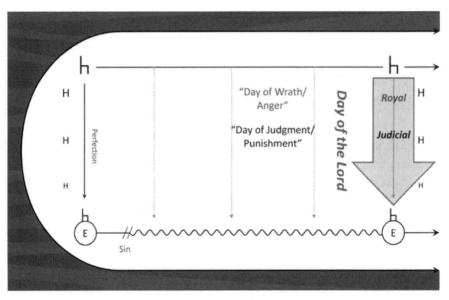

Figure 3.4 – The Judicial Nature of the Day of the Lord

God will then be vindicated in his gubernatorial role, for "he has established his throne for *judgment*" (Ps. 9:7, NRSV). "He will *judge* the world with righteousness" (Ps. 98:9). "He will *judge* the peoples with equity" (Ps. 96:10). "He will execute *judgment* among the nations" (Ps. 110:6), "for he comes to *judge* the earth" (Ps. 96:13). "By fire will the LORD enter into *judgment*, and by his sword, with all flesh; and those slain by the LORD shall be many" (Isa. 66:16; cf. Joel 3:2). Accordingly David cries, "Arise, O LORD! Let not man prevail; let the nations be *judged* before you!" (Ps. 9:19). And another psalmist, "Arise, O God, *judge* the earth; for you shall inherit all the nations!" (Ps. 82:8).

Judgment is also inherently based upon the transgression of a law, for laws are the standard by which judgment is executed. Thus God is a real lawgiver:

"For the LORD is our judge; the LORD is our *lawgiver*; the LORD is our king; he will save us" (Isa. 33:22; cf. James 4:12). He has a real law with real rules, precepts, and statues by which he judges the heavens and the earth. The Mosaic law given to Israel was understood as a temporal expression of the universal and eternal "law of God" (1 Cor. 9:21; cf. Rom. 7:22; Gal. 6:2).

Just as temporal judgments point to the eternal judgment, so also the temporal law pointed to the eternal law by which the earth will be judged (cf. Isa. 2:2–4; 42:1–4; 51:4–5; Mic. 4:1–3). Though the two are different—the former being accommodated to human depravity in historical context—there is an organic continuity between them, for "every one of your righteous rules endures forever" (Ps. 119:160; cf. Matt. 5:17–18). Hence the historical law is given as a "tutor" (Gal. 3:24, NASB), so as to "cultivate" righteousness (cf. Rom. 11:24)—as the psalmist says, "You guide me with your counsel, and afterward you will receive me to glory" (Ps. 73:24; cf. Ps. 25:8; 32:8). Consequently the divine law will go forth on the day of the Lord, judging the nations and establishing righteousness upon the earth. As Isaiah foresaw concerning the last days,

> Many peoples will come and say,
> "Come, let us go up to the mountain of the LORD,
>   to the house of the God of Jacob.
> He will teach us his ways,
>   so that we may walk in his paths."
> *The law will go out from Zion,*
>   the word of the LORD from Jerusalem.
> (Isa. 2:3 NIV)

> Listen to me, my people;
>   hear me, my nation:
> *The law will go out from me;*
>   my justice will become a light to the nations.
> My righteousness draws near speedily,
>   my salvation is on the way,
>   and my arm will bring justice to the nations.
> (Isa. 51:4–5, NIV)

Redemptive history thus has an undeniably penal aspect. The day of the Lord will be the ultimate "day of punishment" (Isa. 10:3; cf. Jer. 50:27).[27] "'The tumult will resound to the ends of the earth, for the LORD will bring *charges* against the nations; he will bring *judgment* on all mankind and put the wicked to the sword,' declares the LORD" (Jer. 25:31, NIV). It will be the climax of the "divine lawsuit" (Heb. *rîb*) against sinful humanity (cf. Isa. 3:13; Jer. 2:9;

Hos. 4:1; Mic. 6:2).[28] "The wickedness of the wicked will be *charged* against him" (Ezek. 18:20, NIV). The day of the Lord is thus presented as a great apocalyptic courtroom in which the divine judge will charge and punish the sins of humanity, restoring righteousness and establishing justice upon the earth.

So David prayed, "Rouse yourself to *punish* all the nations; spare none of those who treacherously plot evil" (Ps. 59:5). And "*Charge* them with crime upon crime; do not let them share in your salvation" (Ps. 69:27, NIV). Hence the punishment of wickedness is one of central facets of the day of the Lord, as Isaiah summarizes: "On that day the LORD will *punish* the host of heaven, in heaven, and the kings of the earth, on the earth. They will be gathered together as prisoners in a pit; they will be shut up in a prison, and after many days they will be *punished*" (Isa. 24:21–22).

Not only is the day of the Lord royal and judicial, but it is also characteristically *economic*. Humanity has done real damage to real things which have real value, and we really owe our Creator for it. The day of the Lord will dispense damages according to damages done. As such the judgment of the divine King is essentially retributive in nature (see figure 3.5).[29] It will be a day of recompense and retribution: "For the LORD is a God of *recompense*, He will fully *repay*" (Jer. 51:56, NASB). Therefore, "Woe to the wicked! Disaster is upon them! They will be *paid back* for what their hands have done" (Isa. 3:11, NIV). "For you *repay* to all according to their work" (Ps. 62:12, NRSV). Projected eschatologically, "The day of the LORD is near upon all the nations. As you have done, it shall be done to you; your deeds shall return on your own head" (Obad. 15). The earth will hear "the sound of the LORD, rendering *recompense* to his enemies!" (Isa. 66:6).

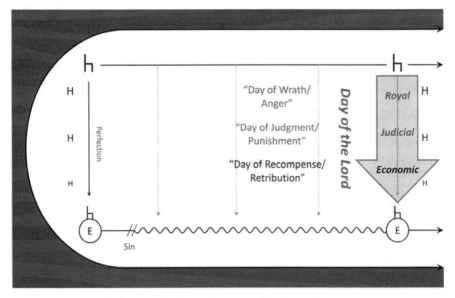

Figure 3.5 – The Economic Nature of the Day of the Lord

Considering that recompense is based upon judgment, the day of the Lord will be an eschatological application of the vengeful aspects of the law: "You shall *pay* life for life, eye for eye, tooth for tooth, hand for hand, foot for foot, burn for burn, wound for wound, stripe for stripe" (Ex. 21:23–24; cf. Deut. 19:21). In other words, "As [the offender] has done it shall be done to him, fracture for fracture, eye for eye, tooth for tooth; whatever injury he has given a person shall be given to him" (Lev. 24:19–20). Hence the psalmist cries, "O God of *vengeance*, shine forth! Rise up, O judge of the earth; *repay* to the proud what they deserve!" (Ps. 94:1–2).

Consequently the day of the Lord will be "the day of *vengeance* of our God" (Isa. 61:2). "For the LORD has a day of *vengeance*, a year of *recompense* for the cause of Zion" (Isa. 34:8). "Behold, your God will come with *vengeance*, with the *recompense* of God" (Isa. 35:4). Wearing "garments of *vengeance* for clothing," God will "*repay* wrath to his enemies and *retribution* to his foes" (Isa. 59:17–18, NIV). So the oracle from Isaiah:

> I stomped on them in my *anger*;
> I trampled them down in my *rage*. . . .
> For I looked forward to the day of *vengeance*,
> and then *payback* time arrived.
> I looked, but there was no one to help;
> I was shocked because there was no one offering support.
> So my right arm accomplished deliverance;
> my *raging anger* drove me on. I trampled nations in my *anger*,
> I made them drunk in my *rage*,
> I splashed their blood on the ground.
> (Isa. 63:3–6, NET)

This threefold classification of the day of the Lord is in simple accord with the nature of creation. Again, if someone smashes my car with a sledgehammer, I get *angry* because that person disrespected me and my bestowed right to own property. Then I press *charges* against him because we live in a land with laws to protect the dignity of life. And if I win the case, then he *repays* me according to the damages done to my car. So it is with God. He is angry concerning humankind's rebellion and the damages done to his creation. Therefore he is pressing charges against humanity for their crimes, and in the end he will make them pay, even with their very lives.

This presentation of the day of the Lord is generally in regard to human depravity, and as such it is highly *negative* in tone (one reason for its neglect in the theological tradition). However, for the righteous, whose sins are atoned for, this day is a positive hope (as outlined above). It will be the final deliverance from the evils of this age. Yet this hope must always be set in context of the gravity of human sinfulness and the substantial negativity associated with the day of the Lord. Thus the exhortation, "Work out your own salvation with fear and trembling . . . holding fast to the word of life, so that in the day of Christ I may be proud that I did not run in vain or labor in vain" (Phil. 2:12–16).

The Day of the Lord in the New Testament

The writers of the New Testament assume this theological framework within which history is envisioned as moving toward an apocalyptic day of the Lord, and which will then usher in a new heavens and new earth.[30] While the phrase "day of the Lord" is often used in full (Acts 2:20; 1 Cor. 5:5; 1 Thess. 5:2; 2 Thess. 2:2; 2 Peter 3:10), its reality is expressed through a variety of phrases: "the day of God" (2 Peter 3:12), "the great day" (Jude 6), "the day of eternity" (2 Peter 3:18), "the day of redemption" (Eph. 4:30), "the day of visitation" (1 Peter 2:12), "the last day" (John 6:39–40,44,54; 11:24; 12:48), "the day when the Son of Man is revealed" (Luke 17:30)—"the great day of God the Almighty" (Rev. 16:14).

Because "the Christ" is God's agent or viceroy, so to speak, the day of the Lord is understood to be "the day of Christ" (Phil. 1:10; 2:16). Thus God will bring his work "to completion at the day of Jesus Christ" (Phil. 1:6). He will sustain us "to the end, guiltless in the day of our Lord Jesus Christ" (1 Cor. 1:8); and we will boast in him "on the day of our Lord Jesus" (2 Cor. 1:14).[31] Because it is assumed that Jesus will initiate the day of the Lord, his "coming" (1 Cor. 15:23; 1 Thess. 3:13; 2 Thess. 2:1), "revealing" (1 Cor. 1:7; cf. 2 Thess. 1:7; 1 Peter 1:5), and "appearing" (1 Tim. 6:14; 2 Tim. 4:8; Titus 2:13) are the anchor of all New Testament "hope" (Rom. 5:2; Eph. 1:18; Col. 1:5).

The day of the Lord is so intrinsic to New Testament thought that it is simply referred to as "the day" or "that day."[32] Accordingly, Jesus said, "On *that day* many will say to me, 'Lord, Lord, . . .'" (Matt. 7:22); "I tell you I will not drink again of this fruit of the vine until *that day* when I drink it new with you in my Father's kingdom" (Matt. 26:29); "I tell you, it will be more bearable on *that day* for Sodom than for that town" (Luke 10:12); "But watch yourselves lest your hearts be weighed down with dissipation and drunkenness and cares of this life, and *that day* come upon you suddenly like a trap" (Luke 21:34).

Likewise, Paul commonly refers to the day of the Lord:

Each one's work will become manifest, for *the Day* will disclose it, because it will be revealed by fire, and the fire will test what sort of work each one has done. (1 Cor. 3:13)

This will take place on *the day* when God will judge men's secrets through Jesus Christ, as my gospel declares. (Rom. 2:16, NIV)

For you yourselves are fully aware that *the day of the Lord* will come like a thief in the night. . . . But you are not in darkness, brothers, for *that day* to surprise you like a thief. For you are all children of light, children of *the day*. (1 Thess. 5:2–5)

When he comes on *that day*, he will receive glory from his holy people—praise from all who believe. (2 Thess. 1:10, NLT)

Let no one deceive you in any way; for *that day* will not come unless the rebellion comes first and the lawless one is revealed, the one destined for destruction. (2 Thess. 2:3, NRSV)

I am convinced that he is able to guard until *that Day* what has been entrusted to me. (2 Tim. 1:12)

May the Lord grant that he will find mercy from the Lord on *that day*!" (2 Tim. 1:18, NIV)

Henceforth there is laid up for me the crown of righteousness, which the Lord, the righteous judge, will award to me on *that Day*, and not only to me but also to all who have loved his appearing. (2 Tim. 4:8)

Let us not give up meeting together, as some are in the habit of doing, but let us encourage one another—and all the more as you see *the Day* approaching. (Heb. 10:25, NIV)

Moreover, the day of the Lord was understood as redemptive history's ultimate "appointed time" (Gk. *kairos*).[33] So the demons shouted, "Have you come here to torment us before *the time*?" (Matt. 8:29). We are called to be watchful, for "you do not know when *the time* will come" (Mark 13:33). Many false Christs will come, claiming, "*The time* is at hand!" (Luke 21:8). Jesus told his disciples, "It is not for you to know *the times or dates* the Father has set by his own authority" (Acts 1:7, NIV). Paul relates these "times and dates" (1 Thess. 5:1, NIV) directly to "the day of the Lord" (v. 2).

Hence we see Paul instructing the Corinthians, "Therefore judge nothing before *the appointed time*; wait till the Lord comes" (1 Cor. 4:5, NIV). For when "*the times* will have reached their fulfillment," God will "bring all things in heaven and on earth together under one head, even Christ" (Eph. 1:10, NIV). We are to keep the good confession "without stain or reproach until the appearing of our Lord Jesus Christ, which He will bring about at *the proper time*" (1 Tim. 6:14–15, NASB). So we are being guarded by God's power "for a salvation ready to be revealed in *the last time*" (1 Peter 1:5). And concerning Jesus' "coming soon" (Rev. 22:12), "*the time* is near" (v. 10, cf. 1:3).

The New Testament carries over from the Old Testament the royal, judicial, and economic characteristics of the day of the Lord. It is "the day of wrath when God's righteous judgment will be revealed" (Rom. 2:5); "for those who are self-seeking and do not obey the truth, but obey unrighteousness, there will be wrath and fury" (v. 8). The wicked will cry out, "Fall on us and hide us from the face of him who is seated on the throne, and from the wrath of the Lamb, for the great day of their wrath has come, and who can stand?" (Rev. 6:17).

As such, the day of the Lord was commonly understood as the final context for "the wrath of God" (John 3:36; Rom. 1:18; 5:9; 12:19; Eph. 5:6; Col. 3:6; Rev. 14:19; 15:1; 19:15). For that reason, John the Baptist threatened the crowds, "You brood of vipers! Who warned you to flee from *the wrath to come?*" (Matt. 3:7). For all people are "by nature children of wrath" (Eph. 2:3), destined "to suffer wrath" (1 Thess. 5:9, NIV) on that day when God will "inflict wrath on us" (Rom. 3:5). On account of our sins, "the wrath of God is coming" (Col. 3:6). Nevertheless, Jesus "delivers us from the wrath to come" (1 Thess. 1:10). All of this was understood in its eschatological context.

Likewise, "the judgment of God" (Rom. 2:2–3; 2 Thess. 1:5) was believed to be ultimately expressed at "the day of judgment" (Matt. 10:15; 11:22,24; 12:36; 2 Peter 2:9; 3:7; 1 John 4:17). It is "the judgment of the great day" (Jude 6), for God "has set *a day* when he will judge the world with justice by the man he has appointed" (Acts 17:31, NIV). This concept was so commonly assumed that it was simply referred to as "the judgment" (Matt. 12:41–42; Luke 10:14; 11:31–32; Heb. 9:27; 2 Peter 2:4).

The day of the Lord is "the coming judgment" (Acts 24:25), or "eternal judgment" (Heb. 6:2), which will take place "on *the day* when God will judge men's secrets through Jesus Christ" (Rom. 2:16, NIV). It will be "the righteous judgment of God" (2 Thess. 1:5), when "the Lord Jesus is revealed from heaven with his mighty angels in flaming fire, inflicting *vengeance* on those who do not know God. . . . They will suffer the *punishment* of eternal destruction" (vv. 7–9). For the wicked are kept "unto the day of judgment to be punished" (2 Peter 2:9, KJV), and they will inherit "eternal punishment" (Matt. 25:46)— namely, "the punishment of eternal fire" (Jude 7). In this way "we will all stand before the judgment seat of God" (Rom. 14:10). "For we must all appear before the judgment seat of Christ, so that each one may receive what is due for what he has done in the body, whether good or evil" (2 Cor. 5:10).

As in the Old Testament, the judgment of God ends in recompense: "Behold, I am coming soon, bringing my *recompense* with me, to *repay* each one for what he has done" (Rev. 22:12). "For the Son of Man is going to come with his angels in the glory of his Father, and then he will *repay* each person according to what he has done" (Matt. 16:27). So Jesus analogizes the day of the

Lord: "Call the laborers and *pay them* their wages, beginning with the last, up to the first" (Matt. 20:8). The righteous will receive their wages in eternal life (John 4:36), for "each will receive his *wages* according to his labor" (1 Cor. 3:8). The wicked receive "the *wages* of sin" (Rom. 6:23), their recompense of eternal death, destruction, and punishment (cf. Matt. 25:46; Heb. 10:27; 2 Thess. 1:9): "Their destruction is their *reward* for the harm they have done" (2 Peter 2:13, NLT). "For after all it is only just for God to *repay* with affliction those who afflict you . . . dealing out *retribution* to those who do not know God and to those who do not obey the gospel of our Lord Jesus" (2 Thess. 1:6–8, NASB).

Thus God will take vengeance on his enemies (cf. Rom. 12:19; Heb. 10:30), for "on the day of wrath . . . he will *repay* according to each one's deeds: to those who by patiently doing good seek for glory and honor and immortality, he will give *eternal life*; while for those who are self-seeking and who obey not the truth but wickedness, there will be *wrath and fury* (Rom. 2:5–8, NRSV). From the unrepentant, God will demand restitution for damages done; and those who cannot pay the debt will pay with their very lives (cf. Matt. 18:25; Rev. 20:15).

The Unity of the Scriptures

The centrality of the day of the Lord is evident not only by the plethora of references, both Old Testament and New, but more importantly by the place it holds as a theological concept. It is literally *the end* of all biblical thought. The day of the Lord is that toward which everything is moving, and it is that to which everything is building.[34]

The most striking illustration of this belief is the use of the Greek alphabet as a metaphor describing redemptive history as a whole (cf. Rev. 1:8; 21:6; 22:13). Creation is portrayed as the first letter of the alphabet, *alpha* (α), while the day of the Lord and the restored creation is thought of as the last letter, *omega* (ω) (see figure 3.6). The Scriptures close with Jesus identifying himself as "the Alpha and the Omega" (Rev. 21:6; 22:13), because he is the primary agent anointed by the Father to restore the heavens and earth when he returns to initiate the day of the Lord.

It is therefore "the beginning and the end" (Rev. 21:6; 22:13) that define biblical history and biblical theology.[35] In the analogy of the alphabet, all of the letters ultimately find their meaning and significance in relation to the α and ω. How do you understand the λ, μ, and ν, apart from the α and ω? To marginalize the α and the ω as alphabetically secondary to the "central alphabetical letters," so to speak, throws the whole arrangement into a shambles. It is the beginning and the end that ultimately inform the whole of our existence, without which we are doomed to be "tossed to and fro by the waves and carried about by every wind of doctrine" (Eph. 4:14). This is why the Bible is so protologically based and eschatologically oriented.[36]

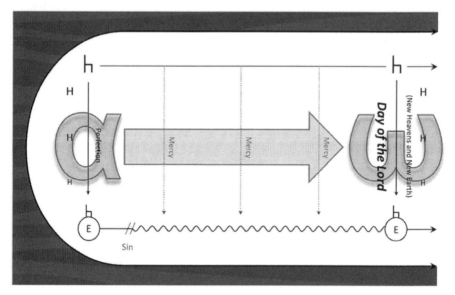

Figure 3.6 – Biblical Theology: Creation to Consummation

This framework gives us an "elementary" theological foundation (Heb. 6:1). It gives context for "the basic principles of the oracles of God" (Heb. 5:12). Returning to a soccer analogy, it is imperative to establish the players on a grass field (cf. the heavens and the earth), with soccer goals (cf. the new heavens and new earth), playing in the right direction (cf. the day of the Lord).[37] Such things are exceedingly elementary, but error concerning these most basic concepts leads to much confusion and grievous errors in the heat of the game.[38]

As the ultimate subject of the oracles of Scriptures and the defining event of redemptive history, the day of the Lord is thus the *theological linchpin* for interpreting all other biblical events and their redemptive implications (see figure 3.7).[39] All theologies have a linchpin, whether stated explicitly or implicitly.[40] Unfortunately, when the day of the Lord is removed or decentralized from its ultimate position, great theological disorder and disarray ensues.

In this way, the day of the Lord is also the primary *unifying reality* of the Scriptures. The Old and New Testaments speak the same message because they end in the same event. Consequently they hold to "the same hope" (Acts 24:15, NIV). They look forward to the same "new heavens and new earth." They believe in the same "resurrection of the dead." They expect the same "glory," the same "salvation," the same "inheritance," the same "kingdom," etc. The New Testament simply asserts that the Messiah had to suffer before entering his eschatological glory (cf. Luke 24:26; Acts 17:3; 1 Peter 1:11), bearing sin before bringing salvation (cf. Acts 3:18–21; Heb. 9:28), being set forward as a propitiation before the day of wrath (cf. Rom. 3:25; 1 John 2:2), providing justification in anticipation of the day of judgment (cf. Rom. 5:9; Titus 3:7), and offering redemption in light of the day of recompense (cf. Eph. 1:7; Col. 1:14).[41]

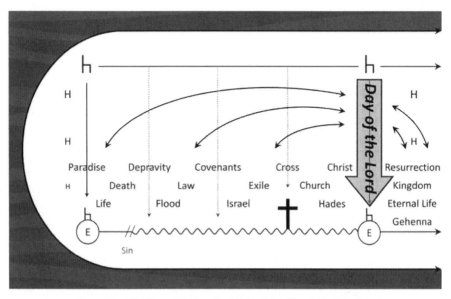

Figure 3.7 – The Day of the Lord as the Unifying Theological Linchpin

We can also observe a simple continuity with the testimony of the Law and Prophets (cf. Luke 24:27; Acts 10:43; Rom. 3:21), which foretold not only "the prize" of eternal life (1 Cor. 9:24; Phil. 3:14) but also the means of receiving that prize—the superior sacrifice and atonement of the new covenant, "poured out for many for the forgiveness of sins" (Matt. 26:28; cf. Acts 13:39). It is this "righteousness from God" (Phil. 3:9; cf. Rom. 10:3) that is discontinuous and sets the old covenant apart from the new (detailed in chapter 8). The eschatological hope which is "attained" by the new covenant is the same (cf. Rom. 9:30–33; Phil. 3:8–11; Heb. 9:15). The idea that the eschatology of the Old Testament was somehow spiritually fulfilled, actualized, or "realized" at the first coming finds precious little real evidence in the Scriptures.[42]

ASPECTS OF THIS AGE
VERSUS THE AGE TO COME

The reality of the day of the Lord inherently creates a *dichotomy of ages*. Because the day of the Lord radically changes so much concerning God, humanity, angels, demons, the heavens, the earth, etc., New Testament writers adopted the language of "this age" (Matt. 12:32; Luke 20:34; 1 Cor. 1:20; 2:6,8; 3:18; Eph. 1:21) versus "the age to come" (Matt. 12:32; Mark 10:30; Luke 18:30; Heb. 6:5).

The relationship between the day of the Lord and the two ages is seen in Jesus' condemnation of the Pharisees: "Anyone who speaks a word against the Son of Man will be forgiven, but anyone who speaks against the Holy Spirit will not be forgiven, either in this age or in the age to come. . . . I tell you that men will have to give account on the day of judgment for every careless word they have spoken" (Matt. 12:32–36, NIV).

It is "the day of judgment" that makes it necessary to speak of two ages. Without the day of the Lord, there is no reason to implement or retain such language.[43]

Time and Eternity

The two-age reality delineated by the day of the Lord assumes a simple *linear view of history*.[44] This age and the age to come lie on the same temporal continuum (see figure 3.8). Thus the same word is used in the New Testament (Gk. *aiōn*) concerning both this "age" and "eternity,"[45] which finds its root in the Old Testament (Heb. *'ôlām*) and is based upon creation's perpetuity (cf. Gen. 3:22; Ps. 78:69; 148:6; Ecc. 1:4; etc.).[46] "Forever" simply assumes the plural form of "age," and as such "eternity" is equivalent to "the coming ages" (Eph. 2:7).

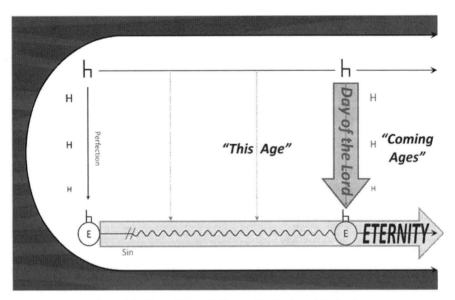

Figure 3.8 – Linear History Delineated by the Day of the Lord

Unlike the Hellenistic view of timeless eternity, we look forward to "an endless succession of ages."[47] The ungodliness of this age will soon come to an end, and God will establish righteousness in the heavens and on the earth "forever and ever" (Gal. 1:5; Eph. 3:21; Phil. 4:20; 1 Tim. 1:17; 2 Tim. 4:18; Heb. 13:21; 1 Peter 4:11; 5:11; Rev. 1:6; 14:11; 15:7; 19:3; 20:10; 22:5)—literally, "for ages and ages" (Gk. *tous aiōnas tōn aiōnōn*). Hence we long for the day when "the kingdom of the world has become the kingdom of our Lord and of his Christ, and he shall reign *forever and ever*" (Rev. 11:15).

This view of history is, above all, *simple*. There is no hidden meaning or agenda, perceptible only to the intellectual or spiritual elite. The biblical presentation of time and history is meant to be taken at face value for God is "patient with you, not wanting any to perish, but all to come to repentance" (2 Peter 3:9, NRSV). Consequently, the Scriptures—the fundamental means by which God communicates this message—must be understood easily by peasant and philosopher alike.

Though the particular elements of redemptive history (the cross, resurrection, holiness of God, depravity of man, etc.) may hold infinite depth, complexity, and mystery, redemptive history itself must remain universally apprehensible, or the very character of God in his governance is compromised. What judge seeks to punish lawlessness throughout the land yet speaks of the coming judgment only to university professors and the political elite? That would be ridiculous. The Bible speaks a simple linear history from creation to consummation that warns sinners of divine judgment and promises eternal life to the penitent.[48]

Linguistic Dichotomies

In light of the coming day, the New Testament develops a host of other phrases. The "present time" (Rom. 8:18), "present age" (1 Tim. 6:17; Titus 2:12; Heb. 9:9), and "present evil age" (Gal. 1:4) are all contrasted with the time and age after the day of the Lord. Moreover, "this life" (Luke 21:34; 1 Cor. 6:3; 15:19), "the present life" (1 Tim. 4:8), "this body" (Rom. 7:24; 2 Peter 1:13), "our lowly body" (Phil. 3:21), and "this perishable . . . mortal body" (1 Cor. 15:53) are contrasted with eternal life and the resurrected body given on the day of the Lord. Likewise, "this world" (Luke 16:8; John 18:36; Rom. 12:2; 1 Cor. 3:19; 5:10; 7:31; 2 Cor. 4:4; Eph. 2:2; 1 John 4:17) and "this present world" (2 Tim. 4:10) are understood in light of "the world to come" (Heb. 2:5).[49] Hence the implied timeline behind Jesus' injunction: "Whoever loves his life [in this age] loses it [in the age to come], and whoever hates his life in this world will keep it for eternal life" (John 12:25; cf. Luke 9:24 and parallels).

Similarly, the prominence of the day of Lord and the twofold chronological view of history gave birth to a wide range of *linguistic dichotomies* in the New Testament (see table 3.1). Such a wide range of temporally dualistic descriptions argues strongly for the apostolic retention of Jewish apocalypticism.

Table 3.1 – Various Linguistic Dichotomies Based upon the Day of the Lord

This Age	*Age to Come*	*References*
Night	Day	Rom. 13:12; 1 Thess. 5:2–8
Evil	Righteous	Gal. 1:4; Acts 2:40; 2 Peter 3:13
Death	Life	Rom. 5:17; 1 Cor. 15:21–22
Mortality	Immortality	Rom. 2:7; 1 Cor. 15:53
Perishable	Imperishable	1 Cor. 9:25; 15:42; 1 Peter 1:23
Suffering	Glory	Rom. 8:18; 2 Cor. 4:17
Not seeing	Appearing	2 Cor. 4:18; 1 Peter 1:7; 1 John 3:2
Time of exile	Time of restoring	Acts 3:21; 1 Peter 1:17
Sojourning	Ruling	1 Cor. 6:2; Heb. 11:13; Rev. 5:10
The world	The kingdom	John 18:36; James 2:5; Rev. 11:15
Things of the flesh	Things of the Spirit	Rom. 8:5; 1 Cor. 3:1
Treasures on earth	Treasures in heaven	Matt. 6:19; 19:21; Luke 16:11

The End of This Age

The two-age reality is also expressed in the phraseology of "the end of the age," referencing the end of *this* age. Consequently Jesus' disciples questioned, "Tell us, when will these things be, and what will be the sign of your coming and of the end of the age?" (Matt. 24:3). So also Jesus concludes their commissioning, "Behold, I am with you always, to the end of the age" (Matt. 28:20).[50] In explaining the parable of the weeds, Jesus likewise summarizes the close of this age, the day of the Lord, and the initiation of the age to come:

> The harvest is the end of the age, and the reapers are angels. Just as the weeds are gathered and burned with fire, so will it be at the end of the age. The Son of Man will send his angels, and they will gather out of his kingdom all causes of sin and all law-breakers, and throw them into the fiery furnace. In that place there will be weeping and gnashing of teeth. Then the righteous will shine like the sun in the kingdom of their Father. (Matt. 13:39–43)

So commonly understood was the apocalyptic framework of redemptive history that the end of this age was simply referred to as "the end." Thus Jesus answers his disciples' question concerning the timing of "the end of the age" (Matt. 24:3): "This gospel of the kingdom will be proclaimed throughout the whole world as a testimony to all nations, and then *the end* will come" (Matt. 24:14). For "the one who endures to *the end* will be saved" (v. 13; cf. Matt. 10:22). And "to him who overcomes and does my will to *the end*, I will give authority over the nations" (Rev. 2:26, NIV).

Therefore the apostles pressed toward the day of the Lord and the end of this age like "those who run in a race" (1 Cor. 9:24, NASB; cf. Heb. 12:1), pressing on "toward the goal" (Phil. 3:14) of the resurrection and eternal life. Hence Paul exhorts the Corinthians to seek the gifts of the Spirit, "as you wait for the revealing of our Lord Jesus Christ, who will sustain you to *the end*, guiltless in the day of our Lord Jesus Christ" (1 Cor. 1:7–8). So also Peter: "*The end* of all things is at hand; therefore be self-controlled and sober-minded for the sake of your prayers" (1 Peter 4:7).[51] And the writer of Hebrews: "For we have come to share in Christ, if indeed we hold our original confidence firm to *the end*" (Heb. 3:14). And "We desire each one of you to show the same earnestness to have the full assurance of hope until *the end*, so that you may not be sluggish, but imitators of those who through faith and patience inherit the promises" (Heb. 6:11–12).

The apocalyptic nature of the Scriptures is further exemplified in the use of *fire* as the means of ending this age. As everything was created in the beginning "out of water and by means of water" (2 Peter 3:5, NRSV), so also will everything be cleansed at the end of this age "by a spirit of judgment and by a spirit of *burning*" (Isa. 4:4). Water is the medium of creation, but fire is the medium of destruction.[52] "For behold, the day is coming, *burning* like an oven, when all the arrogant and all evildoers will be stubble. The day that is coming shall set them *ablaze*, says the LORD of hosts, so that it will leave them neither root nor branch" (Mal. 4:1). So David foresaw,

> Your hand will lay hold on all your enemies;
>> your right hand will seize your foes.
> At the time of your appearing
>> you will make them like a *fiery furnace*.
> In his wrath the LORD will swallow them up,
>> and *his fire* will consume them.
> You will destroy their descendants from the earth,
>> their posterity from mankind.
> (Ps. 21:8–10, NIV)

The day of the Lord will be executed with fire because God himself is a "consuming fire" (Deut. 4:24; 9:3; Isa. 33:14; Heb. 12:29). Accordingly the Lord will descend from heaven "in furious anger and a flame of devouring *fire*"

(Isa. 30:30), for "*fire* goes before him and burns up his adversaries all around" (Ps. 97:3; cf. Ps. 50:3). On "the day of the LORD's wrath . . . all the earth will be devoured in the *fire* of His jealousy" (Zeph. 1:18, NASB), for God's "wrath is poured out like *fire*" (Nah. 1:6). Though humanity labors to build great empires in this age, "the people's labor is only fuel for the *fire*" (Hab. 2:13, NIV). "They are like stubble; the *fire* consumes them" (Isa. 47:14). As Isaiah envisioned,

> See, the LORD is coming with *fire*,
>   and his chariots are like a whirlwind;
> he will bring down his anger with fury,
>   and his rebuke with flames of *fire*.
> For with *fire* and with his sword
>   the LORD will execute judgment upon all men,
>   and many will be those slain by the LORD.
> (Isa. 66:15–16, NIV)

The New Testament amplifies the idea that God will conclude this age with fire. The Gospels introduce John the Baptist warning the people of Israel about "the wrath to come" (Luke 3:7). Those who do not repent will be "thrown into the *fire*" (v. 9), for the Messiah will come and "burn up the chaff with unquenchable *fire*" (v. 17, NASB; cf. Isa. 66:24).[53] Likewise Jesus warns the crowds concerning "that day" (Matt. 7:22): "Every tree that does not bear good fruit is cut down and thrown into the *fire*" (v. 19). Peter proclaims that "the present heavens and earth are being reserved for *fire*, kept for the day of judgment and destruction of ungodly men" (2 Peter 3:7, NASB).[54] Paul adds, "Each one's work will become manifest, for the Day will disclose it, because it will be revealed by *fire*, and the *fire* will test what sort of work each one has done" (1 Cor. 3:13).

This age will end when Jesus appears "in flaming *fire*, inflicting vengeance on those who do not know God" (2 Thess. 1:8). For "as the weeds are gathered and burned with *fire*, so will it be at the end of the age" (Matt. 13:40). The unrepentant have "only a fearful expectation of judgment and of raging *fire* that will consume the enemies of God" (Heb. 10:27, NIV). Jesus warned, "If anyone does not abide in me he is thrown away like a branch and withers; and the branches are gathered, thrown into the *fire*, and burned" (John 15:6). "In the end [they] will be *burned*" (Heb. 6:8, NIV). Evangelism is thus pictured as "snatching [people] out of the *fire*" (Jude 23).

Gehenna and Hades

The language of fire in relation to the day of the Lord is also understood quite *literally*. Real fire will actually burn real people because of real damages done to a real creation which holds real value. Moreover, the real fire will culminate in a real place called "Gehenna," Gk. *gehenna* (Matt. 5:22,29,30; 10:28; 18:9; 23:15,33; Mark 9:43,45,47; Luke 12:5). Gehenna is simply a valley outside of Jerusalem, "currently known as the Wadi er-Rababeh, running S-SW of Jerusalem and also a designation for fiery hell, the opposite of the dominion of God and eternal life."[55] It is known in the Old Testament as the "Valley of Hinnom," Heb. *gê hinnōm* (Josh. 15:8; 18:16; cf. 2 Kings 23:10; 2 Chron. 28:3; 33:6; Neh. 11:30; Jer. 7:31–32; 19:2,6; 32:35), which God will fill with fire, hence turning it into a "lake of fire" (Rev. 19:20; 20:10,14; 21:8).[56]

Isaiah clearly prophesies this relationship:

> The LORD will cause men to hear his majestic voice
> and will make them see his arm coming down
> with raging anger and consuming fire,
> with cloudburst, thunderstorm and hail. . . .
> *Topheth* has long been prepared;
> it has been made ready for the king.
> Its *fire pit* has been made deep and wide,
> with an abundance of fire and wood;
> the breath of the LORD,
> like a stream of *burning sulfur*,
> sets it ablaze.
> (Isa. 30:30,33, NIV)

Topheth is a place within the Valley of Hinnom (cf. 2 Kings 23:10; Jer. 7:31–32; 19:6–14), which Jeremiah prophesied would become "the Valley of Slaughter" (7:32; 19:6).[57] Since these prophecies did not find fulfillment during the exile, the Jews projected them eschatologically during intertestamental times.[58] In Jesus' day it was commonly understood that the Valley of Hinnom (Gehenna) was to be the actual location and *embodiment* of God's final judgment. Thus tradition holds that the valley became for the city of Jerusalem the common receptacle of trash, refuse, and the bodies of dead animals and criminals—kept ever-burning as a sign of the age to come, in keeping with the oracles of God.[59] They were simply stewarding the valley according to its destiny.

Therefore Jesus always speaks of Gehenna as a future reality: "You snakes! You brood of vipers! How will you escape being condemned to *hell* [Gk. *gehenna*]?" (Matt. 23:33, NIV). "And if your hand causes you to sin, cut it off. It is better for you to enter life crippled than with two hands to go to *hell* [Gk. *gehenna*], to the unquenchable fire" (Mark 9:43). This "unquenchable fire" is a reference to the vision of Isaiah, who saw Jerusalem in the age to come. At that time the wicked will be cast outside of the city, and "their worm will not die and their fire will not be quenched; and they will be an abhorrence to all mankind" (Isa. 66:24, NASB).

Gehenna will also be "the furnace of fire, where there will be weeping and gnashing of teeth" (Matt. 13:42,50, NRSV), drawing from the furnace/oven imagery of the prophets (Isa. 31:9; Mal. 4:1; cf. Ps. 21:9). Though this furnace consists of fire, it will be completely enclosed, creating "utter darkness" (2 Peter 2:17; Jude 13). This darkness will be in stark contrast to the brilliant glory of Jerusalem in the age to come (cf. Isa. 60; Rev. 21:23–26), which is understood as the backdrop to "the outer darkness" (Matt. 8:12; 22:13; 25:30). For the righteous will "enter the city by the gates" (Rev. 22:14), but "*outside* are the dogs and sorcerers and the sexually immoral and murderers and idolaters, and everyone who loves and practices falsehood" (v. 15).

The fires of this furnace will also go on *forever*. As Jesus plainly said, "Then [the King] will say to those on his left, 'Depart from me, you cursed, into the *eternal* fire prepared for the devil and his angels'" (Matt. 25:41; cf. Matt. 18:8). Sodom and Gomorrah "serve as an example of those who suffer the punishment of *eternal* fire" (Jude 7, NIV). So the eternal fire will be in accord with eternal punishment (Matt. 25:46), eternal judgment (Heb. 6:2), eternal destruction (2 Thess. 1:9), and eternal torment (Rev. 14:11).[60] Though experiencing a "second death" (Rev. 2:11; 20:6; 20:14; 21:8), unbelievers will never cease to exist, for "they will be tormented day and night forever and ever" (Rev. 20:10).[61]

This torment will be endured eternally because the wicked, like the righteous, will be given resurrected bodies that never die. It will be "a resurrection of both the righteous and the wicked" (Acts 24:15, NASB; cf. Dan. 12:2)—that is, "the resurrection of life" and "the resurrection of judgment" (John 5:29). The wicked will endure eternal death in a resurrected body, while the righteous will enjoy eternal life in a resurrected body. In this way the pain, suffering, and condemnation of the wrath of God will be experienced to its fullest. Thus the fearful injunction of Jesus: "Do not fear those who kill the body but cannot kill the soul; rather fear him who can destroy both soul and body in hell (Gk. *gehenna*)" (Matt. 10:28, NRSV).[62]

Such a corporeal torment is far more terrible than common Platonic notions of incorporeal, ethereal fire. It is *bad news* of the highest order, which consequently heightens the impact of the "good news" of salvation. The greatness of God's severity in Gehenna must be the backdrop for the greatness of God's kindness in the cross; otherwise both are mitigated unto mediocrity. Modern views concerning the severity of divine punishment can be depicted on a spectrum, with unhappiness in this life on one end and eternal bodily torment on the other—with annihilationism, transitional purgatory, and eternal spiritual punishment lying in between (see figure 3.9). It seems clear that only eternal corporeal punishment does justice to both human depravity and the biblical gospel.

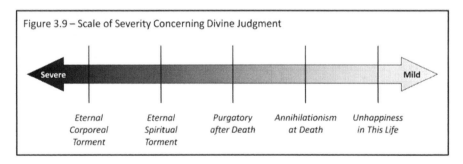

Figure 3.9 – Scale of Severity Concerning Divine Judgment

Severe — Mild

| Eternal Corporeal Torment | Eternal Spiritual Torment | Purgatory after Death | Annihilationism at Death | Unhappiness in This Life |

The day of the Lord will come with fire—a fire that consumes the heavens and the earth and continues on eternally outside of Jerusalem in Gehenna. This is the "literal view" of hell.[63] In this way, God will finally "destroy those who destroy the earth" (Rev. 11:18, NASB). Infinite recompense for infinite damages done.

Those who complain about the severity of the wrath of God simply misunderstand the gravity of human sin. In the beginning creation was deemed "very good" in the sight of God (Gen. 1:31). Human beings brought in every kind of death, pain, suffering, corruption, and perversion. Human beings have done infinite damage to what God created—not only environmentally, but also to the very image of God. As the pinnacle of creation, human beings are of greater worth in the sight of God than anything else (cf. Matt. 6:26; 12:12). Therefore to sin against and pervert the image of God by theft, murder, fornication, etc. is of infinite consequence *in the sight of God*.

Consider two identical cars. One was built on an assembly line in China; the other was built by my own hands in my own garage. Which has more value? To a third-party observer, they are equal. But, in my eyes, there is no comparison. The one I built, pouring my heart and soul into it, is of incomparable worth. Likewise, humanity is fundamentally delusional about the gravity of sin because it lacks a *divine perspective* of the value of human life.[64] Because we are not the ones who poured our very being into creation, designing its apex in our own "image," we have no appreciation for the incomparable worth of a human being in the sight of God and the immeasurable damage done by our sin. It is literally infinite.

So God has chosen *eternal proportionate retribution* as the means of righting the wrong of human sin—damage for damage, pain for pain, suffering for suffering. God himself, in the words of Alva J. McClain, "is the King of hell,"[65] and he will conclude his judgment upon the sin of humankind by literally embodying it forever in a lake of fire (see figure 3.10). In this way God will be eternally vindicated, and all of redeemed humanity will echo the praise of the angel in charge of the waters: "Just are you, O Holy One, who is and who was, for you brought these judgments. For they have shed the blood of saints and prophets, and you have given them blood to drink. It is what they deserve!" (Rev. 16:5–6).[66]

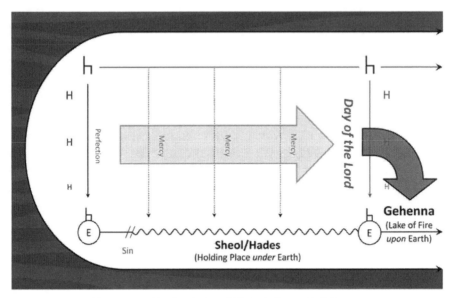

Figure 3.10 – The Conclusion of Divine Judgment in Gehenna

Consequently, in New Testament thought Gehenna "is always in the background, even when the word is not actually present."[67] It is the concrete context of the day of the Lord and the wrath of God. You cannot hold to a theology of new creation without the day of the Lord and Gehenna as its practical *mechanism* and *outworking*, respectively. Using bodily cleansing as an analogy, we could say that it is impossible to attain to the reality of cleanliness (cf. new heavens and earth) without real defecation (cf. day of the Lord) and an actual toilet (cf. Gehenna). Perversion at any of these three points ends in malodor, which indeed often permeates the halls of the modern church.

As seen in figure 3.10, a distinction must be made between Gehenna and Hades (Greek *hadēs*), which translates the Hebrew *sheol* in the Septuagint. Unfortunately, historical English translations use the same word, "hell," to translate both.[68] However, the two terms are mutually exclusive. Hades, or Sheol, is a *temporal* reality that exists *under* the earth as a holding place awaiting the day of the Lord.[69] Gehenna is an *eternal* reality that exists *upon* the earth after the day of the Lord. Nowhere in the Scriptures is Gehenna a present reality; it is only eschatological. Conversely, nowhere is Hades an eternal reality; it is only temporal.[70] Hades itself will be "thrown into the lake of fire" (Rev. 20:14; cf. 2 Peter 2:4; Jude 6).

As with Gehenna, the Bible describes Hades in a variety of ways. Moreover, different areas of Hades are referenced. Generally, Hades is described as the abode of the dead (e.g., Job 21:13; Ps. 9:17; 31:17; 89:48; Eccl. 9:10).[71] It is "under the earth" (Gk. *hupokatō tēs gēs*, cf. Rev. 5:3,13)—that is, "subterranean" (Gk. *katachthonios*, cf. Phil. 2:10). It is in the "lower parts of the earth" (Gk. *katōteros/katōtatos tēs gēs*, cf. Ps. 63:9; 86:13; 88:6; 139:15; Eph. 4:9). It is the "deep" or "depths" (Gk. *bathos/bothros*, cf. Ps. 69:15; 130:1; Isa. 7:11; Ezek. 26:20; 31:14; 32:21–23; Rom. 8:39). Hades is also a "destruction, corruption pit" (Gk. *diaphthora*, cf. Job 33:28; Ps. 16:10; 55:23; Acts 2:27,31; 13:34–36), and it is the "death [place]" (Gk. *thanatos*, cf. Ps. 18:4–5; 116:3; Acts 2:24; Rev. 1:18; 20:13).[72] It is so deep that it is depicted as bottomless, and thus it is referred to as an "abyss" (Gk. *abussos*, e.g., Ps. 71:20; 135:6; Ezek. 31:15; Luke 8:31; Rom. 10:7; Rev. 9:1, 20:1–3), and its lowest levels (Gk. *tartaros*, cf. 2 Peter 2:4) are reserved for Satan and his angels.[73] All of these references are to the same present reality under the earth, and they are clearly distinguished from the future reality of Gehenna upon the earth.[74]

Out of this discussion immediately rises the question of temporal destiny— Where do we go when we die in this age?[75] The answer is contingent upon whether the person asking the question is righteous or unrighteous. Clearly there are unrighteous souls presently held in Hades, since they are raised up and judged in the future (cf. 2 Peter 2:9; Jude 6; Rev. 20:13).[76] The righteous are also clearly held in Hades in the Old Testament (cf. Gen. 37:35; 1 Sam. 28:13–15; 1 Kings 2:2; Ps. 16:10; 49:15).[77] In the New Testament, however, it seems the righteous are kept in the presence of the Lord (cf. 2 Cor. 5:8; Phil. 1:23; Rev. 6:9), where Jesus sits at the right hand of the Father in the height of the heavens until his descension, at which time the righteous will inherit eternal life in the resurrection (cf. 1 Cor. 15:51; 1 Thess. 4:16).

What then accounts for the change between the Old Testament and New Testament? Precisely the *new covenant*, which is enacted through the mediation of Jesus in the heavenly sanctuary (cf. Heb. 8:1–6; 9:10–12,23–26; 10:12–14). This made it possible for the righteous to tarry with the Lord until the resurrection. As the offering of blood by the priests under the Mosaic covenant made it possible for sinful humans to dwell in the presence of the Lord in the earthly sanctuary, so also did the offering of the blood of the new covenant make it possible for sinful humans to dwell in the presence of the Lord in the heavenly sanctuary.

This helps explain numerous New Testament oddities, such as when Jesus "descended into the lower parts of the earth" (Eph. 4:9, NASB), where he "preached to the spirits in prison" (1 Peter 3:19, NIV), and where "the gospel was preached even to those who are dead" (1 Peter 4:6). Moreover, in his ascension "he led captives in his train" (Eph. 4:8, NIV), who also seem to have gone "into the holy city and appeared to many" (Matt. 27:53). Thus, after the cross believers will rest with the Lord while they await the resurrection, but unbelievers will be held in Hades until the day of judgment.

THE NATURE AND CHARACTER OF THIS AGE

The events of the day of the Lord so radically change the nature and character of redemptive history that the apocalyptic language of "this age" versus "the age to come" is necessary to describe life before and after the day. This age involves a fallen order of unrighteousness. The age to come involves a new order of righteousness, both in the heavens and upon the earth. This age involves suffering, sickness, and death—the age to come involves happiness, health, and life. This age involves wickedness, corruption, and evil—the age to come involves righteousness, integrity, and goodness. This age involves divine patience, forbearance, and kindness—the age to come involves "the day of wrath when God's righteous judgment will be revealed" (Rom. 2:5). Hence the age to come is essentially characterized as a reversal of this age.

This Age and Divine Mercy

Such a stark dichotomy of ages ultimately derives from the radical dissimilarity between the nature of God in loving holiness and the nature of humanity in selfish depravity. These contrasting characteristics create the framework for how God relates to humanity in this age. As such, the primary theme of this age is divine "mercy" (see figure 3.11). This age is an age of mercy because God himself is "merciful and gracious" (Ex. 34:6; Ps. 86:15; 103:8)—"For the LORD your God is a merciful God" (Deut. 4:31). "To the Lord our God belong mercy and forgiveness" (Dan. 9:9), and "he exalts himself to show mercy to you" (Isa. 30:18).

The fundamental reason the day of the Lord has not arrived is because of divine mercy: "The Lord is not slow about his promise, as some think of slowness, but is patient with you, not wanting any to perish, but all to come to repentance" (2 Peter 3:9, NRSV). First-century Judaism had lost touch with this ultimate divine agenda, and so Jesus corrected the Pharisees: "Go and learn what this means, 'I desire mercy, and not sacrifice.' For I came not to call the righteous, but sinners" (Matt. 9:13). As such, Jesus embodied the purpose of God in this age: "For the Son of Man came to seek and to save the lost" (Luke 19:10).

Consequently Jesus exhorted his disciples to be merciful, as God is in this age, so that they might inherit the reward of eternal life in the age to come: "But love your enemies, and do good, and lend, expecting nothing in return, and your reward will be great, and you will be sons of the Most High, for he is kind to the ungrateful and the evil. Be merciful, even as your Father is merciful" (Luke 6:35–36).

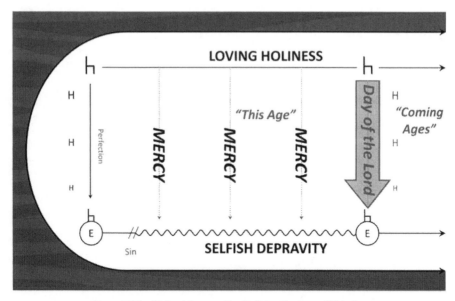

Figure 3.11 – Divine Mercy as the Defining Feature of This Age

Paul described his own life in such terms: "I was shown mercy so that in me, the worst of sinners, Christ Jesus might display his unlimited patience as an example for those who would believe on him and receive eternal life" (1 Tim. 1:16, NIV). He likewise described his ministry within the divine framework of mercy: "God was in Christ reconciling the world to Himself, not counting their trespasses against them, and He has committed to us the word of reconciliation" (2 Cor. 5:19, NASB).

God is forgiving people's sins in this age because of "the riches of his kindness and forbearance and patience" (Rom. 2:4). "In him we have redemption through his blood, the forgiveness of our trespasses, according to the riches of his grace" (Eph. 1:7).[78] This age generally entails God's "divine forbearance" (Rom. 3:25) and the restraint of divine justice. So Paul outlines the cross in anticipation of the age to come:

> But when the goodness and loving kindness of God our Savior appeared, he saved us, not because of works done by us in righteousness, but *according to his own mercy,* by the washing of regeneration and renewal of the Holy Spirit, whom he poured out on us richly through Jesus Christ our Savior, so that being justified by his grace we might become heirs *according to the hope of eternal life.* (Titus 3:4–7)

Thus God, "being rich in mercy" (Eph. 2:4), saved us from the wrath to come, "in order that in the coming ages he might show the incomparable riches of his grace, expressed in his kindness to us in Christ Jesus" (Eph. 2:7, NIV). So also Paul relates the broad movements of God in relation to both Jew and Gentile:

> For just as you were at one time disobedient to God but now have *received mercy* because of their disobedience, so they too have now been disobedient in order that by the mercy shown to you they also may now *receive mercy*. For God has consigned all to disobedience, *that he may have mercy on all*. (Rom. 11:30–32)

Unless we have such a "view of God's mercy" (Rom. 12:1, NIV), we are doomed to live according to "the pattern of this age" (v. 2, AT).[79] The renewing of our minds rests upon an apocalyptic understanding of redemptive history in which the kindness of God expressed in this age will be followed by the severity of God to be expressed at the day of the Lord.

This Age Epitomized by the Cross

The event of the cross is understood as the supreme demonstration of divine love and mercy. It is the epitome of God's dealings with humanity in this age. Thus John describes, "God's love was revealed among us *in this way*: God sent his only Son into the world so that we might live through him" (1 John 4:9, NRSV). Likewise Paul: "For in him all the fullness of God was pleased to dwell, and through him to reconcile to himself all things, whether on earth or in heaven, making peace *by the blood of his cross*" (Col. 1:19–20).

Since the cross typifies the acts of God in this age, we might describe this age as "cruciform," meaning "shaped like a cross."[80] The cross substantially represents how God relates to humanity, from the sin of Adam until the day of the Lord. So Paul summarizes redemptive history, "As one trespass led to condemnation for all men, so one act of righteousness leads to justification and life for all men" (Rom. 5:18). In other words, the sin of Adam and the act of the cross ultimately define all interactions between God and humanity, from creation to the day of the Lord and the inheritance of "eternal life" (v. 21).

Such a cruciform view of this age also lies behind Peter's declaration that the sacrificing of the Messiah "was foreknown before the foundation of the world" (1 Peter 1:20), a theme echoed throughout the New Testament (cf. Rom. 16:25; Eph. 1:4; 3:9; Col. 1:26; 2 Tim. 1:9; Titus 1:2; Rev. 13:8). God's foreknowledge of the cross represents his merciful nature and the merciful manner in which he has always related to humanity. Of course, this cruciform foreknowledge is understood within the apocalyptic context of "the revelation of Jesus Christ" (1 Peter 1:13) and "the day of visitation" (2:12).

In this way, the theology of the Bible is best summarized as *cruciform-apocalypticism* (see figure 3.12). In anticipation of the cataclysmic day of the

Lord, God is relating to humanity in this age according to mercy, as exemplified by the cross. Though some argue that apocalypticism is not a suitable theological environment for the cross,[81] we find just the opposite to be true. The cross finds its cruciality in the context of the day of the Lord.[82] (The interpretation of the cross in sacrificial and atonemental terms will be discussed in detail in chapters 7 and 8). Moreover, the hope of the cross for righteousness and the day of the Lord for salvation exemplify *faith in God alone*, rejecting as anathema all forms of "confidence in the flesh" (Phil. 3:3).[83] God will right the wrongs of humanity, without regard to the strength of human beings.

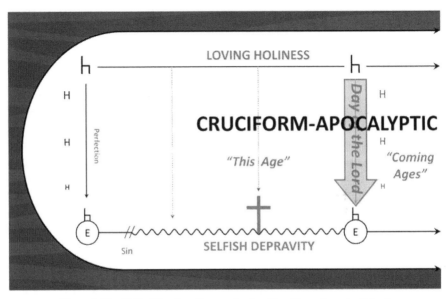

Figure 3.12 – Biblical Theology Summarized as "Cruciform-Apocalypticism"

This approach is simple and straightforward, and it best reflects the general tenor of both Old and New Testament writings. God is showing mercy to sinners before the great day of his wrath, as Paul summarizes: "God demonstrates His own love toward us, in that while we were yet sinners, *Christ died for us*. Much more then, having now been justified by His blood, we shall be *saved from the wrath of God* through Him" (Rom. 5:8–9, NASB). Likewise, we understand, as Luther put it, "the gospel in a nutshell": "For God so loved the world, that he *gave his only Son*, that whoever believes in him should not perish but *have eternal life*" (John 3:16).[84]

If we ask, What is God ultimately doing in this age? then we must answer: He is showing love and offering mercy to his enemies, in light of his coming severity and eternal recompense. Redemptive history is cruciform-apocalyptic, and consequently the mission of the church is simply to "proclaim the Lord's death until he comes" (1 Cor. 11:26).

Temporal versus Eternal Recompense

If this age is so clearly characterized by the restraint of divine justice, then how do we interpret the activity of God *before* the day of the Lord? There are clearly blessings and punishments in this age that are personally administrated by God. Indeed, God does presently punish the wicked (e.g., Ex. 34:7; Deut. 28:15–68; Hos. 8:13). "God is a righteous judge, and a God who feels indignation every day" (Ps. 7:11).

We might describe the divine judgments of this age as "temporal," in contrast to the "eternal" judgment of the age to come. In this way, temporal judgments are never in true accord with what the sins of humanity deserve. "If you, O LORD, kept a record of sins, O Lord, who could stand?" (Ps. 130:3, NIV). In truth, God does keep a record, and this is the psalmist's point. Every human being deserves proportionate retribution—an eternal, corporeal lake of fire—but in this age God's judgment is restrained out of divine mercy. Thus all temporal judgments are actually inherently merciful by nature.

As such, those who lose their homes to fires, earthquakes, and tsunamis are *fortunate* because they are not in a lake of fire. Those who struggle under the oppression of tyrannical regimes are *fortunate* because they are not in a lake of fire. Those who know God and know their own depravity endure all kinds of trial and difficulty, interpreting them as "discipline" from the Lord (Heb. 12:7; cf. Deut. 8:5), because they know they are *fortunate* not to be in a lake of fire. In the end, mercy is the only game being played in this age. So even when bad things happen, they are ultimately designed to point us to the day of judgment and lead us to repentance. Jesus makes this point vividly when speaking about death in this age:

> About this time Jesus was informed that Pilate had murdered some people from Galilee as they were offering sacrifices at the Temple. "Do you think those Galileans were worse sinners than all the other people from Galilee?" Jesus asked. "Is that why they suffered? Not at all! And *you will perish, too, unless you repent of your sins and turn to God.* And what about the eighteen people who died when the tower in Siloam fell on them? Were they the worst sinners in Jerusalem? No, and I tell you again that *unless you repent, you will perish, too.*" (Luke 13:1–5, NLT)

The indictment of the immorality of "that woman Jezebel" also demonstrates this reality (Rev. 2:20–23). The "Son of God" (v. 18) will in this life "strike her children dead," so that at the day of the Lord all the churches will know that he will "give to each of you according to your works" (v. 23). Moreover, the judgments of Revelation illustrate that the temporal wrath of God (6:16; 15:7; 16:1) is ultimately designed to make people "repent" (cf. 9:20; 16:9–11) in light of the eternal wrath of God to come (cf. 11:18; 14:10; 19:15). Therefore, since "God's kindness leads you toward repentance" (Rom. 2:4), temporal judgments are understood to be ultimately merciful.

Conversely, God also blesses the righteous in this age (cf. Deut. 28:1–14; Ps. 5:12; 84:11), for "godliness is of value in every way, as it holds promise for the present life and also for the life to come" (1 Tim. 4:8). But no gift of God in this age compares to the ultimate blessing of the resurrection (cf. Matt. 25:34; James 1:12; Rev. 22:14). The blessings of God in this age, like the judgments of God, are only designed to point us to the ultimate blessing of God in the age to come (see figure 3.13). In this way we receive all blessings (relational, physical, spiritual, etc.) *as divine mercy* to encourage us in perseverance unto the day of the Lord.

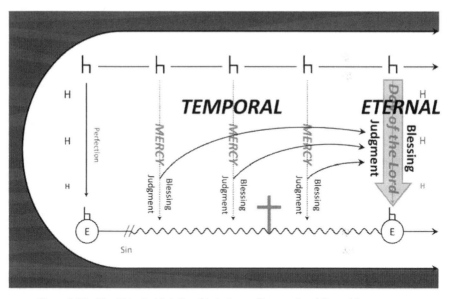

Figure 3.13 – The Historical Relationship between Temporal and Eternal Recompense

When we approach the sovereignty and governance of God in this age as both historical (pointing to the future) and merciful (explaining why the future apocalypse has not yet arrived), it saves us from a great deal of confusion, disillusionment, and despair.

- If the righteous are blessed in this age, *we rejoice*: "Command those who are rich in this present world . . . to be rich in good deeds, and to be generous and willing to share. In this way they will lay up treasure for themselves as a firm foundation for the coming age, so that they may take hold of the life that is truly life." (1 Tim. 6:17–19, NIV)

- If the righteous are not blessed in this age, *we rejoice*: "Has not God chosen those who are poor in the world to be rich in faith and heirs of the kingdom, which he has promised to those who love him?" (James 2:5)

- If the wicked are punished in this age, *we rejoice*: "You are to deliver this man to Satan for the destruction of the flesh, so that his spirit may be saved in the day of the Lord." (1 Cor. 5:5)

- If the wicked are not punished in this age, *we rejoice*: "Since indeed God considers it just to repay with affliction those who afflict you, and to grant relief to you who are afflicted as well as to us, when the Lord Jesus is revealed from heaven with his mighty angels." (2 Thess. 1:6–7)

In this way God can give and take away according to his own prerogative (cf. Job 1:21; 2:10), and we can "give thanks in all circumstances" (1 Thess. 5:18), finding "godliness with contentment" (1 Tim. 6:6) because we have "better and lasting possessions" (Heb. 10:34, NIV). Hence the exhortation: "*Set your hope fully* on the grace that will be brought to you at the revelation of Jesus Christ" (1 Peter 1:13). If you know that "the Lord is coming soon" (Phil. 4:5, NLT), then "you will experience God's peace, which exceeds anything we can understand. His peace will guard your hearts and minds as you live in Christ Jesus" (v. 7, NLT). Otherwise, our hearts become "weighed down with dissipation and drunkenness and cares of this life" (Luke 21:34).

CHRISTOPLATONIC THEOLOGY

When the Christoplatonic worldview is pushed forward in time, it develops into various forms of Christoplatonic theologies. Like soccer players on a basketball court, multitudes of people throughout the history of the church have tried to make the game work. Though specific ideas are innumerable, we can identify four *broad patterns* of thought: 1) escapist Christoplatonism, 2) dominionistic Christoplatonism, 3) dispensational Christoplatonism, and 4) inaugurational Christoplatonism.

Regarding the varied use of the term "Christoplatonism," I do not mean that Christians throughout the history of the church sat around reading Plato's books and then directly reformulated their theology (though this did indeed happen in a few cases). Rather, Plato's ideas were heavily influential on the Hellenistic milieu, which in turn shaped much of the thought of the church during its first few centuries, which in turn set the pattern of thought throughout the Middle Ages, which in turn laid a backdrop for the Reformation, which in turn got dogmatized over centuries (i.e., a series of footnotes to Plato).

The first two patterns listed above dominated throughout much of church history. Instead of a simple futurist-apocalyptic hope, the church has set its hope on an escapist heavenly destiny or a dominionistic materialization of divine sovereignty. So Princeton professor J. Christiaan Beker broadly summarized, "By and large the future apocalyptic dimension of Paul's thought has been misinterpreted in the history of the church. The interpretation of futurist eschatology in the church has been one long process of its transposition into a different key. Especially under the influence of Origen and Augustine future eschatology was made to refer either to the spiritual journey of the believer or to the church as the kingdom of God on earth."[85]

The dispensational pattern was a novel innovation during the nineteenth and twentieth centuries, seeking to solve the Platonic problem through a bifurcation of the plan of salvation. The inaugurational pattern developed in the twentieth century as a melding of the futurist-apocalyptic hope with the present-dominionistic materialization of divine sovereignty.

This historical categorization roughly corresponds to Benedict Viviano's well-articulated, fourfold categorization in *The Kingdom of God in History* (though he conspicuously overlooked the entire dispensational movement, which has had a substantial impact on the church worldwide through the Western missions movement).[86] Let us look at each of these in more detail.

Escapist Christoplatonism

By examining Plato's worldview, we can see many of the themes that were later accommodated by Christian theologians. On the playing field of materiality versus immateriality, the ultimate goal is the "the journey upwards"—that is, "the ascent of the soul into the intellectual world"—for the "world of sight" is a "prison-house" that the immaterial soul seeks to escape.[87] Moreover, the visible world is "timeful," while the intelligible world is *timeless*, for time is simply a copy of the eternal state, wherein the soul ultimately finds rest.[88] Within such a framework, salvation is essentially understood as *the escape of the soul*, which is accomplished temporally through enlightenment and eternally through death (see figure 3.14).[89]

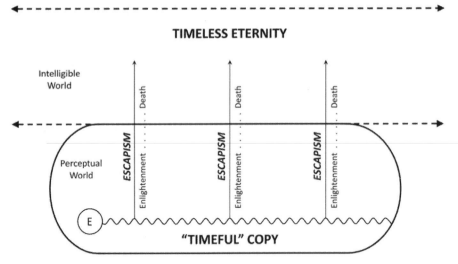

TIMELESS ETERNITY

Figure 3.14 – The Redemptive Framework of Platonism

As Hellenistic thought was accommodated into the early church through the Alexandrian school, the simple linear view of history was forsaken.[90] The hope of the future was transformed into a hope for the "great beyond," and the resurrection of the body was exchanged for the eternal existence of the soul.[91] Origen (c. 182–251) thus details "an incorporeal existence" as the "the end of all things":

> Having sketched, then, so far as we could understand, these three opinions regarding *the end of all things,* and the supreme blessedness . . . we must suppose that *an incorporeal existence is possible,* after all things have become subject to Christ, and through Christ to God the Father, when God will be all and in all; or that when, notwithstanding all things have been made subject to Christ, and through Christ to God (with whom they formed also one spirit, in respect of spirits being rational natures), then the bodily substance itself also being united to most pure and excellent spirits, and being *changed into an ethereal condition* in proportion to the quality or merits of those who assume it (according to the apostle's words, "We also shall be changed"), will shine forth in splendour; or at least that when the fashion of those things which are seen passes away, and *all corruption has been shaken off and cleansed away,* and when the whole of the space occupied by this world, in which the spheres of the planets are said to be, has been left behind and beneath, then is reached *the fixed abode of the pious and the good* situated above that sphere, which is called non-wandering

(ἀπλανής), as in a good land, in a land of the living, which will be inherited by the meek and gentle . . . *which is called truly and chiefly "heaven," in which heaven and earth, the end and perfection of all things, may be safely and most confidently placed.*[92]

This idea of immaterial heaven as "the end and perfection of all things" and "the fixed abode of the pious" became the normative view of the church in the centuries following.[93] The prize of eternal life was understood in terms of an *immaterial heavenly destiny*, due in part to eternity being equated with a realm of immateriality rather than futuristic unending time.[94] As such, timeless immateriality was naturally assumed to be the "heavenly home" of the immaterial soul,[95] which is ultimately achieved through death.[96] So Douglas J. Davies summarizes,

> Though earliest Christianity may have conceived of the eternal future in terms of a restored earth, a second Eden, over the following centuries the Christian afterlife was, largely, interpreted in terms of a heavenly domain. Christian theology, iconography, patterns of worship, the very existence of Easter and its religious celebration, and funerary rites came to speak of human life as a journey through life to the heavenly city. This journey beyond has dominated Christian cultures ever since.[97]

Moreover, a negative view of materiality was also accommodated. The apocalyptic vision of the day of the Lord was changed from the restoration of all things to the annihilation of materiality.[98] The penal aspects of the day of the Lord were also extracted and universalized upon death.[99] Rather than being held for judgment until the day of the Lord (the righteous in the third heaven and the wicked in Hades), all experience judgment upon death (see figure 3.15).[100] Furthermore, the return of Jesus lost its centrality in day-to-day thought, because it became functionally equivalent to death—that is, both end in immaterial heaven.

With the convolution of the day of the Lord also came a fundamental disunity between the Old and New Testaments. Though not as blatant as in Gnosticism,[101] the Old Testament was commonly pitted against the New through various supersessionist reinterpretations (i.e., the New Testament "trumps," "supersedes," or "takes precedence over" the Old Testament). Such "spiritual" hermeneutics became common during the Constantinian era and remain so to this day, as is evident by the many believers who continue to look forward to a *heavenly* promised land, Davidic throne, messianic kingdom, etc.[102]

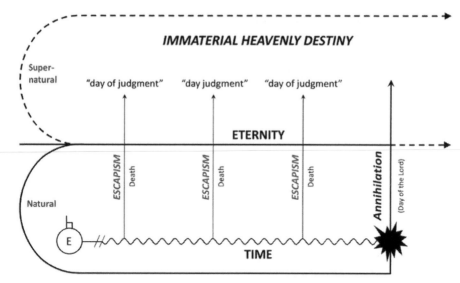

Figure 3.15 – The Modified Redemptive Framework of Christoplatonism

Because human beings inherently live according to their perceived destiny, *monasticism* grew organically out of the seeds of escapist Christoplatonic theology.[103] If materiality is bad, then asceticism and self-discipline are the means by which we separate from the material body and disassociate from the material world.[104] Throughout the Middle Ages, monks and nuns were known as "athletes of Christ," for they were the elites in the race to heaven. Though Luther deemed all such "monkery"[105] as antithetical to a "theology of the cross" (Lat. *theologia crucis*),[106] the Reformation did little to change the overarching heavenly destiny belief.[107]

Dominionistic Christoplatonism

While the ascent and escape of the soul to its heavenly destiny was the primary outworking of the accommodation of Platonic thought, there remained the nettlesome issue of *divine sovereignty*. Within such a framework, how does God rule over both materiality and immateriality? This question was inconsequential to Platonism, since the forms were impersonal and their function was mechanistic. According to Judeo-Christianity, however, God personally governs creation in a dynamic and historical manner. The collision of these two worldviews produced a dominionistic theology in which God *manifests his immaterial reign* into material time and history (see figure 3:16). Rather than the eschatological messianic kingdom as portrayed in the Scriptures, or the immaterial heavenly realm as in Origenistic Christoplatonism, the "kingdom of God" was understood as the materialization of divine sovereignty through Christianized political and ecclesiastical structures.[108]

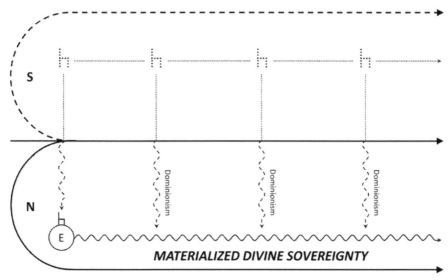

Figure 3.16 – The Manifestation of Divine Sovereignty within Christoplatonism

As such, manifest divine sovereignty was understood as *the end* (i.e., eschatology) to which the prophets spoke. After the conversion of Constantine, therefore, many began to see the Roman emperor, with the church under his authority, as the fulfillment of divine utterance.[109] *Christendom* was the practical outworking of an "eschatology of dominion."[110] Though such thought has often aptly been referred to as "realized eschatology," it lacks a Jewish apocalyptic referent (unlike its twentieth-century descendant; see below), and it fails to describe the heart of the thought pattern—that is, the perpetual materialization of divine sovereignty.

When the Roman Empire began to crumble, the manifestation of divine sovereignty was transferred to the church with the pope functioning as "the Vicar of Christ," extending the rod of divine rule.[111] As the writings of Augustine (354–430) became normative, it was generally accepted that "the Church even now is the kingdom of Christ, and the kingdom of heaven."[112] Nevertheless, with Augustine we have something of a mediating position between Eusebius and Origen—the "church militant," seeking to establish the manifest-sovereignty kingdom in this life, and the "church triumphant," achieving the heavenly-destiny kingdom in the afterlife.[113] Thus escapist Christoplatonism (see figure 3.15) and dominionistic Christoplatonism (see figure 3.16) were awkwardly harmonized (see figure 3.17)—resulting in a view that dominated the Middle Ages and Reformation, and which persists today in many popular circles of the church.[114]

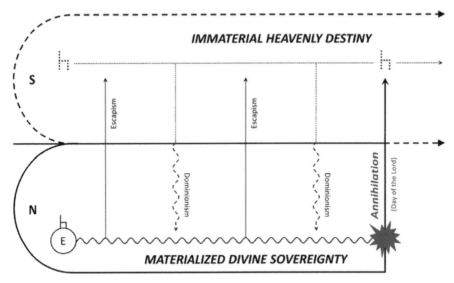

Figure 3.17 – The Augustinian Synthesis of Christoplatonic Salvation and Sovereignty

After the Enlightenment, manifest-sovereignty theology took on a new form within liberalism, wherein the spiritual rule of God produces good moral principles that transform society and hence build the kingdom of God on earth.[115] The functional end of this "social gospel" was similar to its Christendom ancestor, though less belligerent in its mission.[116] But the twentieth century saw the rise of more aggressive forms of dominionistic theology, which openly sought the takeover of government and society.[117]

Throughout the history of the church these two expressions of Christoplatonism (immaterial heavenly destiny and materialized divine sovereignty) have been the primary distortions of the simple cruciform-apocalyptic view found in the Scriptures.[118] Furthermore, these two Christoplatonic expressions inherently set salvation (cf. immaterial heaven) and divine sovereignty (cf. materialized dominion) against one another, since God is trying to take over that which he will ultimately destroy.[119] Within a biblical worldview, salvation (cf. new creation) and sovereignty (cf. cruciform-apocalypticism—i.e., mercy now, recompense to come) work together seamlessly, since Jesus is simply waiting at God's right hand "until the time for restoring all the things" (Acts 3:21), when "his enemies should be made a footstool for his feet" (Heb. 10:13).

These two axes of Christoplatonism also distort the nature and character of God. To those who focus on immaterial heavenly destiny, God is known in practicality as "LORD Escapist." Conversely, to those who emphasize manifest sovereignty, he is understood as "LORD Dominionist." Redemptive history then plays out according to the perceived nature and character of God, and in this way there is little room for a cruciform theology (see figure 3.18).

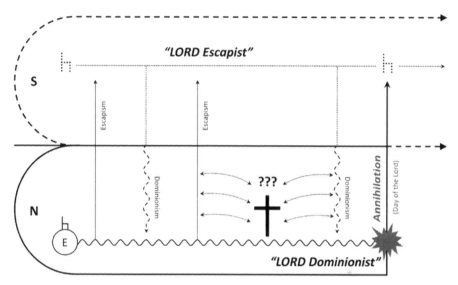

Figure 3.18 – The Distortion of God and the Cross within Christoplatonism

As such, the Bible's commands to "be imitators of God" (Eph. 5:1) and "take up [your] cross" (Luke 9:23) are understood within *monasticism* to be fulfilled by asceticism in all its various forms.[120] Simeon Stylites (c. 390–459), who spent nearly forty years atop a desert pillar, would therefore be the ultimate heavenly destiny disciple. Conversely, bearing your cross, according to *Christendom*, is understood in terms of denying yourself for the cause of executing vengeance upon the enemies of God, as exemplified in the Crusades when banners displaying the cross led the Christian armies in holy war against the infidels. Dominionists to this day continue to receive the same false vision of Constantine: in Latin, *In hoc signo vinces*—meaning, "In this sign, conquer!"[121] Both perversions militate against a true expression of the cross, in both word and deed, regarding the present mercy of God in light of the coming severity of God.

In this way the primary Christoplatonic belief systems compete with the Scriptures for context and meaning. Historically, the language of the Bible (e.g., "gospel," "kingdom," "life," "glory," etc.) has generally fallen into these two patterns of thought (see figure 3.19).[122]

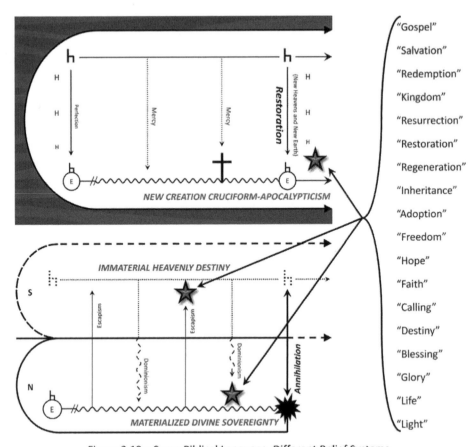

Figure 3.19 – Same Biblical Language, Different Belief Systems

For example, Paul says, "If a law had been given that could give *life*, then righteousness would indeed be by the law" (Gal. 3:21). Given the broader context of Galatians and of Pauline theology, he is simply referring to the age to come and "eternal life" (Gal. 6:8; cf. Rom. 2:7; 5:21)—that is, "the resurrection from the dead" (Phil. 3:11; cf. Rom. 6:5; 1 Cor. 15:12). Within a Christoplatonic framework, however, such a "life" would be associated on the one hand with the eternal sing-along-in-the-sky, or on the other hand with the church's best-life-now.[123]

Dispensational Christoplatonism

From the early church through the Enlightenment, these two patterns of Christoplatonic thought have generally prevailed.[124] During the late nineteenth and early twentieth centuries, however, a new system of interpretation arose in Britain and America known as "dispensationalism."[125] It offered a novel solution to the age-old Platonic problem: *two simultaneous plans of salvation*, one for materiality relating to Israel and the Jews and another for immateriality relating to the church and the Gentiles (see figure 3.20).

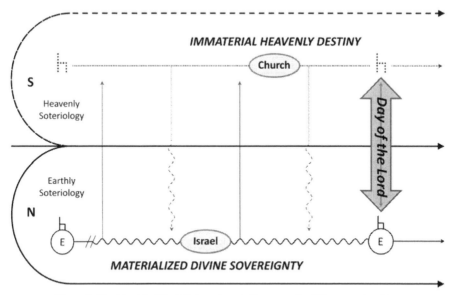

Figure 3.20 – The Modified Christoplatonic Framework of Dispensationalism

Though variously characterized, it is this soteriological dualism that essentially defined dispensationalism as a new theological system.[126] As the first to systematize its theology, Lewis Chafer articulated the eternal metaphysical dualism at the heart of the schema:

> The dispensationalist believes that throughout the ages God is pursuing *two distinct purposes*: one related *to the earth* with earthly people and earthly objectives involved, while the other is related *to heaven* with heavenly people and heavenly objectives involved. Why should this belief be deemed so incredible in the light of the facts that there is a present distinction between earth and heaven *which is preserved even after both are made new*; when the Scriptures so designate an earthly people who go on as such into eternity; and an heavenly people who also abide in their heavenly calling forever? Over against this, the partial dispensationalist, though dimly observing a few obvious distinctions, bases his interpretation on the supposition that *God is doing but one thing*, namely, the general separation of the good from the bad, and, in spite of all the confusion this limited theory creates, contends that the earthly people merge into the heavenly people; that the earthly program must be given a spiritual interpretation or disregarded altogether; and *that there is nothing in eternity but heaven*

and hell. The advocates of this interpretation oppose every earthly feature of the divine program. They disregard or ignore the earthly covenants and promises; they spiritualize or vaporize the vast body of Scripture bearing on the Davidic Throne and Kingdom; they present no specific reason as to why Christ was born as the Son of David; and they recognize no earthly glory or purpose in His second advent. According to their system, Christ comes again to end the world, but, unfortunately for these conceptions, *the world does not end then or ever.*[127]

As seen in Chafer's summary, dispensationalism sought to restore to biblical interpretation not only the new creation reality but also the Jewish ethnic reality (discussed further in chapter 6). Unfortunately, instead of scrapping the whole Platonic snarl, they accommodated it; and in doing so they doubly muddled the theological issues. Not only do the Gentiles inherit a heavenly destiny, but Israel experiences a manifest sovereignty, generally termed "theocracy," mean-ing "a manifestation of the supernatural."[128] The manifestation of divine rule is roughly understood as beginning at Sinai, ending at the exile, and resuming (after a Gentile "intercalation") at the return of Jesus.[129] According to the two plans of salvation, therefore, we generally see dual references applied to the bibli-cal terminology: two "kingdoms," two "inheritances," two "glories," etc.

Being generally a grassroots and popular-level movement, dispensation-alism received little criticism until the mid-twentieth century. At that time, criticism from Reformed circles began to mount,[130] especially concerning the dualistic interpretation of the new covenant—"a defenseless position."[131] Thus, the classical model was modified,[132] but "revised dispensationalism" sought to keep the two plans of salvation *during the millennium* while consolidating them into one plan for eternity.[133] By the late twentieth century, dispensational schol-ars began to abandon their dualistic foundations in favor of more mainstream ideas concerning "inaugurated eschatology."[134]

Inaugurational Christoplatonism

By the turn of the twentieth century, some in European scholarship had come to the conclusion that Jesus and the apostles were thoroughly Jewish in their views of the kingdom, resurrection, salvation, etc.—as reflected in their con-tinued use of apocalyptic language, such as the day of the Lord, the two ages, and the like.[135] This approach came to be known as "consistent eschatology," as it conformed to the thought patterns of the time.[136] However, these scholars' skepticism and lack of cruciform theology led them to conclude that Jesus was a misguided and deluded prophet whom the early church deified and memori-alized by shifting the apocalyptic categories to his return.[137]

In an attempt to save Jesus from such embarrassment, slightly less liberal scholars responded by saying that Jesus spiritually "realized" the Jewish-apocalyptic expectations within himself—and later through the ministry of the church. This approach has been labeled "realized eschatology."[138] The nature of this "realization," however, was *quite Platonic*, very much akin to the manifest-sovereignty pattern of thought which preceded it.[139]

During the mid-twentieth century, a number of scholars took a "mediating position,"[140] incorporating both consistent and realized eschatology—that is, "an eschatology that is in process of realization."[141] More conservative scholars developed this idea,[142] "modifying" the simple Jewish timeline to accommodate the Platonic realized eschatology.[143] This approach was later termed "inaugurated eschatology,"[144] reflecting the "already fulfilled" realized eschatology and the "not yet completed" consistent eschatology.[145] Thus the straightforward, Jewish-eschatological hope was mixed with the Platonic notion of materialized sovereignty.[146]

The underlying assumptions of this schema are that 1) the overarching purpose of God in redemptive history is the manifestation of divine sovereignty and 2) God was doing the same thing at the first coming of the Christ as he will do at the second coming of the Christ. So George Ladd, the evangelical systematizer of inaugurationalism,[147] explained:

> The "history" of the kingdom of God is therefore the history of redemption, *viewed from the aspect of God's sovereign and kingly power.* Before the final and perfect establishment of God's reign there could be a number of mediatorial stages in which *the manifestation of God's sovereignty is realized in varying degrees.* God's reign may be realized less perfectly, partially, but none-the-less really in various realms during the course of this age and before the perfect fulfillment in the age to come. The character of these several *mediatorial manifestations* of God's kingdom can be determined only by careful exegesis of the Scriptural language.[148]

Therefore the only difference between inaugurationalism and its dominionistic ancestor is *the eschatological referent.* The older manifest-sovereignty theology generally had no Jewish-eschatological hope in mind—the Scriptures simply prophesied Christendom.[149] The modern inaugurational message is substantially the same, yet it finds meaning and context in reference to Jewish apocalypticism.[150] Of course, the Bible's eschatology was not realized at the first coming in a plain and straightforward manner—that is, the Messiah is not "already" ruling from an "already" temple in an "already" New Jerusalem with an "already" heavenly glory on an "already" new earth, etc. (to be detailed in chapter 6). Hence the use of the term "realized" is often duplicitous.

Rather than simply referring to the present fulfillment of a future event, it usually refers to a semi-Platonic manifestation of divine sovereignty, which in turn actually redefines the future event. Inaugurationalism is simply partially fulfilled, *Platonically reinterpreted*, Jewish eschatology.[151]

Moreover, the final state of Jewish new-creation eschatology is transformed into a semi-Platonic "final amalgamation of the earthly and heavenly spheres."[152] Inaugurationalism consists of "a semi-eschatological expression incorporating the heavenly realm both in the present and future."[153] In other words, "Final redemption will be the moment when heaven and earth are joined together at last."[154] Thus the material world will be fully "supernaturalized," or "heavenized," so to speak, by the manifestation of divine sovereignty in the age to come, which then becomes the referent for its partial supernaturalization/heavenization in this age. So Ladd summarizes this semi-Platonic, heavenized destiny:

> There is a twofold dualism in the New Testament: God's will is done in heaven; his Kingdom brings it to earth. In the Age to Come, *heaven descends to earth* and lifts historical existence to a new level of redeemed life (Rev. 21:2–3). This is hinted at, although not elaborated on, in the Gospels. . . . This is the will of God: to conquer evil and to bring his people finally into the blessed immortality of the eternal life of the Age to Come.[155]

In this way we could speak of inaugurationalism as a *conflationary soteriology*. God is manifesting his reign both in this age and in the age to come, bringing together the material and immaterial realms (see figure 3.21).[156] Consequently, redemptive history is understood as a continual process of "the inbreaking of the eternal into the temporal,"[157] or put in military terms, "a theology of the invasion of history by the God of heaven."[158]

At this point we must say clearly that to speak of the age to come being inaugurated at the first coming is *substantially equivalent* to saying that "the day of the Lord has come" (2 Thess. 2:2) and "the resurrection has already happened" (2 Tim. 2:18). Few seem as bold as C. H. Dodd, so as to state the obvious: "That the Christian is 'risen from the dead' follows from the 'realized eschatology' of the Gospels. The Kingdom of God has come; the 'Age to Come' has come; the 'life of the Age to Come' is realized."[159] Inaugurationalism is thus bound to its ancient Gnostic roots when it argues for a spiritual realization of the kingdom, resurrection, and the age to come.[160] In the final evaluation, we must conclude that God is not "beyond history," nor does he "break into time," nor is he engaged in an "invasion," nor a "manifestation" of sovereignty—much less an "incision," "incursion," or "realization" of the age to come. All such language is an obvious imposition upon the Scriptures.[161]

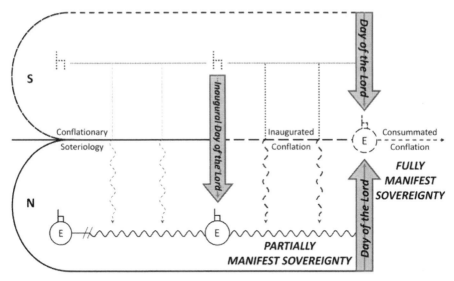

Figure 3.21 – The Modified Christoplatonic Framework of Inaugurationalism

Moreover, like its manifest-sovereignty predecessor, inaugurationalism mars the nature and character of both God and redemptive history. By inaugurating the age to come, *the cross is set aside* as the normative reality of this age, and the purpose of God is interpreted as an ever-increasing realization of divine sovereignty. Furthermore, by spiritually realizing the Jewish-apocalyptic realities, inaugurationalism *mitigates the severity of God* and the coming day of the Lord. As a result, the divine agenda of both advents is truncated, and as such those who embrace inaugurationalism generally avoid apocalypticism and abandon an overt theology of the cross.[162]

Contrary to the prime assumption of inaugurationalism—that the first and second comings are of the same purpose—we must lay hold of the truth that "Christ was sacrificed once *to take away the sins* of many people; and he will appear a second time, not to bear sin, but *to bring salvation* to those who are waiting for him" (Heb. 9:28). Such a fundamental distinction between the nature of this age and the age to come is ubiquitous to the New Testament (cf. Rom. 5:9; 8:17; 2 Cor. 4:17; Phil. 3:9–11; 2 Thess. 1:5–10; 1 Peter 1:4–7; 4:13; Rev. 6:10–11). This age generally entails an expression of the kindness of God, which anticipates the severity of God and the age to come—that is, cruciform-apocalypticism. Thus we understand the apostolic commission: "that repentance and forgiveness of sins should be proclaimed in his name to all nations" (Luke 24:47), resulting in the apostolic proclamation: "[Jesus] commanded us to preach to the people and to testify that he is the one appointed by God *to be judge* of the living and the dead. To him all the prophets bear witness that everyone who believes in him receives *forgiveness of sins* through his name" (Acts 10:42–43).

Such a proclamation stands in stark contrast to the four broad patterns of Christoplatonic thought found throughout the history of the church: escapist, dominionistic, dispensational, and inaugurational. If we remove the Platonic element inherent to each of these, we are left with a simple new-creation theology with a straightforward cruciform-apocalyptic chronology.

Millennial Classification

A concluding note should also be made concerning the deficient classification system of pre-, post-, and a-millennialism. During the early twentieth century, dispensationalists and Reformed theologians sought to distinguish their respective theologies by use of these three labels.[163] "Premillennialists" sought to define themselves according to a "literal" interpretation of the Bible, resulting in an earthly Jewish hope, in contrast to a Reformed "spiritualized" interpretation, resulting in the hopes of heavenly destiny (amillennialism) and/or Christendom (postmillennialism).[164]

Though such a trajectory of theological discussion continues today, belief in the millennium does not define one's belief system as a whole.[165] Millennialism, classically known as "chiliasm" (belief in a thousand-year transitional messianic reign), is an independent doctrine, which may or may not precede a final heavenly destiny, follow an age of Christendom, or pattern an inaugurational realization.[166] Even dispensationalism (in its classical and progressive forms) could function with or without a millennial transition into the eternal state.

Indeed, there are similarities and much overlap between the common millennial labels and the primary worldview patterns (see table 3.2). Historically, postmillennialists have generally been theologically dominionistic,[167] while amillennialists have generally been escapist[168] and premillennialists have generally been new-creationist and/or dispensationalist.[169]

However, such a characterization is increasingly inaccurate, since a consensus is arising concerning the hope of a new creation.[170] Hence the millennial classification system lacks the ability to describe *the basic structure and theological end* of various belief systems. The issue of realized eschatology is generally ignored, and issues of worldview are simply collapsed onto a flat timeline.[171] As such, we find the whole the millennial classification system to be painfully inadequate and in need of immediate retirement.

Concerning chiliasm in general (to be discussed further in chapter 6), we affirm the apostolic hope.[172] Obviously the Scriptures say relatively little about it, and therefore we refrain from a dogmatic declaration. We believe, however, that chiliasm was a minority belief within second-temple Judaism, which was

Table 3.2 – Contrast between Millennial and Worldview Classification Systems

Millennial Label	VS.	Worldview Pattern	Millennial Transition
Premillennialism	~	Apocalyptic New-Creationism	
		Dispensational Christoplatonism	Chiliastic (Millennial)
Amillennialism	~	Escapist Christoplatonism	OR
		Inaugurational Christoplatonism	Non-Chiliastic (Non-Millennial)
Postmillennialism	~	Dominionistic Christoplatonism	

then *confirmed as true* by the Revelation given to the apostle John (cf. Rev. 20:1–6). Thus we hold to what might be described as *chiliastic cruciform-apocalypticism*. We find such a description to represent more accurately the "historic" view of the apostles and much of the early church.[173]

Though missing the mark with his dispensational approach, we conclude with Lewis Chafer: "May the number, already vast indeed, of those who believe the Bible and are subject to its plain teachings continue to increase!"[174]

Chapter Four

❈

THE SPIRIT OF
THE RESURRECTION

The Scriptures open with the declaration that the universe has an absolute and definite "beginning."[1] As such, all things are wholly dependent
upon the Creator: "For from him and through him and to him are all
things" (Rom. 11:36). Creation lives from, to, and through the Creator, and it
is his "spirit," or "breath" (Heb. *rûah*), that animates creation.[2] Moreover, the
Spirit, or "breath," of God is the substance of the word of God, which in turn
becomes the creative power of God. So the psalmist describes creation, "By the
word of the LORD the heavens were made, and by the *breath* [Heb. *rûah*] of his
mouth all their host. . . . For he *spoke*, and it came to be; he *commanded*, and it
stood firm (Ps. 33:6–9; cf. Heb. 11:3).

In this way, the Spirit of God is intimately related to the word of God,
which proceeds from the mouth of God. Thus God's Spirit is synonymous with
the general term for "breath" (Heb. *něšāmâ*), as Elihu says, "The Spirit [Heb.
rûah] of God has made me, and the breath [Heb. *něšāmâ*] of the Almighty gives
me life" (Job 33:4). This understanding undergirds the creation account when
God "formed the man of dust from the ground and breathed into his nostrils
the breath [Heb. *něšāmâ*] of life" (Gen. 2:7). The Spirit/breath/word of God is
the practical agent of life and creation.[3]

Not only does the Spirit of God animate creation, but it also *sustains creation*. So Elihu says, "If it were [God's] intention and he withdrew his spirit
[Heb. *rûah*] and breath [Heb. *něšāmâ*], all mankind would perish together
and man would return to the dust" (Job 34:14–15, NIV). Likewise, Psalm 104
describes the giving and taking of life by the Spirit: "When you take away
their breath [Heb. *rûah*], they die and return to the dust. When you send your

Spirit [Heb. *rûaḥ*], they are created, and you renew the face of the earth" (vv. 29–30, NIV).

Such a *spiritual renewal* is therefore the basis of the eschatological understanding of the new heavens and the new earth (cf. Isa. 65:17; 66:22; Rev. 21:5). As God created the heavens and the earth by his Spirit through his word, so also will he renew and re-create them in the age to come.[4] As a result, those who have "shared in the Holy Spirit" (Heb. 6:4) in this age have a palpable knowledge of "the powers of the age to come" (v. 5). As such, all the workings of the Spirit in this age—miracles, signs, wonders, gifts, etc.—are understood in the context of protological creation and eschatological consummation (see figure 4.1).[5] In other words, the Spirit of God testifies to the work of God— past, present, and future. Thus the Holy Spirit is understood in a historical manner within an apocalyptic framework.

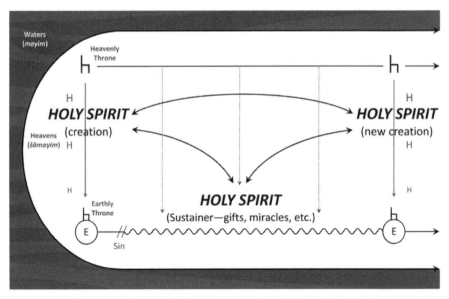

Figure 4.1 – The Apocalyptic Framework of the Activity of God's Spirit

As the Spirit of God gave life to Adam in the beginning, so also will the Spirit of God give life to his righteous descendants in the end. Paul speaks explicitly of this agency of the Spirit in the resurrection in relation to the resurrection of Jesus: "If the Spirit of him who raised Jesus from the dead dwells in you, he who raised Christ Jesus from the dead will also give life to your mortal bodies *through his Spirit* who dwells in you" (Rom. 8:11). Therefore, on the day of the Lord the word will once again be spoken, and "the dead will hear the *voice* of the Son of God. . . . All who are in the tombs will hear his *voice* and come out, those who have done good to the resurrection of life, and those who have done evil to the resurrection of judgment" (John 5:25–29).

In this way, the Scriptures understand the Spirit of God as "the Spirit of the resurrection," as Jürgen Moltmann describes:

> The Spirit of God is the Spirit of Christ, and is as such *the Spirit of the resurrection of the dead*. The Spirit of the Father and the Son is the divine quickening power of the new creation of all things, the power empowering the rebirth of everything that lives. . . . The Spirit does not draw the soul away from the body, nor does it make the soul hasten towards heaven, leaving this earth behind. It places the whole earthly and bodily person in the daybreak colours of the new earth.[6]

THE FIRSTBORN OF THE RESURRECTION

Jesus was understood by the early church to be "the firstborn from the dead" (Col. 1:18; cf. Rev. 1:5). As God raised Jesus from the dead by his Spirit, so then will he also raise all from the dead by his Spirit. And as believers in his resurrection, God promises that we will "be *conformed* to the image of his Son, in order that he might be the *firstborn* among many brothers" (Rom. 8:29). By this Paul means, "We await a Savior, the Lord Jesus Christ, who will *transform* our lowly body to be like his glorious body, *by the power* that enables him even to subject all things to himself" (Phil. 3:20–21). For "he was shown to be the Son of God when he was raised from the dead *by the power* of the Holy Spirit" (Rom. 1:4, NLT). As younger sons (cf. Rom. 8:15; Gal. 4:5), we will be raised from the dead by the same Spirit that raised Christ, the firstborn, from the dead.

The resurrection of Jesus by the Spirit was also understood by the apostles as a "firstfruits" (1 Cor. 15:20,23) of the final resurrection "harvest" (Matt. 13:39; Mark 4:29). Just as worshipers in the Old Testament brought firstfruits of their flocks and fields as an offering to the Lord (cf. Deut. 18:4; 26:2; Neh. 10:35–37), so Jesus was offered and raised as a firstfruits unto the Lord in advance of the final harvest.[7] As Paul outlines, "Christ has been raised from the dead, the *firstfruits* of those who have fallen asleep. For as by a man came death, by a man has come also the resurrection of the dead. For as in Adam all die, so also in Christ shall all be made alive. But each in his own order: Christ the *firstfruits*, then at his coming those who belong to Christ" (1 Cor. 15:20–23).

This emphasis on Christ's individual resurrection in anticipation of the future general resurrection reinforces the simple apocalyptic framework.[8] Because Christ has been raised from the dead, we have an *assurance* of the general resurrection, and thus our faith is not "futile" (1 Cor. 15:17).[9] The day of the Lord will actually come, and the dead will actually be raised. Hence the relevance of Christ's resurrection bears daily upon the struggle and grind of mortality, which slowly breaks down the human psyche with its ruthless accusation that things will forever go on as they are.[10]

Because Jesus alone was "made alive by the Spirit" (1 Peter 3:18, NIV), he is understood to hold *unique divine approval*. So Paul reasoned with the Athenians that God "has fixed a day on which he will judge the world in righteousness by a man whom he has appointed; and of this he has given assurance to all by raising him from the dead" (Acts 17:31). All other sons of Adam are proven to be unrighteous, because they returned to the dust and *stayed there*. This one was raised from the dead so as to demonstrate that he alone is righteous. Accordingly only the "Righteous One" (Isa. 24:16; 53:11; Acts 3:14; 7:52; 22:14) deserves to judge the unrighteous.[11] So Paul concludes that Jesus is "the firstborn from the dead, that in everything he might be preeminent" (Col. 1:18)—that is, "the ruler of kings on earth" (Rev. 1:5).

Thus the bodily resurrection of Jesus pervades apostolic witness (cf. Acts 2:24,32; 3:15,26; 4:10; 5:30; 10:40; 13:30,33–35; 17:3,31; 23:6; 24:21; 25:19; 26:8,23).[12] It held prominence in the early church as well, for the resurrection of Jesus *proved* the apocalyptic nature of the Scriptures.[13] All differing opinions concerning the future (e.g., Pharisaic, Sadducean, Essene, etc.) were silenced in light of Jesus' resurrection and future coming.[14] The early church galvanized its apocalyptic understanding of the Scriptures around the resurrection of Jesus and the gift of the Holy Spirit.

The hope of the Old Testament became "a *living hope* through the resurrection of Jesus Christ from the dead" (1 Peter 1:3). The hope of the resurrection had been confirmed, for a son of Adam had actually come out of the grave. Consequently, "We have the prophetic word more fully confirmed" (2 Peter 1:19). We know Jesus *will* come again, and we *will* "attain the resurrection from the dead" (Phil. 3:11).[15] Therefore, we "press on toward the goal for the prize of the high calling of God in Christ Jesus" (Phil. 3:14, AT).[16]

THE DEPOSIT OF THE RESURRECTION

As Jesus was a firstfruits of the resurrection to come, so also God has given us "the firstfruits of the Spirit" (Rom. 8:23)—the Spirit who will raise us from the dead on the day of Christ Jesus. Likewise, the Holy Spirit is described as a "deposit" (Gk. *arrabōn*) guaranteeing our future resurrection (2 Cor. 1:22; 5:5; Eph. 1:14; cf. 1 Tim. 6:20; 2 Tim. 1:14). In this way Pentecost (Acts 2) was understood as "a payment that obligates the contracting party to make further payments"—that is, "the first installment" of the resurrection to come.[17] So, too, all the gifts of the Holy Spirit are meant to be an "assurance of salvation," so to speak. Paul thus describes the confirmation of the apostolic witness: "The testimony concerning Christ was *confirmed in you*, so that you are not lacking in *any gift*, awaiting eagerly the revelation of our Lord Jesus Christ, who will also *confirm you* to the end, blameless in the day of our Lord Jesus Christ" (1 Cor. 1:6–8, NASB).

The Holy Spirit is meant to confirm the gospel, strengthening believers in their faith unto salvation on the day of the Lord. Therefore the initial Jewish Christians knew the Gentiles would inherit the resurrection, apart from circumcision, because "God, who knows the heart, showed that he accepted them by giving the Holy Spirit to them, just as he did to us" (Acts 15:8, NIV; cf. Acts 10:45; 11:17). Conversely, the lack of the Holy Spirit assures future condemnation, since "anyone who does not have the Spirit of Christ does not belong to him" (Rom. 8:9). Unbelievers inevitably become "scoffers, following their own passions" (Jude 18), because they are "worldly-minded, devoid of the Spirit" (v. 19, NASB). Conversely, the Spirit directs the minds of believers toward the return of Jesus (cf. John 16:13; 2 Peter 1:19–21; 1 John 2:25–27) and helps them fulfill Paul's exhortation: "Set your hearts on things above, where Christ is seated at the right hand of God. . . . When Christ, who is your life, appears, then you also will appear with him in glory" (Col. 3:1,4, NIV).

In this way we are "sealed with the promised Holy Spirit, who is the *guarantee* of our inheritance until we acquire possession of it" (Eph. 1:14). For God has "set his seal of ownership on us, and put his Spirit in our hearts as a deposit, *guaranteeing* what is to come" (2 Cor. 1:22, NIV). Paul summarizes the relationship between our present body, the Holy Spirit, and our resurrected body:

> For we know that if the tent that is our *earthly home* is destroyed, we have a *building from God*, a house not made with hands, eternal in the heavens. . . . For while we are still in *this tent*, we groan, being burdened—not that we would be unclothed, but that we would be *further clothed*, so that what is mortal may be swallowed up by life. He who has prepared us for this very thing is God, who has given us *the Spirit as a guarantee*. (2 Cor. 5:1,4–5)

In this "spiritual body" (1 Cor. 15:44)—that is, "the new body, animated by the Spirit of God"[18]—we will be "like angels . . . being sons of the resurrection" (Luke 20:36, NASB). This spiritual body is in no way referring to a heavenly destiny, but rather a heavenly origin and heavenly quality.[19] As the Messiah will rule upon the earth in heavenly glory (cf. Isa. 4:2; 11:10; Matt. 19:28; 25:31), so also will we receive bodies that radiate heavenly glory, as "star differs from star in glory" (1 Cor. 15:41).

As the agent of both creation and the resurrection, everything the Holy Spirit does inherently testifies to both the original perfection of creation and the eschatological glory of creation (see figure 4.1). Consequently, all activity of the Spirit is by nature a "sign" (Gk. *sēmeion*) pointing to the age to come, which will be a restoration of original glory.[20] As such, the author of Hebrews describes the gifts of the Spirit as "the powers of the age to come" (Heb. 6:5), which are designed to testify to the salvation and divine subjection of the world to come (Heb. 2:3–5). Hence Jesus commissions his disciples:

> Go into all the world and proclaim the gospel to the whole creation. Whoever believes and is baptized *will be saved*, but whoever does not believe *will be condemned*. And *these signs* will accompany those who believe: in my name they will cast out demons; they will speak in new tongues; they will pick up serpents with their hands; and if they drink any deadly poison, it will not hurt them; they will lay their hands on the sick, and they will recover. (Mark 16:15–18)[21]

As the disciples went out and preached, "the Lord worked with them and confirmed the message by *accompanying signs*" (Mark 16:20). The gospel message—concerning the day of the Lord, the salvation of the righteous, and the condemnation of the wicked—was thus accredited by signs and wonders.[22] So Peter (quoting Joel as the prophet spoke for God) summarizes the outpouring of the Spirit: "I will show *wonders* in the heavens above and *signs* on the earth below, blood, and fire, and vapor of smoke; the sun shall be turned to darkness and the moon to blood, before *the day of the Lord* comes, the great and magnificent day. And it shall come to pass that everyone who calls upon the name of the Lord shall be *saved*" (Acts 2:19–21). In this way, the Spirit of God prepares the earth for the coming of the day of God and confirms the message of salvation (see v. 38).

The list given in Mark's "Great Commission" (16:17–18) is typical of the primary signs given by God in this age to testify to the age to come. Exorcisms always accompany the proclamation of the coming kingdom (cf. Matt. 10:7–8; Luke 9:1–2), because Satan and all demons will be driven off the earth in the age to come (cf. Isa. 24:22; Rev. 20:2). So the demonized men of the Gadarenes cried out, "What do you want with us, Son of God? Have you come here to torture us before the appointed time?" (Matt. 8:29, NIV). The demons begged not to be thrown "into the abyss" (Luke 8:31), where they would then be "kept until the judgment" (2 Peter 2:4).

Healings also accompany the proclamation of the gospel (cf. Matt. 4:23; 10:7–8), because sickness and death will be overcome in the resurrection. Therefore the healing of the crippled beggar in Jesus' name (Acts 3:7) was a simple demonstration of the apostolic message: "proclaiming in Jesus the resurrection from the dead" (Acts 4:2). Likewise, the raising of Lazarus (John 11:44) inherently reinforced the message of "the resurrection on the last day" (v. 24), causing many Jews to believe in Jesus as the Christ (v. 45). So also the healing of the paralytic reinforced the reality of the day of judgment and the Son of Man's "authority on earth to forgive sins" (Luke 5:24). But to the Jewish populations who did not repent at the performance of miracles, Jesus said, "It will be more tolerable on the day of judgment for the land of Sodom than for you" (Matt. 11:24).

Akin to healings and exorcisms, many other signs also testify to the age to come. The transfiguration of Jesus' body in appearance "like the sun" (Matt. 17:2) testified to the glory of the resurrection, when the saints will inherit bodies that "shine like the brightness of the heavens" (Dan. 12:3, NIV; cf. Matt. 13:43; 1 Cor. 15:41). Jesus' calming of the storm (Matt. 8:23–27 and parallels) and walking on the lake resulted in the confession, "Truly you are the Son of God" (Matt. 14:33), for it was assumed that the Messiah would tame the wildness of the earth in the age to come (cf. Isa. 11:6–9; 55:12–13; 66:25). Jesus' feeding of the five thousand led the people to respond, "This is indeed the Prophet who is to come into the world" (John 6:14), for he would feed and care for the poor of the earth (cf. Ps. 72:4; Isa. 11:4; Jer. 22:16). The changing of water into aged wine "revealed his glory, and his disciples put their faith in him" (John 2:11, NIV), because on Mount Zion in the age to come "the LORD of hosts will make for all peoples a feast of rich food, a feast of well-aged wine, of rich food full of marrow, of aged wine well refined" (Isa. 25:6). All of the biblical miracles function in the same historical manner as signs, pointing to the eschatological consummation based upon the protological creation (see figure 4.1).[23]

Because God's Spirit sustains what he made, the Spirit is also referred to as the "Helper" (John 14:16,26; 15:26; 16:7; cf. 1 John 2:1). The Holy Spirit helps the saints in their attainment of eternal life, for it is by the gifts of the Spirit that Jesus "will sustain you to the end" (1 Cor. 1:8). The Spirit likewise protects the saints, as Peter encourages in regard to the hope of "an inheritance that can never perish, spoil or fade—kept in heaven for you, who through faith are *shielded by God's power* until the coming of the salvation that is ready to be revealed in the last time" (1 Peter 1:4–5, NIV). Thus we are "kept" and "guarded" (John 17:12) from the evil one in this age, for "he who was born of God protects him" (1 John 5:18). Jesus is *with us* to the end of the age (Matt. 28:20), and the Holy Spirit *intercedes for us* while we hope for future glory (Rom. 8:25–27). Hence the exhortation and benediction of Jude 20–25:

> But you, beloved, building yourselves up in your most holy faith and *praying in the Holy Spirit*, keep yourselves in the love of God, waiting for

the mercy of our Lord Jesus Christ that leads to eternal life. . . . Now to him who is able to *keep you* from stumbling and to *present you* blameless before the presence of his glory with great joy, to the only God, our Savior, through Jesus Christ our Lord, be glory, majesty, dominion, and authority, before all time and now and forever. Amen.

All the gifts of the Spirit (cf. 1 Cor. 12:7–11) are thus designed as a deposit "for the edification of the church" (1 Cor. 14:12, NASB). The "utterance of wisdom" and the "utterance of knowledge" (1 Cor. 12:8) point to the time when we will no longer walk in fallen ways of foolishness and folly, nor will we fumble around in the darkness of depraved reason and understanding (cf. Ps. 14:1–3; 94:8–11; Isa. 11:1–4; 32:1–6).

The gifts of "faith," "healing," and "the working of miracles" (1 Cor. 12:9–10) point to the *boldness and courage* we will have when we see God face to face, no longer consumed by the fear, insecurity, and despair wrought upon our souls by mortality and a body of death. Consequently, the apostolic church prayed, "Grant to your servants to continue to speak your word with all *boldness*, while you stretch out your hand to heal, and signs and wonders are performed through the name of your holy servant Jesus" (Acts 4:29–30). And after praying, "they were all filled with the Holy Spirit and continued to speak the word of God with *boldness*" (v. 31). So Paul concludes, "Since we have such a hope, we are *very bold*" (2 Cor. 3:12).

"Prophecy" and the "distinguishing of spirits" (1 Cor. 12:10, NASB) point to the day when God will judge everything, both in the heavens and on the earth, and there will be a *distinction* between the righteous and the wicked (cf. Mal. 3:18; Matt. 13:30; Rev. 21:6–8). No longer will there be wolves in sheep's clothing (Matt. 7:15; cf. Acts 20:29), and no longer will demons disguise themselves as angels of light (2 Cor. 11:14; cf. Gal. 1:8).

Likewise, the speaking of "various kinds of tongues" and "the interpretation of tongues" (1 Cor. 12:10) points to the time when the pride of humankind and the confounding of languages will be no more (cf. Acts 2:4; Isa. 2:3; Rev. 21:24–27).[24] Ironically, the gift of tongues has become a source of pride and contention in modern times, largely due to the lack of an eschatological orientation and a protological anchor.

As there will be no more need for hope and encouragement of faith in the age to come (cf. Rom. 8:24–26), so the gifts of the Holy Spirit will "cease" and "pass away" (1 Cor. 13:8), for they will find consummation in the resurrection—"when the perfect comes, the partial will pass away" (v. 10).[25] They are temporal helps to keep faith and hope strong to the end (cf. 1 Cor. 1:8; Jude

20–21). We have not been left "as orphans" (John 14:18). Christ loves us, and he will come for us. Moreover, we are not left alone in this age (Matt. 28:20), for God manifests his love to us by his Spirit (Rom. 8:15; Gal. 4:6). Therefore, "We rejoice in hope of the glory of God. . . . And hope does not put us to shame, because God's love has been poured into our hearts *through the Holy Spirit* who has been given to us" (Rom. 5:2,5).

THE UNSEEN HOPE
OF THE RESURRECTION

The gift of the Spirit is therefore understood as a visible confirmation of the future reality of the day of the Lord and the resurrection. The Spirit is given to confirm our divine adoption and inheritance (Rom. 8:16–17), mitigating "the sufferings of this present time" (v. 18) and causing us to "groan inwardly as we wait eagerly for adoption as sons, the redemption of our bodies" (v. 23). However, we do not *presently* see the hope of the resurrection, as Paul concludes, "Now hope that is *seen* is not hope. For who hopes for what he *sees*? But if we hope for what we do not *see*, we wait for it with patience" (vv. 24–25).[26]

Unlike Christoplatonism, which generally interprets "seen" and "unseen" in metaphysical terms (material vs. immaterial), the Scriptures primarily refer to "seen" and "unseen" in historical terms (this age vs. the age to come). Such an approach is based upon the day of the Lord and the "appearing" of God (cf. Ps. 21:9; 102:16; Zech. 9:14; Mal. 3:2), when humanity will "see" him in his glory (cf. Ps. 97:6; Isa. 33:17; 52:8). Such language is assumed in the New Testament and applied to Jesus' own "appearing" (Col. 3:4; 1 Tim. 6:14; Titus 2:13; 1 Peter 5:4; 1 John 2:28). Thus, "when he *appears* we shall be like him, because we shall *see* him as he is" (1 John 3:2), for "he is coming with the clouds, and every eye will *see* him" (Rev. 1:7; cf. Matt. 5:8).

In the New Testament, the dichotomy of that which is seen in this age versus that which is unseen in the age to come is the framework within which faith and hope are exercised (see figure 4.2). As the writer of Hebrews defines, "Now *faith* is being sure of what we *hope for* and certain of what we *do not see*" (Heb. 11:1, NIV).[27] In this age we see sin, suffering, and trials; but we hope for what we do not see—that is, righteousness, peace, and joy—in the age to come. So Paul describes, "Our light and momentary troubles are achieving for us an eternal glory that far outweighs them all. So we fix our eyes not on what is *seen*, but on what is *unseen*. For what is seen is *temporary*, but what is unseen is *eternal*" (2 Cor. 4:17–18, NIV).

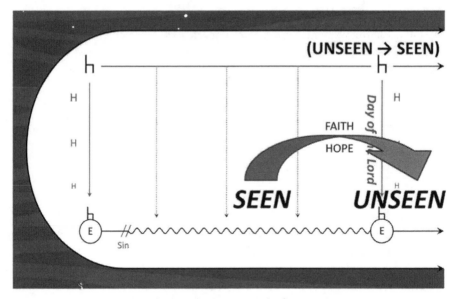

Figure 4.2 – The Apocalyptic Framework of Seen vs. Unseen

Such faith is foundational to the apostolic witness. In light of our coming resurrected body (cf. 2 Cor. 5:1–5) and "the judgment seat of Christ" (v. 10), Paul exhorts us to "walk by faith, not by *sight*" (v. 7). By faith we "see the Day drawing near" (Heb. 10:25), though by sight "our outer self is wasting away" (2 Cor. 4:16). In this way, we are being "guarded *through faith* for a salvation ready to be revealed in the last time" (1 Peter 1:5). Fueled by the gift of the Spirit, our faith in the unseen hope of the resurrection drives us onward to the day of Christ Jesus.

THE LANGUAGE OF THE RESURRECTION

As the Spirit of God is both the agent and sustainer of creation, so also the Spirit of God is the inspirer of the word of God, which sets out the hope of the new creation. The Scriptures develop a number of themes that function symbiotically within this divine testimony. Particularly, the language of life, salvation, blessing, and glory build together unto their consummation on the day of the Lord.

The Life of the Resurrection

Within an apocalyptic framework, the Scriptures develop a *theology of life*, actu- ated by the Spirit of God. It was the spoken word of God that created "every *living* thing" (Gen. 1:28), and it was "the breath of *life*" that made Adam "a *living* creature" (Gen. 2:7). Moreover, it was the "tree of *life*" (Gen. 2:9) that promised perpetual regeneration, for the deprivation of this tree meant death as evidenced in the divine declaration regarding Adam's expulsion from the garden: "lest he reach out his hand and take also of the tree of life and eat, and *live forever*" (Gen. 3:22).[28]

This vision of living forever is recapitulated in the end with the "book of *life*" (Rev. 20:15; 21:27), the "water of *life*" (Rev. 21:6; 22:1), and the restored "tree of *life*" (Rev. 22:2,14,19), which is granted "for the *healing* of the nations" (Rev. 22:2). Moreover, the curse of futility and death upon the earth (cf. Gen. 3:16–19; Rom. 8:20) is lifted—"No longer will there be any curse" (Rev. 22:3, NIV)—and the saints will live and "reign forever and ever" (Rev. 22:5). Thus the Scriptures present a holistic vision of "everlasting *life*" (Dan. 12:2), established protologically and projected eschatologically.[29]

A theology of life develops throughout the Old Testament. Though in this age the dead are universally condemned to Sheol/Hades (cf. Ps. 89:48; Eccl. 9:10), God holds power over both death and Sheol—"The LORD kills and brings to life; he brings down to Sheol and raises up" (1 Sam. 2:6; cf. Rev. 1:18).[30] This is evident not only in the lives of Enoch and Elijah (cf. Gen. 5:24; 2 Kings 2:11), but also in the deaths of Korah and his followers, who "went down alive into Sheol" (Num. 16:33; cf. Ps. 55:15; Prov. 1:12). Moreover, death and Sheol "lie open before the LORD" (Prov. 15:11; cf. Deut. 32:22; Ps. 139:8; Amos 9:2). Hence it is the Lord alone who grants deliverance from Sheol, as David anticipates, "You will not abandon my soul to Sheol" (Ps. 16:10; cf. Ps. 89:48), and rehearses, "You have brought up my soul from Sheol; you restored me to life from among those who go down to the pit" (Ps. 30:3; cf. Ps. 86:12–13).

Consequently it is the Lord alone "who redeems your life from the pit" (Ps. 103:4), as God questions, "Shall I ransom them from the power of Sheol? Shall I redeem them from Death?" (Hos. 13:14). Indeed, God alone can ransom a person's soul, "that he should *live on forever* and never see the pit" (Ps. 49:9). So the psalmist declares, "God will ransom my soul from the power of Sheol, for he will receive me" (v. 15). In this way, the righteous will be raised up and delivered from the realm of the dead and restored to the earth—that is, "the land of the living" (Job 28:13; Ps. 27:13; Isa. 53:8; Ezek. 26:20). "For you have delivered my soul from death, my eyes from tears, my feet from stumbling; I will walk before the LORD *in the land of the living*" (Ps. 116:8–9; cf. Ps. 56:13).

This deliverance from Sheol is the theological framework within which the language of resurrection is developed.[31] So Revelation concludes, "Death and Hades *gave up the dead* who were in them, and they were judged" (20:13). Similarly Isaiah prophesies, "Your dead shall live; their bodies *shall rise*. . . . The earth will give birth to the dead" (Isa. 26:19). And Daniel summarizes, "Many of those who sleep in the dust of the earth *shall awake*, some to everlasting life, and some to shame and everlasting contempt" (Dan. 12:2).[32] In this way, the Bible's theology of life develops simply around the Lord delivering the dead from Sheol by raising them up (i.e. resurrection) to *live forever* on a restored Edenic earth.[33]

The New Testament thus strives toward the singular goal of "eternal life" (Matt. 19:16,29; 25:46; Mark 10:17,30; Luke 10:25; 18:18,30; John 3:15–16,36; 4:14,36; 5:24,39; 6:27,40,47,54,68; 10:28; 12:25,50; 17:2–3; Acts 13:46,48; Rom. 2:7; 5:21; 6:22–23; Gal. 6:8; 1 Tim. 1:16; 6:12; Titus 1:2; 3:7; 1 John 1:2; 2:25; 3:15; 5:11,13,20; Jude 21). The sheer number of references to this phrase is indicative of its prominence in the consciousness of the apostolic church, as Paul declared: "*One thing I do*: forgetting what lies behind and straining forward to what lies ahead, I press on toward the goal for *the prize* of the upward call of God in Christ Jesus" (Phil. 3:13–14). Of course, this prize is eternal life—that is, "the resurrection from the dead" (v. 11), when Jesus "will transform our lowly body to be like his glorious body" (v. 21).

As other terminology was shortened (e.g., "the judgment" for "the day of judgment"), so also eternal life was spoken of simply as "life"—"It is better for you to enter *life* crippled than with two hands to go to hell, to the unquenchable fire" (Mark 9:43). Likewise, "The gate is narrow and the way is hard that leads to *life*, and those who find it are few" (Matt. 7:14). So everyone would have understood Jesus' declaration, "I am the bread of *life*" (John 6:35), for "whoever believes has eternal *life*" (v. 47). Similarly, "I am the light of the world" simply references "the light of *life*" (John 8:12). And "I am the resurrection and the *life*" (John 11:25) is in the context of "the resurrection on the last day" (v. 24).

As such, we believe Jesus is "the Author of *life*" (Acts 3:15), since God "has granted the Son also to have *life* in himself" (John 5:26). Accordingly, "we will also *live* with him" (Rom. 6:8; 2 Tim. 2:11). For by believing we "have *life* in his name" (John 20:31). It is "the *life* of God" (Eph. 4:18)—that is, "the *life* to come" (1 Tim. 4:8), which is "the gracious gift of *life*" (1 Peter 3:7, NRSV). It is "the promise of *life*" (2 Tim. 1:1) and "the word of *life*" (Phil. 2:16), to which we hold fast, knowing we will "reign in *life*" (Rom. 5:17). Indeed, it will be "*life* from the dead" (Rom. 11:15)—that is, "*life* and immortality" (2 Tim. 1:10), because mortality itself will be "swallowed up by *life*" (2 Cor. 5:4; cf. 1 Cor. 15:54). Hence we have been equipped with "all things that pertain to *life*" (2 Peter 1:3) that we may "take hold of the eternal *life*" (1 Tim. 6:12). All of this represents the common *language of life* in the early church that pointed to the anticipated day of the Lord and the coming of Christ Jesus.

Therefore, in no way did the early church believe the resurrection and eternal life had already begun. Those who say that "the resurrection has already happened" (2 Tim. 2:18) actually *destroy* people's faith, for "who hopes for what he already has?" (Rom. 8:24, NIV). This is a gnostic reinterpretation of the gift of the Holy Spirit that tries to extrapolate the individual experience to redemptive history as a whole, thus overturning the fundamental nature of "this age" versus "the age to come" (cf. 1 Cor. 15:12; 2 Thess. 2:2). We still live in "the present evil age" (Gal. 1:4), groaning with "this body of death" (Rom. 7:24), enduring the tyranny of "wicked and evil men" (2 Thess. 3:2). However, "though our outer man is decaying, yet our inner man is being renewed day by day" (2 Cor. 4:16, NASB).

Though signs, wonders, and physical healings were common signs of the resurrection, no one mistook them for the resurrection itself. Though paralytics were healed (Luke 5:25; Acts 3:7) and dead men were raised (John 11:44; Acts 20:9–12), they were still "destined to die once, and after that to face judgment" (Heb. 9:27, NIV). And although debate rages in the academy concerning the spiritual realization of other eschatological concepts in the New Testament (kingdom, Messiah, etc.), one generally accepted point is that the resurrection remains completely apocalyptic.[34] So life and death in this age simply point to the life of the resurrection and the second death of Gehenna in the age to come, which are the final consequence of the protological life and death of creation and the fall (see figure 4.3).

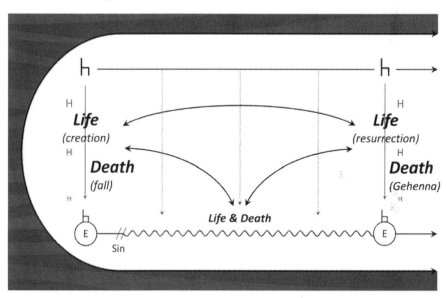

Figure 4.3 – The Apocalyptic Framework of Life and Death

Within such an apocalyptic framework, the sting of death is overcome (1 Cor. 15:55–57). This life is readily forsaken, so that we might "attain to that age and to the resurrection from the dead" (Luke 20:35; cf. Phil. 3:11). We are able to embrace suffering, persecution, and martyrdom, loving not our lives unto death (Rev. 12:11). Without such an approach to life and death, one simply cannot be a disciple of Jesus: "Whoever loves his life loses it, and whoever hates his life in this world will keep it for eternal life" (John 12:25; cf. Matt. 10:39). This is what Jesus meant when he said, "If anyone would come after me, let him deny himself and take up his cross daily and follow me. For whoever would save his life will lose it, but whoever loses his life for my sake will save it" (Luke 9:23–24). Those who walk such a narrow path will receive "the Spirit of life" (Rom. 8:2), which guarantees eternal life—"provided we suffer with him in order that we may also be glorified with him" (v. 17).

The Salvation of the Resurrection

Divine salvation is also interpreted apocalyptically in the Scriptures. The terminology of "salvation" carries the basic connotation of "freedom from limitation."[35] In contrast to "being restricted," salvation in a general sense "connotes freedom from distress."[36] Though finding temporal applications (cf. Ex. 14:13; Judg. 3:9; 1 Chron. 14:11; etc.), salvation is ultimately understood in relation to the restrictive nature of sin and death. Our *condition of mortality* was instituted by God because of the sin of Adam and Eve: "For you are dust, and to dust you shall return" (Gen. 3:19). Death and all of its derivatives are the result of divine condemnation of human sin (cf. Rom. 5:12–18; 1 Cor. 15:21–22). In the end, God is responsible for mortality's introduction, and he is also responsible for its removal: "There will be no more death or mourning or crying or pain, for the old order of things [i.e., mortality] has passed away. . . . *I am* making everything new!" (Rev. 21:4–5, NIV).

In this way, "creation was subjected to *futility*" (Rom. 8:20), by divine design, in order to curb and humiliate the pride of humanity. The limitations of mortality are understood to be a type of *captivity* (see Rom. 7:23), an enslavement from which only God can deliver. So humans are by nature "prisoners of sin" (Gal. 3:22, NLT) and "slaves to sin" (Rom. 6:16,20, NIV; cf. John 8:34). All are "dead in sins" (Eph. 2:5, KJV), and thus "under sin" (Rom. 3:9; 7:14), for "God has *consigned all to disobedience*, that he may have mercy on all" (Rom. 11:32).

Human pride inherently rebels against such an institution. The corporate consciousness of humanity cries out continually, "We are bound by nothing! We have no limits! We are *free!*" Unfortunately, this very proclamation embodies the sin which binds us for condemnation on the last day. Rather than throwing ourselves in the dust and crying, "God, be merciful to me, a sinner!" (Luke 18:13),[37] we harden our calloused hearts to the reality of both our own depravity and the coming wrath of God. To put it another way, those who do not believe they are in need of liberation will not be saved.

Because sin and death are humanity's greatest captivity, salvation is inherently a resurrection concept. Hence Paul summarizes, "For the creation was subjected to futility, not willingly, but because of him who subjected it, in hope that the creation itself will be *set free* from its bondage to corruption and obtain the *freedom* of the glory of the children of God. . . . We ourselves, who have the firstfruits of the Spirit, groan inwardly as we wait eagerly for adoption as sons, the redemption of our bodies. For in this hope we were *saved*" (Rom. 8:20–24).

Note that the Spirit is given as an assurance of our future liberation. And it is the Spirit who helps us and intercedes for us according to that for which we hope—that is, our salvation and resurrection. So Paul continues, "But if we hope for what we do not see, we wait for it with patience. Likewise the Spirit *helps us* in our weakness. For we do not know what to pray for as we ought, but the Spirit himself *intercedes for us* with groanings too deep for words. And he who searches hearts knows what is the mind of the Spirit, because the Spirit intercedes for the saints according to the will of God" (Rom. 8:25–27).

The intercession of the Holy Spirit is in the context of the "futility" and "bondage" of mortality in this life (vv. 20–21). Moreover, it is mortality's "weakness" (Gk. *astheneia*, v. 26)—that is, the "experience of limitation" and "state of debilitating illness"[38]—which the Spirit mitigates while we are in the womb of this age awaiting our birth in the resurrection.[39] Therefore Paul concludes, "And we know that for those who love God all things work together for good, for those who are called according to his purpose. For those whom he foreknew he also predestined to be conformed to the image of his Son, in order that he might be the firstborn among many brothers" (Rom. 8:28–29).

In this way, the activity of the Spirit in this age is designed to help us in the weakness of our mortality until the coming of the Messiah, when the Spirit will liberate us from the tyranny of a body of death (see Rom. 7:23–25).[40] Moreover, God is working out our struggles with mortality in this age for the good of our resurrection (Rom. 8:28), when we will be conformed to the image of his Son (Rom. 8:29) "in a resurrection like his" (Rom. 6:5).

Thus we experience the mechanics of faith, so to speak. The captivity of mortality in this age is designed to drive us to depend upon God, who is the only one able to deliver and save us unto immortality. So God works small deliverances throughout our lives to make us believe in the big deliverance to come, and conversely he allows (and sometimes orchestrates—e.g., Deut. 4:27; Dan. 11:33; Luke 22:31; 2 Cor. 12:7) small captivities in our lives to make us come to terms with our big captivity to sin and death.[41] This causes us to cry out to him by the groaning of the Spirit within us, and he works it all out for our good in the age to come. Consequently, temporal captivity and deliverance (i.e., salvation) point to their protological introduction and eschatological conclusion (see figure 4.4).

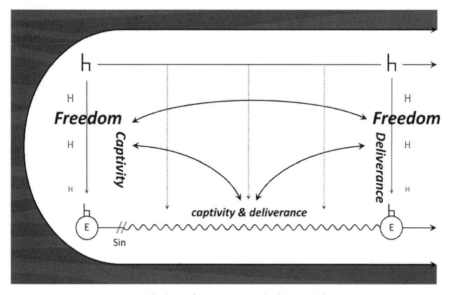

Figure 4.4 – The Apocalyptic Framework of Divine Salvation

Within such an apocalyptic framework, the New Testament assumes salvation to involve a new heavens and new earth, with a resurrection of the righteous and the wicked, inaugurated at the day of the Lord.[42] So an overview of redemptive history can be simply stated: "Christ was sacrificed once to take away the sins of many people; and he will appear a second time, not to bear sin, but to bring *salvation* to those who are waiting for him" (Heb. 9:28, NIV). It is "a *salvation* ready to be revealed in the last time" (1 Peter 1:5), which is reserved for "those who are to inherit *salvation*" (Heb. 1:14). As the first to rise from the dead, Christ Jesus is "the pioneer of their *salvation*" (Heb. 2:10, NRSV); and being perfected in his own resurrection, "he became the source of eternal *salvation* to all who obey him" (Heb. 5:9).

The righteous will "obtain the *salvation* that is in Christ Jesus with eternal glory" (2 Tim. 2:10; cf. 1 Thess. 5:9), for "there is *salvation* in no one else" (Acts 4:12)—faith in Christ crucified is "the way to be *saved*" (Acts 16:17, NIV). "For God did not send the Son into the world to judge the world, but that the world might be *saved* through Him" (John 3:17, NASB). Indeed, "since we have now been justified by his blood, how much more shall we be *saved* from God's wrath through him!" (Rom. 5:9, NIV). This is "the word of truth, the gospel of your *salvation*" (Eph. 1:13). However, only "the one who endures to the end will be *saved*" (Matt. 10:22; 24:13). "But we are not of those who shrink back and are destroyed, but of those who believe and are *saved*" (Heb. 10:39, NIV). In this we greatly rejoice, "for *salvation* is nearer to us now than when we first believed. The night is far gone; the day is at hand" (Rom. 13:11–12).[43]

The Blessing of the Resurrection

The Scriptures also frame divine blessing within an apocalyptic framework. By the word of the Lord, everything with the breath of life was blessed by the Creator in the beginning: "And God *blessed* them, saying, 'Be fruitful and multiply . . .'" (Gen. 1:22). This same divine blessing is reiterated in the new heavens and new earth in the end: "*Blessed* are those who wash their robes, so that they may have the right to the tree of life" (Rev. 22:14).

Conversely, divine cursing is declared in the beginning (Gen. 3:14,17) so as to frustrate creation (Rom. 8:20)[44] and bring about repentance (cf. Ps. 73:3–17; Hos. 5:14–15; Rev. 9:20–21; etc.). This divine cursing culminates in the end with the judgment of the wicked—"Depart from me, you *cursed*, into the eternal fire" (Matt. 25:41)—while the blessing of God culminates in the resurrection, "Come, you who are *blessed* by my Father, inherit the kingdom prepared for you from the foundation of the world" (Matt. 25:34). Thus, "No longer will there be anything *accursed*" (Rev. 22:3), for "the old order of things has passed away" (Rev. 21:4, NIV).

In relation to divine sovereignty, blessing and cursing is roughly equivalent to divine favor and disfavor within a governmental context.[45] Therefore God is favorable to Adam and Eve and delegates governance of the earth by blessing (Gen. 1:26–28). The righteous will likewise be blessed in the age to come when God delegates to them the kingdom (see Matt. 19:28; Luke 22:29–30) on the new earth, "and they will reign forever and ever" (Rev. 22:5).

It is within this broad framework that we are to understand *temporal* divine blessing and cursing. Those who love and obey God are favored and blessed—"Noah found favor in the eyes of the LORD" (Gen. 6:8; cf. Ex. 33:12; Ps. 84:11; Luke 1:30). Those who hate and rebel against God are disfavored and cursed—"On Cain and his offering he did not look with favor. . . . Now you are under a curse and driven from the ground" (Gen. 4:5,11, NIV; cf. Lev. 20; Prov. 12:2; Rev. 2:20–23). So redemptive history plays out according to divine favor and disfavor: "The LORD preserves all who love him, but all the wicked he will destroy. . . . Let all flesh bless his holy name forever and ever" (Ps. 145:20–21). Indeed, "Those blessed by Him shall inherit the earth, but those cursed by Him shall be cut off" (Ps. 37:22, NKJV).[46] And so temporal blessing and cursing point to their protological introduction and their eschatological conclusion (see figure 4.5).

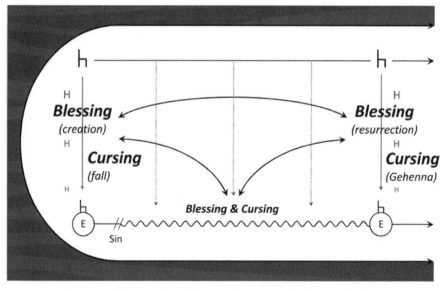

Figure 4.5 – The Apocalyptic Framework of Divine Blessing and Cursing

As such, the blessings and curses of the covenants (Gen. 12:2–3; Deut. 27–28; 2 Sam. 7:11–16) are understood within an apocalyptic context. For example, those who bless Abraham and his descendants will find favor with God; those who curse him will be cursed by God; and in him "all the families of the earth shall be *blessed*" (Gen. 12:3). Though holding a temporal application (see Josh. 21:43–45; 23:14), such words are understood in their ultimate context of deliverance from Sheol, which develops around the day of the Lord and the resurrection.[47]

Thus Peter relates the blessing of the Abrahamic covenant to the restoration of all things: "[Christ] must remain in heaven until the time comes for God to restore everything, as he promised long ago through his holy prophets. . . . And you are heirs of the prophets and of the covenant God made with your fathers. He said to Abraham, 'Through your offspring all peoples on earth will be *blessed.*' When God raised up his servant, he sent him first to you to *bless* you by turning each of you from your wicked ways." (Acts 3:21,25–26, NIV) The Abrahamic covenant is related to the blessing of God throughout redemptive history—*first* by turning Israel from wickedness (Acts 3:26), and *second* by restoring all things (v. 21). This blessing is what it means to be "heirs of the prophets and of the covenant" (v. 25).

Similarly, Paul took for granted that Abraham received "the promise that he would be heir of the world" (Rom. 4:13, NIV). As such, God renamed Abram according to his destiny (Gen. 17:5–8), because he is "the God who gives life to the dead and calls things that are not as though they were" (Rom. 4:17, NIV).[48] So God's "blessing" (vv. 6,9) was understood in the context of "the day of wrath" (Rom. 2:5), "eternal life" (Rom. 5:21), "the glory that is to be revealed" (Rom. 8:18), etc. Within a biblical worldview, everything temporal ultimately relates to its eternal fulfillment, because there is an inherent continuity between the two.

So also the blessing of the Davidic covenant was understood in its ultimate context, wherein all the nations will find favor with God by submission to the Davidic king to come: "Afterward the Israelites will return and seek the LORD their God and David their king. They will come trembling to the LORD and to his *blessings* in the last days" (Hos. 3:5, NIV). So Gabriel declared that Jesus would receive "the throne of his father David, . . . and of his kingdom there will be no end" (Luke 1:32–33), which was confirmed by angels proclaiming, "Glory to God in the highest, and on earth peace to men on whom his *favor* rests" (Luke 2:14, NIV).[49]

In this way we are promised that the favor and blessing of God bestowed in the beginning will be restored in the end by means of the covenants.[50] The blessing of God is the precondition of the resurrection. Those who are favored by God will inherit eternal life, while those who are condemned by God will inherit eternal punishment. So James encourages perseverance, "*Blessed* is the man who remains steadfast under trial, for when he has stood the test he will receive the crown of life" (James 1:12). So also Jesus promises the faithful, "You will be *blessed,* . . . . for you will be repaid at the resurrection of the righteous" (Luke 14:14, NRSV). Moreover, "*Blessed* are the meek, for they shall inherit the earth" (Matt. 5:5). And concerning the martyrs, "*Blessed* are the dead who die in the Lord from now on. . . . For their deeds follow them!" (Rev. 14:13). Indeed, "*Blessed* are those who are invited to the marriage supper of the Lamb" (Rev. 19:9). "*Blessed* and holy is the one who shares in the first resurrection!" (Rev. 20:6).

This *language of blessing* is used throughout the New Testament in relation to "our *blessed* hope, the appearing of the glory of our great God and Savior Jesus Christ" (Titus 2:13).

The Glory of the Resurrection

Related to eternal life, salvation, and divine blessing in the Scriptures is divine glory. God himself is described as "the God of glory" (Ps. 29:3; Acts 7:2), "the king of glory" (Ps. 24:7,10), "the Lord of glory" (1 Cor. 2:8; James 2:1), and "the Majestic Glory" (2 Peter 1:17). Indeed, "the glory of God" (Ps. 19:1; 106:20; John 11:4; Acts 7:55; Rom. 3:23; 2 Cor. 4:6; Rev. 21:23) is a pervasive concept throughout the Scriptures. But what is the ultimate context of divine glory? Why does it appear? How and when is it expressed?

Because God himself is glorious, so also is everything he does. Accordingly, creation—with humanity at its apex—was created in divine glory. So Psalm 8, "O LORD, our Lord, how majestic is your name in all the earth! You have set your glory in the heavens above. . . . You have made man a little lower than the heavenly beings and crowned him with glory and honor" (vv. 1,5, AT).[51] As creation was adorned in divine glory in the beginning, so also will it radiate the glory of God in the end.[52] Thus the vision of Revelation:

> And [the angel] carried me away in the Spirit to a great, high mountain, and showed me the holy city Jerusalem coming down out of heaven from God, having the *glory* of God, its radiance like a most rare jewel, like a jasper, clear as crystal. . . .
>
> And the city has no need of sun or moon to shine on it, for the *glory* of God gives it light, and its lamp is the Lamb. By its light will the nations walk, and the kings of the earth will bring their *glory* into it, and its gates will never be shut by day—and there will be no night there. They will bring into it the *glory* and the honor of the nations. (21:10–11,23–26)

As humanity was crowned in glory and honor protologically, so will the righteous of the nations be laurelled in glory and honor eschatologically. Within such an apocalyptic framework, we understand that temporal revelations of divine glory (cf. Ex. 24:16; 33:22; Num. 14:10) inherently prophesy that "all the earth shall be filled with the *glory* of the LORD" (Num. 14:21). The filling of the tabernacle (Ex. 40:34) and the temple (1 Kings 8:11; 2 Chron. 5:14) anticipate the day when the messianic temple will be filled with glory (Ezek. 43:2–7; Hag. 2:7–9; Mal. 3:1–2), and when "the *glory* of the LORD will be revealed, and all mankind together will see it" (Isa. 40:5, NIV).[53]

The Psalms and Prophets build in anticipation of the glory of God and its eschatological fulfillment. As the psalmist declares, "The nations will fear the name of the LORD, and all the kings of the earth your *glory*. For the LORD will build up Zion; he will appear in his *glory*" (Ps. 102:15–16, NRSV). Hence the Davidic prayer, "Be exalted, O God, above the heavens! Let your *glory* be over all the earth!" (Ps. 57:11; cf. Ps. 108:5). Likewise, "Blessed be the LORD, the God of Israel, who alone does wondrous things. Blessed be his glorious name forever; may the whole earth be filled with his *glory!*" (Ps. 72:18–19). Similarly the royal Psalms (96–99) generally outline the form of the age to come. For example,

> Sing to the LORD, bless his name;
> > tell of his salvation from day to day.
> Declare his *glory* among the nations,
> > his marvelous works among all the peoples! . . .

Worship the LORD in the *splendor* of holiness;
> tremble before him, all the earth! . . .
> For he comes to judge the earth.
He will judge the world in righteousness,
> and the peoples in his faithfulness.
(Ps. 96:2–3,9,13)

The vision of divine glory is particularized in the writings of the prophets. The Messiah will be "given dominion and *glory* and a kingdom" (Dan. 7:14), "for the LORD Almighty will reign on Mount Zion and in Jerusalem, and before its elders, *gloriously*" (Isa. 24:23, NIV). "In that day the branch of the LORD shall be beautiful and *glorious*" (Isa. 4:2), for "then the LORD will create over all of Mount Zion and over its convocations a cloud and smoke by day and a bright flame of fire by night; indeed a canopy will accompany the LORD's *glorious* presence" (v. 5, NET). The nations "shall see the *glory* of the LORD, the majesty of our God" (Isa. 35:2); and therefore "men will fear the name of the LORD, and from the rising of the sun, they will revere his *glory*" (Isa. 59:19, NIV). "In that day the Root of Jesse will stand as a banner for the peoples; the nations will rally to him, and his place of rest will be *glorious*" (Isa. 11:10, NIV). When the glory of God rises upon Jerusalem (Isa. 60:1–3), the nations will gather to see it (Isa. 59:19; 62:2; 66:18), and so "the earth will be filled with the knowledge of the *glory* of the LORD as the waters cover the sea" (Hab. 2:14).

Because the Lord dwells in heavenly glory (cf. Ps. 26:8; 63:2), the day of the Lord will involve the opening of the heavens and the descent of God in divine glory. Hence Isaiah's prayer, "Oh that you would *rend the heavens* and come down, that the mountains might quake at your presence, . . . and that the nations might tremble at your presence!" (Isa. 64:1–2). Likewise David, "*Bow your heavens*, O LORD, and come down! Touch the mountains so that they smoke!" (Ps. 144:5; cf. Ps. 18:9). In this way the glory of God will be revealed, and the darkness of humanity will be exposed.[54]

This scenario of divine glory became common to apocalyptic expectation during New Testament times.[55] So Jesus responds to the messianic declaration of Nathaniel (John 1:49), saying, "Truly, truly, I say to you, you will see *heaven opened*, and the angels of God ascending and descending on the Son of Man" (v. 51). Angels are understood as divine administrators (cf. Ps. 91:11; 103:20–21; Acts 7:53; Gal. 3:19; Heb. 1:14), and as such they will mediate the glory of God in the age to come.[56] The opening of the heavens at Jesus' baptism (Matt. 3:16), the Mount of Transfiguration (Matt. 17:5), and Stephen's stoning (Acts 7:56) would have been interpreted apocalyptically in anticipation of the day of the Lord.[57] Thus Revelation 19:11: "Then I saw *heaven opened*, and behold, a white horse! The one sitting on it is called Faithful and True, and in righteousness he judges and makes war."

Though the heavens are closed in this age, so to speak, they will be opened in the age to come, and the darkness of sinful humanity will be overcome by the glory of God.[58] As with other aspects of divine sovereignty, historical revelations of divine glory point to their protological introduction and their eschatological conclusion (see figure 4.6). Consequently, the gift of the Spirit, and the glory therein (cf. 2 Cor. 3:17–18; 4:4–7), gives us a faint glimpse "in a mirror dimly" (1 Cor. 13:12) into the age to come. As it is in heaven, so it is in the Spirit; as it was in the beginning, so it will be in the end.[59]

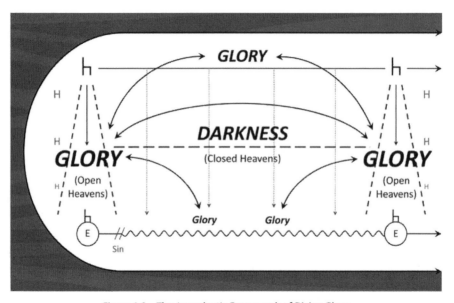

Figure 4.6 – The Apocalyptic Framework of Divine Glory

The thoroughly eschatological orientation of the New Testament is seen in its use of the *language of glory*. Most evident is Jesus' own description of the age to come: "When the Son of Man comes in his *glory*, and all the angels with him, then he will sit on his *glorious* throne" (Matt. 25:31). Indeed, "The Son of Man is going to come with his angels in the *glory* of his Father, and then he will repay each person according to what he has done" (Matt. 16:27; cf. Luke 9:26). The nations "will see the Son of Man coming on the clouds of heaven with power and great *glory*" (Matt. 24:30). For "at the renewal of all things, when the Son of Man is seated on the throne of his *glory*, you who have followed me will also sit on twelve thrones" (Matt. 19:28, NRSV).

Though all human beings have sinned and "fall short of the *glory* of God"

(Rom. 3:23), those who are justified freely by faith in Christ's sacrifice on the cross will be presented blameless "before the presence of his *glory* with great joy" (Jude 24). They will "obtain the salvation that is in Christ Jesus with eternal *glory*" (2 Tim. 2:10), for they have been called "into his kingdom and *glory*" (1 Thess. 2:12, NIV)—that is, "to his eternal *glory* in Christ" (1 Peter 5:10). This glory is "the hope of His calling . . . the riches of the *glory* of His inheritance in the saints" (Eph. 1:18, NASB), for Christ will come "on that day to be *glorified* in his saints, and to be marveled at among all who have believed" (2 Thess. 1:10). Though our present bodies are "sown in dishonor," they will be "raised in *glory*" (1 Cor. 15:43), for Jesus "will transform our lowly body to be like his *glorious* body" (Phil. 3:21). "When Christ who is your life appears, then you also will appear with him in *glory*" (Col. 3:4).

Jesus' disciples asked, "Grant us to sit, one at your right hand and one at your left, in your *glory*" (Mark 10:37), but they didn't understand that "the Messiah should suffer these things and then enter into his *glory*" (Luke 24:26, NRSV). Likewise, our "light momentary affliction is preparing for us an eternal weight of *glory* beyond all comparison" (2 Cor. 4:17). If we "share Christ's sufferings," then we will also "rejoice and be glad when his *glory* is revealed" (1 Peter 4:13). "And when the chief Shepherd appears, you will receive the unfading crown of *glory*" (1 Peter 5:4). The present sufferings "are not worth comparing with the *glory* that is to be revealed to us" (Rom. 8:18)—"the freedom of the *glory* of the children of God" (Rom. 8:21).

All such references to divine glory as eschatological are contextually sound and provide an organic cohesion to the New Testament. Humanity was created in divine glory, and on the last day the heavens will open and the righteous will be raised to life by the Spirit, clothed with bodies of glory, and blessed anew by the Creator. Such glory is the singular prize which the righteous now seek (cf. 1 Cor. 9:22–25; Phil. 3:11–14): the blessing of eternal life in divine glory—that is, "our blessed hope, the appearing of the *glory* of our great God and Savior Jesus Christ" (Titus 2:13).

THE CRUCIFORM-APOCALYPTIC
TESTIMONY OF THE SPIRIT

Within such an apocalyptic framework, the Scriptures declare that Jesus of Nazareth was sent by God and crucified according to divine foreknowledge (cf. Acts 2:23; 3:18; 4:28). After being raised by the Holy Spirit (Rom. 8:11; 1 Cor. 6:14), Jesus interpreted his own death in sacrificial terms (see chapters 7 and 8) for forty days (Acts 1:3) before being taken up. Paul details the progression of this divine impartation of knowledge (1 Cor. 15:3–8), insisting that an atonemental interpretation of the cross was passed on to him *directly* (Gal. 1:12)—that is, "I did not consult any man, nor did I go up to Jerusalem to see those who were apostles before I was" (vv. 16–17, NIV). Thus Paul understands that the sacrificial interpretation of the death of the Messiah "is not of human origin" (v. 11, NRSV).

Therefore, the idea that Jesus' death was accounted by God as an atoning sacrifice in the stead of humanity's sins is not something the apostles figured out. Rather, it came directly from Jesus, being received by the apostles.[60] Justification by faith in anticipation of the day of judgment is the *golden kernel* of apostolic revelation, so to speak—planted by Jesus for forty days and galvanized by the outpouring of the Holy Spirit in Acts 2. Since depraved humanity naturally puts "confidence in the flesh" (Phil. 3:3) to right all that is wrong, the gift of the Holy Spirit was deemed necessary by God to confirm the cruciform revelation. Paul's exhortation to the Galatians is typical of how the apostles understood Pentecost:

> You foolish Galatians! Who has bewitched you? Before your very eyes Jesus Christ was clearly portrayed *as crucified*. I would like to learn just one thing from you: Did you *receive the Spirit* by observing the law, or by believing what you heard? Are you so foolish? After beginning with the Spirit, are you now trying to attain your goal by human effort? . . . Does God *give you his Spirit* and work miracles among you because you observe the law, or because you believe what you heard? (Gal 3:1–5, NIV)

The Spirit was therefore understood as a unique gift from God given to confirm the testimony of Christ crucified in light of the day of the Lord (see figure 4.7). This pattern is seen throughout the book of Acts,[61] and it defines the broad approach of the apostolic witness as a whole.[62] Before Jesus was taken up, he commissioned his disciples as witnesses and promised that they would be clothed with power from on high (Luke 24:48–49; Acts 1:8). This commissioning is then plainly recounted by Peter to Cornelius and his household: "He commanded us to preach to the people and to testify that he is the one appointed by God *to be judge* of the living and the dead. To him all the prophets bear witness that everyone who believes in him receives *forgiveness of sins* through his name" (Acts 10:42–43). The charismatic nature of the apostolic witness is subservient to its cruciform-apocalyptic message, for "while Peter was still *saying these things*, the Holy Spirit fell on all who heard the word" (v. 44).

Likewise Paul prays for the Corinthian church, "I give thanks to my God always for you . . . even as the testimony about Christ was *confirmed among you*—so that you are not lacking in *any gift*, as you wait for the revealing of our

Lord Jesus Christ, who will sustain you to the end, guiltless in the day of our Lord Jesus Christ" (1 Cor. 1:4–8). Such a witness, derived from Jesus himself and fundamentally represented in the epistles of the New Testament, comprised "the apostles' teaching" (Acts 2:42), to which the early church devoted itself.

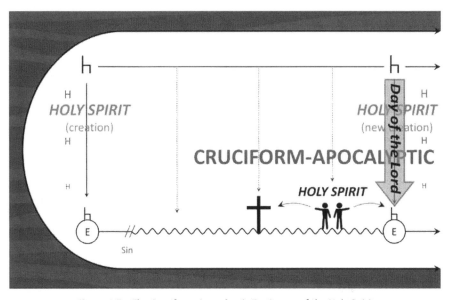

Figure 4.7 – The Cruciform-Apocalyptic Testimony of the Holy Spirit

The message of the cross in light of the day of the Lord is "the standard of teaching" (Rom. 6:17), or "the pattern of sound teaching" (2 Tim. 1:13, NIV), which the apostles sought to pass on to others as they had received it from the risen Christ. So Paul exhorts Timothy, "What you have *heard from me* in the presence of many witnesses *entrust to faithful men* who will be able to teach others also" (2 Tim. 2:2).[63] Such a pattern was thus confirmed by the gift of the Holy Spirit, as Hebrews outlines: "How shall we escape if we ignore such a great salvation? This salvation, which was first announced by the Lord [cf. Acts 1:3], was confirmed to us by those who heard him [cf. 1 Cor. 15:5–7]. God also testified to it by signs, wonders and various miracles, and gifts of the Holy Spirit distributed according to his will [cf. Acts 2; 1 Cor. 12:4–11; Gal. 3:1–5; etc.]" (Heb. 2:3–4, NIV).

THE CHRISTOPLATONIC RESURRECTION

With the accommodation of Hellenistic philosophy, the fundamental Christian hope of the resurrection of the body by the Spirit of God was primarily replaced with the eternal existence of the soul in an immaterial heaven. Though the language of resurrection was incorporated, its reality was denied. As Moltmann summarizes,

> In the degree to which Christianity cut itself off from its Hebrew roots and acquired Hellenistic and Roman form, it lost its eschatological hope and surrendered its apocalyptic alternative to "this world" of violence and death. It merged into late antiquity's gnostic religion of redemption. From Justin onwards, most of the Fathers revered Plato as a "Christian before Christ" and extolled his feeling for the divine transcendence and for the values of the spiritual world. God's eternity now took the place of God's future, heaven replaced the coming kingdom, the spirit that redeems the soul from the body supplanted the Spirit as "the well of life," the immortality of the soul displaced the resurrection of the body, and the yearning for another world became a substitute for changing this one.[64]

Within this dominant form of Christoplatonism, all of the biblical language associated with the resurrection was reinterpreted along escapist lines.[65] "Salvation" became deliverance from materiality unto the liberating "glory" of immateriality. Eternal "life" became the true "blessing" of God that releases us from our bodies (in the Greek tradition of *sōma sēma*—i.e., "the body is a tomb").[66] Therefore immateriality became "the kingdom of heaven," which is our "inheritance," "destiny," "calling," etc. All of this was understood in terms of a "spiritual" resurrection, as Origen argued with ironic condescension:

> We now turn our attention to some of our own believers, who, either from feebleness of intellect or want of proper instruction, adopt a very low and abject view of *the resurrection of the body*. . . . And so also to those who shall deserve to obtain an inheritance in the kingdom of heaven, that germ of the body's restoration, which we have before mentioned, by God's command restores out of the earthly and animal body *a spiritual one, capable of inhabiting the heavens.*[67]

The lack of a vibrant theology of the resurrection has had a crippling effect on the church throughout its history. Though immaterial heaven does hold out some hope for an existence without death, crying, or pain, it lacks an organic connection to *this life*. Because humanity was constitutionally designed for existence *on the earth*, any hope that does not involve an idyllic earthly existence is constitutionally impossible either to understand or to relate to.[68] As the message of the cross and the age to come is often compared to food (cf. Matt. 24:45; 1 Cor. 3:2; Heb. 5:12), the heavenly-destiny gospel is a dry and withered hope that starves believers—gnawing on it as they may—leaving them malnourished and weak in an often debilitating struggle with sin, death, and mortality.

Conversely, the dominionistic Christoplatonic hope—which promises the kingdom *now*, the glory *now*, eternal life *now*, etc.—is something of a fermented and rotten theological food that makes people drunk for a season, but in the end it leaves them nauseated and *diseased*. Though propagated at a popular level in modern times as "health and wealth,"[69] this radical sickness has plagued the church throughout its history. Introduced through Gnosticism (cf. 1 Tim. 6:20; 2 Tim. 2:18; 2 Thess. 2:2), it is a devilish doctrine that took root in Constantinian Christendom and continues strong to the present day.[70]

Because of its perverted worldview, Christoplatonism has primarily produced these two perverted hopes throughout the history of the church. Moreover, its distorted view of creation leaves little room for a theology of the Spirit (technically termed, *pneumatology*). Thus the Spirit of God has generally been neglected in the history of theological reflection.[71] Since the Spirit plays no significant role protologically or eschatologically,[72] he is relegated to a subsidiary function in the attainment of escapist and/or dominionistic ends (see figure 4.8). Without the real historical events of creation and the day of the Lord as anchor points, the gift of the Holy Spirit gets commonly marginalized as a "second blessing," or "second work of grace," given only to the spiritually elite.[73]

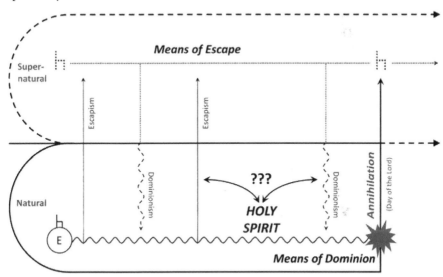

Figure 4.8 – Perversion of the Holy Spirit's Function in Augustinian Christoplatonism

Within dispensationalism, generally speaking, the relationship between the Holy Spirit and the resurrection has been somewhat tenuous.[74] Being relegated mostly to the production of prophecy, the Spirit here also plays a secondary role in redemptive history. Thus dispensationalism has lacked a viable theology and practice of the Spirit, with some going so far as to embrace cessationism, the belief that God retracted the gift of the Spirit when the apostolic witness ended.[75]

Though an emphasis on the Holy Spirit has been revived in modern times, due in part to the advent of the Pentecostal and charismatic movements of the twentieth century,[76] the basic functions of the Holy Spirit in relation to creation and the resurrection are still largely overlooked and disconnected.[77] As inaugurationalism has worked through the ranks, however, many have embraced it as an essential framework for a theology of the Spirit.[78] Gordon Fee thus summarizes the inaugurational approach:

> Through the death and resurrection of his Son Jesus, our Lord, a gracious and loving God has effected eschatological salvation for his new covenant people, the church, who now, as they await Christ's coming, live the life of the future by the power of the Spirit. . . .
>
> Salvation is "eschatological" in the sense that final salvation, which still awaits the believer, is already a present reality through Christ and the Spirit. It is "in Christ" in the sense that what originated in God was effected historically by the death and resurrection of Christ, and is appropriated experientially by God's people through the work of the Holy Spirit—who is also the key to Christian life "between the times," until the final consummation at Christ's *parousia*.[79]

The Spirit is hence understood as *the evidence of realized eschatology*.[80] In this way the Spirit not only has a referent, which informs its meaning and purpose, but it also becomes its own end (see figure 4.9).[81] More than simply "the powers *of* the age to come" (Heb. 6:5), the outpouring of the Spirit embodies the age to come in itself.[82]

Unfortunately, such an approach inherently negates a theology of the cross as the standard of this age. Akin to its dominionistic ancestor, inaugurationalism promises the resurrection and the abundant life *now*.[83] If Jesus truly inaugurated the new creation, wherein the curse is overturned, then we foremost ought to campaign for the deposing of wicked kings, for environmental restoration, for gender equality, etc.[84] If the resurrection has already begun, then where is the impetus to take up our cross in this life (see Luke 9:23 and parallels)? Why should we be those who "endure pain while suffering unjustly" (1 Peter 2:19, NRSV)? Why should we rejoice in persecution (Matt. 5:12; Acts 5:41)? Why should we lay down our lives as Jesus did (John 15:13; 1 John 3:16)? What is the purpose of being the scum of the earth in this age, paraded around like those condemned to die in the arena (1 Cor. 4:9–13)? Why should we love our lives not unto death (Rev. 12:11)? Why should we "always carry around in our body the death of Jesus" (2 Cor. 4:10, NIV)? And why are we

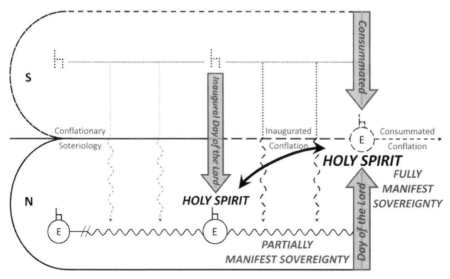

Figure 4.9 – Perversion of the Holy Spirit's Function in Inaugurational Christoplatonism

"always being given over to death for Jesus' sake" (v. 11, NIV)? Why should we "share abundantly in Christ's sufferings" (2 Cor. 1:5), being "united with him in a death like his" (Rom. 6:5), rejoicing "insofar as you share Christ's sufferings" (1 Peter 4:13), "filling up what is lacking in Christ's afflictions" (Col. 1:24), "becoming like him in his death" (Phil. 3:10)? Why should we sell our possessions and give to the needy (Luke 12:33; Acts 2:45), joyfully accepting the confiscation of our property (Heb. 10:34)? Why should we soberly prepare our minds for grievous trials, setting our hope *fully* on the grace to be brought to us at the revelation of Jesus Christ (1 Peter 1:6–13)? If our inheritance has already begun, why then should we heed Paul's *radical* exhortation to forsake living for this age in every way:

> What I mean, brothers, is that *the time is short.* From now on those who have wives should live *as if* they had none; those who mourn, *as if* they did not; those who are happy, *as if* they were not; those who buy something, *as if* it were not theirs to keep; those who use the things of the world, *as if* not engrossed in them. For this world in its present form is passing away. (1 Cor. 7:29–31, NIV)

All of this is the cruciform response to the apocalyptic day. If we do not embrace the cross in this age, then we are, in the sight of God, "illegitimate children" (Heb. 12:8), and we will be "disowned" before the Father on the last day (cf. Matt. 10:33).[85] However, if we follow in the steps of our Master in this life (1 Peter 2:21), then we will be fellow heirs with him in the life to come, "provided we *suffer with him* in order that we may also be glorified with him" (Rom. 8:17).

Inaugurationalism is an insidious denial of the cross, a faithless disowning of Christ crucified. If Paul were alive today, I think he would respond to its dogmatic proclamation the same way he responded to the realized eschatology of his day: "I endure everything for the sake of the elect, that they too may obtain the salvation that is in Christ Jesus, with eternal glory. Here is a trustworthy saying: If we died with him, we will also live with him; if we endure, we will also reign with him. If we *disown* him, he will also disown us; if we are *faithless*, he will remain faithful, for he cannot disown himself" (2 Tim. 2:10–13, NIV).[86]

Chapter Five

❋

THE HOPE
OF THE CHRIST

I n the context of a biblical theology culminating in the day of the Lord, the
resurrection, and a new heavens and new earth, the Scriptures develop a
clear *messianic hope*, which was at the heart of the apostolic witness.[1] Likewise, the question of Jesus' messianic identity pervades the Gospels.[2] Such a
wide usage, with a relative lack of internal debate, communicates a common
understanding of the role and function of the Messiah within redemptive history.[3] Jesus claimed to be "the Expected One" (Matt. 11:3; Luke 7:19, NASB),
but what did this expectation generally entail?

The terms "Messiah" (Heb. *māšîaḥ*) and "Christ" (Gk. *christos*) simply mean
"anointed one" or "consecrated one."[4] In the Old Testament, various "messiahs"
or "christs" were anointed (usually with oil) for different roles and functions—
for example, prophets (1 Kings 19:16; Ps. 105:15), priests (Ex. 29:7; Lev.
4:3–5; 5:16), and kings (1 Sam. 10:1; 1 Kings 1:39; 2 Kings 9:6). People were
ordained to positions of leadership and then anointed to carry out their respon-
sibilities. In this way there is an overlap of meaning between "appointing" and
"anointing" (cf. Num. 1:50; 3:10; 27:16; 1 Sam. 8:1; Ps. 89:27; etc.).

Projected to its eschatological culmination, the Messiah/Christ is the one
appointed and anointed by God to execute the day of the Lord, raise the dead,
judge the wicked, reward the righteous, etc.[5] Thus Peter summarizes the apostolic commissioning: "[God] commanded us to preach to the people and to
testify that [Jesus] is the one *appointed* by God to be judge of the living and the
dead" (Acts 10:42). Paul likewise concludes redemptive history in his preaching to the Athenians: "[God] has set a day when he will judge the world with
justice *by the man he has appointed*" (Acts 17:31, NIV). Similarly, Paul declares

that on that day "God will judge the secrets of men *through Christ Jesus*" (Rom. 2:16, NASB).

In this way the Messiah is understood as *the divine agent*. Representing and working on behalf of God, he is the ultimate mediator of redemptive history.[6] Though God could have chosen to open the heavens and descend upon humanity directly, in an unmediated fashion, he decided according to his own wise counsel to administrate salvation through another. Divine agency is hence the core idea of messianic expectation (or "messianism"), which is seen in all aspects of biblical theology. As God will save his people, so the Messiah is the Savior (cf. Luke 2:11; Phil. 3:20; 1 John 4:14). As God will judge the earth, so the Messiah is the Judge (cf. Acts 10:42; 2 Tim. 4:8; James 5:9). As God will redeem creation, so the Messiah is the Redeemer (cf. Gal. 3:13; Titus 2:14; Heb. 9:15).

So the Messiah/Christ is the divine agent in the apocalyptic mediation of redemptive history (see figure 5.1). Therefore Jesus concludes, "*I am* the Alpha and the Omega, the first and the last, the beginning and the end" (Rev. 22:13).[7] Such a declaration is based upon the arbitration of divine recompense: "Behold, I am coming soon, bringing *my recompense* with me, to repay each one for what he has done" (v. 12).

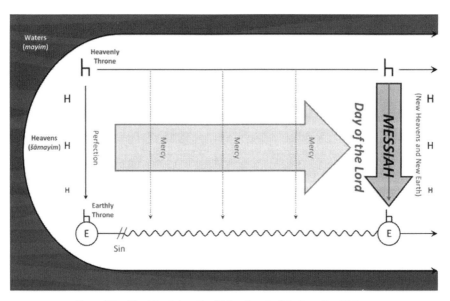

Figure 5.1 – The Messiah as the Divine Agent of Redemptive History

This synergy between God and his Christ is seen throughout the New Testament, especially in relation to the day of the Lord, thus producing the phraseology of "the day of Christ" (Phil. 1:10; 2:16), "the day of Jesus Christ" (Phil. 1:6), and "the day of our Lord Jesus Christ" (1 Cor. 1:8). Likewise divine judgment, as in "the judgment seat of God" (Rom. 14:10), is understood to be administered through the Messiah—that is, "the judgment seat of Christ" (2 Cor. 5:10). In this way the age to come will be a seamless colaboring to establish "the kingdom of Christ *and* God" (Eph. 5:5), for "the throne of God *and* of the Lamb will be in it, and his servants will worship him" (Rev. 22:3).

Since God and Messiah are united in their work, the "Spirit of God" and the "Spirit of Christ" (Rom. 8:9) are one and the same (cf. Eph. 4:3–5). Those who know Messiah, know God, and vice versa (cf. John 8:19; 12:44–50; 14:7–11). And those who follow Messiah, follow God, and vice versa (cf. Matt. 10:32–33; 16:23–27). So those who become disciples by repenting at the preaching of the day of the Lord (cf. Matt. 28:18) are commanded to be baptized "in the name of the Father *and* of the Son *and* of the Holy Spirit" (v. 19)—the Father will judge and restore creation through his Son by the power of his Spirit.[8]

Conversely, those who reject the Messiah, reject God (cf. John 15:23; 16:3)—"Who is the liar but he who denies that Jesus is the Christ? . . . No one who denies the Son has the Father" (1 John 2:22–23). Thus, when persecuted for healing on the Sabbath, Jesus responds, "My Father is working until now, and I am working. . . . I say to you, the Son can do nothing of his own accord, but only what he sees the Father doing" (John 5:17–19).[9] The Messiah does what God does, and this agency was Jesus' justification for violation of the Sabbath traditions. He then further justifies himself by detailing the eschatological conclusion of such agency:

> For as the Father raises the dead and gives them life, *so also the Son gives life* to whom he will. The Father judges no one, but has *given all judgment to the Son*, that all may honor the Son, just as they honor the Father. Whoever does not honor the Son does not honor the Father who sent him. Truly, truly, I say to you, whoever hears my word and believes him who sent me has eternal life. . . .
>
> For as the Father has life in himself, so he has *granted the Son also to have life in himself*. And he has *given him authority to execute judgment*, because he is the Son of Man. Do not marvel at this, for an hour is coming when all who are in the tombs will hear his voice and come out, those who have done good to the resurrection of life, and those who have done evil to the resurrection of judgment. (John 5:21–29)

The Scriptures develop this messianic expectation within an apocalyptic framework culminating in the last day.[10] Though God could have simply come in power and restored creation without mediation, he chose to do it through a man whom he appointed, "the Christ of God" (Luke 9:20; 23:35). Like a golden thread woven through the Scriptures, the "Chosen One" (Luke 9:35) embodies the hope of a new creation, for it is through the Messiah that all will be administrated.[11]

There are two broad approaches in regard to how such a hope developed: the evolution of human expectation[12] and the development of divine oracle.[13] Though the two are, of course, intimately related, liberal commentators generally emphasize the former while conservatives usually stress the latter.[14] My approach assumes the divine inspiration of the Scriptures, calling us to search them with the greatest of care—like the prophets, "inquiring what person or time the Spirit of Christ in them was indicating when he *predicted* the sufferings of Christ and the subsequent glories" (1 Peter 1:11).

THE DEVELOPMENT OF MESSIANIC HOPE

Rather than a conglomeration of arbitrary prophecies, the Scriptures develop the idea of messianic mediation in a more intuitive and organic way. From the beginning of the redemptive narrative, the seed of the messianic idea is planted in the soil of fallen humanity, and it grows progressively according to the covenants God made with men, particularly Adam, Abraham, and David.[15]

The Adamic Messianic Hope

Assuming both the historicity of Genesis and the intentionally messianic orientation of the Old Testament canon as a whole,[16] we find the first revelation of messianic mediation following the sin of Adam and Eve.[17] Speaking to the serpent in the garden, commonly identified as the vessel of Satan,[18] God says,

> Cursed are you above all the livestock and all the wild animals! You will crawl on your belly and you will eat dust all the days of your life. And I will put enmity between you and the woman, and between your offspring and hers; *he will crush your head*, and you will strike his heel. (Gen. 3:14–15, NIV)

This passage is often referred to as the "mother promise" from which all future messianic promises proceed,[19] for God here makes an indirect promise to Adam and Eve, and their progeny, concerning the crushing of Satan's head. It is also called the "protoevangelium," or "first gospel," since it is the first reference of good news to humanity in its fallen state.[20]

Specifically, the singular, masculine pronoun "he" is used to describe the "seed" (Heb. *zera'*), or "offspring," of the woman.[21] This seed of the woman will crush the serpent's "head" (Heb. *rō'š*), which is symbolic of both life and authority.[22] In this way we have the birth of the basic messianic reality—a human being will be born who will mediate God's punishment of Satan and his offspring, or spiritual progeny.[23] The messianic hope is thus fundamentally *genealogical* in nature, which creates a baseline of expectation for future covenants and prophetic oracles.[24]

The relationship of the satanic "head" to the messianic "heel" further portrays the imagery of *military conquest* commonly used in the Old Testament (cf. Josh. 10:24; Ps. 47:3; 89:23), as David sang: "I pursued my enemies and *crushed* them; I did not turn back till they were destroyed. I *crushed* them completely, and they could not rise; they fell beneath my *feet*" (2 Sam. 22:38–39, NIV).[25] Hence we have a protological vision for the rebellion of Satan being brought into militant submission.[26]

With a clear reference to "that ancient serpent" (Rev. 12:9; 20:2), the Scriptures declare the fulfillment of Genesis 3:15 to be an eschatological reality. As the "Christ" (Rev. 20:4,6), Jesus will bring Satan into forceful submission by binding him in Hades for a thousand years and then throwing him, with the wicked, into Gehenna forever (cf. Rev. 20:10,14; 21:8; 22:15). Moreover, Jesus identifies himself protologically as the "Alpha" (Rev. 22:13), who will "repay each one for what he has done" (v. 12). Thus we see the "living seed" of Genesis 3:15 finding full fruition in the day of the Lord, Gehenna, and the resurrection.[27] In this way the messianic seed of Adam is prophesied to be the arbiter of God's apocalyptic day (see figure 5.2).[28]

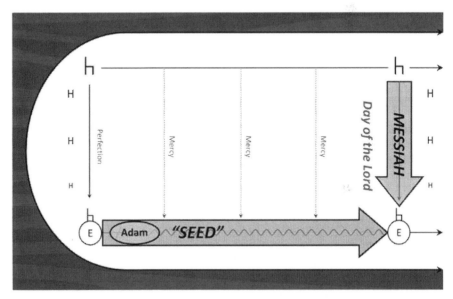

Figure 5.2 – The Adamic Seed as the Divine Agent of Redemptive History

The Old Testament is rife with messianic imagery that references and builds upon Genesis 3:15. David prophesies a messianic "Lord" (Ps. 110:1) at the right hand of God: "He will *crush kings* on the day of his wrath" (v. 5, NIV); indeed, "He will *shatter heads* over the whole earth" (v. 6, NLT). So the Messiah will be the means by which "God will *crush the heads* of his enemies, the hairy crowns of those who go on in their sins" (Ps. 68:21, NIV). As Jeremiah warns, "Behold, the storm of the LORD! Wrath has gone forth, a whirling tempest; it will *burst upon the head* of the wicked" (Jer. 23:19). And Habakkuk prophesies, "You went out for the salvation of your people, for the salvation of your anointed. You *crushed the head* of the house of the wicked, laying him bare from thigh to neck" (Hab. 3:13).

Solomon echoes the cursing language of Genesis 3:14 ("dust you shall eat") when he speaks of "the royal son" (Ps. 72:1): "He will rule from sea to sea and from the River to the ends of the earth. The desert tribes will bow before him and his enemies will *lick the dust*" (Ps. 72:8–9, NIV). The Edenic imagery is also reiterated in Isaiah's vision of the new heavens and new earth in 65:17–25: "The wolf and the lamb shall graze together; the lion shall eat straw like the ox, and *dust shall be the serpent's food*" (v. 25). So too Micah prophesies concerning the day of the Lord:

> The earth will become desolate because of its inhabitants,
>   as the result of their deeds. . . .
> Nations will see and be ashamed,
>   deprived of all their power.
> They will lay their hands on their mouths
>   and their ears will become deaf.
> They will *lick dust like a snake*,
>   like creatures that crawl on the ground.
> They will come trembling out of their dens;
>   they will turn in fear to the LORD our God
>   and will be afraid of you.
> (Mic. 7:13–17, NIV)

Moreover, the heel-to-head imagery is seen when the Messiah treads the "winepress" of the nations on "the day of vengeance" (Isa. 63:4), saying, "In my anger I have *trampled* my enemies as if they were grapes. In my fury I have *trampled* my foes" (v. 3, NLT). Similarly, it is through the messianic "sun of righteousness" (Mal. 4:2) that "the arrogant and the wicked will be burned up like straw" (v. 1, NLT), for the Lord says to the righteous, "You will tread upon the wicked as if they were dust under your feet" (v. 3, NLT).

References and allusions to Genesis 3:15 also abound in the New Testament. Jesus tells his disciples, "I saw Satan fall like lightning from heaven. Behold, I have given you authority to *tread on serpents* and scorpions, and over all the power of the enemy, and nothing shall hurt you" (Luke 10:18–19). And no one would have missed the implications of John's imprecatory preaching: "You brood of *vipers*! Who warned you to flee from the wrath to come?" (Matt. 3:7; Luke 3:7). Jesus reiterates this accusation against the Pharisees (cf. Matt. 12:34) and relates their common destiny with the devil in Gehenna: "You *serpents*, you brood of *vipers*, how are you to escape being sentenced to hell?" (Matt. 23:33).

Moreover, the Pharisees are implicated as "sons of the evil one" (Matt. 13:38), or "children of the devil" (1 John 3:10), whom Jesus exposes as descendants of the lying serpent in the garden: "You are of your father *the devil*, and your will is to do your father's desires. He was a murderer *from the beginning*, and does not stand in the truth, because there is no truth in him. When he lies, he speaks out of his own character, for he is a liar and the father of lies" (John 8:44).

Similarly, Revelation 12–13 is an apocalyptic recapitulation of the Adamic promise, with a "woman" giving birth (12:2) to a "male child" (12:5), and a "great dragon" (12:3)—that is, "that ancient serpent, who is called the devil and Satan" (12:9)—seeking to devour the child (12:4).[29] However, the "beast" (13:1) who is "given authority" by the dragon/serpent (13:4) receives a "fatal head wound" (13:3) as a sign of the ultimate and final head-crushing of Gehenna.[30] So the vision concludes, "If anyone worships the beast and its image . . . he will be tormented with fire and sulfur. . . . And the smoke of their torment goes up forever and ever" (14:9–11).[31]

Paul's references to Genesis 3 abound. For example, he exhorts the Roman church to resist wicked deceivers, whose "smooth talk and flattery" (Rom. 16:18) is akin to that of Satan in the garden. Then he admonishes them "to be wise as to what is good and innocent as to what is evil" (v. 19), an obvious reference to the forbidden tree, for "the God of peace will soon *crush Satan under your feet*" (v. 20). By "soon" he has in mind the coming of Christ and the day of the Lord (cf. Rom. 2:5; 3:6; 4:17; 5:9; 6:5; 8:18–23; 10:9; 11:25–27; 13:12; 14:10–12). Moreover, the "God of peace" (16:20) is understood in light of the messianic passages wherein peace is proclaimed and established upon the earth under the Messiah's rule (cf. Ps. 37:11; Isa. 9:7; 52:7; 60:17; 66:12; Hag. 2:9; Zech. 9:10) and the wicked are tormented forever without peace (cf. Isa. 48:22; 57:21; 66:24).

In 1 Corinthians 15, Paul asserts that in Adam "came death" (v. 21), and death's reversal will come in the resurrection "in Christ" (v. 22). This will initiate the destruction of all satanic "dominion, authority and power" (v. 24, NIV), as Christ will reign "until he has put all his enemies *under his feet*" (v. 25). In light of the discussion of Adam and the entrance of sin, this seems to be a clear reference to the messianic heel of Genesis 3:15. Paul then goes on to loosely quote Psalm 8:6: "God has put all things in subjection *under his feet*" (v. 27). Paul understands the poetic commentary of Genesis 1 to find ultimate fulfillment in the age to come, when the seed of Adam, "the last Adam" (v. 45), brings all things into forceful submission to God as it was in the beginning.[32]

Paul also draws from the head-to-heel imagery of Genesis 3:15 in Ephesians 1. After introducing our blessing and redemption "through his blood, the forgiveness of our trespasses" (v. 7)—trespasses which, of course, entered on account of Adam—Paul sets forth the conclusion of the grand narrative of redemptive history:

> [God] made known to us the mystery of his will according to his kind intention which he purposed in Christ, that in the fullness of the times in the household administration, *to bring together again under the headship of Christ* all things in the heavens and on the earth. (Eph. 1:9–10, AT)[33]

The "household administration" (Gk. *oikonomia*) is in reference to God the Father (being the agent in vv. 3–8) ruling over the heavens and the earth, which are elsewhere inferred as God's "house" (cf. 1 Kings 8:27; 2 Chron. 2:6; Isa. 66:1; Acts 7:48).[34] The fullness of the "times" (Gk. *kairos*) is understood in terms of the "appointed times" of redemptive history, climaxing in the day of the Lord (cf. Ps. 102:13; Dan. 8:19; Hab. 2:3; Acts 1:7; 1 Cor. 4:5; Rev. 11:18). The "all things" in the heavens and on the earth is a direct reference to creation, within which the "bringing together under the headship" of Christ (Gk. *anakephalaioō*, derived from *kephalē*, i.e., "head"),[35] invokes the imagery of Genesis 3:15, since the world in this age is under the rebellious headship of Satan, so to speak (cf. Luke 4:6; Eph. 2:2; 1 John 5:19).

All of this is rearticulated in Paul's following prayer, wherein the church would know Christ and the hope of his calling (Eph. 1:17–18), would know the power of the resurrection of Christ as a firstfruits (vv. 19–20), and would know the enduring dominance of Christ over all creation (vv. 20–23):

> He demonstrated this power in the Messiah by raising Him from the dead and seating Him at His right hand in the heavens—far above every ruler and authority, power and dominion, and every title given, not only in this age but also in the one to come. And He put everything *under His feet* and appointed Him as *head over everything* for the church, which is His body, the fullness of the One who fills all things in every way. (Eph. 1:20–23, HCSB)

Such references to Psalm 8 also provide a simple protological context for the common New Testament phrase "Son of Man," which is applied messianically by Jesus some eighty times in the Gospels.[36] In Psalm 8:4, "son of man"

(Heb. *bēn-'ādām*) refers to the progeny of Adam, since the Hebrew word for "man" and "Adam" are the same. In this way the "Son of Man" is simply the ultimate "Son of Adam,"[37] an approach to the messianic title that cuts through much debate and confusion.[38]

The phrase is commonly used in relation to eschatological judgment—"He has given him authority to execute judgment, because he is the Son of Man" (John 5:27; cf. Matt. 9:6; 12:32; 13:41; 16:27; 24:30; 25:31; Luke 17:24–26).[39] Likewise it is used in relation to protological restoration—"at the renewal of all things, when the Son of Man is seated on the throne of his glory" (Matt. 19:28, NRSV; cf. Matt. 12:8; John 1:51). Thus it is the righteous seed of Adam—that is, the "Last Adam" or "Second Man" (1 Cor. 15:45,47)[40]—who is "appointed the heir of all things" (Heb. 1:2), meaning all that was originally allotted to Adam.[41] He will be anointed judge of all of Adam's progeny—"the living and the dead" (Acts 10:42; 2 Tim. 4:1; 1 Peter 4:5).[42] Moreover, this genealogical approach falls in line with the other messianic titles of "son of Abraham" (Matt. 1:1; cf. Luke 19:9; Gal. 3:16) and "son of David" (Matt. 1:1; 9:27; 12:23; etc.).[43]

The Abrahamic Messianic Hope

The genealogical orientation of Genesis 4–11 is self-evident. Rather than a story with genealogies in it, it is more of a genealogy with stories intermingled. The hope of Adam and Eve rests in the birth of a righteous child. Immediately after the curse of death (Gen. 3:19), therefore, Adam names his wife "Eve" (meaning "life"), in faith that she would become "the mother of all living" (v. 20), so reversing the effects of the serpent's deceit.[44]

Likewise, when Cain is found unrighteous in murdering his brother, the hope is transferred to Seth, for "God has appointed another seed for me instead of Abel" (Gen. 4:25, NKJV). The subsequent genealogy is a reflection of their hope in the imminent childbearing, which would reverse the curse of Genesis 3:17–19.[45] So Lamech names his son "Noah," saying, "This one will give us rest from our work and from the toil of our hands arising from the ground which the LORD has cursed" (Gen. 5:29, NASB). Seth and Noah are the only children in the genealogy whose naming is given commentary, and this commentary is most clearly and simply understood in messianic terms.[46]

Moreover, the imminence of this genealogical-messianic hope is understood within the broader apocalyptic framework of the day of the Lord.[47] As Enoch, "the seventh from Adam" (Jude 14),[48] prophesied, "See, the Lord is coming with ten thousands of his holy ones, to execute judgment on all, and to convict everyone of all the deeds of ungodliness that they have committed in such an ungodly way, and of all the harsh things that ungodly sinners have spoken against him" (Jude 14–15, NRSV).[49]

Following "the genealogy" (Gen. 10:1, NKJV) of Noah and his sons, we see "the genealogy" (11:10, NKJV) from Shem to Abram. The calling of Abram in Genesis 12:1–3 is simply a continuation of the messianic-genealogical narrative.[50] While the nations gave birth to continued wickedness unto divine condemnation (cf. 11:3–9), God called Abram to faith in the birth of the Seed, which would lead to the divine blessing of all the nations—"*In your seed* all the nations of the earth shall be blessed, because you have obeyed My voice" (Gen. 22:18, NASB; cf. Gen. 12:3; 17:7; 18:8).

As discussed in chapter 4, Abraham would have understood the blessing of God ultimately to entail eternal life in the land of the living (cf. Gen. 1:28; 3:22). Though lacking the maturity and detail of the apocalyptic language, Abraham understood the fundamental outcome of the covenant: the salvation of humanity, the restoration of original glory, the judgment of the wicked, and the mediation of a messianic seed. God would create "a great nation" (Gen. 12:2), and through that nation he would bring forth one to mediate his blessing and cursing to all the nations (see figure 5.3).[51]

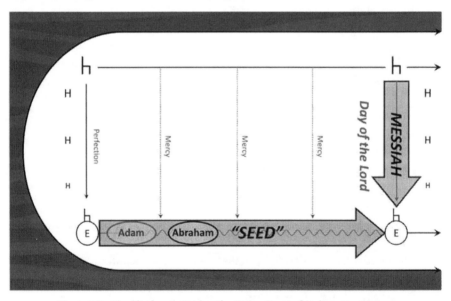

Figure 5.3 – The Abrahamic Seed as the Divine Agent of Redemptive History

Circumcision as the "sign" of the covenant (cf. Gen. 17:9–14) was likewise understood genealogically.[52] Circumcision was instituted after "Abram" was renamed "Abraham," prophesying his becoming "the father of a multitude of nations" (17:5), thus calling "things that are not as though they were" (Rom. 4:17, NIV), as Paul put it. Circumcision was the consecration of the biological means of the messianic birth through the severing of the foreskin, hence constituting the "sign of the covenant" (Gen. 17:11). *How prophetically apropos.* Far more than an ethnic marker or cultural ritual, circumcision was an act of faith by which the Seed was expected to come forth, and through which the promise of the Seed was indeed carried on (cf. Gen. 21:2; 26:4; 28:14; 35:11), since the Seed was literally "in the loins of his ancestor" (Heb. 7:10).

Throughout the Psalms and Prophets, the Abrahamic covenant and its messianic vision are expounded. The "royal son" (Ps. 72:1) will have "dominion from sea to sea, and from the River to the ends of the earth" (v. 8; cf. Ps. 89:25), a clear reference to the land allotment within the Abrahamic covenant—"I will give to you and to your offspring after you the land of your sojournings" (Gen. 17:8; cf. Gen. 12:7; 13:15; 15:18).[53] Similarly, "He shall speak peace to the nations; his rule shall be from sea to sea, and from the River to the ends of the earth" (Zech. 9:10). So the Messiah will rule over the nation of Israel, from the Red Sea to the Mediterranean Sea to the Euphrates River (cf. Ex. 23:31; 1 Kings 4:21–24), administrating divine blessings and glory to all the nations of the earth. Consequently, "All nations will be blessed *through him*, and they will call him blessed" (Ps. 72:17, NIV).

Such a vision is also projected in Isaiah 11, wherein a "Branch" (v. 1) grows ultimately from the Abrahamic root, executing judgment upon the earth (vv. 3–7). "He will raise a banner for the *nations* and gather the exiles of *Israel*" (v. 12), and "of him shall the *nations* inquire, and his resting place shall be glorious" (v. 10). Similarly, if we interpret Psalm 2 traditionally, God speaks to the Messiah: "Ask of me, and I will make the *nations* your inheritance, the *ends of the earth* your possession" (v. 8, NIV). Thus, as "the God of Israel" (Ex. 5:1; Num. 16:9; etc.)[54] and "the God of the whole earth" (Isa. 54:5; cf. Mic. 4:13; Zech. 4:14), he will bless both Jew and Gentile through the Abrahamic Messiah; and in this way "the nations will bless themselves in Him, and in Him they will glory" (Jer. 4:2, NASB).[55]

In such a light, the New Testament writers assume the Abrahamic covenant to be inherently messianic. Hence Paul can state, as if in passing, that "the promise to Abraham and his offspring that he would be *heir of the world* did not come through the law but through the righteousness of faith" (Rom. 4:13). Likewise, Peter relates "the Christ appointed for you" (Acts 3:20) with "the covenant that God made with your fathers, saying to Abraham, 'And in your offspring shall all the families of the earth be blessed'" (v. 25). In this way the "God of Abraham" (Gen. 28:13; Ex. 3:6; Ps. 47:9) will anoint the "son of Abraham" (Matt. 1:1; cf. Luke 3:34) with power and glory, and the nations will rejoice (cf. Ps. 67:4; 97:1; Isa. 24:14–16; 42:10–12)—singing "Blessed be his glorious name forever; may the whole earth be filled with his glory!" (Ps. 72:19).

The Davidic Messianic Hope

The genealogical-messianic expectation continues through the biblical narrative from Abraham to David (cf. Gen. 46:8–24; Ruth 4:18–22; 1 Chron. 1–2). Though there is much to be said concerning messianic promise and prediction between the two, the Messiah is summarily known as "the son of David, the son of Abraham" (Matt. 1:1).[56] Though much time and space within the narrative is devoted to Sinai and the Law, these happened "because of transgressions *until the Seed* to whom the promise referred had come" (Gal. 3:19, NIV).[57] Because the story gets right into the thick of the trees, so to speak, some think the larger messianic forest-view gets lost, which is simply not the case. The larger redemptive narrative remains in the background of consciousness, giving context to the stewardship of the Law, land, monarchy, temple, etc.[58]

The Davidic covenant extends the protologically based, messianic hope into its historical context. Second Samuel 7 (cf. 1 Chron. 17) forms the prophetic pathway upon which the rest of the Scriptures run. Though not initially referenced as a "covenant," the interaction between God, Nathan, and David is later termed as such by David himself (2 Sam. 23:5); by Ethan, the Solomonic temple musician (Ps. 89:3); and by the prophet Jeremiah (Jer. 33:21). Following Genesis 3 and Genesis 12, 2 Samuel 7 is arguably the most important chapter in the Scriptures concerning messianic expectation.[59] So Nathan prophesies:

> When your days are fulfilled and you lie down with your fathers, I will raise up your *offspring* [Heb. *zera* ', "seed," KJV/NKJV] after you, who shall come from your body, and I will establish his kingdom. He shall build a house for my name, and I will establish *the throne of his kingdom forever.* I will be to him a father, and he shall be to me a son. (2 Sam. 7:12–14)

Psalm 89 provides the most direct and comprehensive commentary concerning how the words of 2 Samuel 7 were understood by David and his successors:

> I have made a covenant with My chosen;
> I have sworn to David My servant,
> I will establish *your seed* forever
> And build up *your throne* to all generations. . . .
> But I shall *crush* his adversaries before him,
> And *strike* those who hate him.
> My faithfulness and My lovingkindness will be with him,
> And in My name his horn will be exalted.
> I shall also set his hand on *the sea*

And his right hand on *the rivers.*
He will cry to Me, "You are *my Father,*
My God, and the rock of my salvation."
I also shall make him *My firstborn,*
The highest of the kings of the earth.
(Ps. 89:3–4,23–27, NASB)

The imagery of Genesis 3 is naturally evoked in the references to a seed and the crushing of adversaries. Likewise, the handling of the sea and rivers would be understood in Abrahamic terms—"Our shield belongs to the LORD, our king to the Holy One *of Israel*" (v. 18). Beyond these, the Davidic Seed will be anointed as "the highest of the kings of the earth," thus assuming supreme administration of the age to come. So the divine agent of God's apocalyptic salvation will be the messianic Seed of Adam, Abraham, and David (see figure 5.4).[60]

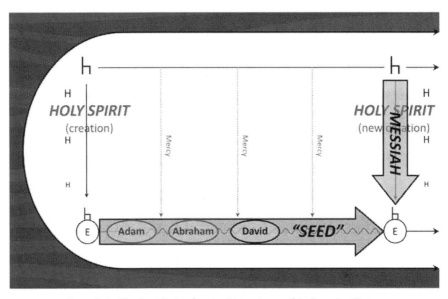

Figure 5.4 – The Davidic Seed as the Divine Agent of Redemptive History

As seen in the diagram, the Spirit of God is the ultimate agent of both creation and redemption. Therefore the Messiah's agency is understood to be under the auspices of a "Spiritual" anointing. In this way God administers his day through his Messiah by means of his Spirit. So Isaiah foresaw:

There shall come forth a shoot *from the stump of Jesse,*
    and a branch from his roots shall bear fruit.
And *the Spirit of the* LORD *shall rest upon him,*
    the Spirit of wisdom and understanding,

the Spirit of counsel and might,
   the Spirit of knowledge and the fear of the LORD. . . .
And he shall strike the earth with the rod of his mouth,
   and with the breath of his lips he shall kill the wicked.
(Isa. 11:1–4)

Similarly Isaiah prophesies: "Here is my servant, whom I uphold, my chosen one in whom I delight; I will *put my Spirit on him* and he will bring justice to the nations" (Isa. 42:1, NIV). And speaking the words of the Messiah, he says, "The *Spirit of the Lord* GOD *is upon me*, because the LORD has *anointed me* to bring good news to the poor; he has sent me . . . to proclaim the year of the LORD's favor, and the day of vengeance of our God" (Isa. 61:1–2).

Thus the Holy Spirit is the ultimate causative agent of the day of the Lord, the new heavens and new earth, the resurrection, and the messianic institution and administration—all of which is assumed in light of the Spirit's original agency in creation. Such a messianic interpretation of the anointing of the Spirit is undoubtedly the context within which Jesus' baptism was understood (see Matt. 3:16 and parallels), when "the Holy Spirit descended on him in bodily form, like a dove" (Luke 3:22).

As the mediator of divine governance, the Messiah is ultimately concerned with the conveyance of divine character. Therefore, since God himself is just and righteous, so also "In love a throne will be established; in faithfulness a man will sit on it—one from the house of David—one who in judging seeks *justice* and speeds the cause of *righteousness*" (Isa. 16:5, NIV). Similarly, "He will reign on David's throne and over his kingdom, establishing and upholding it with *justice and righteousness* from that time on and forever" (Isa. 9:7, NIV).[61]

Jeremiah likewise declares, "I will raise to David a Branch of righteousness; a King shall reign and prosper, and execute *judgment and righteousness* in the earth" (Jer. 23:5, NKJV).[62] Note that the parallel in Jeremiah 33:15 is followed by a reference to the overarching "covenant" with creation, securing the hope of a new heaven and earth under the governance of the Davidic Messiah: "Thus says the LORD: If I have not established my covenant with day and night and the fixed order of heaven and earth, then I will reject the offspring of Jacob and David my servant and will not choose one of his offspring to rule over the offspring of Abraham, Isaac, and Jacob. For I will restore their fortunes and will have mercy on them" (vv. 25–26).[63]

At the heart of the Davidic Covenant is also the concept of the Messiah's *divine sonship*. Note the centrality and repetition of the Messiah being called God's "son":

- "I will be his father, and he will be *my son*." (2 Sam. 7:14, NIV)

- "The LORD said to me, 'You are *my Son*; today I have begotten you.'" (Ps. 2:7)

- "He shall cry to me, 'You are *my Father*, my God.'" (Ps. 89:26)

The Davidic association of divine sonship is likewise seen in the angelic declaration concerning Jesus' birth: "He will be great and will be called the *Son* of the Most High. And the Lord God will give to him the throne of his father *David*, and he will reign over the house of Jacob forever, and of his kingdom there will be no end" (Luke 1:32–33).

Hence the messianic title "Son of God" is primarily derived from the Davidic covenant.[64] He is the descendant of David, whom God approves and deems righteous to rule as his vicar over the earth.[65] As such, the phrase "Son of God" is essentially a messianic title associated with the Davidic King, rather than an ontological phrase concerned with divinity versus humanity.[66] Of course, there is overwhelming evidence for the divinity of Jesus and his onto-logical identification with God Almighty.[67] This is not the main point of the phrase, however, nor is it what people thought of when the heavens opened at Jesus' baptism, the Spirit descended, and the voice spoke, "This is *my Son*, whom I love; with him I am well pleased" (Matt. 3:17, NIV). The same decla-ration is repeated on the Mount of Transfiguration (Matt. 17:5), which was later rehearsed by Peter (2 Peter 1:16–18) and interpreted as "We have the *pro-phetic word* more fully confirmed" (v. 19). The prophetic oracles are primarily concerned with redemptive history, and so also are the messianic titles "Son of God," "Son of Man," etc.

Thus we see the linguistic equation of the titles "Messiah" and "Son of God" in Peter's declaration, "You are the Messiah, the Son of the living God" (Matt. 16:16, NLT), likewise echoed by Martha, "I believe that you are the Messiah, the Son of God" (John 11:27, NRSV). The high priest also charged Jesus, "Tell us if you are the Messiah, the Son of God" (Matt. 26:63, NRSV). Demons even came out of people shouting, "You are the Son of God," because "they knew he was the Messiah" (Luke 4:41, NLT). The Gospels themselves were indeed written "so that you may come to believe that Jesus is the Messiah, the Son of God" (John 20:31, NRSV), and are designed to communicate "the Good News about Jesus the Messiah, the Son of God" (Mark 1:1, NLT). So too Paul uses the phrase "Son of God" functionally, in tandem with "Messiah" (cf. Rom. 1:4; 2 Cor. 1:19; Gal. 2:20; Eph. 4:13).

Moreover, the consistent use of "Messiah," "Son of God," and "Son of Man" *together* in the same passage (cf. Matt. 16:13–17; 26:63–64; John 1:49–51; 3:14–18; 5:22–27) argues strongly for a simple, commonly assumed messianic expectation that incorporated various linguistic expressions—including, for example, "Son of David" (Matt. 9:27; 21:9), "Root of David" (Rev. 5:5; 22:16), "Root of Jesse" (Rom. 15:12; cf. Isa. 11:10), "Morning Star" (2 Peter 1:19; Rev. 22:16), "Expected One" (Matt. 11:3; Luke 7:19, NASB), "Firstborn" (Ps. 89:27; Col. 1:15; Heb. 1:6), "Prophet" (Deut. 18:15; John 6:14; 7:40), "Shepherd" (Ezek. 34:23; John 10:11; 1 Peter 2:24), "Teacher" (Isa. 30:20; Matt. 23:10; John 13:13), "Arm of the Lord" (Isa. 51:9; 53:1; John 12:38), "Savior" (Luke 2:11; Phil. 3:20; 1 John 4:14), "Judge" (cf. Acts 10:42; 2 Tim. 4:8; James 5:9), "Lord" (Luke 2:11; Acts 2:36; Jude 14), "Chosen One" (Isa. 42:1; Luke 9:35; 23:35), "Servant" (Isa. 42:1; 52:13; Matt. 12:18), "Holy One" (Ps. 16:10; Mark 1:24; John 6:69; Acts 2:27), and "Righteous One" (Isa. 53:11; Acts 3:14; 7:52; 22:14).[68] All of these messianic titles draw from oracles in the Old Testament, which also include other titles not mentioned in the New Testament—for example, "Shiloh" (Gen. 49:10), "Star" (Num. 24:17), and "Branch" (Isa. 4:2; 11:1; Zech. 6:12).[69]

The abundance of messianic descriptions is based on the simple underlying genealogical expectation of a "seed" from the line of Adam, Abraham, and David who would mediate God's apocalyptic salvation (see figure 5.5). The many messianic titles are not mysterious, disconnected revelations, but rather simple descriptors of a simple genealogically based messianic expectation.

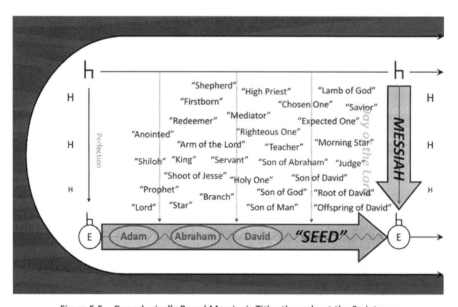

Figure 5.5 – Genealogically Based Messianic Titles throughout the Scriptures

THE CRUCIFORM-APOCALYPTIC
MESSIANIC HOPE

The New Testament begins with "the *genealogy* of Jesus the *Messiah*, the son of *David*, the son of *Abraham*" (Matt. 1:1, NASB). Jesus of Nazareth was "called Christ" (v. 16) by those who followed him, and many "put their faith in him" (John 7:31; 8:3; 11:45). As discussed above, this faith involved mediation of the basic tenets of Jewish apocalypticism: the day of the Lord, the resurrection of the dead, a new heavens and new earth, etc. What then is to be made of the *crucifixion* of the Messiah? Does such an event reinterpret or even overturn the previous messianic expectation?

Jesus and his disciples neither rejected nor rescinded any of the major elements of their Jewish worldview. Jesus' death and resurrection were simply understood as *additional elements* of messianic function, which were somewhat hidden and uncommon to first-century expectation.[70] Thus Jesus had to open the minds of his disciples "to understand the Scriptures" (Luke 24:45), explaining to them "*everything* written about me in the Law of Moses and the Prophets and the Psalms" (v. 44). That which was missing was the expectation that "the Messiah would have *to suffer* all these things before entering his glory" (v. 26, NLT).[71]

In the context of the disciples' discussion concerning the redemption of Israel (v. 21), the eschatological nature of the Messiah's glory was never questioned.[72] In second-temple Judaism, "glory" was the common apocalyptic catchword.[73] Jesus was simply adding to the disciples' expectation that "the Christ *should suffer* and on the third day rise from the dead, and that repentance and forgiveness of sins should be proclaimed in his name to all nations" (Luke 24:46–47). Such repentance and forgiveness of sins were understood by the apostolic tradition in light of the Messiah being "judge of the living and the dead" (Acts 10:42; cf. Acts 17:31). Hence the Messiah's suffering and resurrection was an addition to the common expectation of the mediation of divine judgment and salvation.

The apostolic witness bears out this straightforward approach to the death of the Messiah. The apocalyptic expectations built upon the divine covenants remained ever-present in the apostolic mind. Thus Peter outlines in Acts 3 that God's Christ would suffer (v. 18), repentance would be preached (v. 19), and the Christ would be sent again (v. 20) for the restoration of all things (v. 21). Peter then justifies such an approach by quoting Deuteronomy 18:15 that God would "raise up for you a prophet like [Moses]" (v. 22) who would fulfill the Abrahamic blessing (v. 25). Such a blessing and raising up of the Messiah is interpreted according to redemptive history, finding its fulfillment in both the cross and the day of the Lord: "When God raised up his servant, he *sent him first* to you, to bless you by turning each of you from your wicked ways" (Acts 3:26, NRSV).[74]

In this way the divine program involves *the messianic mediation of both divine mercy and divine judgment.* God will have mercy on humanity through his Messiah, and he will judge humanity through his Messiah. So the apostolic tradition is summarized in Hebrews 9:28: "*Christ,* having been offered once *to bear the sins* of many, will appear a second time, not to deal with sin but *to save* those who are eagerly waiting for him."[75]

Jesus interpreted his own death in the same way. In light of the eschatological kingdom (Luke 22:16,30), he says, "This cup that is poured out for you is the new covenant in my blood" (Luke 22:20). This new covenant is understood in sacrificial terms—that is, "in my blood"—and consequently it is essentially "for the forgiveness of sins" (Matt. 26:28). Superseding the sacrificial aspects of the Mosaic covenant (to be discussed further in chapters 7 and 8), this new covenant in no way affects "the covenants of promise" (Eph. 2:12) made with the forefathers. The new covenant simply provides atonement for that which the Mosaic covenant lacked (cf. Acts 13:39; Heb. 9:13–14). Therefore, "[Christ] is the mediator of a new covenant, so that those who are called may receive the promised eternal inheritance" (Heb. 9:15).

Similarly, the gift of the Holy Spirit was thus understood in light of the common messianic expectation concerning the anointing of the Messiah (cf. Isa. 11:1–3; 42:1; 61:1). As Peter declared at Pentecost, "Exalted at the right hand of God, and having received from the Father *the promise of the Holy Spirit,* he has poured out this that you yourselves are seeing and hearing" (Acts 2:33). The gift of the Spirit was given to confirm the mediation of divine mercy in the cross before the mediation of divine judgment at "the great and glorious day of the Lord" (v. 20, NIV). Indeed, "God has made him both Lord and Christ" (v. 36). Accordingly, Peter concludes, "Repent and be baptized every one of you in the name of Jesus Christ for the forgiveness of your sins, and you will receive the gift of the Holy Spirit" (v. 38). The Holy Spirit was poured out as a confirmation of the apostolic witness concerning the Messiah's role in the atonement of the new covenant and the apocalyptic hope of the day of the Lord (see figure 5.6).

Paul can thus summarize his discussion concerning the mercy and "perfect patience" of God "to those who were to believe in him for eternal life" (1 Tim. 1:16) in this way: "For there is one God, and there is *one mediator* between God and men, the man Christ Jesus, who gave himself as a ransom for all, which is the testimony given at the proper time" (1 Tim. 2:5–6). God has chosen to mediate both atonement and resurrection through the one man, Jesus the Messiah.

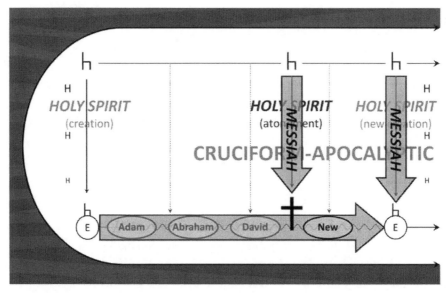

Figure 5.6 – The Gift of the Holy Spirit within Cruciform-Apocalyptic Messianic Hope

Likewise, Paul outlines in Romans 5: "While we were still helpless, at the appointed moment, Christ died for the ungodly" (v. 6, HCSB). And since God "shows his love for us" by the fact that "Christ died for us" (v. 8), "much more shall we be saved *by him* from the wrath of God" (v. 9). So the mediation of reconciliation and salvation is holistically accomplished through God's Messiah: "For if, when we were God's enemies, we were reconciled to him *through* the death of his Son, how much more, having been reconciled, shall we be saved *through* his life! Not only is this so, but we also rejoice in God *through* our Lord Jesus Christ, *through* whom we have now received reconciliation" (vv. 10–11, NIV). Of course, all of this reconciliatory mediation is understood in its broad apocalyptic context: "As one trespass [of Adam] led to condemnation for all men, so one act of righteousness [of Christ] leads to justification and life for all men. . . . so that, as sin reigned in death, grace also might reign through righteousness leading to *eternal life through Jesus Christ* our Lord" (vv. 18,21).

Since the Jewish apocalyptic vision of eternal life remained unchanged by the sacrificial interpretation of the death of the Messiah, the apostolic witness remained tenable within first-century Judaism. Hence the apostles "did not cease teaching and preaching that *the Christ is Jesus*" (Acts 5:42). Likewise Paul "devoted himself exclusively to preaching, testifying to the Jews that *Jesus was the Christ*" (Acts 18:5, NIV). And Apollos "powerfully refuted the Jews in public, showing by the Scriptures that *the Christ was Jesus*" (Acts 18:28).

The simplicity and continuity of the apostolic method and message are demonstrated clearly by Paul in Thessalonica: "And Paul went in, as was his custom, and on three Sabbath days he reasoned with them from the Scriptures, explaining and proving that it was necessary for the Christ to suffer and to rise from the dead, and saying, 'This Jesus, whom I proclaim to you, *is the Christ.*' And some of them were persuaded and joined Paul and Silas" (Acts 17:2–4). The fact that the apostolic witness was readily received by so many Jews (cf. Acts 2:41; 4:4; 5:14; 6:7; 11:19; 13:43; 14:1; 17:4; 18:8; 19:10; 21:20; 24:24; 28:24) argues strongly for an unaltered Jewish-apocalyptic background for the cruciform-messianic message.

CHRISTOPLATONIC CHRISTOLOGY

As previously mentioned, the term "Christ" is little more than Jesus' proper name in much of the popular mind.[76] In the early church, however, one's identity as a believer was dictated by his or her faith and confession that Jesus was "the Christ." As John says, "Everyone who believes that Jesus is the Christ has been born of God" (1 John 5:1). The distortion of messianic expectation robs people of their identity as children of God. Moreover, it robs people of their boldness in bearing the Christian name, as Peter says, "If you suffer as a Christian, do not be ashamed, but praise God that you bear that name" (1 Peter 4:16, NIV). The name that we bear as followers of Jesus inherently confesses our messianic hope.[77]

Though in modern times the term "Christ" has been generally marginalized to Christian jargon, this does not mean Christians have lost all sense of messianic expectation. Rather, their hopes have simply become perverted. All human beings—whether Hindu, Buddhist, Muslim, or naturalist—hold to some form of an "agent of salvation." This can be generalized to humanity as a whole, as with naturalism (or at least to its higher intellectual echelon); or to various incarnated avatars, as in Hinduism; or to historical "awakened ones," as in Buddhism; or to a single eschatological messianic figure (i.e., the Mahdi), as in Islam.

As Christianity accommodated Hellenistic thought, its messianic expectation began to conform to the worldly hopes of salvation within Greek mythology and philosophy. Since salvation in Hellenism is generally interpreted as escaping materiality unto eternal immateriality, the Christ became the grand "Agent of Escapism," so to speak. Jesus was understood as the divine means of achieving incorporeality, which is the defining mark of Gnosticism. George Ladd outlined well the relationship between Platonism and gnostic Christology:

The view found in Plato and in later thinkers, influenced by him, is essentially the same cosmological dualism as is found in later Gnosticism. Like Gnosticism, Platonism is a dualism of two worlds, one the visible world and the other an invisible "spiritual" world. As in Gnosticism, man stands between these two worlds, related to both. Like Gnosticism, Platonism sees the origin of man's truest self (his soul) in the invisible world, whence his soul has fallen into the visible world of matter. Like Gnosticism, it sees the physical body as a hindrance, a burden, sometimes even as a tomb of the soul. Like Gnosticism, it conceives of salvation as the freeing of the soul from its entanglement in the physical world that it may wing its way back to the heavenly world. Two further elements found in Gnosticism do not appear in the Platonic philosophers: that matter is *ipso facto* the source of evil, and that redemption is accomplished by a heavenly redeemer who descends to the earth to deliver the fallen souls and lead them back to heaven.[78]

Though Gnosticism was infantile during New Testament times, its emergence was met with severe opposition. At the end of his life, Paul wrote Timothy: "Avoid the irreverent babble and contradictions of what is *falsely called 'knowledge'* [Gk. *gnōsis*], for by professing it some have swerved from the faith" (1 Tim. 6:20–21; cf. 2 Tim. 2:18). Concerning its application to Christology, John calls Gnosticism "the spirit of the Antichrist," warning, "Every spirit that does not confess that Jesus Christ has come *in the flesh* is not of God" (1 John 4:3, NKJV).

Because of its utterly destructive impact on the faith, identity, and behavior of the believer, Jesus himself gives the gravest condemnation of gnostic Christianity when addressing the Nicolaitans (Rev. 2:6,15), of which he "hates" both their "works" and "teachings"—threatening, "I will come to you soon and *war against them* with the sword of my mouth" (v. 16).[79] According to Irenaeus (c. 130–200), the early church's authority on Gnosticism, the Nicolaitans were followers of Nicolas of Antioch (cf. Acts 6:5),[80] who strayed from the faith and became "an offset of that 'knowledge' falsely so called."[81] The church in Thyatira is also generally believed to have harbored Gnostics, having "learned [Gk. *ginōskō*] what some call the deep things of Satan" (Rev. 2:24).[82] It is this gnostic, "deep-revelatory" approach to the Scriptures, later mitigated and propagated *en masse* by the Alexandrian school of thought, that corrupted the simple messianic faith in Jesus for centuries ensuing.[83] Though Gnostics genuinely believe they hold a superior truth, their faith has actually been *ruined* (cf. 1 Cor. 15:33; 2 Tim. 2:14), and for this reason Jesus and those who follow him despise it.

Though gnostic Christology is enticing on the front end, its end is painfully predictable. As the divine agent of escapism, Christ Escapist takes believers to immaterial heaven through death and finalizes redemptive history at his return by annihilating materiality. Moreover, he calls his followers to "gnostic martyrdom" by forsaking "the world" (i.e., materiality and the body) unto death. So Clement of Alexandria, the first to equate asceticism and martyrdom, said:

> Whence, as is reasonable, the [true Christian] gnostic, when Called, obeys easily, and gives up his body to him who asks; and, previously *divesting himself of the affections of this carcase* . . . He in truth, bears witness to himself that he is faithful and loyal towards God. . . .
>
> If the confession to God is martyrdom, each soul which has lived purely in the knowledge of God, which has obeyed the commandments, is a witness both by life and word, in whatever way it may be *released from the body,—shedding faith as blood* along its whole life till its departure. . . . He is blessed; not indicating simple martyrdom, but *the gnostic martyrdom*, as of the man who has conducted himself according to the rule of the Gospel, in love to the Lord (for the knowledge of the Name and the understanding of the Gospel *point out the gnosis*, but not the bare appellation), so as to leave his worldly kindred, and wealth, and every possession, in order *to lead a life free from passion*. . . .
>
> In living, then, living well is secured. And he who in the body has devoted himself to a good life, is being sent on to *the state of immortality*.[84]

It is this gnostic call based upon gnostic Christology that gave birth to the monastic movement in the deserts of Egypt, which spread throughout the church, dominated its life for over a thousand years, and continues to entice people to this very day. Though not wholly evil (the Spirit and the Scriptures are inherently sanctifying and much good has been accomplished by various monastic individuals throughout church history), monasticism does represent a substantial distortion of the gospel and of a theology of the cross, which calls men and women to embrace the goodness of creation, to hope for its apocalyptic restoration, and to lay down their lives in love *in the midst of an ungodly world* for the salvation of the lost.

Conversely, as dominionistic Christoplatonism developed, Jesus became functionally known as the grand "Agent of Dominionism," as it were. As Christ Dominionist, he calls his followers to become agents of divine sovereignty upon the earth. Thus the church is the "kingdom," and its leaders are "little christs," who function as secondary agents of dominionistic salvation.[85] This side of gnostic Christology gave birth to Christendom during and after the

Constantinian era.[86] So Eusebius of Caesarea (court theologian of Constantine and "radical Origenist"[87]) outlined,

> Thus, as he was the first to proclaim to all the sole sovereignty of God, so he himself, as sole sovereign of the Roman world, *extended his authority over the whole human race.* Every apprehension of those evils under the pressure of which all had suffered was now removed; men whose heads had drooped in sorrow now regarded each other with smiling countenances, and looks expressive of their inward joy. With processions and hymns of praise they first of all, as they were told, *ascribed the supreme sovereignty to God,* as in truth the King of kings; and then with continued acclamations *rendered honor to the victorious Emperor,* and the Caesars, his most discreet and pious sons.[88]

The church welcomed Constantine when he came to power because it had already been primed by the end of the third century through the spread of Christoplatonism.[89] Though monastic-escapist believers and Christendom-dominionistic believers were often antagonistic toward one another (a pattern common till today), Augustine sought to bring the two together (see figure 5.7). The Messiah is both the agent of dominionism for the church militant and the agent of escapism for the church triumphant. Though quite conflicted, this twofold messianic function, expressed practically as "popery and monkery" (as Luther put it), varied little over the next millennium.[90]

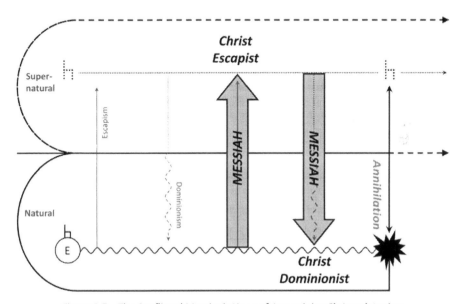

Figure 5.7 – The Conflicted Messianic Hope of Augustinian Christoplatonism

Though the dispensationalist movement restored to Christology a Jewish eschatological emphasis, it retained the Platonic escapism. Jesus' mission as "king of the Jews" is generally unrelated to his heavenly Gentile mission. Therefore we have a doubly confusing messianic expectation: *Christos tōn ethnōn* (Christ of the Gentiles) vs. *Christos tōn Ioudaiōn* (Christ of the Jews). For this reason dispensationalists have emphasized the inane idea of a pretribulational rapture.[91] The Messiah comes twice at the end of the age according to his two messianic roles—secretly the first time to take the Gentilic church to immaterial heaven and openly the second time to rule over the Jewish kingdom on earth. So Lewis Sperry Chafer delineated:

> A clear distinction should be observed between the Scriptures which announce the coming of Christ into the air to receive His Bride, the Church, unto Himself thus to end her pilgrim journey in the world and those Scriptures which announce the coming of Christ to the earth in power and great glory, to judge Israel and the nations and to reign on David's throne from Jerusalem. The first event is in no way whatsoever a part of the second event; it is Christ's way of delivering His people from the *cosmos* world before the divine judgments fall upon it.[92]

Thus Chafer concluded "that in the first event the movement is upward from earth to heaven, as in 1 Thessalonians 4:16–17 . . . and that in the second advent the movement is downward from heaven to earth, as in Revelation

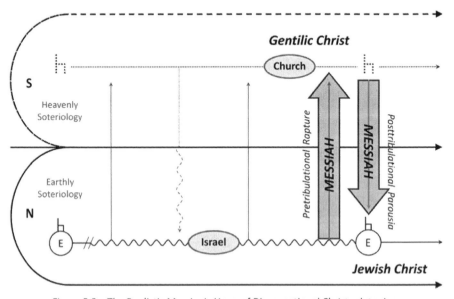

Figure 5.8 – The Dualistic Messianic Hope of Dispensational Christoplatonism

19:11–16."[93] So we see dualistic messianic functions according to the dualistic plans of salvation (see figure 5.8).[94]

Messianic expectation within inaugurationalism is quite similar to its dominionistic predecessor, except with reference to its eschatological conclusion. Within Christendom, Christ's dominionistic mission finds complete fulfillment through the church in this age. Within inaugurationalism, Christ's dominionistic mission finds partial fulfillment through the church in this age and ultimate fulfillment at the second coming.[95] This Christological "already/not yet" tension is articulated by Oscar Cullmann:

> The Kingdom of God will come only at the end of time, but, like the Church itself, the lordship of Christ belongs to the interim between his ascension and return. Thus, as distinguished from the Kingdom of God, the lordship of Christ has already begun. . . .
>
> Just as this lordship has a beginning, so it has also an end. According to the New Testament, the end cannot be described in terms of a date, but it can be described in terms of an event, the return of Christ. The lordship of Christ began with his ascension and will end with his return. . . .
>
> This final act recapitulates in a concentrated and definitive form everything which has already happened before and everything that is taking place in the present—above all the victory over Satan and the "powers." . . .
>
> The period of the Church coincides perfectly with the period of Christ's lordship—also in terms of the characteristic tension between present and future and in terms of what we have said about the invasion of the new aeon.[96]

However, the New Testament everywhere distinguishes different motives and agendas for the first and second comings of Christ. The first is fundamentally to bear sin (cf. John 12:47; 1 Peter 3:18), while the second is ultimately to bring salvation (cf. Heb. 9:28; 1 Thess. 1:10). Indeed Christ has been given all authority in this age (cf. Matt. 28:18; Eph. 1:21), sitting at God's right hand (cf. Acts 2:33; 1 Peter 3:22), but he rules over creation in this age *in mercy* (cf. Eph. 2:4–7; Rom. 2:4–5), *waiting* to make his enemies his footstool (cf. Heb. 10:13; Acts 3:19–21). Inaugurationalism perverts and conflates the agenda of the Messiah into *one homogenous-dominionistic mission* (see figure 5.9).[97] The Messiah came the first time to inaugurate the divine takeover, and he will appear the second time to finish it. Such homology wholly ruins the basic nature of the New Testament gospel, leaving the church with a proclamation that is neither cruciform nor apocalyptic.[98]

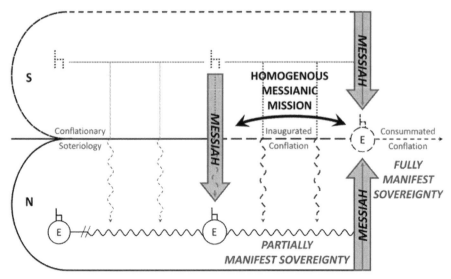

Figure 5.9 – The Homogenous Messianic Hope of Inaugurational Christoplatonism

In conclusion, our faith in Christ Jesus and his return is the very source of our hope. It is "the blessed hope" (Titus 2:13) which fuels the church in its race of faith unto the day of Christ. Furthermore, living in a world "without God and without hope" (Eph. 2:12, NLT), the church is in desperate need of a restoration of biblical hope. Those who get consumed by various Christoplatonic distortions are left with a tawdry hope, often resorting to the strength of depraved human beings who walk in the delusion of a self-imposed messianic complex.[99] Yet even this hope wanes in light of the twentieth century's two world wars, its host of diabolical dictators, various genocides, and rampant multinational-corporate greed (forgetting not the criminal usury of its financiers)—compounded by the threat of famine, overpopulation, terrorism, and nuclear war—not to mention the myriad of energy crises, financial crises, health crises, ecological crises, and the burgeoning global breakdown of the family unit.

Having lost our true messianic hope, we have no real answers for a world wallowing in confusion and despair. Moreover, having put our hope in this life, we have thrown in our lot with a pie-eyed world and have fallen under the curse of the apostle Paul: "If anyone does not love the Lord Jesus Christ, *let him be accursed.* O Lord, come!" (1 Cor. 16:22, NKJV).[100] Conversely, "In the future there is laid up for me the crown of righteousness, which the Lord, the righteous Judge, will award to me on that day; and not only to me, but also to all who have *loved His appearing*" (2 Tim. 4:8, NASB).[101]

Chapter Six

❖

THE GLORY
OF THE KINGDOM

The hope of the Christ is intimately connected with the kingdom he will establish. This messianic kingdom is God's kingdom, or the "kingdom of God" (Mark 1:15), because God is the one responsible for establishing it.[1] It is the "Father's kingdom" (Matt. 26:29), for it is the kingdom of which God the Father approves. It is the "heavenly kingdom" (2 Tim. 4:18), for it is the kingdom which God will anoint with heavenly glory. It is the "kingdom of Christ" (Eph. 5:5)—that is, "the eternal kingdom of our Lord and Savior Jesus Christ" (2 Peter 1:11), which believers inherit as "heirs of God and fellow heirs with Christ" (Rom. 8:17). Thus we long for "his appearing and his kingdom" (2 Tim. 4:1), for it is "the gospel of the kingdom" (Matt. 4:23; 9:35; 24:14), whereby "the kingdom of the world has become the kingdom of our Lord and of his Christ, and he shall reign forever and ever" (Rev. 11:15).

The messianic kingdom is the culmination of biblical hope and expectation, for God will restore what he made in the beginning, and he will do it by means of his appointed Christ, establishing righteousness upon the earth within his everlasting kingdom. Christ's kingdom is the crowning doctrine of the Scriptures, to which all others ultimately gravitate.[2] Here is expressed *finally* the nature and character of God, the inheritance of Christ Jesus, the glory of the Holy Spirit, the destiny of humanity, and the restoration of all creation.

Though theological discussion concerning the messianic kingdom has devolved over the centuries into an endless web of polemical arguments, Christ's kingdom is a simple concept, backed by a simple scriptural testimony, exemplifying a simple Jewish eschatological hope.[3] There is no sign in the New Testament of any confusion concerning the nature of the "kingdom of God."[4]

Like "Christ," the "kingdom of God" was commonly understood. No one questioned what kingdom John was preaching in the wilderness, nor did they question Jesus when he was "teaching in their synagogues and proclaiming the gospel of the kingdom" (Matt. 4:23). None of the disciples asked Jesus what the kingdom entailed when he sent them out preaching, "The kingdom of heaven is at hand" (Matt. 10:7), because it was commonly assumed to coincide with "the day of judgment" (v. 15), salvation (v. 22), the coming of the Messiah (v. 23), Gehenna (v. 28), and eternal life (v. 39).[5]

Moreover, the stunning *lack of commentary* in the New Testament concerning the nature of the kingdom argues strongly for an unaltered Jewish apocalyptic view of the kingdom.[6] Though the meaning of the kingdom is an endless source of contention today, the New Testament is generally unconcerned with its definition (focusing rather on the meaning and contention of the cross). The nature of the kingdom receives little exegetical attention, and when it does it falls in line with Old Testament and intertestamental views (cf. 1 Cor. 15:20–55; 2 Tim. 4:1–18; 2 Peter 1:10–21).[7] If the kingdom, which was the greatest hope of the Jewish mind and heart, had now been "inaugurated," "realized," or "spiritually fulfilled" in some way, would not this grand event be the center of all thought and exhortation? Where is the *fanfare*? Where is the *hoopla*? If the kingdom had finally come, then it seems like a strangely inverted case of "little ado about much."[8]

Rather, the "kingdom of God" is simply the *messianic kingdom*, to which the Jews commonly looked (as they do today) and to which the church sets its hope in the return of Jesus (cf. 1 Cor. 15:50; 2 Tim. 4:1; 2 Peter 2:11).[9] The modern academy has shaped the kingdom of God in its own image, making it so complicated and obtuse that no one outside its esoteric circle can understand it or practically apply it, which makes George Buchanan's oft-quoted characterization of historical research concerning the kingdom painfully true: "Scholars have internalized, de-temporalized, de-historicized, cosmologized, spiritualized, allegorized, mysticized, psychologized, philosophized, and sociologized the concept of the kingdom of God."[10] If an illiterate peasant (which is what most of the New Testament hearers were) cannot understand and immediately respond to the message of the kingdom, then it probably ought not be spoken in the first place![11]

Most of the confusion concerning the nature of the kingdom is the result of two things: linguistics and Platonism. The latter will be addressed at the end of the chapter. The former is rather simply resolved. The linguistic problem derives from the fact that the phrase "kingdom of God" (Gk. *basileia tou theou*) exists only in the New Testament. Thus the linguistic phrase is either a new theological idea or the summation of an old one. From Origen on, many have believed it to be a new spiritualized and/or universalized kingdom. Its common assumption throughout the New Testament, however, suggests that it is simply the summation of the older messianic kingdom idea.

The linguistic problem is further complicated by the general use of "kingdom" (Heb. *malkût*) in the Old Testament referring to God's governance over creation as a whole (cf. 1 Chron. 29:11; Ps. 103:19; 145:11–13; Jer. 10:7; Dan. 4:3,34). Therefore the "kingdom of God" spoken of in the New Testament is often assumed to be a phrase referring to divine sovereignty in general. However, the conflation of the two has no exegetical basis. The "kingdom of God" was phraseology developed during late second-temple Judaism, simply signifying the Jewish messianic kingdom.[12] Most scholars acknowledge this, but then go on to argue that Jesus and the apostles changed or added meaning to the phrase. As we will see, though, nothing suggests that the apostolic witness sought to change its meaning.[13]

The linguistic problem consequently produces a variety of seemingly contradictory linguistic dualisms, which have become commonplace in the debate over the nature of the kingdom. Scholars argue whether the kingdom involves "rule" versus "realm," or whether it is "abstract" versus "concrete," or "present" versus "future," or "eternal" versus "temporal," or "universal" versus "local"; whether it relates to God versus the Messiah; whether its locus is in heaven versus on earth; and so on and so forth.[14] To sort out the confusion, it is helpful to delineate between the *universal* "kingdom" of God, which rules eternally over all of creation, and the *messianic* "kingdom of God," which will rule eschatologically upon the earth.[15] This kind of distinction is often made to help distinguish between general-divine sovereignty and eschatological-messianic governance.[16]

This kind of delineation is ultimately derived from the distinction made in the Scriptures between the heavens and the earth, and the *two thrones* therein. God rules from the heavens (Ps. 2:4; 113:5; Isa. 40:22), while man rules upon the earth (cf. Gen. 1:28; Deut. 32:8; Ps. 8:6). In other words, "The heavens are the LORD's, but the earth He has given to the human race" (Ps. 115:16, HCSB). In the beginning God sat enthroned in the height of the heavens (Gen. 2:2; Isa. 40:22), after enthroning Adam upon the earth (Gen. 1:28; Ps. 8:6). And in like manner he will enthrone the Messiah at the end of the age when he restores all things (cf. Matt. 19:28; 25:31). God's kingdom rules from the highest heaven over all of creation for all time, while the Messiah's kingdom is initiated at the day of the Lord and established upon the earth with its locus in Jerusalem.[17] Such delineations can be applied to the *who, what, when, and where* of the kingdom—all of which are clarified by a universal versus messianic distinction (see figure 6.1).

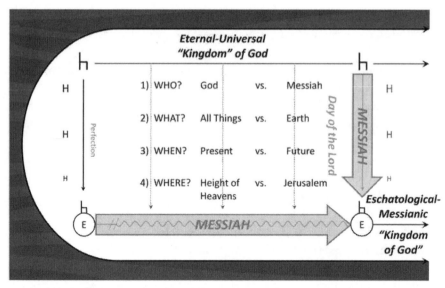

Figure 6.1 – Eternal Universal Kingdom vs. Eschatological Messianic Kingdom

Thus both are true: "The LORD has established *his throne* in the heavens, and *his kingdom* rules over all" (Ps. 103:19), *and* "Of the increase of his government and of peace there will be no end, on the *throne of David* and over *his kingdom*, to establish it and to uphold it with justice and with righteousness from this time forth and forevermore" (Isa. 9:7).[18] Unfortunately, if one's protology and worldview are skewed, this simple observation is impossible to accept. Far from being a theological imposition upon the Scriptures, the delineation between a universal and messianic kingdom is fully in accord with the reality of our existence, its original design, and its intended destiny.[19]

Moreover, the divine and messianic thrones are in no way disconnected or autonomous. As God ruled over Eden before the fall, and as he rules over all of humanity's rebellious kingdoms of men now (cf. Dan. 4:32; John 19:11; Rom. 13:1)—though they may not recognize or appreciate it—so also will he rule over the Messiah's kingdom in the age to come.[20] The two are intimately and organically related—indeed they are functionally "one," as we might say a husband and wife are "one"—but we cannot conflate them into a single homogenous reality, wherein the two lose their individual identities.[21] So the hope of creation lies in the governance of the Trinity and its distinctive-oneness, whereby the Father will anoint the Son in the power of the Spirit to execute judgment upon the nations of the earth, as Psalm 2 summarizes: "The One enthroned in heaven laughs; the Lord scoffs at them. Then he rebukes them in his anger and terrifies them in his wrath, saying, 'I have installed my King on Zion, my holy hill'" (vv. 4–6, NIV).[22]

CHRIST'S KINGDOM:
THE GLORY OF THE NATIONS

The messianic Seed of Adam will establish a kingdom that, because it will incorporate the righteous from all of Adam's progeny, will be ethnically diverse. Moreover, the messianic kingdom will involve the redemption of humanity as it is at the time of eschatological deliverance, which will entail many "nations/ethnicities" (Heb. *gôyim*, Gk. *ethnē*). Thus it will be a *multiethnic, transnational kingdom* (see figure 6.2). Had the day of the Lord come before the Tower of Babel, as Enoch probably expected (see Jude 14–15), then the kingdom would have been singular in its ethnicity. In the age to come, however, the Messiah's kingdom will include "a great multitude that no one could number, from *every nation*, from all tribes and peoples and languages" (Rev. 7:9). For Jesus will return to glorify Jerusalem, and "By [the city's] light will the *nations* walk, and the kings of the earth will bring their glory into it. . . . They will bring into it the glory and the honor of the *nations*" (Rev. 21:24–26).

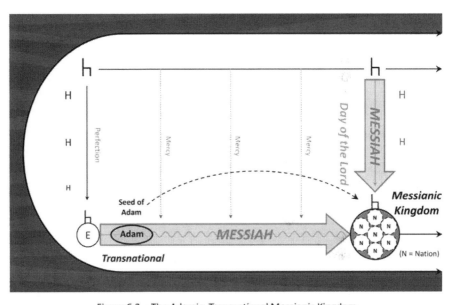

Figure 6.2 – The Adamic, Transnational Messianic Kingdom

The transnational nature of the kingdom is self-evident in most of the common messianic passages. In the last days, the Messiah "shall judge between the *nations*," and thus "nation shall not lift up sword against nation, neither shall they learn war anymore" (Isa. 2:4). After he strikes the earth "with the rod of his mouth" (Isa. 11:4), "The root of Jesse, who shall stand as a signal for the *peoples*—of him shall the *nations* inquire, and his resting place shall be glorious" (v. 10). For "The LORD will lay bare his holy arm in the sight of all the *nations*, and all the ends of the earth will see the salvation of our God" (Isa. 52:10). Indeed, "*Nations* shall come to your light, and kings to the brightness of your rising" (Isa. 60:3).[23] After the suffering of the Messiah, "All the ends of the earth shall remember and turn to the LORD; and all the families of the *nations* shall worship before him" (Ps. 22:27, NRSV). For God has eternally decreed, "My name will be great among the *nations*, says the LORD of hosts" (Mal. 1:11).

Moreover, when establishing the kingdom, God speaks to the Messiah, "Ask of me, and I will make the *nations* your inheritance, the ends of the earth your possession" (Ps. 2:8, NIV). For it is destined that "all kings will bow down to him and all *nations* will serve him" (Ps. 72:11, NIV), and in this way "all *nations* will be blessed through him, and they will call him blessed" (v. 17, NIV). The Messiah is seen in Davidic terms as "the head of the *nations*" (Ps. 18:43) and "a leader among the *nations*" who will "command the *nations*" (Isa. 55:4–5, NLT). When the Messiah comes, "Many *nations* shall join themselves to the LORD in that day, and shall be my people" (Zech. 2:11). As the agent of God Almighty, the Messiah and his kingdom will be the means by which "the LORD will be king over *all the earth*" (Zech. 14:9). And through the Messiah God will receive the promised praise of the nations:

> Clap your hands, all you *nations*;
> > shout to God with cries of joy.
> How awesome is the LORD Most High,
> > the great King over *all the earth!* . . .
> God reigns over the *nations*;
> > God is seated on his holy throne.
> The nobles of the *nations* assemble
> > as the people of the God of Abraham,
> for the kings of the earth belong to God;
> > he is greatly exalted.
> (Ps. 47:1–2,8–9, NIV; cf. Ps. 67:3–7; 96:1–10; 98:2–9; 117:1–2)

As the most defining Old Testament passages concerning the messianic kingdom, Daniel 2 and 7 also portray the Messiah's global reign.[24] In Daniel 7, four kingdoms are presented (vv. 1–8), the last of which incurs divine judgment (vv. 9–14) and is "annihilated and destroyed forever" (v. 26, NASB). In this context, "one like a son of man" (v. 13) is given "dominion and glory and a kingdom, that all peoples, nations, and languages should serve him; his dominion is an everlasting dominion, which shall not pass away, and his kingdom one that shall not be destroyed" (v. 14). As coheirs with the Messiah, "The dominion and the greatness of the kingdoms under the whole heaven shall be given to the people of the saints of the Most High; their kingdom shall be an everlasting kingdom, and all dominions shall serve and obey them" (v. 27).[25]

Similarly, Daniel 2 presents a series of transnational kingdoms (vv. 31–33), which incur divine judgment (v. 34) and which result in the establishment of an eternal messianic kingdom that fills and rules over "the whole earth" (v. 35). At the end of this age, "The God of heaven will set up a kingdom that shall never be destroyed, nor shall the kingdom be left to another people. It shall break in pieces all these kingdoms and bring them to an end, and it shall stand forever" (v. 44). Moreover, as Nebuchadnezzar was "the king of kings" (v. 37) in his day, ruling over a multiethnic kingdom, so also the Messiah will be hailed "the king of kings and lord of lords" (Rev. 19:16; cf. 1 Tim. 6:15), ruling over a benevolent global empire.

Therefore the Scriptures present the messianic kingdom as ethnically diverse and transnational rather than as an *indiscriminate homogeneous assemblage*, as is often the case in the various Christoplatonic distortions. It will be a real kingdom with a real king on a real earth ruling over real nations with real ethnicities. As its source, God takes ethnicity seriously; and indeed he will redeem it, because he is "the God of the whole earth" (Isa. 54:5), "the Lord of the whole earth" (Mic. 4:13; Zech. 4:14), and "the Lord of all the earth" (Ps. 97:5; Zech. 6:5).

Ethnic distinctions in the age to come are based upon the nature of God himself, his design, and his ordained destiny. Thus Jesus concludes his eschatological discourse, "When the Son of Man comes in his glory, and all the angels with him, he will sit on his throne in heavenly glory. *All the nations* will be gathered before him, and he will separate the people one from another as a shepherd separates the sheep from the goats. . . . Then the King will say to those on his right, 'Come, you who are blessed by my Father; take your inheritance, *the kingdom* prepared for you since the creation of the world'" (Matt. 25:31–34, NIV).[26]

CHRIST'S KINGDOM: THE GLORY OF ISRAEL

Not only will the messianic kingdom be universal and multiethnic in scope, but it will also make a *functional distinction between ethnicities* based upon the Abrahamic covenant (cf. Gen. 12:1–3; 15:18–21; 17:3–21; 22:16–18). As the Seed of Abraham, the Christ will rule over one nation—Israel—which in turn will mediate the glory of God to the rest of the nations. God has bound himself ethnically in the unfolding of redemptive history. Though God is "the King of all the earth" (Ps. 47:7), he has revealed himself over three hundred times as "the God of Israel" (including variants "God of Abraham," "God of your fathers," etc.).[27] The messianic Seed will be "the King of *Israel*" (Matt. 27:42; Mark 15:32; John 1:49; 12:13)—that is, "the King of the *Jews*" (Matt. 2:2; 27:11; Mark 15:26; Luke 23:37; John 19:3)—whose rule will extend to the ends of the earth (see figure 6.3). In this way redemptive history is "Israelocentric,"[28] for "salvation comes through the Jews" (John 4:22, NLT).

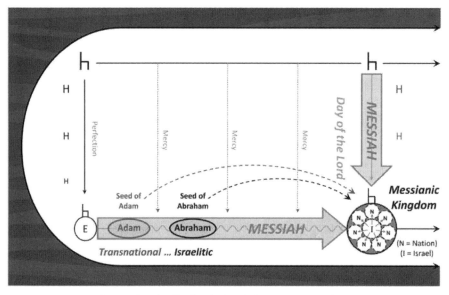

Figure 6.3 – The Abrahamic, Israelitic Messianic Kingdom

Because Abraham was promised that he would inherit the land "from the river of Egypt to the great river, the river Euphrates" (Gen. 15:18), so then his seed will rule "from the River to the ends of the earth" (Ps. 72:8; Zech. 9:10). Such a geographical demarcation between the Euphrates and the ends of the earth confirms the geopolitical demarcation of the kingdom of God in the age to come.[29] Hence the land of Canaan itself is a prophetic oracle, of sorts, inherently prophesying the age to come, and the Jews were and are stewards of that oracle (cf. Matt. 21:33; Rom. 3:2).

The Messiah will be the King of Israel because God himself is "the King of Israel" (Isa. 44:6; Zeph. 3:15). Indeed, the God of the Bible is "the Creator of Israel" (Isa. 43:15). The point that *God* created the nations and *God* created Israel is often overlooked. Why? Was it a benign consequence of the debacle of Babel? No. Was it a temporal necessity for the novelty of the incarnation? No. It was by divine foreknowledge and wisdom with eternal repercussions, which brings us to the crux of the issue—the very point of contention and offense: *God is an ethnicist.* In regard to sin and righteousness, he shows no favoritism or partiality toward any nation or ethnicity (though one could argue that God has actually been harder on the Jews than the Gentiles, as a father might hold his oldest son to a higher standard). However, he has chosen to orchestrate redemptive history in this age (i.e., in the giving and stewarding of the oracles) according to the Jews, and he will administrate redemptive history in the age to come (i.e., in the giving and administrating of eternal life) according to the Jews. Though commonly rejected, ignored, or overlooked, this is a plain fact of the Bible, and the de-ethnicization of the Scriptures borders on hermeneutical schizophrenia.

To most Gentiles, the binding of salvation to Jewish ethnicity is incredibly offensive, since we Irish (as a personal example) fancy ourselves as the "saviors of civilization."[30] But so also do the Koreans, the Egyptians, and the French—and likewise historically the Romans, Mongols, and Germans. Indeed, it is the divine choice concerning one ethnos that offends every other ethnos. Furthermore, it is the divine choice concerning one man, Jesus of Nazareth, that offends every other human being. Why not me? Why not you? Why not the Irish? Why not the Chinese? *Because God chose.* The sovereignty of God simply cannot be overruled on this point.

The Jewish Birthright

In such a light, it was commonly assumed that the messianic kingdom would be an Israelitic kingdom that would benevolently govern the world to come,[31] an idea which has been called "Jewish restoration eschatology."[32] But we must consider the basis of this governance and administration. Many scholars have commented on Israel's "special relation" to God and "special function in history,"[33] or "the priority of Israel in salvation-history."[34] However, such generality is ambiguous and ultimately unhelpful.

The theological driver behind the uniqueness of the Jews is their ethnic "firstborn" position—that is, their "birthright" (Heb. *běkōrâ*, Gk. *prōtotokia*), which was commonly understood as the "inheritance rights as the oldest son" (Heb. 12:16, NIV).[35] In technical terms, this is known as *primogeniture*, the legal right and role of the oldest son for administrating the inheritance of the family estate.[36] The practice has been common throughout time and across cultures because its origin is in the Godhead itself. We delineate between sons in the distribution of our inheritance because God will delineate between sons in the distribution of his inheritance.

Though in modern times we infer little more than birth order to the term "firstborn," its application in the Scriptures clearly implies primogeniture, which in relation to Israel has received little appreciation or attention historically.[37] Yet the Scriptures declare, "Thus says the LORD, Israel is my *firstborn* son" (Ex.

4:22), and "I am a father to Israel, and Ephraim is my *firstborn*" (Jer. 31:9).[38] The idea of Jewish sonship (cf. Deut. 14:1; Isa. 1:2; Hos. 1:10; Mal. 1:6) assumes a theology of birthright, since the Israelites were the first people to be given the privilege of calling the Creator of the heavens and earth "Father" (cf. Deut. 32:6; Isa. 64:8; Mal. 2:10). As God said, "When Israel was a child, I loved him, and out of Egypt I called *my son*" (Hos. 11:1).[39] And so Israel prayed, "You, O LORD, are *our Father*, our Redeemer from of old is your name" (Isa. 63:16).

Intertestamental literature also echoes this view (cf. Sirach 36:17; *Psalms of Solomon* 13:9; 18:4), as Ezra supposedly prayed, "O Lord, these nations, which are reputed to be as nothing, domineer over us and devour us. But we your people, whom you have called your *firstborn*, only begotten, zealous for you, and most dear, have been given into their hands. If the world has indeed been created for us, why do we not possess our world as an inheritance? How long will this be so?" (2 Esdras 6:57–59, NRSV).

As Israel is the firstborn among the nations, so also the Messiah is "the *first-born*, the highest of the kings of the earth" (Ps. 89:27). As the firstborn of all humanity and the ultimate "executor of the estate," so to speak, the Christ will rule over all of the earth and administrate the glory of the age to come. Thus the New Testament identifies Jesus as "the *firstborn* of all creation" (Col. 1:15), and as such he is "appointed the heir of all things" (Heb. 1:2). Moreover, he is "the *firstborn* from the dead, and the *ruler* of the kings of the earth" (Rev. 1:5, NIV), so that "in everything he might be preeminent" (Col. 1:18).

Though all the redeemed are "sons of God," and thus "heirs of God and fellow heirs with Christ" (Rom. 8:17), the supreme role of the administration of the divine inheritance will be upon the shoulders of this one man (cf. Isa. 9:6; Ps. 2:8; 72:17). Hence we seek to be found "in Christ." For "In him we have obtained an *inheritance*. . . . In him you also, when you heard the word of truth, the gospel of your salvation, and believed in him, were sealed with the promised Holy Spirit, who is the guarantee of our *inheritance* until we acquire possession of it, to the praise of his glory" (Eph. 1:11–14).

Similarly, the Messiah, as "the King of Israel," will administrate the glory of God to all the nations through the firstborn nation. This administration will also be reflected in the distribution of the land of the new earth according to ethnicity (see figure 6.4). It was God himself who determined the lands in which the different ethnicities settled in this age (cf. Gen. 10; Deut. 32:8; Acts 17:26), and so too will he determine them in the age to come, according to the mantic promise of the Jewish inheritance of Canaan as "an everlasting possession" (Gen. 17:8; cf. 12:7; 13:5; 26:3; 28:13; 48:4; Ex. 33:1; Num. 32:11; Deut. 1:8; 6:10; 30:20; Ps. 105:10).[40] Such an arrangement of messianic and Jewish primogeniture is exemplified in Psalm 72:

Endow the king with your justice, O God,
   the royal son with your righteousness. . . .
He will rule from sea to sea
   and *from the River to the ends of the earth.* . . .
May his name endure forever;
   may it continue as long as the sun.
All nations will be blessed *through him,*
   and they will call him blessed.
Praise be to the LORD God, *the God of Israel,*
   who alone does marvelous deeds.
Praise be to his glorious name forever;
   may the whole earth be filled with his glory.
(Ps. 72:1,8,17–19, NIV)

Figure 6.4 – Messianic-Israelitic Primogeniture in the Age to Come

Gentiles often disregard or conflate ethnicity when studying redemptive history because they feel somehow slighted, as though they are less loved by God or will not receive equitably from God in the inheritance to come. Indeed, in their depravity Jew and Gentile alike exacerbate this lie from both sides. However, primogeniture is simply a governmental and legal administrative mechanism, devoid of partiality or favoritism.[41] Being the oldest son, I administrated the inheritance of my father's estate when he passed away some years ago, and I can personally testify that the birthright is as much a burden as it is a privilege. Not once did my sister ever think to herself, *I wish I could deal with all of that!* Moreover, though our roles were different, she shared equally in the inheritance. I was *honored* to do the work, and she was *grateful* to be served.

Likewise, no Gentile will envy the role of the Jews in the age to come, for they will serve the nations under their King, who will be revered as "the servant of rulers" (Isa. 49:7; cf. "the one who serves," Luke 22:27). Though it will be a great honor to be "the chief of the nations" (Jer. 31:7) and thus to "judge between the nations" (Isa. 2:4), the result will be universal gratitude to the "Lord of all" (Rom. 10:12), akin to the work of the Spirit in this age—"so that as grace extends to more and more people it may *increase thanksgiving*, to the glory of God" (2 Cor. 4:15).[42]

New Testament Affirmation

At this point we must question whether or not the New Testament seeks to revoke or rescind the birthright of Israel.[43] To say it clearly: Jesus and his disciples never would have dreamed that the God of Israel would forsake the people of Israel (a conclusion that ought to be somewhat self-evident).[44] Jesus assured his disciples, "In the new world, when the Son of Man will sit on his glorious throne, you who have followed me will also sit on twelve thrones, judging *the twelve tribes of Israel*" (Matt. 19:28). It was understood that the Messiah would sit on his glorious throne, administrating the renewal of all things and eternal life through the people of Israel. Moreover, Jesus' calling and sending of "the twelve" (Mark 3:16) is most clearly understood as a sign of his ministry to "the house of Israel" (Matt. 10:6) in light of their destiny in the age to come.

Likewise, during the Last Supper Jesus promised his disciples, "You are those who have stood by Me in My trials; and just as My Father has granted Me a kingdom, I grant you that you may eat and drink at My table in My kingdom, and you will sit on thrones judging *the twelve tribes of Israel*" (Luke 22:28–30, NASB).[45] Here again the context is the eschatological coming of the kingdom of God (vv. 16–18), which is understood simply to be Israelocentric.[46] The issue in both of these situations is not the kind of kingdom that would be inherited but rather the kind of people who would inherit it.[47] The Jewish heirs loved this life more than eternal life (Matt. 6:2; 23:25; Luke 16:14), which made them act like the Gentiles (Matt. 6:31–33; Luke 22:24–26) rather than like true children of God (cf. Matt. 3:9; Luke 6:35).

Similarly, Jesus warned his followers, "Many will come from east and west and will eat with Abraham and Isaac and Jacob in the kingdom of heaven, while the *heirs of the kingdom* will be thrown into the outer darkness, where there will be weeping and gnashing of teeth" (Matt. 8:11–12, NRSV).[48] Here again the kingdom is centered around the Jewish patriarchs, with the threat of expulsion from the messianic feast (cf. Isa. 25:6–9; Matt. 22:1–14; Luke 14:15–24).[49] At another time Jesus even goes so far as to refer to the Jews as "children" and the Gentiles as "dogs" (Mark 7:27 and parallels), thus emphasizing Jewish preeminence at the divine table of redemptive history. The affirmative response of the Canaanite woman—"Yes, Lord, yet even the dogs eat the crumbs that fall from their masters' table" (Matt. 15:27)—then evokes Jesus' declaration, "O woman, great is your faith!" (v. 28).

Various other incidents affirm Jewish peculiarity in the New Testament—for example, Zechariah spoke of God remembering "his holy covenant, the oath that he swore to our father *Abraham*" (Luke 1:72–73); Simeon "was righteous and devout, waiting for the consolation of *Israel*" (Luke 2:25); and Jesus' followers walking on the road to Emmaus "had hoped that he was the one to redeem *Israel*" (Luke 24:21).[50] No evidence, however, is more conclusive than Jesus' own postresurrection teachings. For forty days he appeared to his disciples, "speaking about the kingdom of God" (Acts 1:3). Surely the apostles would have had many questions after such in-depth teaching, yet the *singular question* that gets recorded is "Lord, will you at this time restore the kingdom to *Israel*?" (v. 6). If Jesus was introducing a nonethnic, spiritualized kingdom, it seems he was a fairly obtuse teacher.[51] Again, if it cannot be said clearly in forty days, then it probably ought not to be said. But Jesus *did* say it, and he confirmed it by saying, "It is not for you to know times or seasons that the Father has fixed by his own authority" (v. 7).[52] The Israelitic-messianic kingdom would come, and its timing was "fixed," or "set" (Gk. *tithēmi*), by the Father.[53] Before that day, though, the disciples would receive power from the Holy Spirit to be "witnesses in Jerusalem and in all Judea and Samaria, and to the end of the earth" (v. 8).[54]

Therefore it is this hope in the Israelitic, messianic kingdom which the early church consistently proclaimed (Acts 8:12; 14:22; 20:25; 28:31)—that is, the "same hope" (24:15, NIV) as the unbelieving Jews (cf. 26:7), only the church sought to attain it by faith in an atonemental interpretation of Jesus' death (cf. Rom. 9:30—10:4; Gal. 3:21–29; Phil. 3:8–11). Thus Paul clearly maintains Jewish preeminence in the administration of "the day of wrath when God's righteous judgment will be revealed" (Rom. 2:5). For "There will be trouble and distress for every human being who does evil: *first for the Jew*, then for the Gentile; but glory, honor and peace for everyone who does good: *first for the Jew*, then for the Gentile" (vv. 9–10, NIV). Paul never would have entertained the repudiation of Jewish election. Rather, being sent to the Gentiles, he simply questioned, "Is God the God of Jews *only?* Is he not the God of Gentiles *also?*" (Rom. 3:29–30).

Moreover, in light of Jewish election, priority was given in the preaching and administration of the gospel: "*to the Jew first* and also to the Greek" (Rom. 1:16). This approach is seen throughout Acts (cf. 18:5–6; 19:8–9; 28:23–28) and is exemplified by Paul's declaration to the Jews in Pisidian Antioch: "It was *necessary* that the word of God be spoken *first to you*. Since you thrust it aside and judge yourselves unworthy of eternal life, behold, we are turning to the Gentiles" (Acts 13:46). Such a missiological pattern was not adopted for reasons of efficiency or pragmatism, but rather on the grounds of covenantal obligation.[55] Since the older brother will receive first in the divine inheritance, he ought also to receive first in the good news of the sacrifice which guarantees the promised eternal inheritance.

Furthermore, in Romans 9–11 Paul settles any and all discussion concerning the possible abrogation of the Jewish birthright.[56] Concerning "my kinsmen according to the flesh, who are Israelites" (9:3–4, NASB), Paul emphatically declares, "As regards the gospel, they are enemies for your sake. But as regards election, they are beloved for the sake of their forefathers. For the gifts and the calling of God are *irrevocable*" (11:28–29). It is this "irrevocable calling,"[57] according to the covenants made with the forefathers, which Paul has in mind when he asks, "Has God *rejected* his people?" (11:1). To which he clearly answers, "By no means! . . . God has *not rejected* his people whom he foreknew" (vv. 1–2).[58] Though they rejected their Messiah, this was by divine foreknowledge, so that "through their trespass salvation has come to the Gentiles, so as to make Israel jealous" (v. 11). Yet this "stumble" is by no means a "fall" (v. 11), for the "mystery" (v. 25a) in all of this is not a rejection of Jewish primogeniture but a simple chronological "partial hardening" of the Jews "*until* the fullness of the Gentiles has come in" (v. 25b). Then, indeed, "all Israel will be saved" (v. 26a); and in fulfillment of Isaiah 59:20ff., "The Deliverer will come *from Zion*" (v. 26b).[59]

So "the myth of an undifferentiated humanity,"[60] both in this age and in the age to come, is soundly dismissed.[61] The Bible is clear. As Barry Horner puts it, "God does have a distinctive, ongoing, covenantal regard for Israel after the flesh as beloved enemies (Rom. 11:28)."[62]

Gentile Unity and Inclusion

If redemptive history is differentiated on the basis of ethnicity, how then do we understand Paul when he says, "There is neither Jew nor Greek, there is neither slave nor free, there is no male and female, for you are all one in Christ Jesus" (Gal. 3:28)? Or elsewhere—"Here there is not Greek and Jew, circumcised and uncircumcised, barbarian, Scythian, slave, free; but Christ is all, and in all" (Col. 3:11)? Many take such verses as proof of the revocation of Jewish election, that God no longer regards ethnicity.[63] Paul was not saying this, however. He was simply commenting on the commensurate *quality of salvation* and the subsequent unity of faith.[64] Jew and Gentile alike will enjoy the glory of the new earth and will be richly blessed in the resurrection by their common Lord and Father. Therefore Paul summarizes, "For there is no distinction between Jew and Greek; for the *same Lord* is Lord of all, *bestowing his riches* on all who call on him. For 'everyone who calls on the name of the Lord will be *saved*'" (Rom. 10:12–13).

Though Jew and Gentile are "fellow heirs, members of the same body, and partakers of the promise in Christ Jesus" (Eph. 3:6), the divine inheritance will still delineate different *roles of salvation*.[65] Different children can be fellow heirs and members of the same house yet hold different roles according to birthright and parental commission. So too with the church. Jew and Gentile alike are "fellow citizens" (Eph. 2:19), yet their citizenship is still in relation to "the commonwealth of Israel" (v. 12). Paul is simply battling against the alienation and "hostility" (v. 14) that had grown between Jew and Gentile (as an older and younger sibling might become antagonistic toward one another).

Such animosity between Jew and Gentile was part of a larger trend within late second-temple Judaism. In an attempt to guarantee that Israel would not become apostate (and thus receive a renewed exilic punishment), Jews sought an ever-stricter adherence to the law—which, combined with growing Roman provocation, expressed itself in a progressive condemnation of and separation from the Gentiles.[66] Different groups within Judaism (cf. Pharisees, Sadducees, Zealots, Essenes) held different positions concerning the Gentiles, but the stricter of the Pharisees (i.e., the House of Shammai vs. the House of Hillel[67]) rejected the idea that the Gentiles would participate in salvation.[68] Gentiles would only be blessed *in Abraham* (Gen. 12:3, et al.) if they "became Jews" (Est. 8:17, NASB) and thereby "join themselves to the LORD" (Isa. 56:6; cf. Deut. 23:8; Jer. 50:5; Zech. 2:11).[69]

Those who became Jews were known as "proselytes" (Matt. 23:15; Acts 2:11; 6:5; 13:43),[70] and their conversion was confirmed by "circumcision, baptism, and the offering of a sacrifice in the temple."[71] Those who forsook their pagan idolatry but refrained from becoming Jews were known as "God-fearers" (cf. Acts 10:22; 13:26; 17:4). Such Gentiles were expected to follow the universal laws of God,[72] which were later termed "the Noahide Laws."[73] There was debate within Judaism at the time, though, as to whether or not God-fearing Gentiles would inherit eternal life or be condemned to Gehenna.[74]

The book of Acts seems to indicate that the general sentiment of the early apostolic church was that God-fearers would *not* be saved. Thus the scandal of

Acts 10 is understood: Cornelius was a "God-fearing man" (v. 22), yet "the circumcised believers who had come with Peter were *astonished* that the gift of the Holy Spirit had been poured out even on the Gentiles" (v. 45, NIV). Similarly, when Peter returned to Jerusalem, "the circumcised believers criticized him" for eating with "uncircumcised men" (11:2–3, NRSV). However, when Peter explained his vision and the granting of the gift of the Holy Spirit, they praised God, saying, "Then to the Gentiles also God has granted repentance that leads to life" (11:18).

The Jerusalem council (Acts 15) is best understood in the same light.[75] Some of the stricter Pharisaical believers were adamant: "Unless you are circumcised according to the custom of Moses, you *cannot be saved*" (v. 1). But Peter countered, "God, who knows the heart, bore witness to them, by giving them the Holy Spirit just as he did to us, and he made *no distinction* between us and them, having cleansed their hearts by faith" (vv. 8–9). Thus the Gentiles were shown to be sealed for eternal life apart from becoming Jews, which was deemed to agree (Gk. *sumphōneō*)[76] with the prophets (vv. 15–17, cf. Amos 9:11–12)—Gentiles would inherit eternal life *as Gentiles.*[77] To be included in the body of faith, they did not have to become Jews (see figure 6.5).[78] A supersessionist reading of this text according to realized eschatology seems particularly inane.[79]

As such, it was deemed that the Gentiles would continue to be Gentiles, observing the proto-Noahide laws (vv. 19–21), and the Jews would continue to be Jews, observing the Torah.[80] This straightforward approach to the Jerusalem council (and the issue of Jew and Gentile at large in the New Testament) is further reinforced in Acts 21, where Paul is accused of encouraging Jews to forsake Torah observance (v. 21). Paul silences such criticism, proving his own "observance of the law" (v. 24) and reinforcing the dissimilar standard for Gentiles (v. 25). So Paul concludes simply, "Each one should retain the place in life that the Lord *assigned to him* and to which God has *called him.* This is the rule I lay down in all the churches. Was a man already circumcised when he was called? He should not become uncircumcised. Was a man uncircumcised when he was called? He should not be circumcised" (1 Cor. 7:17–18, NIV).[81]

Jew and Gentile alike will be saved from the wrath to come on the basis of faith in Christ crucified (cf. Rom. 3:30; 4:9–12; 9:30–32). However, Jews should "bear fruit in keeping with repentance" (Matt. 3:8) according to the Torah, while Gentiles should do likewise according to the Noahide laws. Since the former is an expansion of the latter,[82] both are perfected in love and humility (cf. Rom. 13:8–10; Gal. 5:14), and accordingly both have the same broad pattern of discipleship (cf. Rom. 15:5–9; Eph. 4:1–6; Phil. 2:1–13).[83] Paul was generally contending against pride, which approached works of the Torah

Figure 6.5 – Apostolic View of Gentiles Before and After Acts 15

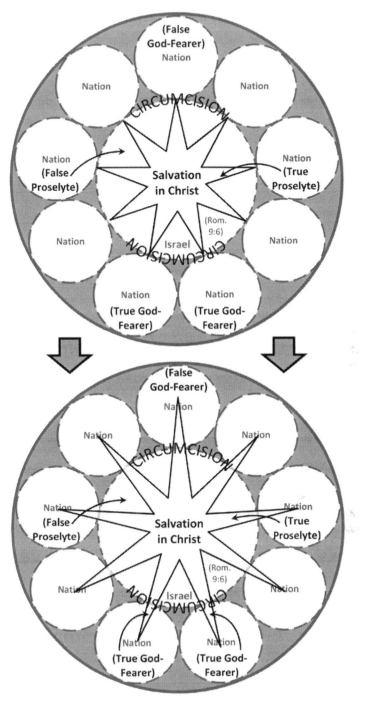

as *the basis* of eschatological salvation (cf. Rom. 4:2; 11:6; Eph. 2:9). This same pride could also corrupt Gentiles (cf. Rom. 11:20; 1 Cor. 1:29), seeking justification on the basis of the Noahide laws, or some other Gentile standard (see chapter 8). Rather, God "will justify the circumcised on the ground of faith and the uncircumcised through that same faith" (Rom. 3:30, NRSV).

CHRIST'S KINGDOM:
THE GLORY OF JERUSALEM

Not only did Jesus' followers believe that he would "restore the kingdom to Israel" (Acts 1:6), but they also expected him to inaugurate a specific kind of Israelitic kingdom: "the coming kingdom of our father *David*" (Mark 11:10). Since the Messiah is the "son of David" (Matt. 1:1; 22:42), God will give him "the throne of his father *David*, and he will reign over the house of Jacob forever, and of his kingdom there will be no end" (Luke 1:32–33). Thus the kingdom of God was expected to be a Davidic-Israelitic, messianic kingdom.

This expectation was simply derived from the Davidic covenant, in which God promised, "I will raise up *your offspring* after you, who shall come from your body, and I will establish *his kingdom*. . . . And I will establish the throne of *his kingdom* forever" (2 Sam. 7:12–13). As discussed in the last chapter, Psalm 89 reiterates the surety and eternality of this covenant: "I have made a covenant with my chosen one; I have sworn to David my servant: 'I will establish your offspring forever, and build your throne for all generations. . . . I will not lie to David. His offspring shall endure forever, his throne as long as the sun before me'" (vv. 3–4,35–36).

Similarly, Isaiah prophesied, "For to us a child is born, to us a son is given. . . . Of the increase of his government and of peace there will be no end, on the throne *of David* and over *his kingdom*, to establish it and to uphold it with justice and with righteousness from this time forth and forevermore" (Isa. 9:6–7). And again, "In love a throne will be established; in faithfulness a man will sit on it—one from the house *of David*—one who in judging seeks justice and speeds the cause of righteousness (Isa. 16:5, NIV). So too Jeremiah said, "In those days and at that time I will raise up for them a righteous descendant *of David*. He will do what is just and right in the land. . . . For I, the Lord, promise: 'David will never lack a successor to occupy the throne over the nation of Israel'" (Jer. 33:15–17, NET; cf. Ezek. 34:23–24; 37:24–25).

The Scriptures therefore assume continuity between the historical Davidic kingdom and the eschatological Davidic kingdom: "The former dominion will be *restored* to you; kingship will come to the Daughter of Jerusalem" (Mic. 4:8, NIV). So Amos prophesied explicitly: "'In that day I will *restore* David's fallen tent. I will repair its broken places, restore its ruins, and build it *as it used to be*, so that they may possess the remnant of Edom and all the nations that bear my name,' declares the LORD, who will do these things" (9:11–12, NIV).

The Messiah will thus sit on David's throne. He will not sit on Nebuchadnezzar's throne—nor Alexander's, nor Augustus', nor Charlemagne's, nor Suleiman's, nor James', nor Washington's. Establishing this simple idea in the mind of a modern believer is tantamount to casting a mountain into the sea (cf. Matt. 21:21). Such is the condition of Gentile depravity that it seems to take a miracle from God wrought by the power of the Holy Spirit to break apart the stronghold of ethnocentrism.

The centrality of the Davidic throne in the prophetic oracles consequently gives rise to the *centrality of Jerusalem*.[84] Because God led David to establish his throne in Jerusalem (2 Sam. 5:6–12; 1 Chron. 11:4–9), the Messiah will take up his throne there, for it is "the city of our God . . . the city of the great King" (Ps. 48:1–2), which Jesus himself reaffirms (cf. Matt. 5:35).[85] Therefore, in accord with the Davidic covenant, God will make new heavens, a new earth, and a *new Jerusalem*, as Isaiah outlines:

> Behold, I will create
>> *new heavens* and a *new earth*.
> The former things will not be remembered,
>> nor will they come to mind.
> But be glad and rejoice forever
>> in what I will create,
> for I will create *Jerusalem* to be a delight
>> and its people a joy.
> I will rejoice over *Jerusalem*
>> and take delight in my people;
> the sound of weeping and of crying
>> will be heard in it no more.
> (Isa. 65:17–19, NIV)

God will reign through the Messiah on the very mount within Jerusalem where David built his palace, "the fortress of Zion, the city of David" (2 Sam. 5:7; 1 Chron. 11:5, NIV). "Mount Zion" is a literal hill in the southeast of Jerusalem.[86] It is here that God prophesied, "I have set my King *on Zion*, my holy hill" (Ps. 2:6).[87] It is "*the mount* that God desired for his abode, yes, where the LORD will dwell forever" (Ps. 68:16)—"For the LORD has chosen *Zion*, he has desired it for his dwelling: '*This* is my resting place for ever and ever; *here* I will sit enthroned, for I have desired it. . . . *Here* I will make a horn grow for David and set up a lamp for my anointed one'" (Ps. 132:13–17, NIV). Indeed,

"The LORD Almighty will reign *on Mount Zion* and in Jerusalem, and before its elders, gloriously" (Isa. 24:23, NIV). And "He will swallow up *on this mountain* the covering that is cast over all peoples. . . . He will swallow up death forever" (Isa. 25:7–8). Hence the relationship between Israel and the nations in the age to come is further specified by its locus in Jerusalem:

> Many nations will come and say,
> "Come and let us go up to *the mountain* of the LORD
> And to the house of the God of Jacob,
> that He may teach us about His ways
> And that we may walk in His paths."
> For *from Zion* will go forth the law,
> even the word of the LORD *from Jerusalem.*
> And He will judge between many peoples
> And render decisions for mighty, distant nations.
> (Mic. 4:2–3, NASB)

In this way, the messianic kingdom will be "Jerusalocentric." That is, the center of the new earth will be the New Jerusalem.[88] God will administrate the restoration of all things through the Messiah reigning on Mount Zion as King of Israel, reigning over all the nations. Thus the Son of David will rule a Jerusalemic kingdom in the age to come (see figure 6.6)—"The LORD will extend your mighty scepter *from Zion*; you will rule in the midst of your enemies" (Ps. 110:2, NIV).

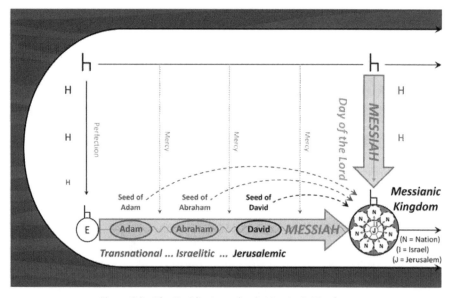

Figure 6.6 – The Davidic, Jerusalemic Messianic Kingdom

Within this covenantal arrangement, the prophets ring in chordal fashion concerning Jerusalem and its future. As Isaiah says, "In that day the Branch of the LORD will be beautiful and glorious. . . . Then the LORD will create over all of *Mount Zion* and over those who assemble there a cloud of smoke by day and a glow of flaming fire by night" (Isa. 4:5, NIV). Likewise, Micah concludes, "The LORD will reign over them in *Mount Zion* from this time forth and forevermore" (Mic. 4:7). And Jeremiah, "At that time *Jerusalem* shall be called the throne of the LORD, and all nations shall gather to it, to the presence of the LORD in *Jerusalem*, and they shall no more stubbornly follow their own evil heart" (Jer. 3:17). And Joel, "The LORD roars from *Zion*, and utters his voice from *Jerusalem*, and the heavens and the earth quake. . . . So you shall know that I am the LORD your God, who dwells in *Zion*, my holy mountain" (Joel 3:16–17). And Zechariah, "Many peoples and strong nations shall come to seek the LORD of hosts in *Jerusalem* and to entreat the favor of the LORD" (Zech. 8:22). Moreover, "On that day living waters shall flow out from *Jerusalem*, half of them to the eastern sea and half of them to the western sea. . . . And the LORD will be king over all the earth" (Zech. 14:8–9).

The restoration of the Davidic throne (cf. Amos 9:11; Mic. 4:8) therefore involves the restoration of Jerusalem. As the psalmist declares, "The nations will fear the name of the LORD, all the kings of the earth will revere your glory. For the LORD will rebuild *Zion* and appear in his glory. . . . So the name of the LORD will be declared in *Zion* and his praise in *Jerusalem* when the peoples and the kingdoms assemble to worship the LORD" (Ps. 102:15–22, NIV). Similarly, Isaiah describes the "good news" (Isa. 52:7) of Jerusalem's redemption:

> The voice of your watchmen—they lift up their voice;
> together they sing for joy;
> for eye to eye they see
> the return of the LORD to *Zion*.
> Break forth together into singing,
> you waste places of *Jerusalem*,
> for the LORD has comforted his people;
> he has redeemed *Jerusalem*.
> The LORD has bared his holy arm
> before the eyes of all the nations,
> and all the ends of the earth shall see
> the salvation of our God.
> (Isa. 52:8–10)

Thus David cries, "Oh, that salvation for Israel would come out of *Zion*!" (Ps. 14:7; 53:6), in accordance with the divine decree: "Out of *Zion*, the perfection of beauty, God will shine forth" (Ps. 50:2, NKJV). For God has promised, "I will grant salvation to *Zion*, my splendor to Israel" (Isa. 46:13, NIV). And he has prophesied, "Awake, awake, O *Zion*, clothe yourself with strength. Put on your garments of splendor, O *Jerusalem*, the holy city. . . . Shake off your dust; rise up, sit enthroned, O *Jerusalem*" (Isa. 52:1–2, NIV). So Isaiah intercedes,

> For *Zion's sake* I will not keep silent,
>   and for *Jerusalem's sake* I will not be quiet,
> until her righteousness goes forth as brightness,
>   and her salvation as a burning torch.
> The nations shall see your righteousness,
>   and all the kings your glory,
> and you shall be called by a new name
>   that the mouth of the LORD will give.
> (Isa. 62:1–2)

God will always "set watchmen," both Jews and Gentiles, who will "give him no rest until he establishes Jerusalem and makes it a praise in the earth" (Isa. 62:6–7). For it is in the establishment of Jerusalem *by the hand of God* that all things will be made new. Because no human hand can restore Jerusalem, we "pray for the peace of Jerusalem" (Ps. 122:6), for "*there* thrones for judgment were set, the thrones of the house of David" (v. 5). Jerusalem's destiny in the age to come informs our prayers in this age. We long for the day when "the ransomed of the LORD shall return and come to *Zion* with singing; everlasting joy shall be upon their heads; they shall obtain gladness and joy, and sorrow and sighing shall flee away" (Isa. 35:10; cf. 51:11).

Jerusalem may be a "barren woman" in this age, but she will "break forth into singing" (Isa. 54:1) when she gives birth to the righteous in the age to come. At that time she will be adorned by God in glory like a bride:

> For your Maker is your *husband*—
>   the LORD Almighty is his name—
> the Holy One of Israel is your Redeemer;
>   he is called the God of all the earth.
> The LORD will call you back
>   as if you were a *wife* deserted and distressed in spirit. . . .
> O afflicted city, lashed by storms and not comforted,
>   I will build you with stones of turquoise,
>   your foundations with sapphires.
> I will make your battlements of rubies,
>   your gates of sparkling jewels,
>   and all your walls of precious stones.

All your *sons* will be taught by the Lord,
    and great will be your *children's* peace.
(Isa 54:5–6,11–13, NIV)

Such prophetic descriptions were engrained in New Testament believers,[89] and they inform our understanding of the future of Jerusalem, especially in relation to Revelation 21–22. God will establish "the holy city, new Jerusalem" (Rev. 21:2; cf. Isa. 52:1; Dan. 9:24), "prepared as a bride adorned for her husband" (Rev. 21:2; cf. Isa. 54:5–6; 62:4–5). It will be "the dwelling place of God" (Rev. 21:3; cf. Ps. 132:13; Ezek. 37:27), where he will "wipe away every tear" (Rev. 21:4a; cf. Isa. 25:8) and where "mourning and crying and pain will be no more" (Rev. 21:4b, NRSV; cf. Isa. 65:18). It will be adorned with jewels and precious metals (Rev. 21:11–21; cf. Isa. 54:11–12; 62:3), and the glory of God will cover it (Rev. 21:23–27; cf. Isa. 4; 60; 62:2). In it will be "the river of the water of life" and "the tree of life," which will be for "the healing of the nations" (Rev. 22:1–2; cf. Ezek. 47:1–12; Zech. 14:8).

To a Jewish believer in the early church, John's vision would have aligned perfectly with the New Jerusalem described by the aggregate of prophetic oracles. No one would have spiritually reinterpreted the Old Testament and its straightforward prophecies in light of such a vision. Rather, the vision with its figurative language and symbolic elements would have simply reinforced the covenants and their derivative prophecies.[90]

Jerusalem was commonly understood to be "the city of the great King" (Ps. 48:2; Matt. 5:35). Hence believing Jews welcomed Jesus *by faith* into the city with palm branches (a sign of victory and fulfillment),[91] saying, "Blessed is the one who comes in the name of the Lord—the King of Israel!" (John 12:13, NRSV). And evoking the pastoral imagery of the Messiah (cf. Jer. 23:4–6; Ezek. 34:23; 37:24; Mic. 5:4), Jesus cried out, "O *Jerusalem, Jerusalem*, the city that kills the prophets and stones those who are sent to it! How often would I have gathered your children together as a hen gathers her brood under her wings, and you were not willing!" (Matt. 23:37).

This cry was then followed by two prophecies: the destruction of the temple ("Your house is left to you desolate," v. 38), and thereafter the ultimate fulfillment of the messianic coronation psalm hailed at the triumphal entry: "I tell you, you will not see me again, until you say, 'Blessed is he who comes in the name of the Lord'" (v. 39; cf. Ps. 118:26). Thus Jesus assumes that Israel *will* see him again; they *will* acknowledge his messiahship; and Jerusalem *will* be gathered under his wing, so to speak. Likewise, Jesus prophesied, in accord with Daniel 7:25 and 9:26: "Jerusalem will be trampled underfoot by the Gentiles, until the times of the Gentiles are fulfilled" (Luke 21:24), implying the messianic rebuilding of Jerusalem after the Son of Man returns (vv. 25–28).

In light of such a commonly understood destiny, how did believers relate to Jerusalem and the land of Israel in this age? Why did God bring the Jews into the land of Canaan? Why did David conquer Jerusalem? Why did Solomon build the temple? Why not just wait for the day of the Lord and the coming of the Messiah while living among the nations? Why not tarry in dispersion? These questions probe to the heart of Jewish calling, and they apply equally to historical as well as modern Israel. The common Christoplatonic answer is that Israel entering and occupying Canaan and Jerusalem was merely typological,[92] illustrating 1) the greater metaphysical entrance and occupation of the immaterial land and heavenly Jerusalem, or conversely, 2) the greater expression of manifest sovereignty through Christendom and her various centers of power.

Neither of these answers reflects the biblical description of Israel's calling in this age, which is essentially a stewardship of the oracles of God. A theology of stewardship is inherent in the biblical narrative as a whole, and it is summarized as such in the New Testament (cf. "steward/manager" [Gk. *oikonomos*], Luke 12:42; 16:1–8; 1 Cor. 4:1–2; 1 Peter 4:10; etc.). Human beings were created to manage the earth (cf. Gen. 1:26–28; 2:15), and we will give an account on the day of judgment for our management (see figure 6.7). If humanity's dominion had ever been lost or lifted (as is often argued in various theologies of manifest sovereignty), then there would be no reason for judgment. Rather, people are held to account on the day of judgment for how they steward their lives in this age (cf. Rom. 14:10; 2 Cor. 5:10).

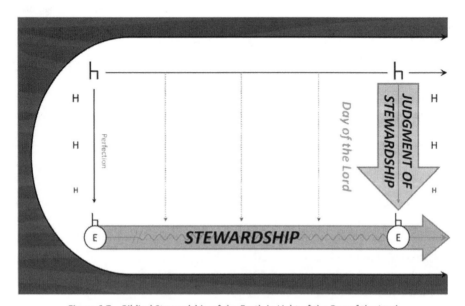

Figure 6.7 – Biblical Stewardship of the Earth in Light of the Day of the Lord

Since stewardship was commonly understood as fundamental to the human constitution, an application of that theology naturally would have carried over to the land of Canaan, the city of Jerusalem, the throne of David, and the temple of the Lord in light of the day of the Lord (see figure 6.8). These things were not ends in themselves, but rather tarrying mechanisms, designed to strengthen hope and faith in God for the age to come.

The steward/tenant relationship between God and Israel concerning the land of Canaan is explicitly stated in Leviticus: "The land must not be sold permanently, because the land is mine and you are but aliens and *my tenants*" (25:23, NIV). Consequently God has chosen Canaan as "his land" (Joel 2:18), because it is the land destined for his glory, the land where he will "gather all the nations and . . . enter into judgment with them there" (Joel 3:2). Though he has repeatedly disciplined his tenants, even removing them from the land altogether, "the LORD will again comfort Zion and again choose Jerusalem" (Zech. 1:17).

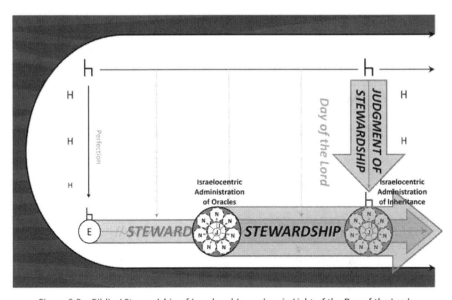

Figure 6.8 – Biblical Stewardship of Israel and Jerusalem in Light of the Day of the Lord

Akin to the land, the Davidic dynasty was considered a stewardship from the Lord. God himself "set up the throne of David over Israel" (2 Sam. 3:10); and because one of David's own descendants would one day sit upon that very throne (cf. 2 Sam. 7:16; Isa. 9:7; Luke 1:32), the Davidic dynasty was essentially "proleptic"—that is, anticipating a future messianic coronation.[93] Thus historical Davidic kings were the "anointed" of the Lord (2 Sam. 22:51; 2 Chron. 6:42; Ps. 18:50; 28:8; 89:38), who like Solomon "sat on the throne of the LORD as king in place of David his father" (1 Chron. 29:23; cf. 1 Kings 2:12).

The throne of the Lord, however, was ultimately designed to accommodate the final "Anointed One" (Ps. 2:2–6; 89:20–37; 132:17; Dan. 9:25), who would establish the Israelitic kingdom in true righteousness and justice (cf. Ps. 72:2; Isa. 9:7; 16:5; Jer. 23:5). Accordingly David prayed at the end of his life, "We are *sojourners* before You, and *tenants*, as all our fathers were" (1 Chron. 29:15, NASB). In this way the historical Davidic kingdom was understood as "the kingdom of the Lord" (1 Chron. 28:5; 2 Chron. 13:8), which was to be kept and stewarded until the coming of the Messiah and the establishment of the everlasting kingdom.[94]

Such a mindset of stewardship is evidenced in Jesus' triumphal entry into Jerusalem and his cleansing of the temple, which evoked the question of the chief priests and elders: "By what authority are you doing these things, and who gave you this authority?" (Matt. 21:23). Jesus responded with a parable about tenants (vv. 33–44). The land of Israel, God, and the Jews are like a vineyard planted by a *master* which is leased to *tenants* (v. 33). The master sent servants (prophets) and his son (the Messiah) to collect the land's fruit (repentance in light of coming judgment; cf. Matt. 3:8; Acts 26:20). The tenants killed them, however, for an illegitimate inheritance (reward in this age; cf. Matt. 6:2; 23:5–7). The primary question is then, "When therefore the owner of the vineyard comes, what will he do to those tenants?" (v. 40). Indeed, he will "put those wretches to a miserable death and let out the vineyard to other tenants" (v. 41). Though the parable was intensely convicting, no one questioned its overall framework. The Jews are indeed called to be tenants, stewarding the land in light of final judgment.

Similarly, Paul affirmed the gamut of Jewish stewardship, saying, "They are Israelites, and to them belong the adoption, the glory, the covenants, the giving of the law, the worship, and the promises" (Rom. 9:4). Though interpreting such a list is difficult,[95] its most straightforward reading implies that Jews are entrusted with a unique birthright ("adoption") established by the covenants unto an apocalyptic glory. Moreover, their calling in this age involves the stewardship of the oracles ("promises"), which include the land, law and temple ("worship"). Indeed some Jews lack faith, and their labors and stewardship will be for naught. But others "earnestly worship night and day" (Acts 26:7), being "zealous for the law" (Acts 21:20), and they will receive their due reward according to their faith.[96]

Such a theology of stewardship weighs heavily in the discussion of the role of the Jews in the land of Israel today. Many argue vehemently that the Jews no longer have a role or calling in the land.[97] Others say the Jews retain a unique calling to steward the land.[98] We must heartily affirm the latter. Though many in the land today are indeed apostate, that too was the case before the exile (cf. Isa. 3:9; Jer. 2:19) and before the AD 70 destruction of Jerusalem (cf. Acts 7:51; Rom. 11:25). Though the Jews have always fallen short (as have all Gentiles!), ought we not support their divine right to promulgate the oracles, of which the land itself stands at the forefront (cf. Ps. 72:8; Zech. 9:10)?

Moreover, just because the Jews cannot steward all of the oracles (e.g., the Davidic dynasty, temple service, etc.), should they not steward as many as possible? Modern Israel engages in many objectionable practices, of course, but should we not support *righteous stewardship* rather than the rejection of Jewish election altogether?[99] If God chooses to discipline his stewards yet again and remove them from the land (as seems anticipated in Isaiah 11:12, Daniel 12:7, Zechariah 14:2, Luke 21:20–24, etc.), so be it.[100] But woe to those who presume upon divine mercy and election.

CHRIST'S KINGDOM:
THE GLORY OF THE TEMPLE

Not only will the Messiah be the King of Israel, and not only will he rule from Mount Zion in Jerusalem, but he will also build the temple of the Lord. At the heart of the Davidic covenant is the building of a temple, or "house," for God. David's decision to build a temple for the ark of the Lord provided the context for the pronouncement of the Davidic covenant (2 Sam. 7:2; 1 Chron. 17:1). Thus the Lord spoke concerning the Davidic offspring, "He shall build *a house* for my name, and I will establish the throne of his kingdom forever" (2 Sam. 7:13; cf. 1 Chron. 17:12).

The prominence of the Jerusalemic temple in the Scriptures cannot be overstated. Because it was the culmination of prophetic history, the "house of the Lord,"[101] or the "house of God,"[102] was the nucleus of Israel's life. So Solomon summarized at its dedication:

> Blessed be the Lord, the God of Israel, who with his hand has fulfilled what he promised with his mouth to David my father, saying, "Since the day that I brought my people out of the land of Egypt, I chose no city out of all the tribes of Israel in which to build *a house*, that my name might be there, and I chose no man as prince over my people Israel; but I have chosen *Jerusalem* that my name may be there, and I have chosen *David* to be over my people Israel." (2 Chron. 6:4–6)

The temple in Jerusalem was also understood to be God's "footstool" (1 Chron. 28:2; Ps. 99:5; Lam. 2:1; cf. "the place of my feet," Isa. 60:13). As such it was *the sign* of his present sovereignty and governance over creation, pointing to his future execution of divine judgment through his appointed Messiah. As Psalm 132 vividly portrays,

> Let us go to *his dwelling place*;
>   let us worship at *his footstool*—
> arise, O LORD, and come to your resting place,
>   you and the ark of your might. . . .
> The LORD swore an oath to David,
>   a sure oath that he will not revoke:
> "One of your own descendants
>   I will place on your throne." . . .
> For the LORD has chosen Zion,
>   he has desired it for his dwelling:
> "*This is my resting place* for ever and ever;
>   *here I will sit enthroned*, for I have desired it." . . .
> "Here I will make a horn grow for David
>   and set up a lamp for my anointed one."
> (Ps. 132:7–8,11,13–14,17, NIV)

The temple was understood as God's "dwelling place" (2 Chron. 36:15; Ezek. 37:27) and "resting place" (cf. 2 Chron. 6:41; Isa. 11:10), the place where he would ultimately come and take up residence forever through his Messiah. Thus the prophetic writings assume the primacy of Jerusalem and Mount Zion, because the eschatological house of the Lord would be built there. So Isaiah describes his vision:

> Now it will come about that
> In the last days
> The mountain *of the house* of the LORD
> Will be established as the chief of the mountains,
> And will be raised above the hills;
> And all the nations will stream to it.
> And many peoples will come and say,
> "Come, let us go up to the mountain of the LORD,
> To *the house* of the God of Jacob;
> That He may teach us concerning His ways
> And that we may walk in His paths."
> For the law will go forth *from Zion*
> And the word of the LORD *from Jerusalem*.
> And He will judge between the nations,
> And will render decisions for many peoples.
> (Isa. 2:2–4, NASB)

As seen in this passage, most references to Zion generally assume the presence of the house of the Lord. Hence Joel would be understood: "The day of the LORD is near. . . . The LORD roars *from Zion*, and utters his voice from Jerusalem, and the heavens and the earth quake" (Joel 3:14–16; cf. Ps. 110:2). Likewise David, "The LORD will extend your mighty scepter *from Zion*; you will rule in the midst of your enemies" (Ps. 110:2, NIV).

In this way Zion and the temple were viewed as the *redemptive epicenter* of the age to come, wherein God would administrate the nations through the Messiah (see figure 6.9).[103] Thus Isaiah describes, "A voice of uproar from the city, a voice *from the temple*, the voice of the LORD who is rendering recompense to His enemies" (Isa. 66:6, NASB). Yet upon the "holy mountain" the redeemed will be made joyful and will receive the blessing of God, "for my house will be called a house of prayer for all nations" (Isa. 56:7, NIV).[104]

Figure 6.9 – The Administration of Divine Glory in the Age to Come

Like the land and the monarchy, the temple was also understood as a stewardship unto the coming of the Messiah and the day of the Lord. The Christ will come to Jerusalem "to bring in everlasting righteousness, to seal up vision and prophecy and to anoint *the most holy place*" (Dan. 9:24, NASB). And "the

Redeemer will come to Zion" (Isa. 59:20, NIV), which will result in the glory of the Lord rising upon it (60:1–2), the nations coming to its light (60:3–12); and their offerings "shall come up with acceptance on my altar, and I will beautify *my beautiful house*" (60:7). Furthermore, the gates of the New Jerusalem will be "open continually . . . that people may bring to you the wealth of the nations. . . . The glory of Lebanon shall come to you . . . to beautify the place of *my sanctuary*, and I will make the place of my feet glorious" (60:11–13; cf. Rev. 21:23–26).

Likewise, Ezekiel ties the resurrection of the dead (37:1–14) and the restoration of Israel (vv. 15–23) to the installation of the Davidic King (vv. 24–25) and the establishment of the eternal divine sanctuary (vv. 26–28): "David my servant shall be their prince forever. . . . And I will set them in their land and multiply them, and will set *my sanctuary* in their midst forevermore. My dwelling place shall be with them, and I will be their God, and they shall be my people. Then the nations will know that I am the LORD who sanctifies Israel, when *my sanctuary* is in their midst forevermore" (Ezek. 37:25–28).

Ezekiel goes on to describe the glory of this sanctuary in chapters 40–47, wherein the continuity between the temple in this age and the temple in the age to come is accentuated.[105] Just as "the glory of the LORD filled the house of the LORD" (1 Kings 8:10) at its dedication, so also in Ezekiel's vision "the glory of the LORD filled the temple" (Ezek. 43:5). Moreover, as the temple is God's "footstool" in this age (1 Chron. 28:2; Ps. 99:5; Lam. 2:1), so also in the age to come God says, "This is the place of my throne and *the place of the soles of my feet*, where I will dwell in the midst of the people of Israel forever" (Ezek. 43:7). Rather than undermining the hope of a future messianic temple, the many similarities between the historical and eschatological temples simply ought to reinforce the stewardship role of the historical temple in preparation for its eschatological glory.

In this regard, the postexilic prophets were chiefly concerned with the establishment and righteous stewardship of the temple. In the book of Haggai, the Jews who had returned to Israel were busying themselves with their own houses while the house of the Lord lay in ruins (1:1–11). They obeyed the voice of the Lord, however, and "came and worked on the house of the LORD of hosts" (1:14). Though the second temple was "as nothing" compared to the "former glory" of Solomon's temple (2:3), the Lord commanded Zerubbabel and Joshua to "be strong" (2:4). For "in a little while" (2:6), "I will shake all nations, so that the treasures of all nations shall come in, and I will fill *this house* with glory, says the LORD of hosts" (2:7). Thus the prophets envisioned three temples: the former Solomonic, the present postexilic, and the eschatological messianic—the present being stewarded unto its eschatological filling. Therefore "the latter glory of *this house* shall be greater than the former, says the LORD of hosts" (2:9). This latter glory is understood within the common expectation of the day of the Lord (cf. "on that day," 2:23), in which God will "shake the heavens and the earth" (2:21) and "overthrow the throne of kingdoms" (2:22).

Similarly, the book of Malachi represents a strong prophetic rebuke concerning poor stewardship of the temple. The priests showed contempt for the name of the Lord (1:6) by bringing sick and lame offerings (1:8), which had become a burden to them (1:13) because of their lack of faith in God as the "great King," who would ultimately "be feared among the nations" (1:14). The priests had violated the covenant with Levi (2:8) by their lack of faith, and Judah "profaned the sanctuary of the LORD, which he loves" (2:11) by being "faithless" (2:16) toward God and toward one another.

All of this "wearied the LORD" because of their root of unbelief, which was ultimately expressed in the question "Where is the God of justice?" (2:17). To this unbelief God answered, "Behold, I send my messenger and he will prepare the way before me. And the Lord whom you seek will suddenly come *to his temple*; and the messenger of the covenant in whom you delight, behold, he is coming, says the LORD of hosts. But who can endure *the day of his coming*, and who can stand when he appears?" (3:1–2).

From the temple this messianic Lord would refine and purify the Levites (3:3–4) and judge the wicked of the land (3:5). This wickedness is ultimately expressed in a lack of temple stewardship (3:7–12), which is rooted in unbelief: "It is vain to serve God" (3:14). But God reassures, "Once more you shall see the distinction between the righteous and the wicked. . . . For behold, the day is coming, burning like an oven, when all the arrogant and all evildoers will be stubble" (3:18—4:1). Consequently we have a holistic view of the relationship between the temple in this age, the coming of the Messiah, and the execution of "the great and awesome day of the LORD" (4:5).

In the same light, the temple priesthood was also understood as a stewardship. Accordingly Joshua, "the son of Jehozadak, the high priest" (Zech. 6:11), was crowned proleptically in anticipation of "the Branch" (6:12) to come. "And he will branch out from his place and build *the temple* of the LORD. It is he who will build the temple of the LORD, and he will be clothed with majesty and will sit and rule on his throne. And he will be *a priest on his throne*. And there will be harmony between the two" (Zech. 6:12–13, NIV).

Thus there is an organic relationship between the Davidic monarchy and the Levitical priesthood, which retains continuity between this age and the age to come based upon stewardship.[106] In this way the prophetic reassurance through Jeremiah is both logical and practical, since it was assumed that the Messiah would restore and glorify the Jerusalemic temple and its priesthood:

David will never fail to have a man to sit on the throne of the house of Israel, nor will *the priests, who are Levites,* ever fail to have a man to stand before me. . . . If you can break my covenant with the day and my covenant with the night, so that day and night no longer come at their appointed time, then my covenant with David my servant—and my covenant *with the Levites* who are priests ministering before me—can be broken and David will no longer have a descendant to reign on his throne. (Jer. 33:17–21, NIV)[107]

Moreover, as discussed in chapter 2, humanity was designed with a priestly nature in the beginning, which will find fulfillment in the age to come (cf. Rev. 5:10; 20:6). As humanity was created to "serve/work" (Heb. *'ābad*) and "guard/keep" (Heb. *šāmar*) the garden (Gen. 2:15), so also the Levites were charged to "serve" and "keep" the tabernacle (Num. 3:7; 8:25–26; 18:5–6) and the temple (1 Chron. 23:32; 26:20).[108] Likewise, in the New Jerusalem we will "serve him day and night in his temple" (Rev. 7:15), for "the throne of God and of the Lamb will be in the city, and his servants will serve him" (Rev. 22:3, NIV).[109] Thus, being the "last Adam" (1 Cor. 15:45; cf. Rom. 5:14), the Messiah will build the final temple and righteously reestablish humanity's eternal priesthood (see figure 6.10), which is in full accord with the Jewish expectations seen in the New Testament.[110]

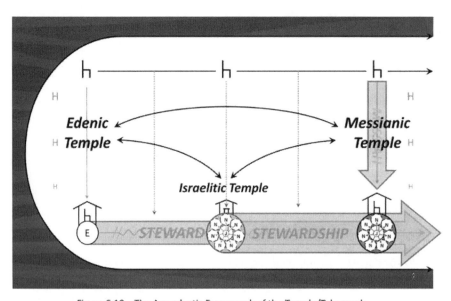

Figure 6.10 – The Apocalyptic Framework of the Temple/Tabernacle

The absolute centrality of the temple in Jesus' day is generally accepted.[111] Anything that takes "forty-six years to build" (John 2:20) implies a great deal of value, meaning, and ambition. Such meaning was simply derived from the

Old Testament and its development of messianic expectation, and that *without question or pretense*. Unfortunately, many assume that Jesus and/or the apostles taught "a complete repudiation of the whole temple-idea."[112] However, there is simply no scriptural evidence for such a claim.[113]

It was in the temple that Zechariah saw his forerunner vision (Luke 1:22) while performing his priestly duty (v. 8). Likewise, Mary and Joseph took Jesus to the temple "to present him to the Lord" (Luke 2:22). There Simeon, who was "waiting for the consolation of Israel" (v. 25), was led by the Spirit into the temple to prophesy Jesus' messianic destiny (v. 34). So too, Anna, who "did not depart from the temple" (v. 37), blessed him and spoke of him to all "who were waiting for the redemption of Jerusalem" (v. 38). And when Jesus as a boy was found in the temple, he simply responded, "Did you not know that I must be in my Father's house?" (v. 49). Surely there was no divine guise involved in the temple being the context of all of these early interactions, which held such strong messianic overtones.

Similarly, after Jesus' baptism, Satan questioned his messiahship three times, culminating in the Lukan account with the quoting of Psalm 91:11–12 at the pinnacle of the temple (Luke 4:9–11). Never in question were the temple, the coming of angels for trampling the serpent underfoot (Ps. 91:13), the inheriting of all the kingdoms of the earth (Ps. 2:8), or the transformation of the earth's stony ecology (Isa. 35:1–2; 55:12–13). It was only the timing and presumption of messianic anointing that was at stake.

While cleansing the temple, Jesus referred to it as "my house" (Matt. 21:13) and "my Father's house" (John 2:16) without the slightest pretense or equivocation. Jesus was actually zealous *for* the temple (John 2:17), not against it. He cleansed it because he cared about it, not because he disparaged it. Moreover, his reference to the resurrection of "the temple of his body" (John 2:21) ought only to *reinforce* the expectation of his establishing an eschatological temple, for it was in response to the question, "What miraculous sign can you show us to prove your authority to do all this?" (v. 18, NIV). Therefore Jesus' resurrection simply proved his authority to sit on his glorious throne in the eschatological Jerusalemic temple.

As previously discussed, the parable of the tenants (Matt. 21:33–46) was addressed to the chief priests and elders in light of Jesus' cleansing of the temple. Though the "vineyard" represented Israel as a whole, the heart of the parable concerned the leaders who were chiefly responsible for stewarding the temple (v. 45). Again, there is no evidence that Jesus questioned the validity of the temple or its purpose for existence. Rather, what was in question was Jesus' messianic "authority" (v. 23) over the temple.

Likewise, when Jesus said, "Something greater than the temple is here" (Matt.

12:6), he did not mean that the temple, "the house of God" (v. 4), had been existentially superseded. He was simply referring to his own authority and exalted position before God (akin to being "above the law," so to speak), which deemed him "guiltless" (v. 7), just as David and the priests were guiltless due to their exalted position (vv. 3–5).

In Jesus' teaching "day after day in the temple" (Luke 22:53; cf. 20:1; 21:37), there is never any record of condescension or controversion toward the temple itself but only toward those who officiated it (cf. Matt. 23:16–22; Luke 20:19). If Jesus was teaching a new supersessionist, self-realized temple, surely this would have been explicitly recorded somewhere! Yet we read nothing of the sort. Furthermore, when the children were "crying out *in the temple*, 'Hosanna to the Son of David!'" (Matt. 21:15), Jesus only affirmed their declaration by quoting Psalm 8 (commonly interpreted in messianic terms, cf. 1 Cor. 15:27; Heb. 2:6–8).

What is more, the entire Olivet Discourse took place "opposite the temple" (Mark 13:3), implying that the temple is the ultimate referent for the entire eschatological drama. Thus the "throwing down" of the stones of the temple (cf. Matt. 24:2 and parallels) does not imply its abrogation or annulment.[114] Akin to the wilderness wanderings or the exile of Israel, the AD 70 destruction of the temple (and the eschatological destruction of the temple) only reflects temporal discipline upon rebellion and hardness of heart. The Jews were not disinherited because of their idolatry and murdering of the prophets, nor was the temple abrogated because of its corruption and spiritual prostitution.[115]

The strongest evidence of continued messianic expectation in relation to the temple is the response of the disciples to Jesus' ascension. When the angels appeared and told them Jesus would return "in the same way as you saw him go into heaven" (Acts 1:11), they returned to Jerusalem and "stayed continually *at the temple*, praising God" (Luke 24:53). In addition, "Every day they continued to meet together *in the temple*" (Acts 2:46, NIV), assumedly observing the traditional hours of prayer (e.g., "going up *to the temple* at the hour of prayer"; Acts 3:1).

Similarly, it was without any sense of guise or subversion that Peter obeyed the angel of the Lord who commanded him, "Go stand *in the temple* and speak to the people all the words of this Life" (Acts 5:20). This was the common practice of the apostles, for "every day, *in the temple* and from house to house, they did not cease teaching and preaching Jesus as the Christ" (5:42). Nowhere does this messianic preaching undermine the existence of the temple, though this was the charge brought against them (e.g., "This man never ceases to speak words against this holy place"; 6:13, cf. 21:28; 24:6). Unfortunately, the church went on in the centuries following to become guilty of this very accusation—instead of being God's "holy place" and the epicenter of redemptive history, the temple was viewed as a carnal Jewish husk to be discarded in lieu of the spiritual kernel of the church militant/triumphant.

Like the other apostles, Paul revered the temple. After his conversion, he immediately "returned to Jerusalem and was praying in the temple" (Acts 22:17), where he fell into a trance and received his call to the Gentiles (v. 21). Again, there is never any sense of renunciation of the temple in his mission to the Gentiles, but rather it was the locus of all such ministry.[116] Moreover, Paul clearly refuted the accusations of temple and Torah abrogation when for seven days "he purified himself along with them and went into the temple, giving notice when the days of purification would be fulfilled and the offering presented for each one of them" (Acts 21:26). The fact that Paul did this without pretense is evident in his later defense before Felix: "I went up to worship in Jerusalem. . . . I came to bring alms to my nation and to present offerings. While I was doing this, they found me purified in *the temple*, without any crowd or tumult" (24:11,17–18). Likewise, Paul tells Festus, "Neither against the law of the Jews, nor against *the temple*, nor against Caesar have I committed any offense" (25:8).

Paul's emphasis on justification by faith in no way contradicts the assumed eschatological program upon which the New Testament hope is based. Paul's references to "the temple service" (1 Cor. 9:13) and the Antichrist taking his seat "in the temple of God" (2 Thess. 2:4) are evidences of this assumption. His reference to the individual believer (cf. 1 Cor. 3:17; 6:19) and to the church as a whole (cf. Eph. 2:21) as a temple is simply analogous, since both contain the Holy Spirit (cf. 2 Cor. 6:16).[117] If Paul was making a radical supersessionist reinterpretation, one would assume he would devote to it more than a few sporadic verses.[118] The present filling of the believer with the Holy Spirit was simply understood as a "deposit" (2 Cor. 1:22; 5:5, NIV), "guaranteeing our inheritance until the redemption of those who are God's possession" (Eph. 1:14, NIV). Thus the filling of the individual believer does not annul or minimize the importance of the temple, but rather confirms the future glory which will envelop the Messiah, his people, his temple, and the whole earth in the resurrection.[119]

Neither does the fulfillment of sacrifice in the new covenant (cf. Heb. 8:13; 9:23; 10:1) annul the purpose of the temple. The temple is not a husk carrying the kernel of sacrifice, so to speak. It is primarily a "footstool" (1 Chron. 28:2; Ps. 99:5; Lam. 2:1)—that is, an earthly throne room. Though the presence of God demands sacrifice in this age for the remission of sin, the ultimate royal design of the temple endures eternally (cf. Ps. 132:7–18; Isa. 60:13; Ezek. 43:7).[120] Such logic, in light of Christ's other royal-eschatological encouragements to the churches in Revelation (cf. Rev. 2:7,11,26; 3:5,21), drives the promise to the Philadelphian church: "The one who conquers, I will make him a pillar in *the temple* of my God. Never shall he go out of it, and I will write on him the name of my God, and the name of the city of my God, *the new Jerusalem*, which comes down from my God out of heaven, and my own new name" (Rev. 3:12).

In summary, we find the New Testament in basic conformity with the common Jewish expectations of the day concerning a future messianic temple. The assumption that Christ and the church have realized and superseded the Jerusalemic temple is unfounded. Jesus will return as the prophets have spoken, executing the day of the Lord, punishing the wicked, rewarding the righteous, ruling over Israel and the nations, raising up Jerusalem and Mount Zion, and sitting on his glorious throne in the house of the Lord.

CHRIST'S KINGDOM:
THE GLORY OF THE MILLENNIUM

So far we have presented a simple Jewish apocalyptic view of the Scriptures—a linear approach to history within an integrated creation (i.e., heavens and earth), wherein this age is delineated from the age to come by the day of the Lord. This day will bring about the judgment of the heavens and earth by fire, restoring it to its original state of perfection and righteousness. This judgment is executed by God's agent of salvation, the Christ, who will raise the dead corporeally, punish the wicked with everlasting torment, and bless the righteous with everlasting life. This blessing is worked out by means of the messianic kingdom (i.e., the kingdom of God), which is the practical framework within which the age to come and the new earth are administrated. This administration is also Israelocentric, executed upon the basis of primogeniture. Moreover, the Christ will rule in heavenly glory from his throne within the Jerusalemic temple raised up on Mount Zion. In this way the glory of the Lord will cover the earth as it was in the beginning (cf. Ps. 72:19; Isa. 11:9; Hab. 2:14).[121]

Even among those who readily accept this basic redemptive framework, there remains the sticky issue of chiliasm (belief in a thousand-year messianic reign, derived from the Gk. *chilias*, meaning "a thousand"). Indeed, the question of whether or not there will be a transitional aspect to the age to come demands an answer. When Jesus returns, will he immediately inaugurate the final state of redemption, or will he progressively make his enemies a footstool for his feet? This is the underlying issue of the "millennial controversy"[122] ("millennialism" is essentially a synonym for chiliasm, since it derives from the Latin *mille* and *annus*, meaning "thousand years").[123]

It is generally agreed that the early church was chiliastic, believing that Jesus would inaugurate a transitional kingdom which would rule from Jerusalem for a thousand years before the final restoration of creation. Such an approach was most often deduced from a plain reading of Revelation 20:1–6: "They came to life and reigned with Christ for a thousand years" (v. 4). Moreover, such a view was buttressed by kingdom passages with a progressive aspect (e.g., Isa. 2:3; 9:7; Dan. 2:35; etc.), in which the culmination of human rebellion is brought increasingly under messianic submission in the age to come, as Paul described:

> Then comes the end, when he delivers the kingdom to God the Father after destroying every rule and every authority and power. For he must reign *until he has put all his enemies under his feet.* The last enemy to be destroyed is death. . . . When all things are subjected to him, then the Son himself will also be subjected to him who put all things in subjection under him, that God may be all in all. (1 Cor. 15:24–28)[124]

Therefore we see a progressive transitional time after the Lord comes and before the final overturning of death—the day when all things will be in perfect submission to God (see figure 6:11). Though chiliasm was a minority belief in first-century Judaism,[125] the Revelation of John was understood to confirm its truth, just as the resurrection of Jesus confirmed the truth of Jewish apocalypticism in general.

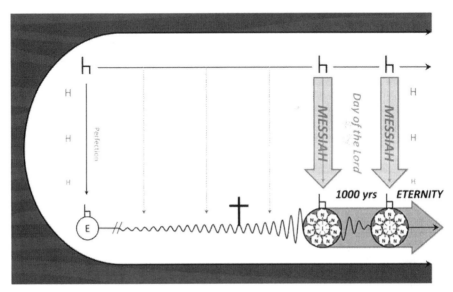

Figure 6.11 – The Chiliastic Transition of the Messianic Kingdom

Revelation 20:1–6 has been shown to stand on its own exegetically,[126] but this was not the real basis of chiliasm in the early church. Millennial thought at the time was ultimately based upon the "cosmic week" or "creation-day world-age" theory, in which each day of creation represented an era of one thousand years of redemptive history.[127] Hence there would be six days (i.e., six thousand years) of divine work before the final day (i.e., one thousand years) of divine rest.[128] In this way, "The seventh day is a sign of the resurrection, the rest of the coming age" (*Life of Adam and Eve* 51.2).[129] After seven thousand years of existence, then comes the "eighth day" (*2 Enoch* 33.1) and the final new creation.[130] Consequently God has given "seven days of ages for repentance" (*Sibylline Oracles* 8.357) before the conclusion of redemptive history.[131]

This chronological formula may sound quaint to the modern ear, but it was based upon substantial biblical exposition, primarily concerning Genesis 2:17: "For *in the day* that you eat of it you shall surely die." Since Adam ate and died short of one thousand years, then "the day" assumedly meant one thousand years by God's reckoning. Thus the pseudepigraphic *Jubilees*:

> And at the end of the nineteenth jubilee in the seventh week, in the sixth year, Adam died. And all of his children buried him in the land of his creation. And he was the first who was buried in the earth. And he lacked seventy years from one thousand years, *for a thousand years are like one day in the testimony of heaven* and therefore it was written concerning the tree of knowledge, "In the day you eat from it you will die." Therefore he did not complete the years of this day because he died in it. (4.29–30)[132]

It was in this light that Psalm 90, the "prayer of Moses," was commonly understood:

> Before the mountains were born
>> or you brought forth the earth and the world,
>> from everlasting to everlasting you are God.
>
> You turn men back to dust,
>> saying, "Return to dust, O sons of men." [cf. Gen. 2:17; 3:19]
>
> *For a thousand years in your sight*
>> *are like a day* that has just gone by,
>> or like a watch in the night.
>
> You sweep men away in the sleep of death;
>> they are like the new grass of the morning—
>
> though in the morning it springs up new,
>> by evening it is dry and withered.
>
> (Ps. 90:2–6, NIV)[133]

Peter thus quotes verse 4 in reference to the coming of God and "the day of judgment" (cf. 2 Peter 3:4–8).[134] Moreover, the use of "[Sabbath] rest" in Hebrews 3–4 fits comfortably within the cosmic-week framework.[135]

Belief in the cosmic week was common in the early church.[136] *The Epistle of Barnabas*,[137] Justin Martyr's *Dialogue with Trypho*,[138] Irenaeus' *Against Heresies*,[139] Commodianus' *Instructions*,[140] Hippolytus' *Commentary on Daniel*,[141] Methodius' *Extracts from the Work on Things Created*,[142] Lactantius' *Epitome of the Divine Institutes*,[143] and Augustine's *City of God*[144] all clearly reflect a chiliastic understanding of redemptive history based upon the creation-day world-age idea—and that often resting upon a chiliastic interpretation of Genesis 2:17.[145] Thus the kingdom of God in the early church was understood apocalyptically, messianically, Israelitically, and chiliastically (see figure 6.12)—as Irenaeus summarized:

> But when this *Antichrist* shall have devastated all things in this world, he will reign for three years and six months, and sit *in the temple at Jerusalem*; and then the Lord will come from heaven in the clouds, in the glory of the Father, sending this man and those who follow him into the lake of fire; but bringing in for the righteous *the times of the kingdom*, that is, the rest, *the hallowed seventh day*; and restoring *to Abraham* the promised inheritance, in which kingdom the Lord declared, that "many coming from the east and from the west should sit down with Abraham, Isaac, and Jacob."[146]

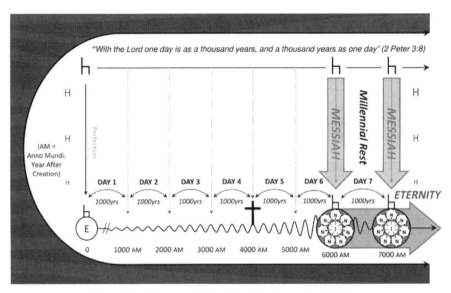

Figure 6.12 – The "Cosmic Week" and the Millennial Sabbath

Such millennial hope suffered greatly during the Constantinian revolution of the fourth century, and Augustine's reinterpretation of Revelation 20 nearly ended all expectation that Jesus would reign upon the earth in the future.[147] So Stanley Grenz summarizes, "By the time of Augustine's death, the nonmillenarian theology of Alexandria and Rome had engulfed the millennialism of Antioch and Ephesus. As a result, at the Council of Ephesus A.D. 431 the church condemned as superstition the belief in a literal, future thousand-year reign on the earth."[148]

Though the Middle Ages were dominated by Augustinian theology, a number of marginal monastic sects, as well as a few Orthodox theologians, sustained the chiliastic heritage.[149] Most of the Protestant Reformers held the Augustinian line, though various Anabaptists, Huguenots, Bohemian Brethren, and English Puritans returned to millennialism.[150] During the Enlightenment, many German Pietists as well as English evangelicals were chiliastic.[151] Though dominionistic zeal overtook and nearly choked out millennial hope during the nineteenth century, dispensationalists spread a novel form of chiliasm in England and America, which took root by the turn of the twentieth century.[152]

Since that time the dispensational bias has been progressively purged, restoring to the modern church its apostolic foundation, such that "[millennialism] is today stronger and more widely spread than at any time in history."[153] Though refraining from a dogmatic statement concerning chiliasm, I heartily affirm the millennial hope of the early church—believing *chiliastic cruciform-apocalypticism* to be the closest approximation of New Testament faith, which was personally delivered to the apostles by our resurrected Lord (cf. Acts 1:3; 1 Cor. 15:3–8; Gal. 1:12; Rev. 1:1). As Justin Martyr, the second-century Christian apologist, asserted: "I and others, who are right-minded Christians on all points, are assured that there will be a resurrection of the dead, and a thousand years in Jerusalem, which will then be built, adorned, and enlarged, as the prophets Ezekiel and Isaiah and others declare."[154]

THE CHRISTOPLATONIC KINGDOM

As Christianity lost its Jewish apocalyptic moorings during the third and fourth centuries, the "kingdom of God" became increasingly associated with immaterial heaven. With Origen, "the inheritance of the kingdom of heaven" is equated with "the departure of the saints from that earth to those heavens,"[155] wherein the "pure in heart" will "quickly ascend to a place in the air, and reach the kingdom of heaven."[156] Thus Neusner and Chilton summarize Origen's theological impact:

> Origen clearly represents and develops a construction of the Christian faith in which eschatology has been swallowed up in an emphasis upon

transcendence. The only time which truly matters is that time until one's death, which determines one's experience in paradise and in the resurrection. *"Heaven" as cosmographic place now occupies the central position once occupied by the eschatological kingdom of God in Jesus' teaching.* That, too, occurs on the authority of progressive dialectics, the refinement of Pauline metaphysics.[157]

Though a "new creation model" has always persisted,[158] this escapist vision has undoubtedly been the dominant understanding of the kingdom throughout the majority of the church's history. On the other hand, the dominionist view of manifest sovereignty has also held great sway—resulting in the assumption that whether God uses kings or popes, he incrementally establishes his messianic kingdom through the (Gentile) political powers of this age.

The progress from Origen to Augustine is well documented,[159] and it was Augustine's teachings on the kingdom of God that "formed the center of the official teaching of the church on the matter through the Middle Ages."[160] The kingdom is both the church triumphant and the church militant—"The Church even now is the kingdom of Christ, and the kingdom of heaven,"[161] though God will ultimately "confer on the human body a property which shall enable it to pass into heaven and dwell there."[162] Though the means of attaining the kingdom (i.e., justification by faith) found great renewal during the Reformation, the distorted hope of the kingdom changed little.[163] Thus, for the majority of church history the interpretation of the kingdom of God has been twofold according to its respective messianic expectation: materialized-sovereignty now and immaterial-heaven upon death (see figure 6.13).

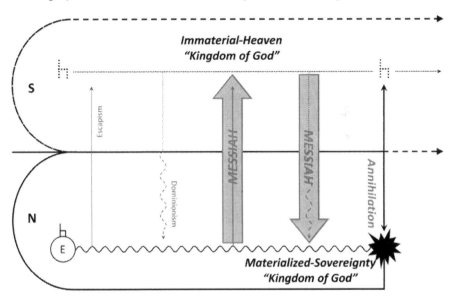

Figure 6.13 – The Conflicted Messianic Kingdom of Augustinian Christoplatonism

As discussed in chapter 4, the idea of an immaterial-heavenly kingdom is difficult to relate to since it has no practical connection to our earthly existence. Though immateriality retains a hope for existence without sin, death, pain, etc., it leaves believers without a concrete hope. Humans were made to rule righteously upon the earth, not in immaterial heaven. Moreover, all ethnic distinctions are erased in the context of immateriality, thus abrogating the basic covenantal framework of the Scriptures.

On the other hand, the dominionistic kingdom idea has led to incalculable damage and disillusionment.[164] Indeed it constitutes an earthly hope, yet it is bound by the depravity of humanity. Moreover, Christendom erases the Israelo-centric focus of the Bible, replacing it with an ethnocentrism of whichever nation or people happens to hold the money, land, and power of their day.[165] Dominion-istic theology also robs believers of the sharp edge of their witness concerning the return of Jesus (cf. Acts 3:21; 10:42; 17:31; etc.).[166] Alva McClain well articulated the inevitable consequences:

> The identification of the Kingdom with the Church has led historically to ecclesiastical policies and programs which, even when not positively evil, have been far removed from the original simplicity of the New Testament *ekklēsia*. It is easy to claim that in the "present kingdom of grace" the rule of the saints is wholly "spiritual," exerted only through moral principles and influence. But practically, once the Church becomes the Kingdom in any realistic theological sense, it is impossible to draw any clear line between principles and their implementation through political and social devises. For the logical implications of a present ecclesiastical *kingdom* are unmistakable, and historically have always led in only one direction, i.e., political control of the state by the Church. The distances down this road traveled by various religious movements, and the forms of control which were developed, have been widely different. The difference is very great between the Roman Catholic system and modern Protestant efforts to control the state; also between the ecclesiastical rule of Calvin in Geneva and the fanaticism of Münster and the English "fifth-monarchy." But the basic assumption is always the same: The Church in some sense is the Kingdom, and therefore has a divine right to rule; or it is the business of the Church to "establish" fully the Kingdom of God among men. Thus the Church loses its "pilgrim" character and the sharp edge of its divinely commissioned "witness" is blunted.[167]

With the advent of dispensationalism, the messianic kingdom took on a dualistic nature, according to the dispensational schema of two redemptive plans. The "kingdom of heaven" relates to the earthly Jewish kingdom (spoken of only in Matthew's Gospel), while the "kingdom of God" relates to the heavenly Gentile kingdom.[168] The kingdom of heaven substantially existed in Israel until the exile.[169] Jesus "offered" the kingdom to the Jews, but they rejected it, which resulted in the kingdom being "postponed."[170] This postponement set into motion a Gentile "intercalation," which will continue until the second coming (pretribulational rapture), at which time the Jewish program will recommence and the kingdom will be reestablished after the final tribulation (see figure 6.14). The complexities of this schema are manifold.[171]

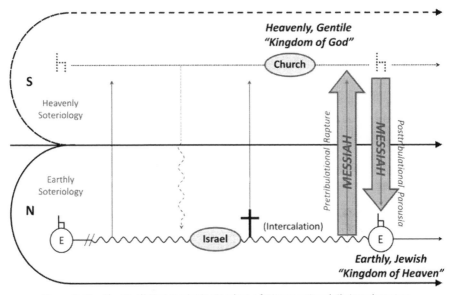

Figure 6.14 – The Dualistic Messianic Kingdom of Dispensational Christoplatonism

As inaugurationalism gradually engulfed the academy during the twentieth century, discussions concerning the kingdom of God became increasingly dominionistic in tone (as opposed to socio-liberal or escapist). This trend is due to the fact that the inaugurationalist kingdom is quite similar to its Christendom ancestor, except it finds its referent in the spiritual realization of the Jewish messianic kingdom. Ultimately, the difference is minor, and history will prove that its application is the same.

At the first coming, heaven began to invade earth, and the conflation of the two will conclude at the second coming (except for those inaugurationalists who still hold to chiliasm, which demands an extra phase of conflict). George Ladd, the great evangelical systematizer of inaugurationalism, describes:

> This is why the Second Coming of Christ is necessary—to complete the work begun in his Incarnation. There are, in other words, two great events

in God's conquest of the powers of evil, two invasions of God into history: the Incarnation and the Second Coming. One scholar has illustrated this by an analogy from World War II. There were two steps in the victory over Nazi Germany: D-Day and V-Day. Once the allies had launched a successful invasion upon the continent and the allied armies had secured a foothold and started their drive across France, the tide of battle turned. The allies were advancing, Germany was in retreat. But there remained much bitter fighting, which lasted until the complete capitulation of the enemy—V-Day. Then the fighting ceased; peace reigned.[172]

Though the church is the obvious vehicle of this spiritual invasion, inaugurationalists continually distance themselves from such conclusions, for obvious reasons. If the messianic missions of the first and second comings are homogenous, then so is the mission of the messianic kingdom (see figure 6.15), and a simple deduction leads to the same mission for the church, which only ever leads in one direction—as McClain noted, to "political control of the state by the Church."

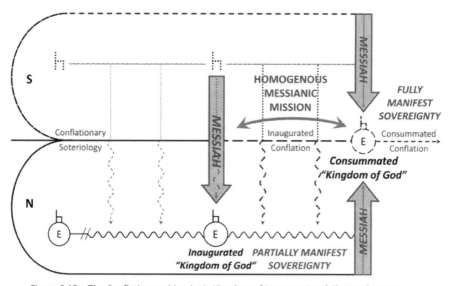

Figure 6.15 – The Conflationary Messianic Kingdom of Inaugurational Christoplatonism

The attempt to argue for a purely "spiritual" kingdom in this age, in contrast to a "visibly manifest" kingdom in the age to come, is Platonism at its finest.[173] There is no immaterial world seeking to manifest itself in materiality. Rather, God sits enthroned over the heavens and earth, waiting in mercy to judge the living and the dead. This age remains this age (Gal. 1:4; Titus 2:12), essentially characterized by the cross (Luke 24:47; Acts 3:19–21); and the age to come remains the age to come (cf. Eph. 1:21; Heb. 2:5), essentially characterized by judgment (Acts 10:42; 2 Tim. 4:1). *Where in the Scriptures does the messianic kingdom ever precede the day of judgment?*[174] Rather, divine judgment always initiates the kingdom (cf. Ps. 2; Isa. 24; Dan. 7; Amos 9; Hab. 2–3; Zeph. 2–3; Zech. 12–14; Mal. 3–4).

The day of the Lord is no insignificant or peripheral event that can be easily spiritualized; it is *the defining event* of redemptive history (see chapter 3). The holy trinity of Jewish eschatology, so to speak, was the day of the Lord, the resurrection of the dead, and the messianic kingdom. No observant first-century Jew would dare to sunder what God had so prophetically joined together! Yet this is exactly the effect of realized eschatology: Jesus and the apostles inaugurated the kingdom and the resurrection before the divine judgment of the last day.

So prominent has inaugurationalism become in the academy that deviation from it is nigh to heresy, as Craig Blomberg insinuates: "One might observe that if a theological perspective is held jointly by such a diverse but impressive array of scholars as Trilling, Kümmel, Jeremias, Ladd, Marshall, Beasley-Murray, Saucy and Blaising, it must almost certainly be true."[175] However, the nearly universal adoption of a theological system does not guarantee correspondence with the truth. Liberalism dominated the academy one hundred years ago; Reformed dogmatics two hundred years before that; and medieval empiricism three hundred years before that.

Though inaugurationalism has received relatively little mainstream criticism, many remain skeptical. Not only are many dispensationalists unconvinced,[176] but many liberals (unbiased by the pressures of tradition) judge the inaugurational schema "a hermeneutical castle built upon exegetical quicksand."[177] As Christopher Rowland describes, "Supporters of the view that Jesus thought of the kingdom as present as well as future point to Luke 16.16 but particularly to sayings like Matthew 11.5f. and to Luke 11.20 and 17.21b. Despite the fact that the consensus of New Testament scholarship accepts that Jesus believed that the kingdom of God had already in some sense arrived in Jesus' words and deeds, the fact has to be faced that the evidence in support of such an assumption is not very substantial."[178]

Liberals find all such spiritual realization to be a form of hermeneutical "trickery,"[179] an attempt to deliver Jesus and the apostles from the embarrassment of Jewish apocalypticism, intentionally avoiding an "at-face-value interpretation" of their words.[180] Indeed, concerning realized eschatology, we must agree. Yet we find *no embarrassment* concerning the Jewish hope of the Law and the Prophets. Liberals simply have no faith (generally due to their naturalistic bias), yet without faith they will be destroyed on the day of his appearing (Heb. 10:37–39).[181] Moreover, liberals have a *chronic lack* of cruciform theology. Assuming that Paul was the primary inventor of an atonemental interpretation of the cross, liberals grossly misunderstand the apostolic tradition.

Not only do dispensationalists and liberals question the inaugurational dogma, but Jewish scholars also find it revolting. The idea that Jesus realized the Old Testament hope without actually doing it is simply ludicrous. All such hermeneutical gymnastics are both unbiblical and *unrealistic*.[182] Ask any devout Jew if the kingdom of God has been inaugurated, and he/she will laugh at you and point to the temple mount as proof of your Gentile ignorance. The world is obviously unredeemed. Truly, it takes a great amount of inaugurational indoctrination to believe that the new heavens and new earth are already happening. Indeed, the question of realized eschatology has fundamentally divided Jews and Christians historically, as Jewish theologian Martin Buber said:

> The church rests on its faith that the Christ has come, and that this is the redemption which God has bestowed on mankind. We, Israel, *are not able* to believe this. . . . We know more deeply, more truly, that world history has not been turned upside down to its very foundations—that the world is not yet redeemed. We *sense* its unredeemedness. The church can, or indeed must, understand this sense of ours as the awareness that *we* are not redeemed. But we know that that is not it. The redemption of the world is for us indivisibly one with the perfecting of creation, with the establishment of the unity which nothing more prevents, the unity which is no longer controverted, and which is realized in all the protean variety of the world. Redemption is one with the kingdom of God in its fulfilment. An anticipation of any single part of the *completed* redemption of the world—for example the redemption beforehand of the soul—is something we cannot grasp, although even for us in our mortal hours redeeming and redemption are heralded.[183]

Of course the New Testament never says that such a redemption of the world has come—only that a greater sacrifice has been made before eschatological salvation (Heb. 9:28), that messianic suffering has come before messianic glory (Luke 24:26), that a propitiation has been put forward before the wrath to come (Rom. 3:25; 1 John 4:10), that justification has been secured in anticipation of the final judgment (Rom. 5:9; Titus 3:7), that a ransom has been offered before the day of redemption (Eph. 4:30; 1 Tim. 2:6). Such a message, devoid of realized eschatology, was readily received by many first-century Jews. The same cannot be said after the church rejected the Jewish eschatological hope in place of an *ersatz* Platonic gospel.

CONCLUSION

In light of the coming kingdom, how then do we relate to the activity of God in this age? As discussed in chapters 3 and 4, God's temporal blessings and curses are understood in light of his eternal blessings and curses. The gifts of the Holy Spirit are likewise understood as a firstfruits of the final harvest, a guarantee of what is to come. Though the firstfruits are essentially of the same substance as the harvest (cf. Rom. 8:23; Heb. 6:5), no one in their right mind would equate the two, for in doing so you might jeopardize the task at hand: the labor necessary before the harvest.

More specifically, let us use the analogy of an *inheritance*, since the kingdom is so often described as such (cf. Matt. 25:34; 1 Cor. 6:9; Gal. 5:21; Eph. 5:5; James 2:5). As a father grooms his child for the ultimate inheritance of the family estate, so also is God grooming the church for its inheritance of the world to come. To speak of the inheritance as a purely future event in no way precludes the involvement of the Father beforehand. What earthly father would declare to his son the futurity of his inheritance, and on such grounds say, "I guess I'll talk to you in forty years!"?[184] Ridiculous. The father's encouragement and discipline *along the way* are absolutely necessary and only reinforce the final passing on or denial of the estate.

The various forms of encouragement and discipline (e.g., an allowance or corporeal punishment) are indeed of the same substance as the final event. However, to refer to the allowance as the inheritance is simply confusing and detrimental to the main point: *The mission of the child is different before and after the inheritance.* The allowance is given for the sake of training and schooling, which qualifies the child for the inheritance. So it is with our inheritance in the kingdom of God. We have received our "allowance" of the Holy Spirit (along with our discipline of hardship and trials; cf. Heb. 12:7) for the purpose of training *in the way of the cross.*

Those who endure the training of the cross will then inherit the kingdom (cf. Matt. 16:24; John 12:26). Those who reject the path of the cross will inherit the lake of fire (cf. Matt. 16:23; 25:41; Gal. 1:8; Phil. 3:18). To conflate the activity of God and the gifts of the Holy Spirit in this age with the activity of God and the kingdom in the age to come confuses the most basic tenet of Christian discipleship: We are not called to receive the kingdom in this age; we are called to take up our cross in this age. Simply put, those who seek their inheritance in this age disqualify themselves for the eternal inheritance (cf. Matt. 16:25; John 12:25).

But it is precisely at this point that inaugurationalism ultimately destroys the faith of the common believer. When the inaugurational doctrine is pressed upon the mind of a believer, the cross generally fades into the background of consciousness.[185] This is due to simple theological and chronological logic. God cannot execute the age to come and wait for it at the same time (though much theological wrangling is exercised to prove this to be true). The return of Jesus is something like a "hostile takeover" of the earth. When Christians digest inaugurational doctrines, they inevitably begin to *already* take over that which Jesus will *not yet* take over until his second coming. Hence unknowing Christians progressively lose sight of the true nature of the cross, perverting it as the means of an inaugurated kingdom in this age, generally in the same theological manner as historical Christendom.[186]

Rather, Jesus is simply waiting to make his enemies his footstool (cf. Acts 2:35; Heb. 10:13), patiently seeking the repentance of the wicked (cf. Rom. 2:4–5; 2 Peter 3:9) and calling the church to proclaim and demonstrate the mercy of God in the cross (cf. Luke 24:47; Acts 10:43; 1 Cor. 2:2; Col. 1:24). Paul thus summarizes our response:

> In the presence of God and of Christ Jesus, who will judge the living and the dead, and *in view of his appearing and his kingdom*, I give you this charge: Preach the Word; be prepared in season and out of season; correct, rebuke and encourage—with great patience and careful instruction. . . . Keep your head in all situations, endure hardship, do the work of an evangelist, discharge all the duties of your ministry. (2 Tim. 4:1–2,5, NIV)

Common logic that corresponds to both reality and the Scriptures argues for a simple chronological progression of events which culminates in the day of the Lord, the resurrection of the dead, and the Jewish messianic kingdom. This was the primal expectation of the early church, as patristic scholar Everett Ferguson summarizes: "The characteristic second-century understanding of the kingdom of God was no threat to Rome because it was heavenly, angelic, and altogether future."[187] Moreover, "The overwhelming usage of 'kingdom' in second-century Christian literature is eschatological. . . . The kingdom is almost uniformly future, heavenly, and eternal."[188]

Even Ladd himself acknowledged, "For Christians of the first three centuries, the Kingdom was altogether eschatological."[189] Unfortunately, he goes on to argue that they were simply ignorant of their new inaugurated status as "a new people of God who are to take the place of Israel."[190] This logic is absurd. If the early church never spoke of realized eschatology, then why do we speak it back into the New Testament?

The theological gravity of the messianic expectation of the early church, especially during the second century, is rarely appreciated. As seen in the Muratorian Fragment, it was the second-century church that primarily formulated the canon of the New Testament.[191] If those who stewarded what we regard as the very oracles of God believed the kingdom to be "altogether future" and "altogether eschatological," then it seems completely inappropriate (and possibly arrogant) to interpret such oracles as portraying an inaugurated kingdom. These men handed to us the very apostolic fountain of truth from which we drink. If they were stewarding the apostolic witness, and believing in the kingdom as such, should we assume their hope to be naïve and their hermeneutic primitive? God forbid! Rather, the second-century witness was simply in accord with the first-century witness, to which we vigorously hold.

The New Testament seeks no new revelation of the kingdom of God, but rather preserves the simple expectation of a Jewish messianic kingdom. The New Testament is primarily concerned with the means of attaining the hope of the kingdom (cf. Acts 26:7; Rom. 9:30; Phil. 3:11; etc.). The new covenant is concerned with the sacrifice of the cross, in contrast to the sacrifices of the old covenant (cf. Rom. 3:25; Heb. 8–10; 1 Peter 3:18; etc.). The "promised eternal inheritance" (Heb. 9:15) of the kingdom is never in question (cf. 1 Cor. 15:50; 2 Tim. 4:1; 2 Peter 1:11; etc.). The New Testament presents a straightforward account of the suffering of the Messiah as an atonement for the forgiveness of sins before the coming of the Messiah in glory for the establishment of his Israelitic kingdom (cf. Luke 24:26; Heb. 9:28; 1 Peter 1:11).

Chapter Seven

✧

THE CRUCIFIXION
OF THE CHRIST

I n light of Jesus' bold proclamation concerning the coming kingdom, messianic expectation surrounding his life and ministry rose to a fever pitch. He had been "accredited by God" as the Messiah by multitudes of "miracles, wonders and signs" (Acts 2:22, NIV). These "deeds of the Christ" (Matt. 11:2) had become commonly known "throughout all Judea" (Acts 10:37), so that only visitors to Jerusalem were ignorant of the "prophet mighty in deed and word before God and all the people" (Luke 24:19). Moreover, "Great crowds followed him" (Matt. 4:25; 8:1; cf. 12:15; 19:2; 20:29), expecting that "the kingdom of God was to appear immediately" (Luke 19:11). The people welcomed him into Jerusalem, shouting, "Hosanna! Blessed is he who comes in the name of the Lord! Blessed is the coming kingdom of our father David!" (Mark 11:9–10); and likewise the children cried out in the temple, "Hosanna to the Son of David!" (Matt. 21:15).

All of this anticipation and excitement hit a wall of disillusionment, however, when the Christ was brutally *crucified.* Though Jesus had expressly and repeatedly warned his disciples that this would happen (cf. Matt. 16:21; 17:22; 20:18; and parallels), common sentiment was that "this shall never happen" (Matt. 16:22) to the Messiah. The people had hoped "that he was the one to redeem Israel" (Luke 24:21), but God had not delivered him (cf. Matt. 27:43). He had clearly been "forsaken" (Matt. 27:46). Beyond the public humiliation of Roman crucifixion,[1] Jesus had been openly humiliated by God himself, for "anyone hung on a tree is under God's curse" (Deut. 21:23, NRSV).[2]

Questions immediately arose concerning why God would allow the suffering and death of his Messiah. These questions are exemplified in the interaction between Jesus and his disciples on the road to Emmaus (Luke 24:13–27). As they were discussing "all these things that had happened" (v. 14), with faces "looking sad" (v. 17), Jesus declared to them, "Oh, how foolish you are, and how slow of heart to believe all that the prophets have declared! Was it not necessary that the Messiah should *suffer these things* and then enter into his glory?" (vv. 25–26, NRSV).

Luke goes on to tell us that "beginning with Moses and all the Prophets, he interpreted to them in all the Scriptures the things concerning himself" (v. 27). We can safely assume that "the things concerning himself" primarily referenced the suffering of the Messiah rather than the glory of the Messiah, for this was the question at hand.[3] Moreover, everyone understood what the messianic glory entailed, since "glory" was the common catchword for Jewish apocalypticism,[4] especially in light of the previous statement concerning the redemption of Israel (v. 21).[5]

Jesus' exposition on the road to Emmaus involved a simple explanation of messianic suffering, which assumed the common expectation of messianic glory. This approach is expressed *prima facie* throughout the New Testament, particularly when we see the phraseology of "suffering" and "glory" used together (cf. Rom. 8:17–18; Heb. 2:8–10; 1 Peter 1:11; 4:13; 5:1). Indeed the Son of Man will come "with power and great glory" (Matt. 24:30), "seated at the right hand of Power and coming on the clouds of heaven" (Matt. 26:64; cf. 16:27; 25:31). And this Jesus, "who was taken up from you into heaven, will come in the same way as you saw him go into heaven" (Acts 1:11)—at which time he will in fact "restore the kingdom to Israel" (v. 6). The apostolic interpretation of the crucifixion of the Messiah begins and ends within the framework of Jewish apocalypticism (see figure 7.1).

In light of such expectation, the New Testament writers often quoted or alluded to Psalm 110 to explain the delay of messianic glory (cf. Acts 2:34–35; 5:31; Rom. 8:34; 1 Cor. 15:25; Eph. 1:20; Col. 3:1; Heb. 1:3; 8:1; 10:12–13; 12:2; 1 Peter 3:22).[6] Contrary to the common inaugurational interpretation, the apostles were simply stating that the first part of the psalm had been fulfilled, which "made more certain" (2 Peter 1:19, NIV) the following verses of the psalm.[7] The same approach is seen in the quotations of Isaiah 61 (cf. Luke 4:18–19); Zechariah 9 (cf. Matt. 21:5; John 12:15); Joel 2 (cf. Acts 2:17–21; Rom. 10:13); and Psalm 2 (cf. Acts 13:33; Heb. 1:5).

Thus, the first verse of Psalm 110 was fulfilled in Jesus' resurrection and ascension: "Sit at my right hand, until I make your enemies your footstool." However, I believe it is assumed by the apostles that verses 2–7 are still yet to happen (cf. "He will shatter kings on the day of his wrath," v. 5).[8] This is the plain meaning of the psalm's quotation at Pentecost (Acts 2:33–34), since its contextual referent is "the great and glorious day of the Lord" (v. 20, NIV), on which we seek to be "saved" (v. 21, cf. vv. 37,40). Likewise, Hebrews 10:12–13 summarizes: "When Christ had offered for all time a single sacrifice for sins, he sat down at the right hand of God, *waiting* from that time until his enemies should be made a footstool for his feet."[9]

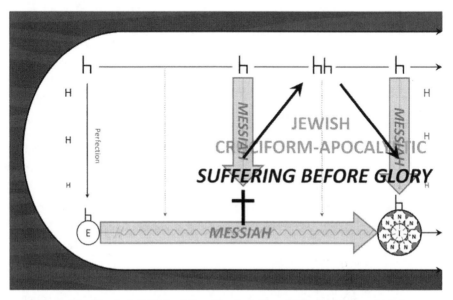

Figure 7.1 – Messianic Suffering Before Messianic Glory within Jewish Apocalypticism

The idea that Jesus is somehow presently "footstooling" his enemies, so to speak, is a "serious mistake,"[10] because it violates the basic nature and purpose of divine mercy in this age. If we inquire as to what God is doing in the present era "until he comes" (1 Cor. 11:26), we must ultimately conclude that he is *waiting* to make his enemies his footstool, "not wanting any to perish, but all to come to repentance" (2 Peter 3:9, NRSV).[11]

THE EMMAUS ROAD EXPOSITION

As Jesus walked with two of his followers (one named Cleopas and the other unnamed) on the road to Emmaus, he "interpreted to them in all the Scriptures the things concerning himself" (Luke 24:27). After this he appeared to the Eleven in Jerusalem and "opened their minds to understand the Scriptures" (v. 45)—that is, "everything written about me in the Law of Moses and the Prophets and the Psalms" (v. 44). But what specifically did Jesus talk about on these two occasions? Based upon later themes in the New Testament, we can infer four areas of discussion: 1) direct prophecies, 2) righteous-suffering typology, 3) calendrical typology, and 4) sacrificial typology. The last of these receives the most attention in the apostolic witness and will be unpacked in the next chapter.

Concerning the direct prophecies of the suffering of the Messiah in the Old Testament, Isaiah 53 is clearly the most referenced prophecy in the New Testament (cf. Matt. 8:17; Mark 9:12; Luke 22:37; John 12:38; Acts 8:32–35; Rom. 10:16; 15:21; 1 Peter 2:22–25).[12] During the Last Supper, Jesus foretold his own death according to Isaiah 53:12: "I tell you that this Scripture must be fulfilled in me: 'And he was numbered with the transgressors'" (Luke 22:37). Earlier, he told his disciples, "The Son of Man must *suffer* many things and be *rejected*" (Luke 9:22)—echoing Isaiah 53:3: "He was despised and *rejected* by others; a man of *suffering*" (NRSV). Putting this suffering and rejection in the context of messianic glory, he also said to them, "As the lightning flashes and lights up the sky from one side to the other, so will the Son of Man be in his day. But first he must *suffer* many things and be *rejected* by this generation" (Luke 17:24–25).

Likewise, when John the Baptist referred to Jesus as "the lamb of God, who takes away the sins of the world" (John 1:29, cf. v. 36), Isaiah 53:6–7 would have been readily apparent: "The LORD has laid on him the iniquity of us all," and he was "like a *lamb* that is led to the slaughter." So also Jesus "remained silent" (Mark 14:61) before his accusers and "made no reply" (Mark 15:5, NIV), recalling Isaiah 53:7: "Like a *sheep* that before its shearers is *silent*, so he opened not his mouth." These circumstances surrounding Jesus' innocent and humiliating death, in light of Isaiah 53, became the primary backdrop for the early church's witness that "it was necessary for the Christ to suffer" (Acts 17:3) and that "God fulfilled what he had foretold through all the prophets, saying that his Christ would suffer" (Acts 3:18, NIV). So Philip interprets the Ethiopian eunuch's reading of Isaiah 53:7–8:

> Now the passage of the Scripture that he was reading was this:
>   "Like a sheep he was led to the slaughter
>   and like a lamb before its shearer is silent,
>   so he opens not his mouth.
>   In his humiliation justice was denied him.
>   Who can describe his generation?
>   For his life is taken away from the earth." . . .
> Then Philip opened his mouth, and *beginning with this Scripture* he told him the good news about Jesus. (Acts 8:32–35)

Isaiah 53 speaks more clearly than any other Old Testament prophetic Scripture concerning the suffering of the Messiah in anticipation of his glory, as the passage concludes: "After the suffering of his soul, he will see the light of life and be satisfied" (v. 11, NIV). Moreover, the glory of his personal resurrection is followed by the glory of Zion as a whole in Isaiah 54 (one of the most referenced Old Testament passages in Revelation 21). In light of its centrality in the New Testament, no wonder Isaiah 53 has been the center of centuries of debate.[13]

Being such a well-known messianic passage, Daniel 9 probably also came up for discussion on the road to Emmaus. Verse 24 summarizes redemptive history: "Seventy weeks are decreed about your people and your holy city, to finish the transgression, to put an end to sin, and to atone for iniquity, to bring in everlasting righteousness, to seal both vision and prophet, and to anoint a most holy place."[14] This verse has "three negatives" followed by "three positives," which naturally fit a chronology of suffering before glory.[15] The transgression, sin, and iniquity of humankind must first be dealt with before the eschatological restoration of righteousness, fulfillment of prophecy, and anointing of the messianic temple.[16]

Verses 25–27 simply elaborate on verse 24. The "anointed one" will come (v. 25), but he "shall be *cut off* and shall have nothing" (v. 26a). The Hebrew word for "cut off" (*kārat*) was commonly associated with sacrifice in the making of a covenant—literally, "cutting a covenant" (cf. Gen. 15:18; 21:27; 31:44; Ex. 23:32; 24:8; Deut. 5:2; 7:2; 29:1; Josh. 9:6,15; 2 Sam. 3:12; 1 Kings 8:9; 2 Chron. 5:10; 34:31; Ezra 10:3; Neh. 9:8; Job 41:4; Ps. 50:5; 89:3; Isa. 55:3; 61:8; Jer. 31:31–33; 34:8; Ezek. 34:25; 37:26; Hos. 2:18; 12:1). The concept of covenant is yoked to *kārat*, for it is sealed by blood and sacrifice—that is, the "blood of the covenant" (Ex. 24:8; Zech. 9:11; Matt. 26:28; Heb. 9:20; 10:29). Thus the cutting off of the Anointed One intimates his death unto the cutting of a new covenant by God (cf. Luke 22:20; 1 Cor. 11:25). After this the city and sanctuary will be destroyed (Dan. 9:26b), and war and desolations will be decreed "to the end" (v. 26c). Furthermore, before the eschatological glory the temple will be desecrated by "an abomination that causes desolation" (v. 27, NIV; cf. 11:31; 12:11), an event of which the New Testament writers are well aware (cf. Matt. 24:15; 2 Thess. 2:4; Rev. 13:6).[17]

Other passages quite probably mentioned in the Emmaus road discussion are referenced in the Gospels themselves. Psalm 22, a lament of David, is best interpreted messianically, since it ends in divine vindication and world redemption (vv. 24–31). Thus Jesus quotes verse 1 from the cross: "My God, my God, why have you forsaken me?" (Matt. 27:46). Those who passed by Jesus "hurled insults at him, shaking their heads" (Matt. 27:39), an allusion to Psalm 22:7: "All who see me mock me; they hurl insults, shaking their heads" (NIV). Moreover, in mocking him they quote Psalm 22:8: "He trusts in the LORD; let him

deliver him; let him rescue him, for he delights in him!" (cf. Matt. 27:43). The
Gospels also allude to Psalm 22:18 in recounting that the soldiers "divided his
garments among them by casting lots" (Matt. 27:35). And of course no one
would have missed Psalm 22:16: "They have pierced my hands and feet" (cf.
John 19:34; 20:25).

On the way to Gethsemane, Jesus also identified himself as "the shepherd"
of Zechariah 13:7, saying, "You will all fall away because of me this night. For
it is written, 'I will strike the shepherd, and the sheep of the flock will be *scattered*'" (Matt. 26:31). Jesus had told his disciples earlier, "You will be *scattered*
. . . and will leave me alone" (John 16:32), which found fulfillment during
his arrest when "all the disciples left him and fled" (Matt. 26:56). Zechariah
11–13 broadly portrays this "shepherd" as being rejected (chap. 11), pierced
(chap. 12), and struck (chap. 13) before the final vindication of the day of the
Lord (chap. 14). So John quotes Zechariah 12:10 concerning the crucifixion:
"These things took place that the Scripture might be fulfilled: . . . 'They will
look on him whom they have pierced'" (John 19:36–37). As with Isaiah 53,
Zechariah 11–13 also leads up to a prophecy of eschatological glory in chapter
14.[18] Therefore Zechariah 12:10 is rightly quoted in light of the return of Jesus:
"Look, he is coming with the clouds, and every eye will see him, even those
who pierced him; and all the peoples of the earth will mourn because of him.
So shall it be! Amen" (Rev. 1:7, NIV).

Psalm 16:10–11 was likewise referenced by the apostles (Acts 2:27–28;
13:35), whose commentary was probably derived from Jesus' forty days of
exposition upon the Scriptures (Acts 1:3). The presence of the Holy One in
"the Pit" (Ps. 16:10, NRSV) clearly speaks of his suffering before the revelation
of "the path of life" (v. 11). The possibility of "abandonment" to Sheol (v. 10)
presupposed death before the enjoyment of "pleasures forevermore" at the right
hand of God (v. 11).

Though these and other direct predictions were probably shared by Jesus
on the Emmaus road, the larger part of the discussion undoubtedly revolved
around typological interpretations of various Old Testament persons, events,
and institutions. For the Scriptures commonly "couched prophecy in typological patterns in which the works of God proceed along identifiable themes."[19]
Thus God worked in the Messiah as he had worked previously in redemptive
history.[20]

BIBLICAL TYPOLOGY

Though the subject of biblical typology received a fair amount of attention in
the twentieth century,[21] throughout church history it has been "one of the most

neglected departments of theological science."[22] Though typology is not overall the "predominant" method of interpretation in the New Testament (especially concerning messianic glory),[23] it does play an important role in interpreting the suffering of the Messiah.

Typology is inherently historical, since people, events, and institutions in the *past* provide a "pattern, example, or type" (Gk. *tupos*) for *future* people, events, and institutions.[24] Therefore a "salvation historical grid" is critical since "some kind of historical sequence under the providence of a sovereign God is necessary for almost any kind of typological hermeneutic."[25] So Adam was "a type of the one who was to come" (Rom. 5:14), for "*as in* Adam all die, *so also* in Christ shall all be made alive" (1 Cor. 15:22). Similarly, Noah's ark and the flood "prefigured" baptism and the deposit of the Spirit (1 Peter 3:21, NRSV), and the Israelites' wanderings took place "as examples for us" (1 Cor. 10:6).[26] Thus biblical typology must be understood *historically* within the greater Jewish apocalyptic framework of redemptive history (see figure 7.2).

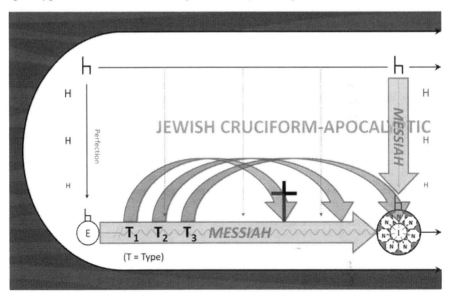

Figure 7.2 – The Jewish Apocalyptic Framework of Biblical Typology

Though varied in its specific application, the ultimate end of all biblical typology is found in the "restoration of all things" (Acts 3:21, NASB), for in it we find the final destiny of everything. As we discussed in the last chapter, creation week was understood typologically, representing redemptive history as a whole—"with the Lord one day *is as* a thousand years" (2 Peter 3:8; cf. Ps. 90:4).[27] The cataclysm of the flood anticipated the eschatological "day of judgment" (2 Peter 3:7), for "*as were* the days of Noah, *so will be* the coming of the

Son of Man" (Matt. 24:37). The destruction of Sodom and Gomorrah gave us "an *example* of what is going to happen to the ungodly" (2 Peter 2:6)—that is, "a punishment of eternal fire" (Jude 7). The exodus of Israel finds ultimate fulfillment in the deliverance of humanity from sin and tyranny (cf. Ex. 12:27; Rom. 8:20–21; 1 Thess. 1:10). The conquest of the land under Joshua (Heb. *yĕhôšûă'* or *yēšûă'*) prefigured the greater Yeshua and the messianic conquest of the earth (cf. Josh. 11:16–23; 1 Cor. 15:24–25; Rev. 19:11–16). The occupation of the land, settlement of Jerusalem, and building of the Davidic throne (i.e., "Davidic typology")[28] likewise point to the Messiah's rule in the age to come (cf. Ps. 132:11–18; Luke 1:33; 22:30; Acts 1:6). The exile and return of Israel anticipates the final regathering in the resurrection (cf. Isa. 11:10–12; Matt. 24:31; 1 Thess. 4:17).

Even temporally limited prefigurations—such as the faithfulness of Moses over the tabernacle patterning the faithfulness of Jesus over the church in this age (Heb. 3:3–6), or the celebration of the Passover patterning pure relations within the church in this age (1 Cor. 5:6–8), or the veil of Moses patterning the blindness of unbelieving Jews in this age (2 Cor. 3:13–16)—find their redemptive end in the age to come, since these temporal realities exist for the sake of their eternal destiny (see figure 7.3).[29] Typology is thus made sane and safe within the bounds of a redemptive history anchored in the day of the Lord.[30] Within such an apocalyptic framework, we approach the typology that underlies the suffering of the Messiah.

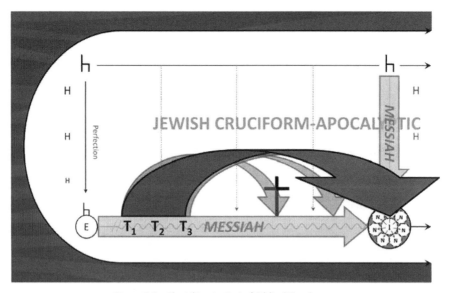

Figure 7.3 – The Ultimate End of Biblical Typology

THE FULFILLMENT
OF RIGHTEOUS SUFFERING

In the lives of righteous individuals throughout the Bible, we find a pattern of suffering which prefigures the suffering of the Christ. For example, Jesus twice calls the life of Jonah a "sign" (Matt. 12:39; 16:4). "For *just as* Jonah was three days and three nights in the belly of the great fish, *so will* the Son of Man be three days and three nights in the heart of the earth" (Matt. 12:40). And as Jonah later preached to Nineveh, so also Jesus, "one greater than Jonah" (v. 41, NIV), has been "proclaimed among the nations" (1 Tim. 3:16; cf. Luke 11:30). However, "the men of Nineveh will rise up at the judgment" and condemn many, "for they repented at the preaching of Jonah" (Matt. 12:41). Hence we see in the life of Jonah a general progression of suffering before glory, which roughly corresponds to the life of Christ in the context of redemptive history as a whole.

The prophets of old were also types of the messianic suffering, for all the prophets were "persecuted for righteousness' sake" (Matt. 5:10). Indeed, the wicked "persecuted the prophets" (Matt. 5:12) and "murdered the prophets" (Matt. 23:31; cf. Luke 13:34). So Stephen concluded before his martyrdom, "Which of the prophets did your ancestors not persecute? They killed those who foretold the coming of the Righteous One, and now you have become his betrayers and murderers" (Acts 7:51–52, NRSV). Therefore, the Messiah suffers "because suffering is the inevitable fate of the prophet."[31]

Not only have all the prophets suffered, but righteous saints suffer in general, which provides a typological pattern for the suffering of "the Righteous One" (Isa. 24:16; 53:11; Acts 3:14; 7:52). Because of the order of this age, the righteous commonly suffer, while the wicked commonly prosper. Because God in his great mercy is restraining his wrath and delaying the day of justice, "the wicked sprout like grass and all evildoers flourish" (Ps. 92:7). They are "always at ease, they increase in riches" (Ps. 73:12). Indeed, "Evildoers not only prosper but they put God to the test and they escape" (Mal. 3:15). "Why does the way of the wicked prosper?" (Jer. 12:1). "Why do the wicked live, reach old age, and grow mighty in power?" (Job 21:7). Because God is full of "kindness and forbearance and patience" (Rom. 2:4), "not wishing that any should perish" (2 Peter 3:9). Thus in this age the earth is *not* a home of righteousness (cf. 2 Peter 3:13), and because of this the righteous inevitably suffer.

Though a theology of righteous suffering is plainly drawn from the historical figures of the Old Testament (cf. 2 Tim. 3:8; Heb. 11:35–37; 2 Peter 2:5–7)—particularly Job (cf. Job 2:13; 9:17; 14:22; 21:6; 30:17–23)—it is developed extensively in the Psalms (cf. esp. Pss. 9; 22; 31; 69; 118).[32] The righteous are "stricken" (cf. Ps. 73:5,14; 109:22), "attacked" (cf. Ps. 56:2; 62:3; 69:4; 109:3), "hated" (cf. Ps. 9:13; 18:17; 25:19; 34:21; 35:19; 38:19; 41:7; 44:7; 69:4; 86:17; 118:7; 129:5), "afflicted" (cf. Ps. 9:12; 10:12; 22:24; 31:7; 34:19; 44:24; 69:29; 82:3; 94:5; 116:10; 129:2; 140:12), and "oppressed" (cf. Ps. 9:9; 10:18; 42:9; 43:2; 55:3; 56:1; 72:14; 73:8; 103:6; 119:122; 146:7). Because of the nature of this age, this is the normal experience of the righteous.

Would the righteous throughout history suffer, yet the Anointed One be spared? No. Rather, "It was *fitting* that God, for whom and through whom all things exist, in bringing many children to glory, should make the pioneer of their salvation perfect through sufferings" (Heb. 2:10, NRSV).

The idea of righteous suffering in the Old Testament carries over directly into the New Testament, as Paul summarized: "We *must* go through many hardships to enter the kingdom of God" (Acts 14:22, NIV). And "all who desire to live a godly life in Christ Jesus *will* be persecuted" (2 Tim. 3:12). Believers should not be "disturbed" or "surprised" by their afflictions, "as though something strange were happening" (1 Peter 4:12), because "we are destined for this" (1 Thess. 3:3). As Jesus said, "In the world you *will* have tribulation" (John 16:33). But we know that if we "suffer for righteousness' sake" (1 Peter 3:14), then we will be "blessed" and "considered worthy of the kingdom of God, for which [we] are also suffering" (2 Thess. 1:5).

This "sober-minded" (1 Peter 1:13) approach to life helps believers stand firm in their faith, "knowing that the same kinds of suffering are being experienced by your brotherhood throughout the world" (1 Peter 5:9). For "it has been granted to you that for the sake of Christ you should not only believe in him but also suffer for his sake" (Phil. 1:29).

Consequently the suffering of the righteous is the divinely ordained *pattern* of this age, which the Messiah fulfilled perfectly and which the church seeks to emulate. As Paul put it, "I rejoice in what was suffered for you, and I fill up in my flesh what is still lacking in regard to Christ's afflictions, for the sake of his body, which is the church" (Col. 1:24, NIV). Indeed, the body of Christ is called to "share abundantly in Christ's sufferings" (2 Cor. 1:5), "always being given over to death for Jesus' sake" (2 Cor. 4:11). Far from being a morbid or masochistic approach to life, this is a faith-based approach, whereby we find our identity and joy in the hope of eternal life which is set before us (cf. Heb. 12:2).

The cruciform message is pictured as "the aroma of Christ" (2 Cor. 2:15), which the regenerate breathe deeply as "a fragrance from life to life," while the unregenerate choke upon it as "a fragrance from death to death" (v. 16). He who "hates his life" (John 12:25; cf. Luke 14:26) for the sake of eternal life is not ashamed of the crucified Messiah (cf. Matt. 10:33; Luke 9:26), for in him is typified the divine pattern of righteous suffering: "When he was reviled, he did not revile in return; when he suffered, he did not threaten, but continued entrusting himself to him who judges justly" (1 Peter 2:23). Thus the church is left with "an *example*, so that you might follow in his steps" (v. 21).[33]

THE FULFILLMENT
OF THE CALENDAR

The second area of typological fulfillment that Jesus probably referenced on the road to Emmaus revolved around the Jewish "calendar of sacred time."[34] Paul summed up the Jewish calendar as "festivals, new moons, or sabbaths" (Col. 2:16, NRSV). This threefold reference to the calendar is common in the Old Testament (cf. 1 Chron. 23:31; 2 Chron. 31:3; Neh. 10:33; Isa. 1:13; Ezek. 45:17; Hos. 2:11), representing the weekly, monthly, and yearly patterns of devotion (cf. Gal. 4:10: "You observe days and months and seasons and years").[35]

The Sabbath was the weekly observance of creation (cf. Ex. 20:11; 31:17),[36] which anticipated "the renewal of all things" (Matt. 19:28, NRSV; cf. Isa. 56:6–7; 58:13–14).[37] Hence it became "a symbol of the time of salvation . . . an anticipation of the joyous eschatological age."[38] Likewise, the "new moon" celebration (Num. 10:10; 29:6; cf. Ezra 3:5; Ps. 81:3), often referenced in conjunction with the Sabbath (cf. 2 Kings 4:23; Ezek. 46:1; Amos 8:5), was a monthly reminder of the coming new age:

> For as the new heavens and the new earth
>   that I make
> shall remain before me, says the LORD,
>   so shall your offspring and your name remain.
> From *new moon to new moon*,
>   and from *Sabbath to Sabbath*,
> all flesh shall come to worship before me,
>   declares the LORD.
> (Isa. 66:22–23)

The Jewish calendar also included three annual festivals: *Pesach* (Passover/ Unleavened Bread), *Shavuot* (Pentecost/Weeks/Harvest), and *Sukkot* (Tabernacles/Ingathering):

> Three times in the year you shall keep a feast to me. You shall keep the Feast of Unleavened Bread. As I commanded you, you shall eat unleavened bread for seven days. . . . You shall keep the Feast of Harvest, of the

firstfruits of your labor, of what you sow in the field. You shall keep the Feast of Ingathering at the end of the year, when you gather in from the field the fruit of your labor. (Ex. 23:14–16)

Three times a year all your men must appear before the LORD your God at the place he will choose: at the Feast of Unleavened Bread, the Feast of Weeks and the Feast of Tabernacles. (Deut. 16:16, NIV)

These festivals coincided with the harvests of the agricultural cycle: spring (barley), summer (wheat), and autumn (fruit).[39] Passover was celebrated in the spring (approximately early April), fifty days before Pentecost, which celebrated "the firstfruits of wheat harvest" (Ex. 34:22), while Tabernacles was celebrated in the fall (approximately early October), "at the end of the [Jewish] year" (Ex. 23:16). Therefore the annual festivals were clearly divided between spring and fall. The other festivals and days of commemoration revolved around and inter-related the three major festivals.[40]

Jewish tradition relates this calendar to redemptive history, since God created and instituted the reality of time itself.[41] So Paul refers to the calendar in Colossians 2:16 and says, "These are a shadow of the things to come, but the substance belongs to Christ" (v. 17). In this way redemptive history (executed by Christ) is the true calendar, which is seen in the shadowy outline of the Jewish calendar. Jesus thus interprets the Passover: "I will not eat it again until it finds fulfillment in the kingdom of God" (Luke 22:16, NIV).[42] Likewise, the outpouring of the Spirit on Pentecost (Acts 2:1) is understood as "the first-fruits" (Rom. 8:23), a clear allusion to the Festival of Weeks (cf. Ex. 23:16; 34:22; Lev. 23:17; Num. 28:26).

If Passover and Pentecost were fulfilled *in redemptive history*, then surely Tabernacles, "the preeminent annual festival"[43]—that is, "the Temple festival *par excellence*"[44]—will be typologically fulfilled "at the year's end" (Ex. 34:22; cf. Zech. 14:16) with the great eschatological "ingathering" of Israel and the nations (cf. Ps. 102:22; Isa. 11:12; 66:18; Jer. 23:3; Ezek. 37:21; Mic. 4:6; Zeph. 3:18–20; Matt. 24:31; 2 Thess. 2:1). This will be in full accord with traditional Jewish expectation—that is, "the eschatological expectation of God's final tabernacling with his people forever."[45] Consequently we see the annual cycle of festivals fulfilled typologically in redemptive history within the greater apocalyptic framework (see figure 7.4). Because the Messiah is God's agent in executing redemptive history and because the calendar is inter-preted typologically according to that timeline, it is logical that the Messiah would suffer in fulfillment of Passover before entering his glory in fulfillment of Tabernacles.[46]

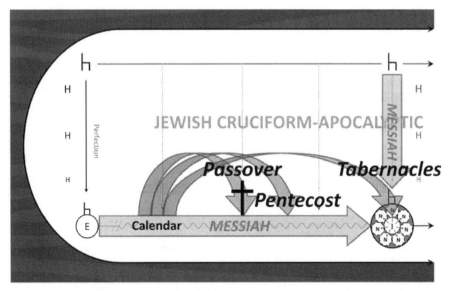

Figure 7.4 – The Typological Fulfillment of the Jewish Calendar

Beyond the calendar as a whole, the Passover event itself anticipates a messianic suffering before glory. Many interpreters only see in Passover a type of messianic suffering—as the lambs were sacrificed at twilight and their blood spread on the doorposts (Ex. 12:6–7), so also "Christ, our Passover lamb, has been sacrificed" (1 Cor. 5:7). Indeed, this is true. However, a clear eschatological tradition of messianic glory and *deliverance* surrounding Passover had developed by the first century.[47] As Joachim Jeremias summarizes,

> The Jewish passover celebration at the time of Jesus is both retrospect and prospect. At this festival the people of God remember the merciful immunity granted to the houses marked with the blood of the paschal lamb and the deliverance from the Egyptian servitude. But that is only one aspect. At the same time the passover is *a looking forward to the coming deliverance* of which the deliverance from Egypt is the prototype. This typology is a concept which "most comprehensively determined already in early times, as no other did, the form that the doctrine of final salvation took." . . . So the night of the Passover is called the "sign" through which God guarantees the coming of the Messiah. The passover traditions variously reflect the vitality of this Messianic hope, just as do the revolts against Rome which repeatedly took place at the passover.[48]

The night of Passover became a night of commemoration in expectation of the messianic deliverance. Because the exodus happened on the night of Passover—"a night of watching by the Lord"—so the Israelites obeyed the command, "This same night is a *night of watching* kept to the LORD by all the people of Israel throughout their generations" (Ex. 12:42). Jesus affirmed this tradition by concluding the Olivet Discourse, "Therefore, *keep watch*" (Matt. 24:42, NIV; cf. 25:13), an allusion no one would have missed with Passover "two days away" (26:2).[49]

The serving of wine, bread, and bitter herbs (Ex. 12:8; Num. 9:11) also held eschatological significance, which Jesus affirmed: "I will not drink again of this *fruit of the vine* until that day when I drink it new with you in my Father's kingdom" (Matt. 26:29).[50] Similarly, he parallels the Passover meal with the eschatological feast—"that you may *eat and drink* at my table in my kingdom and sit on thrones judging the twelve tribes of Israel" (Luke 22:30).[51] Moreover, Jesus' command, "Do this in remembrance of me" (v. 19; cf. 1 Cor. 11:24), was spoken in light of the messianic tradition of God remembering the Messiah, Jerusalem, and the people of Israel.[52] For example:

> O LORD God, do not turn away the face of your anointed one!
>> *Remember* your steadfast love for David your servant.
> (2 Chron. 6:42)

> LORD, *remember* David
>> and all that he suffered.
> (Ps. 132:1, NLT)

> *Remember* your congregation, which you have purchased of old. . . .
>> *Remember* Mount Zion, where you have dwelt.
> (Ps. 74:2)

Thus Passover is by nature an "eschatological banquet,"[53] a tradition which the early church carried on in Communion (Acts 2:42,46; 20:7,11; 1 Cor. 10:16; 11:20–25).[54] This weekly celebration is also thereby an *intercession* by which we remember Jesus and his death, calling upon God the Father to likewise remember his Son, "that he may send the Christ" (Acts 3:20) at the appointed time which the Father has "fixed by his own authority" (Acts 1:7; cf. 1 Tim. 6:15). So in our remembrance of Jesus we call upon God to remember the covenants and bring to completion that which he has spoken by the prophets; and in this way, "As often as you eat this bread and drink the cup, you proclaim the Lord's death until he comes" (1 Cor. 11:26).[55]

Furthermore, the singing of a "hymn" (Matt. 26:30; Mark 14:26) refers to the conclusion of the Passover meal, which involved the antiphonal singing of the second half of the Hallel (i.e., Psalms 113–118).[56] In Jewish tradition, the Hallel was assumed to be the "Hallelujah Chorus" that the saints would sing to welcome the Messiah into Jerusalem.[57] This messianic interpretation is plainly seen at the triumphal entry when the climax of the Hallel (Ps. 118:25–26) is jubilantly declared, "Hosanna! Blessed is he who comes in the name of the Lord!" (Mark 11:9).[58]

The apostles understood the crucifixion in light of Jesus' typological explanation of Passover during the Last Supper (Luke 22:15–20). So John points out that Jesus was delivered over to be crucified on "the day of Preparation of the Passover" (John 19:14). Moreover, the Roman soldiers "did not break his legs" (v. 33) in order to hasten his death, which took place to fulfill the Passover pattern: "that the Scripture might be fulfilled: 'Not one of his bones will be broken'" (v. 36; cf. Ex. 12:46; Num. 9:12).[59] As the Passover lamb was sacrificed at dusk before the midnight judgment (Ex. 12:3–13), so also the Messiah was sacrificed before the eschatological judgment and great messianic deliverance (see figure 7.5).

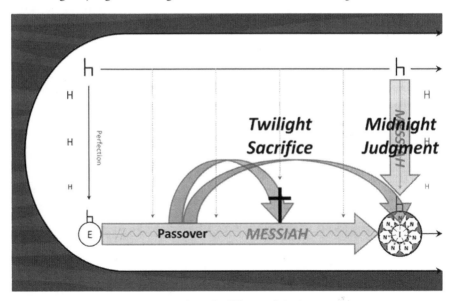

Figure 7.5 – The Typological Fulfillment of the Passover Event

For this reason Paul can state rather casually (as if it was common knowledge), "Christ, our Passover lamb, has been sacrificed" (1 Cor. 5:7).[60] As such, the church is now called to "celebrate the festival, not with the old leaven, the leaven of malice and evil, but with the unleavened bread of sincerity and truth" (v. 8). And in this way we are to put out of our fellowship anyone who lacks sobriety concerning the coming judgment (cf. vv. 9–11), "that his spirit may be saved in the day of the Lord" (v. 5). Such an exhortation assumes a common typological interpretation of the death of Jesus before the day of the Lord in accord with the Passover pattern.[61]

THE FULFILLMENT
OF THE SACRIFICIAL SYSTEM

The final and greatest typological pattern that would have been referenced on the road to Emmaus was the sacrificial system. Intimately related to the calendar, the sacrificial system was at the heart of Jewish life.[62] Israel's inception as a nation was based upon a ratification sacrifice (cf. Ex. 24:4–8), and its maintenance in righteousness was contingent upon its faithfulness to the sacrificial system (cf. Ex. 29:38–42; Lev. 1–7; Num. 28–29). Sacrifices were offered "day by day" (Ex. 29:38; Num. 28:3; cf. Dan. 12:11; Heb. 7:27; 10:11), "morning and evening" (1 Chron. 16:40; 2 Chron. 13:11; Ezra 3:3), on the Sabbath (Lev. 23:38; Num. 28:9–10; Ezek. 46:4), on new moons (Num. 10:10; 28:11–15; 2 Chron. 31:3), and at all the yearly festivals (Ex. 23:18; 34:25; Lev. 23:37; Num. 29:39). Sacrifices were thus couched within the calendar as a whole, as later summarized in the Old Testament narratives (cf. 1 Chron. 23:31; 2 Chron. 2:4; 8:13; 31:3; Ezra 3:5; Neh. 10:33) and in the prophets (cf. Isa. 1:13; Ezek. 45:17):

> And [the Levites] were to stand every morning, thanking and praising the LORD, and likewise at evening, and whenever *burnt offerings* were offered to the LORD on Sabbaths, new moons, and feast days, according to the number required of them, regularly before the LORD. (1 Chron. 23:30–31)

> Behold, I [Solomon] am about to build a house for the name of the LORD my God . . . for *burnt offerings* morning and evening, on the Sabbaths and the new moons and the appointed feasts of the LORD our God, as ordained forever for Israel. (2 Chron. 2:4)

> We also take on ourselves the obligation to give yearly a third part of a shekel for the service of the house of our God: for the showbread, the regular grain offering, the regular *burnt offering*, the Sabbaths, the new moons, the appointed feasts, the holy things, and the *sin offerings* to make atonement for Israel, and for all the work of the house of our God. (Neh. 10:32–33)

The calendar and sacrifices were thus two sides of the same devotional coin, so to speak, and all of these culminated on the Day of Atonement, or Yom Kippur (Heb. *yôm hakkippurîm*; cf. Ex. 30:10; Lev. 16:29–34; 23:26–32; Num. 29:7–11). The Day of Atonement is the tenth and final day of the "high holy days," which follows the celebration of the New Year, or Rosh Hashanah (Heb. *rōʾš haššānâ*; Ezek. 40:1; cf. Lev. 23:24; Num. 29:1).[63] The Day of Atonement was "the most important day in the religious calendar of Israel,"[64] and it remains to date the highest of holy days in Judaism.[65] Referred to simply as "the day" or "the great day" from the late second-temple period,[66] Yom Kippur is "the cultic climax" of Israel's year.[67] It demands such reverence because it epitomizes all the sacrifices made throughout the year "to make atonement for the people of Israel once in the year for all their sins" (Lev. 16:34, NRSV).[68]

Therefore the New Year, in accord with the Sabbath and the festivals, is understood both protologically and eschatologically, for "Rosh Hashanah also prefigures the end of days, the Last Judgment, when all souls shall appear before God."[69] Jewish tradition holds that in the beginning, God created Adam and Eve on Rosh Hashanah; in ancient Israel, the kings were coronated on Rosh Hashanah; and in the end, God will crown the Messiah and judge humanity on Rosh Hashanah.[70] The New Year was celebrated with the blowing of a horn, or trumpet (Heb. *shôphār*, cf. Lev. 23:24; Num. 29:1), a tradition also projected eschatologically (cf. Isa. 27:13; Matt. 24:31; 1 Cor. 15:52; 1 Thess. 4:16; Rev. 11:15).

And furthermore, according to Jewish tradition, God will come on Rosh Hashanah to judge the living and the dead, consummating atonement for his people on Yom Kippur, and thereby inaugurating the Feast of Tabernacles and the eternal dwelling of God with humankind.[71] Thus we have a broad typological pattern of sacrifices throughout the year culminating in Rosh Hashanah and the Day of Atonement, which prefigures the ultimate sacrifice of the Messiah before the consummation of the day of judgment and the age to come (see figure 7.6).

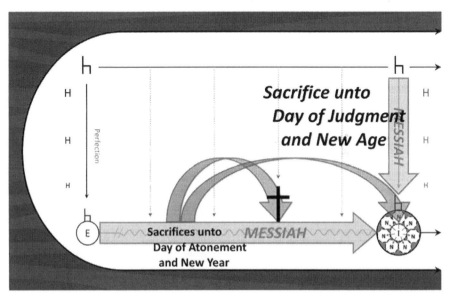

Figure 7.6 – The Typological Fulfillment of the Sacrificial System

This typological approach to the sacrificial system, within an apocalyptic framework, is seen throughout the New Testament. John the Baptist called people to flee from the wrath to come (cf. Matt. 3:1–12; Luke 3:1–17), declaring, "Behold, the *Lamb of God*, who takes away the sins of the world!" (John 1:29; cf. v. 36).[72] Likewise, the apostolic witness generally proclaimed, "Christ loved us and gave himself up for us, a fragrant *offering and sacrifice* to God" (Eph. 5:2). Indeed, every reference to "the blood of Christ" (1 Cor. 10:16; Eph. 2:13; Heb. 9:14; 1 Peter 1:19; cf. 1 Cor. 11:27; Heb. 10:19; 1 John 1:7; Rev. 7:14; 12:11) is a sacrificial reference.[73] And the preaching of the "forgiveness of sins" in Jesus (cf. Acts 2:38; 5:31; 10:43; 13:38; 26:18) assumes a sacrificial interpretation, for "without the shedding of blood there is no forgiveness of sins" (Heb. 9:22).

Nowhere is a typological approach to the sacrificial system more evident than in Hebrews 8–10, for as a whole that system was seen as "a shadow of the good things to come but not the reality itself, and is therefore completely unable, by the same *sacrifices* offered continually, year after year, to perfect those who come to worship" (10:1, NET). Rather, "When Christ had offered for all time a single *sacrifice* for sins, he sat down at the right hand of God, waiting from that time until his enemies should be made a footstool for his feet. For by a single *offering* he has perfected for all time those who are being sanctified" (10:12–14).

The earthly sanctuary and its accompanying sacrificial system served as a "pattern" (8:5), or type (Gk. *tupos*), of the heavenly sanctuary (8:1–5; 9:1–5), from which would come a greater messianic priest (8:6; 9:11,24) who would make a new covenant (8:8,13; 9:15) by providing a better sacrifice (8:6; 9:12,26), "thus securing an eternal redemption" (9:12). Or as summarized in 9:13–15:

> The *blood of goats and bulls* and the ashes of a heifer sprinkled on those who are ceremonially unclean sanctify them so that they are *outwardly clean*. How much more, then, will the *blood of Christ*, who through the eternal Spirit offered himself unblemished to God, *cleanse our consciences* from acts that lead to death, so that we may serve the living God!
>
> For this reason Christ is the mediator of a *new covenant*, that those who are called may receive the promised *eternal inheritance*—now that he has died as a ransom to set them free from the sins committed under the first covenant. (NIV)

Hence the priestly sanctuary, duties, and sacrifices were understood typologically, finding their fulfillment in the suffering of the Messiah sacrificially before the glorifying of the Messiah eschatologically—"So Christ was sacrificed once to take away the sins of many people; and he will appear a second time, not to bear sin, but to bring salvation to those who are waiting for him" (9:28, NIV).

Assuming that the epistles of the New Testament basically represent what Jesus taught his disciples after his resurrection (cf. Luke 24:44–48; Acts 1:3), we can essentially deduce that the justification for messianic suffering before glory, as expounded on the road to Emmaus (Luke 24:25–27), was based upon direct prophecies and a typological understanding of righteous suffering, the calendar, and the sacrificial system.[74] The various aspects and implications of the messianic sacrifice (e.g., righteousness, reconciliation, propitiation, justification, redemption, etc.) will be discussed in the next chapter.

CHRISTOPLATONIC TYPOLOGY

Throughout the history of the church, the Emmaus road encounter has been understood in accordance with the presupposed theological tradition of the interpreter. These traditions have generally fallen within the two primary eschatological categories of Christoplatonism: immaterial-heavenly destiny (church triumphant) and material-manifest sovereignty (church militant), each of which *redefines* the eschatological and Israelitic "glory" of the Messiah. One of the main hermeneutical tools used to justify this reinterpretation has been typology, for at typology's core we see "the struggle to properly interpret the OT that can be traced to the beginnings of the church."[75] Simply put, we interpret the Old Testament according to our theological endgame, and then we apply typology to it (see figure 7.7).

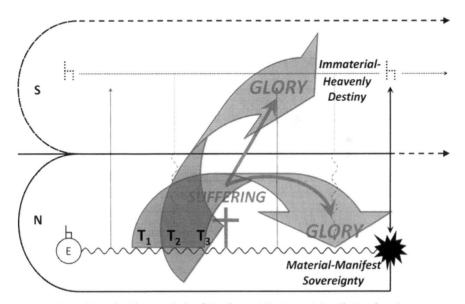

Figure 7.7 – The Ultimate Ends of Typology within Augustinian Christoplatonism

Origen exemplifies the common corruption of typology (in an exposition of Passover, no less): "We ought not to suppose that historical events are types of other historical events, and material things of other material things; rather material things are types of *spiritual things* and historical events of *intelligible realities*."[76] Accordingly, Adam and Eden are types of our immaterial body in an immaterial paradise; Abraham and Canaan are types of our heavenly calling and the spiritual promised land; Moses and the exodus are types of our freedom from the tyranny of materiality; and so on and so forth. [77]

On the other hand, according to manifest sovereignty Adam and paradise are typical of the church militant (the manifestation of Jesus' resurrected glory); Abraham is a type of the consummated promised land of Christendom (Jesus' inheritance of the nations); Moses is a type of the emperor and/or the pope (Jesus' vicar upon the earth), freeing the world from pagan idolatry; and so on and so forth.[78]

Within the Augustinian synthesis, these ends work in tandem—the Old Testament typologically prophesies the church militant in this life unto the church triumphant in the next life.[79] This twofold typological interpretation of a realized kingdom and a heavenly destiny in turn justified the aberrant practices of monasticism and Christendom throughout the Middle Ages.[80] Once typology drifts from its Jewish eschatological moorings, its flights of fancy know no end.[81] Moreover, the distortion of typology promoted the increased use of allegory, following the Alexandrian school of thought.[82] As typified by Origen,[83] bizarre interpretations of the Scriptures spread throughout the church under the guise of spiritual "revelation."[84]

The bottom line of all this aberration is the eradication of a simple Jewish apocalyptic hope. The Old Testament is wholly dismissed as typologically/allegorically fulfilled and superseded by the first coming. Rather than a fulfillment of suffering at the first coming before a fulfillment of glory at the second coming, we find the oxymoronic fulfillment of both at the first coming, thus negating any eschatological hope. As Origen scholar Jean Daniélou expresses, "The Old Testament had at one time a function to fulfil, but that function was to prefigure and prepare for the New. Once the New Testament was in force, the Old Testament lapsed as far as its literal meaning was concerned but kept its value as a figure."[85]

This hermeneutical approach of the Alexandrian school of thought dominated the church for more than a millennium, as Leonhard Goppelt summarizes: "In the West, Hilary, Ambrose, Augustine, and Jerome were influenced by Alexandria. Their very arbitrary exegesis, which made use of both allegorical and typological interpretation, was the authoritative model for the Middle Ages."[86] Though Luther and the Reformers drew back from the use of allegory and typology, their interpretation concerning the ultimate eschatological realities changed little (though their renewed emphasis on the cross is more than commendable).

Not until the rise of dispensationalism do we find a fundamentally different theological framework and corresponding use of typology. Its dualistic soteriology results in suffering before twofold glory—the Gentile immaterial glory of the heavenly redemptive plan and the Jewish material glory of the earthly redemptive plan (see figure 7.8).[87] Dispensationalists have historically avoided typology because of its potential infringement upon a "literal hermeneutic,"[88] a fact that non-dispensationalists have exploited.[89] If typology were logically applied within dispensationalism, however, we would see the same twofold result as seen in the dualistic interpretation of the new covenant.[90] The incorporation of typology into dispensationalism would only exacerbate its manifold complexity.[91]

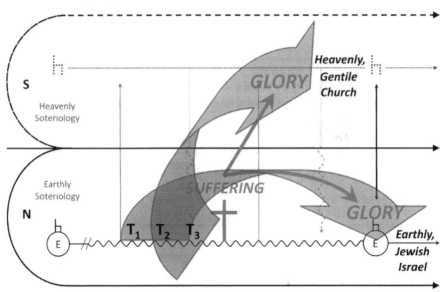

Figure 7.8 – The Ultimate Ends of Typology within Dispensational Christoplatonism

With the rise of inaugurationalism in the twentieth century, we have yet another approach to interpreting the sufferings of Christ before his entrance into glory—"a semi-eschatological expression incorporating the heavenly realm both in the present and future."[92] This "realized" eschatology (again, a term with duplicitous meanings) involves a messianic glory in this age (represented by Jesus' resurrection and Pentecost) and a messianic glory in the age to come.[93] Typology is thus interpreted within this framework. Persons, events, and institutions in the Old Testament find their end both in this age and the supernaturalized age to come (see figure 7.9).[94]

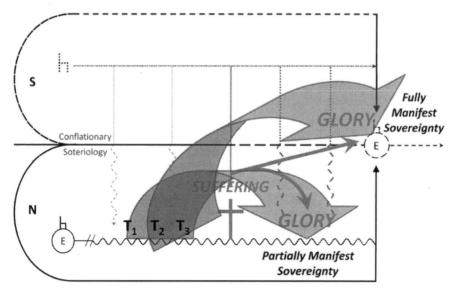

Figure 7.9 – The Ultimate Ends of Typology within Inaugurational Christoplatonism

Within inaugurationalism, though, the present fulfillment of Old Testament typological realities is not primarily related to the cross but rather to the present spiritual realization of the Jewish eschatological hope. God is establishing the kingdom now, in part, which will be fully manifest in the age to come. In this way modern inaugurationalism is quite akin to its Christendom ancestor, since the cruciform nature and purpose of this age is similarly obscured and neglected. The obvious conclusion cannot be escaped: God is extending the inquisitional rod, so to speak, to his enemies both now and in the age to come.[95]

Moreover, the so-called "realization" of Jewish eschatology is not a straightforward fulfillment of the Old Testament hope. Rather, Jewish eschatology is "rethought," "redefined," "reworked," and "reimagined."[96] Indeed, inaugurated eschatology is simply *reimagined Gentilic eschatology,* an imaginary system of thought that does not actually correspond to reality, neither presently nor eschatologically.

Therefore inaugurationalists commonly seek to spiritually realize only the overtly Jewish aspects of Old Testament eschatology. The more ethnically generalized aspects (e.g., resurrection of the dead, new earth, day of the Lord, etc.) are retained.[97] However, in the Bible even these events are cast within the greater covenantal framework of Jewish election (cf. Isa. 65; Ezek. 37; Joel 3; etc.). Thus inaugurationalists seem driven toward a systematic campaign of *theological ethnic cleansing.*[98] Yet the God of Israel does not change.

In this way realized eschatology also drives an unnecessary and detrimental wedge between Judaism and Christianity, as Jewish theologian David Ariel articulates,

> What is it, after all, that marks the difference between Christians and Jews? . . . Jews believe in the eventual fulfillment of an elusive dream of a perfect world. Christians believe that the world has already been saved by the crucifixion and resurrection of the Messiah Jesus. The difference between the belief in future redemption and realized redemption is the chasm that separates Jewish from Christian thinking.[99]

Indeed, "realized redemption" does create a chasm of thought between us and the Scriptures, yet the apostles knew nothing of the sort. Their hope remained thoroughly Jewish-apocalyptic, as Acts 1:3–11 plainly reveals. The division between Jews and the Jesus-following "sect" (Acts 24:5,14; 28:22) of the New Testament simply concerned the sacrificial interpretation of the cross, not a spiritual realization of Jewish eschatology.

Unfortunately, confusion immediately arises in the comparison of Jewish "future redemption" and Christian "realized redemption," because the two are fundamentally different in nature. The former is Israelitic and Jerusalemic, while the latter is Gentile and quite Romish. Realized eschatology does not actually inaugurate the Jewish Old Testament hope, but rather it transforms and redefines Jewish eschatology.[100] N. T. Wright claims, for example, that Jesus "had not come to rehabilitate the symbol of holy land, but to subsume it within a different fulfilment of the kingdom, which would embrace the whole creation."[101] This redefined fulfillment has dramatic consequences for our interpretation of the Old Testament, however, because the new definition inherently negates the old definition.

This negation is called "supersessionism," which is variously termed "replacement theology" or "displacement theology."[102] R. Kendall Soulen outlines its basic tenets:

> For most of the past two millennia, the church's posture toward the Jewish people has come to expression in the teaching known as supersessionism, also known as the theology of displacement. According to this teaching, God chose the Jewish people after the fall of Adam in order to prepare the world for the coming of Jesus Christ, the Savior. After Christ came, however, the special role of the Jewish people came to an end and its place was taken by the church, the new Israel.[103]

Such language of the church as "the new Israel" is ubiquitous in modern inaugurationalist writings, because realized eschatology necessarily results in supersessionism (see figure 7.10).[104] If the Law and the Prophets envision an

Israelitic eschatology, and Jesus and the apostles redefine and fulfill that eschatology, then supersessionism is the result.[105] The old reality is replaced with a new and different reality.[106]

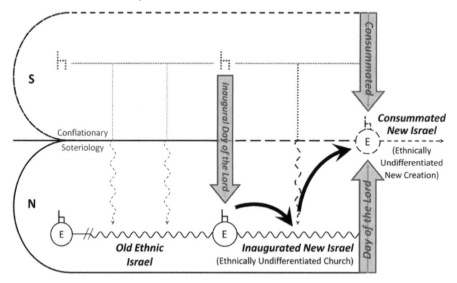

Figure 7.10 – Supersessionism as the Necessary Product of Realized Eschatology

With examples too many to cite, inaugurationalists always come to the same conclusion: "National Israel is nothing other than the empty shell from which the pearl has been removed and which has lost its function in the history of redemption."[107] Indeed, it is "the hard fact that national Israel and its law have been permanently replaced by the church and the New Covenant."[108] The church is "a new people of God who are to take the place of Israel,"[109] for "the concern of the New Testament is a relationship with Jesus Christ, not a restoration of the types of the Old Testament."[110] If in the first coming "Israel's history had reached its intended fulfillment," then the church can rightly claim to be "the continuation of Israel in a new situation."[111]

Based on these ideas, Israel committed (and consequently continues to commit) the "meta-sin" of carnal ethnocentric nationalism.[112] Though not as flagrant and abusive as Origen,[113] or Luther,[114] modern supersessionists continue to do violence to the covenants by rifling them of their fundamentally ethnic nature, based upon the interpretive logic that "the coming of the kingdom of God through Jesus the Messiah has transformed and reinterpreted all the promises and prophecies in the Old Testament."[115] Indeed, "The implication is that the Jewish nation has no longer a place as the special people of God; that place has been taken by the Christian community, and in them God's purposes for Israel are to be fulfilled."[116]

I doubt that any of these supersessionists would be so bold if they were speaking face to face with a modern orthodox Jew, who would probably *spit in their face*—not for the offense of Jewish nationalism, but for offense of the Jewish Scriptures themselves. Such ideas are repugnant to modern Jews,[117] and indeed they are inherently contradictory to the biblical hope. It is one thing, as is often done in the New Testament, to confront a Jewish man with his arrogance and self-righteousness (an issue common to Jew and Gentile alike; see Romans 11:17–32); it is quite another to call his hope, explicitly or implicitly, *archaic and carnal.*[118] In the New Testament, what divided Jews who believed in Jesus from Jews who did not was the atonemental suffering of the Messiah, not differing views of Jewish election, the kingdom, the temple, Jerusalem, etc. The spiritual realization, transformation, and supersession of these things are simply baseless.[119]

Can we not accept the straightforward, face-value teaching of the Old Testament? As a whole, it is clearly apocalyptic, messianic, and Israelitic. In the context of a new heavens and new earth, these things constitute the "glory" of the age to come.[120] Nowhere in the New Testament is this glory questioned; rather it is universally assumed and affirmed (cf. Matt. 19:28; 24:30; 25:31; Rom. 8:18; 1 Cor. 15:43; 2 Cor. 4:17; Eph. 1:18; Phil. 3:21; Col. 3:4; 2 Thess. 1:10; 2 Tim. 2:10; Titus 2:13; 1 Peter 4:13; 5:10; Jude 24). The Messiah came the first time to suffer and bear sin. Why would this simple fact alter the Jewish eschatological hope?

The various Christoplatonic eschatologies held throughout the church's history inherently contradict the Old Testament's unequivocal vision of divine glory. Conversely, the New Testament affirms the hope of the Old Testament, arguing simply that God sent his Messiah first as a sacrifice for the sin of humanity before sending his Messiah again to execute judgment upon the sin of humanity (cf. Acts 3:18–26; Rom. 5:1–9; Heb. 10:12–13). Therefore Jew and Gentile alike must repent of their sins, accept God's predetermined atonement as the means of escaping divine wrath, and thus together inherit the glory of eternal life. Though lacking the theological sophistication of the modern academy and its inaugurational refinement, I find this to be the common-sense approach to the Scriptures that most reasonably corresponds to the apostolic witness in its premodern, first-century Jewish context.

Chapter Eight

❖

THE RIGHTEOUSNESS
OF GOD

Peter's response to the declaration of the death of the Messiah is probably characteristic of the general tenor of first-century messianic
expectation—"Far be it from you, Lord! This shall *never* happen to you"
(Matt. 16:22).[1] God's Messiah would come, establish a throne in Jerusalem,
be anointed with divine glory, raise the dead, and judge the nations. Yet God
chose, "in all wisdom and insight" (Eph. 1:8), to hand him over to death. His
crucifixion was "determined" (Luke 22:22) by God, "predestined to take place"
(Acts 4:28), for it was "foretold by the mouth of all the prophets" (Acts 3:18).
He was "delivered over by the predetermined plan and foreknowledge of God"
(Acts 2:23, NASB), because "it was the LORD's will to crush him and cause him
to suffer" (Isa. 53:10, NIV).

The answer to *why* the Messiah was handed over by God "according to the
counsel of his will" (Eph. 1:11) constitutes the essential center of New Testament thought and meditation.[2] In light of the apocalyptic hope of the day of
the Lord, the resurrection of the dead, and the kingdom of God, why was it
"necessary for the Christ to suffer" (Acts 17:3)? What did the death of the Messiah *mean*, and why was his death different than the death of any other human
being? Many prophets had been martyred in the past, yet God deemed—in his
own system of accounting—that this martyrdom was different, unique, and
necessary.[3]

Based upon Paul's descriptions of divine revelation (cf. 1 Cor. 15:3–8; Gal.
1:12), we can assume that Jesus interpreted to his disciples his own death in detail
during the forty days of teaching (Acts 1:3) prior to his ascension. I believe this
teaching concerning the divine interpretation of messianic suffering is substantially

represented in the epistles of the New Testament. The death of the Messiah was understood sacrificially: atoning for human sin, propitiating the wrath of God, justifying the sinner, and redeeming that which was primordially lost.

THE SACRIFICIAL NATURE
OF THE MESSIAH'S DEATH

As discussed in the previous chapter, the suffering of the Messiah was understood by the apostles as a sacrifice, typologically fulfilling the sacrificial system. The ultimate purpose of the sacrifices and offerings was to "make atonement on your behalf for your sin" (Lev. 5:6, NRSV; cf. Lev. 4:20,26,31,35; 5:10,13,16,18; 6:7; 8:34; 9:7; 10:17; 12:7; 14:18–20,29–31; 15:15,30; 16:6,11,16–18,32–34; 19:22; 23:28; Num. 6:11; 8:12,19; 15:25,28; 16:46; 28:22,30; 29:5). Here we note the inherently vicarious and substitutional nature of sacrifice, which is made "on your behalf." Such substitutionality is clearly portrayed by the laying on of hands (cf. Lev. 1:4; 3:2,8,13; 4:4,15,24,29,33; 8:14,22; 16:21; Num. 8:12) and the confession of sins—especially on the Day of Atonement (Lev. 16:21; cf. Lev. 5:5; 26:40; Num. 5:7)—symbolizing the *transference of iniquity* onto the head of the animal.[4] Those who transgress the law will "bear [their] iniquity" (Lev. 5:1,17; 7:18; 17:16; 19:8; 20:17,19; 22:16; Num. 5:31; 14:34; 18:1; 30:15) and "bear [their] sin" (Lev. 20:20; 22:9; 24:15; Num. 9:13; 18:22). But for those who repent, confess their sins, and offer the ordained sacrifice, the animal "shall bear all their iniquities" (Lev. 16:22; cf. Lev. 10:17).[5] Thus by sacrifice a person's sins are borne away, "and he shall be *forgiven*" (Lev. 4:26,31,35; 5:10,13,16,18; 6:7; 19:22; Num. 15:28).[6]

God, by his own initiative and mercy, makes the provision of atonement for the forgiveness of sin: "*I have given it* for you on the altar to make atonement for your souls, for it is the blood that makes atonement by the life" (Lev. 17:11; cf. Lev. 4:2; 6:7; etc.). So God ultimately provides deliverance from sin, a theme common throughout the Scriptures (e.g., Gen. 22:14; Deut. 32:36; Ps. 22:4; Matt. 1:21). Accordingly, it is God who offered his Messiah as a sacrifice for the forgiveness of sins: "Christ was sacrificed once to take away the sins of many people; and he will appear a second time, not to bear sin, but to bring salvation to those who are waiting for him" (Heb. 9:28, NIV). "For Christ, our Passover lamb, has been sacrificed" (1 Cor. 5:7; cf. John 1:29), "a fragrant offering and sacrifice to God" (Eph. 5:2). Therefore, "When Christ had offered for all time a single sacrifice for sins, he sat down at the right hand of God, waiting from that time until his enemies should be made a footstool for his feet" (Heb. 10:12–13; cf. Heb. 7:27; 9:26).

Throughout the Scriptures *blood signifies sacrifice.* Hence every reference to "the blood of Christ" (1 Cor. 10:16; Eph. 2:13; Heb. 9:14; 1 Peter 1:19; cf. 1 Cor.

11:27; Heb. 10:19; 1 John 1:7; Rev. 7:14; 12:11), or "his blood" (Rom. 3:25; 5:9; Eph. 1:7; Heb. 9:12; 13:12; 1 Peter 1:2; Rev. 1:5; cf. Col. 1:20; Rev. 5:9), is a sacrificial reference. It is "the blood of the covenant" (Matt. 26:28; Heb. 10:29; 13:20; cf. 1 Cor. 11:25) that "purifies" and "cleanses" us from sin (cf. Acts 15:9; Eph. 5:26; Titus 2:14; Heb. 9:14; 10:2; 1 Peter 1:22; 1 John 1:7–9). Though the Old Testament sacrifices purified the flesh, "how much more will the *blood of Christ*, who through the eternal Spirit offered himself without blemish to God, *purify our conscience* from dead works to serve the living God. Therefore he is the mediator of a new covenant, so that those who are called may receive the promised eternal inheritance" (Heb. 9:14–15).

Akin to the language of blood, the *vicarious language* of the New Testament assumes a sacrificial framework.[7] As the sacrifice was offered in lieu of the worshiper, so also the Messiah died "for" (Gk. *anti*), or "on behalf of" (Gk. *huper*), sinners.[8] Indeed, it is "of first importance," Paul said, "that Christ died *for* our sins in accordance with the Scriptures" (1 Cor. 15:3). Similarly, Peter declared, "Christ also suffered once *for* sins, the righteous *for* the unrighteous, that he might bring us to God" (1 Peter 3:18). And John stated that Christ "laid down his life *for* us" (1 John 3:16) and that God "loved us and sent his Son to be the atoning sacrifice *for* our sins" (1 John 4:10, NRSV). The apostolic witness is saturated with such vicarious-sacrificial declarations concerning the death of the Messiah.[9] Moreover, Jesus used the same language concerning his own death: "This is my blood of the covenant, which is poured out *for* many for the forgiveness of sins" (Matt. 26:28).[10]

Jesus' declaration during the Last Supper exemplifies the sacrificial presuppositions of the New Testament: 1) The blood of the Messiah was shed; 2) on behalf of many; 3) for the forgiveness of sins.[11] Divine forgiveness only happens on the basis of the sacrificial shedding of blood (Heb. 9:22), and consequently the apostolic proclamation of the forgiveness of sins through faith in Jesus (cf. Acts 2:38; 5:31; 10:43; 13:38; 26:18) also assumed a sacrificial interpretation. The idea that the earliest apostolic church, as revealed in the book of Acts, lacked a developed theology of atonement is groundless.[12] In light of the temple and the sacrificial system, which was still operational at the time, the apostolic declaration concerning the forgiveness of sins would have been commonly understood as fundamentally sacrificial.

The forgiveness of sins and a sacrificial interpretation of the cross were predicated on a belief in the depravity of man in light of the holiness of God. Following the sin of Adam, "all have sinned and fall short of the glory of God" (Rom. 3:23). For "sin came into the world through one man" and "all sinned" (Rom. 5:12), which "led to condemnation for all men" (v. 18). Thus "by a man came death" (1 Cor. 15:21), and "in Adam all die" (v. 22).[13] Being "ungodly" (Rom. 4:5; 5:6; Jude 15) and "sinners" (Rom. 5:19; Gal. 2:17; 1 Tim. 1:15), all humans—Jew and Gentile alike—are "by nature children of wrath" (Eph. 2:3), and "sons of disobedience" (Eph. 2:2; cf. Rom. 11:32).[14] Because all are "alienated and hostile in mind, doing evil deeds" (Col. 1:21), the Scriptures declare all to be "prisoners of sin" (Gal. 3:22, NLT) and "slaves to sin" (Rom. 6:20; cf. John 8:34).

Such a depraved condition necessarily results in alienation and estrangement from our Creator, "the Holy One" (Ps. 89:18; Isa. 40:25; Hos. 11:9). Holiness and sinfulness cannot coexist. Therefore all are considered to be "under sin" (Rom. 3:9; 7:14) and "under condemnation" (James 5:12; cf. Rom. 5:16–19). Apart from God, we are metaphorically "dead in our trespasses" (Eph. 2:5; cf. 1 Tim. 5:6), and hence "alienated from the life of God" (Eph. 4:18). Because all are "hostile to God" (Rom. 8:7), all are deemed "God's enemies" (Rom. 5:10, NIV).

However, the Scriptures declare that by faith in the sacrificial death of the Messiah our sins are forgiven and we are *reconciled* to God. Such reconciliation (Gk. *katallagē*) is also called "atonement," which means "to bring together in mutual agreement," for it was originally broken into two words: "at onement."[15] To make at-one-ment is to make reconciliation, for "in the New Testament the basic idea of the Atonement is that of reconciliation."[16] Various modern translations have sought to incorporate the word "atonement," so as to emphasize this idea (cf. Rom. 3:25; 5:11; Heb. 2:17; 9:5; 1 John 2:2; 4:10).[17] Throughout the New Testament, this reconciliation was understood within the preexisting apocalyptic framework. Thus, in light of the day of the Lord, the apostles proclaimed that sinful humans could be reconciled to their holy Creator by means of faith in the sacrificial death of the Messiah (see figure 8.1).[18]

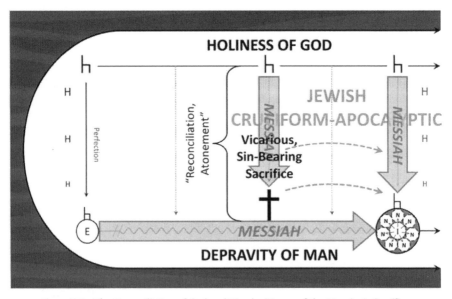

Figure 8.1 – The Reconciliation of God and Man by Means of the Messianic Sacrifice

For example, in the context of the Jewish eschatological "judgment seat of Christ" (2 Cor. 5:10), Paul declares, "The love of Christ controls us, because we have concluded this: that one has *died for all*, therefore all have died. . . . In Christ God was *reconciling* the world to himself, not counting their trespasses against them, and entrusting to us the message of reconciliation" (vv. 14,19). Similarly, the apostle says, "You, who once were alienated and hostile in mind, doing evil deeds, he has now *reconciled* in his body of flesh *by his death*, in order to present you holy and blameless and above reproach before him" (Col. 1:21–22). So also, in Romans, Paul summarizes the sacrificial death of the Messiah unto our reconciliation with God and salvation from the coming wrath:

> God shows his love for us in that while we were still sinners, Christ *died for us*. Since, therefore, we have now been justified *by his blood*, much more shall we be *saved* by him from the wrath of God. For if while we were enemies we were *reconciled* to God by the death of his Son, much more, now that we are reconciled, shall we be *saved* by his life. (Rom. 5:8–10)

Though humanity seeks reconciliation with the divine in a multitude of ways, God has determined that there is only one way to assuage the hostility: through faith in the sacrificial death of his Messiah. In this way, Christ Jesus stands between the sin of humanity and the holiness of God: "For there is one God, and there is *one mediator* between God and men, the man Christ Jesus, who gave himself as a ransom for all, which is the testimony given at the proper time" (1 Tim. 2:5–6).

Though the idea of sacrifice is often revolting to modern ears (no one offers animals to appease the gods), it was the foundational reality by which the suffering of the Messiah was understood. A naturalistic bias deems sacrificial ideas to be "primitive." And all attempts to "spiritualize," "christologize," or otherwise change the basic understanding of sacrifice, carried over from the Old Testament, are baseless.[19] Moreover, the marginalization of sacrificial realities as linguistic "metaphors," "motifs," or "figures of speech" do violence to the apostolic witness.[20] The Messiah's death was constitutionally sacrificial, and thereby vicarious and sin-bearing.[21] Either Christ Jesus bears our sins before God on the last day, or we bear our own sins eternally.[22]

The messianic sacrifice is thus understood as the only means of escaping divine wrath and inheriting eternal life (cf. Rom. 8:1–24; Eph. 1:3–14; 2 Tim. 1:8–12; Titus 3:4–7; 1 Peter 1:13–21; 1 John 4:7–18; etc.). It is the means of *attaining* the long-awaited Jewish eschatological hope (cf. Acts 26:7; Rom. 9:30–32; Phil. 3:7–11). The apostolic writers (especially Paul) therefore refer to the Messiah's sacrificial death in a shorthand style as "the gospel" (cf. Rom. 1:16; Gal. 1:11; Col. 1:23; 1 Tim. 1:11), since it is "the power of God *for salvation* to everyone who believes, to the Jew first and also to the Greek" (Rom. 1:16).[23]

GOD'S RIGHTEOUSNESS
AND SACRIFICIAL ATONEMENT

The language of "righteousness" in the New Testament rests upon sacrificial realities.[24] Simply put, the sacrifices of the Old Testament were given to rectify sin and make worshipers righteous in the sight of God. This remediation was accomplished by the *transference of sin* from the worshiper to the animal (cf. Lev. 5:6; 10:17; 16:22), while the innocence of the animal was "credited to him" (Lev. 7:18). The animal was accepted "on his behalf" (Lev. 1:4, NIV) *if* the worshiper offered it in faith and with repentance (note the cry of the prophets concerning sacrifices without repentance; see Isa. 1:11–20; Amos 5:21–27; Mic. 6:6–8). In this way the worshiper was united with the animal, which functioned vicariously—bearing his sin—while he himself was accounted "before the LORD" (Lev. 10:17; 16:30; 19:22) according to the innocence of the animal. Thus the conclusion, "He will be *forgiven* for any of these things he did that made him guilty" (Lev. 6:7, NIV).[25]

In such a light, the sacrifice of the Messiah was understood in the New Testament as a "sin offering" (Rom. 8:3, NIV).[26] Those who put their faith in him as a sacrifice will be "declared righteous" (Rom. 2:13; 3:20, NIV) in God's sight. Based upon the mechanism of the transference of sin in God's accounting, we are "counted as righteousness" (Rom. 4:5), and on the last day we will be qualified to inherit eternal life. This divine transference is "reckoned as a gift" (Rom. 4:4, NRSV)—that is, not of our own doing but "the gift of God" (Eph. 2:8), also summarized as "the free gift of righteousness" (Rom. 5:17).[27] In this way we have received "the righteousness that comes from God" (Rom. 10:3, NRSV).[28] So Paul stated his emphatic desire to "be found in him, not having a righteousness *of my own* that comes from the law, but that which comes through faith in Christ, the righteousness *from God* that depends on faith" (Phil. 3:8–9).

Such reckoning and crediting of righteousness (or "imputing," as in the older English), derives directly from the sacrificial system, which was the commonly understood framework for the death of the Messiah. Thus the revelation of "a righteousness from God" (Rom. 1:17, NIV) was simply the revelation of the sacrificial offering of the Messiah (see figure 8.2). In light of "the judgment seat of Christ" (2 Cor. 5:10), Paul summarized, "For our sake [God] made him to be sin who knew no sin, so that in him we might become the righteousness of God" (v. 21).[29] As the sacrificial animal was "made to be sin," so to speak, on behalf of the worshiper, so also the Messiah was made to be sin on behalf of sinners that we might be declared righteous before God and therefore be "guilt-less in the day of our Lord Jesus Christ" (1 Cor. 1:8; cf. Eph. 5:27; Phil. 1:10; Col. 1:22; 1 Thess. 3:13; 5:23).

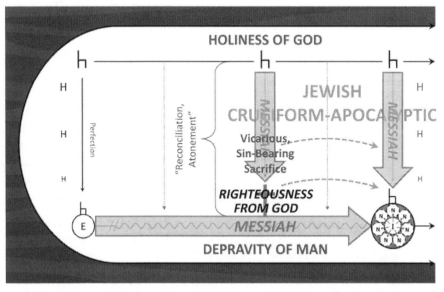

Figure 8.2 – Righteousness Reckoned by God through Faith in the Messianic Sacrifice

Similarly, Paul speaks in Romans 3:21–25 of "a righteousness from God" (vv. 21,22, NIV) that has been revealed "by his blood" (v. 25).[30] In light of the eschatological day (cf. 2:5,16; 3:5,6,19), Paul understands the messianic sacrifice to accomplish righteousness in three ways: propitiation, justification, and redemption. Note the integration of these realities within a sacrificial framework:

> But now the *righteousness of God* has been manifested apart from the law, although the Law and the Prophets bear witness to it—the righteousness of God through faith in Jesus Christ for all who believe. For there is no distinction: for all have sinned and fall short of the glory of God, and are *justified* by his grace as a gift, through the *redemption* that is in Christ Jesus, whom God put forward as a *propitiation* by his blood, to be received by faith. (Rom. 3:21–25)

As we will see, these three words roughly represent royal, judicial, and economic realities within the character of God and redemptive history. However, they are all built upon vicarious sacrifice, accomplishing in each of these areas a righteous status. By his blood propitiation is made (Rom. 3:25; cf. 1 John 1:7; 2:2; 4:10). By his blood we are justified (Rom. 5:9; cf. Titus 3:7). By his blood redemption is achieved (Eph. 1:7; Heb. 9:14–15; 1 Peter 1:18–19). By his blood we are reconciled to God (Col. 1:20; cf. 2 Cor. 5:19; Eph. 2:13). The cumulative force of these passages cannot be overstated. Again, all atonement realities build upon the foundation of substitutional sacrifice.[31] Moreover, it is the sacrificial blood that enables and enacts all of the other aspects of the atonement, which establishes human beings as righteous in the sight of God.[32]

Propitiation

The concept of propitiation is almost completely absent from modern culture and terminology. No one uses propitiatory language in everyday conversation; it has become Bible rhetoric with little meaning to the common believer. In fact, at the very mention of the word most people disengage, their eyes glazing over. Nevertheless, propitiation lies at the heart of biblical faith and thought.

Propitiation, more than any other atonemental term, is associated with sacrifice. Though relatively rare in the New Testament (Luke 18:13; Rom. 3:25; Heb. 2:17; 9:5; 1 John 2:2; 4:10), the Greek word (*hilasmos*) and its cognates are used extensively in the Septuagint (some 150 times) to translate the Hebrew terms for atonement (*kippūr/kāphar*). Though commonly translated "make atonement," verses like Leviticus 6:7 literally read, "The priest shall *make propitiation* for him before the LORD."[33] Likewise, the sacrificial calendar culminated with the Day of Atonement (Lev. 16), or "Day of Propitiation," wherein the wrath of God toward the sin of Israel was appeased.[34] This relationship is seen in New Testament, where *hilasmos* is alternatively translated "atoning sacrifice" (1 John 2:2; 4:10, NRSV, NIV) and "sacrifice of atonement" (Rom. 3:25, NRSV, NIV).

The term "propitiation," inside and outside the Scriptures, simply means "an appeasement of anger."[35] Inherent to the term are royal connotations, for God is angry *in his gubernatorial role* (cf. Ps. 21:9; 110:5; Matt. 22:7; Rev. 6:16).[36] Because he is so disrespected among the nations (cf. Ps. 2:1; 46:6; Rev. 11:18) and because his righteous ways are disregarded (cf. Ezek. 22:26; 2 Peter 2:2), the nations are "storing up wrath against [themselves] for the day of God's wrath" (Rom. 2:5, NIV).

The language of appeasement assumes the reality of divine wrath, an idea inherently offensive to many.[37] However, God is not like fallen angry humans,[38] nor like the pagan gods they worship.[39] He is not a "pitiless ogre" who lashes out arbitrarily.[40] Rather, he is *holy* in his anger, which is driven by *love* for that which he created and for that over which he rules.[41]

If my son beats his siblings, I should rightly get angry, because I love his siblings and desire their well-being. This idea is commonly termed "righteous anger"—that is, as Leon Morris describes, "a burning zeal for the right coupled with a perfect hatred for everything that is evil."[42] So "the LORD is a jealous and avenging God; the LORD is avenging and wrathful; the LORD takes vengeance on his adversaries and keeps wrath for his enemies" (Nah. 1:2; cf. Deut. 4:24; 6:15). Or a Paul states summarily, "the wrath of God is revealed from heaven against all ungodliness and unrighteousness of men" (Rom. 1:18).

For this reason the wrath of God "pervades the entire corpus" of the Old Testament.[43] Its references are too numerous to cite.[44] God hates sin, and he is in "total opposition to every form of sin."[45] Likewise, in the New Testament the anger and wrath of God lie as a backdrop to the drama of the life, death, and resurrection of Jesus (cf. Matt. 3:7; 18:34; 22:7; Luke 14:21; John 3:36). Jesus understood the "cup" he was drinking (Matt. 26:39 and parallels)—that is, "the cup of [God's] wrath" (Isa. 51:17; cf. Ps. 75:8; Jer. 25:15; 49:12; Rev. 14:10; 16:19).[46] Even now God is clearly angry with the sins of humanity (cf. Rom. 2:5; 3:5; 5:9; 12:19; 13:4; Eph. 5:6; Col. 3:6; 1 Thess. 2:16; Heb. 10:27; Rev. 6:16; 19:15). How then is his wrath appeased, his anger assuaged, and his fury placated? How does God become "propitious" toward us when we have so clearly sinned?

This cry for propitiation is universal. The tax collector literally prayed, "O God, *be propitiated* for me, the sinner" (Luke 18:13).[47] Deep within every human being is a longing that our Creator, in whose image we are made, would be pleased with us. He is pleased, however, with only one man—Jesus of Nazareth (cf. Matt. 3:17; 17:5)—and God has shown this to be so by raising him, and only him, from the dead (Acts 17:31). The fact that all human beings remain in the grave proves the divine disapproval of their lives. This is a depressing fact only for those who refuse to acknowledge their condition, turn, and bind themselves by faith to Christ crucified. For God has answered our cry for divine approval by putting forward his Son "as a propitiation by his blood, to be received by faith" (Rom. 3:25).

The propitiatory sacrifice of the Messiah to assuage the wrath of God was ultimately understood in light of the eschatological "day of wrath" (Zeph. 1:15; Rom. 2:5; cf. Ps. 110:5; Rev. 6:17). Though his anger has been appeased *presently* toward those in Christ—that is, "We have peace with God" (Rom. 5:1; cf. Eph. 2:13; Col. 1:20)—this present experience of peace with God is in *anticipation* of being saved "from the wrath to come" (1 Thess. 1:10; cf. Rom. 5:9). So John says that God "loved us and sent his Son to be the propitiation for our sins" (1 John 4:10); and as a result we have "confidence for the day of judgment" (v. 17). Thus we see the propitiatory relationship between the cross and the day of the Lord (see figure 8.3).

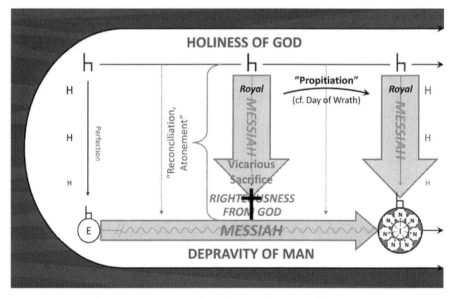

Figure 8.3 – The Propitiative Nature of the Messianic Sacrifice

Justification

Unlike "propitiation," the term "justification" is quite common in modern English. We say things like "He was justified in what he did" and "How do you justify that?" Though ideas of necessity, reasonableness, and generic ethicality are assumed in the Scriptures, the biblical terms (Heb. *tsādēq* and Gk. *dikaios*, and their cognates) carry a fundamental *legal sense*.[48] Moreover, these words produce two different English word groups—"justified" and "righteous"—to which we often assign different meanings.[49] This delineation is foreign to both Greek and Hebrew.[50] If you are "righteous," then you are legally just; and if you are "justified," then you are legally in-the-right (i.e., "innocent"), rather than legally in-the-wrong (i.e., "guilty").[51]

The concepts of justice and righteousness are therefore bound up inextricably with legal and judicial concepts such as law, ordinances, charges, judgment, guilt, etc. Justice is the effect of judgment based upon law, which results in righteousness. So, throughout the Scriptures, righteousness and judgment are used in tandem, too many times to quote.[52] God is a "righteous Judge" (Ps. 7:11; 2 Tim. 4:8), and he will indeed "judge the world with righteousness" (Ps. 98:9; cf. Ps. 9:8; 67:4; 72:2; 96:13). When applied to the greater apocalyptic narrative of the Scriptures, we see that God has "fixed a day on which he will *judge* the world in *righteousness* by a man whom he has appointed" (Acts 17:31)—"the day of wrath when God's *righteous judgment* will be revealed" (Rom. 2:5; cf. 2 Thess. 1:5).[53] Thus we know that the earth is headed for "the day of *judgment*" (2 Peter 3:7), which will result in "new heavens and a new earth in which *righteousness* dwells" (v. 13).

In this way, the closest biblical synonym (or at least parallel) of "righteousness" is "justice."[54] The legal and judgmental *sense* of biblical righteousness cannot be ignored or brushed aside.[55] So pervasive is the legal reality that God can rightly be spoken of as "a God of law,"[56] for "God works by the way of law."[57] God administrates creation by "the fixed laws of heaven and earth" (Jer. 33:25, NIV; cf. Jer. 31:35; Ps. 74:16), which are reflected in the laws given at Sinai (cf. Deut. 6; Ps. 78:5–8; 1 Tim. 1:8–11).

Because divine law dictates redemptive history, the day of judgment was expected to be an orderly event (though, of course, still apocalyptic). God would judge the nations according to his righteous laws (cf. Isa. 2:2–4; 42:4; 51:4; Joel 3:2) and make atonement for the sins of his people (cf. Deut. 32:43; Ps. 79:9; Dan. 9:24). This was reflected in every New Year celebration (Rosh Hashanah) leading up to the Day of Atonement (Yom Kippur).[58] God will charge humanity with the guilt of their crimes and they will receive their due punishment, which, as we saw in chapter 3, involves eternal conscious torment (Gehenna). As we also saw earlier in this chapter, God established sacrifice as the prescribed means to forgive and "pardon" (Heb. *sālaḥ/nāśā*) transgression and iniquity (cf. Ex. 23:21; 34:9; Num. 14:19; Deut. 29:20; Job 7:21; Ps. 25:11; Isa. 40:2; 55:7; Mic. 7:18). In this way we are absolved of "guilt" (Heb. *ʾāšam*), another pervasive legal concept in the Scriptures.[59]

Those who are forgiven are thus "acquitted" (cf. Ex. 23:7; Deut. 25:1; Ps. 69:27; Isa. 5:23; Mic. 6:11), the same word in both Greek and Hebrew for "justify/declare righteous"—now applied to the sinner. To "justify" the guilty is to "acquit" them, which means they are "declared righteous." First-century believers would have understood "justification" along such simple lines: *a legal term indicating the verdict of acquittal read by a judge, announcing the accused as "not guilty."* These are the judicial categories into which the apostles placed the sacrificial death of the Messiah in relation to the apocalyptic day of judgment (see figure 8.4).[60]

When we understand justification in the sense of legal acquittal, as Paul clearly does in 1 Corinthians 4:4,[61] many New Testament passages become much more straightforward (as seen by the addition of the bracketed language of acquittal in the following Scripture quotations). By faith in Jesus' death, "we seek to be justified [acquitted] in Christ" (Gal. 2:17, NIV). Since "we have now been justified [acquitted] by his blood, much more shall we be saved by him from the wrath of God" (Rom. 5:9). It is God who "justifies [acquits] the ungodly" (Rom. 4:5), "so that being justified [acquitted] by his grace we might become heirs according to the hope of eternal life" (Titus 3:7). "Therefore, since we have been justified [acquitted] by faith, we have peace with God through our Lord Jesus Christ" (Rom. 5:1). In light of the day of judgment, justification is a simple legal term, which is synonymous with acquittal when applied to the guilty. So Paul explains, in light of the various eschatological themes of Romans 8 (cf. vv. 11,18,23,29):

> If God is for us, who is against us? He who did not withhold his own Son, but gave him up for all of us, will he not with him also give us everything else? Who will bring any *charge* against God's elect? It is God who *justifies* [acquits]. Who is to *condemn*? It is Christ Jesus, who died, yes, who was raised, who is at the right hand of God, who indeed *intercedes* for us. (Rom. 8:31–34, NRSV)

Here the Messiah is understood as a legal advocate in a trial interceding for a defendant who is accused and condemned—that is, declared guilty. Because of Christ's death, we have been acquitted of the charges against us, thus averting the judgment and punishment due us on the last day.

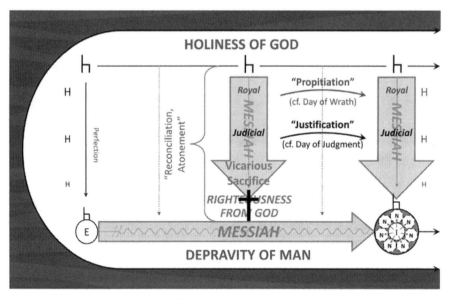

Figure 8.4 – The Justificative Nature of the Messianic Sacrifice

This reality is universal for Jew and Gentile alike. As a result of Adam's "transgression" (i.e., breaking of a law), "death reigned" (Rom. 5:14). "For the judgment following one trespass brought condemnation, but the free gift following many trespasses brought justification [acquittal]" (Rom. 5:16). Note Paul's straightforward forensic logic:

Therefore, as one *trespass* led to *condemnation* for all men, so one act of *righteousness* leads to *justification* [acquittal] and life for all men. For as by the one man's *disobedience* the many were made *sinners*, so by the one man's *obedience* the many will be made *righteous*. Now the *law* came in to increase the *trespass*, but where *sin* increased, grace abounded all the more, so that, as *sin* reigned in death, grace also might reign through *righteousness* leading to eternal life through Jesus Christ our Lord. (Rom. 5:18–21)

This is the legal terminology into which the death of the Messiah is placed. By the sinful act of one man all are declared sinners. By the righteous act of one man all are declared righteous and acquitted of their sins, that on the day of Christ they might inherit the kingdom of God and eternal life.[62]

So we find ourselves at the heart of Paul's argument: *On what basis, in the sight of God, are we acquitted of our sins*—by our righteous acts or by the Messiah's righteous act in the cross? This is the context for the "sharp disagreement" (Acts 15:39) between Paul and his adversaries concerning the "works of the law" (Rom. 3:20,28; Gal. 2:16; 3:2,5,10).[63] These works of the law refer simply to "works of righteousness" (Titus 3:5, NRSV)—that is, generic obedience to the commands of the Mosaic Law, especially the Decalogue (cf. Rom. 2:17–23; 4:2–4; 7:7–12; 9:11; Gal. 3:10; 2 Tim. 1:9; Titus 3:5; James 2:14–26; etc.).[64]

On what basis will we be acquitted and forgiven of the charges against us on the day of judgment—upon our obedience to the divine statutes or upon faith in the obedience of the Messiah?[65] The apostle's assertion is that "it is no longer on the basis of works; otherwise grace would no longer be grace" (Rom. 11:6), for "a person is not justified [acquitted] by works of the law but through faith in Jesus Christ" (Gal. 2:16). So Paul reasons: "For all who *rely on works of the law* are under a curse; for it is written, 'Cursed be everyone who does not abide by all things written in the Book of the Law, and do them.' Now it is evident that no one is justified [acquitted] before God *by the law*, for 'The righteous shall live by faith'" (Gal. 3:10–11).

Since the whole world will be "held accountable to God" (Rom. 3:19), Paul says, "*By works of the law* no human being will be justified [acquitted] in his sight" (v. 20), a reference not only to God's present eye upon humanity but also to his "appearing" (Ps. 102:16; Mal. 3:2; Titus 2:13) and our "seeing" God (Ps. 97:6; Isa. 52:8; 1 John 3:2). Justification and acquittal cannot happen on the basis of our works of righteousness, "for all have sinned and fall short of the glory of God" (Rom. 3:23). According to these sins alone, we will give account. (What murderer stands before a judge and argues his charity?)[66] Therefore, God has provided a means of justification/acquittal by the vicarious sacrificial death of the Messiah, which results in our being "justified [acquitted] by his grace as a gift" (Rom. 3:24). This is the common-sense approach and interpretation of, arguably, the most debated passage in church history:

> For *by works of the law* no human being will be *justified* [acquitted] in his sight, since through the law comes knowledge of sin.
>
> But now the righteousness of God has been manifested apart from the law, although the Law and the Prophets bear witness to it—the righteousness of God *through faith* in Jesus Christ for all who believe. For there is no distinction: for all have sinned and fall short of the glory of God, and are *justified* [acquitted] *by his grace* as a gift, through the redemption that is in Christ Jesus, whom God put forward as a propitiation by his blood, to be received *by faith*. This was to show God's righteousness, because in his divine forbearance he had passed over former sins. (Rom. 3:20–25)[67]

This approach to Romans 3 is confirmed in Romans 4, which is Paul's point when he introduces the passage: "What then shall we say that Abraham, our forefather, discovered in this matter?" (Rom. 4:1, NIV). As Abraham "believed God" and it was "reckoned to him as righteousness" (v. 3, NRSV), so also "to one who *without works* trusts him who justifies [acquits] the ungodly, such faith is *reckoned as righteousness*" (v. 5, NRSV). This "reckoning" (Gk. *logizomai*), or "counting" (ESV, KJV), or "crediting" (NASB, NIV), is applied in anticipation of the day of judgment, when we will be considered righteous in the eyes of the Judge, and declared as such before his court.[68] Hence we will be acquitted of our sins and "declared righteous in his sight" (Rom. 3:20, NIV).

Elsewhere Paul likewise summarizes our present justification in anticipation of the day of the Lord and eternal life:

> For we ourselves were once foolish, disobedient, led astray, slaves to various passions and pleasures, passing our days in malice and envy, hated by others and hating one another. But when the goodness and loving kindness of God our Savior appeared, he saved us [from eschatological judgment, cf. 1:2; 2:11–13], not because of *works done by us* in righteousness, but according to *his own mercy*, by the washing of regeneration and renewal of the Holy Spirit, whom he poured out on us richly through Jesus Christ our Savior, so that being *justified* [acquitted] *by his grace* we might become heirs according to the hope of eternal life. (Titus 3:3–7)

Lack of clarity and simplicity concerning the idea of justification is largely due to a failure in understanding the day of the Lord and its forensic nature. We are not justified from a theological concept of human depravity into a nebulous theological system of atonement. Rather, we are justified from real sins that have done real damage to a real creation before a real Judge in anticipation of a real day of judgment. That day will not be "like" a law court; it will be a *real courtroom*, with real charges brought against real transgressions, which have really angered a real King and Judge.[69] In this real future context, one thing will be clear to all: "No one living is righteous before you" (Ps. 143:2). The only means of justification and acquittal before God will be faith in the messianic sacrifice, that he might bear our sins and punishment in our stead.[70] Thus will the oracle be ultimately fulfilled:

> But he was pierced for our transgressions,
> he was crushed for our iniquities;
> the punishment that brought us peace was upon him. . . .
> After the suffering of his soul,
> he will see the light of life and be satisfied;
> by his knowledge my righteous servant will justify many,
> and he will bear their iniquities.
> (Isa. 53:5,11, NIV)

Redemption

Like justification, "redemption" is an English word that is still in common usage. In the financial realm, we seek the redemption of bonds, vouchers, or coupons. We might ask, "Can we redeem this situation?" We speak of honor being redeemed or tell "stories of redemption." Though the word has a marginal secular usage, for many Christians redemption remains almost entirely a religious concept. "Redemption" is viewed as just another Bible word representing the whole of the Christian life and experience in a generic sense. When a deeper meaning is applied, it is usually seen as little more than a synonym for "deliverance."[71] While deliverance and redemption in the Scriptures are related concepts (cf. Ex. 6:6; Job 6:23; Isa. 50:2; Jer. 15:21), deliverance is the implication of redemption, not its equivalent. The release from bondage is accomplished by redemption.

"Redemption" (Gk. *lutrōsis*) and "to redeem" (Gk. *lutroō*) are based upon the idea of "ransom" (Gk. *lutron*)—that is, a *payment price* for the release of something.[72] Though the term "redemption" is sometimes used in the Scriptures without direct reference to a ransom payment (e.g., Luke 21:28; Rom. 8:23; Eph. 4:30), the fact that a ransom has been paid is implied and assumed.[73] Redemption is inherently an economic idea, wherein payment is made or a debt is repaid.[74] This was commonly understood both inside and outside the Scriptures.[75]

In the Old Testament redemption is variously associated with the buying back of family property and/or slaves by the payment of money (cf. Lev. 25:29–34,47–55; Jer. 32:7–12), the receiving of firstborns by the payment of sacrifice and offerings (cf. Ex. 13:11–16; Lev. 27:26–27; Num. 18:15–17), and the purchasing of Israel by the payment and cost of God's exertion of power and effort (cf. Ex. 6:6; Deut. 7:8; Ps. 77:14–15). Much theological wrangling surrounds these passages, but as Leon Morris states clearly: "Redemption consistently signifies deliverance by payment of price. . . . As a stubborn substratum in every case there is the basic price-paying conception."[76]

In biblical thought this price-paying conception of redemption is ultimately applied to the broad redemptive narrative. Humanity has rebelled against God and broken his laws, which has caused objective, measurable damages to creation. In response, God has handed human beings over to the slavery of their sin until their debt should be repaid. This recompense ultimately takes place on the day of the Lord, when all people are judged according to their deeds and either make restitution for their wrongs or pay the debt with their very lives— that is, in Gehenna. Only when that debt is paid are individuals redeemed from their miserable circumstances.[77]

This narrative is assumed in the New Testament and applied to the death of Jesus. God attributes value to the sacrifice of the Messiah, which is then counted toward the debt of humanity to purchase and liberate them from their bondage and slavery.[78] When seen through the apocalyptic lens of salvation history, the redemption passages of the New Testament become clearer (see figure 8.5). For those who put their faith in Christ crucified, the day of recompense will become "the day of redemption" (Eph. 4:30), because "in him we have redemption through his blood, the forgiveness of our trespasses, according to the riches of his grace" (Eph. 1:7).

As with justification and propitiation, the present redemptive payment of our debt has been made in anticipation of our future deliverance. Thus the heavenly song expounds: "Worthy are you to take the scroll and to open its seals, for you were slain, and by your blood you *ransomed* people for God from every tribe and language and people and nation, and you have made them a kingdom and priests to our God, and they shall reign on the earth" (Rev. 5:9–10).[79]

Likewise Peter describes, "If you call on him as Father who judges impartially according to each one's deeds, conduct yourselves with fear throughout the time of your exile, knowing that you were *ransomed* from the futile ways inherited from your forefathers, not with perishable things such as silver or gold, but with the precious *blood of Christ*, like that of a lamb without blemish or spot" (1 Peter 1:17–19). Here we see the sacrificial "blood of Christ" being counted by God as "precious," and hence applied in anticipation of the judgment to come toward the debt of our "futile ways."

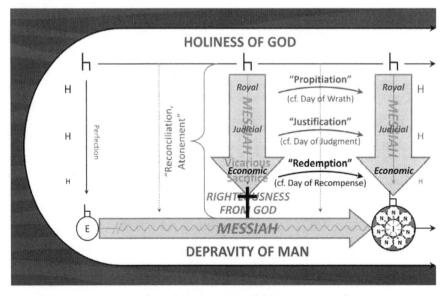

Figure 8.5 – The Redemptive Nature of the Messianic Sacrifice

Likewise Paul says, "There is one God, and there is one mediator between God and men, the man Christ Jesus, who gave himself *as a ransom* for all, which is the testimony given at the proper time" (1 Tim. 2:5–6).[80] Such a mediation is in the context of "those who were to believe in him for eternal life" (1 Tim. 1:16). Thus we wait for "our blessed hope, the appearing of the glory of our great God and Savior Jesus Christ, who gave himself for us *to redeem us* from all lawlessness and to purify for himself a people for his own possession" (Titus 2:13–14).

This apostolic interpretation is derived from Jesus' own declaration that "the Son of Man came not to be served but to serve, and to give his life *as a ransom* for many" (Mark 10:45). Jesus clearly understood his death in terms of a payment for the transgressions of "the many" (cf. Isa. 53:11–12). The eschatological orientation of redemption is also seen when Jesus references "the Son of Man coming in a cloud with power and great glory" (Luke 21:27), saying, "When these things begin to take place, straighten up and raise your heads, because your *redemption* is drawing near" (v. 28).[81]

Likewise Paul, in speaking of "the glory that is to be revealed to us" (Rom. 8:18), eagerly awaits our "adoption as sons, the *redemption* of our bodies" (v. 23). And by the sacrifice of Christ we have "obtained eternal *redemption*" (Heb. 9:12, NASB), for "he is the mediator of a new covenant, so that those who are called may receive the promised eternal inheritance, since a death has occurred that *redeems* them from the transgressions committed under the first covenant" (v. 15).

Of course this eternal redemption, inheritance, and salvation is understood in light of the Israelocentric vision of the Old Testament, therefore corresponding to "the redemption of Jerusalem" (Luke 2:38; cf. Isa. 52:3), wherein Jesus is "the one to redeem Israel" (Luke 24:21; cf. Acts 1:6).[82] Those who disintegrate redemption by separating the redemption of creation and the body from the redemption of Israel and the nations fall into no small error. Jesus will indeed "restore *everything*, as he promised long ago through his holy prophets" (Acts 3:21, NIV).

Our being "bought with a price" (1 Cor. 6:20; 7:23) and "purchased with his own blood" (Acts 20:28, NASB) is the driving force behind our being "*justified* by his grace as a gift, through the *redemption* that is in Christ Jesus, whom God put forward as a *propitiation* by his blood, to be received by faith" (Rom. 3:24–25). So the three atonemental realities are interrelated and cooperative. The redemptive payment of the blood of Jesus justifies/acquits us of our sins and propitiates/assuages the wrath of God toward us. As sin creates the threefold progression of emotive anger unto penal charges unto fiscal retribution, so the substitutional sacrifice satisfies the debt, allowing the charges to be dropped, and thus resolves the wrath of the King/Judge/Creator.[83] In this way the substitutional nature of the death of the Messiah is multifaceted (see figure 8.6).

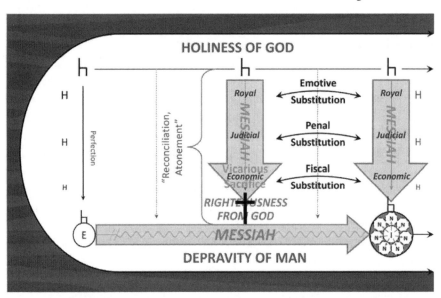

Figure 8.6 – The Threefold Substitutional Nature of the Messianic Sacrifice

As stated above, the various royal, judicial, and economic aspects of the cross are based upon the foundational interpretation of the death of the Messiah as a vicarious sacrifice. Moreover, the different aspects of the cross are based upon the apocalyptic realities of the day of the Lord (see chapter 3). They are not mere metaphors, images, or figures of speech. They are different aspects of real history, based upon real events, involving real persons, culminating in a real day.[84] At two points in redemptive history are the wrath, judgment, and retribution of God satisfied: the cross and the day of the Lord. Righteousness is fulfilled only at Calvary and in Gehenna. Where humanity will be found on that day is the great choice facing each individual.

THE CHALLENGE OF FAITH

Nothing has been more challenging to the modern mind than the Jewish apocalyptic nature of Jesus' second coming (discussed in chapters 3–6) and the sacrificial nature of his first coming. Both have been deemed "embarrassing," the product of "primitive" religion. These two defining characteristics of the apostolic witness have been either avoided or ridiculed by most within the modern academy. Through Platonism, realized eschatology, supersessionism, a naturalistic approach to the Old Testament, and the rejection of sacrificial atonement, the modern church continues to drift from its apostolic moorings.

Though human depravity surely plays a role, God has intentionally made the gospel challenging to confront human pride and strength. For this reason, the New Testament proclaims the death of the Messiah as a sin-bearing sacrifice in light of the judgment to come as a reality to be received "by faith" (Rom. 3:25; 5:1; 9:30–32; Gal. 2:16; 3:8,22–26). Unfortunately, "faith" is another one of those Bible words that has lost much of its original meaning in modern times. It is commonly associated with abstract "belief" (the same Greek word translates both), which in turn is assumed to be little more than mental assent to cognitive categories that often have little impact on everyday life.[85] This could not be further from the biblical understanding of faith.

In the Scriptures, faith (Gk. *pistis*, Heb. *'āman*) involves a heart-level commitment that expresses itself in faithfulness to the One to whom it is committed.[86] Because the day of the Lord will begin with a revealing of people's hearts (cf. Rom. 2:16; 1 Cor. 4:5) and proceed to a judgment of their words (cf. Matt. 12:36; Jude 15) and deeds (cf. Rom. 2:6; 2 Cor. 5:10), issues of the heart demand the utmost attention (Prov. 4:23). Indeed, sin begins within the heart in the form of pride (Isa. 14:13; 1 Tim. 3:6), diversifying to other forms of iniquity (James 1:15; 4:2), proceeding from the mouth into every area of life (Matt. 15:18–19; James 3:6). Because our lives generate from the heart, so the reckoning of our lives in the eyes of God, and the accounting of our sins, will begin with the heart. Likewise, the accounting of the divine provision of sacrifice unto atonement will be based upon the heart response: "For *with the heart* one believes and is justified, and with the mouth one confesses and is saved" (Rom. 10:10).

Because of its "heart-felt" nature, biblical faith carries the connotation of "trust" and "reliance."[87] So Paul argues concerning the faith of Abraham: "To the one who does not work *but trusts* [Gk. *pisteuō*] him who justifies the ungodly, his faith is counted as righteousness" (Rom. 4:5). The force of Romans 4:1–8 is hard to overstate. Those who trust their very selves to divine mercy are the ones "to whom God counts righteousness" (v. 6). Those who trust God's provision of sacrifice are "those whose lawless deeds are forgiven, and whose sins are covered" (v. 7), for "the Lord will not count [their] sin" (v. 8). It is the wholehearted entrusting of oneself to God that will result in pardon on the day of judgment.

This kind of faith is quite confrontational, because it requires a heart response. Comparing faith in Christ's sacrifice to those living under the sacrificial system of the Old Testament, it took faith to actually believe that God accounted one's sin to the animal. Imagine standing over a young bull with a repentant heart concerning sins common to humankind. After laying your hands upon the animal and killing it, what has changed? The memory of the sin still remains. The effect upon family and friends still remains. Faith was demanded of the worshiper to trust and believe that God truly accounted the sin forgiven.

The same applies to every atonemental circumstance in the Scriptures. Judgment is coming at midnight (Ex. 12:12)—Will God really pass over us on account of a little blood on the door? Snakes are biting, and people are actually dying (Num. 21:6)—Will God really heal us if we look at the snake on the pole? The same dynamics apply to the greater redemptive narrative (cf. Luke 22:15–16; John 3:14–15). So Paul relates the hope of salvation from the wrath of God to our faith in the sacrifice: "Therefore, since we have been justified *through faith*, we have peace with God through our Lord Jesus Christ, through whom we have gained access *by faith* into this grace in which we now stand. . . . Since we have now been justified by his blood, how much more shall we be saved from God's wrath through him!" (Romans 5:1–2,9, NIV).

Inherent to atonemental faith is identification and participation. The worshiper must identify with the object of atonement and participate with it by faith. This is the intent of Communion, a regular "remembrance" for the purpose of identification and participation in the event of the cross. So Paul states explicitly, "The cup of blessing that we bless, is it not a *participation* in the blood of Christ? The bread that we break, is it not a *participation* in the body of Christ?" (1 Cor. 10:16). Because it is a participation in the death of Jesus, "whoever eats the bread or drinks the cup of the Lord in an unworthy manner will be guilty of sinning against the body and blood of the Lord" (1 Cor. 11:27, NIV). Thus they will "eat and drink judgment against themselves" (v. 29, NRSV).

Such participatory language ultimately derives from the sacrificial system. Those who offered sacrifices were united with the sacrifice by faith. The animal experienced death on behalf of the worshiper, and the worshiper died with the animal, so to speak. So Paul, in light of the sacrificial death of the Messiah (cf. Rom. 5:6–21) declares,

> Do you not know that all of us who have been baptized into Christ Jesus were baptized into his death? We were buried therefore *with him* by baptism into death, in order that, just as Christ was raised from the dead by the glory of the Father, we too might walk in newness of life. For if we have been united *with him* in a death like his, we shall certainly be united *with him* in a resurrection like his. (Rom. 6:3–5)

Such participatory thought defines much of the language of atonement in the New Testament. As Paul continues in Romans 6, "If we have died *with Christ*, we believe that we will also live *with him*" (v. 8). Likewise, he tells the Colossians, "You have died, and your life is hidden *with Christ* in God. When Christ who is your life appears, then you also will appear *with him* in glory" (Col. 3:3–4). As one offering a sacrifice sought to be found in the animal before the eyes of God, so Paul sought to be "found in [Christ], not having a righteousness of my own" (Phil. 3:9). Therefore he sought to "know Christ," to become "like him in his death," so as to "attain the resurrection from the dead" (vv. 10–11).

The drive to live this life by atonemental faith, so as to inherit eternal life, lies behind the apostle's classic declaration: "I have been crucified *with Christ*. It is no longer I who live, but Christ who lives in me. And the life I now live in the flesh I live *by faith* in the Son of God, who loved me and gave himself for me" (Gal. 2:20). So participation in the sacrifice by faith in this age was understood as the means of participation in the resurrection in the age to come.

Real events evoke real participatory faith. Unfortunately, the Platonic delusion robs people of the reality of redemptive history, for when life's ultimate end is immaterial heaven, accountability for sin and deeds done in materiality are diminished and the gravity of sin is lifted. When faith is uprooted from its historical context and bound in an unholy union to theological abstractions, the human heart quickly disengages. Rather, God calls us to truly *trust him* in light of a real history of human sin, its real consequences, and the real day when humanity will be judged.

In life's volatile situations, we call to others, "Trust me, and I will lead you through this!" Similarly, our faith and trust are in God, who calls to us, "Trust me, that when my Son comes and consumes the heavens and earth in fire, I will pass over you on the basis of faith in his blood!" We have real historical events—creation, the cross, and the day of the Lord—in which our hearts can trust and engage.

Moreover, these real events are every bit as challenging as they are encouraging. In a time and culture in which personal accountability is diminished by relativistic thinking, the message of the day of the Lord smacks of brash primitivism. Just like every generation before us, we question, "Where is the God of justice?" (Mal. 2:17). We live in a wicked culture that renounces God and says in its heart, "You will not call to account" (Ps. 10:13). We are like those complacent people "who say in their hearts, 'The LORD will not do good, nor will he do ill'" (Zeph. 1:12). Indeed we are the scoffers to come in the last days who say, "Where is the promise of his coming? For ever since the fathers fell asleep, all things are continuing as they were from the beginning of creation" (2 Peter 3:4). In the midst of the grinding "cares of this life" (Luke 21:34), true belief and faith in the day of the Lord is indeed "difficult" (Mark 10:24).[88]

Even more difficult to believe is that the judgment of God on that day will be determined by faith. Maybe God *will* judge the wicked; surely people who commit heinous sins, like Jeffrey Dahmer, deserve his judgment! As seen in the common reaction to Dahmer's conversion, however, many say to themselves, *How can God not judge people like Jeffrey Dahmer?*[89] How can God forgive upon the basis of faith alone? To the broken and repentant, this is wonderful news. But to the haughty and self-righteous, this is impossible to accept. Thus, the twofold confrontation of faith concerning the cross and the day of the Lord faces every human being (see figure 8.7). The whole world is under sin (Rom. 3:9; Gal. 3:22); Jesus will judge the living and the dead (Acts 10:42; 2 Tim. 4:1); but those who put their faith in Christ crucified will find mercy (Rom. 3:24; Gal. 2:16). Those who "set aside the grace of God" (Gal. 2:21, NIV), on the other hand, "will suffer the punishment of eternal destruction" (2 Thess. 1:9).

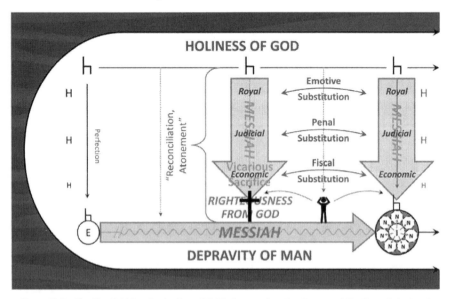

Figure 8.7 – The Twofold Confrontation of Faith Concerning the Cross and the Day of the Lord

Perseverance

This tension of faith concerning the imputed righteousness of the cross in anticipation of the judgment of the day of the Lord defined the life and functioning of the early church. *Perseverance* in justification by faith was at the heart of all apostolic exhortation. Being found in Christ, "not having a righteousness of my own" (Phil. 3:9), was the "one thing" that Paul sought to obtain:

> Not that I have already obtained *it* [atonemental faith, vv. 7–11] or have already become *perfect* [in atonemental faith], but I press on so that I may lay hold of *that* [faith in the cross] for which also I was laid hold of by Christ Jesus. Brethren, I do not regard myself as having laid hold of *it* [faith in the cross] yet; but one thing I do: forgetting what *lies behind* [self-righteous faith, vv. 4–6] and reaching forward to what *lies ahead* [being found in Christ in the resurrection, vv. 9–11], I press on toward the goal, for the prize of the upward call of God in Christ Jesus. (Phil. 3:12–14, NASB)

Perseverance of faith in Christ crucified defines most of the New Testament's controversies (cf. 1 Cor. 1:23; Gal. 3:1) and exhortations (cf. 1 Cor. 1:8; Phil. 1:6). Life lived by faith in Christ's sacrifice is therefore analogous to a "race" (cf. 1 Cor. 9:24; Gal. 5:7; 2 Tim. 4:7), wherein conversion is the starting line and the day of the Lord is the finish line. How you start is not as important as how you finish, though obviously you cannot finish without starting. Who puts blood on their door at dusk, but then goes down to frolic in the Nile before midnight? Who looks at the snake on the pole once, but then goes about tending to his wounds? The dead man does. The atonement only applies if faith is held *unto the time of judgment*. The Scriptures leave no room for the popular notion of "once saved, always saved."[90]

Thus Paul projects upon the church his personal drive to take hold of Christ crucified, forgetting his former life of self-righteousness: "I am sure of this, that he who began a good work in you [i.e., faith in Christ crucified] will *bring it to completion* at the day of Jesus Christ" (Phil. 1:6). Likewise, Paul labored for the gifts of the Holy Spirit to strengthen the church in the way of the cross unto eternal life: "I give thanks to my God always for you because of the grace of God that was given you in Christ Jesus . . . even as *the testimony about Christ* was confirmed among you—so that you are not lacking in any gift, as you wait for the revealing of our Lord Jesus Christ, who will *sustain you to the end*, guiltless in the day of our Lord Jesus Christ" (1 Cor. 1:4–8).

Moreover, Paul declares to the Colossians that in light of their having been "alienated and hostile" toward God, Christ "has now reconciled in his body of flesh by his death, in order to present you holy and blameless and above reproach before him, if indeed you *continue in the faith*, stable and steadfast, not shifting from the hope of the gospel that you heard, which has been proclaimed in all creation under heaven" (Col. 1:22–23). The only guarantee of salvation is *persevering atonemental faith*, which depends not on human strength but casts itself continually upon God's mercy unto the day of Lord. Thus we see why Paul so emphasizes the life of faith lived "in the flesh" (Gal. 2:20)—that is, in this age before the resurrection.

In this way, New Testament discipleship is also understood to be cruciform, for our whole life is meant to be conformed to the cross. Those who embark upon the journey of faith in Christ crucified endure its complexities. In the cross is revealed God's righteousness and man's depravity. Why did God deem it necessary to crush his Servant? Because of the punishment that was due us. As Paul encapsulates, "Here is a trustworthy saying that deserves full acceptance: Christ Jesus came into the world to save sinners—of whom I am the worst" (1 Tim. 1:15, NIV). This "trustworthy saying" is meant to serve as a theological summation. The crucifixion happened in order to save sinners from the wrath of God (which, of course, was understood within the Jewish apocalyptic framework of redemptive history).

Before receiving a revelation of the cross, all human beings assume a general righteousness and a lack of need for atonement. Ask someone on the street, "Will you go to heaven when you die?" (or some question of acceptability in the sight of God), and you will usually get a confident "Yes." The assumption is a basic correspondence between the righteousness of God and the righteousness of mankind. At conversion comes a revelation of sin, depravity, and the need for divine mercy. God is understood as holy, while we are wicked—the cross being the solution. However, this is not a one-time revelation. It is a progressive disclosure of the holiness of God and the depraved state into which we have all been born (see figure 8.8).

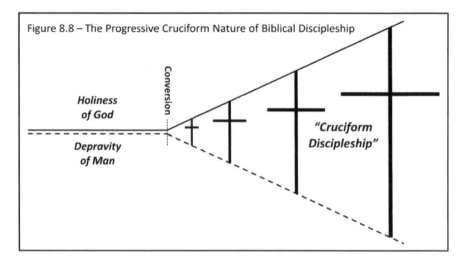

Figure 8.8 – The Progressive Cruciform Nature of Biblical Discipleship

Holiness of God

Conversion

Depravity of Man

"Cruciform Discipleship"

Thus we have a pattern for understanding the Christian life as exemplified by the apostle Paul, who before conversion was "a Pharisee, a son of Pharisees" (Acts 23:6)—"the strictest party of [the Jewish] religion" (Acts 26:5)—and "as to righteousness under the law, blameless" (Phil. 3:6, NRSV). The cross, however, reveals our being "foolish, disobedient, led astray, slaves to various passions and pleasures, passing our days in malice and envy, hated by others and hating one another" (Titus 3:3). So Paul can declare at the end of his life, "I was shown mercy so that in me, *the worst of sinners*, Christ Jesus might display his unlimited patience as an example for those who would believe on him and receive eternal life" (1 Tim. 1:16).

If we overlay figure 8.8 with the previous figures of redemption history (see figure 8.9), we see the process of the delusion of human righteousness being broken in light of the day of the Lord, when "the haughtiness of man shall be humbled, and the lofty pride of men shall be brought low" (Isa. 2:11) and when "God will judge men's secrets through Jesus Christ, as my gospel declares" (Rom. 2:16, NIV).

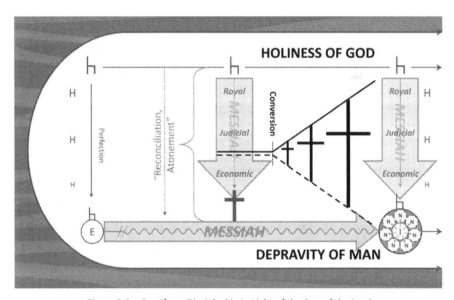

Figure 8.9 – Cruciform Discipleship in Light of the Day of the Lord

Disqualification

Though salvation is "the gift of God" (Eph. 2:8)—that is, "the free gift of righteousness" (Rom. 5:17)—we face the perennial threat of *disqualification* (Gk. *adokimos*) in our discipleship race unto the day of the Lord (cf. 2 Cor. 13:5–7; 2 Tim. 3:8; Titus 1:16). So Paul relates his life of consecration to the gospel:

Do you not know that in a *race* all the runners compete, but only one receives the prize? So run that you may obtain it. Every athlete exercises self-control in all things. They do it to receive a perishable wreath, but we an imperishable. So I do not run aimlessly; I do not box as one beating the air. But I discipline my body and keep it under control, lest after preaching to others I myself should be *disqualified* [Gk. *adokimos*]. (1 Cor. 9:24–27)

This idea of disqualification, or becoming "reprobate" (KJV), is again rooted in the sacrificial system. When we walk in known sin we are disqualified in the eyes of God because *there is no sacrifice for intentional sin,* according to both Old Testament and New.[91] The only sin that is atoned for is "unintentional sin" (cf. Lev. 4:2; 5:15; Num. 15:24; Heb. 9:7).[92] Intentional sins—such as idolatry, adultery, murder, rebellion, and the like—resulted in being "cut off" from the people of Israel (Lev. 7:20; 17:4; 18:29; etc.) and/or death (Lev. 20; 24:14–23; Deut. 17:1–7).[93]

Likewise, excommunication (Matt. 18:17; 1 Cor. 5:2) and/or divine judgment (1 Cor. 11:29; Rev. 2:23) is the New Testament standard. So Paul threatens believers who continue willfully in their sin: "Do you not know that the unrighteous will not inherit the kingdom of God?" (1 Cor. 6:9; cf. Gal. 5:21; Eph. 5:5).[94] Thus he quotes from the Law: "Purge the evil person from among you" (1 Cor. 5:13; cf. Deut. 13:5; 17:7; 21:21; 22:21–24). Because those who willfully sin will be disqualified in the end, Paul's injunction is considered merciful: "You are to deliver this man to Satan for the destruction of the flesh, so that his spirit may be saved in the day of the Lord" (1 Cor. 5:5).

The very purpose of this age is to bring to light the gravity of human sin. Therefore when we "realize our guilt" (cf. Lev. 4:13,22,27; 5:2; 6:4) and repent of our sin, God forgives according to the sacrifice. Intentional sin becomes to us, and to God, unintentional—we hate it and *intend not to do it again.* So God forgives and relents from impending judgment, a common theme throughout the Scriptures (cf. 1 Kings 21:29; Ps. 106:45; Jer. 18:8; Jonah 3:10; 1 John 1:9). However, "If we go on *sinning deliberately* after receiving the knowledge of the truth, there no longer remains a sacrifice for sins, but a fearful expectation of judgment, and a fury of fire that will consume the adversaries" (Heb. 10:26–27). So "no one who abides in [Christ] keeps on sinning; no one who keeps on sinning has either seen him or known him" (1 John 3:6; cf. 1 John 5:18). The call of God is thus a continually repentant heart before God unto the day of Christ Jesus (cf. Phil. 1:6; Heb. 12:1–4; 2 Peter 1:10)—or, in other words: "Work out your own salvation with fear and trembling" (Phil. 2:12).

Hence there is no place among believers for the all-too-common Western phenomenon of "Sunday Christianity." Those who think they can deliberately sin throughout the week and go to church on the weekend to find forgiveness will find their guilt remaining on the day of judgment. Hear the fearful indictment of Hebrews 6:

> For it is impossible, in the case of those who have once been enlightened
> . . . and then have *fallen away* [Gk. *parapipto*, "to fail to follow through
> on a commitment"[95]], to restore them again to repentance, since they are
> crucifying once again the Son of God to their own harm and holding him
> up to contempt. For land that has drunk the rain that often falls on it, and
> produces a crop useful to those for whose sake it is cultivated, receives a
> blessing from God. But if it bears thorns and thistles, it is *worthless* [Gk.
> *adokimos*] and near to being cursed, and its end is to be burned. (vv. 4–8)

Though we do indeed wrestle continually with a body of death in this age (cf. Rom. 7:7–25), the answer is not to give in and resign to compromise. Rather, we must continually cast our sin upon God and his sin offering (cf. Rom. 8:1–4). Though we sin against God a thousand times, he will yet forgive us, *if* we repent at a heart level (cf. Matt. 18:22; Col. 3:13). If we sin and do not repent, it will result in disqualification. Therefore, "*Examine yourselves* as to whether you are in the faith. *Test yourselves*. Do you not know yourselves, that Jesus Christ is in you?—unless indeed you are *disqualified*" (2 Cor. 13:5, NKJV). Let us continue to run the race faithfully unto the day of Christ Jesus.

THE CIRCUMCISION GROUP

It was commonly assumed in the New Testament that the openly unrepentant and disobedient would not inherit eternal life (cf. 1 Cor. 6:9; Gal. 5:21; Eph. 5:5). Less obvious, however, was the disqualification of many who were outwardly obedient and righteous yet *inwardly unrepentant*. This was the plague that consumed the Pharisaical movement (cf. Matt. 23:25–28; Luke 16:15). Those who lack inward repentance are also excluded from atonement and acquittal in the sight of God.

This plague entered into the early church, unfortunately, primarily through a distinct group called "the circumcision party" (Acts 11:2; Gal. 2:12; Titus 1:10). So Paul describes them, "For there are many rebellious people, mere talkers and deceivers, especially those of the circumcision group" (Titus 1:10, NIV). Moreover, "both their minds and their consciences are defiled" (v. 15), for though they "profess to know God," they are "detestable, disobedient, *unfit* [Gk. *adokimos*] for any good work" (v. 16). Though their good works give the outward "appearance of godliness" (2 Tim. 3:5), they are, literally, "*disqualified* with reference to any good deed."[96]

Whether referenced directly (Acts 11:2; Gal. 2:12; Eph. 2:11; Titus 1:10) or indirectly (Acts 15:5; 21:20; Rom. 2:17–29; 3:8; 16:17; Gal. 6:12; Phil. 3:2; Col. 2:11–19; 1 Tim. 1:3–7; 2 Tim. 3:5), the circumcision group was the primary human enemy of the gospel in the New Testament (the Gnostics were only a budding movement at the time). Though calling themselves followers of Christ, they were in truth "severed from Christ" (Gal. 5:4), having "lost connection with the Head" (Col. 2:19, NIV). They "belonged to the party of the Pharisees" (Acts 15:5) and demanded of Gentile believers, "Unless you are circumcised according to the custom of Moses, you cannot be saved" (Acts 15:1).[97] They were influential enough that both Peter and Barnabas were "led astray" (Gal. 2:13). Pictured in Acts 15 as a minority sect within the larger Jewish Christian church, it appears (according to Paul's descriptions) that most of them contradicted the core message of the gospel and hence were "enemies of the cross of Christ" (Phil. 3:18).

In all the debate about who the circumcision group was and what their motivations were, Galatians 6:12 gives us a clear window into their world.[98] The first part of the verse says that they were "trying to compel [believers] to be circumcised" (NIV), which could only reasonably happen within "the household of faith" (v. 10; cf. 2:12). Thus we know they were Christians, albeit "false brothers" (Gal. 2:4) led by "false apostles, deceitful workmen, disguising themselves as apostles of Christ" (2 Cor. 11:13). The first part of Galatians 6:12 also reveals their unholy motivations, as Paul refers to them as "those who want to make a *good impression outwardly*" (NIV), which parallels v. 13: "They desire to have you circumcised that they may boast in your flesh."

Such outward evidences of success are highly motivating to the unregenerate (cf. Matt. 23:15; Gal. 4:17) and fit well with Paul's other descriptions of the circumcision group: serving "their own appetites" (Rom. 16:18), preaching Christ "from envy and rivalry" (Phil. 1:15), teaching "for shameful gain" (Titus 1:11), etc.[99] The second part of Galatians 6:12—where Paul says the false teachers forced the Galatian believers to be circumcised "only in order that they may not be *persecuted* for the cross of Christ"—reveals the social dynamics between the circumcision group and unbelieving Jews. Paul's emphasis on their avoidance of persecution as the "sole" or "only" (Gk. *monon*) motivation should not be taken literally, but it should be appreciated as their defining social feature.

The circumcision group was based in Jerusalem (Gal. 2:1–12), highly connected to the party of the Pharisees (Acts 6:7; 15:5). Unlike Paul, it seems they were afraid to tell the religious leaders in Jerusalem that they were destined for Gehenna apart from faith in Christ crucified, for persecution concerning the message of the cross was an ever-present threat (cf. Acts 5:18; 8:1; 1 Thess. 2:14). The tension between Paul and the church in Jerusalem is clearly evident from passages such as Galatians 2.[100]

This tension is most clearly seen in Acts 21 when Paul and his companions arrive in Jerusalem. Being warmly received by the brothers (v. 17), they were taken to James and the elders (v. 18). After hearing Paul's account of the work of God among the Gentiles (v. 19), the elders all praised God (v. 20). Yet they warned Paul concerning the rumors assumedly spread by the circumcision group: "You see, brother, how many thousands there are among the Jews of those who have believed. They are all zealous for the law, and they have been *told about you* [assumedly by the circumcision group] that you teach all the Jews who are among the Gentiles to forsake Moses, telling them not to circumcise their children or walk according to our customs" (vv. 20–21). Paul and his companions were encouraged to engage in purification rites to prove their obedience to the law (v. 24), which they did for seven days (26).[101] However, unbelieving Jews stirred up a riot against Paul (v. 27–30), with a notable absence of a Jewish Christian presence.

The circumcision group's avoidance of persecution revolved around the "offense of the cross" (Gal. 5:11). To understand the theology behind this offense, it is useful to rehearse a few prominent ideas and address a few issues previously untouched. The offense essentially involved how we are acquitted on the day of judgment.[102] Like many unbelieving Jews, those within the circumcision group "rely on works of the law" (Gal. 3:10) for eschatological vindication, for unless you "obey the law" (Rom. 2:25) you "cannot be saved" (Acts 15:1). This heart-reliance concerning the basis of forgiveness is the crux of the contention. Those "trying to be justified *by law* have been alienated from Christ" (Gal. 5:4, NIV), "for *by works* of the law no human being will be justified in his sight" (Rom. 3:20).[103] This was Paul's battle line which created much of the offense: "For we *hold* that one is justified *by faith* apart from works of the law" (Rom. 3:28).

We know that both believing and unbelieving Jews held "the same hope" (Acts 24:15, NIV) concerning salvation (cf. Rom. 11:26; Heb. 9:28; etc.). The contention of the New Testament simply concerned the basis of attaining that hope. Everyone knew righteousness before God was the door to eternal life (cf. Ps. 24:3–5; Isa. 33:15; 56:1). But how was righteousness to be attained? Was it by faith in the sacrifice provided by God, or was it by faith in "our works" (2 Tim. 1:9)—that is, "works of righteousness" (Titus 3:5, NRSV), or "works of the law" (Rom. 3:20,28; Gal. 2:16; 3:2,5,10)?[104] Was salvation at the day of the Lord "on the basis of works" (Rom. 11:6), or was it "through faith in Jesus Christ" (Gal. 2:16)? Was it not "by Christ's physical body through death" (Col. 1:22, NIV)—that is, "through his blood" (Eph. 1:7)? Indeed, it is not "human will or exertion" which determines our destiny, but rather "God, who has mercy" (Rom. 9:16).

At the heart of the offense also lay the question of how to relate to the Mosaic law (in the narrow sense of a body of commands) in light of eschatological salvation. We know the law was designed to reveal, condemn, and discipline sin (cf. Rom. 3:20; Gal. 3:24; 1 Tim. 1:9). It was not designed, however, to establish a righteous standing before God unto the inheritance of eternal life. This was the purpose of the sacrificial system (cf. Acts 13:39; Heb. 9:13–15). So Paul asserts, "If a law had been given that could give life, then righteousness would indeed be by the law" (Gal. 3:21). Rather, the law "imprisoned everything under sin, so that the promise [of eternal life] by faith in Jesus Christ might be given to those who believe" (Gal. 3:22). Obedience to the commands of the law was never meant to be the basis of acquittal before God. Conversely, the law was given "because of transgressions" (v. 19), functioning as a "disciplinarian" (v. 24, NRSV) to curb our tendencies toward sin in this age. Thus "the law is good if one uses it properly" (1 Tim. 1:8, NIV), for it is "profitable for teaching, for reproof, for correction, and for training in righteousness" (2 Tim. 3:16).

Instead of "rightly handling the word of truth" (2 Tim. 2:15), the circumcision group (and unbelieving Jews) perverted the law, relying on it for a righteous standing before God in light of the eschatological judgment. This defies the fundamental relationship between God's mercy and human sinfulness (cf. Rom. 9:14–29). When this relationship is healthy, our "pursuit" (Gk. *diōkō*; cf. Rom. 9:30; Phil. 3:14) of righteousness is regulated and channeled toward substitute-justification (based upon sacrifice) rather than self-justification (based upon works). So Paul relates the general difference between Jew and Gentile in their pursuit of righteousness:

> What shall we say, then? That Gentiles who did not pursue righteousness have attained it, that is, a righteousness that is *by faith*; but that Israel who pursued a law that would lead to righteousness did not succeed in reaching that law. Why? Because they did not pursue it by faith, but as if it were *based on works*. (Rom. 9:30–32)

This pursuit of righteousness is clearly carried out with the ultimate goal of being "saved" (Rom. 10:1,9,10,13), since there is no indication of a break in thought between chapters 9 and 10. Paul can testify that the Jews in their pursuit of righteousness "have a zeal for God," but it is not "according to knowledge" (Rom. 10:2). "For, being ignorant of the righteousness that comes *from God*, and seeking to establish *their own*, they did not submit to God's righteousness. For Christ is the end of the law for righteousness to everyone who believes" (vv. 3–4). Here Christ as the "end" (Gk. *telos*) of the law refers simply to his sacrifice as the attained goal in humanity's pursuit of righteousness.[105]

Though the circumcision group self-identified as Christians, Paul places them in the same category as the unbelieving Jews (though maybe even worse since they claimed to have knowledge of Christ crucified). They are "false brothers" (Gal. 2:4), "deceitful workmen" (2 Cor. 11:13), "dogs" and "evildoers" (Phil. 3:2). They are "empty talkers and deceivers" (Titus 1:10), who "want to be teachers of the law, but they do not know what they are talking about or what they so confidently affirm" (1 Tim. 1:7, NIV). They "proclaim Christ out of selfish ambition" (Phil. 1:17, NRSV). They "disqualify" others from the prize, because they have an "unspiritual mind" that "delights in false humility" (Col. 2:18, NIV).[106] They have "minds set on earthly things" (Phil. 3:19), flattering with words as a "pretext for greed" (1 Thess. 2:5).[107] They are "peddlers of God's word" (2 Cor. 2:17), "teaching for shameful gain" (Titus 1:11; cf. 2 Cor. 11:20). They "practice cunning" and "tamper with God's word," employing "disgraceful, underhanded ways" (2 Cor. 4:2). They practice hypocrisy (Gal. 2:13), enslaving people (2 Cor. 11:20; Gal. 2:4), throwing them into confusion (Gal. 1:7; 5:10), and causing divisions (Rom. 16:17; 1 Tim. 1:4). Because their god is their "appetite," their future is "destruction" (Phil. 3:19, NASB).[108] Since they try to "pervert the gospel of Christ," Paul's wish is that they would be "eternally condemned" (Gal. 1:7–9, NIV). "Their end will correspond to their deeds" (2 Cor. 11:15).[109]

Such aggressive language would scarcely be tolerated, much less received, by modern hearers, but it reflects the severity of divine judgment concerning self-righteousness. Like their unbelieving Pharisaical counterparts, those of the circumcision group were ultimately concerned with exalting themselves (cf. Matt. 23:12; 2 Cor. 11:17), winning the approval of others (cf. Matt. 23:5; Gal. 4:17), and lining their pockets with money (cf. Matt. 23:25; 2 Cor. 2:17). On the day of the Lord, however, they will be "sentenced to hell" (Matt. 23:33; cf. Gal. 1:8; Phil. 3:19).

In the final analysis, there are only two groups of people: those who will inherit "eternal punishment" and those who will inherit "eternal life" (Matt. 25:46). The latter will have their names written in the book of life (Phil. 4:3; Rev. 20:12), based upon faith in the cross, while the former will be thrown into the lake of fire (Rev. 20:15), based upon unforgiven sin. For this reason, the issues become both *black and white* and *life and death.*

Thus Paul draws a sharp line between faith in Christ crucified and faith in works of the flesh—that is, substitute-righteousness versus self-righteousness (see figure 8.10). In the same vein, Paul contrasts "the one who works [for] his wages" (Rom. 4:4) with "the one who does not work but trusts him who justifies the ungodly" (v. 5). The circumcision group was the primary threat to Paul's presentation of the death of the Messiah as the necessary vicarious sacrifice for human sin. The rejection of this belief was the effective *nullification* of the grace of God, for "if justification were through the law, then Christ died for no purpose" (Gal. 2:21). So there are two groups of people associated with the name of Christ whose sin will remain at the day of the Lord: those who presume upon the sacrifice and those who set aside the sacrifice.

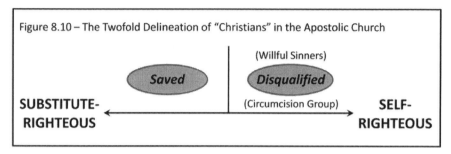

Figure 8.10 – The Twofold Delineation of "Christians" in the Apostolic Church

FAITH AND BOASTING

Because faith involves the entrusting of one's very being to another, the natural result is "boasting" (Gk. *kauchaomai, kauchēsis*).[110] Whatever you commit yourself to is the thing in which you will boast, as commonly seen in such things as knowledge, money, career, relational connections, social impact, etc. The circumcision group boasted in their righteous deeds, while Paul boasted in the cross (cf. Rom. 3:27; Gal. 6:13–14; Eph. 2:8–11). The boasting of the former was common in first-century Judaism,[111] as is evident in Jesus' parable concerning "some who trusted in themselves that they were righteous" (Luke 18:9; cf. Luke 7:41–47). The justifying of self (cf. Luke 10:29; 16:15), based upon pride (cf. Matt. 23:12; Rom. 11:17–23), is at the heart of all self-righteous boasting. The condemnation of, and condescension toward, fellow Jewish "sinners" (cf. Matt. 11:19; Mark 2:15–17; Luke 7:39; 15:2) was indicative of the culture (see especially Luke 19:7).

This self-righteous boasting—that is, becoming "arrogant" (Rom. 11:18)—resulted in the "breaking off" (vv. 17,19) of many Jews from the covenants and the hope of the resurrection. Such arrogant boasting was not limited to Jews, however, but was understood as a universal reality, common to Jew and Gentile alike. So Paul warns the Gentiles in Rome:

> But if some of the [Jewish] branches were broken off, and you [Gentiles], although a wild olive shoot, were grafted in among the others and now share in the nourishing root of the olive tree, do not *be arrogant* [Gk. *katakauchaomai*; "boast," KJV, NKJV, NRSV, NIV] toward the branches. . . . They were broken off because of their unbelief, but you stand fast through faith. So do not become *proud*, but stand in awe. For if God did not spare the natural branches, neither will he spare you. (Rom. 11:17–21)

Paul goes on to say, more or less, that redemptive history is directed by God according to the responses of pride and humility in the human heart. When the Jews repent of their arrogance toward the cross, they will be "grafted back into their own olive tree" (v. 24). Moreover, they have experienced such a "hardening" (v. 25), or "blindness" (KJV, NKJV), for the purpose of God extending mercy to the Gentiles (vv. 30–32).[112] However, such self-righteousness will indeed be reversed, "and in this way all Israel will be saved" (v. 26).

The cross inherently militates against pride and self-righteous boasting. In the eyes of the haughty, the cross represents both weakness and failure. As Paul summarized, "We preach Christ crucified, a stumbling block to Jews and folly to Gentiles" (1 Cor. 1:23). Nevertheless, it was designed by God to be this way:

> God chose what is *foolish* in the world to shame the *wise* [cf. Gentile pride]; God chose what is *weak* in the world to shame the *strong* [cf. Jewish pride]; God chose what is low and despised in the world, even things that are not, to bring to nothing things that are, so that no human being might *boast* in the presence of God. (1 Cor. 1:27–29)

Christ Jesus has become *for us* "righteousness and sanctification and redemption" (v. 30), so that the Scripture might be fulfilled, "Let the one who boasts, boast in the Lord" (v. 31, cf. Jer. 9:24). Though the circumcision group claimed to "boast in God" (Rom. 2:17), this was by vicarious reliance upon the law.[113] It was an unrighteous boasting, perverting the gift of God for self-exaltation (cf. Matt. 6:5; John 5:39). Their "boasted mission" (2 Cor. 11:12) sought to "boast about outward appearance" (2 Cor. 5:12)—that is, "boast according to the flesh" (2 Cor. 11:18; cf. Gal. 6:13). Paul saw this as contrary to the character of God and to the nature of the cross. Thus he sought to "boast of the things that show my weakness" (2 Cor. 11:30), the greatest being his gospel concerning Christ crucified. Because God revealed the path to righteousness by the cross, all boasting is "excluded" (Rom. 3:27), for if we are "justified by works," then we have "something to boast about, but not before God" (Rom. 4:2).

Hence Paul, out of a fear of God, summarized his letter to the Galatians: "Far be it from me to boast except in the cross of our Lord Jesus Christ" (6:14). Similarly, he told the Corinthians: "I decided to know nothing among you except Jesus Christ and him crucified" (1 Cor. 2:2). The relationship between Paul's theology and his cruciform boast is spelled out explicitly in his letter to the Ephesians: "For by grace you have been saved through faith. And this is not your own doing; it is the gift of God, not a result of works, so that no one may boast" (Eph. 2:8–9).[114]

Within this tension between self-righteousness and substitute-righteousness, the gift of the Holy Spirit is understood. Because the Spirit was sent to lead us into all truth (John 15:26; 16:13), so that we might inherit eternal life (1 John 2:24–27), *walking according to the Spirit in the New Testament is understood as walking according to the cross and justification by faith.* Though Paul, like the circumcision group, had "reason for confidence in the flesh" (Phil. 3:4), he sought to "worship in the Spirit of God and boast in Christ Jesus and have no confidence in the flesh" (v. 3, NRSV). Note the relationship between the Spirit, the flesh, and boasting. This is how we worship God: by casting ourselves continually upon the cross unto the day of Christ Jesus, putting no confidence in "a righteousness of my own" (v. 9). When we boast in the cross, we are walking according to the Holy Spirit, for it is assumed that the Spirit himself boasts in Christ crucified alone: "These things [concerning the cross, cf. 1 Cor. 1:18—2:5] God has revealed to us *through the Spirit.* For the Spirit searches everything, even the depths of God" (1 Cor. 2:10).

In Romans 8, Paul outlines in detail what it means to walk "according to the Spirit" (vv. 4,5). If we assume that the circumcision group are those who "set their minds on the things of the flesh" (v. 5), the message of verses 3–5 stands out clearly:

> God has done what the law, weakened by the flesh, could not do [i.e., attain righteousness before God]. By sending his own Son in the likeness of sinful flesh and for sin ["a sin offering," NIV/HCSB], he condemned sin in the flesh, in order that the righteous requirement of the law might be fulfilled in us [vicarious righteousness], who walk not *according to the flesh* [to attain righteousness] but *according to the Spirit* [to attain righteousness]. For those who live *according to the flesh* [i.e., unbelieving Jews and the circumcision group] set their minds on the things of the flesh [cf. Gal. 6:13; Phil. 3:18], but those who live *according to the Spirit* set their minds on the things of the Spirit [cf. 1 Cor. 2:12–16; Col. 3:2]. (Rom. 8:3–5)[115]

Similarly, Paul questioned the Galatians, who had been "bewitched" (Gal. 3:1) by the circumcision group (cf. 2:12): "Did you receive *the Spirit* by works of the law or by hearing with faith?" (3:2). This "hearing with faith" clearly concerned "Jesus Christ . . . publicly portrayed as crucified" (v. 1). So Paul reasons, "Having started with *the Spirit*, are you now ending with *the flesh*?" (v. 3, NRSV). Walking according to the Spirit meant faith in Christ crucified; walking according to the flesh meant reliance on "works of the law" (v. 10).[116] If we sow to the flesh, we will ultimately "reap destruction"; but if we sow to the Spirit, we will "reap eternal life" (Gal. 6:8, NIV). Let us then "fight the good fight of the faith," so as to "take hold of the eternal life to which [we] were called" (1 Tim. 6:12).[117]

CHRISTOPLATONIC RIGHTEOUSNESS

As Paul made clear, pride and self-righteousness are universal to humanity (cf. Rom. 3:9; 1 Cor. 1:23), deriving from our forefather Adam (cf. Rom. 5:12; 1 Cor. 15:21) and affecting every generation (cf. Rom. 3:23; Gal. 3:22). It was a problem for both Jew and Gentile in the first century, and it is a problem for both Jew and Gentile today. One's hope and eschatology may encourage or deter pride and self-righteousness, but the two can function somewhat independently. Many throughout history have held a highly distorted Christoplatonic hope, yet remained markedly repentant and humble. Others have held more closely to the biblical revelation when it comes to eschatology, yet reeked of self-aggrandizement (the Pharisees serving as the model).

That being said, one's view of redemptive history *inevitably affects* the response of the heart. When judgment and reward are distorted, or altogether removed from the picture, issues of righteousness are affected. Given our fallen state, we will always tend toward self-exaltation, self-justification, self-righteousness, etc. But the severity of God in the day of the Lord is meant to curb such tendencies. For example, my children may love me and generally seek to please and obey me. Yet every parent *knows* that without the ever-present persuasion of reward for good behavior and punishment for bad behavior, children will tend to run wild.

So also does the history of Christianity unfold. As the biblical view of the day of the Lord is transformed into a spiritualized, universalized, or realized eschatology, our view of both the severity and kindness of God are mitigated, and the church generally loses its spiritual fervor and focus. Both the reward of eternal life and the punishment of eternal fire are designed to awaken the human heart to the realities of righteousness, sin, and judgment. Thus self-righteousness latent in the human heart went unchecked in the early church as it progressively broke from its Jewish eschatological moorings. So Leon Morris describes,

> Even in the early church it was not long before some people began to speak of Christianity as "the new law" and to subject themselves to a legalism every bit as trying as that of which the New Testament writers complained in Judaism. And this has continued in the history of the church. Again and again it is not liberty in Christ which has characterized believers, but strict conformity to some new rule they have made or found. This may involve a rigorous asceticism or the firm conviction that the way forward is by observance of some sacramental discipline or the like. . . . Mankind has a fiendish ingenuity in discovering ways of bringing itself into bondage. Paul's words are far from being out of date.[118]

In both its monastic and Christendom expressions, Christoplatonic Christianity increasingly suffered from self-justification. Monasticism generally sought self-justification by asceticism and its corollary "righteous deeds," while Christendom self-justified its worldly power and wealth (for the glory of God, of course) based upon that age-old principle, "might is right."[119]

Over time monasticism became the dominant expression of what righteousness was understood to mean in the Western church. As it developed and spread from the Egyptian deserts to the European countryside, it began to codify its way of life. This codification took the form of a "rule,"—that is, a rule of religious life. The most influential rule was that of Saint Benedict (Latin, *Regula Benedicti*), written about 540. Radical self-discipline was the foundation of all monastic rules, unto the production of personal and corporate holiness. The stated goal of this holiness was the attaining of eternal life, as the Rule of Saint Benedict makes clear in its closing lines:

> Now, we have written this Rule that, observing it in monasteries, we may show that we have acquired at least some *moral righteousness*, or a beginning of the monastic life. . . . Thou, therefore, who hastenest to the *heavenly home*, with the help of Christ fulfil this least rule written for a beginning; and then thou shalt with God's help attain at last to the greater heights of knowledge and virtue which we have mentioned above.[120]

Throughout the Middle Ages, monasticism generally sought the attainment of moral righteousness in this life unto entrance into immaterial heaven at death. The former often rose to fever pitch, and it was against such abuses of monastic self-righteousness that the Augustinian monk Martin Luther primarily reacted.[121] After fifteen years of ardent moral pursuit, Luther found himself crushed by legalism and plagued by a guilty conscience, crying out, "How may I find a gracious God?"[122] The answer came by a "theological breakthrough" (c. 1515) concerning "the righteousness of God."[123] Luther realized that when Paul spoke of the righteousness of God (e.g., Rom. 1:7; 3:21; 10:3; Phil. 3:9) he meant "a righteousness which is *a gift from God*, rather than a righteousness *which belongs to God*."[124] The judgmental righteousness of God spoken of throughout the Scriptures (e.g., Ps. 50:6; 98:9; Isa. 5:16; 51:5) was *bad news* for the sinner, but the atonemental righteousness of God spoken of by Paul was *good news* for the sinner. Though still couched within a redemptive framework of heavenly destiny, Luther found peace with God and recovered the essential substitutional heart of the gospel (see figure 8.11). People are acquitted of their sins and saved from the wrath of God by faith in Christ's sacrifice.

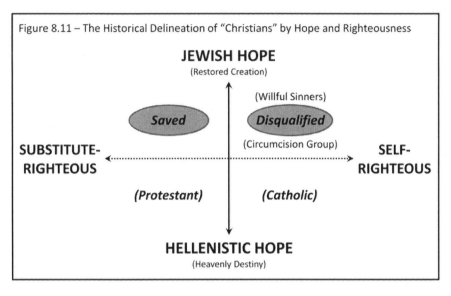

Figure 8.11 – The Historical Delineation of "Christians" by Hope and Righteousness

JEWISH HOPE
(Restored Creation)

(Willful Sinners)

Saved *Disqualified*

(Circumcision Group)

SUBSTITUTE-RIGHTEOUS

SELF-RIGHTEOUS

(Protestant) *(Catholic)*

HELLENISTIC HOPE
(Heavenly Destiny)

Of course, not all Catholics during the time of the Reformation were self-righteous, just as there were believers within Pharisaical movement during Paul's day.[125] However, the general spiritual culture of Catholicism during the time of the Reformation had clearly degenerated into a meritorious system of works-righteousness (technically faith *plus* works), which had crippled the gospel and the church's witness.[126] Within such an arid spiritual climate, Luther's theology of the cross (justification by faith *alone*) spread like wildfire, disrupting the structures of the Catholic Church and the very fabric of European society.[127]

Over time, the theology of the Reformation was codified and dogmatized many times over in various forms, providing a defined platform for Protestant missions and evangelism for the next four hundred years. As historical and archeological evidence began to mount in the early twentieth century, however, Protestants began to grapple with the Jewish background of the gospel. With the rediscovery of apocalyptic eschatology (Schweitzer, et al.) and the proposal of its "realization" at the first coming of Jesus (Dodd, et al.), the centrality of the cross began to veer.[128] As inaugurationalism (whether full or partial) came into vogue, many of the traditional categories for interpreting the cross began to be redefined.

Since Paul is the most prominent interpreter of the cross in the New Testament, this redefinition centered on his writings and came to be known as "the new perspective on Paul."[129] This so-called New Perspective (also referred to as NPP, for New Perspective on Paul) found its roots in the Jewish studies of the early twentieth century,[130] and it developed in the wake of the Holocaust.[131]

Though concerning itself with every area of theology and history, the New Perspective focused its attention on Martin Luther's supposed anachronistic misreading of Paul.[132] It is said that Paul did not have an "introspective conscience," as did Luther, characteristic of "late medieval piety and theology."[133] Instead, he had a robust conscience, fundamentally in line with his previous Pharisaical life.[134] In fact, Judaism as a whole had been misconstrued by Luther as a legalistic religion of works-righteousness, rather than as a religion of grace with provisions for sin.[135] Moreover, Paul was not primarily concerned, as was Luther, with issues of personal salvation (i.e., soteriology and eschatology), but rather he was concerned with "the place of the Gentiles in the Church" (i.e., sociology and ecclesiology).[136]

Within this framework, Paul's references to "justification by faith" are reinterpreted to answer the question, "On what grounds can Gentiles participate in the people of God in the last days?"[137] Furthermore, the "works of the law" (i.e., circumcision, Sabbath observance, and food laws) are understood to be simply Jewish "identity markers" or "ethnic badges," which kept the Gentiles excluded from the covenant community.[138] According to this view, Paul never really experienced a "conversion," as such, but was simply called as an apostle to take the gospel beyond the Jewish confines.[139] Additionally, since Paul is not primarily concerned with issues of salvation, there is no need to read into his writings a substitutional righteousness. Instead, the "righteousness of God" is simply "God's faithfulness" to his covenants, thus speaking of the qualities that God *possesses* rather than the status that he *imputes* as a gift to sinners.[140] Therefore Luther's fundamental "theological breakthrough" is overturned.

Such a radical dismissal of traditional Lutheran and Reformed theology obviously created a firestorm of controversy, drawing heavy criticism at both the academic level[141] and the popular level.[142] Though recent debate has degenerated into something of a "quagmire,"[143] one thing is for certain: The New Perspective has been greatly "overstated."[144] Some aspects of the New Perspective are helpful, but Paul's primary emphasis is soteriological, not sociological.[145] It is the vertical relationship between God and persons that dominates Paul's thinking, rather than the horizontal relationship between person and person.[146] Moreover, Judaism, like Christianity, *is* a religion of grace, yet the ideal is easily perverted in both by the same prideful self-righteousness derived from the fall.[147]

Paul clearly characterized the unbelieving Jews of his day as "arrogant" (Rom. 11:18), a condition likewise plaguing the Gentiles (cf. Rom. 1:30; 1 Cor. 4:18). Jesus too condemned many of the Jews of his day for exalting themselves (Matt. 23:12; Luke 14:11), for justifying themselves (Luke 10:29; 16:15), for acting in pretense (Matt. 23:5; Luke 20:47), and for being confident in their own righteousness (Luke 18:9). It is pride that ultimately determines our salvation—that is, our being "broken off" or "grafted in" (Rom. 11:19). And it is salvation that remains the driving question of the apostolic witness: "What must I do to be saved?" (Acts 16:30; cf. Acts 2:21,37–38; 3:19; 4:12; 10:42; 11:14; 15:1,11; 16:17; 17:31; 24:25).

The New Perspective has two major problems. First, in line with its liberal leanings, it generally rejects a sacrificial interpretation of the cross, and thus any reference to substitutional atonement is anathema. Second, it generally holds to a highly inaugurational approach to Jewish eschatology.[148] Therefore both the cross and the day of the Lord are distorted, resulting in the same old liberal conclusion: Salvation and the kingdom are established now through the church and social justice.

The New Perspective is somewhat the logical consequence of inaugurationalism; and to the degree that it is embraced, sociological and ecclesiological issues become prominent. Thus extreme inaugurationalism produces extremely sociologically oriented interpretations.[149] Since the majority of Paul's discussion concerning the cross takes place in an eschatological context, those who embrace the realization of eschatology in this age logically place Paul's thought in the context of ecclesiology in this age.[150] Those who hold more closely to a future realization/judgment tend to interpret Paul's thought along more traditional lines (see figure 8.12).[151]

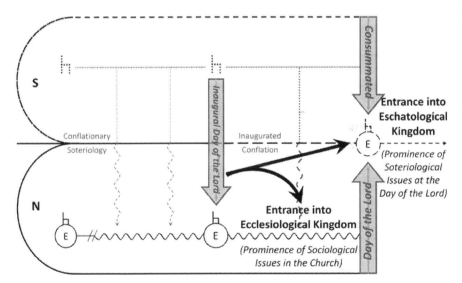

Figure 8.12 – The Inaugurational Framework behind the New Perspective

Though Luther's theology lacked an apocalyptic framework for redemptive history, culminating in the day of the Lord and the resurrection of the body, his fundamental "theological breakthrough" of substitutional righteousness based upon sacrificial atonement remains sound.[152] On the last day when God opens the books of history and charges each and every human being with the crimes they committed while in the body, only those whose names are written in the book of life (by faith in the God's sacrifice on their behalf) will be acquitted. Those without faith in Christ crucified will bear their own sin, and thus they will be thrown into the lake of fire. Then the acquitted will inherit eternal life and will be rewarded according to their righteous deeds. But all of the righteous deeds of the guilty will be for naught, since they will be disqualified.

Chapter Nine

❀

THE WITNESS
OF THE CHURCH

The explanation of the death of the Messiah as a sacrifice for the forgive-ness of sins in light of eschatological judgment certainly predominated the forty days of apostolic teaching (Acts 1:3; cf. Luke 24:45–51). At the end of this time, the apostles asked about the close of this age and the res-toration of the kingdom to Israel (Acts 1:6). Jesus confirmed the Father's set time for the coming of the kingdom (v. 7) but then he commissioned them to the task of this age: "You will be *my witnesses* in Jerusalem and in all Judea and Samaria, and to the end of the earth" (v. 8). The apostolic church consistently understood itself in terms of its commission to "testify" and "bear witness" (Gk. *marturia, martureō*).[1]

Our concern lies in the content of this commission. What does it mean to be a witness? To what are we testifying? What is involved in this testimony? And more importantly, what is *not* involved? These are the questions that have stirred diligent disciples of Jesus throughout the history of the church.

The clearest reference and explanation of Jesus' commission in Acts 1:8 is given by Peter when he addresses Cornelius:

> You know the *message* God sent to the people of Israel, telling the *good news* of peace through Jesus Christ, who is Lord of all. . . . He was not seen by all the people, but by *witnesses* whom God had already chosen—by us who ate and drank with him after he rose from the dead. He commanded us to preach to the people and to *testify* that he is the one whom God appointed as *judge of the living and the dead*. All the prophets testify about him that everyone who believes in him receives *forgiveness of sins* through his name. (Acts 10:36–43, NIV)

273

This passage clarifies the basic twofold purpose of the church's witness in this age: 1) testimony of the coming judgment by Jesus, and 2) testimony of the means of forgiveness through Jesus. This is how Peter summarizes "the message"—that is, "the good news of peace through Jesus Christ, who is Lord of all" (v. 36). God has given Jesus all authority and power to judge the earth at the day of the Lord, and God has ordained the sacrificial death of Jesus as the means of escaping divine judgment at the day of the Lord. These two events—the first coming and the second coming of the Messiah—are the two primary elements of the apostolic witness.

These two events are also inherent in the accounts of Jesus' commission found in the Gospels (Mt. 28:18–20; Mk. 16:15–16; Lk. 24:46–49). Before the ascension, Matthew records,

> Jesus came and said to them, "*All authority* in heaven and on earth has been given to me. Go therefore and make disciples of all nations, *baptizing* them in the name of the Father and of the Son and of the Holy Spirit, teaching them to observe all that I have commanded you. And behold, I am with you always, to the end of the age." (28:18–20)

Jesus' declaration of being endowed with all authority references the day of judgment, while the command to baptize and make disciples references the forgiveness and cleansing of sins, which is to be carried until the end of this age.[2]

The Gospel of Mark likewise concludes: "Go into all the world and proclaim the gospel to the whole creation. Whoever believes and is *baptized* will be *saved*, but whoever does not believe will be *condemned*" (16:15–16).[3] Again, baptism was understood in light of the purification rites of the law, and the day of the Lord would have been the assumed context for salvation and condemnation.

So also Jesus declares in Luke, "Thus it is written, that the Christ should suffer and on the third day rise from the dead, and that repentance and *forgiveness of sins* should be proclaimed in his name to all nations, beginning from Jerusalem. You are *witnesses* of these things" (24:46–48). The sufferings of Christ and the witness to the nations were understood in light of the redemption of Israel (v. 21) and the glory to come (v. 26).

When we consider the apostolic witness as a whole, therefore, its emphasis is generally upon both the cross and the day of the Lord. It can be characterized broadly as both *cruciform* and *apocalyptic*. This twofold focus on the first and second comings of the Messiah is also based upon a *creational* understanding. God created the heavens and the earth without sin and death, while Adam and his progeny are to blame for its fallen state. Via the cross God has worked for our reconciliation, which he will consummate when he makes a new heavens and new earth (cf. Rom. 5; 1 Cor. 15; 2 Peter 3).

Moreover, this universal restoration assumes a *covenantal* framework. Both this age and the age to come are Israelocentric in their administration of the grace of God (cf. Rom. 1:16; 2:9; 3:5; 9:4–5). The covenants with the Jewish forbearers (Abraham, Moses, David, etc.) will never be revoked (Rom. 11:11–29), and the kingdom will indeed be restored to Israel (Luke 24:21–26; Acts 1:6–8). Concerning these things, God gave the gift of the Holy Spirit to confirm his message (cf. Acts 2:33; 3:16; 4:30; etc.). Thus the apostolic witness is inherently *charismatic*. Without the active working of the Spirit of God, the church's proclamation lacks substantive confirmation. So we see the characteristic elements of the apostolic witness: creational, covenantal, cruciform, charismatic, and apocalyptic (see figure 9.1).[4]

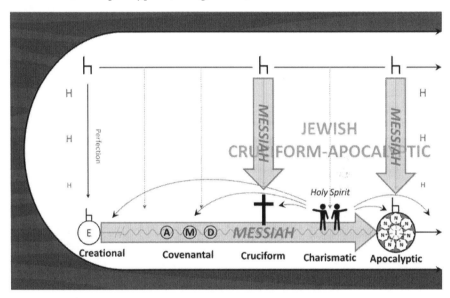

Figure 9.1 – The Characteristic Elements of the Apostolic Witness

The apostles held these elements together organically and holistically. Though involving infinite depth and mystery, they were easily apprehended by even the least educated. Hence the apostolic witness bears no resemblance to the abstract speculations of the Gnostics (1 Tim. 6:20) or the endless arguings of the philosophers (Acts 17:21). Rather, in light of the judgment to come (Acts 2:35; 10:42; 17:31; 24:25), the thrust of their message was ardently moral: "Repent!" (Acts 2:38; 3:19; 5:31; 11:18; 17:30; 20:21; 26:20). Those who repent of their sins and believe in Christ crucified will be saved from the wrath to come and will be rewarded in the resurrection in accordance with their deeds. Those who reject the message of Christ crucified will find their names blotted out of the book of life, and all their righteous deeds will be forfeited.

Unfortunately, throughout the history of the church various movements and traditions have distorted and/or failed to hold together the primary elements of the apostolic witness. We trace such distortions to their Christoplatonic root. Rather than a simple historical witness from creation to consummation, the Christoplatonic witness tends to become metaphysical in nature—that is, a testimony concerning *the interplay between the material and immaterial.* The escapist witness etherealizes into "five principles" of this, or "three keys" to that—a particularizing of ideals before death and our release from the tyranny of the body. Conversely, the dominionist witness degenerates the historical narrative into types and prefigurations of manifest sovereignty, unto the gratification of a temporal inheritance (see figure 9.2).[5]

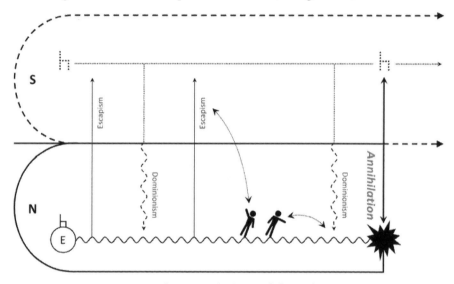

Figure 9.2 – The Distorted Witness of Christoplatonism

Instead, the biblical witness shows us how we come to know God—not by the gnostic revelation of an esoteric circle (whether cultic or academic), nor by the arm of the flesh in amassing power and wealth in the name of God. We come to know God, rather, simply by hearing and believing in his historical acts which culminate on his day. Paul demonstrates this most clearly when preaching to the pagans in Athens who worshiped an "unknown god" (Acts 17:23). That which is unknown Paul makes known by proclaiming creation (v. 24), Gentile history (vv. 25–28), Gentile depravity (v. 29), divine mercy (v. 30), and eschatological judgment (v. 31). Every recorded apostolic proclamation assumes such a timeline (cf. Acts 2:17–36; 3:17–26; 4:24–30; 5:30–32; 7:2–53; 10:34–43; 13:16–41,46–48; 14:15–17; 15:7–11; 16:31; 17:3; 20:25–35; 24:14–15,25; 26:19–23). In regard to this timeline, with its beginning, middle, and end points (creation, covenants, cross, and consummation), the apostles repeatedly declared, "We are witnesses" (Acts 2:32; 3:15; 5:32; 10:39).

THE FAITHFUL VERSUS
FALSE WITNESS

Though being a witness involves the straightforward proclamation of historical facts and events, there is an underlying and assumed legal reality, which is based upon the Old Testament and the common secular usage of "witness/ testimony."[6] Before the pronouncement of a verdict, human trials demanded the testimony of two or three witnesses (Num. 35:30; Deut. 17:6; 19:15), a practice assumed throughout the New Testament (Matt. 18:16; John 8:17; 2 Cor. 13:1; 1 Tim. 5:19; Heb. 10:28). When a second witness was unavailable, other things were used—for example, seven lambs (Gen. 21:30), a heap of stones (Gen. 31:48), or God himself (Gen. 31:50; cf. 1 Sam. 20:12). God used a song (Deut. 31:19) and the Book of the Law (Deut. 31:26) to testify against the deeds of Israel. Likewise, he called the heavens and the earth as witnesses against them (Deut. 4:26; 30:19; 31:28). And God himself often testified against their sin (cf. Jer. 29:23; 42:5; Mic. 1:2; Mal. 2:14; 3:5). Similarly, Israel was called to be a witness against the idolatry of the nations (Isa. 43:10; 44:8), and so also the prophetic tradition took up the theme of being a witness on behalf of God (cf. Isa. 6:8; Jer. 1:7; Ezek. 2:3).[7]

> The LORD, the God of their fathers, sent word to them *through his messengers* again and again, because he had pity on his people and on his dwelling place. But they mocked *God's messengers*, despised his words and scoffed at his prophets until the wrath of the LORD was aroused against his people and there was no remedy. (2 Chron. 36:15–16, NIV)

So the word of the Lord came to the prophets again and again as a testimony concerning sin, righteousness, and divine judgment (cf. Isa. 1:1ff.; Jer. 2:1ff.; Ezek. 7:1ff.). Similarly, the word of the Lord came to John the Baptist calling Israel to repentance in light of the wrath to come (Luke 3:2–9), a theme often reiterated by Jesus (cf. Matt. 4:17; 11:20; 23:13) and summarized as "bearing witness" (cf. John 1:7; 3:11,32; 5:36; 8:14; 18:37).[8] The whole of their ministries was understood as a witness bringing forth *testimonial evidence* within the greater narrative of God's eschatological lawsuit.

On the last day, not only the words of Jesus and the prophets will bear witness (John 12:48). Moses himself will bear witness (John 5:45); careless words will bear witness (Matt. 12:36–37; cf. Luke 19:22); dust shaken in protest will bear witness (Luke 9:5; cf. Matt. 10:14–15); one's own conscience (Rom.

2:15–16) and judgmental pronouncements (Matt. 7:2) will bear witness; the blood of the righteous will bear witness (Matt. 23:35–36); even the people of Nineveh and the queen of the South will bear witness (Matt. 12:41–42). And the acquitted will inherit eternal life, while the guilty will be "sentenced to hell" (Matt. 23:33). On the day of judgment, those who are forgiven will be eternally vindicated, while those who remain guilty will be eternally condemned, *substantiated* by the testimony of multiple witnesses. God is building his case, so to speak, for the eschatological verdict, since such a "condemnation" (Gk. *krima, krinō*) assumes a law-court context (cf. Luke 24:20; Rom. 5:16).[9]

Thus Jesus is the ultimate and "faithful witness" (Rev. 1:5)—that is, "the faithful and true witness" (Rev. 3:14)—concerning the righteousness of God, the depravity of humanity, the coming judgment, eternal life, etc. "For this purpose I was born and for this purpose I have come into the world—to *bear witness* to the truth" (John 18:37). The antithesis of the faithful and true witness, however, is the *false witness* who gives untrue and inaccurate testimony (cf. Matt. 26:60) based upon unrighteous motivations (cf. Matt. 15:19). According to the Old Testament, false witnesses destroyed the integrity of the law (cf. Ex. 23:1–7; Deut. 19:16–21), and false prophets spoke lies that deluded their hearers (cf. Isa. 9:15–16; Jer. 14:14; 23:14; Ezek. 22:28).

God has appointed Jesus as Judge in the eschatological lawsuit against humanity, and Jesus has called his disciples to testify as true witnesses in anticipation of that day—"He commanded us to preach to the people and to *testify* that he is the one appointed by God to be *judge* of the living and the dead" (Acts 10:42). So Allison A. Trites incisively summarizes, "Jesus has a lawsuit with the world. His witnesses include John the Baptist, the Scriptures, the words and works of Christ, and later the witness of the apostles and the Holy Spirit."[10]

The dichotomy between true and false witnesses in the New Testament is stark. Not only are there some who pervert the reality of the judgment to come—that is, the Gnostics (cf. 1 Cor. 15:12; 2 Thess. 2:2; 1 Tim. 6:20; 2 Tim. 2:18), but there are also some who pervert the means of forgiveness in the judgment to come—that is, the circumcision group (cf. Acts 11:2; Gal. 2:12; Eph. 2:11; Titus 1:10). The former say the day of the Lord and the resurrection have already been realized. The latter set aside the grace of God by boasting in the flesh. *Both are equally false witnesses because they delude their hearers concerning the reality of who God is, who we are, and how the future will play out.*[11] The apostolic message radically condemns all forms of false witness (cf. Gal. 1:8; 2 Tim. 2:16–19; 2 Peter 2:1; 1 John 4:1), because the eternal destiny of human beings is at stake—"Knowing the fear of the Lord, we persuade others" (2 Cor. 5:11).

Therefore, the apostolic witness is received as "the testimony of God" (1 Cor. 2:1)—that is, "the testimony about Christ" (1 Cor. 1:6) or "the testimony about our Lord" (2 Tim. 1:8). Note the common theme of "*testifying* to the kingdom of God" (Acts 28:23), "*testifying* to the gospel of God's grace" (Acts 20:24, NIV), "*testifying* . . . that the Christ was Jesus" (Acts 18:5), "giving their *testimony* to the resurrection of the Lord Jesus" (Acts 4:33), etc. So Paul summarized the purpose of his calling:

> This is good, and pleases God our Savior, who wants all men to be saved and to come to a knowledge of the *truth*. For there is one God and one mediator between God and men, the man Christ Jesus, who gave himself as a ransom for all men—the *testimony* given in its proper time. And for this purpose I was appointed a herald and an apostle—I am telling the truth, I am not lying—and a teacher of the true faith to the Gentiles. (1 Tim. 2:3–7, NIV)

Here again we see "the truth" comprised of a few elements in the context of a simple redemptive timeline: the holiness of God, the depravity of humanity, salvation from the wrath to come, and the atonement of the cross (note 1 Tim. 1:15–17).[12] These elements in proper relation (chronological and apocalyptic) comprise "the testimony" heralded by the true and faithful apostolic witness—"I am telling the *truth*, I am not *lying*."

Similarly, Paul exhorts Timothy: "I charge you in the presence of God and of Christ Jesus, who is to judge the living and the dead, and by his appearing and his kingdom: *preach the word*; be ready in season and out of season; reprove, rebuke, and exhort, with complete patience and teaching" (2 Tim. 4:1–2). This charge is then followed by a warning concerning the temptations of the false witness: "For the time is coming when people will not endure *sound teaching*, but having itching ears they will accumulate for themselves teachers to suit their own passions, and will turn away from listening to the *truth* and wander off into *myths*" (vv. 3–4). The "truth" and "sound teaching" are here equated with a patient and zealous witness to the coming kingdom and salvation from its judgment (cf. also 2 Tim. 2:10; 3:15). The false witness negates both for the sake of ungodly ambition and desire.

The conflict between the true and false witness will culminate at the end of the age when God's restraint of human wickedness is removed (cf. Zech. 5:8; 2 Thess. 2:7). The Antichrist will come forth (Dan. 7:20; 2 Thess. 2:3), and the testimony of God's holiness, humanity's sin, coming judgment, and present mercy will come to a climax.[13] Though the divine testimony will be clearer and louder than at any other point in human history, people still will not repent of their wickedness (Rev. 9:20; 16:9–11). Thus God will finish building his case against the progeny of Adam, which will then be presented before all on the last day.

The eschatological climax of the divine witness spoken through his saints and prophets is outlined in the Olivet Discourse (esp. Matt. 24:9–14 and parallels). In accord with Daniel 7:21–25, the saints will be handed over and "hated by all nations" (Matt. 24:9). The ultimate reason for this persecution, however, will be "to *bear witness* before them" (Mark 13:9) so that "this gospel of the kingdom will be proclaimed throughout the whole world as a *testimony* to all nations, and then the end will come" (Matt. 24:14). Though commonly interpreted as a positive testimony,[14] context suggests that this gospel is an *indictment* upon the "all nations" (v. 9) who are hating and persecuting the saints.[15] Akin to John the Baptist's preaching of "the gospel" (Luke 3:18, NASB), the proclamation of the kingdom of God is often characterized by the punishment of the wicked (cf. Matt. 13:42; 1 Cor. 15:24; Rev. 11:15–18), which of course is good news to the poor, broken, and persecuted (cf. Matt. 5:10; Luke 6:20; 2 Thess. 1:5; James 2:5).

This indicting witness is expounded upon throughout the book of Revelation, which is meant to be viewed as "the revelation of Jesus Christ" (1:1) given to his servant John, "who bore witness to the word of God and to the testimony of Jesus Christ" (1:2).[16] The book of Revelation accords with a predominantly negative interpretation of Matthew 24:9–14. The testimony of the saints, accompanied by divine temporal judgments, will escalate in anticipation of the day of the Lord. Hence the persecution and martyrdom of the saints is one of the dominant themes of the book (cf. 2:9,13; 3:9; 6:9; 7:14; 11:7,18; 12:11,17; 13:7; 14:12,16; 15:2; 16:6; 17:6; 18:20; 19:2; 20:4).

The multitude of martyrs "who come out of the great tribulation" (7:14, NASB) are those "who had been slain for the word of God and for the *witness* they had borne" (6:9). The "two witnesses" (11:3) typify the church as a whole, for "when they have finished their *testimony*, the beast that rises from the bottomless pit will make war on them and conquer them and kill them" (11:7). Indeed the dragon makes war "on those who keep the commandments of God and hold to the *testimony* of Jesus" (12:17). Yet "they have conquered him by the blood of the Lamb and by the word of their *testimony*, for they loved not their lives even unto death" (12:11). Like Antipas, who died as a "faithful witness" (2:13), the church is called to testify with "patient endurance" (1:9; cf. 2:2,19; 3:10; 13:10; 14:12). Those who are killed "for the *testimony* of Jesus and for the word of God" (20:4)—even all who suffer "on account of the word of God and the *testimony* of Jesus" (1:9)—will receive their reward in the age to come. Thus God will conclude his case against humanity by speaking through his saints and prophets, "who hold to the *testimony* of Jesus" (19:10). "For the essence of prophecy is to give a clear *witness* for Jesus" (19:10, NLT). This is the witness that Jesus initiated (Acts 1:8), and when it is finished he will descend from heaven and judge the earth.

THE WITNESS OF THE CHURCH
IN WORD AND DEED

Though God seeks to warn the world of impending judgment, his ultimate desire is to communicate his love for mankind (cf. John 3:16; Rom. 5:8; Eph. 2:4). The true testimony of the church always involves the judgment of God and the love of God—that is, "the kindness and the severity of God" (Rom. 11:22). But in order to be understood rightly these must be placed on the timeline of redemptive history, typified in the cross and the day of the Lord. Otherwise they become theological jargon, detached from reality and irrelevant to human experience. God actually showed mercy to human beings in the cross in order to save them from the wrath and judgment due them on the day of the Lord.

The apostolic church consecrated itself wholeheartedly to this simple witness. Many liberals and academicians view such evangelical zeal as naïve—and indeed the apostolic witness was markedly unsophisticated. As Jesus said, though, "Wisdom is justified by her deeds" (Matt. 11:19). Of course when Jesus said this he had in mind "the day of judgment" (v. 22), and it is precisely this evangelical conviction that drove the apostolic church: *That which will matter most on the day of judgment is the salvation of human beings from the wrath of God through faith in the cross.* To this end God has commissioned the church (cf. Acts 10:42–43; 1 Tim. 1:15–16; 2 Peter 3:9), and those who reject such a commission reject God and the totality of his purpose for this age.

The primary means of this evangelical witness is the proclamation of truth by *words*. This is seen throughout the Gospels and the book of Acts. The spoken word is presumed to be the principal medium by which individuals are informed of redemptive history.[17] Therefore, after relating to the salvation of his own people, the people of Israel, in Romans 10:1–13, Paul questions, "But how are they to call on him in whom they have not believed? And how are they to believe in him of whom they have never heard? And how are they to hear without someone *preaching*? And how are they to preach unless they are sent? As it is written, 'How beautiful are the feet of those who preach the good news!'" (vv. 14–15).

The engine behind the apostolic witness was public preaching and teaching.[18] As seen in other movements throughout history—the Irish *peregrini*, the Franciscan mendicants, the Wesleyan revivalists, etc.—the Word of God bears upon societal consciousness by sustained, zealous public proclamation.[19]

Paul fully consecrated his life to this end, likening his life to an athletic race (cf. 1 Cor. 9:24–27) and seeking to "become all things to all people, that by all means I might save some" (v. 22). Paul's apostleship was inherently tied to preaching (cf. Acts 26:16–18; 1 Tim. 2:7; 2 Tim. 1:11), so that rejection of the latter implied rejection of the former: "Woe to me if I do not preach the gospel!" (1 Cor. 9:16). Thus his apostolic calling was to be "set apart for the gospel of God" (Rom. 1:1), which involved his wholehearted service "in preaching the gospel of his Son" (v. 9, NIV). Paul's ministry reflects the heart of the apostolic church, signified in Peter and John's declaration, "We cannot but *speak* of what we have seen and heard" (Acts 4:20).

To empower the ministry of public proclamation God promised "the gift" (Acts 1:4) of the Holy Spirit: "You will receive power when the Holy Spirit has come upon you, and you will be my witnesses" (v. 8). The relationship between preaching and the Holy Spirit is most evident in Jesus' commission recorded in Luke:

> This is what is written: The Christ will suffer and rise from the dead on the third day, and repentance and forgiveness of sins will be *preached* in his name to all nations, beginning at Jerusalem. You are *witnesses* of these things. I am going to send you what my Father has promised; but stay in the city until you have been clothed with *power* from on high. (24:46–49, NIV)

The event of Pentecost was then understood as the divine seal upon the public proclamation of Christ crucified, symbolically represented in the loosing of the tongue for divine utterance (Acts 2:4) and tangibly represented in Peter's proclamation of repentance and forgiveness in light of the day of the Lord (Acts 2:17–40). So the early church prayed, "Grant to your servants to continue to *speak* your word with all boldness" (Acts 4:29). And so God answered: "When they had prayed, the place in which they were gathered together was shaken, and they were all filled with the Holy Spirit and continued to *speak* the word of God with boldness (Acts 4:31). Put simply, the Holy Spirit is given to embolden the proclamation of the gospel, a pattern seen throughout the book of Acts (cf. 4:13; 9:27; 13:46; 14:3; 18:26; 19:8; 26:26; 28:31).

Unfortunately, the misuse of the gift of the Holy Spirit for purposes other than the proclamation of the gospel is a universal phenomenon. As often found in modern charismatic and Pentecostal movements, the apostolic church encountered gross perversions of the gifts of the Holy Spirit. Simon sought to buy the gift with money (Acts 8:20). Itinerant Jewish exorcists tried to cast out demons in Jesus' name (Acts 19:13–14). Some in the circumcision group boasted of angelic visitations (Gal. 1:8; Col. 2:18). Others preached the gospel out of selfish ambition (Phil. 1:15–17), peddling the word of God for profit (2 Cor. 2:17). And it was not uncommon for miracles to be used for selfish ends (cf. Matt. 7:22; 1 Cor. 13:2). This is the very point of the *false prophet* (cf. Deut. 13:1–5)—his miracles are real, yet in the end they lead to destruction (cf. Matt. 24:24; 2 Thess. 2:9).

Thus the words of the gospel, even right words anointed by the Holy Spirit, must be *substantiated and demonstrated* by righteous deeds produced by righteous intentions. Those who proclaim the hope of the age to come must actually live for the age to come. Believers are repeatedly exhorted to "walk in a manner worthy of the calling to which you have been called" (Eph. 4:1; cf. Phil. 1:27; Col. 1:10; 1 Thess. 2:12). If we proclaim that the saints will rule the earth in the age to come, then what happens when unbelievers see us squabbling over the trivial things of this age (cf. 1 Cor. 6:1–6)? When we proclaim that the age to come will be full of righteousness, peace, and love, and yet we tear one another down with our words, then we "grieve the Holy Spirit of God, by whom [we] were sealed for the day of redemption" (Eph. 4:30). When we tell people that Jesus is the Messiah—that "God has highly exalted him and bestowed on him the name that is above every name" (Phil. 2:9)—and yet we follow after human personalities (cf. 1 Cor. 1:12; 3:4), what becomes of our witness? When we condemn greed yet show favoritism to the rich, we deceive ourselves (James 1:22), for "has not God chosen those who are poor in the world to be rich in faith and heirs of the kingdom, which he has promised to those who love him?" (James 2:5). Those who say they live for the age to come yet truly live for this age "bring the way of truth into disrepute" (2 Peter 2:2, NIV). They will be assigned a place with the unbelievers (Luke 12:46) and the hypocrites (Matt. 24:51).

Similarly, those who proclaim the cross must actually live out the cross. To preach the cross without actually taking up your cross (cf. Luke 9:23 and parallels) results in the message of the cross being "emptied of its power" (1 Cor. 1:17).[20] Those who say they follow Christ crucified yet lord it over those they lead (Luke 22:25; cf. 1 Peter 5:3), masquerading as kings (1 Cor. 4:8), will be "revealed" by fire, "for the Day will disclose it" (1 Cor. 3:13). What becomes of the message of the cross if we set aside the grace of God (Gal. 2:21) and impose a harsh asceticism on others (Col. 2:16–23)? Instead of "one beggar telling another beggar where to find bread,"[21] we become bankers passing by beggars, scolding them for their lack of a work ethic. Rather, our words must be demonstrated by our lives.[22] In this way the church witnesses to Christ Jesus, concerning both his first and second coming, by word and deed.

THE WITNESS OF THE CHURCH TYPIFIED IN MARTYRDOM

One of the defining features of the early church was its embracing of martyrdom.[23] According to tradition, all of the apostles, except John, were martyred.[24] As Tertullian is known for saying, "The blood of Christians is the seed of the

Church."[25] Even unbelievers recognize the centrality of martyrdom in the rise of early Christianity, for in it "a person sets the highest imaginable value upon a religion and communicates that value to others."[26] This is not the biblical reasoning behind martyrdom, though.

The Greek terms for "martyr" and "witness" are one and the same (Gk. *martus*). The martyr is simply one who *witnesses unto death*. Jesus' commissioning of his disciples as "witnesses" (Acts 1:8) would have thus carried the edge of death, especially in light of his previous statements concerning martyrdom: "If anyone would come after me, let him deny himself and take up his *cross* and follow me" (Matt. 16:24; cf. Mark 8:34; Luke 9:23). And even more categorically: "Whoever does not bear his own *cross* and come after me cannot be my disciple" (Luke 14:27).

Unfortunately, at a popular level the "cross" has come to mean anything unpleasant in a believer's life.[27] Jesus' hearers, however, would have understood the cross to refer to crucifixion, the Roman means of execution—which in the post-Maccabean era signified Jewish revolt and *martyrdom*.[28] Jesus' call to take up the cross is a simple and bald command to embrace martyrdom.[29] Accordingly it follows: "Whoever would save his life will lose it, but whoever loses his life for my sake will find it" (Matt. 16:25).

This call to martyrdom is seen throughout Jesus' ministry. He taught his disciples that the suffering of the prophets—which included martyrdom—was an example to be followed (Matt. 5:12; Luke 6:23). The prophets had been beaten and stoned (cf. Matt. 21:35 and parallels). They had been mistreated and killed (Matt. 22:6). They had been rejected and murdered (Matt. 23:31,37). And all of this for the witness they maintained (cf. Luke 11:49; Acts 7:52).

Likewise, Jesus repeatedly told his disciples that he would suffer persecution and be killed (Mark 8:31; 9:12,31; 10:33). He accepted a bloody "cup" and a "baptism" of death (Mark 10:38; Luke 12:50), which in turn he extended to his disciples: "The cup that I drink you will drink, and with the baptism with which I am baptized, you will be baptized" (Mark 10:39). Thus he sent his disciples out to preach "as sheep in the midst of wolves" (Matt. 10:16), warning them,

> A disciple is not above his teacher, nor a servant above his master. It is enough for the disciple to be *like his teacher*, and the servant *like his master*. If they have called the master of the house Beelzebul, how much more will they malign those of his household. . . .
>
> Do not fear those who *kill the body* but cannot kill the soul. Rather fear him who can destroy both soul and body in hell. . . .
>
> Whoever does not *take his cross* and follow me is not worthy of me. Whoever finds his life will lose it, and whoever *loses his life* for my sake will find it. (Matt. 10:24–25,28,38–39)

Martyrdom was the clear implication of what it meant to be a follower and witness of Jesus.[30] Those who want to be "like their teacher" will relinquish their life in this age, while those who seek to keep their life will lose it in the resurrection. So Jesus made clear elsewhere:

> Truly, truly, I say to you, unless a grain of wheat falls into the earth and *dies*, it remains alone; but if it *dies*, it bears much fruit. Whoever loves his life loses it, and whoever *hates his life* in this world will keep it for eternal life. If anyone serves me, he must *follow me*; and where I am, there will my servant be also. If anyone serves me, the Father will honor him. (John 12:24–26)

In this way Jesus equates service to God with hating life in this age and being led unto martyrdom—these the Father will honor with eternal life.

Hence the relationship between witnessing and martyrdom is simply this: Those who would follow Jesus and proclaim him as judge of the living and the dead must be prepared to die for their faith. Not all will die as martyrs, of course, but *all must embrace martyrdom at a heart level.*[31] This is the "cost" of being a disciple (cf. Luke 14:25–35). The completion of the tower (v. 28) and the winning of the war (v. 31) are analogous to the inheriting of eternal life (cf. vv. 14–24). Unless you "count the cost" (v. 28) on the front end, you will fail to accomplish your goal. The cost of eternal life is bearing the cross (v. 27), which is then interpreted, "Any one of you who does not renounce all that he has cannot be my disciple" (v. 33). At the heart of all Christian discipleship lies this forsaking of all for the sake of following and witnessing to Jesus unto death.

At this point it should be clear that Jesus called his disciples to martyrdom. But why? Did Jesus simply seek to test the fidelity of his followers? Or was there a greater meaning to be conveyed through martyrdom? The Maccabees had bravely faced martyrdom, seeking "to die nobly" (2 Maccabees 7:5, NRSV)—but unto what? A cursory reading reveals the message being conveyed: God hates his enemies and will vindicate the righteous by punishing them eternally:

> And when he [the second son] was at his last breath, he said, "You accursed wretch, you dismiss us from this present life, but the King of the universe will raise us up to an everlasting renewal of life, because we have died for his laws." (2 Maccabees 7:9, NRSV)

> When he [the fourth son] was near death, he said, "One cannot but choose to die at the hands of mortals and to cherish the hope God gives of being raised again by him. But for you there will be no resurrection to life!" (2 Maccabees 7:14, NRSV)

But he [the fifth son] looked at the king, and said, "Because you have authority among mortals, though you also are mortal, you do what you please. . . . Keep on, and see how his mighty power will torture you and your descendants!" (2 Maccabees 7:16–17, NRSV)

And when he [the sixth son] was about to die, he said, "Do not deceive yourself in vain. . . . Do not think that you will go unpunished for having tried to fight against God!" (2 Maccabees 7:18–19, NRSV)

The young man [the seventh son] said, "What are you waiting for? . . . But you, unholy wretch, you most defiled of all mortals, do not be elated in vain and puffed up by uncertain hopes, when you raise your hand against the children of heaven. You have not yet escaped the judgment of the almighty, all-seeing God. For our brothers after enduring a brief suffering have drunk of ever-flowing life, under God's covenant; but you, by the judgment of God, will receive just punishment for your arrogance. (2 Maccabees 7:30,34–36, NRSV)

Indeed such a message is true. It is spoken throughout the New Testament (cf. Matt. 25:31–46; Rom. 2:5–11; 2 Thess. 1:6–10; 2 Peter 2:9), and it is a valid motivation for martyrdom in itself.[32] The cause of justice, however, is not what Jesus ultimately wanted to communicate through his own martyrdom and that of his disciples. Jesus' martyrdom was meant to convey *the love and mercy of God toward his enemies.* Thus Jesus, in marked contrast to the Maccabees, prayed before his death: "Father, *forgive them*, for they know not what they do" (Luke 23:34).

In line with his teaching concerning the enemies of God—for example, "Love your enemies and pray for those who persecute you" (Matt. 5:44), and "Bless those who curse you, pray for those who abuse you" (Luke 6:28)—Jesus did not seek to call down fire from heaven (Luke 9:54), nor did he call upon the twelve legions of angels at his disposal (Matt. 26:53). Rather, "When he was reviled, he did not revile in return; when he suffered, he did not threaten, but continued entrusting himself to him who judges justly" (1 Peter 2:23). All of this was done to demonstrate his love for the world (Eph. 2:4–7), his kindness toward sinners (Rom. 5:8–11), and his mercy to his enemies (Col. 1:20–22).

The call to be "like his master" (Matt. 10:25) was taken up by Stephen, the first Christian "martyr" (Acts 22:20, NIV). When facing death, he mimicked his Lord: "Falling to his knees he cried out with a loud voice, 'Lord, do not hold this sin against them'" (Acts 7:60). This heart to see the forgiveness and salvation of the enemies of God sets Christian martyrdom apart from every other kind of martyrdom. It is death *for the sake of love* that makes a disciple like Jesus. Without love martyrdom is worthless, as Paul makes clear: "If I deliver up my body to be burned, but have not love, I gain nothing" (1 Cor. 13:3). Therefore martyrdom is only Christian if it communicates the love and mercy of God.

God has chosen martyrdom as the ultimate means of demonstrating his love. "For God so loved the world, that *he gave* his only Son" (John 3:16). God has ordained voluntary self-sacrifice for the sake of others as the greatest proof of divine intentions. "God *proves his love* for us in that while we still were sinners Christ died for us" (Rom. 5:8, NRSV). There is no greater vehicle for such communication. "Greater love has no one than this, that someone *lay down his life* for his friends" (John 15:13; cf. 10:11). Because of the character of God, this is how he has chosen to make himself known (cf. 1 John 3:16; 4:8–10). Those who have not embraced the cross simply do not know God, and they cannot make him known.

For this reason Jesus commissioned his disciples as "martyr-witnesses." They were sent for the same purpose that he was sent, and they were sent in the same manner that he was sent. "As the Father has sent me, even so I am sending you" (John 20:21). Similarly, Jesus prayed, "As you sent me into the world, so I have sent them into the world" (John 17:18). As the Father handed over his Son out of mercy, so also has he chosen to hand over the saints as a testimony of his mercy (see figure 9.3).

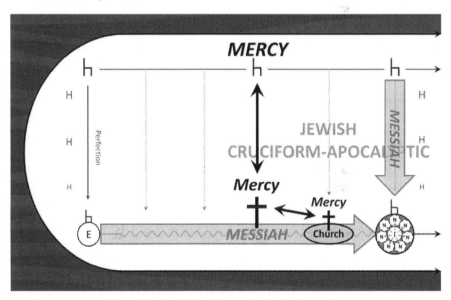

Figure 9.3 – The Biblical Witness Typified in Martyrdom

As the church seeks to testify to the mercy of God in light of the judgment to come, its words and actions must align, and the ultimate action that demonstrates the message of mercy is loving martyrdom: "For it has been granted to you that *for the sake of Christ* you should not only believe in him but also suffer for his sake" (Phil. 1:29). It is for the sake of a witness to Christ Jesus and to the cross that we welcome "the sharing of his sufferings by becoming like him in his death" (Phil. 3:10, NRSV). Indeed we "share abundantly in Christ's sufferings" (2 Cor. 1:5), "always carrying in the body the death of Jesus" (2 Cor. 4:10). So we should not be "surprised at the fiery trial" (1 Peter 4:12), but rather "rejoice insofar as [we] share Christ's sufferings" (v. 13).

As Jesus suffered "to seek and to save the lost" (Luke 19:10), so also the church embraces suffering. We seek to honor Christ Jesus and his cross so that as many people as possible might come to know him and be found in him at the judgment. Thus Paul summarized his apostolic commissioning:

> Now I rejoice in my sufferings *for your sake*, and in my flesh I am filling up what is lacking in Christ's afflictions *for the sake of his body*, that is, the church, of which I became a minister according to the stewardship from God that was given to me for you, *to make the word of God fully known*, the mystery hidden for ages and generations but now revealed to his saints. (Col. 1:24–26)

In his preaching of the gospel, Paul accepted and even rejoiced in his afflictions, because they were for the sake of Christ and his body, the church. Paul's "filling up what is lacking in Christ's afflictions" is by the command of the Father, who is "filling up" the divine testimony, so to speak, through the self-sacrifice of both his Son and his church.[33] By imitating Christ, Paul is the *prototypical martyr-witness*. In his desire to follow Jesus and "make the word of God fully known," he offers his very life for the sake of those to whom he preaches.

Such self-sacrifice defined Paul's apostolic ministry. He would give his own life for the sake of others, that they might be saved from divine wrath: "Therefore I endure everything [cf. "suffering, bound with chains," v. 9] *for the sake of the elect*, that they also may obtain the salvation that is in Christ Jesus with eternal glory" (2 Tim. 2:10). He would even take upon himself the divine wrath to see others saved: "For I could wish that I myself were accursed and cut off from Christ for the sake of my brothers, my kinsmen according to the flesh" (Rom. 9:3; cf. 10:1). Such "unceasing anguish" (Rom. 9:2) over the salvation of others is only created by the Holy Spirit, who imparts to us the love of Christ, which in turn compels us to lay down our lives for the gospel and for those to whom we preach (2 Cor. 5:14–20). Paul provides a shining example of someone who takes up their cross daily (Luke 9:23); that is, he daily consecrated himself to God and the divine mission—making the gospel of Christ Jesus, his cross, and his return known to the ends of the earth unto death. "And as for us, why do we endanger ourselves every hour? *I die every day*—I mean that, brothers—just as surely as I glory over you in Christ Jesus our Lord" (1 Cor. 15:30–31).

As noted earlier, the divine witness will culminate at the end of this age, which will also be in accord with a culmination of martyrdom. God will make his final plea with humanity, and the church will have a final opportunity to display Christ crucified to the world. As God handed over his Son to death to prove his great love for his enemies, so also will he hand over his church as a faithful witness of his mercy. As wicked men were given authority from above (cf. John 19:11) to deliver up Jesus "according to the definite plan and fore-knowledge of God" (Acts 2:23), so also will the Antichrist be given authority (cf. Dan. 7:21; Rev. 13:7), and the saints will be delivered over to him (cf. Dan. 7:25; Matt. 24:9). As Jesus endured the cross (Heb. 12:2), so also must the saints patiently endure (Rev. 1:9; 3:10; 13:10; 14:12). As the blood of Jesus was shed (Matt. 26:28), so too will the blood of the saints be spilled (Rev. 16:6; 17:6; 18:24). As Jesus was offered as a sacrifice (Heb. 9:12; 10:12), the saints are likewise pictured as a slain offering under the heavenly altar (Rev. 6:9; cf. Rom. 12:1; Phil. 2:17; 2 Tim. 4:6).[34] The similarities are striking, because God designed them both to be part of a greater testimony concerning his mercy and judgment in redemptive history.

Being the ultimate expression of this testimony, martyrdom is one of the main themes—if not the primary theme—of the book of Revelation.[35] Because this age will conclude when the testimony of God is complete, the culmination of martyrdom will be the primary *timing indicator* for its conclusion. This is stated explicitly in God's interaction with the slain souls under the altar:

> I saw under the altar the souls of those who had been slain for the word of God and for the witness they had borne. They cried out with a loud voice, "O Sovereign Lord, holy and true, *how long* before you will judge and avenge our blood on those who dwell on the earth?" Then they were each given a white robe and told to rest a little longer, *until the number of their fellow servants and their brothers should be complete*, who were to be killed as they themselves had been. (Rev. 6:9–11)

Of course, martyrdom is not the only timing indicator. God will testify of himself by many other means (e.g., wars, calamities, true versus false mira-cles, etc.), which will likewise culminate eschatologically. Martyrdom, however, seems to be the primary sign. The saints will be handed over for "time, times, and half a time" (Dan. 7:25; 12:7; cf. Rev. 11:2; 12:14; 13:5), and when this time is complete they will receive the kingdom (Dan. 7:27; Rev. 20:4). God will testify about himself through his saints and through their treatment. They are mistreated in this age, while the wicked prosper—*because* God is mercifully refraining from righteous judgment, desiring all to be saved. In such light he has chosen his saints to display his merciful, kind, and patient character through martyrdom.

Not only is martyrdom a timing indicator, but it is also the primary *mechanism* for the culmination of God's activity at the end of the age. As his saints are persecuted (cf. Rev. 7:14; 13:7; 16:6; 17:6), temporal judgments escalate (cf. Rev. 8:5; 14:7; 16:7; 18:2). The progression of the book can be seen in the climax of the declaration of fallen Babylon: "Rejoice over her, O heaven, and you saints and apostles and prophets, for God has given judgment for you against her!" (18:20).

More specifically, it is the intercession of the saints in tribulation that causes God to pour out his judgments—a theme seen throughout the Old Testament (e.g., Gen. 18:20; Ex. 3:7; Ps. 9:12; Isa. 5:7). This is vividly portrayed when the angel stands at the altar with a golden censer (Rev. 8:3), which is then filled with incense and the prayers of the saints (assumedly the saints under the same altar and those who have come out of the great tribulation; cf. 6:9; 7:14). The incense and prayers rise before God (8:4), and then they are filled with fire and hurled upon the earth (8:5). This same pattern of intercession resulting in temporal judgment is seen throughout the book (cf. 6:10–14; 11:15–19; 15:2–8; 16:7–9; 19:1–16).

God will avenge all unrighteousness, but the greatest evil is the murdering of the righteous. The image of God is of the highest value in all creation, and the destroying of the righteous image will incur the greatest of divine wrath. Even the blood of the righteous cries out from the ground (Gen. 4:10; cf. Matt. 23:35). Therefore the intercession of the martyrs triggers the temporal judgments, which are themselves a sign of the ultimate punishment of the wicked on the day of judgment. Martyrdom, intercession, and temporal judgments all come to a crescendo in the opening of the heavens and the descent of Jesus, who "judges and makes war" (Rev. 19:11).

Since human history is progressing toward this end, one would think martyrdom would be foremost in the modern church's consciousness and seen as its highest honor—*as it was in the early church*,[36] which had a clearly developed "theology of martyrdom."[37] However, discussions about martyrdom are almost nonexistent in the church today (except in some frontier-missions circles, but even then its significance is rarely considered). A "theology of martyrdom" is difficult to come by, and when it is presented it is usually marred by inaugurationalism.[38] The age to come and the new creation were not inaugurated by the suffering and death of Jesus, nor are they furthered by the pacifistic suffering of the church.[39] Such theology is painfully counterproductive.

The church must have a *future* eternal weight of glory in order to embrace a *present* light and momentary affliction (2 Cor. 4:17).[40] Moreover, it must have a theology of the cross that dictates its self-sacrificial mission in this age. Our practice of taking up the cross must be driven by a theology that tells us that this is what God is doing. God is thus extending the cross—that is, preaching repentance and forgiveness of sins in light of the day of the Lord (Luke 24:47; Acts 2:38; 3:19; etc.). In other words, the theology and practice of the church needs to be both cruciform and apocalyptic. Otherwise its sharp witness is blunted and its holy ambition is compromised.

When the mission of God in this age (and thereby the mission of the church) becomes the inauguration of the kingdom and the age to come, the cross ceases to be the standard of this age. Instead it serves only a subsidiary role unto the saints' present inheritance. In such a light, is there any reason to wonder why martyrdom is so overlooked in the contemporary church? At best, inaugurationalism views martyrdom as a waste; more realistically, it views martyrdom as a failure.

I would argue that there is a direct correlation between the rise of inaugurationalism in the modern church and its neglect of martyrdom, because the former inherently militates against the latter. In real life, those who are already inheriting the hope of the kingdom will never voluntarily lay down their lives. The theology of present glory will always be justification for rejecting anything negative in this life. In this way, martyrdom is the great measuring rod of theological truth. In the days to come inaugurationalism will be tested, and *it will be found wanting*. And here lies the catastrophe of today's theology: In its greatest hour of need, on the eve of global persecution, it has robbed the church of its most necessary theological training. The prospect of martyrdom is the first thing the Chinese church teaches its disciples,[41] and it is "the issue of utmost importance" for any church under persecution.[42]

The measure of the church throughout history is its production of true and faithful martyrs.[43] The Christian witness is a martyr-witness, and the Christian church is a martyr-church. To this church God has given the Holy Spirit (Acts 1:8). But those who will not receive martyrdom as a distinct possibility of God's will and leadership over their lives cannot be Jesus' disciples (cf. Luke 14:27–33; John 12:25–26), and thus they are not part of the true church which will inherit eternal life.

It does not matter if *we think* we are Christians. Jesus only considers someone his disciple if that person is willing to lay down his or her life for the same reason he laid down his own life. Saving people from the wrath to come is worth dying for. Jesus is fully committed to it. Are we?

AN ANALYSIS OF PASSAGES COMMONLY ASSOCIATED WITH REALIZED ESCHATOLOGY

F rom its earliest origins in the New Testament (cf. 2 Thess. 2:2; 1 Tim. 6:20; 2 Tim. 2:18), the plague of realized eschatology has persisted throughout the history of the church. It has seen a significant resurgence in modern times, however, becoming the standard of much theological exposition across a wide spectrum of denominations and theological camps. This resurgence is largely due to the writings of C. H. Dodd[1] and those who have accommodated his ideas.[2]

Dodd's desire was to counter the rising tide of ultracritical scholars (Schweitzer, et al.) who said that Jesus was nothing but a common Jew who believed and hoped in the common Jewish eschatology of his day. Being unbelievers, these scholars contended that Jesus was simply mistaken, and so his delusions came to a crashing end when the Romans killed him. (Of course the early church resurrected his delusions to cover over his failure.) Thus Dodd, to his credit, sought a noble end by restoring to Jesus a sense of divine identity and mission.

Realized eschatology was the tool Dodd used to save Jesus from the embarrassment of his failed Jewish dreams. Though Jesus was well aware of the eschatology of his day, he was supposedly unique in that he believed he was spiritually realizing those hopes within himself and his own ministry.[3] As stated previously, Dodd's belief in this realization was based largely on a Platonic framework in which the "wholly other" transcendental order is manifested into material time and space.[4] This belief in a present manifestation was justified by selective quotations of particular verses (Mark 1:15; Matt. 12:28; Luke 17:21; etc.) and a radical dismissal of the majority of Jesus' apocalyptic sayings.[5]

Dodd's critical method of writing off so many blatantly apocalyptic passages was untenable, and therefore, few followed him wholeheartedly.[6] However, a mediating position, which sought to hold both apocalypticism and realized eschatology in tandem (i.e., inaugurated eschatology), began to take hold in

Europe after World War II.[7] This inaugurationalist approach eventually made its way into American evangelicalism (G. E. Ladd, et al.), and from there it has spread to the ends of the earth.

Unfortunately, the only people who have questioned the inaugurationalist dogma hold either a liberal or dispensational bias. I firmly reject both, holding to the divine inspiration of the Bible and the divine identity of Jesus, while also holding to a single redemptive plan involving both Jew and Gentile. I find no embarrassment in Jesus' Jewish apocalyptic worldview, but rather embrace it wholeheartedly, for in it we find the fullness of truth and life. God ordained the cross as the sacrificial means of attaining the glorious hope of the resurrection and eternal life—to the Jew first and then to the Gentile.

Multitudes who have followed in Dodd's footsteps, however, have rejected such Jewish eschatology (note also Dodd's notorious rejection of propitiatory atonement). And, like Dodd, they use the exact same verses to justify their rejection (Mark 1:15; Matt. 12:28; Luke 17:21; etc.).[8] Of course, as Johannes Weiss noted in his day, liberal scholarship of the nineteenth century used the same verses to prove a present moralistic kingdom.[9] This appendix will examine these verses in context, along with some of Jesus' parables and Paul's sayings that are also quoted out of context.[10] The goal of this study is to demonstrate that, far from indicating a belief in the realization of Jewish eschatology, these verses are actually potent reinforcements of the apocalyptic worldview.

THE SAYINGS OF JESUS

At the heart of all controversy concerning realized eschatology are Jesus and his sayings. Did he affirm the Jewish hope of the Law and Prophets, or was he the Lone Ranger of second-temple Judaism who proclaimed the present spiritual fulfillment of the kingdom?[11] Common sense suggests the former.[12] Since the inception of realized eschatology, however, a number of sayings have consistently been referenced as proof that Jesus was the pioneer in proclaiming the spiritual realization of Jewish eschatology.

Johannes Weiss identified the classic strongholds of Matthew 12:28 ("The kingdom of God has come upon you") and Luke 17:21 ("The kingdom of God is within you," KJV).[13] C. H. Dodd embraced these wholeheartedly, as well as Mark 1:15 ("The kingdom of God is at hand") and Matthew 11:12 ("The kingdom of heaven has suffered violence").[14] Dodd confidently declared, moreover, that Jesus' parables reinforced the "mystery" (Mark 4:11, KJV) of realized eschatology contained in these sayings.[15] Unfortunately, multitudes have blindly followed Dodd's "hermeneutical castle built upon exegetical quicksand,"[16] parroting nearly verbatim his supposed evidences for realized eschatology.

Before examining the sayings of both Jesus and Paul, a word must be said about the relationship between realized eschatology and Greek verbs. Historically, the entire edifice of realized eschatology has been primarily built upon the use of eschatological concepts (especially the kingdom of God) with *past-tense or present-tense* Greek verbs. Something of a revolution has happened in recent New Testament linguistic studies, however, concerning the Greek verb.[17] Rather than communicating *time* (past, present, and future), Greek verbs primarily communicate *aspect* (perfective, imperfective, and stative).[18] Akin to Hebrew verbs, Greek verbs generally do not communicate the time of the action, but rather describe "the way the user of the verb subjectively views the action."[19] The time of the action is chiefly determined by its *context*, including adverbs, genre, and historical references.[20]

This approach to Greek verbs solves the historical problem of so many supposed "present-tense" verbs referring to realities both in the past ("historic present") and in the future ("futuristic present"), and of so many supposed "past-tense" verbs referring to realities both in the present ("dramatic aorist") and in the future ("proleptic aorist").[21] When Greek verbs are approached as aspectual, all the complicated terminology and elaborate systems of exceptions can be done away with, and translations of tense/time can be made according to appropriate context. The bottom line theologically is that supposed present-tense and past-tense verbs can no longer be used as proof of realized eschatology.

The Kingdom Is at Hand

The initial proclamation of both John the Baptist and Jesus was "Repent, for the kingdom of heaven is at hand" (Matt. 3:2; 4:17).[22] Following Dodd, many believe this to be a statement declaring the spiritual inauguration (i.e., reinterpretation) of the Jewish messianic kingdom.[23] The context of this statement, however, is clearly apocalyptic. It involves "the wrath to come" (3:7), bad trees being axed and "thrown into the fire" (v. 10), and chaff being burned "with unquenchable fire" (v. 12). All of these references were borne out of the Prophets, and no one would have mistaken the quotation of Isaiah 40 as anything but the day of the Lord.[24]

Jesus and John the Baptist were simply reiterating the heart of the prophetic declaration: "The Day of the Lord is at hand" (Isa. 13:6; Joel 1:15; Zeph. 1:7, NKJV; cf. Ezek. 30:3; Obad. 15; Mal. 4:5). Everyone understood that the day of the Lord and the kingdom of God were functionally synonymous, because the day initiated the kingdom. Thus Jesus sent out his disciples to preach the coming kingdom (Luke 10:1–9), warning them:

> When you enter a town and are not welcomed, go into its streets and say,
> "Even the dust of your town that sticks to our feet we wipe off against

you. Yet be sure of this: *The kingdom of God is near.*" I tell you, it will be more bearable *on that day* ["on the day of judgment," Matt. 10:15] for Sodom than for that town. (vv. 10–12, NIV)

In like manner, Jesus concludes his eschatological discourse: "Now when these things begin to take place, straighten up and raise your heads, because your redemption is drawing near. . . . When you see these things taking place, you know that the kingdom of God is near" (Luke 21:28–31).

The same message of the temporal nearness of the day of the Lord and kingdom of God is likewise reiterated throughout the New Testament. Peter declares, "The end of all things is *at hand*; therefore be self-controlled and sober-minded" (1 Peter 4:7). James says, "Establish your hearts, for the coming of the Lord is *at hand*" (James 5:8). Paul states, "Salvation is nearer to us now than when we first believed. The night is far gone; the day is *at hand*" (Rom. 13:11–12). In light of the Lord's coming (Phil. 3:20), our resurrection (3:21), and the "book of life" (4:3), Paul also exhorts, "The Lord is *at hand*; do not be anxious about anything" (4:5–6). Likewise, the writer of Hebrews urges corporate meetings and encouragement—"all the more as you see the Day *drawing near*" (Heb. 10:25). And the entire book of Revelation is given on the premise that "the time *is near*" (1:3; 22:10), for Jesus Christ "is coming with the clouds" (1:7; cf. 22:20).

In light of the prior language of the Prophets and its continued use throughout the New Testament, it is clear that Jesus was not changing the commonly understood Jewish eschatology of his day when he declared the nearness of the kingdom. He was simply urging *repentance* and a devout, wholehearted response to that kingdom.[25] This same urgency for repentance in light of the day of the Lord is mirrored throughout the apostolic witness (cf. Acts 2:38; 3:19; 5:31; etc.).

What then is to be said about the much-debated "delay" of Jesus' return? Because Jesus and the apostles declared the imminence of the kingdom, does it mean they were mistaken?[26] By no means! Was Isaiah mistaken when he declared the imminence of the day of the Lord over seven centuries prior to Jesus and the apostles? Or Zephaniah a century later? Or Malachi two centuries after that? Of course not. They were simply functioning in their prophetic role and speaking the message they had received from God.

Why then would the prophets, Jesus, and the apostles uniformly declare the nearness of the day of the Lord when its coming was actually thousands of years in the future? *Because time is relative to God, and thus the oracles prove true in relation to their Author.* This is the explanation given by Peter concerning the delay of the day of judgment (about thirty years at that time). Peter states the core question of the scoffers: "Where is the promise of his coming?" (2 Peter 3:4).[27] Then he responds, declaring that they overlook the simple fact "that with the Lord one day is as a thousand years, and a thousand years as one day" (v. 8). In other words, time is relative to God, and likewise to his oracles. Therefore, "The Lord is not slow to fulfill his promise *as some count slowness*, but is patient toward you. . . . But the day of the Lord will come like a thief" (vv. 9–10).

Though humans may count the delay in God's coming as slowness, God counts it as imminence because of his transcendence of time. In this way, the oracles remain true regardless of the time or means of their delivery. Those who speak on behalf of God have always had, and always will have, one driving message: *Repent, for the day of the Lord is at hand.*

The Kingdom Has Come upon You

If one of Jesus' sayings has become the "hermeneutical cornerstone" for realized eschatology, it would be Matthew 12:28 (cf. Luke 11:20),[28] where Jesus states, "If it is by the Spirit of God that I cast out demons, then the kingdom of God has come upon you."[29] Based upon a rigid tense translation of the Greek verb *ephthasen* ("has come"), inaugurationalists claim absolute proof of the spiritual realization of the kingdom.[30] When we look at the passage as a whole and interpret the verb according to aspect, however, we actually find a *forceful affirmation* of the commonly understood Jewish messianic kingdom.

This saying was spoken in the context of Jesus healing a demon-oppressed man (Matt. 12:22). Everyone was amazed and asked, "Can this be the Son of David?" (v. 23). Clearly they took this exorcism to mean that the restored Davidic kingdom was in view. The Pharisees rejected Jesus' messiahship and accused him of driving out the demon by the power of Satan (v. 24). Jesus' response to this accusation (vv. 25–37) was threefold: 1) it was illogical; 2) it was immoral; and 3) it was the basis of their eternal judgment.

Since space prohibits a detailed commentary of Jesus' response, we can only summarize the main point Jesus was making—*people will be judged according to their words on the day of the Lord.* Consequently the Pharisees' present accusation makes certain their eternal damnation, as Jesus concludes, "I tell you, on the day of judgment people will give account for every careless word they speak, for by your words you will be justified, and by your words you will be condemned" (vv. 36–37). If the exorcisms happened by the Spirit of God, then Jesus is actually the Jewish Messiah (i.e., the Son of David). And if he is the Jewish Messiah, then the careless accusation of the Pharisees secures their eternal judgment.

This certainty lies behind the perfective aspect (traditionally aorist/past tense) of the verb *ephthasen*. Jesus is simply communicating the completed and finalized reality of their judgment based upon their careless words.[31] A better translation of verse 28 would thus be: "If I cast out demons by the Spirit of God, then the kingdom of God *will most certainly come upon you!*" Though some have previously acknowledged the possibility of a "proleptic aorist,"[32] I find the context of the passage to be most obviously eschatological.[33] As such, "the day of judgment" (v. 36), "the age to come" (v. 32), "the kingdom of God" (v. 28), and "the Son of David" (v. 23) all refer to the same Jewish apocalyptic reality. Hence the perfective aspect of *ephthasen* simply communicates the certainty of this future reality.

This common-sense approach coincides with the fearful and negative use of the same phraseology throughout the Old Testament.[34] Based upon violations of the law, "all these curses shall *come upon* you and overtake you" (Deut. 28:15). The prophets regularly rehearsed the same language, as Jeremiah declared, "Because you sinned against the LORD and did not obey his voice, this thing has *come upon* you" (40:3). Or as Zephaniah exhorted, "Gather together, yes, gather, O shameless nation, before the decree takes effect—before the day passes away like chaff—before there *comes upon* you the burning anger of the LORD, before there *comes upon* you the day of the anger of the LORD" (2:1–2). Or as Daniel prayed, "As it is written in the Law of Moses, all this calamity has *come upon* us; yet we have not entreated the favor of the Lord our God, turning from our iniquities and gaining insight by your truth" (9:13).

The idea of divine judgment coming upon the wicked is similarly seen throughout the New Testament. So Jesus warns, "But watch yourselves lest your hearts be weighed down with dissipation and drunkenness and cares of this life, and that day *come upon* you suddenly like a trap. For it will *come upon* all who dwell on the face of the whole earth" (Luke 21:34–35). Likewise, the scribes and Pharisees of Jesus' day will be "sentenced to hell" (Matt. 23:33), for "all these things will *come upon* this generation" (v. 36). Therefore "the wrath of God *comes upon* the sons of disobedience" (Eph. 5:6). For "sudden destruction will *come upon* them as labor pains *come upon* a pregnant woman, and they will not escape" (1 Thess. 5:3). Thus the rich should "weep and howl for the miseries that are *coming upon* you" (James 5:1). Yet, for the righteous, "I will also keep you from the hour of trial that is going to *come upon* the whole world to test those who live on the earth" (Rev. 3:10, NIV).

In such light, 1 Thessalonians 2:16—"God's wrath has *come upon* them at last"—stands out as particularly important, since it most closely corresponds grammatically to Matthew 12:28 (i.e., both have an aorist *ephthasen* with the preposition *epi*). Moreover, Jesus' situation and Paul's situation are quite similar. Both are being persecuted by unbelieving Jews, and both are declaring that the present actions of those Jews are securing their future damnation. Some claim that Paul's use of the aorist within such a clear eschatological context (cf.

1 Thess. 1:10; 2:19; 3:13; 4:15–17; 5:1–9) makes this verse "one of the more problematic passages in the entire Pauline corpus."[35] Of course, it is only problematic if *ephthasen* is translated as past tense rather than as perfective aspect. A better translation (quite akin to Matthew 12:28) would thus be: "God's wrath *will most certainly come upon* them in the end!"[36]

In this way both Jesus and Paul use the perfective form of *ephthasen* to forcefully affirm the Jewish apocalyptic end of their enemies.[37] Far from being proof of realized eschatology, they speak in the perfective (like the Hebrew prophets) to communicate the complete surety of the future reality.[38] Furthermore, the cumulative effect of the "come upon" phraseology throughout prophetic witness would have created a compounded *negative emotional response* within the hearer. The mere mention of the kingdom coming upon someone, in light of the day of judgment, was meant to instill fear and trembling, leading to repentance. If the kingdom comes upon you (Matt. 12:28), it means you have been shut off from divine forgiveness (v. 32), and at the day of judgment (v. 36) "you will be condemned" (v. 37).

The Kingdom Is within You

Perhaps no other saying of Jesus has been more misunderstood and distorted throughout the church's history than Luke 17:21: "Behold, the kingdom of God is in the midst of you." Assumedly derived from the Gnostic tradition,[39] Anthony[40] and Origen[41] propagated a spiritualistic interpretation of this saying that continues to date, supported by a number of English translations (e.g., "The kingdom of God *is within you*," KJV, NKJV, NIV). Modern commentaries offer a multitude of interpretive options,[42] yet the most common-sense approach is tragically absent.[43]

In this passage (Luke 17:20–37), Jesus is simply correcting *Jewish zealotry* and its perverted expectation of the kingdom of God.[44] Within first-century Pharisaism (especially within the House of Shammai) there was sympathy with the Jewish insurgent movements, which distorted their view of the Law and the Prophets. Instead of a radically apocalyptic expectation of the kingdom (cf. Isa. 13; 65; Dan. 7; Joel 3; etc.), a mixture of hope was introduced that incorporated the strength of the flesh in synergy with the coming of God. Patterned after the Maccabean revolt,[45] it was supposed that God would anoint a descendant of David, who would gather an army and come forth from the wilderness (and/or inner rooms) and progressively grow in power, with heaven approving and the angels attending.[46] Such insurgent movements were relatively common at the time (cf. Acts 5:36–37; 21:38).[47]

When asked when the kingdom of God would come (Luke 17:20), Jesus responded, "The kingdom of God is not coming *with signs to be observed*"

(NASB).[48] There is much dispute concerning the nature of these "signs," but Jesus makes clear he is speaking about Jewish insurgencies by qualifying, "Nor will they say, 'Look, here it is!' or, 'There it is!'" (v. 21, NASB). The Matthean parallel elaborates: "So, if they say to you, 'Look, he is *in the wilderness*,' do not go out. If they say, 'Look, he is *in the inner rooms*,' do not believe it" (24:26). Such an insurgent hope, which organized itself in the wilderness or in the inner rooms, is countered in both Gospel accounts with Jesus' declaration, "As the lightning flashes and lights up the sky from one side to the other, so will the Son of Man be in his day" (Luke 17:24; cf. Matt. 24:27). Simply put, the Pharisaical vision for the day of the Lord had become polluted. It was not apocalyptic *enough*.

We must therefore interpret this passage, as well as the entire Olivet Discourse (Matt. 24 and parallels), as a *polemic against zealotry*.[49] The strength of the flesh is corrupt beyond measure, and as such it will play no part in the redemption of the earth. Conversely, it only degenerates an already miserable situation, adding fuel to the coming fire. The kingdom of God will not come progressively by the strength of the flesh, but rather *suddenly* by the power of God, "as the lightning flashes" (v. 24), "as it was in the days of Noah" (v. 26), and "as it was in the days of Lot" (v. 28). Moreover, that day will not require observation; it will be *obvious* to all, just as the existence of a corpse is obvious when vultures circle overhead (v. 37).

What then is to be said about the statement in verse 21 that "the kingdom of God *is* [Gk. *estin*] in the midst of you"? Unfortunately, modern debate has focused on the tense of the verbs in verses 20–21. Rather than the "present tense," the imperfective aspect is used throughout to highlight the dramatic actions unfolding. To resolve the awkwardness created by a strict tense translation, some have suggested a "futuristic present tense" for all of the verbs, since the thrust of the original question concerns the future (thus, "the kingdom of God *will be* in the midst of you").[50] Most of this debate, however, seems to be generally tangential, since neither Jesus nor the Pharisees would have questioned the futurity of the kingdom. Rather, the contention concerned *how* that futurity would unfold. The Pharisees saw it coming progressively from men out of the wilderness or inner courts, while Jesus saw it coming suddenly from God out of the heavens.

Consequently, the ultimate contention regards the origin of the kingdom (God vs. man), which in turn determines the timing of the kingdom (suddenly vs. progressively). As such, the translation of verse 21 should turn on the alternative meaning of *estin*: "to have a point of derivation or origin, *be/come from somewhere*."[51] As *estin* is elsewhere translated "come" (cf. Matt. 21:25; John 1:46; 7:27–29; 1 Cor. 11:8) and taken in its commonly understood futuristic context, we would thus translate Luke 17:21b: "Behold, the kingdom of God *comes into* your midst."[52]

In this way, Jesus' statement naturally leads into verses 22–37, for the kingdom will come into their midst just as it happened during the days of Noah and Lot.[53] The strength of the flesh played no part in the execution of divine judgment then, and the strength of the flesh (as embodied in Jewish insurgent movements) will play no part in the enthronement of the Son of Man on the last day. Far from being a pronouncement of realized eschatology (and some sort of internal or spiritualistic kingdom), Jesus' statement is actually a radical indictment of all nonapocalyptic eschatology. The Jewish messianic kingdom will come suddenly with divine power and glory.

The Kingdom Has Been Forcefully Advancing

The great irony of realized eschatology is that it relies on texts which in truth perfectly contradict its message. Realized eschatology argues that the texts above communicate 1) a good thing of divine blessing, 2) aimed at believers, 3) individually, 4) in the present. However, the kingdom being at hand, coming upon you, and coming into your midst is very much 1) a bad thing of divine judgment, 2) aimed at unbelievers, 3) corporately, 4) in the future.[54] Realized eschatology actually turns Jesus' message on its head and robs it of its strength and conviction. Instead of inducing fear and trembling, leading to repentance and conversion, it deludes its hearers into believing a lie.[55] In the end, those who do not work out their salvation with fear and trembling will not inherit eternal life.

Similarly, realized eschatology has inverted Matthew 11:12—"From the days of John the Baptist until now the kingdom of heaven has suffered violence, and the violent take it by force." Though the tone of the entire passage is quite negative (vv. 7–19), followed by declarations of woe (vv. 20–14), many interpret this verse as something positive. It is maintained that Jesus is declaring the spiritual realization of Jewish eschatology, which is attained by a spiritually aggressive (i.e., "violent") way of life.[56]

Though Dodd admitted that the meaning of this passage was "exceedingly difficult to determine,"[57] he nonetheless maintained (leaning on the questionable parallel in Luke 16:16) that it clearly reveals that Jesus "proclaimed that the Kingdom of God, the hope of many generations, had at last come."[58] Concerning such a radical declaration, should we not take a more prudent approach? If the meaning of a passage is "exceedingly difficult to determine," should we not err on the more conservative and traditional side? The burden of proof rests on realized eschatology to evidence its revolutionary claims, and if Jesus did indeed proclaim such a radical reinterpretation of the Law and Prophets, then we should expect an *elaborate exposition.* Without such an expounding, we should assume—by default—the Jewish understanding of the kingdom.

Though this passage does contain many difficulties, it is not too difficult to determine its basic meaning: *Before the day of the Lord, the righteous will suffer and be persecuted* (as was the common apocalyptic expectation). In the context of the previous warning about the coming persecution (Matt. 10:16–39) and the current imprisonment of John the Baptist (11:2), Jesus affirms his own messianic identity (vv. 2–6). Then he turns to the crowds and exalts the greatness of John's prophetic identity (vv. 7–11). And just like all the prophets before them, both Jesus and John will suffer persecution at the hands of violent men (v. 12), for John fully embodied the prophetic calling (vv. 13–15). Moreover, just as in previous generations, the generation of Jesus and John is hostile because of its rebellious attitudes, akin to "childish brats" in the marketplace (vv. 16–19).[59] Therefore the basic meaning of the passage concerns the relationship between Jesus and John and their shared persecution.

When we focus on verses 11–12, we are confronted with a number of issues. There are two variables for interpretation in verse 11 (kingdom now vs. future and the identity of least vs. greater), and there are two variables in verse 12 (positive vs. negative violence statement and positive vs. negative violence response). Thus there are four options of interpretation for each verse (a mind-boggling sixteen interpretive possibilities in all!).[60] It is no wonder that interpretation of this passage commonly devolves into confusion and conflict.

Concerning verse 11, it seems clear that we ought to identify "the one who is *least* in the kingdom of heaven" as Jesus himself.[61] Assumedly based on Daniel 4:17 ("The Most High rules the kingdom of men and gives it to whom he will and sets over it the lowliest of men"), Jesus elsewhere identifies himself as the least in this world, sent as the servant of all.[62] The world views the servant as the least; God views the servant as the greatest. Hence, "Whoever *humbles* himself like this child is the *greatest* in the kingdom of heaven" (Matt. 18:4), and "He who is *least* among you all is the one who is *great*" (Luke 9:48). Similarly, after the mother of the two sons of Zebedee asked that her sons be given the highest positions in the coming kingdom (Matt. 20:20–21), Jesus explained to his disciples,

> You know that the rulers of the Gentiles lord it over them, and their *great* ones exercise authority over them. It shall not be so among you. But whoever would be *great* among you must be your *servant,* and whoever would be *first* among you must be your *slave,* even as the Son of Man came not to be served but to serve, and to give his life as a ransom for many. (vv. 25–28)

The Lukan parallel adds, "Let the *greatest* among you become as the *youngest* ["lowest rank," NLT], and the leader as one who serves" (22:26), thus concluding with the eschatological exaltation: "that you may eat and drink at my table in my kingdom and *sit on thrones* judging the twelve tribes of Israel" (v. 30). In this way, we have abundant evidence for the use of "least" and "greatest" in light of the eschatological judgment, which will result in a radical reversal of the hierarchies of the earth (cf. "many who are first will be last, and the last first"; Matt. 19:30).[63]

Therefore Matthew 11:11 is simply saying that John the Baptist is indeed the greatest born among women (i.e., the greatest of the prophets and the culmination of the prophetic witness; cf. vv. 13–15),[64] yet Jesus is even greater than he, because Jesus humbled himself like a submissive child (i.e., became least) even more than did John (unlike the rebellious children of his generation; cf. vv. 16–19).[65] The common inaugurational interpretation of this verse is nonsensical,[66] since the beginning of a spiritually realized kingdom is impossible to determine, and John the Baptist would be logically excluded from the kingdom, or denigrated at best.[67]

Concerning verse 12, there are four options in regard to the kingdom of heaven and the realities of "inflicting violence" (Gk. *biazō*), "violent men" (Gk. *biastēs*), and "forceful seizure" (Gk. *harpazō*). Either both parts of the verse are positive (NIV), both are negative (KJV, NKJV, NAB, NASB, NRSV, ESV), one is positive and the other is negative (NLT), or vice versa.[68] Since the idea of "violence" is almost universally negative in the Scriptures (cf. Gen. 6:11; Ps. 58:2; 140:1–5; Ezek. 22:26; etc.), I interpret the verse as a double negative, wherein the second part of the verse explicates the first: "The kingdom of heaven *suffers violence*, and violent people *attack it*."[69] We can see that this is a simple statement concerning the bold prophetic proclamation of John and Jesus and the violent response of their enemies.[70]

I interpret the parable of the children in the marketplace (vv. 16–19) similarly. Those who see verse 12 as a positive statement generally interpret the singing children as John and Jesus, while those who view verse 12 negatively generally associate the children with "this generation" (v. 16).[71] The latter is clearly what Jesus meant, for it is the accusations of this generation which are highlighted in verses 18–19. Moreover, statements concerning "this generation" are elsewhere generally negative (cf. Matt. 12:39–45; 16:4; 17:17).

Thus the parable falls in line with the preceding passage concerning the persecution of John and Jesus and sets up the following passage concerning the condemnation of unrepentant cities (vv. 20–24).[72] Far from a proclamation of realized eschatology, the kingdom suffering violence is simply a declaration concerning persecution of John and Jesus, assuming the apocalyptic destruction of their enemies "on the day of judgment" (vv. 22,24).[73] In this way, Jesus' saying accords with the common Jewish apocalyptic expectation that the righteous will suffer before the day of the Lord.[74]

The Kingdom Is Mysterious and Parabolic

If realized eschatology were pictured as a tent, its poles would be the individual sayings of Jesus (discussed above), and its covering would be Jesus' parables. According to Dodd and those who have followed him, the revealing of realized eschatology is the primary purpose of the parables. Hence the core element of "the mystery of the kingdom of God" (Mark 4:11, KJV) is believed to be realized eschatology.[75] As Dodd summarized:

> This is the "mystery of the Kingdom of God"; not only that the *eschaton*, that which belongs properly to the realm of the "wholly other," is now a matter of actual experience, but that it is experienced in the paradoxical form of the suffering and death of God's representative.[76]

Therefore the Jewish messianic kingdom is transformed into a nebulous spiritualistic reality somehow expressed through the crucifixion of the Messiah. Moreover, the implication is that the Jews of Jesus' day had a false hope in the commonly hoped-for messianic kingdom, and as such Jesus had to tell them rudimentary parables to help them see the spiritualistic nature of the kingdom. In light of a common-sense reading of the parables, however, I find this approach both absurd and offensive.

The foreign interpolation of realized eschatology into Jesus' parables confounds their basic purpose: *the concealing of truth from the unrepentant*. The parables are not primarily meant to reveal some kind of new truth, but rather to conceal the plain truth from the ungodly. Jesus thus explains the context of the mystery/secret of the kingdom: "And he said to them, 'To you has been given the secret of the kingdom of God, *but for those outside* everything is in parables, so that "they may indeed see but not perceive, and may indeed hear but not understand, lest they should turn and be forgiven"'" (Mark 4:11–12). Again, though Jesus speaks to his disciples plainly (cf. Matt. 5–7; 10:5–42; 18:1–9; etc.), he speaks to the unrepentant (those who will not "turn and be forgiven") in parables—"This is why I speak *to them* in parables, because seeing they do not see, and hearing they do not hear, nor do they understand" (Matt. 13:13).

In this way, the parables are not designed to impart new knowledge to believers concerning God and redemptive history. Rather, they are spoken *polemically against unbelievers* as a condemnation of their sin, pride, and hardheartedness. Of course, believers can receive instruction and encouragement from the parables, but we must not lose sight of their overall orientation (something that happens quite often, especially in relation to the disputed parables). Most of the parables make a simple contrast of good versus bad responses to God, and as such we must always be mindful that Jesus primarily spoke the parables as an indictment of the bad response.

For example, the first major parable found in the Gospels is the wise versus foolish builders (Matt. 7:24–27). This parable certainly includes an encouragement to believers to build their metaphorical houses upon the rock. But the overall orientation and purpose of the parable is toward unbelieving Jews and their leaders, who are repeatedly highlighted in the previous chapters (cf. 5:20; 6:2,5, 16; 7:5,15). Consequently, "on that day" (7:22)—that is, the day of the Lord—divine judgment will come upon the world like a storm. Those who have lived out their repentance will endure the day, while those who have lived for the age to come *in pretense* (cf. "Lord, Lord, did we not prophesy in your name . . . "; v. 22) will fall "with a great crash" (v. 27, NIV). The parable of the builders is thus primarily spoken as an indictment of foolish builders and secondarily as an encouragement to wise builders.

Similarly, the major parables of Matthew 13 (the shorter, debatable parables will be discussed at the end of this section) are aimed at "this wicked generation" (12:45), especially "the Pharisees and teachers of the law" (12:38), who "plotted how they might kill Jesus" (12:14). The parable of the sower and the seeds (13:3–9) is primarily aimed at those who hear the message of the kingdom (i.e., eternal life) yet reject it or receive it halfheartedly, choosing to live mostly for "this life" (v. 22, NIV). The parable of the wheat and tares (vv. 24–30) is similarly spoken to "the sons of the evil one" (v. 38), those who will be "gathered and burned with fire . . . at the end of the age" (v. 40). Likewise, the parable of the good and bad fish (vv. 47–50) is meant to be a warning to "the wicked" (v. 49, NIV), who are in danger of being thrown into "the fiery furnace" (v. 50) at the end of the age. Again, the parables were spoken "to them" (v. 13), because "they look, but they don't really see" (v. 13, NLT). The parables concern people's response to the message of the day of the Lord, not a realization of the day of the Lord.

The parables of the unforgiving servant (Matt. 18:23–35), the vineyard workers (Matt. 20:1–16), the two sons (Matt. 21:28–32), the wicked tenants (Matt. 21:33–41), and the wedding banquet (Matt. 22:1–14) were all spoken publicly, so as to highlight and delineate righteous versus wicked behavior in light of the final judgment. Far from communicating any kind of realized eschatology, the aim of these parables is simply to communicate that "many who are first will be last, and the last first" (19:30; cf. 20:16). That is to say, many who were commonly thought to be righteous (thus inheriting a first place of glory in the age to come) were actually wicked (thus inheriting a last place of punishment with the pagans), while many who were commonly thought to be wicked (i.e., the sinners and tax collectors; cf. 9:11; 11:19) would actually inherit the greatest glory in the coming kingdom (cf. "The tax collectors and prostitutes will get into the kingdom of God before you"; 21:31, NASB).[77] So all of these parables culminate with the denunciation of the scribes and Pharisees in Matthew 23, summarized by the statement: "Whoever exalts himself will be humbled, and whoever humbles himself will be exalted" (v. 12).[78]

Those parables which involve or highlight only one thing, person, or group (often righteous) are no less designed "for those outside." The parable of the persistent widow (Luke 18:1–8) is aimed at the Pharisees who had become sympathetic to the Zealots (cf. 17:20–37), and as such they had stopped praying and lost heart in the day of the Lord (18:1). The parable of the shrewd manager (Luke 16:1–13) is designed to mock the Pharisees, "who were lovers of money" (v. 14), because "the sons of this age are more shrewd in relation to their own kind than the sons of light" (v. 8, NASB). In light of the coming judgment, unbelievers often use their wealth to love people more than those who supposedly live for eternal life! Similarly, the parables of the lost sheep (Luke 15:3–7) and the lost coin (vv. 8–10) are aimed at the lack of compassion and joy on the part of the Pharisees and teachers of the law, who "muttered" (v. 2) about Jesus' welcoming of the tax collectors and sinners. The parable of the lost son (vv. 11–32) delineates multiple players, but communicates the same thing. These parables about the kindness and mercy of God were primarily spoken to expose the judgmental arrogance of the Jewish leaders.[79]

The more controversial parables of Matthew 13 should also be understood in this light. Akin to the parables of the lost sheep and lost coin (Luke 15:3–10), the parables of the hidden treasure and pearl (Matt. 13:44–46) were meant to expose the greedy and unwise way of life created by the Jewish leaders of the time (cf. Matt. 6:1–18; 23:5–28). Though outwardly they claimed to live for the age to come, inwardly they were actually "full of greed and self-indulgence" (Matt. 23:25). Though the parables of the hidden treasure and pearl exemplify righteousness, they are still spoken concerning "those outside,"[80] and never for a moment would they have been understood as realizing or overturning the common apocalyptic expectations concerning the inheritance of eternal life.

Likewise, the parables of the mustard seed and leaven (Matt. 13:31–33) would have been understood *negatively*, spoken "to them" (v. 13), and interpreted apocalyptically, in light of "the end of the age" (v. 40). These two terse parables are simply negative teaching devices with a single player, akin to the parables of the rich fool (Luke 12:16–21), the barren fig tree (Luke 13:6–9), and the counting of the costs (Luke 14:28–33). Leaven was commonly understood as a bad thing, Old Testament and New (cf. Ex. 12:15–20; 34:25; Lev.

2:11; Matt. 16:6,11–12; 1 Cor. 5:6–8; Gal. 5:9); and the allusion to Daniel 4:12 concerning the mustard seed (Matt. 13:32) probably would not have been heard by Jesus' hearers in a positive light. Thus the leaven and the mustard seed most likely would have been associated with the preceding and following "weeds" (vv. 25,38), which were destined to be "burned" (vv. 30,40)—especially since the mustard seed and leaven parables are given no explanation (a point rarely appreciated). In this way, they simply communicate that God, in his great mercy, will allow the wickedness to grow to its full measure (an idea seen throughout the Scriptures; cf. Gen. 15:16; Dan. 8:23; Zech. 5:5; Matt. 23:32; 1 Thess. 2:16) until the judgment at the end of the age. Again, if the mustard seed and leaven parables are bookended by a parable concerning God allowing evil to continue to maturity, then should we not assume the unexplained parables in the middle to communicate the same message?

To justify interpreting the mustard seed and leaven as positive parables elaborating a realized eschatology, you have to 1) go against the prevailing Jewish understanding; 2) go against the common apocalyptic theme of Jesus' preaching; 3) go against the overall context of the chapter; 4) go against the immediately adjacent verses; and 5) go against the passages and elements that are referenced in the parables themselves.[81] Of course, this never seems to stop proponents of realized eschatology, who treat the sayings addressed above in like manner.[82] The interpretation of Jesus' parables in a nonapocalyptic manner, exalting the strength of the flesh (and ultimately justifying Constantinian Christianity), is completely anathema to the message and ministry of Jesus and the apostles.

THE SAYINGS OF PAUL

Inaugurationalists look to Paul as the primary successor of Jesus' teachings on realized eschatology. If Jesus was the Lone Ranger of second-temple Judaism, then surely Paul was his Tonto. A systematic study of Paul's writings, though, reveals a consistent apocalyptic emphasis.[83] Conversely, Dodd and his followers maintain that Paul and the apostles "reflected upon" the outpouring of the Spirit and progressively preached the realization of Jewish eschatology.[84] In this way, the church, composed of both Jews and Gentiles, became the new and true Israel, realizing the blessings foretold by the prophets in the "here and now."[85]

Some look to Paul's relative lack of reference to "kingdom" and his emphasis on "righteousness" and the Spirit as a sign that "God's eschatological rule was already being manifested in the present."[86] Nonsense! *If Paul was redefining the kingdom and Jewish eschatology, then he would have focused his language on the Jewish eschatological terms and expounded upon them, so as to fill them with new meaning.* Rather, he simply assumed the common Jewish eschatology and focused on the means of inheriting the kingdom (righteousness before God by faith in Christ's sacrifice) and the confirmation of that means (in the deposit of the Spirit).[87]

Paul's lack of emphasis on the kingdom is compensated by his consistent emphasis on the day of the Lord (cf. Acts 17:31; Rom. 2:5; 1 Cor. 3:13; Phil. 1:10; 1 Thess. 5:2; 2 Tim. 4:8), the resurrection (cf. Rom. 6:5; 1 Cor. 15:42; 2 Cor. 5:4; Phil. 3:11), and the return of Jesus (cf. 1 Cor. 15:23; Col. 3:4; 1 Thess. 3:13; 2 Thess. 2:1; 2 Tim. 4:1; Titus 2:13). Moreover, *most of his references to the kingdom are clearly eschatological* (cf. 1 Cor. 6:9–10; 15:24,50; Gal. 5:21; Eph. 5:5; Col. 4:11; 1 Thess. 2:12; 2 Thess. 1:5; 2 Tim. 4:1,18). Only a few references—namely Romans 14:17, 1 Corinthians 4:20, and Colossians 1:13— are debatable, and we will examine them next.[88] On the whole, Paul's message is simple and clear: Put faith in the cross, so as to be accounted righteous before God on the last day, thus inheriting the kingdom, resurrection, and eternal life.

The Kingdom Is Righteousness, Peace, and Joy in the Holy Spirit

Concerning the supposed apostolic belief in realized eschatology, Romans 14:17 is commonly quoted as the clearest example: "For the kingdom of God is not a matter of eating and drinking but of righteousness and peace and joy in the Holy Spirit." Outlining the history of modern interpretation subsequent to Schweitzer and Dodd, George Ladd concluded emphatically, "The Word of God *does* say that the Kingdom of God is a present spiritual reality. 'For the kingdom of God is not eating and drinking but righteousness and peace and joy in the Holy Spirit' (Rom. 14:17). Righteousness and peace and joy are fruits of the Spirit which God bestows now upon those who yield their lives to the rule of the Spirit. They have to do with the deepest springs of the spiritual life, and this, says the inspired apostle, is the Kingdom of God."[89]

Many modern interpreters would agree with Ladd, but is this really Paul's point in Romans 14? I do not think so. Nothing about Romans 14:17 communicates the timing of the kingdom. The verb (*eimi*) is simply referring to the Jewish messianic kingdom, which is understood as a future reality (as evidenced by the numerous eschatological references surrounding the verse).[90] We often do the same thing today when we speak of a future reality: "Your inheritance *is* a serious matter," or "The future *is* unknown," or "His death *is* imminent." Paul is speaking the same way in Romans 14:17, using the verb "to be" to describe the future Jewish kingdom, rather than describing a present spiritualized reality.[91]

To understand Romans 14, we need to see that Paul is expounding upon the end of Romans 13. In light of our salvation being nearer now than when we first believed (13:11), Paul is arguing that "the day is at hand" (v. 12) and the night of this age is almost over. How then should we live, and what holds *eternal significance*? Paul answers,

So then let us cast off the works of darkness and put on the armor of light. Let us walk properly *as in the daytime*, not in orgies and drunkenness, not in sexual immorality and sensuality, not in quarreling and jealousy. But put on the Lord Jesus Christ, and make no provision for the flesh, to gratify its desires. (vv. 12–14)

Romans 14 is simply an exposition of the phrase "as in the daytime." The age to come will not involve drunkenness, immorality, or strife. Thus we should not engage in those things, because we are not *destined* for those things. Moreover, we were not *designed* for those things in the beginning. They are fruitless and hold no eternal value.

Similarly, arguments between Jewish and Gentile believers concerning dietary laws (14:2–4,14–16,20–21) and calendar observance (vv. 5–9) are fruitless and hold no value when we all "stand before the judgment seat of God" (v. 10). Though we may "pass judgment" (vv. 3,4,10,13,22) on each other in this age concerning these things, they will hold little weight on the last day, when "each of us will give an account of himself to God" (v. 12).

In essence, "the kingdom of God" (v. 17) and "the judgment seat of God" (v. 10) are *functionally synonymous*.[92] What we eat and drink in this age will be of little consequence on the day of the Lord and in the kingdom of God. The age to come will consist of righteousness, peace, and joy in the Holy Spirit, and the judgment seat of God will not be a matter of eating and drinking. Therefore, in this age "let us pursue what makes for peace and for mutual upbuilding" (v. 19). In this way, "strong" believers will not be dragged into the meaningless toils of "weak" believers, who in turn will not divide the body of Christ by their vain judgments.

Far from redefining the common Jewish eschatology, Paul is simply describing its future reality, hence reinforcing the sobriety and eternal perspective inherent in Jewish apocalypticism.[93] Thus, to summarize: "Let us walk properly as in the daytime," and not "quarrel over opinions" which hold little eternal significance, since the age to come "is not a matter of eating and drinking but of righteousness and peace and joy in the Holy Spirit." This futurist approach squares with both the passage as a whole and with common expectations of the kingdom.[94] Interposing realized eschatology into Romans 14 is both illogical and counterproductive to Paul's argument that eschatology (cf. "salvation," "the day," "judgment seat," "kingdom") is the primary driver of Christian discipleship.[95]

The Kingdom Is Not a Matter of Talk but of Power

Similar to Romans 14:17, Paul also describes the coming kingdom in 1 Corinthians 4:20: "The kingdom of God is not a matter of talk but of power" (NIV).[96] Many interpreters understand this statement to be a clear declaration of realized eschatology. As with Romans 14, however, the context does not even come close to supporting this interpretation. Eschatological references abound, both preceding (cf. 1:8,29; 2:6; 3:13; 4:5) and following (cf. 5:5; 6:2–3,14; 7:29; etc.) the statement. Moreover, Paul's use of "kingdom of God" elsewhere in the letter is clearly eschatological (cf. 6:9–10; 15:24, 50). His "very casual" use of the phrase also indicates that it was a commonly understood term to both Paul and his readers. [97] If realized eschatology had become so commonly associated with the phrase, where is the evidence (i.e., long discourses and elaborations) that its meaning had been so radically redefined *and* commonly accepted?

Rather, Paul had in mind the Jewish messianic kingdom, and the coming of this kingdom does not consist of talk but of power. As I once heard it preached, "Jesus will not cleanse the earth of wickedness by striking it with footnotes!" He will come, instead, *with a rod* (cf. Ps. 2:9; Isa. 11:4; Rev. 19:15) and punish the wicked for their evil words and deeds. This is the kind of "power" Paul is speaking of in reference to the kingdom (cf. 1 Cor. 3:13; 4:5; 5:13; 6:9–10). Similarly, Paul threatens to execute a temporal judgment by coming "with a rod" (4:21). As such, *Paul understands that temporal judgments within the church are meant to bring sobriety concerning God's eternal judgment.*

This pattern is repeated in the following verses concerning the excommunication of the sexually immoral man, to be done with the hope "that his spirit may be saved in the day of the Lord" (5:5). As Paul justifies, "What business is it of mine to judge those outside the church? Are you not to judge those inside? God will judge those outside. 'Expel the wicked man from among you'" (vv. 12–13, NIV).

Paul reiterates this approach again in relation to lawsuits among believers (6:1–8). Because believers will "judge the world" (v. 2) in the age to come, they ought to be able to judge within the church in matters "pertaining to this life" (v. 3). Moreover, the Lord's Supper (11:17–34) is also designed to maintain repentance "until he comes" (v. 26). Anyone who partakes of Communion without repentance "eats and drinks judgment on himself" (v. 29). Such temporal judgments (e.g., being "weak and ill"; v. 30) are meant to shake us, "so that we may not be condemned along with the world" (v. 32).

This pattern of temporal judgment awaking the unrepentant to eternal judgment is what Paul has in mind when he says that "the kingdom of God does not consist in talk but in power" (4:20). Consequently, Paul follows with the question, "What do you wish? Shall I come to you with a rod, or with love in a spirit of gentleness?" (v. 21). Paul is here implicitly contrasting God's gentleness in this age with his severity at the day of the Lord. The "power" of the "arrogant people" (v. 19) simply refers to their judging and administrating within the church, which may indeed involve a public display of the Spirit's judgment (cf. Ananias and Sapphira; Acts 5:1–10).

Paul's reference to the eschatological kingdom coming in power (and the implied divine judgment therein) makes much more sense than a present realized kingdom.[98] (If that were the case, it seems Paul would refer to handing the sexually immoral man over to a present realization of the day of the Lord in 5:5 and to believers exercising a present judgment of the world and the angels in 6:2–3!) Thus, the reading of realized eschatology into Paul's reference to the kingdom of God in 4:20 is completely out of line with 1) commonly held expectations of the kingdom; 2) the rest of Paul's uses of "kingdom" in the letter; and 3) the immediate context of chapters 4–6, which highlight temporal judgment in light of eternal judgment.[99]

We Have Been Transferred into the Kingdom

The last of the verses commonly quoted as proof of Paul's belief in a realized eschatology is Colossians 1:13: "He has delivered us from the domain of darkness and transferred us to the kingdom of his beloved Son."[100] Unfortunately, we have here another example of simplistic reliance upon a tense-based translation of the Greek verb to prove realized eschatology. The verbs "deliver" and "transfer" are primarily understood as past tense instead of perfective aspect.[101] Some even go so far as to claim that Paul has no future reality in mind at all![102]

The surrounding context of Paul's thought, however, is clearly eschatological, for in the previous verse the Colossians have been qualified "to share in the *inheritance* of the saints in light." Everywhere else in Paul's letters the inheritance of the saints is understood as eschatological (cf. 1 Cor. 6:9–10; 15:50; Gal. 3:18; 5:21; Eph. 1:11,14,18; 5:5; Col. 3:24).[103] Moreover, Paul's use of "light" (v. 12) and "darkness" (v. 13) is elsewhere in line with the Jewish apocalyptic understanding of this age and the age to come (cf. Rom. 13:12; 1 Cor. 4:5; Eph. 5:8; Phil. 2:15; 1 Thess. 5:5).[104] Thus Paul would understand our deliverance and "the forgiveness of sins" (v. 14) in light of "the Lord Jesus Christ, who gave himself for our sins to deliver us from the present evil age" (Gal. 1:3–4).

Because of the striking similarity of language, Acts 26:15–18 is helpful when discussing Colossians 1:12–14. Paul describes when Jesus appeared and commissioned him by saying,

> I have appeared to you for this purpose . . . delivering you from your people and from the Gentiles—to whom I am sending you to *open their eyes,* so that they may *turn from darkness to light* and from the *power of Satan to God,* that they may receive *forgiveness of sins* and a *place* among those who are sanctified by faith in me. (Acts 26:16–18)

Both passages contain the same basic elements. The opening of the eyes of the Gentiles is echoed in the prayer of Colossians 1:9–12. The turning from darkness to light and from the power of Satan to God is the main point of verses 13–14.[105] And the receiving of forgiveness of sins and "a place" (cf. "the *inheritance* among all those who are sanctified"; Acts 20:32) is the result of such repentance. No one would read realized eschatology into Acts 26 (cf. "my hope in the promise made by God to our fathers"; v. 6), yet it is so confidently and forcefully interjected into Colossians 1.

Paul's point in Colossians 1:12–14 is simply that of Acts 26:16–18. Because we have been qualified to share in the eternal inheritance by the sacrifice of Christ, *we will most certainly be delivered* (perfective aspect) from this present evil age and brought into the coming kingdom of Christ.[106] This eschatological approach accords with the rest of the letter (cf. 1:5,22,27; 3:4,6,24) and the rest of Paul's writings. The interposing of realized eschatology into Colossians 1:13 runs perfectly counter to Paul's thought and his later exhortation:

> Set your minds on things that are above, not on things that are on earth. For you have died, and your life is hidden with Christ in God. When Christ who is your life appears, then you also will appear with him in glory. (3:2–4)

Those who lay down their lives in this age and put no confidence in the flesh will inherit the coming kingdom. Realized eschatology shuts the kingdom of God in people's faces by telling them they have something to live for in this age. This is a deathtrap which will only "lead people into more and more ungodliness" (2 Tim. 2:16) and ultimately destroy their faith.

CONCLUSION

The vast majority of Jewish eschatological references in the New Testament clearly remain as such. The few verses discussed above are commonly cited as proof that Jesus and the apostles reinterpreted and transformed the Jewish eschatology of their day. But as we have seen, these verses—read in the context of their surrounding passages—are actually forceful affirmations of the plain reading of the Law and Prophets. If realized eschatology (i.e., the "already" of inaugurationalism) is nonexistent in the New Testament, what then are we left with? Precisely—*Jewish apocalypticism*, which must be augmented with a *cruciform theology*. Such a worldview lies behind Jesus' rhetorical question, "Was it not necessary that the Messiah [Jewish] should suffer these things [cruciform] and then enter into his glory [apocalyptic]?" (Luke 24:26, NRSV).

Why then speak so forcefully against realized eschatology? It is often claimed that believers will not engage the world and act apart from the motivation of realized eschatology. However, I find this logic to be both flawed and lethal. It is *flawed* in that motivation is driven by conviction of truth and falsehood, love and hate, reward and punishment, etc. Such conviction can apply equally to things of this age (realized eschatology) or things of the age to come (Jewish eschatology). Motivation derived from eternal realities creates holy ambition; motivation derived from temporal realties creates vain ambition. An eternal inheritance is actually a better motivator than a temporal inheritance (or at least it ought to be!).

As such, realized eschatology is also *lethal*, primarily for three reasons. First, it destroys believers' joy in the blessed hope by setting their minds and hearts on an inheritance in this age, while simultaneously mitigating their urgency concerning the imminence of the day of the Lord. This approach erodes an eternal perspective and creates a fundamental worldliness within the church. Second, it disqualifies believers from the eternal inheritance by changing the standard of discipleship in this age from the cross to a spiritually realized kingdom (i.e., the cross is no longer the embodiment of the will of God in this age but rather a historical event which only enabled the present kingdom). This approach inevitably leads to believers laying down their crosses, so to speak, and rejecting a theology of suffering. Third, it deludes believers into supersessionist beliefs concerning the spiritualization of Israel and the jettisoning of the unique calling of the Jews in redemptive history. The church becomes the "new Israel," and Jews are too often held in contempt. Again, realized eschatology irreparably damages the biblical timeline, particularly concerning 1) the day of the Lord, 2) the cross, and 3) Jewish election. Thus, at every turn realized eschatology contradicts the Jewish cruciform-apocalyptic nature of the Bible.

For this reason, Paul described the realized eschatology of his day as "irreverent babble" (1 Tim. 6:20; 2 Tim. 2:16). It is *babble* because it usually goes on and on, with little or no correspondence with reality. For centuries Orthodox Jews have consistently pointed out that Gentile Christians are fundamentally out of touch with reality: The wicked still rule the earth, the nations still surround Israel with raging hatred, Jerusalem has not been glorified, the messianic temple has not been built, the Messiah is not sitting on the Davidic throne, the light of God's day has not dawned, the dead have not been raised, the earth has not been restored, and so on and so forth. Nor does such a realized vision line up with the Old Testament. Where do we find such a spiritualization of these things in the Law and the Prophets? Common sense (the basic ability of reason and deduction given by God) should lead us to the simple conclusion that the resurrection, kingdom, and day of the Lord are a future reality anchored in the parousia of Christ.

Moreover, realized eschatology is *irreverent* because it treats trivially that which God deems most holy. God spoke and revealed himself to the prophets, and as such his self-revelation is bound to his vision for the future. His mantric self-declaration as "the God of Israel" is likewise inextricably tied to "the hope of Israel" (Acts 28:20). The restoration of Israel (Acts 1:6), the redemption of Jerusalem (Luke 2:38), the coming Davidic kingdom (Mark 11:10)—these are not small things to be reimagined, minimized, and marginalized. Rather, Jesus taught his disciples to pray with a holy fear: "Our Father in heaven, hallowed be your name. *Your kingdom* come, *your will* be done, on earth as it is in heaven" (Matt. 6:9–10). The Jewish messianic kingdom is God's kingdom. It is God's will. It is *holy*. Realized eschatology is the product of Gentile arrogance (Rom. 11:17–25). It disrespects the God of Israel. It is *unholy*.

Thus Paul declared that Hymenaeus and those who embraced the realized eschatology of their day had "made shipwreck of their faith" (1 Tim. 1:19), and as such they ought to be "handed over to Satan that they may learn not to *blaspheme*" (v. 20). The trivialization of Jewish eschatology through various techniques of reinterpretation under the banner of realized eschatology is tantamount to blasphemy. Therefore Paul likened the teaching of Hymenaeus and Philetus to "gangrene" (2 Tim. 2:17), which quite literally "overturns" (Gk. *anatrepō*) people's faith (v. 18). So Paul declared concerning such teaching: "Everyone who confesses the name of the Lord must turn away from wickedness" (v. 19, NIV).

ABBREVIATIONS

AB   Anchor Bible

ABD   *The Anchor Bible Dictionary*, ed. David N. Freedman, 6 vols. (Doubleday, 1992).

ANF   *The Ante-Nicene Fathers: The Writings of the Fathers Down to A.D. 325*, ed. A. Roberts, J. Donaldson, and A. C. Coxe, 10 vols. (CLC, 1885–87; reprint Hendrickson, 1994).

APOT   *The Apocrypha and Pseudepigrapha of the Old Testament*, ed. R. H. Charles, 2 vols. (Clarendon, 1913).

BA   *Biblical Archaeologist*

BBR   *Bulletin for Biblical Research*

BDAG   W. Bauer, F. W. Danker, W. Arndt, and F. W. Gingrich, *A Greek-English Lexicon of the New Testament and Other Early Christian Literature*, 3rd ed. (Univ. Chicago, 2001).

BDF   F. Blass, A. Debrunner, and R. W. Funk, *A Greek Grammar of the New Testament and Other Early Christian Literature* (Univ. Chicago, 1961).

BECNT   Baker Exegetical Commentary on the New Testament

BSac   *Bibliotheca Sacra*

CBQ   *Catholic Biblical Quarterly*

CC   Continental Commentaries

CTJ   *Calvin Theological Journal*

DJG   *Dictionary of Jesus and the Gospels*, ed. Joel B. Green and Scot McKnight (InterVarsity, 1992).

DP   The *Dialogues of Plato*, trans. Benjamin Jowett, 3rd ed., 5 vols. (Clarendon, 1892)

EBC   Expositor's Bible Commentary

EDNT   *Exegetical Dictionary of the New Testament*, ed. H. R. Balz and G. Schneider, 3 vols. (Eerdmans, 1990).

Gk.   Greek

HALOT   *The Hebrew and Aramaic Lexicon of the Old Testament*, L. Koehler, W. Baumgartner, and J. J. Stamm, 3rd ed., 4 vols. (E. J. Brill, 1994–99).

Heb.   Hebrew

HTR	*Harvard Theological Review*
ICC	International Critical Commentary
ISBE	*The International Standard Bible Encyclopedia,* ed. Geoffrey W. Bromiley, rev. ed., 4 vols. (Eerdmans, 1979–88).
JBL	*Journal of Biblical Literature*
JE	*The Jewish Encyclopedia,* ed. Isidore Singer, 12 vols. (Funk & Wagnalls, 1901–06).
JETS	*Journal of the Evangelical Theological Society*
JPSTC	The JPS Torah Commentary
JSNT	*Journal for the Study of the New Testament*
JSOT	*Journal for the Study of the Old Testament*
JTS	*Journal of Theological Studies*
LSJ	H. G. Liddell, R. Scott, H. S. Jones, and R. McKenzie, *A Greek-English Lexicon,* 9th ed. (Oxford, 1996).
LW	*Luther's Works,* American Edition, ed. J. Pelikan and H. T. Lehman, 55 vols. (Muehlenberg, Fortress, and Concordia, 1955–86).
LXX	Septuagint (Old Testament in Greek, third century BC)
NAC	New American Commentary
NBD	*New Bible Dictionary,* ed. D. R. W. Wood and I. Howard Marshall, 3rd ed. (InterVarsity, 1996).
NHLE	*The Nag Hammadi Library in English*, ed. James M. Robinson, 4th ed. (E. J. Brill, 1996).
NIB	The New Interpreter's Bible
NICNT	New International Commentary on the New Testament
NICOT	New International Commentary on the Old Testament
NIDCC	*New International Dictionary of the Christian Church*, ed. J. D. Douglas, Earle E. Cairns, and James E. Ruark (Zondervan, 1978).
NIDNTT	*New International Dictionary of New Testament Theology*, ed. Colin Brown, 4 vols. (Zondervan, 1986).
NIDOTTE	*New International Dictionary of Old Testament Theology and Exegesis*, ed. Willem A. VanGemeren, 5 vols. (Zondervan, 1997).
NIGTC	New International Greek Testament Commentary
NIVAC	NIV Application Commentary
NovT	*Novum Testamentum*
NPNF1	*A Select Library of the Nicene and Post-Nicene Fathers of the Christian Church*, First Series, ed. Philip Schaff, 14 vols. (CLC, 1886–89; reprint Hendrickson, 1994).

NPNF2	*A Select Library of the Nicene and Post-Nicene Fathers of the Christian Church*, Second Series, ed. Philip Schaff and Henry Wace, 14 vols. (CLC, 1890–1900; reprint Hendrickson, 1994).
NT	New Testament
NSBT	New Studies in Biblical Theology
NTS	*New Testament Studies*
OTP	*The Old Testament Pseudepigrapha*, ed. James H. Charlesworth, 2 vols. (Doubleday, 1983–85).
OT	Old Testament
par.	(and) parallel passage(s)
PNTC	Pillar New Testament Commentary
PTR	*Princeton Theological Review*
SBJT	*The Southern Baptist Journal of Theology*
TDNT	*Theological Dictionary of the New Testament*, ed. G. Kittel and G. Friedrich, 10 vols. (Eerdmans, 1964–76).
TWOT	*Theological Wordbook of the Old Testament*, ed. R. L. Harris, G. L. Archer Jr., and B. K. Waltke, 2 vols. (Moody, 1980).
TynBul	*Tyndale Bulletin*
TNTC	Tyndale New Testament Commentary
TOTC	Tyndale Old Testament Commentary
WBC	Word Biblical Commentary
WTJ	*Westminster Theological Journal*
ZECNT	Zondervan Exegetical Commentary on the New Testament

NOTES

Chapter One

1. See G. W. Bromiley, "Truth," *ISBE*, 4:926–28; cf. Roger Nicole, "The Biblical Concept of Truth," in *Scripture and Truth*, ed. D. A. Carson and John D. Woodbridge (Grand Rapids: Baker, 1992), 287–98.

2. Concerning the OT apocryphal writings, T. W. Davies notes, "The Jews in the early Christian centuries had really two Bibles: (1) There was the Hebrew Bible which does not include the Apocrypha, and which circulated in Palestine and Babylon; (2) there was the Greek version (LXX [which did include the Apocrypha]) used by Greek-speaking Jews everywhere" ("Apocrypha," *ISBE*, 1:163). Since the apostolic church relied on the latter, this work will reference apocryphal books in more of a deuterocanonical ("second canon") sense, lying somewhere between protocanonical (OT and NT) and noncanonical (e.g., pseudepigrapha); see also David A. deSilva, *Introducing the Apocrypha: Message, Context, and Significance* (Grand Rapids: Baker, 2002).

3. See an introduction to pluralism in Lesslie Newbigin, *The Gospel in a Pluralist Society* (Grand Rapids: Eerdmans, 1989).

4. Early Christianity never sought to part ways with Judaism, but was only regarded as a Jewish "sect" (Acts 24:5,14; 28:22). Thus, Judeo-Christianity was originally "a territory without border lines" (Daniel Boyarin, *Border Lines: The Partition of Judaeo-Christianity* [Philadelphia: University of Pennsylvania Press, 2004], 1).

5. In modern times the liberal tradition has largely rejected the bodily resurrection of Jesus, as typified by the Jesus Seminar (e.g., J. D. Crossan, R. Funk, M. J. Borg, S. L. Harris, B. Mack, etc). By undermining the definitive event of Christianity, they "destroy the faith of some" (2 Tim. 2:18, NIV). See rebuttals by Michael J. Wilkins and J. P. Moreland, eds., *Jesus Under Fire: Modern Scholarship Reinvents the Historical Jesus* (Grand Rapids: Zondervan, 1995); Craig A. Evans, *Fabricating Jesus: How Modern Scholars Distort the Gospels* (Downers Grove, IL: InterVarsity, 2006); and N. T. Wright, *The Resurrection of the Son of God* (Minneapolis: Fortress, 2003).

6. John H. Gerstner observes,

   > Despite the dominant usage of *euangellismos* in the New Testament, its derivative, evangelical, was not widely or controversially employed until the Reformation period. Then it came into prominence with Martin Luther precisely because he reasserted Paul's teaching on the *euangellismos* as the indispensable message of salvation. Its light, he argued, was hidden under a bushel of ecclesiastical authority, tradition, and liturgy. The essence of the saving message for Luther was justification by faith alone, the article by which not only the church stands or falls but each individual as well. Erasmus, Thomas More, and Johannes Eck denigrated those who accepted this view and referred to them as "evangelicals." ("The Theological Boundaries of Evangelical Faith," in *The Evangelicals: What They Believe, Who They Are, Where They Are Changing*, ed. David F. Wells and John D. Woodbridge [Nashville: Abingdon, 1975], 23)

7. Kenneth S. Kantzer writes,

> Theology, therefore, must not be drawn from reason (though for the most part the evangelical acknowledges his dependence on consistent reason and logical processes), not from experience (though he recognizes that without experience by which it is personally appropriated, good theology is not only unattainable but is utterly worthless), and not from tradition (though he treasures it with gratitude and freely acknowledges that without tradition his spiritual understanding would be impoverished and he might never come to faith). The evangelical, rather, seeks to construct his theology on the teaching of the Bible, the whole Bible, and nothing but the Bible; and this formative principle represents a basic unifying factor throughout the whole of contemporary evangelicalism. ("Unity and Diversity in Evangelical Faith," in Wells and Woodbridge, eds., *The Evangelicals*, 52)

8. For a well-articulated history of Protestant evangelicalism, see Stanley J. Grenz, "Nurturing the Soul, Informing the Mind: The Genesis of the Evangelical Scripture Principle," in *Evangelicals and Scripture: Tradition, Authority, and Hermeneutics*, ed. V. Bacote, L. C. Miguélez, and D. L. Okholm (Downers Grove, IL: InterVarsity, 2004), 19–41.

9. Moisés Silva, "Who Needs Hermeneutics Anyway?" in *Introduction to Biblical Hermeneutics: The Search for Meaning*, ed. Walter C. Kaiser Jr. and Moisés Silva (Grand Rapids: Zondervan, 2007), 17.

10. See the helpful introductory handbook by W. Randolph Tate, *Handbook for Biblical Interpretation: An Essential Guide to Methods, Terms, and Concepts*, 2nd ed. (Grand Rapids: Baker Academic, 2012).

11. Paul Feinberg describes the hermeneutical difficulties:

> Scripture is the product of dual authorship. Which author's intention, man's or God's, is determinative? If it is the human author's intention, then the interpreter is dealing with a finite mind in a historical and cultural context. Here the author's intention can be determined. On the other hand, if it is the divine author's intention, then, since God is infinite and omniscient, it would appear that the meaning could go beyond the concrete, historical understanding of the text. He could mean things that human interpreters would miss. It would seem that almost any statement, no matter how simple, might have nuances that we would miss. In sum, if you limit meaning to the human author's intention, then you are faced with his ignorance and possible error. While, on the other hand, if meaning is expanded to the divine author's intention, you are up against our ignorance and the superiority of God's ways to ours. ("Hermeneutics of Discontinuity," in *Continuity and Discontinuity: Perspectives on the Relationship Between the Old and New Testaments*, ed. J. S. Feinberg [Westchester, IL: Crossway, 1988], 112–13)

12. See J. I. Packer, "Infallible Scripture and the Role of Hermeneutics," in *Scripture and Truth*, 325–56.

13. Thus I agree with the Chicago Statement on Biblical Inerrancy (published in C. F. H. Henry, *God, Revelation and Authority*, vol. 4 [Waco: Word, 1979], 211–19) that the Scriptures are both inerrant and infallible: "*Infallible* signifies the quality of neither misleading nor being misled and so safeguards in categorical terms the truth that Holy Scripture is a sure, safe, and reliable rule and guide in all matters. Similarly, *inerrant* signifies the quality of being free from all falsehood or mistake and so safeguards the truth that Holy Scripture is entirely true and trustworthy in all its assertions" (217).

14. Here we are forced into some form of *sensus plenior* (literally, "the fuller sense"), as clearly evidenced in passages such as Dan. 12:6–9, John 11:49–52, Eph. 5:29–33, and 1 Peter

1:10–12; see an introduction in R. E. Brown, "The History and Development of the Theory of a *Sensus Plenior*," *CBQ* 15 (1953): 141–62; and W. S. LaSor, "Prophecy, Inspiration, and *Sensus Plenior*," *TynBul* 29, no. 1 (1978): 48–60.

15. See a concise history of development by F. F. Bruce and J. J. Scott Jr., "Interpretation of the Bible," in *Evangelical Dictionary of Theology*, 2nd ed., ed. Walter A. Elwell (Grand Rapids: Baker, 2001), 611–15.

16. See an introduction by Gordon D. Fee and Douglas K. Stuart, *How to Read the Bible for All Its Worth*, 3rd ed. (Grand Rapids: Zondervan, 2003), 17–31.

17. Concerning pretheoretical and presuppositional aspects of worldview, see James W. Sire, *Naming the Elephant: Worldview as a Concept* (Downers Grove, IL: InterVarsity, 2004), 75–86.

18. As is evident by a cursory study of the use of the Old Testament in the New; see Gregory K. Beale, ed., *The Right Doctrine from the Wrong Texts? Essays on the Use of the Old Testament in the New* (Grand Rapids: Baker Academic, 1994).

19. Norman L. Geisler and William D. Watkins, *Worlds Apart: A Handbook on World Views*, 2nd ed. (Grand Rapids: Baker, 1989), 11.

20. N. T. Wright, *The New Testament and the People of God* (London: SPCK, 1992), 123.

21. As Francis Schaeffer concluded, "There is one worldview which can explain the existence of the universe, its form, and the uniqueness of people—the worldview given to us in the Bible" (Francis A. Schaeffer, *The Complete Works of Francis A. Schaeffer: A Christian Worldview* [Westchester, IL: Crossway, 1982], 5:357).

Moreover, "The Christian system (what is taught in the whole Bible) is a unity of thought. Christianity is not just a lot of bits and pieces—there is a beginning and an end, a whole system of truth, and this system is the only system that will stand up to all the questions that are presented to us as we face the reality of existence" (ibid., 1:178).

22. Though we affirm a *general confluence* between the human authors and divine author, especially concerning historical/gospel narratives and pastoral/poetical writings, the transcendence of the divine author must be maintained, especially in the prophetical/apocalyptical writings. See a summary of evangelical approaches in W. Edward Glenny, "The Divine Meaning of Scripture: Explanations and Limitations," *JETS* 38, no. 4 (December 1995): 481–500.

23. Thus, our goal is not to replicate the worldview of the early church or of ancient Israel, but to understand reality as it really is—the assumption being that the worldview of the biblical writers, though not perfect, is closer, in an ultimate sense, to correspondence with reality than our own post-Enlightenment worldview. This is contrary to common naturalistic sentiment, which regards ancient Near Eastern thought as fundamentally "primitive."

24. David K. Naugle, *Worldview: The History of a Concept* (Grand Rapids: Eerdmans, 2002), 4.

25. A term coined by Immanuel Kant in *Critique of Judgment* (1790) and expounded upon by the nineteenth-century German philosophers G. W. F. Hegel (1770–1831), Wilhelm Dilthey (1833–1911), and Friedrich Nietzsche (1844–1900); see Naugle, *Worldview*, 68–107.

26. "The word is used in a great many areas, ranging from the natural sciences to philosophy to theology. Authors who use it often do so without concern for proper definition, and even when definitions are given they tend to be far from precise" (Sander Griffioen, "The Worldview Approach to Social Theory: Hazards and Benefits," in *Stained Glass: Worldviews and Social Science*, ed. Paul A. Marshall, Sander Griffioen, and Richard J. Mouw

[Lanham, MD: University Press of America, 1989], 83; quoted in Sire, *Naming the Elephant*, 23).

27. *Concise Oxford English Dictionary*, 11th ed., s.v. "world view."

28. See the definitive study of the term's history and usage in Naugle's *Worldview*, which covers Protestant evangelicalism (chap. 1), Roman Catholicism and Eastern Orthodoxy (chap. 2), philological history (chap. 3), philosophical history (chaps. 4–6), and the various scientific disciplinary histories (chaps. 7–8). Naugle concludes that "in the entire history of 'worldview,' no single philosophic school or religious community has given more sustained attention to or taken more advantage of this concept than Protestant evangelicals" (p. 31).

29. The two primary Reformed headwaters of worldview thinking (with much overlap, even from the beginning) are James Orr, *The Christian View of God and the World* (Edinburgh: Andrew Elliot, 1893); and Abraham Kuyper, *Calvinism* (New York: Revell, 1899). From Orr have generally flowed the major works of Carl F. H. Henry, Arthur Holmes, and Ronald Nash. From the Kuyperian tradition we have the works of Herman Dooyeweerd, Cornelius Van Til, Francis Schaeffer, James Olthius, and Albert Wolters. All modern discussion of worldview owes greatly to the Reformed tradition (see esp. Naugle, *Worldview*, 4–32).

30. Note also the contributions of Protestant missiologists: Paul G. Hiebert, *Transforming Worldviews: An Anthropological Understanding of How People Change* (Grand Rapids: Baker, 2008); Charles H. Kraft, *Christianity in Culture: A Study in Dynamic Biblical Theologizing in Cross-Cultural Perspective* (Maryknoll, NY: Orbis, 1979); and David J. Hesselgrave, *Communicating Christ Cross-Culturally* (Grand Rapids: Zondervan, 1978), esp. 190–285.

31. Sire hits this in his first two worldview questions: "1. *What is prime reality—the really real? . . . 2. What is the nature of external reality, that is, the world around us?*" (James W. Sire, *The Universe Next Door: A Basic Worldview Catalog*, 5th ed. [Downers Grove, IL: InterVarsity, 2009], 22).

32. "A world view is a *macro*-model; it is a model that attempts to explain *all* of reality, not just some aspect of it. . . . [It] is designed to explain *all* relationships of all things and/or events in the *whole* of reality" (Geisler and Watkins, *Worlds Apart*, 14).

33. Within naturalism, the "theory of everything" has become the holy grail of modern physicists, a concept first introduced by John Ellis, "The Superstring: Theory of Everything, or of Nothing?" *Nature* 323 (1986): 595–98.

34. Thus, Corliss Lamont (1902–1995), the leading humanist spokesman of the twentieth century, entitled chap. 4 of *The Philosophy of Humanism* "Humanism's Theory of the Universe," explaining,

> Any complete philosophy of existence requires a carefully worked out theory of the universe, in technical terms a *metaphysics*, an ontology, or a world-view. As we have already seen, Humanism believes that Nature itself constitutes the sum total of reality, that matter-energy and not mind is the foundation stuff of the universe, and that supernatural entities simply do not exist. This nonreality of the supernatural means, on the human level, that human beings do not possess supernatural and immortal souls; and, on the level of the universe as a whole, that our cosmos does not possess a supernatural and eternal God. (Corliss Lamont, *The Philosophy of Humanism*, 8th ed. [Amherst, NY: Humanist Press, 1997], 126)

35. Acknowledging that all worldviews have a great internal diversity of thought and practice—*especially* Hinduism—we will proceed with broad generalizations that roughly

represent the majority. For an introduction to Hinduism's *Brahman*, see R. C. Zaehner, *Hinduism*, 2nd ed., OPUS Series (Oxford: Oxford University Press, 1966), 36–56. For an overview of the origin and construction of the cosmos, as defined by the later Puranic tradition, see Cornelia Dimmitt and J. A. B. van Buitenen, eds., *Classical Hindu Mythology: A Reader in the Sanskrit Purānas* (Philadelphia: Temple University Press, 1978), 32–54.

36. Edward Conze observes, "In their views on the structure and evolution of the universe, the Buddhists were, however, content to borrow from the traditions of contemporary Hinduism" (*Buddhism: Its Essence and Development* [Oxford: Bruno Cassirer, 1951], 34).

According to Akira Sadakata, these "three worlds" are drawn from Brahmanistic sources and are mirrored in the early Vedic tripartite universe of *bhur* (earth), *bhuva* (moon), and *svar* (sun), which composed the lower, middle, and upper regions of the Brahmanic universe, respectively. By their sacrifices, the gods had attained to the upper regions of *svar*, which humans too could reach through their sacrifices. This in turn defined the practice of early Brahminic tradition. Later Vedic and Puranic tradition developed this construct into many heavens and hells, but retained the same vertical universe. See Akira Sadakata, *Buddhist Cosmology: Philosophy and Origins*, trans. Gaynor Sekimori (Tokyo: Kōsei Publishing, 1997), 25–47.

37. Buddhist cosmology is exceedingly complex; see an excellent overview by Rupert Gethin, *The Foundations of Buddhism*, OPUS series (Oxford: Oxford University Press, 1998), 112–32.

38. The full progression is outlined in chap. 42 of the classical text *Tao Te Ching*: "The Tao gives birth to One [*chi*, the primordial manifestation of cosmic energy]. One gives birth to Two [*yin/yang*, complementary existential principles]. Two gives birth to Three [*sanqing*, the "Three Pure Ones," the three highest deities in the Taoist pantheon]. Three gives birth to all things [*wanwu*]" (Lao Tzu, *Tao Te Ching: A New English Version*, trans. Stephen Mitchell [New York: Harper & Row, 1988], 42; information in brackets added).

"This passage describes the cosmogonic process as moving from Nonbeing or the Dao to Oneness; the One then spontaneously divides into the two complementary principles (yin/yang) which in turn generate the 'ten thousand things' (*wanwu*) or the manifest cosmos" (Fabrizio Pregadio and Lowell Skar, "Inner Alchemy (*Neidan*)," in *Daoism Handbook*, ed. Livia Kohn [Leiden, Netherlands: Brill, 2000], 483).

39. "Naturalism," *The Encyclopedia of Philosophy: Supplement*, ed. Donald M. Borchert (New York: MacMillan, 1996), 372. However, the definition of "nature," or the oft-referred to "physical realm," is something of a philosophical quandary, since its parameters are assumedly defined by human sensibility—that is, what we can observe, measure, test, etc.

40. Though "Christian Platonist" has long been used to describe a Platonist who wears a Christian mask, "Christoplatonism" is a term recently popularized by Randy Alcorn (see *Heaven* [Wheaton: Tyndale, 2004], 52, 110, 459–66).

41. Of course it is "God" (Gen. 1:1a) who is truly the ultimate reality, from which the heavens and earth are then created (see Sire's discussion in chap. 3 of *Naming the Elephant*). For the purposes of understanding the nature and function of worldview, we will limit our metaphysical discussion to creation.

42. Sigmund Mowinckel explains the working of these elements in a biblical context:

Eschatology is a doctrine or a complex of ideas about 'the last things', which is more or less organically coherent and developed. Every eschatology includes in some form or another a dualistic conception of the course of history, and implies that the present state of things and the present world order will suddenly come to an end and be superseded by another of an essentially different kind. As a rule this new order has the character of a fresh beginning, a *restitutio in integrum*, a return to the origins, without the corruption which subsequently overtook and deformed the original creation. Eschatology also includes the thought that this drama has a universal, cosmic character. The universe itself, heaven and earth, is thrown into the melting pot. It follows that this is not brought about by human or historical forces, or by any immanent, evolutionary process. The transformation is definitely catastrophic in character, and is brought about by supernatural, divine, or demonic powers. (*He That Cometh: The Messiah Concept in the Old Testament and Later Judaism*, trans. G. W. Anderson [Nashville: Abingdon, 1956], 125–26)

43. Thus the common tradition cataloged by Mircea Eliade, *The Myth of the Eternal Return: Or, Cosmos and History*, trans. W. R. Trask (Princeton: Princeton University Press, 1971).

44. So N. T. Wright observes that "all worldviews contain an irreducible narrative element, which stands alongside the other worldview elements" (*New Testament and the People of God*, 38). Moreover, "Worldviews provide the *stories* through which human beings view reality. Narrative is the most characteristic expression of worldview, going deeper than the isolated observation or fragmented remark" (ibid., 123).

45. Ibid. Wright slightly modified these questions from Brian J. Walsh and J. Richard Middleton in *The Transforming Vision: Shaping a Christian World View* (Downers Grove, IL: InterVarsity, 1984), 35. See also the updated edition of *Transforming Vision*, which addresses postmodernity and contains an extended discussion of "metanarrative" (*Truth Is Stranger Than It Used to Be: Biblical Faith in a Postmodern Age* [Downers Grove, IL: InterVarsity, 1995], esp. 63–107).

46. See also Sire's list of existential questions in *The Universe Next Door*, 22–23.

47. Wright, *New Testament and the People of God*, 42.

48. Naugle, *Worldview*, 303.

49. "Implicit in all of this is the additional point that these beliefs must cohere in some way to form a system. A fancy term that can be useful here is *conceptual scheme*, by which I mean a pattern or arrangement of concepts (ideas). A worldview, then, is a conceptual scheme by which we consciously or unconsciously place or fit everything we believe and by which we interpret and judge reality" (Ronald H. Nash, *Worldviews in Conflict: Choosing Christianity in a World of Ideas* [Grand Rapids: Zondervan, 1992], 16).

50. As Sire's definition begins, "A worldview is a *commitment*, a fundamental orientation of the heart, that can be expressed as a story or in a set of presuppositions (assumptions which may be true or entirely false) which we hold (consciously or subconsciously, consistently or inconsistently) about the basic constitution of reality, and that provides the foundation on which we live and move and have our being" (*Naming the Elephant*, 122; italics added).

51. Wendy Doniger O'Flaherty articulates the perpetual cycle of perfection, sin, destruction, and recreation:

> The myth of the Fall, or the loss of the Golden Age, entails three presuppositions: there was a beginning of human action, a first wicked act, and a previous period in which God had created everything in perfection. But how can this be used to qualify the cycle of rebirth, which has no beginning? . . .
>
> The Indian answer to this paradox is simple, and brilliant: the Fall itself is cyclical; it happens again and again, over and over, within the cycle of rebirth. . . .

The world begins over and over again; each time, it is created out of water, and the Golden Age takes place. This Age degenerates until finally the fourth Age is reached, the present Kali Age, which is destroyed by fire and flood; all is once again water, out of which the world is created anew. (*The Origins of Evil in Hindu Mythology* [Berkeley: University of California Press, 1976], 17–18)

52. Gautama Buddha (c. 563–483 BC) assumedly accepted the Hindu framework for reality (though this is greatly debated in modern times). He clearly assumed the soteriological cycle of *samsara* and the goal of *moksha*, which attains *nirvana*—that is, the extinction of desire, suffering, and self-consciousness (see Gethin, *Foundations of Buddhism*, chaps. 3 and 5). The primary difference between the two worldviews lies in the Buddhist response and praxis. The emphasis is more upon *the practicing of holiness* that leads to enlightenment (i.e., the "Noble Eightfold Path"), rather than speculating about the nature of reality.

"Buddhism regards itself as presenting a system of training in conduct, meditation, and understanding that constitutes a path leading to the cessation of suffering. Everything is to be subordinated to this goal. And in this connection the Buddha's teachings suggest that preoccupation with certain beliefs and ideas about the ultimate nature of the world and our destiny in fact hinders our progress along the path rather than helping it" (Gethin, *Foundations of Buddhism*, 65–66).

In this way, the role of the gods is greatly subordinated to Buddha's example and "teachings" (the *Dharma*, distinguished from the lower-case cosmic law *dharma*). Along with the *Satigha* ("assembly, community"), these become the *tri-ratna* ("three jewels") by which one is distinguished as a Buddhist, saying upon conversion, "To the Buddha I go for refuge; to the Dharma I go for refuge; to the Satigha I go for refuge" (ibid., 34).

53. As Richard Dawkins is known for saying, "In a universe of electrons and selfish genes, blind physical forces and genetic replication, some people are going to get hurt, other people are going to get lucky, and you won't find any rhyme or reason in it, nor any justice. The universe that we observe has precisely the properties we should expect if there is, at bottom, no design, no purpose, no evil, no good, nothing but pitiless indifference" ("God's Utility Function," *Scientific American* [November 1995]: 85).

54. On the direct relationship between biblical protology and eschatology, "the old and new creations," see Warren A. Gage, *The Gospel of Genesis: Studies in Protology and Eschatology* (Winona Lake, IN: Eisenbrauns, 1984).

55. The inherent conflict between naturalism and these "primitive" apocalyptic elements has led many in modern times to "demythologize" the Scriptures, following the lead of Martin Heidegger (1889–1976) and Rudolf Bultmann (1884–1976)—and to an extent Paul Tillich (1886–1965). The existentialist movement of the twentieth century, both within and without the church, was essentially an ideological movement that articulated various aspects of modern life within a naturalistic framework (though of course claiming to explore human existence without metaphysical presuppositions).

Bultmann's work (see esp. "New Testament and Mythology," in *New Testament and Mythology and Other Basic Writings*, ed. and trans. S. M. Ogden [Philadelphia: Fortress, 1984], 1–43) is thus summarized:

The term dymythologization [more commonly rendered "demythologization"] means the decoding of myth or the reinterpretation of ancient mythical patterns of thought in the Bible into contemporary thought patterns. Bultmann believes that contemporary thought demands a modern scientific view of the universe which interprets reality in terms of a closed cause and effect natural order. Such a view excludes the possibility of miracles defined as supernaturally caused events; every event has a natural cause. . . .

Therefore, Bultmann asserts that the biblical myths, such as the three-level universe, with heaven above, the flat earth with hell below, angels, Satan, incarnation, resurrection, ascension, second coming, judgment, and all miracles, require an existential interpretation to be meaningful for modern man. (Alfred A. Glenn, "Rudolf Bultmann: Removing the False Offense," *JETS* 16, no. 2 [1973]: 73–74; information in brackets added)

56. Historical rabbinic Judaism and modern Judaism hold the same basic framework and timeline, yet reject a suffering Messiah (see chaps. 7 and 8).

57. The Demiurge ("Artisan/Craftsman") was the intermediary who used the forms to create materiality. Plato's theory of the forms is found scattered throughout his dialogues; cf. *Timaeus*, 27–52; *Phaedo*, 73–80; *Republic*, 3:402–3; 5:472–83; *Cratylus*, 389–90, 439–40; *Phaedrus*, 248–50; *Theaetetus*, 184–86; *Sophist*, 246–59.

58. As portrayed by Plato's parable of the cave:

This entire allegory, I said, you may now append, dear Glaucon, to the previous argument; *the prison-house is the world of sight*, the light of the fire is the sun, and you will not misapprehend me if you interpret *the journey upwards to be the ascent of the soul into the intellectual world* according to my poor belief, which, at your desire, I have expressed—whether rightly or wrongly God knows. But, whether true or false, my opinion is that *in the world of knowledge the idea of good appears last of all*, and is seen only with an effort; and, when seen, is also inferred to be the universal author of all things beautiful and right, parent of light and of the lord of light in this visible world, and the immediate source of reason and truth in the intellectual; and that this is the power upon which he who would act rationally either in public or private life must have his eye fixed. (Plato, *The Republic*, 7:517 [*DP*, 3:217]; italics added)

59. As exemplified by the death of Socrates (see Plato's *Phaedo*), who on his last day expounded upon the immortality of the soul and embraced death with peace and joy. On the contrast between Socrates and Jesus, see Oscar Cullmann, *Immortality of the Soul or the Resurrection of the Dead? The Witness of the New Testament* (London: Epworth Press, 1958), 19–27.

60. "*Until philosophers are kings, or the kings and princes of this world have the spirit and power of philosophy, and political greatness and wisdom meet in one, and those commoner natures who pursue either to the exclusion of the other are compelled to stand aside, cities will never have rest from their evils—no, nor the human race, as I believe—and then only will this our State have a possibility of life and behold the light of day*" (Plato, *The Republic*, 5:473 [*DP*, 3:170–71]).

61. Alfred N. Whitehead, *Process and Reality: An Essay in Cosmology*, ed. David R. Griffin and Donald W. Sherburne, corrected ed. (originally published in 1929; New York: Free Press, 1979), 39.

62. The crystallized concept of "nature" as a materialistic metaphysical whole developed out of the resurgence of Aristotelian thought in late medieval scholasticism (c. 1250–1350); see "Nature" and "Physical" in *The Oxford Dictionary of English Etymology*, ed. C. T. Onions (Oxford: Oxford University Press, 1966), 604 and 677, respectively. The Platonic contrast of the immaterial "supernatural" developed in tandem, esp. during the Renaissance; see "Supernatural," *Chambers Dictionary of Etymology*, ed. Robert K. Barnhart (Edinburgh: Chambers, 1988), 1093.

63. J. Christiaan Beker, *Paul's Apocalyptic Gospel: The Coming Triumph of God* (Philadelphia: Fortress, 1982), 108.

64. As classically outlined by Richard Bell, *The Origin of Islam in Its Christian Environment* (London: Macmillan, 1926); cf. David Cook, *Studies in Muslim Apocalyptic* (Princeton, NJ: Darwin Press, 2002).

65. J. Christiaan Beker observes,

> It must be pointed out that the interpretation of the future eschatological dimension of the hope has been largely a stream of misinterpretation in the history of the church. To be sure, both Albert Schweitzer and Martin Werner have drawn attention to the de-eschatologizing of the early Christian message in the history of the church. However, their basic insights have until recently been neglected by systematic theology and biblical scholarship alike. The history of futurist eschatology in the church has been one long process of spiritualization and/or ecclesiologizing or institutionalizing, especially under the influence of Origen and Augustine. From the condemnation of Montanism in the second century and the exclusion of chiliastic apocalypticism at the Council of Ephesus (A.D. 431) through its condemnation by the reformers (in the Augsburg Confession) and until today, future eschatology was pushed out of the mainstream of church life and thus pushed into heretical aberrations. The impact of this spiritualizing process and the distaste for apocalyptic speculations made by sectarian groups have no doubt contributed to the overwhelmingly negative estimate of apocalyptic by biblical and theological scholarship since the Enlightenment. (*Paul the Apostle: The Triumph of God in Life and Thought* [Philadelphia: Fortress, 1980], 138–39)

66. See an introduction in John H. Walton, *Ancient Near Eastern Thought and the Old Testament: Introducing the Conceptual World of the Hebrew Bible* (Grand Rapids: Baker, 2006), 15–40.

67. See a survey of the rise of apocalyptic research in Klaus Koch, *The Rediscovery of Apocalyptic*, trans. M. Kohl (London: SCM Press, 1972).

68. Wright, *New Testament and the People of God*, 286.

69. For example, David Flusser, *Jesus* (New York: Herder and Herder, 1969); and Geza Vermes, *Jesus the Jew: A Historian's Reading of the Gospels* (London: Collins, 1973). See an early summary of the movement by Donald A. Hagner, *The Jewish Reclamation of Jesus: An Analysis and Critique of Modern Jewish Study of Jesus* (Grand Rapids: Zondervan, 1984). The characteristic element of the so-called "third quest" for the historical Jesus has concerned his Jewish background; see esp. Ben Witherington III, *The Jesus Quest: The Third Search for the Jew of Nazareth* (Downers Grove, IL: InterVarsity, 1997).

70. So Bultmann states,

> It is entirely possible that in a past mythical world picture truths may be rediscovered that were lost during a period of enlightenment; and theology has every reason to ask whether this may be possible in the case of the world picture of the New Testament. But it is impossible to repristinate a past world picture by sheer resolve, especially a *mythical* world picture, now that all of our thinking is irrevocably formed by science. A blind acceptance of New Testament mythology would be simply arbitrariness; to make such acceptance a demand of faith would be to reduce faith to a work, as Wilhelm Herrmann made clear, one would have thought, once and for all. Any satisfaction of the demand would be a forced *sacrificium intellectus*, and any of us who would make it would be peculiarly split and untruthful. For we would affirm for our faith or religion a world picture that our life otherwise denied. Criticism of the New Testament is simply a given with modern thinking as it has come to us through our history. (*New Testament and Mythology*, 3–4)

71. Though Albert Schweitzer jettisoned a theology of the cross and though his mystical conclusions went awry, his basic Jewish-eschatological premise holds true:

> The thoroughgoing application of Jewish eschatology to the interpretation of the teaching and work of Jesus has created a new fact upon which to base the history of dogma. . . . The teaching of Jesus does not in any of its aspects go outside the Jewish world of thought and project itself into a non-Jewish world, but represents a deeply ethical and perfected version of the contemporary Apocalyptic.
>
> Therefore the Gospel is at its starting-point exclusively Jewish-eschatological. . . . The history of dogma has to show how what was originally purely Jewish-eschatological has developed into something that is Greek. (Schweitzer, *Paul and His Interpreters: A Critical History*, trans. W. Montgomery [London: A. & C. Black, 1912], ix–x)

Likewise Schweitzer's assessment of the academic tradition remains true: "Theological science has in fact been dominated by the desire *to minimise as much as possible the element of Jewish Apocalyptic* in Jesus and Paul, and so far as possible to represent the Hellenisation of the Gospel as having been prepared for by them. It thinks it has gained something when in formulating the problem it has done its best *to soften down the antitheses to the utmost* with a view to providing every facility for conceiving the transition of the Gospel from one world of thought to the other" (ibid., ix; italics added).

Unfortunately, Schweitzer commonly associated Jewish-apocalyptic with "the end of the world," which is inaccurate, as many, including N. T. Wright, have pointed out: "The events, including the ones that were expected to come as the climax of YHWH's restoration of Israel, remained within (what we think of as) the this-worldly ambit. The 'kingdom of god' has nothing to do with the world itself coming to an end. That makes no sense either of the basic Jewish worldview or of the texts in which the Jewish hope is expressed. It was after all the Stoics, not the first-century Jews, who characteristically believed that the world would be dissolved in fire" (*New Testament and the People of God*, 285).

72. The embarrassment of the apocalyptic was highlighted by Klaus Koch, *Ratlos vor der Apokalyptik* (Gütersloh, Germany: Mohn, 1970), roughly translated "At a Loss over Apocalyptic," published in English as *The Rediscovery of Apocalyptic*.

73. Clayton Sullivan, *Rethinking Realized Eschatology* (Macon, GA: Mercer University Press, 1988), 4.

74. So Beker writes,

> Indeed, although scholars usually concede that apocalyptic terminology is an important building block in Paul's theology, its future-imminent aspect represents an obstacle to our modern mentality, to the extent that it is either demythologized in an existentialist fashion or neutralized.
>
> Here, if anywhere, the interpretive tension between "what it meant" and "what it means" is obvious. The so-called primitive world view of apocalyptic and the delay of the parousia are, for most interpreters, such an overwhelming problem, and the utopian distortions and delusions of apocalyptic fanatics such an embarrassment, that Paul's emphasis on the imminent parousia is for all practical purposes either treated as peripheral, or existentially reinterpreted, or subjected to developmental theories. (*Paul's Apocalyptic Gospel*, 45)

75. See a comprehensive history of the movement by Ronald L. Numbers, *The Creationists: The Evolution of Scientific Creationism* (New York: Alfred A. Knopf, 1992). The expanded edition (Harvard University Press, 2006) addresses the intelligent design movement.

76. See Hal Lindsey, et al.; cf. Bart D. Ehrman, *Jesus: Apocalyptic Prophet of the New Millennium* (Oxford: Oxford University Press, 1999), 3–19. But as Beker points out, "Legitimate

criticism, however, should not make us complacent or blind to the sad fact that respectable theologies of the established church have continuously dismissed apocalyptic from their own theological agenda and are thus indirectly responsible for the distortions of neo-apocalypticism among us. For the apocalyptic silence of the established church certainly left the vacuum that this movement now fills" (*Paul's Apocalyptic Gospel*, 28).

77. As Dale C. Allison acknowledges, "In like fashion, when the Jesus tradition envisions the Son of man coming on the clouds or foretells the general resurrection, we should, *even if this puts us in the disagreeable company of modern fundamentalists*, think of the redeemer literally flying upon the clouds and of the redeemed literally coming forth from their graves—and also of all that those events represent: the vindication of Jesus, the triumph of believers, the judgment of the wicked, the fulfillment of prophecy, etc. The literal and the symbolic need not be sundered" (*Jesus of Nazareth: Millenarian Prophet* [Minneapolis: Fortress, 1998], 164; italics added).

Moreover, Allison asserts,

Beginning with Origen, most of the church fathers disparaged chiliasm and literal eschatological expectations as "judaizing." They were right—not to disparage, but to make the association with Judaism. For the literal interpretation corresponds to the original intention of the texts, which were forged within the Jewish tradition, a tradition that so often anticipated a literal messianic kingdom in Jerusalem. In other words, the prophecies of a millennium or golden age were originally taken at more or less face value, and this continued to be the case through much of the second century. But as Christianity became an almost wholly Gentile phenomenon and the elapse of the years saw the fires of eschatological enthusiasm die down, things changed. Eventually the fathers, like the rationalist Maimonides after them, and like some New Testament scholars today, came to regard eschatological prophecy as "merely a parable and a figure of speech" (*Mishneh Torah* 14). (Ibid., 169)

78. See the mounting criticisms by Michael Denton, *Evolution: A Theory in Crisis* (Bethesda, MD: Adler & Adler, 1985); Phillip E. Johnson, *Darwin on Trial* (Downers Grove, IL: InterVarsity, 1991); William A. Dembski, ed., *Uncommon Dissent: Intellectuals Who Find Darwinism Unconvincing* (Wilmington, DE: ISI Books, 2004); and the particularly incisive David Berlinski, *The Devil's Delusion: Atheism and Its Scientific Pretensions* (New York: Crown Forum, 2008).

79. See Michael J. Behe, *Darwin's Black Box: The Biochemical Challenge to Evolution* (New York: The Free Press, 1996).

80. "To claim that life evolved is to demand a miracle. The simplest conceivable form of single-celled life should have at least 600 different protein molecules. The mathematical probability that even one typical protein could form by chance arrangements of amino acid sequences is essentially zero—far less than 1 in 10^{450}. To appreciate the magnitude of 10^{450}, realize that the visible universe is about 10^{28} inches in diameter" (Walt Brown, *In the Beginning: Compelling Evidence for Creation and the Flood*, 8th ed. [Phoenix: Center for Scientific Creation, 2008], 17).

81. See Jonathan Wells, *Icons of Evolution: Why Much of What We Teach About Evolution Is Wrong* (Washington, DC: Regnery Publishing, 2000).

82. Radiometric dating is based upon three assumptions: 1) the *original amount* of both parent and daughter elements is known, 2) the *decay rate* has remained constant, and 3) the sample has remained in a *closed system* (i.e., no leaching, diffusion, and/or metamorphism). See a summary in John Morris, *The Young Earth*, rev. ed. (Green Forest, AR: Master Books, 2007), 48–70. All three assumptions have problems. See Larry Vardiman,

Andrew A. Snelling, and Eugene F. Chaffin, eds., *Radioisotopes and the Age of the Earth: A Young-Earth Creationist Research Initiative*, 2 vols. (El Cajon, CA: Institute for Creation Research; St. Joseph, MO: Creation Research Society, 2000, 2005); archived at http://www.icr.org/rate. See a summary in Donald DeYoung, *Thousands . . . Not Billions: Challenging an Icon of Evolution, Questioning the Age of the Earth* (Green Forest, AR: Master Books, 2005).

83. Average dinosaur body size is exceedingly difficult to calculate. However, based on 63 dinosaur genera, Nicholas Hotton estimated an average generic mass in excess of 850 kg and a median generic mass of nearly two tons. This contrasts sharply with extant mammals (788 genera), whose average generic mass is 863 grams, with a median mass of 631 grams; see Nicholas H. Hotton, "An Alternative to Dinosaur Endothermy: The Happy Wanderers," in *A Cold Look at the Warm Blooded Dinosaurs*, eds. R. D. K. Thomas and E. C. Olson (Boulder, CO: Westview Press, 1980), 311–50. Though this estimate has been disputed (see Robert Bakker in the same volume, pp. 351–462), it generally represents the massive difference between ancient and modern animals. For a survey, see Gregory S. Paul, *The Princeton Field Guide to Dinosaurs* (Princeton: Princeton University Press, 2010).

84. Though explanations have been attempted (e.g., P. Martin Sander, et al., "Biology of the Sauropod Dinosaurs: The Evolution of Gigantism," *Biological Reviews of the Cambridge Philosophical Society* 86, no. 1 [February 2011]: 117–55), there remains the glaring ecological problem of limited land mass. Only an earth with far greater habitable land mass could sustain such animals (see Brown, *In the Beginning*, 117–31).

85. As Brown explains,

> If evolution happened, the fossil record should show continuous and gradual changes from the bottom to the top layers. Actually, many gaps or discontinuities appear throughout the fossil record. At the most fundamental level, a big gap exists between forms of life whose cells have nuclei (eukaryotes, such as plants, animals, and fungi) and those that don't (prokaryotes, such as bacteria and blue-green algae). Fossil links are also missing between large groupings of plants, between single-celled forms of life and invertebrates (animals without backbones), among insects, between invertebrates and vertebrates (animals with backbones), between fish and amphibians, between amphibians and reptiles, between reptiles and mammals, between reptiles and birds, between primates and other mammals, and between apes and other primates. In fact, *chains* are missing, not *links*. The fossil record has been studied so thoroughly that it is safe to conclude that these gaps are real; they will never be filled. (*In the Beginning*, 11–12)

86. "If the sedimentary deposits around the world formed over hundreds of millions of years, we would expect to find evidence of erosion over time, resulting in the periodical creation of irregular surfaces. But many times when sedimentary layers are exposed, such as in road highway cuttings, beach cliffs, and river canyons, there is very little evidence of erosion between the layers. . . . If the millions of years had actually occurred, why are the tops of the under layers not highly irregular like the present topography that we now observe?" (John F. Ashton, *Evolution Impossible: 12 Reasons Why Evolution Cannot Explain the Origin of Life on Earth* [Green Forest, AR: Master Books, 2012], 102).

See also Ariel A. Roth, "'Flat Gaps' in Sedimentary Rock Layers Challenge Long Geologic Ages," *Journal of Creation* 23, no. 2 (August 2009): 76–81.

87. See Brown's discussion on liquefaction as the means of stratification and fossilization (*In the Beginning*, 169–81); cf. Guy Berthault, "Experiments on Lamination of Sediments," *Journal of Creation* 3, no. 1 (April 1988): 25–29. Also notable is the formation

of polystrate fossils, which are found all over the world and indicate rapid burial (see Tas Walker, "Polystrate Fossils: Evidence for a Young Earth," *Creation* 29, no. 3 [June 2007]: 54–55). Evolutionists argue that these and other rapid burial fossils (e.g., fossilized jellyfish, worms, eggs, scales and fins) are caused by local catastrophes such as landslides, river floods, volcanic ash, or blown sand dunes (cf. http://www.talkorigins .org/indexcc/CC/CC363.html). However, the size of many of these fossils (e.g., whales and sauropods), their complete remains, their contorted positions (sometimes in mass graves), and their global placement indicate a large-scale, global event (cf. Michael Oard, "Dead Whales: Telling Tales?" *Creation* 26, no. 4 [September 2004]: 10–14). See a summary in Morris, *The Young Earth*, 96–119.

88. See M. Schweitzer and T. Staedter, "The Real Jurassic Park," *Earth* (June 1997), 55–57; and M. H. Schweitzer, J. L. Wittmeyer, J. R. Horner, and J. K. Toporski, "Soft-tissue Vessels and Cellular Preservation in *Tyrannosaurus Rex*," *Science* 207 (2005): 1952–55. Mary Schweitzer, student of the famous paleontologist "Dinosaur" Jack Horner, describes the incident as it happened at Montana State University: "The lab filled with murmurs of amazement, for I had focused on something inside the vessels that none of us had ever noticed before: tiny round objects, translucent red with a dark center. Then a colleague took one look at them and shouted, 'You've got red blood cells. You've got red blood cells!'"

Unfortunately, Schweitzer's evolutionary worldview completely distorted a reasonable interpretation of the evidence: "It was exactly like looking at a slice of modern bone. But of course, I couldn't believe it. I said to the lab technician: 'The bones are, after all, 65 million years old. How could blood cells survive that long?'" (quoted in Carl Wieland, "Sensational Dinosaur Blood Report!" *Creation* 19, no. 4 [September 1997]: 42–43).

89. Such materials, known to break down rapidly under common conditions, require special pleadings to sustain an old earth timescale. See Shaun Doyle, "The Real 'Jurassic Park'?" *Creation* 30, no. 3 (June 2008): 12–15; and Carl Wieland, "Ancient DNA and the Young Earth," *Journal of Creation* 8, no. 1 (1994): 7–10; cf. Brown's detailed list (*In the Beginning*, 35–36).

90. See Don DeYoung, "Is the Moon Really Old?" *Creation* 14, no. 4 (September 1992): 43; and Jonathan Sarfati, "The Moon: The Light That Rules the Night," *Creation* 20, no. 4 (September 1998): 36–39.

91. Michael J. Oard observes,

It was discovered about 40 years ago that in the evolutionary origin of the solar system the sun would have been significantly less luminous with the earth receiving about 20 to 30% less sunlight than today. . . . On this basis, the earth should have been totally glaciated from near its beginning, after it cooled down from its initially hot state within evolutionary scenarios. . . .

This glaciation should have continued indefinitely to this day with no possible biological evolution, unless something drastic occurred to warm the earth. . . .

Evolutionary scientists need the earth relatively warm for the evolution of life, which would be impossible within their paradigm if the earth is totally frozen over. ("Is the Faint Young Sun Paradox Solved?" *Journal of Creation* 25, no. 2 [August 2011]: 17–19; cf. Danny R. Faulkner, "The Young Faint Sun Paradox and the Age of the Solar System," *Journal of Creation* 15, no. 2 [2001]: 3–4)

92. See D. Russell Humphreys, "Can Evolutionists Now Explain the Earth's Magnetic Field?" *Creation Research Society Quarterly* 33, no. 3 (December 1996): 184–85; and Humphreys, "The Earth's Magnetic Field Is Still Losing Energy," *Creation Research Society Quarterly* 39, no. 1 (June 2002): 3–13.

93. See Brown, *In the Beginning*, 148–61.

94. From its infantile beginnings in Tim M. Berra, *Evolution and the Myth of Creationism* (Stanford, CA: Stanford University Press, 1990), to its mature development in Mark Isaak, *The Counter-Creationism Handbook* (Berkeley: University of California Press, 2007), which is a published form of *The TalkOrigins Archive*, available at http://www.talkorigins.org/indexcc/. See a systematic response by *CreationWiki*, available at http://creationwiki.org/index_to_creationist_claims.

95. See Brown's overview of the earth's twenty-five major features (esp. oceanic ridges, mountain ranges, earthquakes, plateaus, and overthrusts) that are better explained by flood geology (*In the Beginning*, 105–41).

96. See John F. Ashton, ed., *In Six Days: Why Fifty Scientists Choose to Believe in Creation* (Green Forest, AR: Master Books, 2000).

   Morris recounts, "Recently, a group of professors from a major, conservative evangelical seminary met with scientists from ICR. Every one of them had abandoned the recent creation position, usually in favor of the framework hypothesis. . . . The theologians admitted they held to an old earth in spite of the obvious sense of Scripture and would adopt a young-earth belief only if the consensus view of secular scientists shifted to recent creation" (*The Young Earth*, 125).

   Of course, scientists who do question the Darwinian dogma face stiff consequences; see Jerry Bergman, *Slaughter of the Dissidents: The Shocking Truth about Killing the Careers of Darwin Doubters*, 2nd ed. (Southworth, WA: Leafcutter Press, 2011).

97. Clayton Sullivan, for example, echoes the conclusions of Schweitzer, et al.: "Having expressed these caveats, I conclude this chapter by observing that scholars such as Johannes Weiss, Albert Schweitzer, and Martin Dibelius were correct: Jesus' Kingdom preaching was predicated on a mistake. His fervent belief that the Kingdom would appear on earth within his listeners' lifetime was an error, an illusion, an unfulfilled hope" (*Rethinking Realized Eschatology*, 64).

98. As exemplified by Bruce K. Waltke's essay "Kingdom Promises as Spiritual," in *Continuity and Discontinuity: Perspectives on the Relationship Between the Old and New Testaments*, ed. John S. Feinberg (Wheaton: Crossway, 1988), 260–87.

Chapter Two

1. The association of the "waters" (Heb. *mayim*) with the "deep" (Heb. *tĕhôm*) in Gen. 1:2 is straightforward. *Tĕhôm* is used some thirty-six times in the OT, and most of the references clearly refer to waters in the form of oceans, seas, lakes, and fountains (cf. Gen. 7:11; 8:2; Ex. 15:5,8; Deut. 8:7; Job 28:14; 38:16,30; Ps. 33:7; 42:7; 77:16; 78:15; 104:6; 106:9; 107:26; 135:6; Prov. 3:20; 8:24; Isa. 51:10; 63:13; Ezek. 26:19; 31:4,15; Jonah 2:5; Hab. 3:10).

2. Though most English translations (e.g., KJV, NKJV, NASB, ESV) translate here the plural *šāmayim* into the singular ("heaven"), this is purely arbitrary. The same word is generally translated as plural ("heavens") in vv. 1, 9, 14, 15, etc. The translation of *šāmayim* in v. 8 as "sky" (NRSV, NIV, NLT) does not fit with the cosmological nature of the passage as introduced in v. 1. Moreover, other references to God creating and stretching out the *šāmayim* (e.g., Ps. 104:2; Isa. 42:5; Zech. 12:1) are nearly universally translated "heavens."

3. Gordon J. Wenham, *Genesis 1–15*, WBC (Dallas: Word, 1998), 20.

4. Though the etymology of *šāmayim* is claimed to be "obscure" (G. von Rad, "οὐρανός," *TDNT*, 5:502), its derivation from the compound *ša* and *mayim*—i.e., "the space in the waters" or "the place of the waters" (*NIDOTTE*, 4:160)—is contextually sound.

5. Though the earth has an infinitesimally small amount of water relative to the cosmic waters, the point being made is the centrality of water to the life created in the following verses, though water in and of itself is rather unique and wonderful; see Lyall Watson and Jerry Derbyshire, *The Water Planet: A Celebration of the Wonder of Water* (New York: Crown Publishers, 1988).

6. Though "white hole cosmology" seems speculative, note the cosmological interpretation of Gen. 1:3–8 in D. Russell Humphreys, *Starlight and Time: Solving the Puzzle of Distant Starlight in a Young Universe* (Green Forest, AR: Master Books, 1994), 31–38.

7. Fully aware of the limitations of a two-dimensional diagram, especially its circular nature, we must simply acknowledge the limitations of mortality. Though the biblical language of the heavens being "up" or "above" is incompatible with a spherical earth, there may be an issue of dimensionality at work, akin to how a three-dimensional coordinate would relate to a two-dimensional coordinate. The diagram is simply an attempt to portray faithfully the primary aspects of the nature and relations of the heavens and the earth, which ultimately find meaning and import in their theological extrapolation—i.e., "new heavens and new earth" (Isa. 65:17; cf. 2 Peter 3:13; Rev. 21:1).

8. The justification for the singular translation is the Hebrew use of the plural as superlative—e.g., "It probably does not mean a number of different heavens but is an expression for the superlative" ("שָׁמַיִם," *HALOT*, 4:1521). However, the commonly held view of the plurality of the heavens, both in the Scriptures and Jewish intertestamental texts (see n. 10 below), nullifies this statement. The judgment of when a word is superlative becomes quite arbitrary, as is seen between the various translations (cf. Gen. 1:1; 11:4; Deut. 10:14; 1 Kings 8:27; Job 22:12; 38:29; etc.).

9. The Greek word for heaven(s), *ouranos*, is used almost three hundred times in the NT, approximately one-third in the plural and two-thirds in the singular. This is not because the writers were sloppy or because they had converted to a Hellenistic understanding of the universe. The singular use is simply referencing one heaven of the heavens (usually God's dwelling place) or the heavens as a "collective singular"—i.e., referring to all that is above. The distinction is clear when both noun forms are used together (e.g., Matt. 6:9–10; 24:29; 2 Cor. 5:1–2). For example, in the Lord's Prayer, "our Father" is in "the heavens" (plural), while the hope of the kingdom is that the will of God would be done

on earth as it is in "heaven" (singular)—that is, the heaven of heavens where God sits enthroned, since the will of the Lord is not fully obeyed presently in other parts of the heavens.

10. The exact number of heavens is not stated explicitly in the Scriptures. Jewish tradition varies from three (*Testament of Levi* 2–3) to five (*3 Baruch* 11–17) to seven (*Apocalypse of Abraham* 10:8; 19:4; *Ascension of Isaiah* 7–10; *Life of Adam and Eve* 35:2) to ten (*2 Enoch* 20–22). As color classifications of a rainbow vary, so also might the delineation of the heavenly realms. Though Paul may have had in mind more than three strata to the heavens (2 Cor. 12:2), this arrangement—upper, middle, and lower heavens—preserves plurality while allowing for further dissection. See also discussions in Christopher Rowland, *The Open Heaven: A Study of Apocalyptic in Judaism and Early Christianity* (London: SPCK, 1982), 78–93; and Adela Yarbro Collins, *Cosmology and Eschatology in Jewish and Christian Apocalypticism* (Leiden, Netherlands: Brill Academic, 1996), 21–54.

11. For intertestamental background—e.g., *1 Enoch, 2 Enoch, Testament of Levi, Apocalypse of Zephaniah, Apocalypse of Abraham, Ascension of Isaiah*, and *3 Baruch*—see Martha Himmelfarb, *Ascent to Heaven in Jewish and Christian Apocalypses* (Oxford: Oxford University Press, 1993), esp. 29–71. Himmelfarb seems to miss the mark, however, concerning the eschatological orientation of apocalypticism, believing the ultimate apocalyptic purpose to be "that human beings can become the equals of angels" (p. 4).

12. Because of the Platonic distortion, it is commonly assumed in modern times that heaven is not designed to host human bodies, but this assumption is not supported by the Scriptures. Jesus clearly sits enthroned in heaven with a resurrected body. Enoch and Elijah went up in their bodies. And Paul might have been caught up in his body—"whether *in the body* or out of the body I do not know" (2 Cor. 12:2). Corporeal ascension was neither foreign nor beyond plausibility.

13. The naturalistic critic finds the biblical language insufferable. For example, Rudolf Bultmann wrote, "These mythological conceptions of heaven and hell are no longer acceptable for modern men since for scientific thinking to speak of 'above' and 'below' in the universe has lost all meaning, but the idea of the transcendence of God and of evil is still significant" (*Jesus Christ and Mythology* [New York: Charles Scribner's Sons, 1958], 20). Though Bultmann calls this significance the "deeper meaning" (p. 18), one finds the transcendence of God magnified within a straightforward reading of the biblical worldview.

14. A fuller list would include Gen. 6:17; 7:19; 11:4; 28:12; Ex. 20:4; Deut. 4:39; 5:8; 11:21; 30:12; Josh. 2:11; 1 Kings 8:23; 2 Chron. 7:1; Job 28:24; Ps. 50:4; 85:11; 113:6; Isa. 14:12; 24:21; 44:23; 51:6; Jer. 10:11; Matt. 3:16; 28:2; John 1:51; 3:13; 6:33ff.; Acts 1:9ff.; 2:19; 7:55f.; 10:11ff.; Eph. 4:8ff.; 1 Thess. 4:16; Rev. 12:10ff.; 18:1; 21:2.

15. The supposed naïveté of popular conception will surely be vindicated in the end. D. L. Moody recounted,

> Soon after I was converted, an infidel asked me one day why I looked *up* when I prayed. He said that heaven was no more above us than below us; that heaven was everywhere. Well, I was greatly bewildered, and the next time I prayed, it seemed almost as if I was praying into the air. Since then I have become better acquainted with the Bible, and I have come to see that heaven is above us; that it is upward, and not downward. The Spirit of God is everywhere, but God is in heaven, and heaven is above our heads. It does not matter what part of the globe we may stand upon, heaven is above us. (*Heaven: Where It Is, Its Inhabitants, and How to Get There*, Rev. ed. [Chicago: Revell, 1884], 15–16)

16. A fuller list would include Gen. 28:12f.; Deut. 26:15; 1 Kings 8:30,39,43,49; 1 Chron. 16:31; 21:26; 2 Chron. 2:6; 6:18–39; 30:27; Neh. 9:27; Job 22:12,14; Ps. 2:4; 11:4;

20:6; 29:9f.; 33:13; 68:5; 102:19; 103:19; 104:2f.; 113:5; 123:1; 135:6; Eccl. 5:2; Isa. 40:22; 57:15; 63:15; 66:1; Jer. 23:24; 25:30; Lam. 3:41,50; Dan. 4:35; 5:23; Zech. 2:13; Matt. 6:9; 23:9; Acts 2:33; 3:21; 7:49,55; Rom. 8:34; Eph. 1:20; Col. 3:1; Heb. 1:3; 10:12; Rev. 4:2; 20:11; 22:3.

17. W. Michaelis, "παντοκράτωρ," *TDNT*, 3:914; cf. Hab. 2:13; Zeph. 2:10; Zech. 1:3 in the LXX.

18. This will be discussed further in chap. 6 and distinguished from the eschatological messianic kingdom—the restored kingdom of Adam upon the earth (cf. "son of Man," "last Adam," etc.)—referred to in the NT as the "kingdom of God" (cf. Mark 9:47; 10:23–25; 14:25; etc.).

19. For a survey of the heavenly temple in intertestamental literature, see Martha Himmelfarb, "Apocalyptic Ascent and the Heavenly Temple," *Society for Biblical Literature 1987 Seminar Papers*, ed. Kent H. Richards (Atlanta: Scholars, 1987), 210–17.

20. Concerning this tradition in intertestamental literature, see *Wisdom of Solomon* 9:8; *2 Baruch* 4:3ff.; and *Testament of Levi* 5:1.

21. See the discussion on the reality of the heavenly temple and its earthly pattern (Heb. *tabnith*) in Allen P. Ross, *Recalling the Hope of Glory: Biblical Worship from the Garden to the New Creation* (Grand Rapids: Kregel, 2006), 187–90.

22. Though I believe John H. Walton is errant concerning his rejection of creation *ex nihilo* (see chap. 4, n. 1), his point concerning temple functionality in ancient Near Eastern thought is well-put:

> In the traditional view that Genesis 1 is an account of material origins, day seven is mystifying. It appears to be nothing more than an afterthought with theological concerns about Israelites observing the Sabbath—an appendix, a postscript, a tack on.
>
> In contrast, a reader from the ancient world would know immediately what was going on and recognize the role of day seven. Without hesitation the ancient reader would conclude that this is a temple text and that day seven is the most important of the seven days. . . .
>
> How could reactions be so different? The difference is the piece of information that everyone knew in the ancient world and to which most modern readers are totally oblivious: *Deity rests in a temple, and only in a temple.* This is what temples were built for. We might even say that this is what a temple is—a place for divine rest. (*The Lost World of Genesis One: Ancient Cosmology and the Origins Debate* [Downers Grove, IL: InterVarsity Academic, 2009], 71; italics added)

23. Thus we see vividly the two axes of apocalyptic thought: heavenly revelation and eschatological consummation. See the formative article by John J. Collins, "Introduction: Towards the Morphology of a Genre," in *Apocalypse: The Morphology of a Genre*, ed. John J. Collins (Semeia 14; Missoula, MT: Scholars Press, 1979), 1–20; cf. Collins, *The Apocalyptic Imagination* (Grand Rapids: Eerdmans, 1998).

24. This presentation of the heavenly sanctuary is in no way in agreement with the novel and unfounded views of the Adventists. Though strumming a sound close to the Bible, they are completely out of tune. Adventists believe that the failed prophecy of Jesus' return in 1844, as prophesied by William Miller and others, was simply a misinterpretation of Daniel 8:14. Instead of cleansing the earthly sanctuary after 2,300 symbolic "days" (i.e., years), Jesus actually began the final phase of his "atoning ministry" by moving from the heavenly Holy Place to the Most Holy Place and cleansing the heavenly sanctuary through "sin transfer" (in fulfillment of the antitypic "Day of Atonement"). This action

also inaugurated a time of "investigative judgment" against the Babylonian, non-Adventist church. This time will come to fulfillment at the end of the age when the Babylonian church will fall away and only the "remnant" of Adventists will be saved. See General Conference of Seventh-day Adventists, *Beliefs*, "24. Christ's Ministry in the Heavenly Sanctuary"; available at http://www.adventist.org/beliefs/.

For more on the Adventist doctrine of the "heavenly sanctuary," see Marc Rasell, *Exploring the Heavenly Sanctuary: Understanding Seventh-day Adventist Theology* (Milton Keynes, England: AuthorHouse, 2009); and Samuele Bacchiocchi, *God's Festivals in Scripture and History*, 2 vols. (Berrien Springs, MI: Biblical Perspectives, 1995–1996). For a rebuttal, see Russell Earl Kelly, *Exposing Seventh-Day Adventism*, 2nd ed. (Lincoln: Writer's Club Press, 2005), 55–101.

25. The nature, purpose, and effects of the death of the Messiah as an atonement will be discussed in chap. 8.

26. "In Re 2.7 ἐν τῷ παραδείσῳ τοῦ θεοῦ 'in the paradise of God,' the reference may reflect somewhat more closely the historical background of this term, which is derived from an Old Persian word meaning 'enclosure,' and thus was applied to a 'garden' or 'park.' For that reason, a number of commentators have believed that in Re 2.7, it is appropriate to translate 'the garden of God,' especially since in the context the reference is to the fruit of the tree of life" ("1.14 παράδεισος," *Greek-English Lexicon of the New Testament: Based on Semantic Domains*, ed. J. P. Louw and E. A. Nida, 2nd ed., vol. 1 [New York: United Bible Societies, 1988], 5).

27. See J. Jeremias, "παράδεισος," *TDNT*, 5:765–73; esp. 770. Note *2 Enoch* 8:1: "And those men took me from there, and they brought me up to the third heaven, and set me down there. Then I looked downward, and I saw Paradise. And that place is inconceivably pleasant" (*OTP*, 1:114). And *2 Enoch* 42:3: "And I ascended to the east, into the paradise of Edem, where rest is prepared for the righteous. And it is open as far as the 3rd heaven; but it is closed off from this world" (*OTP*, 1:168).

28. See Gregory K. Beale's overall discussion of the garden of Eden, the third heaven, and the new heavens and new earth as a "paradisal city-temple" in *The Temple and the Church's Mission: A Biblical Theology of the Dwelling Place of God*, NSBT 17 (Downers Grove, IL: InterVarsity, 2004), 23–80. Beale summarizes his argument in "Eden, the Temple, and the Church's Mission in the New Creation," *JETS* 48, no. 1 (2005): 5–31.

29. See Ioan Petru Colianu, "Ascension," in *Encyclopedia of Religion*, ed. Mircea Eliade (New York: Macmillan, 1987), 1:435–41; and Mircea Eliade, *Shamanism* (Princeton, NJ: Princeton University Press, 1964), 259–87.

30. Following in the footsteps of Rudolf Bultmann, who wrote,

> The cosmology of the New Testament is essentially mythical in character. The world is viewed as a three-storied structure, with the earth in the centre, the heaven above, and the underworld beneath. Heaven is the abode of God and of celestial beings—the angels. The underworld is hell, the place of torment. Even the earth is more than the scene of natural, everyday events, of the trivial round and common task. It is the scene of the supernatural activity of God and his angels on the one hand, and of Satan and his daemons on the other. . . .
>
> All this is the language of mythology, and the origin of the various themes can be easily traced in the contemporary mythology of Jewish Apocalyptic. . . .
>
> Can Christian preaching expect modern man *to accept the mythical view of the world as true*? To do so would be both senseless and impossible. It would be senseless, because there is nothing specifically Christian in the mythical view of the world as such. It is simply the cosmology of a pre-scientific age. Again, it

would be impossible, because no man can adopt a view of the world by his own volition—it is already determined for him by his place in history. ("New Testament and Mythology," in *Kerygma and Myth: A Theological Debate*, ed. H. W. Bartsch [London: SPCK, 1953], 1–3)

31. So John H. Walton articulates, "We must first recognize that the garden of Eden was not, strictly speaking, a garden for man, but was the garden of *God* (Isa. 51:3; Ezek. 28:13). The garden of Eden is not viewed by the author of Genesis simply as a piece of Mesopotamian farmland, but as an archetypical sanctuary, that is, a place where God dwells and where man should worship him. Many of the features of the garden may also be found in later sanctuaries, particularly the tabernacle or Jerusalem temple. These parallels suggest that the garden itself is understood as a sort of sanctuary'" (*Ancient Near Eastern Thought and the Old Testament: Introducing the Conceptual World of the Hebrew Bible* [Grand Rapids: Baker Academic, 2006], 124; quoting Gordon J. Wenham, "Sanctuary Symbolism in the Garden of Eden Story," in *Proceedings of the Ninth World Congress of Jewish Studies* [Jerusalem: World Union of Jewish Studies, 1986], 19).

32. The plural usage of sanctuary in Ezekiel 28:18 is found elsewhere in reference to the tabernacle (Lev. 21:23) and temple (Jer. 51:51; Ezek. 7:24), as Beale explains: "The plural reference to the one temple probably arose because of the multiple sacred spaces or 'sanctuaries' within the temple complex (e.g., courtyard, Holy Place, Holy of Holies)" ("Eden, the Temple, and the Church's Mission," 10).

33. Some scholars argue that the glorious being who had "fallen" in Ezekiel 28 is Adam, based on the Septuagint's rendering of being anointed *with* (v. 14) and being banished *by* (v. 16) the guardian cherub (see Norman C. Habel, "Ezekiel 28 and the Fall of the First Man," *Concordia Theological Monthly* 38 [1967]: 516–24). This would picture Adam in all of his priestly wisdom (v. 12) and blamelessness (v. 15), ordained on the Edenic mount of God (v. 14), and adorned with the same precious stones (v. 13) that later priests wore (cf. Ex. 28:17–20; 39:10–13); see also Beale, *Temple and the Church's Mission*, 75–76.

34. See Wenham, "Sanctuary Symbolism," 19–25; Beale, *Temple and the Church's Mission*, 66–80; Ross, *Recalling the Hope of Glory*, 81–108; T. Desmond Alexander, *From Eden to the New Jerusalem: An Introduction to Biblical Theology* (Grand Rapids: Kregel, 2009), 20–24; and J. V. Fesko, *Last Things First: Unlocking Genesis 1–3 with the Christ of Eschatology* (Fearn, Scotland: Mentor, 2007), 57–75.

35. Diagram used by consent of Timothy Miller; see *Poised for Harvest, Braced for Backlash: Birthing New Testament Movements When Jesus Disrupts the Systems* (Maitland, FL: Xulon Press, 2009).

36. On the "arboreal lampstand" representing light and life, see Carol L. Meyers, *The Tabernacle Menorah: A Synthetic Study of a Symbol from the Biblical Cult* (Piscataway, NJ: Gorgias Press, 2003). On the law representing wisdom and death to those who touch it, see Beale, *Temple and the Church's Mission*, 73–74.

37. Robert Hayward explains, "Both ben Sira and Jubilees, in their different ways, bring Adam into direct association with the Temple understood as Eden. According to Jubilees, the first ritual act of worship was offered by Adam immediately after his expulsion from the garden. . . . Adam is thereby constituted the first priest in a succession which will lead to Levi, and then to Aaron and his sons" (C. T. R. Hayward, *The Jewish Temple: A Non-Biblical Sourcebook* [London: Routledge, 1996], 90).

Testament of Levi 18:6–14 and *1 Enoch* 24–27 also closely relate the temple and the garden of Eden (see Beale, *Temple and the Church's Mission*, 77–79). For further study, see also Margaret Barker, *The Gate of Heaven: History and Symbolism of the Temple in Jerusalem* (London: SPCK Publishing, 1991), esp. 68–72.

38. Leonhard Goppelt summarizes, "Behind Ex. 25 stands the ancient oriental idea of a mythical analogical relation between the two worlds, the heavenly and the earthly, the macrocosm and the microcosm, so that lands, rivers, cities and esp. temples have their heavenly originals" ("τύπος as the Heavenly Original according to Exodus 25:40," *TDNT*, 8:256–57).

The astute reader will here recognize the apparent similarity to Platonism (as Goppelt and others have pointed out; see esp. Leonhard Goppelt, *Typos: The Typological Interpretation of the Old Testament in the New* [Grand Rapids: Eerdmans, 1982], 42–60). However, Platonism is simply a perversion. The Bible teaches earthly "images" (Heb. *tselem*, i.e., "representation"; see "צֶלֶם," *HALOT*, 1028–29) of heavenly originals, both qualitatively real and metaphysically substantial. Platonism teaches earthly "copies" of heavenly "forms," differing qualitatively and metaphysically. Ironically, modern supernaturalism views materiality as more substantial, whereas Platonism viewed materiality as the dreamlike-state from which we awake into the more "real" ideal world (though the latter is portrayed in the modern allegory by C. S. Lewis, *The Great Divorce: A Dream* [New York: HarperCollins, 1946]).

39. C. R. Schoonhoven aptly observes,

> The popular conception of heaven revolves around clouds, harps, and angels, with humanity marching through the Pearly Gates to live a life of bliss. This conception is far removed from the biblical witness. Rather, the Bible depicts heaven under the wrath of God, the scene of cosmic warfare, and finally subject to dissolution prior to the creation of a new heaven. This ambivalence surrounding heaven is to be expected because of the fundamental antithetical structure of biblical eschatology, which is conceived in terms of this present evil age and the age to come. It must be stressed that in this framework this whole age experiences turbulence, disquiet, and flux; both heaven and earth experience the wrath of God, the powers of evil, personal incompleteness, and temporality. Only the age to come is "heaven" in any idyllic sense. ("Heaven," *ISBE*, 2:654)

40. "The term *divine council* is used by Hebrew and Semitic scholars to refer to the heavenly host, the pantheon of divine beings who administer the affairs of the cosmos. All ancient Mediterranean cultures had some conception of a divine council. The divine council of Israelite religion, known primarily through the psalms, was distinct in important ways" (Michael S. Heiser, "Divine Council," in *Dictionary of the Old Testament: Wisdom, Poetry & Writings*, ed. Tremper Longman III and Peter Enns [Downers Grove, IL: InterVarsity, 2008], 112).

See also E. Theodore Mullen, *The Assembly of the Gods: The Divine Council in Canaanite and Early Hebrew Literature*, Harvard Semitic Monographs 24 (Chico, CA: Scholars Press, 1980); and Mullen, "Divine Assembly," *ABD*, 2:214–17.

41. As in the pseudepigraphic *2 Enoch* 31:1–2, "And I created a garden in Edem, in the east, so that he might keep the agreement and preserve the commandment. And I created for him an open heaven, so that he might look upon the angels, singing the triumphal song. And the light which is never darkened was perpetually in paradise" (*OTP*, 1:154).

42. Cf. Gregory A. Boyd, *God at War: The Bible and Spiritual Conflict* (Downers Grove, IL: InterVarsity, 1997).

43. The Platonic intrusion distorts divine sovereignty by relegating it to a static state within the material/immaterial construct. Thus, instead of a *dynamic governance*, it is framed as an abstract existential "providence," an unbiblical concept which implies a mechanistic relationship between God and creation (cf. Paul J. Achtemeier, "Providence," *Harper's Bible Dictionary* [San Francisco: Harper & Row, 1985], 832).

The overlaying of sovereignty upon the material realm (dynamic and timely) versus the immaterial realm (static and timeless) creates the problem of "causation," which in turn devolves into the endless debate concerning predestination and foreknowledge—that is, causative (Calvinist) versus historical (Arminian). The rejection of divine foreknowledge by the open theists (cf. C. Pinnock, G. Boyd, J. Sanders, W. Hasker, etc.) only exacerbates the situation and denigrates the truth of divine sovereignty (see John Piper, J. Taylor, and P. K. Helseth, eds., *Beyond the Bounds: Open Theism and the Undermining of Biblical Christianity* [Wheaton: Crossway, 2003]; and Thomas R. Schreiner and B. A. Ware, eds., *Still Sovereign: Contemporary Perspectives on Election, Foreknowledge, and Grace* [Grand Rapids: Baker, 2000]).

Note that I agree with the open theists concerning Augustine's systematization of sovereignty within the Platonic framework; I disagree, however, regarding their solution of rejecting a straightforward understanding of divine foreknowledge. One cannot believe in limited-particular foreknowledge apart from universal foreknowledge, since all events happen within a tightly interconnected existential web (i.e., foreknowledge of one event demands foreknowledge of events directly connected, and so on and so forth).

It is only in its restoration within a biblical worldview that the cognitive dissonance concerning the paradox of human free will and divine foreknowledge is resolved. As the functioning of a child in a house is radically affected by the proximity and intent of his/her father, so also is our relating to our heavenly Father and his sovereignty affected by his metaphysical proximity and benevolent intent. When God is in the same metaphysical "house," our hearts are set at rest with his intimate, loving sovereignty, and we can come to terms with his foreknowledge. Divine foreknowledge does not relieve us of our responsibility to respond or lessen our accountability when we choose to disobey. His foreknowledge of our choices is *his* problem, not ours. A biblical worldview, with its holistic integration and "closeness" of metaphysical proximity, helps us let go of control and let God be God.

44. See M. W. Chavalas, "Assyriology and Biblical Studies: A Century of Tension," in *Mesopotamia and the Bible*, ed. M. W. Chavalas and K. L. Younger Jr. (Grand Rapids: Baker, 2002), 21–67.

45. Beginning with the publication of the Babylonian creation account found in the *Enuma elish* tablets (see George Smith, *The Chaldean Account of Genesis* [London: Thomas Scott, 1876]), many OT scholars followed suit, and soon it was the general consensus of critical opinion that the Hebrew creation story depended on a Babylonian original (cf. Hermann Gunkel, *The Legends of Genesis* [Chicago: Open Court, 1901]; and John Skinner, *Genesis*, ICC [New York: Scribner, 1910]).

46. See Luis I. J. Stadelmann, *The Hebrew Conception of the World* (Rome: Pontifical Biblical Institute, 1970); Richard J. Clifford, *Creation Accounts in the Near East and in the Bible* (Washington, DC: Catholic Biblical Association, 1994); and Wayne Horowitz, *Mesopotamian Cosmic Geography* (Winona Lake, IN: Eisenbrauns, 1998). Evangelical scholars have likewise conceded to this approach to the Scriptures; cf. John Walton, *Genesis 1 as Ancient Cosmology* (Winona Lake: Eisenbrauns, 2011), esp. 159–61.

47. See James P. Holding, "Is the *raqiya'* ('firmament') a solid dome? Equivocal language in the cosmology of Genesis 1 and the Old Testament: a response to Paul H. Seely," *Technical Journal* (now *Journal of Creation*) 13, no. 2 (November 1999): 44–51.

48. This phrase seems to have been coined first by T. H. Gaster, "Cosmogony," in *Interpreter's Dictionary of the Bible*, vol. 1 (Nashville: Abingdon, 1962), 702.

49. See George L. Robinson, "Figure 2: The Ancient Hebrew Conception of the Universe," *Leaders of Israel* (New York: Association Press, 1913), 2; and Denis O. Lamoureux, *Evolutionary Creation: A Christian Approach to Evolution* (Eugene, OR: Wipf & Stock, 2008), 108.

50. See esp. Noel K. Weeks, "Cosmology in Historical Context," *WTJ* 68, no. 2 (Fall 2006): 283–93; in contrast, see Paul H. Seely, "The Geographical Meaning of 'Earth' and 'Seas' in Genesis 1:10," *WTJ* 59, no. 2 (Fall 1997): 240–46; Seely, "The Firmament and the Water Above, Part 1," *WTJ* 53, no. 2 (Fall 1991): 227–40; and Seely, "The Firmament and the Water Above, Part 2," *WTJ* 54, no. 1 (Spring 1992): 31–46.

51. See a survey of ancient Near Eastern creation myths in James B. Pritchard, ed., *The Ancient Near East: An Anthology of Texts and Pictures*, 3rd ed. with supplement (Princeton: Princeton University Press, 1969), 1–155. See a survey of specifically Mesopotamian myths in Horowitz, *Mesopotamian Cosmic Geography*.

52. See the introductory diagram in Horowitz, *Mesopotamian Cosmic Geography*, xii.

53. H. F. Vos, "Flood," *ISBE*, 2:319–21. For a listing of flood legends, see Byron C. Nelson, *The Deluge Story in Stone*, 2nd ed. (Minneapolis: Bethany, 1968), 165–76; and James B. Frazer, *Folk-lore in the Old Testament*, vol. 1 (London: Macmillan, 1918), 107–331 (though Frazer is highly critical).

54. See R. Laird Harris, "The Bible and Cosmology," *Bulletin of the Evangelical Theological Society* 5, no. 1 (March 1962): 11–17. "It is modern Bible students who have travestied the Biblical picture, paralleled it to Babylonian nonsense, then informed a secular public that the Bible is not believable by a modern mind. . . . Destructive criticism has sold the world a shabby substitute for the Biblical cosmology. We need to re-emphasize the Biblical teaching. The foolish notions of a three-storied universe or a flat square earth or a geo-centric universe are not Biblical. And we need to say so as loudly as possible" (pp. 11–12).

55. I agree with Walter C. Kaiser Jr. that the use of *stereōma* in the Septuagint simply reflects the Greek view of the heavens at the time the translators did their work; see "The Literary Form of Genesis 1–11," in *New Perspectives on the Old Testament*, ed. J. Barton Payne (Waco: Word, 1970), 48–65.

Kaiser also gives numerous reasons to believe Genesis 1–11 is "historical narrative"—i.e., a story relating historical facts, rather than poetry or nonhistorical narrative (allegory, parable, myth, etc.) designed simply to communicate generic principles or ideas. For example, in Genesis 2–11 are found "64 geographical terms, 88 personal names, 48 generic names, and at least 21 identifiable cultural items (such as gold, bdellium, onyx, brass, iron, gopher wood, bitumen, mortar, brick, stone, harp, pipe, cities, towers)" (p. 59). All of these indicate historical rather than nonhistorical literature and argue for a straightforward historical reading of Genesis.

56. H. J. Austel writes:

The heavens are frequently described in figurative language as having windows (Gen 7:11; II Kgs 7:2; Mal 3:10 . . .), gates (Gen 28:7), doors (Ps 78:23), pillars (Job 26:11), and foundations (II Sam 22:8). They are stretched out and spread out like a tent or a curtain (Isa 40:22).

The use of such figurative language no more necessitates the adoption of a pagan cosmology than does the modern use of the term "sunrise" imply astronomical ignorance. The imagery is often phenomenological, and is both convenient and vividly forceful. Thus a disobedient Israel would find the heavens to be like iron (Lev 26:19) or like bronze (Deut 28:23), not yielding the much-needed rain. Note that if the heavens were conceived of as a metallic vault, as is commonly suggested from Gen 1:8, 14 etc., the above passages would be meaningless, since the skies would already be metal. The word *rāqîa* (q.v.) comes from the verb meaning "to hammer out" and "stretch (a piece of metal) out" as an overlay. It is the idea of spreading out that carries over to the noun, not the idea of a metallic substance. "Expanse" is an acceptable translation. ("2407a שָׁמַיִם (*šāmayim*)," *TWOT*, 935)

57. Einstein recapitulated Newtonian physics within the framework of "space-time," space relating to Newton's three-dimensional calculations and time being the fourth dimension based on the speed of light. The theory of general relativity explained the mechanism of gravity (space-time curvature), which Newton lacked, with time and space functioning like a flexible "fabric" upon which objects of mass lie. For an introduction, see Steve Adams, *Relativity: An Introduction to Space-Time Physics* (London: Taylor & Francis, 1997).

58. Concordism is the belief that there is "a correspondence or alignment between Scripture and science" (Lamoureux, *Evolutionary Creation*, xv.) The accusation of concordism has become the means of invalidating the work of anyone who would suggest that God might communicate through the Bible any post-Enlightenment knowledge. It also seems to have become the rallying cry of those bent on "reinterpreting" biblical inerrancy. Those who reject concordism argue that God "accommodated" the ignorance of the ancient Hebrews by speaking to them according to the false science of their time, because the Bible is supposedly designed to give redemptive truth rather than scientific truth. As Paul Seely made clear early in his career, "*The Bible assumes that the universe is three-storied; but, we do not believe that Christians are bound to give assent to such a cosmology, since the purpose of the Bible is to give redemptive, not scientific truth. The relationship of science to Scripture is this: The Bible gives redemptive truth through the scientific thoughts of the times without ever intending that those scientific thoughts should be believed as inerrant*" (Paul H. Seely, "The Three-Storied Universe," *Journal of the American Scientific Affiliation* 21, no. 1 [1969]: 18; italics in the original).

59. Total occurrences of *rāqia`* are as follows: Gen. 1:6ff., 14f., 17, 20; Ps. 19:2; 150:1; Ezek. 1:22f., 25f.; 10:1; Dan. 12:3. Its use in Ezekiel is irrelevant, since the vision does not concern the cosmos as a whole. Its use in Daniel is clearly equated with the heavens (note that the LXX translates *rāqia`* with *ouranos*).

60. According to Seely, "The fact that it was named 'heaven(s)' in Gen 1:8 and birds fly in the heaven(s) (Deut 4:17) seems to imply the *raqia^c* was not solid. But the word *samayim* (heaven[s]) is broader in meaning than *raqia^c*. It encompasses not only the *raqia^c* (v. 8; Ps 19:6; 148:4) but the space above the *raqia^c* (Ps 2:4; 11:4; 139:8) as well as the space below (Ps 8:8; 79:2)" ("The Firmament and the Water Above, Part I," 237). There is a reason Seely only cites these verses and does not quote them. None of them say anything about the heavens being distinct from or extending beyond the firmament. Moreover, the firmament is not even mentioned in any of them. James Holding summarizes,

> The problem with this argument is that the claim that shamayim is "broader in meaning" than *raqiya`* in Genesis is simply groundless—the result of circular reasoning. In Genesis 1:8, the implication is that the *raqiya`* has the name *shamayim* in an exact one-to-one correspondence, just as is the case for the "Earth" and the "Seas" when they are named (v. 10). There is no reason to see a broader meaning of *shamayim* than an exact equation with *raqiya`*.
>
> In fact, Seely's only reason for saying that *shamayim* and *raqiya`* are not equal seems to be that it would result (because of verses like Deuteronomy 4:17, and other [*sic*] like Psalm 11:4) in the absurd conclusion that the birds fly or God sits enthroned "inside" a solid structure! In other words . . . he has started with the idea of the solid sky, based on the views of ancient people, and forced onto the text divisions in the *shamayim* that are simply not specified, and in the case of Genesis 1, not even permitted, by the text. ("Is the *raqiya`* ('firmament') a solid dome," 46)

61. See Lamoureux, *Evolutionary Creation*, 129–31. This framework is also assumed by M. J. Kline, "Space and Time in the Genesis Cosmogony," *Perspectives on Science and Christian Faith* 48, no. 1 (March 1996): 2–15.

62. Psalm 104 and Psalm 29 are often quoted as evidence that God dwells above the cosmic waters, pitching his tent "on the waters" (104:3) and sitting enthroned "over the engulfing waters" (29:11, NET). However, the heavens as a whole are referenced as a "tent" in 104:2, and the "chambers" of verse 3 are the Heb. *'ăliyâ*, which speaks of the "roof-room." For this reason the NASB, NKJV, and NIV translate it "upper chambers," and thus the "beams" (Heb. *qārâ*) of those chambers would logically be the ceiling "rafters" (NLT) set "in the waters" (NASB, KJV, NKJV) rather than the floor joists set "on the waters" (ESV, NRSV, NIV). Psalm 29 is cosmologically irrelevant, since it primarily speaks of the sovereignty of God over creation, particularly in times of judgment. The Lord "thundering over the waters" (v. 3) is paralleled by breaking the cedars of Lebanon (v. 5), striking with flashes of lightening (v. 7), shaking the desert of Kadesh (v. 8), and stripping the forest bare (v. 9). These judgments are concluded by God's sovereignty over *the historical flood* (v. 10; Heb. *mabbûl*), which is used elsewhere only in reference to the flood of Noah (cf. Gen. 6:17; 7:6–7,10,17; 9:11,15,28; 10:1,32; 11:10).

63. "Considering that the Hebrews were a scientifically naive people who would accordingly believe the *raqia*ᶜ was solid, that both their Babylonian and their Egyptian background would influence them to believe the *raqia*ᶜ was solid, and that they naturally accepted the concepts of the peoples around them so long as they were not theologically offensive, I believe we have every reason to think that both the writer and original readers of Genesis 1 believed the *raqia*ᶜ was solid. The historical meaning of *raqia*ᶜ in Gen 1:6–8 is, accordingly, 'a solid sky'" (Seely, "The Firmament and the Water Above, Part I," 235; cf. 228, 230, 231, 234).

64. This was Bultmann's cherished phrase, though he believed demythologization to be a third option.

> It is, of course, true that de-mythologizing takes the modern world-view as a criterion. To de-mythologize is to reject not Scripture or the Christian message as a whole, but the world-view of Scripture, which is the world-view of a past epoch, which all too often is retained in Christian dogmatics and in the preaching of the Church. To de-mythologize is to deny that the message of Scripture and of the Church is bound to an ancient world-view which is obsolete.
>
> The attempt to de-mythologize begins with this important insight: Christian preaching, in so far as it is preaching of the Word of God by God's command and in His name, does not offer a doctrine which can be accepted either by reason or by a *sacrificium intellectus*. Christian preaching is *kerygma*, that is, a proclamation addressed not to the theoretical reason, but to the hearer as a self. In this manner Paul commends himself to every man's conscience in the sight of God (II Cor. 4:2). De-mythologizing will make clear this function of preaching as a personal message, and in doing so it will eliminate a false stumbling-block and bring into sharp focus the real stumbling-block, the word of the cross.
>
> For the world-view of the Scripture is mythological and is therefore unacceptable to modern man whose thinking has been shaped by science and is therefore no longer mythological. (*Jesus Christ and Mythology*, 35–36)

65. For a primer, see Colin Brown, *Christianity and Western Thought: A History of Philosophers, Ideas and Movements* (Downers Grove, IL: InterVarsity, 1990).

66. Though Plato and Aristotle agreed on a dualistic split between material and immaterial, Aristotle disagreed with his teacher concerning the relationship between the two. Aristotle argued that the universals ("forms") did not produce the particulars ("copies"), but rather the universals were present in the particulars (see esp. *Metaphysics*, Book VII)—i.e., materiality is real in and of itself without the need of a separate metaphysical pattern.

67. Many attribute Alexander's superhuman ambition to egotism, power hunger, or madness. Akin to Hitler, however, his intentionality and calculated approach seem to argue for ideology and philosophy as his primary motivation. He conquered the world so that he could Hellenize, civilize, and enlighten the world.

68. See chap. 1, n. 57. For example, Plato stated:

> And having been created in this way, the world has been framed in the likeness of that which is apprehended by reason and mind and is unchangeable, and must therefore of necessity, if this is admitted, be a copy of something. Now it is all-important that the beginning of everything should be according to nature. And in speaking of the copy and the original we may assume that words are akin to the matter which they describe; when they relate to the lasting and permanent and intelligible, they ought to be lasting and unalterable, and, as far as their nature allows, irrefutable and immovable—nothing less. But when they express only the copy or likeness and not the eternal things themselves, they need only be likely and analogous to the real words. As being is to becoming, so is truth to belief. (*Timaeus* 29; *DP*, 3:449)

69. As such, a better pictorial representation (cf. figure 2.6) would entail dotted lines for the perceptual world and solid lines for the intelligible world. However, for consistency of communication, as related to its later accommodation into Judeo-Christian thought (cf. figures 3.14, 3.15, etc.), lines representing a simple material versus immaterial framework are retained.

70. *Theaetetus* 156 (*DP*, 4:210). Socrates' characterization is preceded by this description, "Take a look round, then, and see that none of the uninitiated are listening. Now by the uninitiated I mean the people who believe in nothing but what they can grasp in their hands, and who will not allow that action or generation or anything invisible can have real existence" (*Theaetetus* 155; *DP*, 4:210).

71. This view is most famously portrayed in the "Allegory of the Cave" (*Republic* 7.514a–520a), which is related to the "Metaphor of the Sun" (6.507b–509c) and the "Analogy of the Divided Line" (6.509d–513e), both of which immediately precede it at the end of Book 6. The common theme in these parables is the "sun," a metaphor for the source of illumination, which Plato held to be the "Form of the Good," generally interpreted as his notion of God.

72. See John M. Dillon, "Platonism," *ABD*, 5:378–81.

73. As Alfred North Whitehead articulates in his famous statement: "The safest general characterization of the European philosophical tradition is that it consists of a series of footnotes to Plato. I do not mean the systematic scheme of thought which scholars have doubtfully extracted from his writings. *I allude to the wealth of general ideas scattered through them*" (*Process and Reality: An Essay in Cosmology*, ed. David R. Griffin and Donald W. Sherburne, corrected ed. [New York: Free Press, 1979; originally published 1929,], 39; italics added).

74. Tertullian (c. 160–230) speaks of the demonization of Socrates as though it were widely known and commonly understood, "Socrates, as none can doubt, was actuated by a different spirit. For they say that a demon clave to him from his boyhood" (*A Treatise on the Soul*, chap. 1). This no doubt refers to the "inner voice" that Socrates frequently relied upon, which he referred to as the "Daimonion" but has been modernly equated with the conscience.

Socrates, though, claimed divine inspiration from the Daimonion (*Phaedrus*, 242) and related to it as a "monitor" assigned uniquely to him among humanity (*Republic*,

496). Having never heard of the Daimonion, Socrates' fellow Athenians regarded it as a new divinity, and Xenophon equated it to divination (*Memorabilia*, 4.3.12). Generalizing some passages in Xenophon and Plato, where Daimonion is employed metaphorically, as a symbolic expression for the inner conviction, "The attempt has been made to deliver Socrates from an embarrassing and, for a wise man and pattern of virtue, unworthy eccentricity by explaining the Daimonion as a figure of speech" (Abraham J. Heschel, *The Prophets*, vol. 2 [New York: Harper, 1971], 591; quoting K. Joel, *Der Xenophon-tische und der echte Socrates* [Berlin, 1893], 67).

75. Note Philip Schaff's concise and timeless testimony:

> The Alexandrian theology aims at a reconciliation of Christianity with philosophy, or, subjectively speaking, of *pistis* with *gnosis*; but it seeks this union upon the basis of the Bible, and the doctrine of the church. . . . Clement came from the Hellenic philosophy to the Christian faith; Origen, conversely, was led by faith to speculation. The former was an aphoristic thinker, the latter a systematic. The one borrowed ideas from various systems; the other followed more the track of Platonism. But both were Christian philosophers and churchly gnostics. As Philo, long before them, in the same city, had combined Judaism with Grecian culture, so now they carried the Grecian culture into Christianity. (*History of the Christian Church*, vol. 2 [New York: Charles Scribner's Sons, 1910], 779)

Likewise, James Orr summarized,

> Alexandria was, next to Athens, the city of the Greek world in which intellectual tendencies of every sort met and commingled. It was to be expected, therefore, that in this busy centre the attempt would early be made to unite Christianity with what was best in the thought and culture of the time. This, accordingly, is what we see taking place in the famous Catechetical School at Alexandria. It is characteristic of the Alexandrian School that it takes up a genial attitude to heathen learning and culture; regards Greek philosophy and science as in its way also a providential preparation for the Gospels; seeks to meet an antichristian Gnosis by a better Gnosis, which grows out of faith and love. It is speculative, liberal, idealistic in spirit; in its Scriptural methods allegorical, though not to the subversion of the history, as in the heretical Gnosticism. (*The History and Literature of the Early Church* [London: Hodder and Stoughton, 1913], 116)

76. J. M. Dillon describes Christoplatonism, "All Christian theology is dependent, to an extent at least, on contemporary Greek philosophy, primarily Platonism, but some Christian thinkers fall particularly strongly under Platonic influence, and properly merit the title of Christian Platonists." ("Platonism," *ABD*, 5:380).

However, Tertullian's cry at the end of the second century concerning the distance between Athens and Jerusalem (cf. *Prescription Against Heretics*, VII) argues that the "extent" of dependence in the apostolic church is quite small, if not nonexistent (cf. Acts 17:18–32).

77. See the timeless and comprehensive treatments by Charles Biggs, *The Christian Platonists of Alexandria: Eight Lectures* (Oxford: Claredon Press, 1886); and Edwin Hatch, *The Influence of Greek Ideas and Usages upon the Christian Church*, 6th ed. (London: Williams and Norgate, 1897).

78. See John Chryssavgis, *In the Heart of the Desert: The Spirituality of the Desert Fathers and Mothers*, revised ed. (Bloomington, IN: World Wisdom, 2008). Beyond their direct influence on medieval monasticism, the "desert fathers" substantially influenced many modern movements, including the German evangelicals, the Pennsylvania Pietists, and

the Methodist revival in England (see Douglas Burton-Christie, *The Word in the Desert: Scripture and the Quest for Holiness in Early Christian Monasticism* [Oxford: Oxford University Press, 1993], 7–9).

79. Quoted in Chryssavgis, *In the Heart of the Desert*, 15; see Athanasius, *Life of Anthony* 14 (*NPNF2*, 4:200).

80. Thomas C. Oden summarizes the relationship:

> This point must be savored unhurriedly to sink in deeply: The Christians to the south of the Mediterranean were teaching the Christians to the north. Africans were informing and instructing and educating the very best of Syriac, Cappadocian and Greco-Roman teachers. This flow of intellectual leadership in time matured into the ecumenical consensus on how to interpret sacred Scripture and hence into the core of Christian dogma.
>
> The common misperception is directly the opposite—that intellectual leadership typically moved from the north to the south, from Europe to Africa. But in Christian history, contrary to this common assumption, the flow of intellectual leadership demonstrably moved largely from Africa to Europe—south to north. (*How Africa Shaped the Christian Mind: Rediscovering the African Seedbed of Western Christianity* [Downers Grove, IL: InterVarsity, 2007], 28–29)

81. Tertullian, "Pagan Philosophy the Parent of Heresies," *Prescription Against Heretics*, Chap. 7 (*ANF*, 3:246–47); italics added.

82. See Thorlief Boman, *Hebrew Thought Compared with Greek* (London: SCM Press, 1960). After Boman's idiosyncratic work (though we might say that many of his conclusions were true despite his faulty linguistic approach), many have followed the pendular lead of James Barr: *The Semantics of Biblical Language* [Oxford: Oxford University Press, 1961]; and *Old and New in Interpretation: A Study of the Two Testaments* (London: SCM Press, 1966).

83. See G. E. Ladd, *The Pattern of New Testament Truth* (Grand Rapids: Eerdmans, 1968), esp. 9–40.

84. See, for example, Marvin R. Wilson, *Our Father Abraham: Jewish Roots of the Christian Faith* (Grand Rapids: Eerdmans, 1989), 135–92.

85. Ladd, *The Pattern of New Testament Truth*, 40.

> For our present purpose, the important thing to note is the difference between the Hebrew and the Greek views of reality. For the Greek, the world, nature, human history—in sum, the sphere of the visible—formed the realm of flux and change, of becoming, of the transient. Reality belonged to the realm of the invisible, the good, the unchanging, which could be apprehended only by the mind of the soul transcending the visible. Thus salvation was found in the flight of the soul from the world to the invisible world of God.
>
> For the Hebrew, reality was found in God who makes himself known in the ebb and flow of both nature and historical events by his acts and by his words. God comes to men in their earthly experience. Thus the final redemption is not flight from this world to another world; it may be described as the descent of the other world—God's world—resulting in a transformation of this world. (Ibid., 36–37)

86. "Origen clearly represents and develops a construction of the Christian faith in which eschatology has been swallowed up in an emphasis upon transcendence. The only time which truly matters is that time until one's death, which determines one's experience in paradise and in the resurrection. '*Heaven' as cosmographic place now occupies the central position once occupied by the eschatological kingdom of God in Jesus' teaching.* That, too, occurs

on the authority of progressive dialectics, the refinement of Pauline metaphysics" (Jacob Neusner and Bruce Chilton, *Jewish and Christian Doctrines: The Classics Compared* [New York: Routledge, 2000], 183; italics added).

87. See a history of the "spiritual vision model" by Craig A. Blaising, "Premillennialism," in *Three Views on the Millennium and Beyond*, ed. Darrell L. Bock (Grand Rapids: Zondervan, 1999), 160–74.

88. Origen, *On First Principles*, 2.11.5–6 (*ANF*, 4:299); italics and bracketed portions added.

89. Modern theologians likewise drift into such categories—e.g., Jürgen Moltmann: "Finally, compared with the invisible heaven in which the glory of God dwells, the earth means the whole visible and temporal world in which God does not dwell—or not as yet. In this symbolic sense, the earth is not merely this planet. It is the whole material world of which this planet is a part" (*God in Creation: A New Theology of Creation and the Spirit of God*, trans. M. Kohl [Minneapolis: Fortress, 1993], 160).

Moltmann continues, "Heaven is, as it were, the preparing and making available of the potentialities and potencies of the world's creation, redemption and glorification" (p. 166). This view of heaven as "the space of the possible" (p. 167) is rather Platonic, as is evident in Moltmann's interaction with Plato's Ideas (pp. 167–68): "That is the essential reason why the Greek Fathers of the church took over the Platonic doctrine of Ideas, appropriating them for Christian theology. The archetypes for all created realities are also prepared in the kingdom of *the Creator's* potentialities" (p. 167).

90. The Bible is completely devoid of the metaphysical concepts of "natural" and "supernatural." There is no word in the Hebrew language that can be translated as "nature" or "natural"; and the Greek *phusis/phusikos*, sometimes translated "nature/natural," universally refers to something's inherent quality or makeup (cf. Rom. 1:26f.; 2:14; 11:21ff.; 1 Cor. 11:14; Gal. 2:15; 4:8; Eph. 2:3; James 3:7; 2 Peter 2:12), thus carrying no metaphysical connotations. Moreover, the term *supernatural*, which is so commonly used to describe the heavens and all therein, is *never* used in the Bible. How can a word that is so unbiblical, both conceptually and linguistically, find such consistent use in the modern church? Its use is highly symptomatic and reveals the bedrock of our Hellenistic worldview.

91. Thus believers are encouraged to participate in a "supernatural fast"—no verbalizing of the term *supernatural* for at least thirty days. This helps break the habitual use of nonbiblical terminology.

92. Craig Keener articulates the linguistic struggle, "I felt I had to use the category of supernatural because, to address the questions as they exist in our culture, I needed to articulate it in terms that were at hand. But the category of supernatural really isn't a biblical perspective. It's using Hume's paradigm. If we believe that God is the Creator and is sovereign, then he is at work in the whole world around us" ("It's Okay to Expect a Miracle," *Christianity Today*, December 9, 2011, http://www.christianitytoday.com/ct/2011/december/okay-to-expect-miracle.html [accessed January 2012]). See also Keener, *Miracles: The Credibility of the New Testament Accounts*, 2 vols. (Grand Rapids: Baker Academic, 2011).

Chapter Three

1. "Apocalyptic" can refer to both *theology*, a type of thought involving climactic and devastating eschatology, and *literature*, a genre of writings during second-temple Judaism and early Christianity. Hence the consensus definition: "a genre of revelatory literature with a narrative framework, in which a revelation is mediated by an otherworldly being to a human recipient, disclosing a transcendent reality which is both temporal, insofar as it envisages eschatological salvation, and spatial insofar as it involves another, supernatural world" (John J. Collins, *The Apocalyptic Imagination: An Introduction to Jewish Apocalyptic Literature*, 2nd ed. [Grand Rapids: Eerdmans, 1998], 5).

2. Though Klaus Koch describes eight common features of apocalyptic thought (*The Rediscovery of Apocalyptic*, trans. M. Kohl [London: SCM Press, 1972], 28–33), the day of the Lord is strangely absent in his discussion, a pervasive phenomenon in modern discussions concerning the apocalyptic.

3. Apocalyptic thought is characterized not only by cataclysm but by the *suddenness* of such cataclysm. This is unmistakably portrayed by the imagery of the NT. The cataclysm will be sudden and all-consuming, like the torrent of a raging storm (Matt. 7:27; Luke 6:48), esp. as in the flood of Noah (Matt. 24:37; Luke 17:26; 2 Peter 3:6), like fire and sulfur raining down on Sodom and Gomorrah (Luke 17:28; 2 Peter 2:6), like lightning spreading across the sky (Matt. 24:27; Luke 17:24), like a thief breaking into a house in the middle of the night (Matt. 24:43; 1 Thess. 5:2; 2 Peter 3:10; Rev. 3:3; 16:15), and like a woman gripped by hard labor (Matt. 24:8; Mark 13:8). The radical nature of apocalyptic language is designed to awaken the human heart from the stupor of familiarity with sin and unrighteousness in this age, as is evident from Jesus' injunction to "keep watch" (Matt. 24:42; cf. Mark 13:33; Luke 12:37) that we might not be "weighed down with dissipation, drunkenness and the anxieties of this life" (Luke 21:34).

4. Apocalypticism is generally a hermeneutical approach which sees the broad view of redemptive history in such terms. So Jürgen Moltmann relates apocalypticism to the OT prophets: "The apocalyptic picture of history is rooted in the historic thinking of Israel and bound up with the prophetic eschatology. . . . In place of a historic theology we have a theology of history and in place of a historic eschatology comes an eschatological contemplation of history" (*Theology of Hope: On the Ground and the Implications of a Christian Eschatology*, trans. M. Kohl [Minneapolis: Fortress, 1993], 134–35).

5. Thus the controversy concerning the "origins" of apocalyptic thought seems generally tangential. Most modern studies of apocalyptic thought are built upon naturalistic assumptions—i.e., apocalypticism as a mode of thought evolved from nonapocalypticism over time. More conservative commentators find the source of this evolution in the OT prophets; see Leon Morris, *Apocalyptic*, 2nd ed. (London: InterVarsity, 1973); D. S. Russell, *The Method and Message of Jewish Apocalyptic: 200 BC – AD 100* (Philadelphia: Westminster Press, 1964); and to a large extent H. H. Rowley, *The Relevance of Apocalyptic: A Study of Jewish and Christian Apocalypses from Daniel to the Revelation*, rev. ed. (New York: Harper & Brothers, 1946). More liberal commentators derive apocalypticism from Persia, Babylon, and the Greco-Roman milieu (see P. D. Hanson, et al., "Apocalypses and Apocalypticism," *ABD*, 1:279–88; and David Hellholm, ed., *Apocalypticism in the Mediterranean World and the Near East* [Tübingen: Mohr-Siebeck, 1983]); or from even older Mesopotamian, Akkadian, and Canaanite mythology (see Frank M. Cross, *Myth and Hebrew Epic* [Cambridge: Harvard University Press, 1973]; and Lester L. Grabbe and Robert D. Haak, eds., *Knowing the End from the Beginning: The Prophetic, the Apocalyptic and their Relationships* [New York: T & T Clark, 2003]); see an introduction in Collins, *Apocalyptic Imagination*, 1–42.

6. Even naturalists, who believe death and corruption to be constitutional to existence, project such realities to their ultimate end by extrapolating population growth in the struggle for resources, or by studying the probabilities of asteroids impacting the earth, or by pushing climatology models centuries into the future, etc. All humans seek an ultimate end to their existence, which I believe is set forth plainly in the Scriptures centered around the day of the Lord.

7. "Sections of both the Old and New Testaments, known as apocalyptical writings, offer a third view of history. This perspective views history to be like an arrow that moves toward a target called 'the day of the LORD' (Amos 5:18) or 'the kingdom of God' (Mark 1:15). In this view, history has direction and meaning. Caught up in the struggles of the present age, the faithful may not always be able to 'see the big picture,' but there is one" (Kenneth E. Bailey, *Jesus Through Middle Eastern Eyes: Cultural Studies in the Gospels* [Downers Grove, IL: IVP Academic, 2008], 114).

8. The Greek *apokatastasis*, "restoration," in its lone usage here in Acts 3:21, derives from *apokathistēmi*, meaning "to restore to an earlier state" (BDAG, 111). Thus *apokatastasis*—"restoring everything to perfection" (BDAG, 112)—references the former state of mankind in Eden.

9. The Greek *paliggenesia* is a compound of *palin*, "anew, again," and *genesis*, "source, origin" (see BDAG, 752). Thus, God is going to "again-Genesis" at the day of the Lord. Jürgen Moltmann sets *paliggenesia* in context:

> The word παλιγγενεσία derives from oriental cosmology, which was introduced into the ancient world by the Pythagoreans. . . .
>
> In Jewish apocalyptic, however, this concept was refashioned eschatologically. There it meant the unique and final "rebirth" for the eternal kingdom of the creation which had become old, transient and mortal. . . . What Daniel and the apocalyptists who followed him expected of the coming of the Son of man and his enduring righteousness and justice was just such a universal new birth of the world (Daniel 7). We meet this cosmic, apocalyptic interpretation of "rebirth" in Matt. 19:28: "In the rebirth (παλιγγενεσία; RSV: 'new world'), when the Son of man shall sit on his glorious throne, you who have followed me will also sit on twelve thrones, judging the twelve tribes of Israel." The Son of man who suffers here will there be exalted; the Son of man who is judged here will there himself be the judge, the Son of man put to death here will there live eternally. His followers will be drawn into his humiliation here and his exaltation there. (*The Spirit of Life: A Universal Affirmation*, trans. M. Kohl [Minneapolis: Fortress, 2001], 145)

10. Craig A. Blaising observes,

> The *new creation model* of eternal life draws on biblical texts that speak of a future everlasting kingdom, of a new earth and the renewal of life on it, of bodily resurrection (especially of the physical nature of Christ's resurrection body), of social and even political concourse among the redeemed. The new creation model expects that the ontological order and scope of eternal life is essentially continuous with that of present earthly life except for the absence of sin and death. Eternal life for redeemed human beings will be an embodied life on earth (whether the present earth or a wholly new earth), set within a cosmic structure such as we have presently. It is not a timeless, static existence but rather an unending sequence of life and lived experiences. It does not reject physicality or materiality, but affirms them as essential both to a holistic anthropology and to the biblical idea of a redeemed creation. ("Premillennialism," in *Three Views on the Millennium and Beyond*, ed. Darrell L. Bock [Grand Rapids: Zondervan, 1999], 162)

11. So Jürgen Moltmann describes, "This horizon embraces on the one hand 'creation in the beginning' and, on the other, 'the creation of the End-time.' It takes its definition from the creation of the heavens and the earth 'in the beginning' (Gen. 1:1), and from the creation of 'the new heavens and the new earth' (Isa. 65:17) at the end. But this means that Israel did not merely develop a *protological* understanding of creation; in the process of so doing it also arrived at an *eschatological* view of creation. Both dimensions are necessarily present in 'the soteriological understanding of creation'" (*God in Creation: A New Theology of Creation and the Spirit of God*, trans. M. Kohl [Minneapolis: Fortress, 1993], 54).

12. In his commentary on Genesis, John H. Sailhamer notes,

> By commencing his history with a "beginning" (*rē'šît*), a word often paired with "the end" (*'aḥarît*), the author also prepares the way for the consummation of that history at "the end of time," *'aḥarît*. . . .
>
> The growing focus within the biblical canon on the "last days" (*'aḥărît hayyāmîm*) is an appropriate extension of the "end" (*'aḥărît*) already anticipated in the "beginning" (*rē'šît*) of Genesis 1:1. The fundamental principle reflected in 1:1 and the prophetic vision of the future times of the "end" in the rest of Scripture is that the "last things will be like the first things." ("Genesis," in *The Expositor's Bible Commentary: Genesis–Leviticus*, rev. ed., ed. Tremper Longman III and David E. Garland, vol. 1 [Grand Rapids: Zondervan, 2008], 51)

13. Oscar Cullmann aptly states,

> The belief in the resurrection presupposes the Jewish connexion between death and sin. Death is not something natural, willed by God, as in the thought of the Greek philosophers; it is rather something unnatural, abnormal, opposed by God. . . . The Genesis narrative teaches us that it came into the world only by the sin of man. Death is a curse, and the whole creation has become involved in the curse. . . .
>
> The Greek doctrine of immortality and the Christian hope in the resurrection differ so radically because Greek thought has such an entirely different interpretation of creation. (*Immortality of the Soul or the Resurrection of the Dead? The Witness of the New Testament* [London: Epworth Press, 1958], 28–29)

14. Though the use of hyperbole is clear, the apostolic father Papias paints such a picture of the age to come:

> [As the elders who saw John the disciple of the Lord remembered that they had heard from him how the Lord taught in regard to those times, and said]: "The days will come in which vines shall grow, having each ten thousand branches, and in each branch ten thousand twigs, and in each true twig ten thousand shoots, and in every one of the shoots ten thousand clusters, and on every one of the clusters ten thousand grapes, and every grape when pressed will give five-and-twenty metretes of wine. And when any one of the saints shall lay hold of a cluster, another shall cry out, 'I am a better cluster, take me; bless the Lord through me.' In like manner, [He said] that a grain of wheat would produce ten thousand ears, and that every ear would have ten thousand grains, and every grain would yield ten pounds of clear, pure, fine flour; and that apples, and seeds, and grass would produce in similar proportions; and that all animals, feeding then only on the productions of the earth, would become peaceable and harmonious, and be in perfect subjection to man." . . . These, then, are the times mentioned by the prophet Isaiah: "And the wolf shall lie down with the lamb," etc. (Isa. 11:6ff.). (*Fragments of Papias*, 14; *ANF*, 1:153–54)

15. So J. Jeremias,

> The exclusive starting-point of all later Jewish statements about the Paradise of the first age is the Paradise story in Gn. 2f. If this alone offered rich materials for imaginative adornment, this tendency was increased even further by the combination of Paradise with the eschatological hope. . . .
>
> The site of reopened Paradise is almost without exception the earth, or the new Jerusalem. Its most important gifts are the fruits of the tree of life, the water and bread of life, the banquet of the time of salvation, and fellowship with God. The belief in resurrection gave assurance that all the righteous, even those who were dead, would have a share in reopened Paradise. ("παράδεισος," *TDNT*, 5:766–67)

16. Similarly, Psalm 8, a hymn of creation, is quoted messianically in reference to the age to come (cf. 1 Cor. 15:27; Heb. 2:8). Creation conforms to its leadership, both in this age and the age to come, for "the creation itself will be set free from its bondage to corruption and obtain the freedom of the glory of the children of God" (Rom. 8:21).

17. Though the concept of "nature" does not correspond to the biblical terminology of "creation," T. Desmond Alexander rightly comments, "All of these passages describing a transformed environment look forward to a time when nature and humanity will be in harmony as God originally intended. When this happens, the earth will be very different, for God's disfavor and curses will be removed" (*From Eden to the New Jerusalem: An Introduction to Biblical Theology* [Grand Rapids: Kregel, 2009], 163).

18. Rom. 8:18–25 is a quintessential apocalyptic passage, for the stark dichotomy of the two ages is punctuated by "the glory that is to be revealed [lit. "apocalypsed," Gk. *apokaluptō*] to us. For the creation waits with eager longing for the revealing [lit. "apocalypsing," Gk. *apokalupsis*] of the sons of God" (vv. 18–19).

> Present suffering in light of future glory was common in second-temple Judaism (see a summary in James D. G. Dunn, *Romans 1–8*, WBC [Dallas: Word, 1998], 468–69). For example, "And the Lord answered and said to me . . . With regard to the righteous ones, those whom you said the world has come on their account, yes, also that which is coming is on their account. For this world is to them a struggle and an effort with much trouble. And that accordingly which will come, a crown with great glory" (2 Baruch 15.7–8; *OTP*, 1:626). Such a crown of eschatological glory is assumed by all the NT authors (cf. 1 Cor. 9:25; 2 Tim. 4:8; James 1:12; 1 Peter 5:4; Rev. 2:10), giving context to present suffering.

19. "The Old Testament nowhere holds forth the hope of a bodiless, nonmaterial, purely 'spiritual' redemption as did Greek thought. The earth is the divinely ordained scene of human existence. Furthermore, the earth has been involved in the evils which sin has incurred. There is an interrelation of nature with the moral life of man; therefore the earth must also share in God's final redemption. . . . A new universe is to be created which will replace the old. This is no new thought but is the summation of a whole aspect of prophetic theology" (George Eldon Ladd, *The Presence of the Future: The Eschatology of Biblical Realism* [Grand Rapids: Eerdmans, 1974], 59–60).

20. Jürgen Moltmann summarizes (critically) this simple approach, "Creation was from the beginning perfect. Human sin spoilt it. Grace is the divine expedient designed to remedy the predicament of sin. And at the end the goodly, primal creation will be restored as it in truth always was and will be: eschatology is the doctrine of the *restitutio in integrum*, the return to the pristine beginning" (*The Coming of God: Christian Eschatology*, trans. M. Kohl [Minneapolis: Fortress, 2004], 262).

21. Anthony A. Hoekema summarizes, "The New Testament believer, therefore, is aware that history is moving toward the goal of this final consummation. This consummation of

history, as he sees it, includes such events as the Second Coming of Christ, the general resurrection, the Day of Judgment, and the new heavens and new earth. Since the new heavens and new earth will be the culmination of history, we may say that all history is moving toward this goal" (*The Bible and the Future* [Grand Rapids: Eerdmans, 1979], 32).

22. "So the time of the world as a whole takes the form of the *circulatio*, the circle. If the end corresponds to the beginning, and if this beginning returns again in the end, then the time of the world has a splendid symmetrical conformation. What happens at the end can then only be the 'restoration' of the beginning" (Moltmann, *Coming of God*, 263).

23. See similar themes in Warren Austin Gage, *The Gospel of Genesis: Studies in Protology and Eschatology* (Winona Lake, IN: Eisenbrauns, 1984): "First, God is considered as the protological Creator and the eschatological Redeemer. Second, Adam as the first man is compared with Christ as the last Man. Third, the protological fall of man into cursing is considered in view of the prophecy of the eschatological restitution of man to blessing. Fourth, the earthly Edenic beginning is compared with the promise of Edenic Zion in the end. Fifth, the protological pattern of the Noahic judgment is considered with regard to its eschatological recurrence" (p. 5).

24. "From Genesis to Revelation we feel that this book is in a real sense a unity. It is not a collection of fragments, but has, as we say, an organic character. It has one connected story to tell from beginning to end; we see something growing before our eyes; there is plan, purpose, progress; the end folds back on the beginning, and, when the whole is finished, we feel that here again, as in the primal creation, God has finished all his works, and behold, they are very good" (James Orr, *The Problem of the Old Testament* [New York: Scribner's, 1907], 32; quoted in Daniel P. Fuller, *The Unity of the Bible: Unfolding God's Plan for Humanity* [Grand Rapids: Zondervan, 1992], 22).

25. Though lacking a protological emphasis (due to a naturalistic bias), Moltmann well articulates:

> From first to last, and not merely in the epilogue, Christianity is eschatology, is hope, forward looking and forward moving, and therefore also revolutionizing and transforming the present. The eschatological is not one element *of* Christianity, but it is the medium of Christian faith as such, the key in which everything in it is set, the glow that suffuses everything here in the dawn of an expected new day. For Christian faith lives from the raising of the crucified Christ, and strains after the promises of the universal future of Christ. . . . A proper theology would therefore have to be constructed in the light of its future goal. Eschatology should not be its end, but its beginning. (*Theology of Hope*, 16)

26. For example, "fury" (Ex. 15:7; Lev. 26:28; Deut. 29:28; Ps. 2:5; 7:6; Isa. 10:5,25; 26:20; 30:27; 66:15; Jer. 21:5; Lam. 2:4; Ezek. 5:13,15; 6:12; 19:12; 21:17; 23:25; 24:13; Hab. 3:12); "wrath" (Ex. 32:11; Lev. 10:6; Num. 16:46; Deut. 9:7f.,22; 29:23,28; 1 Sam. 28:18; 2 Kings 22:13,17; 23:26; 2 Chron. 12:7,12; 19:2,10; 24:18; 28:11,13; 29:8; 32:26; 34:21,25; 36:16; Ezra 7:23; 8:22; 10:14; Neh. 13:18; Job 20:28; Ps. 6:1; 21:9; 38:1; 56:7; 59:13; 78:21,59; 89:46; 110:5; Isa. 9:19; 10:6; 13:9,13; 51:17,20,22; Jer. 4:4; 6:11; 7:20,29; 10:10; 21:12; 23:19; 25:15; 30:23; 36:7; 42:18; 50:13,25; Lam. 2:2; 4:11; Ezek. 7:19; 9:8; 13:13; 20:33; 22:22,31; 25:14; 36:6; 38:18; Dan. 9:16; Hos. 11:9; Nah. 1:2; Hab. 3:2,8; Zeph. 1:18; Zech. 8:2,14); "anger/angry" (Gen. 18:30,32; Ex. 4:14; 34:6; Num. 11:1,10,33; 12:9; 14:18; 22:22; 25:3f.; 32:10,13f.; Deut. 1:37; 3:26; 4:21,25; 6:15; 7:4; 9:8,18ff.; 11:17; 13:17; 29:20,23f.,27f.; 31:17,29; 32:16,21; Josh. 7:1,26; 22:18; 23:16; Judg. 2:12,14,20; 3:8; 6:39; 10:7; 14:19; 2 Sam. 6:7; 24:1; 1 Kings 11:9; 14:9,15; 15:30; 16:7,13,26,33; 22:53; 2 Kings 13:3; 17:11,17f.; 21:6; 22:17; 23:19,26; 24:20; 1 Chron. 13:10; 2 Chron. 25:15; 28:9,25; 29:10; 30:8; 33:6; 34:25; Neh. 9:17;

Job 4:9; 9:13; 20:23; 21:17; 42:7; Ps. 6:1; 7:6; 27:9; 38:1; 74:1; 77:9; 78:21,31; 79:5; 80:4; 86:15; 103:8; 106:29,40; 145:8; Prov. 22:14; 24:18; Isa. 5:25; 9:17; 12:1; 13:9,13; 30:27,30; 54:8; 64:9; 66:15; Jer. 3:12; 4:8,26; 7:18,20; 8:19; 10:24; 11:17; 12:13; 18:23; 23:20; 25:6f.,37; 30:24; 32:29f.; 36:7; 42:18; 44:3,8; 49:37; 51:45; 52:3; Lam. 1:12; 2:1,22; 3:66; 4:11; Ezek. 5:13,15; 13:13; 25:14; 35:11; 38:18; Dan. 9:16; Hos. 11:9; Joel 2:13; Jonah 3:9; 4:2; Mic. 7:18; Nah. 1:3; Hab. 3:8; Zeph. 2:2f.; 3:8; Zech. 1:2,12; 7:12; 10:3; Mal. 1:4).

27. Again, because of the temporal nature of the Scriptures, historical events organically "point" to their protological introduction and eschatological conclusion. Thus historical judgments upon human sin inherently prophesy the eschatological judgment. This is how much of the prophetical language and imagery concerning the day of the Lord is developed (cf. Jer. 46:21; Ezek. 21:29; Hos. 5:9; Amos 3:14; Mic. 7:4; Zeph. 1:9).

28. "רִיב," *HALOT*, 1226; cf. John M. Bracke, "רִיב (rîb I)," *NIDOTTE*, 3:1105–6.

29. Note the usage of Heb. *gāmal/gĕmûl* ("to recompense/recompense") (Ps. 28:4; 94:2; 103:10; 116:12; 137:8; Isa. 3:11; 35:4; 59:18; 66:6; Jer. 51:6; Lam. 3:64; Joel 3:7; Obad. 15); see J. P. Lewis, "360 לָמַג (*gāmal*)," *TWOT*, 166–67.

30. Ernst Käsemann is known for stating (critically): "Apocalyptic was the mother of all Christian theology" (*New Testament Questions of Today*, trans. W. J. Montague [London: SCM Press, 1969], 102). I agree (though I reject Käsemann's naturalistic bias), for the resurrection of Jesus confirmed the apocalyptic approach to the Scriptures. Apocalypticism is thus the theological framework within which the severity of God and the kindness of God are embodied in the day of the Lord and the cross, respectively.

31. Unfounded is the dispensational attempt to distinguish between the "day of the Lord" and the "day of Christ" (akin to its delineation between the "kingdom and God" and the "kingdom of heaven"), finding in them "two separate [salvific] programs" (J. Dwight Pentecost, *Things to Come: A Study in Biblical Eschatology* [Grand Rapids: Zondervan, 1965], 232).

32. "Sometimes it is called 'that day' (Matt. 7:22; 1 Thess. 5:4; 2 Tim. 4:8), and again it is called 'the day' without any qualification whatever, as if it were the only day worth counting in all the history of the world and of the race (1 Cor. 3:13). . . . All Pauline literature is especially suffused with this longing for the Parousia, the day of Christ's glorious manifestation. The entire conception of that day centers therefore in Christ and points to the everlasting establishment of the kingdom of heaven, from which sin will be forever eliminated" (H. E. Dosker, "Day of the Lord," *ISBE*, 1:879).

33. "In spite of the attempts of OT prophets (1 Pt. 1:11), Christians cannot calculate these times (Mk. 13:33; 1 Th. 5:1f.; Ac. 1:7). God Himself will put them in an absolute schedule in accordance with the requirements of salvation history, and a prior fixing of the year or the day would be opposed to the divine sovereignty (Ac. 1:7). καιρός then becomes a technical term for the last judgment or the end" (Gerhard Delling, "καιρός," *TDNT*, 3:461).

34. "The apocalypticists believed in God, and believed that He had some purpose for the world He had made, and that His power was equal to its achievement. Their faith goes beyond the faith in the divine control of history, indeed. It is a faith in the divine initiative in history for the attainment of its final goal. Such a belief is fundamental to the Christian view of God and the world" (Rowley, *Relevance of Apocalyptic*, 152).

Indeed, "They would have smiled at the idea so widespread in our day that God is of all beings the most helpless. Few, indeed, would formulate their faith in those words, but many would appear to cherish their substance. For they believe that man is vastly powerful to influence the course of the world by his acts, or to launch ideas that will change the course of history, while God is shut outside the circle of history, a mere spectator, and powerless to intervene" (ibid.).

35. Though rejecting a literal interpretation of Genesis 1–3, J. V. Fesko well articulates,

> The categories of the beginning are embedded in eschatology, the creation of the heavens and earth become the *new* heavens and earth (Isa. 65:17; 66:22) and the garden of Eden reappears in the book of Revelation (2:7; cf. Isa. 51:3; Zech. 1:17). The broader category of protology enables one to consider matters of ontology, or systematic theology, but also redemptive history, or biblical theology. Under this broader rubric of protology one can see the connections between anthropology and christology, the first and second Adams, and protology and eschatology, Genesis and Revelation, the beginning and the end, the alpha and omega. (*Last Things First: Unlocking Genesis 1–3 with the Christ of Eschatology* [Fearn, Scotland: Mentor, 2007], 33–34)

36. So the assertion that Geerhardus Vos makes concerning Paul's eschatological orientation holds: "It will appear throughout that to unfold the Apostle's eschatology means to set forth his theology as a whole. Through a conceptual retroversion the end will be seen to give birth to the beginning in the emergence of truth. . . . The presence of this antithetical orientation is clearly seen in the correspondence of the two names for Christ, 'the eschatos Adam' and 'the deuteros Man,' the opposite to the former no less than to the latter being the 'protos Man'" (*The Pauline Eschatology* [Princeton: Princeton University Press, 1930], 11). Of course, Paul's "theology as a whole" also emphasized the cross and justification by faith in light of the coming judgment—i.e., "cruciform-apocalypticism."

37. Based on this apostolic foundation, the early church developed its common eschatological doctrines, as patristic scholar Brian E. Daley summarizes:

> Risky though it always is to speak of a consensus among theologians, one may at least discern the outlines of a common eschatological *doctrine*, as well as these common axioms or presuppositions, emerging in the writings we have studied, despite many variations of interpretation and emphasis on the part of individual writers.
>
> (a) Central, for instance, to the early Christian theological tradition is what has been called a "*linear" view of history*: the conviction that history has an origin and an end, both rooted in the plan and the power of God. . . .
>
> (b) Equally central to Patristic eschatological thought is the insistence that the fulfillment of human history must include the *resurrection of the body*. . . .
>
> (c) Following the expectations of both the Jewish Scriptures and the New Testament, early Christian writers also agreed on the prospect of God's *universal judgment*. . . . And it is Christ, God's Word made flesh, who will embody and execute that judgment by coming to be visibly present again at the end of its history. (*The Hope of the Early Church: A Handbook of Patristic Eschatology* [New York: Cambridge University Press, 1991], 219–20; italics in the original)

38. As N. T. Wright laments,

> I have become convinced that most people, including most practicing Christians, are muddled and misguided on this topic, and that this muddle produces quite serious mistakes in our thinking, our praying, our liturgies, our practice, and perhaps particularly our mission to the world. . . . Often people assume that Christians are simply committed to a belief in 'life after death' in the most general terms and have no idea how the more specific notions of resurrection, judgment, the second coming of Jesus, and so on fit together and make any sense—let alone how they relate to the urgent concerns of today's real world.

(*Surprised by Hope: Rethinking Heaven, the Resurrection, and the Mission of the Church* [New York: HarperOne, 2008], 6)

39. Though I disagree with their incorporation of "realized eschatology" (see the introduction; to be discussed further at the end of this chap.), I am indebted to Clifford and Johnson for the "linchpin" phraseology (see Ross Clifford and Philip Johnson, *The Cross Is Not Enough: Living as Witnesses to the Resurrection* [Grand Rapids: Baker, 2012], chap. 1).

40. In theological discussion, this is more commonly referred to as the "center" of biblical theology (see chap. 8, n. 2).

41. The incorporation of realized eschatology tends to break the simple unity of the Scriptures (i.e., communicating that the NT is talking about something fundamentally different than the OT), as seen in the works of Fuller, *Unity of the Bible*; Walter C. Kaiser Jr., *Recovering the Unity of the Bible: One Continuous Story, Plan, and Purpose* (Grand Rapids: Zondervan, 2009); and G. K. Beale, *A New Testament Biblical Theology: The Unfolding of the Old Testament in the New* (Grand Rapids: Baker Academic, 2011).

42. Passages commonly associated with "realized eschatology" (e.g., Matt. 12:28; Luke 17:21; etc.) are addressed in the appendix.

43. Thus the spiritual realization of the day of the Lord and the resurrection incurs such harsh apostolic condemnation (cf. 2 Thess. 2:2; 2 Tim. 2:18; 1 Cor. 15:12ff.). Realized eschatology breaks the basic apocalyptic framework of redemptive history.

44. See Oscar Cullmann, *Christ and Time: The Primitive Christian Conception of Time and History*, trans. Floyd V. Filson (Philadelphia: Westminster, 1950); and Cullmann, *Salvation in History*, trans. S. G. Sowers (New York: Harper & Row, 1967). Though I applaud Cullmann's emphasis on the Jewish, linear view of history (along with his spirited condemnation of Platonism), I reject his perversion of that simple timeline through realized eschatology (see esp. *Christ and Time*, 81–93; and *Salvation in History*, 166–85).

45. "The word used to express eternity, αἰών ('age'), is *the same word* that is also applied to a limited division of time; otherwise expressed, between what we call eternity and what we call time, that is, between everlasting continuing time and limited time, the New Testament makes absolutely no difference in terminology. Eternity is the endless succession of the ages (αἰῶνες)" (Cullmann, *Christ and Time*, 62).

46. "The LXX generally translates *ʿōlām* by *aiōn* which has essentially the same range of meaning. That neither the Hebrew nor the Greek word in itself contains the idea of endlessness is shown both by the fact that they sometimes refer to events or conditions that occurred at a definite point in the past, and also by the fact that sometimes it is thought desirable to repeat the word, not merely saying 'forever,' but 'forever and ever'" (Allan A. Macrae, "1631a עוֹלָם [*ʿōlām*]," *TWOT*, 673).

47. As C. R. Schoonhoven points out,

> In Platonic and Hellenistic thought eternity was often conceived of as timelessness. According to this tradition man's final goal is to seek to escape from time into timelessness, i.e., into eternity (cf. Plato *Phaedo* 79, 106e–108a; *Symposium* 208a; *Republic* 611a–b; *Timaeus* 27d–28a [contrast 37d]). . . .
>
> From the biblical perspective such a dualism, which posits an exclusive and qualitative difference between time and eternity, is false. In the understanding of the writers of the OT and NT, eternity is not timelessness but endless time. . . .
>
> The NT, like the LXX, used Gk *aiōn* (translated 'age') for eternity. This same word is used for a long but limited duration of time. The use of identical terms for both everlastingly continuing time and limited time emphasizes the notion of eternity as an endless succession of ages. Time is not demeaned in the NT, but rather exalted. ("Eternity," *ISBE*, 2:162–63)

48. This simplicity is one of the reasons J. Christiaan Beker preferred the term *apocalyptic*: "The reader may well ask: Why use the term apocalyptic at all? My reasons for using 'apocalyptic' are twofold: first of all, the term 'apocalyptic' guards against the multivalent and often chaotic use of the concept of 'eschatology' in modern times. . . . The use of the term apocalyptic clarifies the future-temporal character of Paul's gospel. Second, apocalyptic denotes an end-time occurrence that is both cosmic-universal and definitive. . . . The term 'apocalyptic' refers more clearly than the general term 'eschatology' to the specificity and extent of the end-time occurrence" (*Paul's Apocalyptic Gospel: The Coming Triumph of God* [Philadelphia: Fortress, 1982], 14). In other words, apocalypticism clearly emphasizes the realities of the day of the Lord and leaves no room for the unending ambiguities of existentialism and realized eschatology.

49. There has been extensive theological debate over the interpretation and translation of "age" (Gk. *aiōn*) and "world" (Gk. *kosmos*). The reason for the linguistic overlap between *aiōn* and *kosmos* (cf. esp. Matt. 13:22; Luke 16:8; Rom. 12:2; 1 Cor. 2:6; 2 Cor. 4:4; 1 Tim. 6:17; 2 Tim. 4:10; Heb. 1:2; 11:3) is due to the fact that "this world" and "this age" hold *historical continuity* with "the world to come" and "the age to come," and thus they hold many assumed commonalities. The introduction of metaphysical dualism (i.e., "this world" versus "the world beyond") breaks the continuum and confounds the commonalities.

50. By telling his disciples, "All authority in heaven and on earth has been given to me" (Matt. 28:18), Jesus is simply saying that he has been entrusted with judging the living and the dead at the day of the Lord (cf. John 5:22–27; Acts 10:42). Until that day, therefore, they are to preach "repentance and forgiveness of sins . . . to all nations" (Luke 24:47), "baptizing them" (Matt. 28:19) as a confirmation of their forgiveness and salvation from the coming wrath. The complete lack of reference to the day of the Lord in modern commentaries concerning Matt. 28:18 is astonishing; cf. France (NICNT), Hagner (WBC), Turner (BECNT), Carson (EBC), Nolland (NIGTC), Davies and Allison (ICC), Luz (Hermeneia), Wilkins (NIVAC), Blomberg (NAC), Morris (PNTC), etc. Such is the product of realized eschatology.

51. The "all things" here refers historically, rather than metaphysically, to the things of this age. So the NET renders, "For *the culmination* of all things is near." As Peter H. Davids points out, "The phrase used here points to this linear concept of history in the NT and therefore the end of this historical age with all that is associated with it (therefore, 'the end of *all* things')" (*The First Epistle of Peter*, NICNT [Grand Rapids: Eerdmans, 1990], 155–56).

52. Note the pseudepigraphic *Life of Adam and Eve*: "Indeed, six days after Adam died, Eve, aware that she would die, gathered all her sons and daughters, Seth with thirty brothers and thirty sisters, and Eve said to (them) all, 'Listen to me, my children, and I will tell you that I and your father transgressed the command of God, and the archangel Michael said to us, "Because of your collusion, our LORD will bring over your race the wrath of his judgment, first by water and then by fire; by these two the LORD will judge the whole human race"'" (49.1–3; *OTP*, 2:292).

53. Note the metaphor of "chaff," which is also used extensively in the OT to refer to the wicked in relation to divine judgment and the day of the Lord (Ps. 1:4; 35:5; 83:13; Isa. 17:13; 29:5; 33:11; 40:24; 41:15; Jer. 13:24; Dan. 2:35; Hos. 13:3; Zeph. 2:2; Mal. 4:1). The scriptural context of John's imprecation upon the Pharisees and teachers of the law would have been obvious to everyone.

54. Many assume that 2 Peter 3 speaks of the annihilation of materiality unto a heavenly destiny. However, the "destruction," Gk. *apoleia/apollumi* (vv. 6,7,9), described concerns sin and unrighteousness, both in the heavens and upon the earth. Just as the earth was

destroyed by water in the flood (v. 6), so also will the heavens and earth be destroyed by fire on the day of the Lord (v. 7). The earth was not annihilated in the flood, but rather *cleansed*. The passing away (Gk. *parerchomai*, v. 10a) of the heavens and the burning with intense heat (Gk. *kausoō*, v. 10b) of the earth and its works are simply summarized in v. 11 as "all things are to be destroyed" (NASB). The "all things" are the evil entities in the heavens and upon the earth that make them a "home of unrighteousness," so to speak. As seen elsewhere in the NT, the "all things" are ultimately in reference to that which dwells within the heavens and the earth (cf. Rom. 11:36; 1 Cor. 8:6; Eph. 1:10; Col. 1:16–18).

The "elements," Gk. *stoicheion*, of the earth (v. 10, NASB) and of the heavens (v. 12) are generally understood in the NT as "sinful ways" or "principles" (cf. Gal. 4:3,9; Col. 2:8,20; Heb. 5:12). It is the base depravity of demonic powers in the heavens and demonized human beings upon the earth that will be destroyed on the day of the Lord. The heavens and the earth will endure this destruction and become a "home of righteousness" (v. 13, NIV), just as the earth endured the destruction of ungodly people during the flood.

55. D. F. Watson, "Gehenna (Place)," *ABD*, 2:926.

56. As William V. Crockett explains,

> Southwest of the city was the Valley of Hinnom, an area that had a long history of desecration. The steep gorge was once used to burn children in sacrifice to the Ammonite god Molech (2 Kings 23:10; Jer. 7:31; 32:35). Jeremiah denounced such practices by saying that Hinnom Valley would become the valley of God's judgment, a place of slaughter (Jer. 7:32; 19:5–7). As the years passed, a sense of foreboding hung over the valley. People began to burn their garbage and offal there, using sulfur, the flammable substance we now use in matches and gunpowder. Eventually, the Hebrew name *ge-hinnom* (canyon of Hinnom) evolved into *geenna* (*gehenna*), the familiar Greek word for hell (Matt. 5:22,29; 10:28; 18:9; 23:33; Mark 9:43,45; Luke 12:5). Thus when the Jews talked about punishment in the next life, what better image could they use than the smoldering valley they called *gehenna*? . . .
>
> Some Jews, of course, took the fiery images literally, supposing that Hinnom Valley itself would become the place of hellfire and judgment (1 Enoch 27:1–2; 54:1–6; 56:3–4; 90:26–28; 4 Ezra 7:36). ("The Metaphorical View," in *Four Views on Hell* [Grand Rapids: Zondervan, 1996], 58)

Though Crockett says this last view "was minor and not widely held in Judaism," and that "the New Testament also rejects this view" (ibid.), this statement is unsubstantiated. The opposite is actually true, since the burden of proof lies upon the metaphorical interpretation. Nowhere is there any direct evidence for a changing of expectation in the NT, and the intertestamental references used by Crockett for justifying a metaphorical interpretation were noncanonical to first-century Jews, who would have defaulted to the plainly understood words of the prophets (cf. Isa. 30:30–33; 66:24; Jer. 7:32; 19:5–7).

57. Because of the linear-temporal nature of the Scriptures, historical events organically "point" to their protological introduction and eschatological conclusion. Thus historical judgments upon human sin inherently prophesy the eschatological judgment. This is how much of the prophetical language and imagery concerning the day of the Lord is developed (cf. Jer. 46:21; Ezek. 21:29; Hos. 5:9; Amos 3:14; Mic. 7:4; Zeph. 1:9).

58. See 4 Ezra 7:35–38; *Assumption of Moses* 10:10,19; *2 Baruch* 59:10; *1 Enoch* 27:2f.; 48:9; 54:1; 90:26f.; 103:8. See a summary of intertestamental descriptions in Dale C. Allison, *Resurrecting Jesus: The Earliest Christian Tradition and Its Interpreters* (New York: T & T Clark, 2005), 81–82. Although the second-temple Jewish belief in Gehenna is widely acknowledged by modern commentators, most go on to argue that it was reinterpreted by

the apostles and the early church (akin to the reinterpretation of other Jewish apocalyptic concepts, such as the kingdom, resurrection, messianic expectation, etc.).

59. Rabbi David Kimhi references this common tradition in his commentary on Psalm 27 (c. 1200): "Gehenna is a repugnant place, into which filth and cadavers are thrown, and in which fires perpetually burn in order to consume the filth and bones; on which account, by analogy, the judgment of the wicked is called 'Gehenna'" (quoted in Lloyd R. Bailey, "Gehenna: The Topography of Hell," *Biblical Archeologist* 49 [September 1986]: 188). Modern scholarship increasingly rejects this testimony (see Watson, "Gehenna," 2:926–28, and Bailey, "Gehenna," 189).

However, as Joachim Jeremias points out,

Road sweepers may be referred to in b.B.M. 26a (cf. b. Pes. 7a): "According to R. Shemaiah b. Zeira the streets of Jerusalem were swept every day," evidently to secure the levitical purity of the city. The fact that the Valley of Hinnom was a dump for filth and rubbish agrees with this statement. The upper end of the valley, between the tower of Hippicus and the Gate of the Essenes in the south, was called βηθσώ or βησου (*BJ* 5.145); according to A. Neubauer's etymological explanation, this means "place of filth". The gate called the Dung Gate M. Eduy, i.3 (cf. p. 5), the quarter of the despised weavers, gave immediately on to the Valley of Hinnom at its debouchment into the Kidron Valley. This accords with the fact that the Valley of Hinnom was a place of abomination from ancient times, since it was connected with the worship of Moloch (II Kings 23.10; Jer. 2.23 and elsewhere), and was supposed to be the same as Gehenna (Hell), which took its name from it. It was still in modern times the place for rubbish, carrion and all kinds of refuse. (*Jerusalem in the Time of Jesus*, trans. F. H. and C. H. Cave [London: SCM Press, 1969], 16–17)

60. A plain reading of these texts contradicts the annihilationist arguments of Edward W. Fudge, *The Fire That Consumes: A Biblical and Historical Study of the Doctrine of Final Punishment*, 3rd ed. (Eugene, OR: Cascade Books, 2011); Clark H. Pinnock, "The Destruction of the Finally Impenitent," *Criswell Theological Review* 4 (Spring 1990): 243–59; and Pinnock, "The Conditional View," in *Four Views on Hell*, 135–66. Why would the fire remain forever yet its purposes pass away? Why are eternal life and eternal judgment consistently contrasted (cf. Matt. 13:42–43; 25:46; John 3:16; 5:29; Rom. 2:7–8) if they are not functional and existential opposites? Similarly, how can *aionios* (eternal) refer to one thing in relation to *zoē* (life) and something completely different in relation to *kolasis* (punishment), *olethros* (destruction), and *krima* (judgment)? Moreover, to deny infinite divine punishment because of human finitude (thus assuming finite consequences of human sin) is illogical, since God is the referent.

For a thorough criticism of annihilationism, see Robert Peterson, *Hell on Trial: The Case for Eternal Punishment* (Phillipsburg, NJ: Presbyterian and Reformed, 1995); and Christopher Morgan and Robert Peterson, eds., *Hell Under Fire: Modern Scholarship Reinvents Eternal Punishment* (Grand Rapids: Zondervan, 2004).

61. Note the clear references to eternal conscious torment in the Apocrypha (Judith 16:17; Sirach 7:17; 4 Ezra 2:29; 7:26–42; 4 Maccabees 9:9; 10:10–15; 12:12; 13:15), the Pseudepigrapha (*1 Enoch* 10.13; 18.9–16; 26–27; 48.8–10; 54.1–6; 56.1–4; 90.24–27; 100.7–9; 103.7–8; 108.4–7; *2 Enoch* 10.1–3; 40.12–13; 63.4; *2 Baruch* 30.4–5; 44.12–15; 51.6; 59.2; 64.7–10; 83.8; 85.12–13; *Assumption of Moses* 10:10; *Jubilees* 36.9–11; *Sibylline Oracles* 1.100–103, 349–50; 2.283–312; 4.179–91), and the apostolic fathers (*2 Clement* 6:7; 17:7; *Martyrdom of Polycarp* 2:3; 11:2; *Epistle to Diognetus* 10:7–8; Ignatius, *Ephesians* 16:2; *Apocalypse of Peter* 20–33).

So Crockett summarizes,

> Annihilationists often construct awkward scenarios where the wicked are consumed but the fire burns forever, or where the wicked suffer greatly but temporarily in an unquenchable fire. To solve a problem they construct a fire that rages endlessly, even though the wicked would have been consumed during the first moments of eternity. Is this what the second-century writers were trying to say? That the wicked will be destroyed in eternal, indestructible fires? Or were they following that line of thought that speaks of eternal, conscious punishment for the wicked? Is seems to me that some annihilationists look for any straw in the wind to keep from admitting that early Christians affirmed eternal, conscious punishment. (*Four Views on Hell*, 66)

62. Daley continues his summary of thinking in the early church: "With judgment comes also *retribution*. Following the Jewish apocalyptic tradition, as reflected in the New Testament, early Christian writers almost universally assumed that the final state of human existence, after God's judgment, will be permanent and perfect happiness for the good, and permanent, all-consuming misery for the wicked. Apocalyptic imagery continued to dominate the conception of both these states throughout the Patristic period, especially in the portraits drawn of the suffering of the damned" (*Hope of the Early Church*, 220–21).

63. See John F. Walvoord, "The Literal View," in *Four Views on Hell*, 11–28. Though Walvoord argues for eternal punishment by real fire, his presentation lacks the substantiality of a real place.

64. Naturalism is the most devaluing of belief systems, for human beings are understood to be no more than a sophisticated sack of protoplasm—as Ernst Haeckel understood the first cell, or "Monera," to evolve from nonlife: "a shapeless, mobile, little lump of mucus or slime, consisting of albuminous combination of carbon" (*The History of Creation: Or the Development of the Earth and Its Inhabitants by the Action of Natural Causes*, vol. 1 [New York: D. Appleton, 1876], 184). In practicality, this view of the constitution of life remains commonly assumed within the Western secular mind.

65. Though conflating the realities of Hades and Gehenna, McClain articulates well the popular misconception of a cosmic struggle between God and Satan:

> The strange notion that the devil is the king of hell has no basis in divine revelation. *God* is the King of hell, just as He is the King of everything else in time and space. And because this is so, that everlasting prison-house of the lost will not be the noisy and disorderly place that is sometimes imagined by the popular mind. There is no more orderly place than a well-disciplined prison, even under imperfect human government. There will be no riots in hell. For all those who reject the mercy of God in Christ and recognize no final argument but force, there will be force without stint or limit, the force of a divine government from which there can be no escape, either now or hereafter. (*The Greatness of the Kingdom: An Inductive Study of the Kingdom of God* [Winona Lake, IN: BMH Books, 1959], 25)

66. Moreover, Gehenna will ultimately be a source of rejoicing for the righteous. Akin to a high school next to a prison where all the drug pushers, thugs, and pedophiles are locked up, so will the righteous rejoice in the cleansing of the earth (cf. Ps. 101:8; Isa. 35:8; 52:1; Joel 3:17; Rev. 21:27). With the great multitude we will eternally resound, "*Hallelujah!* Salvation and glory and power belong to our God, for true and just are his judgments. He has condemned the great prostitute who corrupted the earth by her adulteries. . . . *Hallelujah!* The smoke from her goes up for ever and ever. . . . *Hallelujah!*

For our Lord God Almighty reigns. Let us rejoice and be glad and give him glory!" (Rev. 19:1–7, NIV).

67. O. Böcher states,

> In other places in the NT where the eternal punishment of fire is considered, the idea of γέεννα is always in the background, even when the word is not actually present. This is true especially for the use of κάμινος (Matt 13:42,50; cf. Rev 9:2) or λίμνη τοῦ πυρός (Rev 19:20; 20:10,14f.; 21:8; cf. 14:10); not only the godless (cf. also Luke 16:24) but also Satan with his demons will be destroyed in it by eternal fire (Matt 25:41; Rev 19:20; 20:10,14; cf. T. Jud. 25:3; ἄβυσσος 2). Perhaps 1 Cor 3:10–15; 2 Pet 3:5–13 (cf. Mark 9:49; Luke 17:29f.) teach that these expressions assume the purifying power of fire. Early Christianity shares this view of eschatology with contemporary Judaism. ("Gehenna; hell," EDNT, 1:240)

68. If we are going to continue to use the term "hell," then it must be reserved for either hadēs or gehenna. I prefer the latter for evangelical consistency (most modern translations have followed this path by transliterating sheol and hadēs). This is fine as long as we actually associate "hell" with a future reality upon the earth. However, the Old English and Germanic roots (hel, helle, hölle, holja) almost universally refer to the present "underworld" or "nether world," which corresponds to sheol/hadēs (see "Hell," The Oxford Dictionary of English Etymology, ed. C. T. Onions [Oxford: Oxford University Press, 1966], 435).

69. Though not authoritative, firsthand accounts of near-death survivors who testify of the wicked being held within the earth do accord with the testimony of the Scriptures (see Bill Wiese, 23 Minutes in Hell [Lake Mary, FL: Charisma House, 2006]; Mary K. Baxter, A Divine Revelation of Hell [New Kensington, PA: Whitaker House, 1993]; and Maurice S. Rawlings, To Hell and Back: Life After Death–Startling New Evidence [Nashville: Thomas Nelson, 1993]).

70. So Joachim Jeremias explains,

> Fundamental for an understanding of the γέεννα passages in the NT, which occur only in the Synoptists and John, is the sharp distinction made by the NT between ᾅδης and γέεννα. This distinction is a. that Hades receives the ungodly only for the intervening period between death and resurrection, whereas Gehenna is their place of punishment in the last judgment; the judgment of the former is thus provisional but the torment of the latter eternal (Mk. 9:43 and par.; 9:48). It is then b. that the souls of the ungodly are outside the body in Hades, whereas in Gehenna both body and soul, reunited at the resurrection, are destroyed by eternal fire (Mk. 9:43 and par., 45, 47 and par., 48; Mt. 10:28 and par.). ("γέεννα," TDNT, 1:658)

71. The reality of sheol/hadēs as a tarrying place for the dead is also reinforced by the common ancient practice of necromancy (cf. Lev. 19:26,31; 20:6; Deut. 18:10; 1 Chron. 10:13; Isa. 8:19; 29:4).

72. Because Gehenna is equated with the "second death" (Rev. 20:14; 21:8), it seems that the deuteros thanatos, "second death," is primarily a reference to the first thanatos of Hades rather than the death of human mortality. Hence the second death is more a place than an event (cf. Rev. 20:13–15), though the latter meaning may also be implied.

73. Tartaros may also be a separate area beneath Hades, but not the place of final judgment (see "ταρταρόω," BDAG, 991).

74. Note the dichotomy of various expressions concerning present Hades and future Gehenna:

Present Hades – Temporal *Under* the Earth	Future Gehenna – Eternal *Upon* the Earth
Gk. *hadēs* (Heb. *sheol*) – "Hades, underworld, abode of dead" (Gen. 37:35; 42:38; 44:29,31; Num. 16:30,33; Deut. 32:22; 1 Sam. 2:6; 1 Kings 2:6,9,34; Ps. 6:5; 9:17; 16:10; 18:5; 30:3; 31:17; 49:15f.; 55:15; 86:13; 88:3; 89:48; 139:8; 141:7; Prov. 1:12; 2:18; 5:5; 7:27; 9:18; 14:12; 15:11,24; 27:20; 30:16; Eccl. 9:10; Isa. 5:14; 14:9,11,15,19; 28:15,18; 38:10,18; 57:9; Ezek. 31:15–17; 32:27; Hos. 13:14; Amos 9:2; Jonah 2:3; Hab. 2:5; Matt. 11:23; 16:18; Luke 10:15; 16:23; Acts 2:27,31; Rev. 1:18; 6:8; 20:13f.)	Gk. *gehenna* (Heb. *gehinnōm*) – "Gehenna, hell, Valley of Hinnom"[i] (Matt. 5:22,29f.; 10:28; 18:9; 23:15,33; Mark 9:43,45,47; Luke 12:5; Jas. 3:6)[ii] Gk. *gehennan tou puros* – "fire of *Gehenna*, hell fire" (Matt. 5:22; 18:9) Gk. *Tapheth* (Heb. *topheth*) – "place of fire [within *gehenna*]" (2 Kings 23:10; Isa. 30:33; Jer. 7:31f.; 19:6,11–13)
Gk. *abussos* (Heb. *tehom*) – "abyss, deep, depths, bottomless pit" (Job 28:14; 38:16; Ps. 71:20; 107:26; 135:6; Ezek. 31:15; Amos 7:4; Jonah 2:6; Hab. 3:10; Luke 8:31; Rom. 10:7; Rev. 9:1f.,11; 11:7; 17:8; 20:1,3)	Gk. *limnē tou puros* – "lake of fire" (Rev. 19:20; 20:10,14f.; 21:8; cf. Isa. 30:33) Gk. *kaminos tou puros* – "furnace of fire" (Matt. 13:42,50; cf. Ps. 21:9; Isa. 31:9; Mal. 4:1)
Gk. *diaphthora* (Heb. *shachath*)– "pit [of *sheol*], destruction" (Job 33:28; Ps. 9:15; 16:10; 55:23; 107:20; Acts 2:27,31; 13:34–36)	Gk. *puri asbestos* – "unquenchable fire" (Matt. 3:12; Mark 9:43,48; Luke 3:17; cf. Isa. 34:9f.; 66:24)
Gk. *hupokatō tēs gēs* – "under, underneath the earth" (Ex. 20:4;[i] Deut. 4:18;[i] 5:8;[i] Rev. 5:3,13) Gk. *katōteros tēs gēs* – "lower (parts) of the earth" (Eph. 4:9) Gk. *katōtatos* – "lowest (parts)" (Ps. 86:13; 88:6) Gk. *katōtatos tēs gēs* – "lowest (parts) of the earth" (Ps. 63:9; 139:15) Gk. *katachthonios* – "subterranean" (Phil. 2:10)	Gk. *pur to aiōnion* – "everlasting fire" (Matt. 18:8; 25:41; Jude 7; cf. Isa. 33:14) Gk. *kolasin aiōnion* – "everlasting punishment" (Matt. 25:46; cf. Isa. 24:21f.; Dan. 12:2) Gk. *krimatos aiōniou* – "everlasting judgment" (Heb. 6:2; cf. Isa. 9:6; Jer. 23:5) Gk. *aiōnios olethros* – "everlasting destruction" (2 Thess. 1:9; cf. Ps. 2:12; Isa. 11:9)
Gk. *bathos* – "deep, depth" (Ps. 69:15;[ii] 130:1;[ii] Isa. 7:11*; Rom. 8:39) Gk. *bathos tēs gēs* – "deep, depth of the earth" (Ezek. 26:20; 31:18; 32:24) Gk. *bothros* – "deep pit, grave" (Ezek. 26:20; 31:14,18; 32:21–23,* 29f.)	Gk. *skotos to exōteron* – "outside, outer darkness" (Matt. 8:12; 22:13; 25:30; cf. Ps. 107:14) Gk. *zophos tou skotous* – "utter, blackest darkness" (2 Peter 2:17; Jude 13; cf. Joel 2:2; Zeph. 1:15)
Gk. *tartaroō* – "cast into Tartaros ['Netherworld, depths of Hades']" (2 Peter 2:4)	Gk. *anastasin kriseōs* – "resurrection of judgment, damnation" (John 5:29; cf. Dan. 12:2; Acts 24:15)
Gk. *thanatos* (Heb. *maveth*) – "Death, realm of dead" (2 Sam. 2:26; Ps. 6:5; 18:4f.; 49:14; 88:6 [LXX]; 107:14; 116:3; Prov. 5:5; 7:27; 14:12 [LXX]; 16:25 [LXX]; Isa. 28:15,18; 38:18; Hos. 13:14; Acts 2:24; Rev. 1:18; 20:13)	Gk. *deuteros thanatos* – "second death" (Rev. 2:11; 20:6; 20:14; 21:8)

Present Hades – Temporal *Under* the Earth	Future Gehenna – Eternal *Upon* the Earth
i. Combines with Gk. *hudor*, "water," i.e., "water under the earth" ii. Variant of *bathos* * Translates Heb. *sheol* in LXX	i. References to the Valley of Hinnom in this age include Josh. 15:8; 18:16; 2 Kings 23:10; 2 Chron. 28:3; 33:6; Neh. 11:30; Jer. 7:31f.; 19:2,6; 32:35 ii. Intertestamental references include 4 Ezra 7:36ff.; *1 Enoch* 27:2f.; 48:9; 54:1–6; 90:26f.; 103:8; *2 Baruch* 59:10; *Assumption of Moses* 10:19

75. Helpful discussions on this subject are found in Hoekema, *The Bible and the Future*, 92–108; George Eldon Ladd, *A Theology of the New Testament*, ed. Donald A. Hagner, 2nd ed. (Grand Rapids: Eerdmans, 1993), 597–99; and Wayne Grudem, *Systematic Theology: An Introduction to Biblical Doctrine* (Grand Rapids: Zondervan, 1994), 810–27.

76. The doctrine of "soul sleep," as held by Jehovah's Witnesses and Seventh Day Adventists, deviates from the Scriptures. Jehovah's Witnesses teach the annihilation of the soul at death and its recreation at the resurrection, while the Adventists teach that the soul is simply inert, residing in the "memory of God." The poetic language of Ecclesiastes (cf. 9:5; 12:7) is not a reliable theological base for either of these beliefs. Human souls are clearly conscious in the intermediate state, both in Hades (cf. 1 Sam. 28:15; Isa. 14:9; Luke 16:23) as well as heaven (cf. 2 Cor. 5:8; Rev. 6:9; 20:4). Moreover, the killing of the body but not the soul (cf. Matt. 10:28, par.) argues for the continuance of the soul after the death of the body. The description of death as "sleep" (1 Cor. 15:16; 1 Thess. 4:13; etc.) is figurative, as Ladd explains: "Sleep was a common term for death both in Greek and Hebrew literature [cf. R. Bultmann, *TDNT*, 3:14] and need not carry any theological significance" (*Theology of the New Testament*, 599).

77. Though a separation between the wicked and righteous within Sheol is implied in the OT, it is more clearly articulated in second-temple Judaism. In the *Apocalypse of Zephaniah* (see *OTP*, 1:514–15), the prophet is taken to Hades and shown the state of humanity before "the day of the Lord" (12:6). The righteous are pictured as crossing over a river chasm: "You have escaped from the Abyss and Hades, now you will cross over the crossing place . . . to all the righteous ones, namely Abraham, Isaac, Jacob, Enoch, Elijah and David" (9:2–4). Abraham is portrayed as an intercessor "beseeching the Lord" for those in the fiery area of Hades (11:1–6). In 4 Maccabees, the martyrs are also pictured as tarrying with Abraham until the judgment: "For if we so die, Abraham and Isaac and Jacob will welcome us, and all the fathers will praise us" (13:17, NRSV).

Moreover, Ezra supposedly asks God directly, "O Lord, show this also to your servant: whether after death, as soon as everyone of us yields up the soul, we shall be kept in rest until those times come when you will renew the creation, or whether we shall be tormented at once?" (2 Esdras 7:75, NRSV). To which God gives a detailed answer (vv. 76–99), which boils down to the righteous receiving "rest" (v. 91) in seven ways, while the wicked "shall not enter into habitations, but shall immediately wander about in torments, always grieving and sad, in seven ways" (v. 80).

This gives some context to Jesus' teaching on Lazarus and the rich man in Hades (Luke 16:19–31). Though the eschatological judgment is not immediately referenced, it is part of the surrounding context, i.e., "give an account" (16:2), "eternal dwellings" (16:9), "heaven and earth to pass away" (16:17). Moreover the Synoptic parallels to Luke 17:1–3 (cf. Matt. 18:1–9; Mark 9:42–50) clearly incorporate the eschatological realities of the kingdom of God, eternal life, Gehenna, and eternal fire.

78. "The tracing of the concept of mercy in the Eng. Bible is complicated by the fact that 'mercy', 'merciful' and 'have mercy upon' are translations of several different Heb. and Gk. roots, which are also variously rendered in other occurrences by other synonyms, such as 'kindness', 'grace', 'favour' (and cognate verbs)" (J. W. L. Hoad, "Mercy, Merciful," *NBD*, 751).

79. "After urging his audience to offer their bodies to God as a 'spiritual act of worship,' Paul adds, [*and*] *do not conform to the pattern of this world* (lit. 'and do not be conformed to this age'). The NIV omits 'and,' adds 'the pattern of,' and substitutes 'this world' for the more literal sense, 'this age'" (Colin G. Kruse, *Paul's Letter to the Romans*, PNTC [Grand Rapids: Eerdmans, 2012], 463–64).

80. Though the "new perspective on Paul" (discussed in chap. 8) disproportionately emphasizes "participation" in Christ (a theme resurrected by E. P. Sanders and esp. Richard Hays from the "Christ-mysticism" of Albert Schweitzer, et al.), "cruciformity" is a concept that applies well to redemptive history in general (see Michael J. Gorman, *Cruciformity: Paul's Narrative Spirituality of the Cross* [Grand Rapids: Eerdmans, 2001]; and Gorman, *Inhabiting the Cruciform God: Kenosis, Justification, and Theosis in Paul's Narrative Soteriology* [Grand Rapids: Eerdmans, 2009]).

81. Take Leon Morris, for example:

> It may be doubted whether apocalyptic is a very good vehicle for the expression of the characteristic Christian message. Christianity puts its emphasis on the cross. . . .
>
> In the apocalyptic literature, on the other hand, the emphasis is always on the last judgment and the events associated with it. . . .
>
> We cannot have it both ways. Granted that both the incarnation and the End are important, both cannot be the really significant thing. For the apocalypses there is the concentration on the future. In Christianity there is the recognition that the incarnation, with the atonement as its high point, is the most important event of all time. That is why, as Burkitt puts it, an apocalypse is not the proper literary form for setting forth the essential Christian message. (*Apocalyptic*, 2nd ed. [London: InterVarsity, 1973], 96–97)

82. Morris exemplifies the bias against apocalypticism so prevalent in Reformed theology:

> Apocalyptic is not a good medium for expressing "the cruciality of the cross" and in fact it does not express it. Where the New Testament writers are concerned with the last things and final judgment they can use apocalyptic vividly and forcefully. But where they deal with Christ's saving work they use categories like justification by faith, reconciliation, the new covenant sealed with Christ's blood, and others. Here apocalyptic is not helpful. The New Testament writers do not use it and we can see why. Apocalyptic is simply not suitable as a way of bringing out such truths. And since Christ's atoning work is the central doctrine of New Testament Christianity, apocalyptic fails us at the heart of the faith. (Ibid., 100)

83. As Paul rejected the humanistic approach of the circumcision group in regards to atonement (cf. Gal. 2:12ff.; Eph. 2:11ff.; Titus 1:10ff.), so Jesus rejected the humanistic, nonapocalyptic approach to salvation which arose out of the Maccabean tradition (cf. Matt. 16:22ff.; Luke 17:20ff.; John 3:3ff.). As Johannes Weiss well articulated,

> How can one expect even the slightest inclination on Jesus' part towards any kind of revolutionary act? By force and insurrection men might establish a Davidic monarchy, perhaps even as glorious a kingdom as David's had been; but God will establish the Kingdom of God without human hands, horse, or rider, with only his angels and celestial powers. To hope for the Kingdom of God in the

transcendental sense that Jesus understood it and to undertake revolution are as different as fire and water. . . .

This is not to say that he did not believe in any kind of political restoration; but that only God should bring it about. (*Jesus' Proclamation of the Kingdom of God*, trans. R. H. Hiers and D. L. Holland [German original, 1892; Philadelphia: Fortress, 1971], 102–3)

84. See Martin Luther, "A Brief Instruction on What to Look for and Expect in the Gospels (1521)," *LW*, 35:113–24.

85. Beker, *Paul's Apocalyptic Gospel*, 61.

86. Benedict T. Viviano, *The Kingdom of God in History* (Wilmington, DE: Michael Glazier, 1988). Viviano's four categories (eschatological, spiritual-mystical, political, and ecclesial) are here condensed into three (eschatological, escapist, and dominionistic), since "the political stream" (pp. 45–51) and "the ecclesial stream" (pp. 51–56) basically derive from the same theology/ideology. Generally, the same streams played out in the Middle Ages (pp. 57–80) and the "early modern period" (pp. 81–122). Only in the twentieth century (pp. 123–48) was the Jewish apocalyptic vision resurrected, and so Viviano traces "the recovery or retrieval of the original eschatological kingdom proclamation of Jesus" (p. 123).

87. *The Republic*, 7:517 (*DP*, 3:217).

88. As Plato stated,

Now the nature of the ideal being was everlasting, but to bestow this attribute in its fulness upon a creature was impossible. Wherefore he ["the creator"] resolved to have a moving image of eternity, and when he set in order the heaven, he made this image eternal but moving according to number, while eternity itself rests in unity; and *this image we call time.* For there were no days and nights and months and years before the heaven was created, but when he constructed the heaven he created them also. They are all parts of time, and *the past and future are created species of time, which we unconsciously but wrongly transfer to the eternal essence*; for we say that he "was," he "is," he "will be," but the truth is that "is" alone is properly attributed to him, and that "was" and "will be" are only to be spoken of becoming in time, for they are motions, but that which is immovably the same cannot become older or younger by time, nor ever did or has become, or hereafter will be, older or younger, nor is subject at all to any of those states which affect moving and sensible things and of which generation is the cause. These are *the forms of time, which imitates eternity* and revolves according to a law of number. (*Timaeus*, 37–38 [*DP*, 3:456]; italics added)

89. George E. Ladd summarizes,

The Greeks—at least many of them who followed in the philosophical tradition of Plato—believed in a cosmic dualism. There were two worlds—the seen and the unseen, the visible and the invisible, the phenomenal and the noumenal. The visible world was a realm of ebb and flow, flux and change, instability, having only the appearance of reality. The unseen world was the world of permanence, of ultimate reality. In the same way man was a dualism of body and soul. The body belongs to the phenomenal world, the soul to the noumenal world. . . . "Salvation"—a biblical, not a Greek concept—meant that at death the soul would be liberated from the body and take its flight to the noumenal world. (*The Last Things* [Grand Rapids: Eerdmans, 1978], 29–30)

90. "For Plato, eternity is not endlessly extended time, but something quite different; it is timelessness. Time in Plato's view is only the copy of eternity thus understood. How

much the thinking of our days roots in Hellenism, and how little in Biblical Christianity, becomes clear to us when we confirm the fact that far and wide the Christian Church and Christian theology distinguish time and eternity in the Platonic-Greek manner. This then has important consequences, and when the New Testament perspective of redemptive history is thereby affected, it leads to a radical transformation of the Primitive Christian preaching" (Cullmann, *Christ and Time*, 61–62).

91. Moltmann describes the transition,

> The first reduction of heaven to something quite different was made in the Christian church itself. As the realistic eschatology of the kingdom of God receded, heaven was increasingly—and to the same degree—declared to be the place of salvation for the soul. The prayer for the coming of the kingdom "on earth as it is in heaven" was replaced by the longing "to go to heaven" oneself. The kingdom of God's glory and the salvation of the whole creation was reduced to heaven; and heaven was reduced to the salvation of the soul.
>
> This religious reduction led to the heedless neglect of the earth and to the surrender of its future. Anyone who confuses the kingdom of God with heaven transforms his hope into resignation. (*God in Creation*, 181)

92. Origen, *On First Principles*, 2.3.7 (*ANF*, 4:274–75; italics added). Therefore, "It is simply assumed that the word *heaven* is the appropriate term for the ultimate destination, the final home, and that the language of resurrection, and of the new earth as well as the new heavens, must somehow be fitted into that" (Wright, *Surprised by Hope*, 19).

93. See an account in Blaising, *Three Views on the Millennium and Beyond*, 160–74.

94. Concerning Origen, Hans Bietenhard also observed, "The whole hope of the Christian is therefore a hope of heaven: the earth is not worthy of a Christian's hope. But this meant a complete abandonment of the Christian conception of time. A Greek dualism of above and below replaced the NT contrast between this world and the world to come" ("The Millennial Hope in the Early Church," *Scottish Journal of Theology* 6, no. 1 [1953]: 21).

95. As rehearsed in Alister E. McGrath, *A Brief History of Heaven* (Oxford: Blackwell, 2003); and Peter Stanford, *Heaven: A Guide to the Undiscovered Country* (New York: Palgrave Macmillan, 2004).

96. Unlike the biblical hope in which death is "swallowed up" by life in the resurrection (cf. Isa. 25:8; 1 Cor. 15:54; 2 Cor. 5:4), the Christoplatonic hope actually glorifies and immortalizes death. Because death is the means of salvation and the practical agency of escaping material existence, Christoplatonism is in truth a "theology of death," so to speak, as is evident by the longing for death found commonly within the monastic tradition. So Wright articulates, "Death will not simply be redefined, but defeated. God's intention is not to let death have its way with us. If the promised final future is simply that immortal souls will have left behind their mortal bodies, why then death still rules—since that is a description, not of the *defeat* of death, but simply of death itself, seen from one angle" (*Surprised by Hope*, 15).

97. Douglas J. Davies, *A Brief History of Death* (Oxford: Blackwell, 2005), 7.

98. Such a view naturally leads to the denigration of all things earthly, including Jewish thinking—as we see in Origen:

> For which reason, now, we may also see of a truth that *all the doctrines of the Jews of the present day are mere trifles and fables*, since they have not the light that proceeds from the knowledge of the Scriptures; whereas those of the Christians are the truth, having power to raise and elevate the soul and understanding of man, and to persuade him to seek a citizenship, *not like the earthly Jews here below,*

but in heaven. And this result shows itself among those who are able to see the grandeur of the ideas contained in the law and the prophets, and who are able to commend them to others. (*Against Celsus*, 2.5 [*ANF*, 4:431–32]; italics added)

99. So Daley notes, "From the end of the second century (Tertullian), Patristic writers begin also to suggest the prospect of a *judgment* pronounced by God *at the end of each individual's life.* . . . From Tertullian on . . . most Greek and Latin Patristic authors confidently accept Platonic philosophical arguments that the soul, as the conscious and self-determining core of the human person, is indestructible, and so anticipates its eternal fate, through a preliminary personal judgment, from the moment of death" (*Hope of the Early Church*, 220; italics in the original).

100. Within this view, Gehenna and Hades are melded into one homogenous, static, and immaterial reality, which exists eternally and is experienced by the wicked universally upon death. Unfortunately, damages done *in the body* lose their proportionate retribution in an incorporeal hell. Why would God punish us for destroying that which he is ultimately going to destroy? If everyone's body is going to be destroyed anyway, what is the harm of rape, murder, fornication, etc.?

By analogy, if I have a rusty antique car in my backyard that I am planning to restore to mint condition and someone comes and destroys it with a sledgehammer, then I am inclined to destroy that person with a sledgehammer. However, if I am planning on towing the car to the junkyard in a couple of months to have it crushed, then why should I seek vengeance if it is wrecked? The same logic applies to redemptive history. God created something beautiful and valuable; human beings wrecked it, and God will be vindicated when he makes them pay *corporeally* for what they have wrecked.

101. Marcion, for example, pushed Christoplatonism to its logical end by bifurcating not only redemptive history but also God himself, asserting that the OT presents a deity of materiality ("the Demiurge"), a god of wrath and judgment, while the NT reveals a deity of immateriality ("the Heavenly Father"), a god of compassion, mercy, and love, "alien" to this world. Though few technically believe this in modern times, it is the practical reality of many. For an insightful reading, see Tertullian's *Adversus Marcionem* (*ANF*, 3:269–475) and Adolf von Harnack's classic, *Marcion: The Gospel of the Alien God* (1924), trans. John E. Steely and Lyle D. Bierma (Jamestown, NY: Labyrinth Press, 1990).

102. So E. R. Craven (oft-quoted by dispensationalists) argued for a "normal interpretation of the prophecies":

Normal is used instead of *literal* (the term generally employed in this connection) as more expressive of the correct idea. No terms could have been chosen more unfit to designate the two great schools of prophetical exegetes than *literal* and *spiritual*. These terms are not antithetical, nor are they in any proper sense significant of the peculiarities of the respective systems they are employed to characterize. They are positively misleading and confusing. *Literal* is opposed not to *spiritual* but to *figurative; spiritual* is in antithesis on the one hand to *material*, on the other to *carnal* (in a bad sense). The *Literalist* (so called) is not one who denies that *figurative* language, that *symbols*, are used in prophecy, nor does he deny that great *spiritual* truths are set forth therein; his position is, simply, that the prophecies are to be *normally* interpreted (i.e. according to the received laws of language) as any other utterances are interpreted—that which is manifestly literal being regarded as literal, that which is manifestly figurative being so regarded. The position of the Spiritualist (so called) is not that which is properly indicated by the term. He is one who holds that whilst certain portions of the prophecies are to be *normally* interpreted, other portions are to be regarded as having a *mystical* (i.e. involving some secret meaning) sense. Thus, for instance, Spiritualists (so called) do not deny that when the Messiah is spoken of as "a man of sorrow and acquainted with grief," the prophecy is to be *normally* interpreted; they affirm, however, that when He is spoken of as coming "in the clouds of heaven" the language is to be "spiritually" (mystically) interpreted. . . . The terms properly expressive of the schools are *normal* and *mystical*. (J. P. Lange, et al., *A Commentary on the Holy Scriptures: Revelation*, trans. E. Moore [New York: Scribner's Sons, 1874], 98; italics in the original)

103. For a detailed history of monastic thought and practice, see Bernard McGinn, *The Presence of God: A History of Western Christian Mysticism*, 5 vols. (New York: Crossroad, 1991–2012).

104. As Anthony, the father of monasticism, described,

We have lived *in the discipline* a long time: but rather as though making a beginning daily let us increase our earnestness. . . . Whenever, therefore, we live full fourscore years, or even a hundred *in the discipline*, not for a hundred years only shall we reign, but instead of a hundred we shall reign for ever and ever. And though we fought on earth, we shall not receive our inheritance on earth, but we have *the promises in heaven*; and having *put off the body which is corrupt*, we shall receive it incorrupt. . . .

Nor let us think, as we look at the world, that we have renounced anything of much consequence, for the whole earth is very small compared *with all the heaven*. Wherefore if it even chanced that we were lords of all the earth and gave it all up, it would be nought worthy of comparison with *the kingdom of heaven*. . . .

So let us daily *abide firm in our discipline*, knowing that if we are careless for a single day the Lord will not pardon us, for the sake of the past, but will be wrath against us for our neglect. . . .

Wherefore, children, let us *hold fast our discipline*, and let us not be careless. . . . To avoid being heedless, it is good to consider the word of the Apostle, "I die daily." For if we too *live as though dying daily*, we shall not sin. (*Life of Anthony* 16–19 [*NPNF2*, 4:200–201]; italics added)

105. Luther incisively observed,

Quite clearly, once you think the matter over, you can see that by this kind of talk Satan has thought up this figment about counsels and the state of perfection so as to adorn this perverted monkery. When he saw that nothing is vowed or ever could be vowed in monkery which Christians had not already vowed in their baptism (with the exception of continence), he began to think up the idea of perfection and counsels to make the ordinary way despised and by a lot of make-believe make this extraordinary way very glamorous. He did this so that men would not see that the vows concerned trivialities. And he succeeded in fostering this error. ("The Judgment of Martin Luther on Monastic Vows (1521)," *LW*, 44:265; cf. Luther, "Avoiding the Doctrines of Men (1522)," *LW*, 35:125–53)

106. As most clearly articulated in the Heidelberg Disputation of 1518; see Gerhard O. Forde, *On Being a Theologian of the Cross: Reflections on Luther's Heidelberg Disputation, 1518* (Grand Rapids: Eerdmans, 1995).

107. For example, Luther declared,

The outward life of the Turks [Muslims] is said to be marked by a semblance of piety. They pray, fast, give alms, establish charitable institutions, and build churches. They are ready to help others. And with this appearance of holiness they deceive many people. Thus the pope also duped us. At the time we did not know better, but we believed that monastic orders and monkeries were *the proper and correct way to heaven*. Anyone who is not well armed with this article of faith and has not pressed it deep into his heart falls easy prey to the shining external gleam of holiness as well as to the prominent names of prophets and teachers. But because they have devised such *a variety of ways to heaven*, we will tell them: "We will stick to *the one Way to heaven* and adhere to Him who descended and simultaneously remained above." (*LW*, 22:335; italics added)

108. See a history of the development of this theological pattern in Viviano, *The Kingdom of God in History*, 45–56.

109. So Eusebius, Constantine's court historian, described,

Our Saviour's mighty power destroyed at once the many governments and the many gods of the powers of darkness, and proclaimed to all men, both rude and civilized, to the extremities of the earth, *the sole sovereignty of God himself.* Meantime *the Roman empire*, the causes of multiplied governments being thus removed, effected an easy conquest of those which yet remained; its object being to unite all nations in one harmonious whole; an object in great measure already secured, and destined to be still more perfectly attained, even to *the final conquest of the ends of the habitable world*, by means of the salutary doctrine, and through the aid of that Divine power which facilitates and smooths its way. . . .

In short, *the ancient oracles and predictions of the prophets were fulfilled*, more numerous than we can at present cite, and those especially which speak as follows concerning the saving Word. "He shall have dominion from sea to sea, and from the river to the ends of the earth." And again, "In his days shall righteousness spring up; and abundance of peace." "And they shall beat their swords into plough-shares, and their spears into sickles: and nation shall not take up sword against nation, neither shall they learn to war any more." These words, predicted ages before in the Hebrew tongue, *have received in our own day a visible fulfillment*, by which the testimonies of the ancient oracles are clearly confirmed. (*Oration in Praise of Constantine*, 16.6–8 [*NPNF2*, 1:606–7]; italics added)

110. See David Chilton, "Appendix A. The Eschatology of Dominion: A Summary," in *Paradise Restored: A Biblical Theology of Dominion* (Tyler, TX: Dominion Press, 1985), 223–35. Modern dominionists thus often look to Constantine as the exemplar of the faith and the first major breakthrough of the dominionistic "kingdom of God."

111. "Ecclesiastically the term applies to Christ's earthly representatives. In the Roman Church it means the pope, who (as the 'Vicar of Christ') claims universal jurisdiction from Christ's words to Peter (John 21:16ff.), and until the ninth century it referred also to emperors" (C. G. Thorne Jr., "Vicar," *NIDCC*, 1016).

112. So Augustine claimed in *City of God*,

Therefore the Church even now is the kingdom of Christ, and the kingdom of heaven. Accordingly, even now *His saints reign with Him*. . . .

It is then of *this kingdom militant*, in which conflict with the enemy is still maintained, and war carried on with warring lusts, or government laid upon them as they yield, until we come to that most peaceful kingdom in which we shall reign without an enemy, and it is of *this first resurrection in the present life*, that the Apocalypse speaks in the words just quoted. For, after saying that the devil is bound a thousand years and is afterwards loosed for a short season, it goes on to give a sketch of what the Church does or of what is done in the Church in those days, in the words, "And I saw seats and them that sat upon them, and judgment was given." It is not to be supposed that this refers to the last judgment, but to the seats of the rulers and to the rulers themselves *by whom the Church is now governed.* (*City of God*, 20.9.1–2 [*NPNF1*, 2:430]; italics added)

The impact of *City of God* is difficult to calculate, as its theology became ubiquitous to Catholics and Protestants alike (see an excellent analysis in Dan Gruber, *The Church and the Jews: The Biblical Relationship* [Hanover, NH: Elijah Publishing, 1997], 213–32).

113. "The Middle Ages on the whole did not understand well the this-worldly future dimension of the kingdom of God. This was so due to three factors: a widespread ignorance of the apocalyptic Jewish background of this expectation, together with an acute Platonizing longing for the eternal, for a place outside of time and history. This is the first factor. To it we must add the Augustinian transformation of the kingdom into the church militant and triumphant, and lastly the imperial ideology of the Christian empire as the kingdom of God on earth" (Viviano, *Kingdom of God in History*, 57).

114. See Viviano, ibid., 57–99. Viviano describes the tensions of Augustine's theology:

Indeed, ultimately, for Augustine, the kingdom of God consists in eternal life with God in heaven. That is the *civitas dei*, the city of God, as opposed to the *civitas terrena*. That is his basic view. But, unlike Origen, he lived in the Christian empire. He could not ignore its claims to theological attention. Again, unlike Origen, he was a Roman who shared the Latin outlook of practical administration. . . .

Henceforward Christendom would have two practical rival theories as to where the kingdom was on earth: the empire and the church. Augustine's view would dominate and become the normal Roman Catholic view down to our own times. It would grow and develop, sometimes into exaggerated forms, especially among clergymen and those laymen interested in resisting the emperor. The imperial view would prevail in the East, but also in the West, at those times when the Western empire felt strong and sure of itself and among those circles which cherished the ideal of the Christian empire under an anointed priest-king. Whenever the papacy grew weak or disorganized the old ideal would rise up as an alternative. (pp. 53–54)

115. As articulated by Albrecht Ritschl (1822–1889) and his disciple Adolf von Harnack (1851–1930); see esp. Ritschl, *The Christian Doctrine of Justification and Reconciliation* (1900), and Harnack, *What Is Christianity?* (1901).

116. The social gospel movement of the early twentieth century was generally a practical application of liberal kingdom theology, spearheaded in America by Washington Gladden (1836–1918) and Walter Rauschenbusch (1861–1918); see esp. Gladden, *Social Salvation* (1902), and Rauschenbusch, *A Theology for the Social Gospel* (1917).

117. Modern dominionistic theologians employ highly figurative hermeneutics, typologically reinterpreting the OT to support taking over the earth in this age—i.e., by faith "taking the land," "sitting enthroned," etc.—producing modern movements with labels such as "Christian reconstructionism," "theonomy," "Kingdom Now," "dominionism," "kingdom theology," etc. These movements are split distinctly into two groups, Reformed and charismatic (see the complex interrelationships in Bruce Barron, *Heaven on Earth? The Social and Political Agendas of Dominion Theology* [Grand Rapids: Zondervan, 1992]). The former includes R. J. Rushdoony, G. Bahnsen, G. North, K. Gentry, R. Sutton, and G. DeMar. The latter includes K. Hagin, K. Copeland, B. Mumford, J. Hayford, and C. P. Wagner. Foremost dominionist practitioner C. P. Wagner estimates that by 2025 "almost 50 percent" of the church worldwide will be dominionistic in their theology and practice (C. Peter Wagner, *Dominion! How Kingdom Action Can Change the World* [Grand Rapids: Chosen, 2008], 73).

All such theological wranglings are radically naïve and nearsighted in their approach to the restoration of all things, as exemplified by Wagner:

> Acts 3:21 talks of Jesus being in heaven "until the times of restoration of all things, which God has spoken by the mouth of all His holy prophets since the world began." Restoration also means "transformation," and this dates back to the beginning, when Adam and Eve were in the garden of Eden. Even though Jesus came and changed history, He is waiting for us to do our part in bringing restoration to pass in real life. Meanwhile, He is reigning through us until "He puts an end to all rule and all authority and power. For He must reign till He has put all enemies under His feet" (1 Corinthians 15:24–25). (*Dominion*, 73)

118. So Moltmann summarizes the basic twofold distortion of the early church's eschatological hope:

> Ever since Augustine, "God and the soul" have gone together and, following his lead, people have put the fate of the soul at the centre of the ultimate questions. There are two reasons for this. On the one hand, we have the well-known condemnation of the millenarian historical hope by the mainline churches. If there is no longer any historical future worth hoping for, all that is left is the vista of eternity, an eternity equally close to every time, and equally far off. But on the other hand, the Constantinian imperial churches condemned early Christian millenarianism only because they saw themselves in the Christian imperium as "the holy rule" of Christ's Thousand Years' empire. So every future hope for a different, alternative kingdom of Christ was feared and condemned as heresy. (*Coming of God*, xv)

119. Moreover, throughout the history of the church these two theological patterns have created the conflicting practices of monasticism and Christendom, which reached their height during the "golden age" of monasticism and high popery (c. 1100–1300). Modern pietists and dominionists alike ought to learn the many lessons of the High Middle Ages. At no other time was there such a refined system of monastic righteousness as seen in adherence to the Benedictine, Cistercian, Franciscan, and Dominican rules. And at no other time was there such a universal rule of the church, wherein the pope picked the kings of Europe and the church owned over 30 percent of its lands. Yet Luther rightly deemed (in his customary brash style) all such "popery and monkery" (*LW*, 41:85) to be "the true, erring, apostate, shameless whore of the devil" (ibid., 215). Those who seek to walk these roads ought to consider those who have walked them in times past.

120. The Bible indeed calls for meaningful asceticism (Matt. 6:17; 1 Cor. 9:27; Col. 3:5; 1 Peter 2:11), but not as an imitation or means of salvation. Akin to the snake on the pole (Num. 21:9; John 3:14), asceticism is used to crucify the flesh in order to keep our hope set fully on the return of Jesus (Rom. 13:11–14; 1 Peter 1:13–17) and to walk out this life according to the cross (Gal. 2:20; Phil. 3:9).

121. Eusebius relates that while marching with his army Constantine looked up into the sky and saw "a cross of light in the heavens" with the Greek words "εν τούτῳ νίκα," which renders the common Latin phrase. The following night he had a dream. "In his sleep the Christ of God appeared to him with the same sign which he had seen in the heavens, and commanded him to make a likeness of that sign which he had seen in the heavens, and to use it as a safeguard in all engagements with his enemies" (*Life of Constantine* 1.29; *NPNF2*, 1:490). Constantine's sign of Chi-Rho atop a cross, the "labarum," has been used throughout history in various mottos, seals, and coats of arms to invoke militant imagery.

122. Note Wright's "two quite different ways of looking at the future of the world" (*Surprised by Hope*, 81): divinized "evolutionary optimism" (pp. 81–87) and Platonized "souls in transit" (pp. 88–91). Thus the conclusion, "Redemption is not simply making creation

a bit better, as the optimistic evolutionist would try to suggest. Nor is it rescuing spirits and souls from an evil material world, as the Gnostic would want to say. It is the remaking of creation, having dealt with the evil which is defacing and distorting it" (p. 97).

123. The modern "prosperity gospel" is simply a popular recapitulation of Augustinianism, in which the two axes of Christoplatonism work in tandem. See David W. Jones and Russell S. Woodbridge, *Health, Wealth & Happiness: Has the Prosperity Gospel Overshadowed the Gospel of Christ?* (Grand Rapids: Kregel, 2011); and Simon Coleman, *The Globalisation of Charismatic Christianity: Spreading the Gospel of Prosperity* (Cambridge: Cambridge University Press, 2000).

124. Of course there have always been pockets of cruciform and apocalyptic thought, though less often held together.

125. See esp. John N. Darby, Cyrus I. Scofield, Lewis S. Chafer, and Arno C. Gaebelein.

126. Dispensationalist historian Larry Crutchfield summarizes,

> What is it exactly that makes a person a dispensationalist? What are the indispensable ingredients of dispensational theology? As Ryrie puts it, "What is the *sine qua non* of the system?"
>
> It is not the issue of distinguishably different economies in God's governance of world affairs, for nondispensationalists frequently employ the term "dispensation" in the development of their own dispensational schemes. . . .
>
> The number of dispensations to which one holds and the question of premillennialism—belief in Christ's return to reign over a literal thousand year earthly kingdom—are not the deciding factors either. . . .
>
> Neither are the doctrines of the pretribulation rapture of the saints and the parenthetical nature of the church the essential ingredients of dispensational theology. . . . They are not that which reduces it to its lowest common denominator. They are not the heart of the system.
>
> Ryrie suggests that there are three essential factors—the *sine qua non* of the system—in determining who is and is not a dispensationalist.
>
> First, a dispensationalist makes a sharp distinction between Israel and the church. It is the dispensationalist's belief that throughout history, God has purposed two distinct purposes. One program involves the earthly people—Israel (Judaism), while the other involves a heavenly people—the church (Christianity). According to Ryrie, this distinction between Israel and the church "is probably the most basic theological test of whether or not a man is a dispensationalist, and it is undoubtedly the most practical and conclusive." (*The Origins of Dispensationalism: The Darby Factor* [Lanham, MD: University Press of America, 1992], 28–29)

127. Lewis S. Chafer, "Dispensationalism," *BSac* 93 (1936): 448; italics added; article reprinted as *Dispensationalism* (Dallas: Dallas Seminary Press, 1936). Chafer also wrote, "The distinction between the purpose for Israel and the purpose for the Church is about as important as that which exists between the two Testaments. Every covenant, promise, and provision for Israel is earthly, and they continue as a nation with the earth when it is created new. Every covenant or promise for the church is for a heavenly reality, and she continues in heavenly citizenship when the heavens are recreated" (*Systematic Theology*, vol. 4 [Grand Rapids: Kregel, 1993], 47).

128. George N. H. Peters, *The Theocratic Kingdom of Our Lord Jesus, the Christ*, vol. 1 (New York: Funk & Wagnalls, 1884), 88. Peters articulates the metaphysical framework for the theocratic kingdom: "The Word begins with the supernatural (the presence of God) and the natural in harmony. It shows how an antagonism was produced, causing the

withdrawal of the supernatural from the sight of man, and yet how in mercy it at times exhibited itself to man, in and through and for man, especially in giving revelations of its will. . . . Now the kingdom being designed to restore and manifest the original concord once existing between the natural and supernatural, the Bible closes with that kingdom *in such accordance*" (ibid., 80; italics in the original).

129. So Chafer states,

> In fact, the new, hitherto unrevealed purpose of God in the outcalling of a heavenly people from Jews and Gentiles is so divergent with respect to the divine purpose toward Israel, which purpose preceded it and will yet follow it, that the term *parenthetical*, commonly employed to describe the new age-purpose, is inaccurate. A parenthetical portion sustains some direct or indirect relation to that which goes before or that which follows; but the present age-purpose is not thus related and therefore is more properly termed an *intercalation*. The appropriateness of this word will be seen in the fact that, as an interpolation is formed by inserting a word or phrase into a context, so an intercalation is formed by introducing a day or a period of time into the calendar. The present age of the Church is an intercalation into the revealed calendar or program of God as that program was foreseen by the prophets of old. Such, indeed, is the precise character of the present age. (*Systematic Theology*, 4:41; italics in the original)

130. See Oswald T. Allis, *Prophecy and the Church* (Philadelphia: Presbyterian and Reformed, 1945).

131. Bruce A. Ware, "The New Covenant and the People(s) of God," in *Dispensationalism, Israel and the Church: The Search for Definition*, ed. Craig A Blaising and Darrell L. Bock (Grand Rapids: Zondervan, 1992), 91; cf. Craig A. Blaising, "Development of Dispensationalism by Contemporary Dispensationalists," *BSac* 145 (1988): 278.

132. See esp. Charles C. Ryrie, John F. Walvoord, Alva J. McClain, and J. Dwight Pentecost. For a history of dispensationalism and its three phases—classical, revised, and progressive—with excellent diagrams, see Craig A. Blaising and Darrell L. Bock, *Progressive Dispensationalism* (Wheaton: Victor, 1993), 21–56; cf. Blaising, "Dispensationalism: The Search for Definition," in Blaising and Bock, *Dispensationalism, Israel and the Church*, 13–34.

133. Thus the common emphasis on the "millennial kingdom" (cf. esp. John F. Walvoord, *The Millennial Kingdom* [Findlay, OH: Dunham, 1959]), though there was disagreement as to where eternity would play out—Ryrie argued for "heaven" (*Dispensationalism Today* [Chicago: Moody, 1965], 147), while Pentecost argued for a "new earth" (*Things to Come*, 561–62).

134. On "progressive dispensationalism," see Blaising and Bock, *Progressive Dispensationalism*; Blaising and Bock, *Dispensationalism, Israel and the Church*; and Robert L. Saucy, *The Case for Progressive Dispensationalism: The Interface between Dispensational & Non-Dispensational Theology* (Grand Rapids: Zondervan, 1993). Bruce K. Waltke summarizes the movement as a "restructuring of dispensationalism within the framework of inaugurated eschatology" ("A Response," in Blaising and Bock, *Dispensationalism, Israel and the Church*, 347).

135. See Weiss, *Jesus' Proclamation of the Kingdom of God*; Albert Schweitzer, *The Quest of the Historical Jesus*, trans. W. Montgomery, 2nd ed. (London: A. & C. Black, 1911); and Schweitzer, *The Mystery of the Kingdom of God*, trans. W. Lowrie (London: A. & C. Black, 1914).

136. This approach is fundamentally rearticulated in Dale C. Allison, *Jesus of Nazareth: Millenarian Prophet* (Minneapolis: Fortress, 1998); and Bart D. Ehrman, *Jesus: Apocalyptic Prophet*

of the New Millennium (Oxford: Oxford University Press, 1999); cf. Scot McKnight, *A New Vision for Israel: The Teachings of Jesus in a National Context* (Grand Rapids: Eerdmans, 1999), esp. 70–155.

137. Like so many before him, Schweitzer concluded by redefining the straightforward Jewish hope:

> The Baptist appears, and cries: "Repent, for the Kingdom of Heaven is at hand." Soon after that comes Jesus, and in the knowledge that He is the coming Son of Man lays hold of the wheel of the world to set it moving on that last revolution which is to bring all ordinary history to a close. It refuses to turn, and He throws Himself upon it. Then it does turn; and crushes Him. *Instead of bringing in the eschatological conditions, He has destroyed them.* The wheel rolls onward, and the mangled body of the one immeasurably great Man, who was strong enough to think of Himself as the spiritual ruler of mankind and to bend history to His purpose, is hanging upon it still. *That is His victory and His reign.* (*Quest of the Historical Jesus*, 368–69; italics added)

In the final analysis, Schweitzer et al. simply recapitulated the former liberal dogma. Concerning the commonality between Schweitzer and the liberalism he so vehemently criticized, Paul Schubert observed, "Both drop Jesus' faith in the future consummation to the bottom of the ocean of outdated mythology, while they sail on the smooth but treacherous surface of this ocean in the same boat of Jesus' social ethics toward the promised land of a Christian civilization" ("The Synoptic Gospels and Eschatology," *Journal of Bible and Religion*, 14, no. 3 [1946], 155).

138. C. H. Dodd, *The Parables of the Kingdom*, 3rd ed. (London: Nisbet, 1936); cf. Gustaf Dalman, *The Words of Jesus*, trans. D. M. Kay (Edinburgh: T & T Clark, 1902).

139. Dodd's work leaned heavily on Dalman, who generally rejected the Jewish hope in place of a generic and transcendental "sovereignty of heaven" (*Words of Jesus*, 92). Dodd's realized eschatology was likewise based upon "the transcendent order beyond space and time" (*Parables of the Kingdom*, 56). Thus it is generally acknowledged that "Dodd's thought is more platonic than biblical" (Ladd, *Theology of the New Testament*, 56). Dodd's revised thought falls along the same lines, with the kingdom consummating "beyond history" (*The Founder of Christianity* [London: Macmillan, 1971], 115). J. D. Crossan's "sapiential eschatology" (*The Historical Jesus: The Life of a Mediterranean Jewish Peasant* [San Francisco: HarperSanFrancisco, 1991]) has carried on the basic tenets of this tradition to the present day.

140. C. K. Barrett, "New Testament Eschatology," *Scottish Journal of Theology* 6, no. 2 (June 1953): 155.

141. Joachim Jeremias, *The Parables of Jesus*, trans. S. H. Hooke, rev. ed. (New York: Scribner's, 1963), 230; cf. W. G. Kümmel, *Promise and Fulfillment*, trans. D. M. Barton (London: SCM Press, 1957); and Norman Perrin, *The Kingdom of God in the Teaching of Jesus* (Philadelphia: Westminster, 1963).

142. See Oscar Cullmann, *Christ and Time*, trans. F. V. Filson (Philadelphia: Westminster, 1950); and Herman Ridderbos, *The Coming of the Kingdom*, trans. H. de Jongste (Philadelphia: Presbyterian and Reformed, 1962); cf. similar lines of thought in Geerhardus Vos, *The Pauline Eschatology* (Princeton, NJ: Princeton University Press, 1930).

143. Note the contrasting timelines in Vos (*Pauline Eschatology*, 38) and Culmann (*Christ and Time*, 82), upon which Ladd built (*Theology of the New Testament*, 66–67).

144. See a discussion concerning the phrase in Hoekema, *The Bible and the Future*, 1–22; and Thomas R. Schreiner, *New Testament Theology: Magnifying God in Christ* (Grand Rapids: Baker, 2008), 41–116.

145. Phrases that Oscar Cullmann coined: "The *new element* in the New Testament is not eschatology, but what I call the tension between the decisive 'already fulfilled' and the 'not yet completed,' between present and future" (*Salvation in History*, 172). Cullmann illustrated this view with his World War II D-day, V-day analogy: "The present period of the Church is the time between the decisive battle, which has already occurred, and the 'Victory Day'" (*Christ and Time*, 145; cf. p. 84, where the analogy is laid out in full).

146. So Jürgen Moltmann summarizes, "C. H. Dodd and Rudolf Bultmann developed different forms of what has been called presentative or realized eschatology. This is a partly Platonizing, partly existential interpretation of the early Christian message, which stresses the presence of salvation in the Spirit, in the proclamation and in faith. It attempts to eliminate early Christian apocalyptic as being a mythical view of history belonging to its own time" (*The Future of Creation: Collected Essays*, trans. M. Kohl [Minneapolis: Fortress, 2007], 18–19).

147. See the fascinating background of Ladd's life (raised a Baptist dispensationalist) in John A. D'Elia, *A Place at the Table: George Eldon Ladd and the Rehabilitation of Evangelical Scholarship in America* (New York: Oxford University Press, 2008).

148. George E. Ladd, *Crucial Questions About the Kingdom of God* (Grand Rapids: Eerdmans, 1952), 84–85; italics added. Of course this "careful exegesis" is based upon a mistaken realized interpretation of Matt. 11:12; 12:28; Luke 17:21; etc. (cf. ibid., 85–94). See the appendix for a rebuttal.

149. Some equate Constantinian imperial theology with realized eschatology, but I hesitate to do so since Christendom is generally without reference to Jewish apocalypticism—i.e., the OT simply prophesies Christendom. It is the *self-awareness* of changing the Jewish eschatological hope that defines realized eschatology. It must be granted, however, that many early Christian theologians were actually conscious of this transformation (see esp. R. Kendall Soulen, *The God of Israel and Christian Theology* [Minneapolis: Fortress, 1996], 25–56). Whatever the degree of intentionality, all such reinterpretation must simply be deemed *Gentile arrogance* (cf. Rom. 11:18–25).

150. Inaugurationalists talk out of both sides of their mouth when they insist (in an attempt to distance themselves from the atrocities of historical Christendom) that the kingdom is not equivalent to the church. However, if the kingdom is the rule of God in the hearts of believers, and the church is comprised of believers, how then can the kingdom not be equated with the church? It is therefore a short road to Christendom. As Alva J. McClain warned, "Once the Church becomes the Kingdom in any realistic theological sense, it is impossible to draw any clear line between principles and their implementation through political and social devises. For the logical implications of a present ecclesiastical *kingdom* are unmistakable, and historically have always led in only one direction, i.e., political control of the state by the Church" (*The Greatness of the Kingdom: An Inductive Study of the Kingdom of God* [Winona Lake, IN: BMH Books, 1959], 438).

151. Thus N. T. Wright articulates his inaugurationalism (more honestly than most) as the "rethinking and reworking of traditional Jewish theology," "redefinition of Jewish eschatology," "reworking of the central Jewish doctrines," and "reimagining of Jewish eschatology" (*Paul: Fresh Perspectives* [London: SPCK, 2005], 130, 136, 150, and 151, respectively).

152. Koch, *Rediscovery of Apocalyptic*, 32.

153. Bruce K. Waltke, "Kingdom Promises as Spiritual," in *Continuity and Discontinuity: Perspectives on the Relationship Between the Old and New Testaments*, ed. John S. Feinberg [Wheaton: Crossway, 1988], 275.

154. Wright, *Surprised by Hope*, 123. Wright elsewhere describes "an integrated vision of new creation in which 'heaven' and 'earth,' the twin halves of created reality, are at last united" (N. T. Wright, *The Resurrection of the Son of God* [London: SPCK, 2003], 470).

155. Ladd, *Theology of the New Testament*, 67; italics added. Of course, heaven itself does not descend to the earth, but rather the New Jerusalem descends "out of heaven from God" (Rev. 21:2). The heavens and the earth endure eternally, only in a righteous state.

156. Though worldview issues are poorly articulated, Ladd's well-known diagram, with its two merging lines in a chronological manner, is the clearest representation of the inaugurational schema (see *Theology of the New Testament*, 67).

157. "C. H. Dodd made a new kind of interpretation with his 'realized eschatology.' He accepted the sayings of the present as the most meaningful and interpreted eschatological language as symbolizing the inbreaking of the eternal into the temporal, the wholly other into the historical" (G. E. Ladd, "Kingdom of God," *ISBE*, 3:24). Though common in the academy, Ladd greatly furthered the language of "inbreaking" in evangelicalism (cf. *The Presence of the Future*, 7–9, 26, 55, 89, 101, 125, 131, esp. 180–90, 256, 271, 284, 317–19, 335–37).

158. "The theology of the kingdom of God is a theology of the invasion of history by the God of heaven in the person of Jesus of Nazareth to bring history to its consummation in the age to come beyond history. The age to come may be spoken of as 'beyond history' because heaven has invaded history and raised it to a higher level in the redeemed order" (G. E. Ladd, *Pattern of New Testament Truth* [Grand Rapids: Eerdmans, 1968], 57).

159. Dodd, *Parables of the Kingdom*, 157, n. 2.

160. See, for example, N. T. Wright: "God had acted in Jesus the Messiah to usher in the new age, to inaugurate the new covenant, to plant the seeds of new creation. The preaching of the gospel was the means whereby the Spirit worked in the hearts and minds of both Jews and Gentiles not just to give them a new religious experience, not even just to bring them salvation, but to make them the people in whom the new age, the Age to Come of Jewish eschatological expectation, had come to birth" (*Paul: Fresh Perspectives*, 147). Or Ladd, summarily, speaks of "a present spiritual resurrection and a future bodily resurrection" ("Historic Premillennialism," *The Meaning of the Millennium: Four Views*, ed. Robert Clouse [Downers Grove, IL: InterVarsity, 1977], 32). See a systematic presentation in Beale, *New Testament Biblical Theology*.

161. The relatively few Scriptures that are superficially interpreted in an inaugurational manner (e.g., Matt. 12:28; Luke 17:21; Rom. 14:17) are addressed in the appendix.

162. As reflected in *The Presence of the Future*—Ladd's "magnum opus" (D'Elia, *A Place at the Table*, 121)—which never even mentions the cross.

163. This threefold classification is an early-twentieth century invention, as is evident by the lack of definitions in the final edition of the *International Standard Bible Encyclopedia* (Eerdmans, 1939) and the testimony of Louis Berkhof: "The name [amillennialism] is new indeed, but the view to which it is applied is as old as Christianity. . . . It has ever since [the early church fathers] been the view most widely accepted, is the only view that is either expressed or implied in the great historical Confessions of the Church, and has always been the prevalent view in Reformed circles" (*Systematic Theology* [Grand Rapids: Eerdmans, 1938], 708).

164. See esp. the instrumental work of Charles L. Feinberg, *Premillennialism or Amillennialism?* (Grand Rapids: Zondervan, 1936).

165. As seen in Ladd's further delineation between "dispensational premillennialism" and "historic premillennialism" (cf. Clouse, *Meaning of the Millennium*, 17–114), which is simply chiliastic inaugurationalism.

166. Thus two inaugurationalists may be virtually identical in all theological convictions yet differ in relation to a millennial transition into the age to come, as was the case with Anthony Hoekema and George Ladd (see Hoekema, "An Amillennial Response," in Clouse, *Meaning of the Millennium*, 55–59).

167. See Loraine Boettner, *The Millennium* (Phillipsburg, NJ: Presbyterian and Reformed, 1957); Kenneth L. Gentry Jr., *He Shall Have Dominion: A Postmillennial Eschatology* (Tyler, TX: Institute for Christian Economics, 1992); David Chilton, *Paradise Restored: A Biblical Theology of Dominion* (Tyler, TX: Dominion Press, 1985); and Marcellus J. Kik, *An Eschatology of Victory* (Philadelphia: Presbyterian and Reformed, 1974).

168. Since amillennialists and postmillennialists hold the same figurative view of the millennium, the terms "optimillennialism" and "pessimillennialism" have been coined to distinguish the broader framework of thought (see Gary North, *Millennialism and Social Theory* [Tyler, TX: Institute for Christian Economics, 1991], 136–37; David Chilton, "Optimistic Amillennialism," *The Geneva Review* 20 [July 1985]: 5–6; and Richard B. Gaffin Jr., "Theonomy and Eschatology: Reflections on Postmillennialism," in *Theonomy: A Reformed Critique*, ed. William S. Barker and W. Robert Godfrey [Grand Rapids: Zondervan, 1990], 197–224).

So Greg L. Bahnsen, "*In short*, postmillennialism is set apart from the other two schools of thought by its essential *optimism* for the kingdom in the *present age.* This confident attitude in the power of Christ's kingdom, the power of its gospel, the powerful presence of the Holy Spirit, the power of prayer, and the progress of the great commission, sets postmillennialism apart from the essential pessimism of amillennialism and premillennialism" ("The Prima Facie Acceptability of Postmillennialism," *Journal of Christian Reconstructionism* 3, no. 2 [Winter 1976–77]: 66–67; italics in the original).

169. Though new-creationism persisted throughout the history of the church, it was generally assimilated into the dispensational movement in America and Britain; see a history of the "new creation model" in Blaising, *Three Views on the Millennium and Beyond*, 164–92.

170. So Kenneth L. Gentry Jr., "Although Blaising associates the arising of the spiritual model of eternity with the birth of amillennialism and postmillennialism, both of these non-premillennial eschatologies now strongly affirm a new creation model. . . . Indeed, amillennialist Hoekema provides a thorough presentation of the new creation model in his 1979 book, *The Bible and the Future*" ("A Postmillennial Response to Craig A. Blaising," in *Three Views on the Millennium and Beyond*, 231).

171. See Grudem, *Systematic Theology*, 1109–13.

172. On the chiliastic beliefs of the early church, see Hans Bietenhard, "The Millennial Hope in the Early Church," *Scottish Journal of Theology* 6, no. 1 (1953): 12–30; and Dietrich H. Kromminga, *The Millennium in the Church: Studies in the History of Christian Chiliasm* (Grand Rapids: Eerdmans, 1945), 17–113.

173. In contrast to "dispensational premillennialism" and "historic premillennialism" (i.e., chiliastic inaugurationalism). Ladd's use of "historic" is both presumptive and nondescriptive.

174. Chafer, "Dispensationalism," 449.

Chapter Four

1. Contrary to the rising trend of *creatio ex material* (cf. H. Gunkel, S. R. Driver, G. von Rad, C. Westermann, V. P. Hamilton, B. K. Waltke, and J. H. Walton), a view commonly held in ancient Near East cosmogonies. See the traditional view (*creatio ex nihilo*) defended in Gordon J. Wenham, *Genesis 1–15*, WBC (Dallas: Word, 1998), 12–15; and K. A. Mathews, *Genesis 1–11:26*, NAC (Nashville: Broadman & Holman, 1996), 137–44.

2. See J. Barton Payne, "2131a רוּחַ (*rûaḥ*)," *TWOT*, 836–37.

3. Thus John's equating of Jesus with the Word would have been understood (cf. John 1:1ff.), as Jürgen Moltmann summarizes, "As Christians understand it, creation is a trinitarian process: God the Father creates through the Son in the power of the Holy Spirit. So all things are created 'by God,' are formed 'through God' and exist 'in God'" (*The Source of Life: The Holy Spirit and the Theology of Life*, trans. M. Kohl [Minneapolis: Fortress, 1997], 115).

4. Though distorted by a natural/supernatural lens, Geerhardus Vos well articulates, "On the one hand the Spirit is the resurrection-source, on the other He appears as the substratum of the resurrection-life, the element, as it were, in which, as in its circumambient atmosphere the life of the coming aeon shall be lived. He produces the event and in continuance underlies the state which is the result of it. He is Creator and Sustainer at once, the *Creator Spiritus* and the Sustainer of the supernatural state of the future life in one" (*The Pauline Eschatology* [Princeton: Princeton University Press, 1930], 163). See also Vos's earlier article, "The Eschatological Aspect of the Pauline Conception of the Spirit," in *Biblical and Theological Studies* (New York: Scribner's Sons, 1912), 209–59.

5. So Wolfhart Pannenberg: "The Spirit is at work already in creation as God's mighty breath, the origin of all movement and all life, and only against this background of his activity as the Creator of all life can we rightly understand on the one hand his work in the ecstatics of human conscious life, and on the other hand his role in the bringing forth of the new life of the resurrection of the dead" (*Systematic Theology*, trans. G. W. Bromiley, vol. 3 [Grand Rapids: Eerdmans, 1998], 1).

6. Jürgen Moltmann, *The Spirit of Life: A Universal Affirmation*, trans. M. Kohl (Minneapolis: Fortress, 2001), 94–95; italics in the original; cf. also pp. 9, 88, 94, 152f., 189, 192, and 270.

7. Likewise the gift of the Spirit to the believer in this age is understood as a "firstfruits" (Rom. 8:23) of the final gift of the Spirit in the resurrection. However, instead of humans giving a firstfruits to God, it is God giving a firstfruits to humans: "In Rom. 8:23 the relationship of giver and recipient is reversed and ἀπαρχή is the first-fruits of God to man (cf. 2 Cor. 5:5). The gift of the *pneuma* is only provisional. It is only the beginning which will ultimately be followed by υἱοθεσία, by the gift of the σῶμα πνευματικόν" (Gerhard Delling, "ἀπαρχή," *TDNT*, 1:486).

8. Note that Paul explains the resurrection in this way as *a polemic against realized eschatology*. In 1 Cor. 15:12, he asks, "How can some of you say that there is no resurrection of the dead?" These believers had not become Epicureans, for Paul's reference in v. 32 is simply a mocking of the functional similarity of their conclusions with that of the world. Rather, "Some Corinthians, influenced by an 'over-realized eschatology,' believed that they had already experienced resurrection (cf. 2 Tim. 2:16–18). They understood Jesus' being raised as exaltation to heaven, not as bodily resurrection, and concluded that they were exalted with Jesus through the sacraments (cf. Rom. 6:4). These Corinthians would be the theological forerunners of the second-century gnostics who appear to adapt and rebut Pauline statements" (David E. Garland, *1 Corinthians*, BECNT [Grand Rapids: Baker, 2003], 699).

9. As Moltmann poetically writes,

> With the rebirth of Christ from death to eternal life we also expect the rebirth of the whole cosmos. Nothing that God has created is lost. Everything returns in transfigured form. So we expect that the Spirit of the new creation of all things will vanquish human violence and cosmic chaos. More than that: we expect that the power of time and the power of death will be vanquished, too. Finally, we expect eternal consolation when "the tears are wiped away" from our eyes. We expect eternal joy in the dance of fellowship with all created being and with the triune God. (*Source of Life*, 123)

10. So Rudolf Bultmann foundered, "*The mythical eschatology* is untenable for the simple reason that the parousia of Christ never took place as the New Testament expected. History did not come to an end, and, as every schoolboy knows, it will continue to run its course" ("New Testament and Mythology," in *Kerygma and Myth: A Theological Debate*, ed. H. W. Bartsch [London: SPCK, 1953], 5).

> Translating "sane person" for "schoolboy," Jürgen Moltmann counters, "Today the notion that world history will continue to run its course is nothing more than wishful thinking. 'Every sane person' is aware of the nuclear, ecological and economic catastrophes that threaten the modern world. The apocalyptic eschatology which Bultmann considered 'mythical' is more realistic than his faith in the inexorable onward course of world history. The belief that things will 'always go on' and that no end is in sight—at least not for us—is one of the fairytales of 'the modern world,' the fairytale of its endlessness and its lack of an alternative. That is secularized millenarianism" (*The Coming of God: Christian Eschatology*, trans. M. Kohl [Minneapolis: Fortress, 2004], 135).

11. Here it becomes exceedingly clear that mortality is the result of divine condemnation. If mortality is the result of the devil or of human error, or if it is just inherent to creation, then the logic of divine approval in the overcoming of mortality by resurrection breaks down.

12. Though lacking a cruciform balance, Joel B. Green summarizes, "The resurrection of Jesus by God is the central affirmation of the Christian message in the Acts of the Apostles" ("'Witnesses of His Resurrection': Resurrection, Salvation, Discipleship, and Mission," in *Life in the Face of Death: The Resurrection Message of the New Testament*, ed. Richard N. Longenecker [Grand Rapids: Eerdmans, 1998], 227). See also Kevin L. Anderson, *"But God Raised Him from the Dead": The Theology of Jesus' Resurrection in Luke-Acts* (Waynesboro, GA: Paternoster, 2006).

13. For a survey of the doctrine of the resurrection in the early church, see N. T. Wright, *The Resurrection of the Son of God* (London: SPCK, 2003), 480–552.

14. N. T. Wright describes,

> The early Christians hold firmly to a two-step belief about the future: first, death and whatever lies immediately beyond; second, a new bodily existence in a newly remade world. . . .
>
> Within early Christianity there is virtually no spectrum of belief about life beyond death. . . . Whereas the early Christians were drawn from many strands of Judaism and from widely differing backgrounds within paganism, and hence from circles that must have held very different beliefs about life beyond death, they all modified that belief to focus on one point on the spectrum. Christianity looks, to this extent, like a variety of Pharisaic Judaism. There is no trace of Sadducean view or of that of Philo. . . .
>
> We have plenty of evidence of debates about all sorts of things, and the virtual unanimity on resurrection stands out. Only in the late second century, a good

150 years after the time of Jesus, do we find people using the word *resurrection* to mean something quite different from what is meant in Judaism and early Christianity, namely, a spiritual experience in the present leading to a disembodied hope in the future. For almost all of the first two centuries, resurrection in the traditional sense holds not just center stage but the whole stage. (*Surprised by Hope: Rethinking Heaven, the Resurrection, and the Mission of the Church* [New York: HarperOne, 2008], 41–42)

15. Though frightfully inaugurational, Sidney Greidanus articulates well the confidence generated by such events:

The way of redemptive-historical progression sees every Old Testament text and its addressees in the context of God's dynamic history, which progresses steadily and reaches its climax in the life, death, and resurrection of Jesus Christ and ultimately in the new creation. The whole Old Testament throbs with a strong eschatological beat. Every passage in some way or in some degree voices or echoes the message: "God is acting! God is coming! God is faithful to his covenant promises! His mercy indeed endures forever! God will not cast off His chosen people! God is preparing salvation." From our position later in redemptive history, we should not only hear this eschatological beat but also recognize its fulfillment in the First and Second Coming of Jesus. (*Preaching Christ from the Old Testament: A Contemporary Hermeneutical Method* [Grand Rapids: Eerdmans, 1999], 237)

16. "Called me heavenward" (NIV), "calling us up to heaven" (NLT), and "the heavenly call" (NRSV) are all Platonic distortions of the simple translation of *avō*, meaning "above, up, high." The only use of *ouranos* in the book of Philippians is found in 3:20, which simply references the residence of our Lord and our resurrected body, which we will receive at Jesus' coming (v. 21). It is clear that Paul has in mind attaining the resurrection of the dead (v. 11). Thus the "upward call" (NASB, ESV, NKJV, NET) is fair, but "high calling" (KJV) is preferred.

17. See "ἀρραβών," BDAG, 134.

18. C. K. Barrett describes, "*Spiritual* does not describe a higher aspect of man's life; the noun spirit (πνεῦμα) on which it is based refers to the Spirit of God, and the *spiritual body* is the new body, animated by the Spirit of God, with which the same man will be clothed and equipped in the age to come, which he reaches (supposing him to die before the *parusia*) by way of resurrection" (*The First Epistle to the Corinthians* [London: Continuum, 1968], 372–73).

19. As Wright explains,

Heaven is the place where *God's purposes for the future are stored up*. It isn't where they are meant to stay so that one would need to go to heaven to enjoy them; it is where they are kept safe against the day when they will become a reality on earth. If I say to a friend, "I've kept some beer in the fridge for you," that doesn't mean that he has to climb into the fridge in order to drink the beer. God's future inheritance, the incorruptible new world and the new bodies that are to inhabit that world, are already kept safe, waiting for us, not so that we can go to heaven and put them on there but so that they can be brought to birth in this world or rather in the new heavens and new earth. (*Surprised by Hope*, 151–52)

20. See "σημεῖον," BDAG, 920–21.

21. Though modern textual scholarship is virtually unanimous in its verdict that the so-called longer ending of Mark (16:9–20) is spurious, I am quoting it here as a representative

conflation of apostolic themes found in the Gospels and Acts (see a comparison of these themes in Craig A. Evans, *Mark 8:27–16:20*, WBC [Dallas: Word, 2001], 546).

22. Likewise, the Messiah was expected to come with signs demonstrating the approval of God and the certainty of prophesied future events (cf. Matt. 12:38; 1 Cor. 1:22). Thus the crowds questioned, "When the Christ appears, will he do more *signs* than this man has done?" (John 7:31). Jesus had plainly answered such a question previously: "The works that the Father has given me to accomplish, the very works that I am doing, bear witness about me that the Father has sent me" (John 5:36). And when John the Baptist sent disciples to inquire if Jesus was "the Expected One" (Matt. 11:3, NASB), Jesus responded with the common signs of the resurrection: "the blind receive their sight and the lame walk, lepers are cleansed and the deaf hear, and the dead are raised up, and the poor have good news preached to them" (Matt. 11:5; cf. Isa. 35:4ff.; 61:1ff.). As such, Peter declared to his fellow Israelites, "Jesus of Nazareth was a man *accredited by God* to you by miracles, wonders and signs, which God did among you through him, as you yourselves know" (Acts 2:22, NIV).

23. In his monumental treatment of the age to come, George N. H. Peters summarizes,

> The miracles then are *assurances* vouchsafed that the kingdom will come as it is predicted. The miracles of Jesus are so varied and significant in the light of the kingdom that it can be readily perceived *how* they give us the needed confidence in its several requirements and aspects. The resurrection of dead ones is connected with the kingdom; that the keys of death hang at Christ's girdle is shown in the miracles of the raising of the daughter of Jairus, the widow's son, and of Lazarus, when just dead, carried out to burial, and already in the corrupting embrace of the tomb. Sickness and death are banished from the inheritors of the kingdom; the numerous miracles of healing various sicknesses and of restoring the dying, establish the power existing that can perform it. The utmost perfection of body is to be enjoyed in the kingdom; this is foreshadowed by the removal of blindness, lameness, deafness, and dumbness. Hunger, thirst, famine, etc., give place to plenty in the kingdom; the miracles of feeding thousands attest to the predicted power that will accomplish it. The natural world is to be completely under the Messiah's control in that kingdom; the miracles of the draught of fishes, the tempest stilled, the ship at its destination, the walking on the sea, the fish bringing the tribute money, the barren fig-tree destroyed, and the much-ridiculed one of water changed into wine, indicate that He who sets up this kingdom has indeed power over nature. The spiritual, unseen, invisible world is to be, as foretold, in contact and communication with this kingdom; and this Jesus verifies by the miracles of the transfiguration, the demoniac cured, the legion of devils cast out, passing unseen through the multitude, and by those of His own death, resurrection and ascension. Indeed there is scarcely a feature of this kingdom foretold which is to be formed by the special work of the Divine, that is not also confirmed to us by some glimpses of the Power that shall bring them forth. The kingdom—the end—is designed to remove the curse from man and nature, and to impart the most extraordinary blessings to renewed man and nature, but all this is to be done through One who, it is said, shall exert supernatural power to perform it. It is therefore reasonable to expect that *as part* of the developing of the plan itself, that when He first comes, through whom man and nature are to be regenerated, a manifestation of power—more abundant and superior to everything preceding—over man and nature should be exhibited, *to confirm our faith in Him and in His kingdom.* This is done, and an appeal is made to it. We are confident that the best, most logical defence of the miracles of Christ and of

the Bible is in the line here stated, viz., regarding them *as indicative and corroborative of God's promises relating to the future destiny of the Church and world.* The miracles are thus found to be *essential,* to answer a divine purpose, to supply a requisite evidence; and hence in the Scriptures they are called "signs" (σημεία) of something else intended; signs that the Word shall be fulfilled in the exertion of power. (*The Theocratic Kingdom of Our Lord Jesus, the Christ,* vol. 1 [New York: Funk & Wagnalls, 1884], 89–90; italics in the original)

Of course, the concept of "power over nature" is not a biblical one; and this distortion of the first verse of the Bible is the foundation for Peters's concept of "theocracy": "The Word begins with the supernatural (the presence of God) and the natural in harmony. It shows how an antagonism was produced, causing the withdrawal of the supernatural from the sight of man. . . . Now the kingdom being designed to restore and manifest the original concord once existing between the natural and supernatural, the Bible closes with that kingdom *in such accordance*" (p. 80). It is not a "theocratic kingdom" that will conquer nature and manifest divine sovereignty, but rather it is simply a "messianic kingdom" that will punish rebellion and restore what humanity has broken (see further discussion in chap. 6).

24. Few things have caused more division and difficulty upon the earth than the Tower of Babel. Those who have lived their entire lives in a monolingual culture are often unable to appreciate this reality, and therefore an authentic connection between Genesis 11 and Acts 2 is lacking. This disconnect is often reinforced by a naturalistic bias that negates the historicity of Babel. The lack of any real evidence for the evolution of language, however, argues strongly for its reality. As Philip E. Ross observes, "It was Charles Darwin who first linked the evolution of languages to biology. In *The Descent of Man* (1871), he wrote, 'the formation of different languages and of distinct species, and the proofs that both have been developed through a gradual process, are curiously parallel.' But linguists cringe at the idea that evolution might transform simple languages into complex ones. Today it is believed that no language is, in any basic way, 'prior' to any other, living or dead. Language alters even as we speak it, but it neither improves nor degenerates" ("Hard Words," *Scientific American* 264 [April 1991]: 144; quoted in Walt Brown, *In the Beginning: Compelling Evidence for Creation and the Flood,* 8th ed. [Phoenix: Center for Scientific Creation, 2008], 58).

25. First Corinthians 13:8–12 is not speaking of the completion of the New Testament canon, as cessationists claim. It is referring to the day of the Lord and the age to come, which is the theme to which Paul refers both before and after this passage. The gifts of the Holy Spirit are to be earnestly desired (12:31; 14:1) for the common good and strengthening of the church (12:7; 14:3,26). See Jon M. Ruthven, *On the Cessation of the Charismata: The Protestant Polemic on Post-biblical Miracles,* rev. ed. (Tulsa: Word & Spirit, 2011), esp. 107–67.

26. The language of "waiting" in the New Testament (cf. 1 Cor. 1:7; Gal. 5:5; Phil. 3:20; 1 Thess. 1:10; Titus 2:13; Heb. 9:28; James 5:7f.; 2 Peter 3:12ff.; Jude 21) is also inherently apocalyptic, drawn from the prophetic writings in the context of the day of the Lord (cf. Isa. 25:9; 26:8; 30:18; 40:31; 49:23; 64:4; Lam. 3:25f.; Hos. 12:6; Mic. 7:7; Zeph. 3:8; Ps. 25:3ff.; 27:14; 31:24; 37:7ff.; 40:1; 62:1ff.; etc.). Concerning the wickedness of this age, therefore, believers are repeatedly exhorted to patience, endurance, and perseverance, trusting that God will soon execute his righteous judgments at the return of Jesus (cf. Rom. 5:2–4; Col. 1:11–12; 2 Thess. 1:4–7; Heb. 10:35–37; James 1:12; Rev. 2:2–7; 13:7–10).

27. A cursory reading of Hebrews 11 shows such faith and hope to be historical rather than metaphysical, looking *forward* to the age to come rather than upward to immateriality. Thus Noah's faith condemned the world because he responded in holy fear "when warned about things *not yet seen*" (v. 7, NIV). Abraham too "was *looking forward* to the city that

has foundations, whose designer and builder is God" (v. 10). Likewise, Moses "considered abuse suffered for the Christ to be greater wealth than the treasures of Egypt, for he was *looking ahead* to the reward" (v. 26, NRSV). "Others were tortured, refusing to accept release, in order to obtain a *better resurrection*" (v. 35, NRSV). In this way, faith is pictured as "the race that is set before us" (Heb. 12:1), since it involves a simple linear movement from point A (creation) to point B (consummation).

28. Here the naturalistic bias is seen in full glory, as the lack of commentary on סלעל יחו ("and live forever") is appalling. Of the major modern commentaries, few even reference the phrase, and those who do view it as an interpolation derived from Babylonian sources (cf. Claus Westermann, *Genesis 1–11*, CC [Minneapolis: Fortress, 1994], 272–73).

29. As Alister E. McGrath puts it,

> The whole of human history is thus enfolded in the subtle interplay of sorrow over a lost paradise, and the hope of its final restoration. . . .
>
> Deep within the human soul there nestles a sense that something is wrong with the world as we know it. The world we know is somehow not quite what it ought to be. It seems to cry out for restoration or renewal. . . . The history of human culture demonstrates a "repeated attempt to re-establish the paradisal situation lost at the dawn of time" (Eliade). This is often expressed in terms of the interplay of two eras—the paradise that was lost in the early mists of time, and to which we shall one day be restored. (*A Brief History of Heaven* [London: Blackwell, 2003], 40–41)

30. The phrase "gathered to his people" (Gen. 25:8,17; 35:29; 49:33; Num. 20:24,26; Deut. 32:50), or "go to your fathers" (Gen. 15:15; cf. Gen. 47:30; Judg. 2:10), refers to the dead in Sheol, as seen in the channeled testimony of Samuel: "Tomorrow you and your sons shall be *with me*" (1 Sam. 28:19). See Victor P. Hamilton, *The Book of Genesis, Chapters 18–50*, NICOT (Grand Rapids: Eerdmans, 1995), 168.

> So Jewish theologian Nahum M. Sarna comments,

> It is not the same as burial in an ancestral grave, because it is employed of Abraham, Aaron, and Moses, none of whom was buried with his forefathers. It is also not identical with interment in general because the report of burial follows this phrase, and the difference between the two is especially blatant in the case of Jacob, who was interred quite a while after being "gathered to his kin." It would seem, therefore, that the existence of this idiom, as of the corresponding figure "to lie down with one's fathers," testifies to a belief that, despite his mortality and perishability, man possesses an immortal element that survives the loss of life. Death is looked upon as a transition to an afterlife where one is united with one's ancestors. This interpretation contradicts the widespread, but apparently erroneous, view that such a notion is unknown in Israel until later times. (*Genesis*, JPSTC [Philadelphia: Jewish Publication Society, 1989], 174)

31. So R. A. Muller, "The OT provides the context of belief from which the idea of resurrection comes and according to which it must be understood. The roots of the concept are there, both positively and negatively, although the terminological apparatus is not" ("Resurrection," *ISBE*, 4:145). Contrary to the common liberal sentiment that the OT holds no theology of resurrection, see G. W. E. Nickelsburg, "Resurrection," *ABD*, 5:680–91; and Nickelsburg, *Resurrection, Immortality, and Eternal Life in Intertestamental Judaism* (Cambridge, MA: Harvard University Press, 1972).

32. Likewise, a theology of resurrection develops in the intertestamental literature; see esp. 2 Maccabees 7, 14; 4 Ezra 7; *1 Enoch* 22, 46, 51, 62, 67, 90, 92; *Testament of Benjamin* 10; *Apocalypse of Baruch* 49ff.; and *Sibylline Oracles* 4:176–92.

33. The national resurrection of Israel (cf. Ezek. 37:1–14; Hos. 6:1–3) naturally presumes upon the knowledge of individual resurrection, for where else would meaning be derived? So the individual precedes the national, and the two are therefore bound together: "Thus says the Lord GOD: Behold, I will open your graves and raise you from your graves, O my people. And I will bring you into the land of Israel. And you shall know that I am the LORD, when I open your graves, and raise you from your graves, O my people. And I will put my Spirit within you, and you shall live, and I will place you in your own land" (Ezek. 37:12–14).

34. "Thus far he [Jesus] is exactly on the map of first-century Jewish belief. Unlike his re-defining of kingdom and messiahship, on the question of resurrection he seems to have little or nothing new to say" (Wright, *Surprised by Hope*, 38). If only Wright continued his "disciplined historical imagination" (p. 50), the idea of redefining the kingdom and messiahship would "blow away" along with so much historical criticism.

35. B. A. Milne, "Salvation," *NBD*, 1047.

36. J. E. Hartley, "929 יָשַׁע (yāša)," *TWOT*, 414.

37. The self-identification of "sinner" in the NT draws from a wealth of usage in the OT, particularly in the Psalms (cf. Gen. 13:13; Num. 27:3; 32:14; Deut. 29:18; 1 Kings 1:21; 2 Chron. 19:2; Ps. 1:1,5; 3:8; 7:10; 9:17f.; 11:2,6; 28:3; 32:10; 34:21–22; 36:12; 37:10,12,14,16f.,20f.,32,34,40; 39:1–2; 50:16; 55:3; 58:4,11; 68:2; 71:4; 73:3,12; 75:8,10; 82:2,4; 84:10; 90:8; 91:8; 94:3,13; 97:10; 101:8; 104:35; 106:18; 109:2,6; 112:10; 119:53,61,95,110,119,155; 125:3; 129:3–4; 139:19; 140:5,9; 141:5,10; 145:20; 146:9; 147:6; Prov. 11:31; 12:13; 23:17; 24:19; Amos 9:8,10; Isa. 1:4,28,31; 13:9; 14:5; 65:20; Ezek. 33:8,19; Dan. 12:10).

38. "ἀσθένεια," BDAG, 142.

39. Note the same analogy in the apocryphal book 4 Ezra, given in response to Ezra's question concerning the end of the age: "In Hades the chambers of the souls are like the womb. For just as a woman who is in labor makes haste to escape the pangs of birth, so also do these places hasten to give back those things that were committed to them from the beginning. Then the things that you desire to see will be disclosed to you" (2 Esdras 4:41–43, NRSV).

40. The deliverance of our souls from bodies of death is the assumed meaning behind "the salvation of your souls" (1 Peter 1:9)—i.e., "an inheritance that is imperishable, unde-filed, and unfading, kept in heaven for you, who by God's power are being guarded through faith *for a salvation* ready to be revealed in the last time" (vv. 4–5).

41. Note Paul's simple logic, "For we do not want you to be ignorant, brothers, of the afflic-tion we experienced in Asia. For we were so utterly burdened beyond our strength that we despaired of life itself. Indeed, we felt that we had received the sentence of death. But that was to make us rely not on ourselves but on God who raises the dead. *He delivered us from such a deadly peril, and he will deliver us.* On him we have set our hope that he will deliver us again" (2 Cor. 1:8–10).

42. See the building testimony of salvation in the Psalms (3:7f.; 7:10; 9:14ff.; 14:7; 18:46–50; 20:5f.; 21:5–9; 24:5; 28:8f.; 37:39; 40:10f.; 50:23; 51:12; 53:6; 65:2–5; 67:2; 68:19ff.; 69:29; 72:13; 76:9; 79:9f.; 85:7ff.; 91:16; 96:2; 98:1ff.; 116:13; 118:14–26; 132:16; 140:7; 145:19; 146:3; 149:4) and Prophets (Isa. 12:2f.; 25:9; 26:1; 33:6; 45:17; 46:13; 49:6ff.; 51:5–8; 52:7–10; 56:1; 59:11–18; 60:18; 61:10; 62:1,11; 63:5; Jer. 3:23; Lam. 3:26; Jonah 2:9; Mic. 7:7; Hab. 3:13; Zech. 9:9; 12:7), which culminates in the apostolic witness.

43. The present and past tense usage of salvation in the NT (cf. Acts 2:47; Rom. 8:24; 1 Cor. 1:18; 15:2; 2 Cor. 2:15; Eph. 2:5,8; 2 Tim. 1:9; Titus 2:11; 3:5) simply assumes the

clause "from the wrath to come," as evidenced by the surrounding context in each usage (see also the discussion on verbal aspect in the appendix). Commenting on the aorist tense in Rom. 8:24, Douglas Moo says, "It is somewhat unusual for Paul to use the σῴζω word group of a past experience (although see Eph. 2:5,8; 2 Tim. 1:9; Tit. 3:5), but there is nothing inconsistent in his doing so. While final salvation from God's wrath will not take place until the last day (see 5:9,10), deliverance in principle from that wrath *has* already taken place when we were justified by faith" (*The Epistle to the Romans*, NICNT [Grand Rapids: Eerdmans, 1996], 521, n. 71).

44. So we read in the apocryphal book 4 Ezra:

> I made the world for their sake, and when Adam transgressed my statutes, what had been made was judged. And so the entrances of this world were made narrow and sorrowful and toilsome; they are few and evil, full of dangers and involved in great hardships. But the entrances of the greater world are broad and safe, and yield the fruit of immortality. Therefore unless the living pass through the difficult and futile experiences, they can never receive those things that have been reserved for them. Now therefore why are you disturbed, seeing that you are to perish? Why are you moved, seeing that you are mortal? Why have you not considered in your mind what is to come, rather than what is now present? (2 Esdras 7:11–16, NRSV)

45. See John N. Oswalt, "285 בָּרַךְ (*bārak*)," *TWOT*, 132–33.

46. On blessing and cursing in the Psalms in light of the coming Messiah and the day of the Lord, see 1:1ff.; 2:12; 21:6; 37:10–22; 45:2ff.; 67:7; 72:17; 84:5; 112:1ff.; 115:12–18; 118:26; 132:15ff.; 133:3; 144:15; 146:5. For an eschatological introduction to the Psalter, see esp. David C. Mitchell, *The Message of the Psalter: An Eschatological Programme in the Book of Psalms*, (Sheffield, UK: Sheffield Academic, 1997). See also the classic article by Geerhardus Vos, "Eschatology of the Psalter," *The Princeton Theological Review* 18 (1920): 1–43 (later published as an appendix in *Pauline Eschatology*, 321–65).

47. Likewise, the Deuteronomic blessings (see Deut. 30:1–20) are understood in light of their ultimate fulfillment in the resurrection (see Rom. 10:5–13), and the Deuteronomic curses are understood in relation to eschatological fulfillment (cf. Deut. 21:23 with Gal. 3:13; Deut. 24:7 with 1 Cor. 5:13; Deut. 27:26 with Gal. 3:10; and Deut. 29:4 with Rom. 11:8).

48. So Abraham is commanded to walk in a manner worthy of his calling, so to speak (cf. Phil. 1:27; Eph. 4:1; Col. 1:10; 1 Thess. 2:12)—the scriptural pattern of discipleship, as Paul elsewhere relates (cf. Rom. 13:12ff.; 1 Cor. 6:2ff.; Eph. 5:5ff.).

49. The terrifying assumption is that "there is no peace for the wicked" (Isa. 48:22, NASB; 57:21; cf. Rev. 14:11), and hence the angelic host is prophesying the future destiny of the child to execute divine vengeance. "The proclamation of 'glory (*doxa*) to God in the highest,' and that of the eschatological 'peace on earth' are nothing but a summary of the future bliss that will be realized in and by the coming of the kingdom" (Herman N. Ridderbos, *The Coming of the Kingdom*, trans. H. de Jongste [Philadelphia: Presbyterian and Reformed, 1962], 28).

Moreover, the context of the song assumes military imagery, as Verlyn D. Verbrugge has noted,

> The song sung on the fields of Bethlehem is not being sung by a heavenly choir, complete with long robes, arranged in neat rows with sopranos, altos, tenors, and basses and singing a song of victory—or even a song of simple praise and "glory to God." This στρατιά is rather an army of angels—a multitude of the heavenly

army (we can infer from Matthew 26:53 that there may be as many as twelve legions)—and they are singing their song in full battle array, and the words that they sing are, in essence, a celestial version of "Hail to the Chief." ("The Heavenly Army on the Fields of Bethlehem (Luke 2:13–14)," *CTJ* 43, no. 2 [November 2008]: 311)

50. Thus the Davidic and Abrahamic covenants are woven together in their eternal destiny, as Solomon prophesied, "Endow the king with your justice, O God, the royal son with your righteousness. . . . In his days the righteous will flourish; prosperity will abound till the moon is no more. He will rule from sea to sea and from the River to the ends of the earth. . . . May his name endure forever; may it continue as long as the sun. *All nations will be blessed through him*, and they will call him blessed. . . . Praise be to his glorious name forever; may the whole earth be filled with his glory. Amen and Amen" (Ps. 72:1,7–8,17–19, NIV).

51. The heavens here parallel the earth, both of which reflect the glory of God. Thus the NET reads, "You reveal your majesty in the heavens above!" So Hans-Joachim Kraus, "Corresponding to 'the world' (ארץ), in which the glory of the name radiates, there are (in the parallelism) שמים, the heavens, on which the brightness of God is reflected. For the interpretation of these statements of choral verse, cf. Pss. 104:1f. and 19:1" (*A Continental Commentary: Psalms 1–59* [Minneapolis: Fortress, 1993], 181).

52. Note the quotations of Ps. 8 in eschatological context (1 Cor. 15:27; Heb. 2:6–8). As creation was set in divine order under the feet of Adam in the beginning, so will it be restored under the last Adam (1 Cor. 15:45). As such, the new heavens and new earth will express the glory of God in fullness.

53. Thus the assumption underlying the declaration of perpetuity by Solomon, "I have indeed built you an exalted house, a place for you to dwell in *forever*" (1 Kings 8:13). And the divine response of perpetuity, "I have consecrated this house that you have built, by putting my name there *forever*" (1 Kings 9:3). Likewise the worshipers sang, "For he is good, for his steadfast love endures *forever*" (2 Chron. 5:13).

54. So the *language of light* is also associated with divine glory. For example, "Arise, shine, for your *light* has come, and the *glory* of the LORD has risen upon you" (Isa. 60:1). And in response to the vision of Isa. 2:2–4: "O house of Jacob, come, let us walk *in the light* of the LORD" (v. 5). Thus the apostolic exhortation, "For you yourselves are fully aware that *the day of the Lord* will come like a thief in the night. . . . But you are not in darkness, brothers, for that day to surprise you like a thief. For you are all *children of light*, children of the day. We are not of the night or of the darkness" (1 Thess. 5:2–5; cf. Rom. 13:11–14; Eph. 5:5–10).

55. As Klaus Koch summarizes,

The catchword *glory* is used wherever the final state of affairs is set apart from the present and whenever a final amalgamation of the earthly and heavenly spheres is prophesied. Glory is the portion of those who have been raised from the dead, who will thus become as the angels or the stars of heaven (Dan. 12.3; I Enoch 50.1; 51.4). Glory is then the mark not only of man, however, but also of conditions, the "state" in which they live, the heavenly Jerusalem (Rev. 21.1ff.; II Bar. 32.4), or of the eschatological ruler (II Bar. 30.1) who is above them. (*The Rediscovery of Apocalyptic*, trans. M. Kohl [London: SCM Press, 1972], 32)

56. Jesus' pronouncement to Nathaniel would also evoke Jacob's dream in which he saw angels ascending and descending on a stairway "reaching to the heavens" (Gen. 28:12, NET), thus confirming the promise of a messianic offspring in whom "shall all the families of the earth be blessed" (v. 14).

57. See *Testament of Levi* 18:4–11:

> This one will shine forth like the sun in the earth; *he shall take away all darkness from under heaven*, and there shall be peace in all the earth. The heavens shall greatly rejoice in his day and the earth shall be glad; the clouds will be filled with joy and the knowledge of the Lord will be poured out on the earth like the water of the seas. And the angels of glory of the Lord's presence will be made glad by him. *The heavens will be opened*, and from the temple of glory sanctification will come upon him, with a fatherly voice, as from Abraham to Isaac. . . . In his priesthood sin shall cease and lawless men shall rest from their evil deeds, and righteous men shall find rest in him. *And he shall open the gates of paradise*; he shall remove the sword that has threatened since Adam, and he will grant to the saints to eat of the tree of life. The spirit of holiness shall be upon them. (*OTP*, 1:794–95; italics added)

And *Testament of Judah* 24:1–6:

> And a man shall arise from my posterity like the Sun of righteousness, walking with the sons of men in gentleness and righteousness, and in him will be found no sin. And *the heavens will be opened upon him* to pour out the spirit as a blessing of the Holy Father. . . . This is the Shoot of God Most High; this is the fountain for the life of all humanity. Then he will illumine the scepter of my kingdom, and from your root will arise the Shoot, and through it will arise the rod of righteousness for the nations, to judge and to save all that call on the Lord. (*OTP*, 1:801; italics added)

58. Though concluding inaugurationally, Jürgen Moltmann comments,

> Ever since the story of the Fall, the symbol of "the closed heaven" has been an emblem of the divine judgment and the exile into which human beings have been cast out. "The closed heaven" is a sign that God hides his face. "The darkened heaven" is ultimately a portent of the last, apocalyptic judgment. Against this background, "the opened heaven" means that the era of grace is beginning, that God is turning his face towards men and women in kindness, that the alienation from true life has been overcome, and that "the gateway" to the paradise of an achieved and harmonious life has now been opened. (*God in Creation: A New Theology of Creation and the Spirit of God*, trans. M. Kohl (Minneapolis: Fortress, 1993], 170–71)

59. Note the creation account in pseudepigraphic *2 Enoch*, "I created a garden in Edem [*sic*], in the east, so that he might keep the agreement and preserve the commandment. And I created for him an open heaven, so that he might look upon the angels, singing the triumphal song. And the light which is never darkened was perpetually in paradise" (31:1–2; *OTP*, 1:152). Elsewhere, Eden is described as "open as far as the 3rd heaven" (42:3).

60. Contrary to the common idea that Paul, in regard to a theology of atonement, was the founder of Christianity; see esp. William Wrede, *Paul*, trans. E. Lummis (London: Philip Green, 1907); and Joseph Klausner, *From Jesus to Paul*, trans. W. F. Stinespring (New York: Macmillan, 1943). See an introduction in David Wenham, *Paul: Follower of Jesus or Founder of Christianity?* (Grand Rapids: Eerdmans, 1995).

61. See 1:6–11; 2:17–40; 3:12–26; 4:8–12; 5:29–32; 8:5–13; 10:34–46; 13:16–48; 15:7–11; 17:22–31; 20:18–35; 24:14–25; 26:4–23; 28:23–31.

62. The fact that the apostolic witness was readily received by so many Jews argues strongly for an unaltered Jewish apocalyptic background to the cruciform message (see Acts 2:41; 4:4; 5:14; 6:7; 11:19; 13:43; 14:1; 17:4; 18:8; 19:10; 21:20; 24:24f.; 28:24).

63. Paul here has in mind "the promise of life" (2 Tim. 1:1, NRSV), i.e., "life and immortality" (1:10), which we receive "not because of our works but because of his own purpose and grace" (1:9)—a clear reference to the cross (cf. Rom. 4:5; 11:6; Gal. 2:16; Eph. 2:9; Titus 3:5)—all of which is consummated "on that Day" (2 Tim. 1:18).

64. Moltmann, *Spirit of Life*, 89.

65. To this day escapist Christoplatonism remains the dominant hope of the church, as Oscar Cullmann lamented,

> If we were to ask an ordinary Christian today (whether well-read Protestant or Catholic, or not) what he conceived to be the New Testament teaching concerning the fate of man after death, with few exceptions we should get the answer: "The immortality of the soul." Yet this widely-accepted idea is one of the greatest misunderstandings of Christianity. There is no point in attempting to hide this fact, or to veil it by reinterpreting the Christian faith. This is something that should be discussed quite candidly. The concept of death and resurrection is anchored in the Christ-event . . . and hence is incompatible with the Greek belief in immortality; because it is based in *Heilsgeschichte* ["salvation history"] it is offensive to modern thought. (*Immortality of the Soul or the Resurrection of the Dead? The Witness of the New Testament* [London: Epworth Press, 1958], 15)

66. "Greek thought, and in consequence many Hellenizing Jewish and Christian sages, regarded the body as a prison-house of the soul: *sōma sēma* 'the body is a tomb.' The aim of the sage was to achieve deliverance from all that is bodily and thus liberate the soul" (M. H. Cressey, "Dualism," *NBD*, 284).

67. Origen, *On First Principles*, 2.10.3 (*ANF*, 4:294); italics added.

68. Note Randy Alcorn's forceful analogy,

> We do not desire to eat gravel. Why? Because God did not design us to eat gravel. Trying to develop an appetite for a disembodied existence in a non-physical Heaven is like trying to develop an appetite for gravel. No matter how sincere we are, and no matter how hard we try, it's not going to work. Nor should it. What God made us to desire, and therefore what we *do* desire if we admit it, is exactly what he promises to those who follow Jesus Christ: a resurrected life in a resurrected body, with the resurrected Christ on a resurrected Earth. (*Heaven* [Wheaton: Tyndale, 2004], 7)

69. See Gordon D. Fee, *The Disease of the Health and Wealth Gospels* (Vancouver: Regent College Publishing, 1985).

70. Convincing people trapped in this delusion that they are *alienated* from Christ crucified is quite difficult. For a systematic approach, see David W. Jones and Russell S. Woodbridge, *Health, Wealth & Happiness: Has the Prosperity Gospel Overshadowed the Gospel of Christ?* (Grand Rapids: Kregel, 2010). Note the fascinating firsthand account of disillusioned dominionist Colonel V. Doner in *Christian Jihad: Neo-Fundamentalists and the Polarization of America* (Littleton, CO: Samizdat Creative, 2012).

71. So Jürgen Moltmann summarizes, "After the West committed itself to the *filioque* in the Nicene Creed by separating itself from the Eastern church in 1054, and after the persecution of the so-called Enthusiasts by both the Protestant and the Catholic churches at the time of the Reformation, the experience and theology of the Spirit of God ceased to play much of a part in our churches" (*The Church in the Power of the Spirit: A Contribution to Messianic Ecclesiology*, trans. by M. Kohl [London: SCM Press, 1977], xv).

72. Moltmann makes a valiant attempt at incorporating the Spirit protologically (see *God in Creation*), though his view of "heaven and earth" (chap. 7) is still markedly Platonic.

73. As commonly seen in the traditions of early Methodism, nineteenth-century Holiness movements, early twentieth-century Pentecostalism, and modern charismatic movements. See John Wesley, *A Plain Account of Christian Perfection* (1766); Charles Finney, "Christian Perfection," in *Lectures to Professing Christians* (1837); Andrew Murray, *The Two Covenants: And the Second Blessing* (1899); Dennis Bennett, *Nine O'clock in the Morning* (1970); etc. See an introduction in James D. G. Dunn, *Baptism in the Holy Spirit: A Re-examination of the New Testament on the Gift of the Spirit* (London: SCM Press, 1970).

74. As reflected in Robert L. Saucy, "An Open But Cautious View," in *Are Miraculous Gifts for Today? Four Views*, ed. Wayne A. Grudem (Grand Rapids: Zondervan, 1996), 97–155.

75. For example, John MacArthur, *Charismatic Chaos* (Grand Rapids: Zondervan, 1992). Cessationism is generally found in Reformed circles; see B. B. Warfield, *Counterfeit Miracles* (New York: Charles Scribner's, 1918); Anthony Hoekema, *What About Tongues Speaking?* (Grand Rapids: Eerdmans, 1966); and Richard B. Gaffin Jr., *Perspectives on Pentecost: Studies in New Testament Teaching on the Gifts of the Holy Spirit* (Grand Rapids: Baker, 1979).

76. See Stanley M. Burgess and Eduard M. van der Maas, eds., *New International Dictionary of Pentecostal and Charismatic Movements*, rev. ed. (Grand Rapids: Zondervan, 2002).

77. See William W. Menzies and Stanley M. Horton, *Bible Doctrines: A Pentecostal Perspective* (Springfield, MO: Gospel Publishing House, 1971); and J. Rodman Williams, *Renewal Theology: Systematic Theology from a Charismatic Perspective*, 3 vols. (Grand Rapids: Zondervan, 1988–92).

78. C. H. Dodd worked out his realized eschatology concerning the Spirit and Paul's theology in *The Apostolic Preaching and Its Developments* (London: Hodder & Stoughton, 1936). Many have since mitigated and accommodated a realized eschatological approach to the Spirit; see esp. Neill Q. Hamilton, *The Holy Spirit and Eschatology in Paul* (Edinburgh: Oliver & Boyd, 1957); James D. G. Dunn, *Jesus and the Spirit* (London: SCM Press, 1975); Gordon D. Fee, *God's Empowering Presence: The Holy Spirit in the Letters of Paul* (Peabody, MA: Hendrickson, 1994); and Moltmann, *Spirit of Life*.

79. Fee, *God's Empowering Presence*, 13.

80. "The gift of the out-poured Spirit meant that the messianic age had already arrived. The Spirit is thus the central element in this altered perspective, the key to which is Paul's firm conviction that the Spirit was both the *certain evidence* that the future had dawned, and the *absolute guarantee* of its final consummation" (Fee, *God's Empowering Presence*, 806; italics in the original). And, "The Spirit is the evidence that the *eschatological promises of Paul's Jewish heritage have been fulfilled*" (Ibid., 808; italics in the original). The radical implications of this last statement will be discussed further in chapters 6 and 7.

81. So Moltmann,

> The new foundation of the eschatology which takes its bearings from the future by way of the 'theology of hope,' does away with the Platonic time-eternity pattern. . . . The new approach now develops eschatology as the horizon of expectation for the historical experience of the divine Spirit. The Holy Spirit is not simply the subjective side of God's revelation of himself, and faith is not merely the echo of the Word of God in the human heart. The Holy Spirit is much more than that. It is the power that raises the dead, the power of the new creation of all things; and faith is the beginning of the rebirth of human beings to new life. (*Spirit of Life*, 7)

82. See Gordon Fee's diagram (which overlooks the metaphysical issues) in *Paul, the Spirit, and the People of God* (Peabody, MA: Hendrickson, 1996), 50.

83. John 10:10 is in the context of God's judgment upon the blind and wicked shepherding of the Pharisees (cf. 9:39–41), i.e., "a thief and a robber" (10:1), unto the assumed eschatological salvation of the righteous—"If anyone enters by me, *he will be saved* and will go in and out and find pasture" (10:9).

84. Therefore Moltmann was a vocal proponent of liberation, ecologist, and feminist theologies, criticizing the Pentecostal/charismatic movements for not applying the gift of the Spirit to social, political, and ecological concerns:

> Some theologians have discovered a new love for the charismatic movements; but this can also be an escape, a flight from the politics and ecology of the Spirit in the world of today. What is behind this trend, which must undoubtedly be termed purely individualistic? One reason is certainly the continuing Platonization of Christianity. Even today this still puts its mark on what is termed "spirituality" in the church and religious groups. It takes the form of a kind of hostility to the body, a kind of remoteness from the world, and a preference for the inner experiences of the soul rather than the sensory experiences of sociality and nature. (*Spirit of Life*, 8)

The answer to the "continuing Platonization of Christianity" is not inaugurationalism, but rather cruciform-apocalypticism.

85. So the NIV translates *arneomai*, i.e., "to disclaim association with a person or event" ("ἀρνέομαι," BDAG, 132). The reference to "Father" favors this translation, and the context favors being found *in the likeness of God*, enduring persecution and martyrdom as he does (cf. Matt. 10:14–28), for "a disciple is not above his teacher, nor a servant above his master" (v. 24).

86. Paul has in mind here sharing in the sufferings of Christ (2 Tim. 2:3), with perseverance like a good soldier (v. 4), a competent athlete (v. 5), and a hard-working farmer (v. 6). So too we are to "remember Jesus Christ" (v. 8), "for which I am suffering, bound with chains as a criminal" (v. 9). Thus to deny him and become faithless is to deny his cross and his call to perseverant suffering in this age. The connection to Hymenaeus and Philetus (vv. 16–19) and their assumed forsaking of the cross and suffering by means of realized eschatology seems straightforward.

Chapter Five

1. As is evident in Paul's conversion and immediate preaching in the synagogues "that Jesus was *the Christ*" (Acts 9:22). Likewise in Thessalonica, "This Jesus, whom I proclaim to you, is *the Christ*" (17:3). In general, he was "occupied with the word, testifying to the Jews that *the Christ* was Jesus" (18:5). Likewise Apollos "powerfully refuted the Jews in public, showing by the Scriptures that *the Christ* was Jesus" (18:28). The messianic identity of Jesus was a prominent theme in the apostolic witness (cf. Acts 2:36; 3:20; 8:5; 10:36; etc.), for "every day, in the temple and from house to house, they kept right on teaching and preaching Jesus as *the Christ*" (Acts 5:42, NASB).

2. The presentation of Jesus as "the Christ" (Matt. 1:17; Luke 3:15; John 4:29), i.e., the one "who is called Christ" (Matt. 1:16), is a central purpose of the recorded Gospels, as John says, "These are written so that you may believe that Jesus is *the Christ*, the Son of God, and that by believing you may have life in his name" (John 20:31). So the angel told the shepherds at his birth, "Unto you is born this day in the city of David a Savior, who is *Christ* the Lord" (Luke 2:11). Accordingly, Peter's confession was, "You are *the Christ*, the Son of the living God" (Matt. 16:16). So also Martha declared, "I believe you are *the Christ*, the Son of God, who is coming into the world" (John 11:27). Even the demons "knew that he was *the Christ*" (Luke 4:41). However, Jesus warned them and his disciples "to tell no one that he was *the Christ*" (Matt. 16:20).

   Many questioned if John the Baptist "might be *the Christ*" (Luke 3:15), but he confessed freely, "I am not *the Christ*, but I have been sent before him" (John 3:28; cf. John 1:20). In the same way, the ministry of Jesus was marked by the controversy of the people asking, "Can this be *the Christ*?" (John 4:29). On occasion the Jews confronted Jesus directly, "If you are *the Christ*, tell us plainly" (John 10:24). To which Jesus responded, "I told you, and you do not believe" (v. 25). Likewise, at his trial they demanded, "Tell us if you are *the Christ*, the Son of God" (Matt. 26:63). To which he replied, "Yes, it is as you say" (v. 64, NIV). Pilate later asked the crowd, "Whom do you want me to release for you: Barabbas, or Jesus who is called *Christ*?" (Matt. 27:17). Even on the cross, people passed by and hurled insults, saying, "He saved others; let him save himself, if he is *the Christ* of God, his Chosen One!" (Luke 23:35). So also the criminals being crucified with him questioned, "Are you not *the Christ*? Save yourself and us!" (v. 39).

3. As opposed to a generally convoluted expectation (cf. Jacob Neusner, William S. Green, and Ernest Frerichs, eds., *Judaisms and Their Messiahs at the Turn of the Christian Era* [Cambridge: Cambridge University Press, 1987]); and E. P. Sanders, *Jesus and Judaism* [Philadelphia: Fortress, 1985]).

4. See V. P. Hamilton, "1255 מָשַׁח (*māšaḥ*)," *TWOT*, 530–32; and "Χριστός," BDAG, 1091.

5. Unfortunately, at a popular level the term "Christ" means little more than a sort of last name for Jesus. His proper name was "Jesus son of Joseph from Nazareth" (John 1:45, NRSV; cf. Matt. 26:71; Luke 24:19; John 19:19). When his followers ascribed to him the name "Jesus Christ," or "Jesus the Messiah" (Matt. 1:1,18; Mark 1:1, NLT), they had in mind a whole host of things that are generally absent from the consciousness of the modern church.

   This phenomenon, however, is not new: "Although we cannot be sure, it seems that *Christos* became a proper name when the gospel of Jesus as the Messiah first moved into the Gentile world that did not understand the Jewish background of anointing and for whom therefore 'the anointed one' was a meaningless term. This is suggested by the fact that disciples were first called 'Christians' (*Christianoi*) in Antioch (Acts 11:26); and this word designates partisans of a certain group" (George Eldon Ladd, *A Theology of the New*

Testament, 2nd ed., ed. Donald A. Hagner [Grand Rapids: Eerdmans, 1993; first published 1974 by Eerdmans], 133–34).

6. "We have seen that it is characteristic of New Testament Christology that Christ is connected with the total history of revelation and salvation, beginning with creation. There can be no *Heilsgeschichte* without Christology; no Christology without a *Heilsgeschichte* which unfolds in time. Christology is the doctrine of an 'event,' not a doctrine of natures" (Oscar Cullmann, *The Christology of the New Testament*, trans. S. C. Guthrie and C. A. M. Hall [Philadelphia: Westminster, 1963], 9).

7. Protological messianic agency would have thus been understood: "He was in the beginning *with God*. All things were made *through him*, and without him was not any thing made that was made" (John 1:2–3). Paul speaks even more explicitly: "There is one God, the Father, from whom are all things and for whom we exist, and one Lord, Jesus Christ, *through whom* are all things and *through whom* we exist" (1 Cor. 8:6). Likewise, when Paul said, "*By him* all things were created" (Col. 1:16), he meant "thrones or dominions or rulers or authorities," which were delegated according to messianic function, "that in everything he might be preeminent" (v. 18). Similarly Heb. 1:2: "In these last days he has spoken to us by his Son, whom he appointed the heir of all things, *through whom* also he created the world."

8. Though divinity is clearly implied, the messianic connotations of the Trinitarian formula are commonly lost to the modern church. The Trinitarian doctrine is inextricably bound to the eschatological denouement (cf. Rom. 8:15ff.; Phil. 2:9ff.; 1 Thess. 1:10), for the end comes when the Son "delivers the kingdom to God the Father after destroying every rule and every authority and power. For he must reign until he has put all his enemies under his feet" (1 Cor. 15:24–25).

   Therefore, "The whole Christian eschatology ends in this inner-trinitarian process, through which the kingdom passes from the Son to the Father. Eschatology accordingly is not simply what takes place in the Last Days in heaven and on earth; it is what takes place in God's essential nature" (Jürgen Moltmann, *The Trinity and the Kingdom: The Doctrine of God*, trans. M. Kohl [Minneapolis: Fortress, 1993], 92).

9. Throughout the Scriptures, creation and redemptive history are described as the "work(s)" of God (cf. Gen. 2:2f.; Ex. 34:10; Deut. 11:7; Judg. 2:7; 1 Sam. 14:6; Ps. 19:1; 28:5; 33:4; 92:4; 102:25; 145:4f.; Prov. 8:21; Isa. 5:12; 10:12; 19:25; 28:1; 45:11; 64:8; Jer. 50:25; 51:10; Dan. 4:37; 9:14; Hab. 1:5; 3:2; Matt. 11:20ff.; John 4:34; 5:17,36; 9:3f.; 10:37f.; 14:10; Rom. 14:20; Phil. 2:13; Col. 2:12; Heb. 4:3f.; 13:21). Hence the Messiah is the *agent of divine work* who accomplishes the will of God (cf. John 5:17–37; 6:30–40; 10:25–38; 14:8–14; 15:23f.; 17:4).

   Similarly, a man would "strip for work" in the ancient world by taking off his outer garment (cf. John 21:7), thus "baring his arms," so to speak (cf. Isa. 52:10; Ezek. 4:7). Since God is the archetypal Worker, his Messiah, as a functional extension, is pictured as the revealed "arm of the LORD" (Isa. 53:1; cf. Isa. 30:30; 40:10; 59:16; 63:5). Consequently Jesus is identified as the messianic conduit of divine activity: "Though he had done so many signs before them, they still did not *believe in him*, so that the word spoken by the prophet Isaiah might be fulfilled: 'Lord, who has believed what he heard from us, and to whom has *the arm of the Lord* been revealed?' [Isa. 53:1] . . . Isaiah said these things because he saw his glory and spoke of him" (John 12:37–41). Jesus responds by affirming his messianic agency: "Whoever believes *in me*, believes not in me but *in him* who sent me. And whoever *sees me sees him* who sent me" (vv. 44–45).

10. Similarly, Jesus presented himself to Martha as the agent of the resurrection: "*I am* the resurrection and the life. Whoever believes in me, though he die, yet shall he live. . . . Do

you believe this?" (John 11:25–26). To which Martha simply affirms, "Yes, Lord; I believe that *you are the Christ*, the Son of God, who is coming into the world" (v. 27). So also Jesus declared to Thomas, "*I am* the way, and the truth, and the life. No one comes to the Father except *through me*" (John 14:6).

11. Being anchored in the *parousia* of Jesus, the faith and hope of the apostolic church was thus "irreducibly eschatological" (John T. Carroll, *The Return of Jesus in Early Christianity* [Peabody, MA: Hendrickson, 2000], 4).

12. For example, W. O. E. Oesterley, *The Evolution of The Messianic Idea: A Study in Comparative Religion* (London: Pitman & Sons, 1908); Sigmund Mowinckel, *He That Cometh: The Messiah Concept in the Old Testament and Later Judaism*, trans. G. W. Anderson (Nashville: Abingdon, 1954); Joseph Klausner, *The Messianic Idea in Israel: From Its Beginnings to the Completion of the Mishnah*, trans. W. F. Stinespring (New York: Macmillan, 1955); Joachim Becker, *Messianic Expectation in the Old Testament*, trans. D. E. Green (Edinburgh: T & T Clark, 1980); J. H. Charlesworth, ed., *The Messiah: Developments in Earliest Judaism and Christianity* (Minneapolis: Fortress, 1992); and Antti Laato, *A Star Is Rising: The Historical Development of the Old Testament Royal Ideology and the Rise of the Jewish Messianic Expectations* (Atlanta: Scholars Press, 1997).

13. For example, Alfred Edersheim, *Prophecy and History in Relation to the Messiah* (London: Longmans, 1885); Franz Delitzsch, *Messianic Prophecies in Historical Succession*, trans. S. I. Curtiss (New York: Scribner's Sons, 1891); Willis J. Beecher, *The Prophets and the Promise* (New York: Thomas Y. Crowell, 1905); J. Barton Payne, *Encyclopedia of Biblical Prophecy: The Complete Guide to Scriptural Predictions and Their Fulfillment* (Grand Rapids: Baker, 1973); Gerard van Groningen, *Messianic Revelation in the Old Testament* (Grand Rapids: Baker, 1990); Walter C. Kaiser Jr., *The Messiah in the Old Testament* (Grand Rapids: Zondervan, 1995); and Michael Rydelnik, *The Messianic Hope: Is the Hebrew Bible Really Messianic?* (Nashville: B&H Academic, 2010).

14. See an introductory survey in Ronald E. Clements, "Messianic Prophecy or Messianic History?" *Horizons of Biblical Theology* 1 (1979): 87–104; and Clements, "The Messianic Hope in the Old Testament," *JSOT* 43 (1989): 3–19.

15. Though the Scriptures do not expressly state that God made a covenant with Adam, many (especially within the Reformed tradition) have identified such a covenant in light of contrasts made in Hos. 6:7, Rom. 5:14, and 1 Cor. 15:22 (cf. Louis Berkhof, *Systematic Theology* [Grand Rapids: Eerdmans, 1938], 211–18; and Westminster Confession of Faith [1647], chap. 7). Moreover, God's relationship with Adam falls under the broader "covenant with creation," so to speak (cf. Jer. 33:20–25 and Ps. 89:11; 104:5; 119:90; etc.).

16. See an introduction in Rydelnik, *Messianic Hope*, 65–82; and John H. Sailhamer, "The Messiah and the Hebrew Bible," *JETS* 44, no. 1 (March 2001): 5–23.

17. Unfortunately, many modern scholars believe Jewish messianism arose as a response to social oppression during the exile and postexilic milieu, hoping for the restoration of the former glory of the Davidic kingdom. The Scriptures, however, are by definition of divine origin, and as such "Messianic prophecy was thus not a product of a human yearning for a better life, but the result of a 'supernatural' revelation" (Sailhamer, "Messiah and the Hebrew Bible," 6). Moreover, Sailhamer adds,

> What I have tried to suggest is that it can be argued that the books of the OT are messianic in the full NT sense of the word. The OT is the *light* that points the way to the NT. The NT is not only to cast its light back on the Old, but more importantly, the light of the OT is to be cast on the New. The books of the OT were written as the embodiment of a real, messianic hope—a hope in a

future miraculous work of God in sending a promised Redeemer. This was not
an afterthought in the Hebrew Bible. This was not the work of final redactors.

I believe the messianic thrust of the OT was the *whole* reason the books of the
Hebrew Bible were written. In other words, the Hebrew Bible was not written
as the national literature of Israel. It probably also was not written to the nation
of Israel as such. It was rather written, in my opinion, as the expression of the
deep-seated messianic hope of a small group of faithful prophets and their followers. (Ibid., 23)

18. As in the NT (cf. 2 Cor. 11:14; Rev. 12:9; 20:2), intertestamental literature identifies the
Edenic serpent as Satan (cf. *4 Maccabees* 18:8; *Jubilees* 3:17ff.; *Psalms of Solomon* 4:11),
and *Apocalypse of Moses* 16:4–5 specifically relates the serpent as the "vessel" of Satan:
"The devil said to him [the serpent], 'Do not fear; only become my vessel, and I will
speak a word through your mouth by which you will be able to deceive him [Adam]'"
(*OTP,* 2:277).

19. See Anthony A. Hoekema, *The Bible and the Future* (Grand Rapids: Eerdmans, 1979), 5.

20. The referencing of Genesis 3:15 as the *protoevangelium* is attributed to Irenaeus of Lyons
(c. 135–202), *Against Heresies*, 3.23.7 and 5.21.1. However, a messianic reading of Gen.
3:15 is seen in the translation of the LXX (see R. A. Martin, "The Earliest Messianic Interpretation of Gen 3:15," *JBL* 84 [1965]: 425–27) and the earliest Aramaic translations
of Genesis. Compare Jewish Targums of Pseudo-Jonathan, Neofiti, and Fragmentary (see
John Skinner, "The 'Protevangelium,'" *Genesis*, ICC [New York: Scribner, 1910], 80–88),
where Satan is defeated in the age of the messianic kingdom (see also M. B. Shepherd,
"Targums, the New Testament, and Biblical Theology of the Messiah," *JETS* 51, no. 1
[March 2008]: 45–58). These early readings suggest a common messianic interpretation
of the OT stemming from Genesis.

21. Since *zera'* is always in singular form in the Hebrew Bible, Gen. 3:15 also introduces us
to the idea of "corporate solidarity," that is, "The *one* who represents the group and the
many who are represented are equally a part of the same single meaning intended by the
author" (Kaiser, *Messiah in the Old Testament*, 25). In other words, many offspring can be
represented by the single offspring of Adam and Eve, which is then carried through the
rest of the OT covenants (cf. Gen. 17:7; 2 Sam. 7:12; Gal. 3:16,29). Thus the English
word "offspring," being a collective singular noun, is an adequate translation for *zera'*
(contrary to "descendant[s]"). Unfortunately, the Greek *genos* is also used as a messianic
title, "Offspring of David" (Rev. 22:16, NIV). So it seems the translation of Heb. *zera'*
[Gk. *sperma*, LXX] is best left as "seed," which also carries protological associations (cf.
Gen. 1:11,12,29) commonly assumed in the mind of the ancient reader.

22. The Hebrew language has no specific word for "head," but rather *rō'š* refers to the "upper
part," e.g., the "heads" of the mountains (Gen. 8:5), the "head" of the Tower of Babel
(Gen. 11:4), the "heads" of the clans of Israel (Num. 1:16), the "head" of the tribes of
Israel (1 Sam. 15:17), etc. (see W. White, "2097 ראשׁ [*rō'š*]," *TWOT*, 825–26). Consequently, the "head" of the serpent could naturally be interpreted governmentally.

23. Contrary to the nonmessianic interpretation of John Skinner (ICC), Claus Westermann
(CC), Ephraim Speiser (AB), and John Walton (NIVAC). See John Sailhamer's insightful discussion of this passage in *The Pentateuch as Narrative* (Grand Rapids: Zondervan,
1992), 106–9. "Consequently, more is at stake in this brief passage than the reader is at
first aware. A program is set forth. A plot is established that will take the author far beyond this or that snake and his 'seed'" (p. 107).

24. Thus messianism is characterized by Walter Kaiser as "epigenetical," a biological term
meaning "the progressive development of an embryo from an undifferentiated egg cell"

(*Concise Oxford English Dictionary*, 11th ed. [Oxford: Oxford University Press, 2004], s.v. "epigenesis").

> The unity that Scripture exhibited was not static—a flat-Bible type of uniformity; it had an organic or epigenetical aspect to it that defied an easy categorization or simplification. Even in its earliest OT statements, that divine word . . . had within it seminal ideas that only later amplifications would unfold from the germs of thought that were just barely visible when first announced. That is why the metaphor from biology is an apt one: prophetic truth had an organic, epigenetical nature. The fixed core of ideas connected with the promise-plan of God and the representative of that promise remained constant. But as time went on, the content of that given word of blessing, promise, or judgment grew in accordance with seed thoughts that were contained within its earliest statements, much as a seed is uniquely related to the plant that it will become if it has life at all. (Kaiser, *Messiah in the Old Testament*, 27)

25. See also the fuller discussion of OT language that references Genesis 3:15—including "head crushing," "broken enemies," "stricken serpents," and those who "lick the dust" and are "trampled underfoot"—in James Hamilton, "The Skull Crushing Seed of the Woman: Inner-Biblical Interpretation of Genesis 3:15," *SBJT* 10, no. 2 (Summer 2006): 30–54.

26. For more on the hermeneutical issues surrounding Gen. 3:15, see T. D. Alexander, "Messianic Ideology in the Book of Genesis," in *The Lord's Anointed: Interpretation of the Old Testament Messianic Texts*, ed. P. E. Satterthwaite, R. S. Hess, and G. J. Wenham (Grand Rapids: Baker, 1995), 19–39.

27. As Jewish theologian Adolph Saphir summarized,

> The Protoevangelion; the first promise is justly so called, because it contains the Gospel in germ. Scripture, or rather the Revelation, of which it is a record, is an organic growth; not an aggregate of successive teaching, added in a mechanical way, but a development of "living seed." Known unto God are all his works from the beginning of the world; especially His central work of Redemption. Hence every part of God's revelation is complete, containing the seed. . . . And so far from our having fully comprehended it, only the end will explain the beginning; only the Millennial age will disclose Genesis. When Satan is finally bruised under our feet we shall understand the Protoevangelion. (*Christ Crucified: Lectures on I Corinthians II* [London: James Nisbet, 1873], 2–3)

28. See also the timeless exposition of Gen. 3:15 by E. W. Hengstenberg, *Christology of the Old Testament*, trans. T. Meyer and J. Martin, vol. 1 (orig. 1872; Grand Rapids: Kregel, 1956), 14–29.

29. Here it seems that *drakōn megas* (Rev. 12:3) draws from use in the LXX where *drakōn* translates Heb. *tannîn*, i.e., "serpent" (Ex. 7:9ff.; Deut. 32:33; Job 7:12 [cf. 20:16; 26:13]; Ps. 74:13; 91:13; Amos 9:3; Jer. 51:34). See the discussion of OT usage in W. Foerster, "δράκων," *TDNT*, 2:281–83.

30. "God must be the unmentioned agent of the beast's 'wound.' . . . Such a wound on the head of the grand nemesis of God's people reflects Gen. 3:15, especially when seen together with Rev. 12:17" (Gregory K. Beale, *The Book of Revelation: A Commentary on the Greek Text*, NIGTC [Grand Rapids: Eerdmans, 1999], 687–88).

31. Note that the "worship" of the dragon (13:4; also referred to as the serpent in 12:9), and vicarious worship of the beast (13:4,8,12,15; 14:9,11), is the culmination of sin, which accords with the account of the original satanic sin in the pseudepigraphic *Life of Adam and Eve*, 12–16.

32. Psalm 8:4–6 is also quoted messianically in Hebrews 2:6–8. It is clear that "putting everything in subjection under his feet" (v. 8) references God's subjection of "the world to come" (v. 5) by means of the Messiah. The "bringing many sons to glory" (v. 10) and the forceful submission of Satan under the heel of Christ will surely come to pass, even though "at present, we do not yet see everything in subjection to him" (v. 8).

33. On the history and difficulties of translating this passage, see Frank Thielman, *Ephesians*, BECNT (Grand Rapids: Baker, 2010), 63–70. The author's translation roughly accommodates the NASB (*oikonomia* = "administration," cf. BDAG, 697–98) and the NIV (*anakephalaioō* = "bring together under one head," cf. BDAG, 65). On the latter, see esp. Clinton Arnold's translation of 1:10b, "to bring everything under the headship of Christ, everything in heaven and everything on earth, in Christ" (*Ephesians*, ZECNT [Grand Rapids: Zondervan, 2010], 88).

34. "In the Greek world οἰκονομία was regularly used for God's ordering and administration of the universe. Here in 1:10 it also appears to have that active force (cf. also 3:9), while elsewhere (cf. 3:2; 1 Cor 4:1; 9:17; Col 1:25) it refers to Paul's apostolic role and office" (Andrew T. Lincoln, *Ephesians*, WBC [Dallas: Word, 1990], 31–32). Note a similar logic in Eph. 3:14–15, "For this reason I kneel before *the Father*, from whom his *whole family* in heaven and on earth derives its name" (NIV).

35. Though the translation of this phrase has a long and contentious history (see H. Schlier, "ἀνακεφαλαιόομαι," *TDNT*, 3:681–82), its meaning is fairly straightforward within a biblical worldview and a cruciform-apocalyptic theology. The first part of the passage (Eph. 1:3–8) primarily references the work of the cross, while the second part (vv. 9–14) speaks primarily of the day of the Lord—both of which are "according to the purpose of his will" (v. 5), i.e., "the mystery of his will, according to his purpose" (v. 9).

36. The protological context also explains its varied usage in the OT, both messianic (cf. Dan. 7:13; Ps. 80:17; 144:3) and non-messianic (cf. Num. 23:19; Job 25:6; Dan. 8:17; and some ninety references in Ezekiel). Just as the OT prophet is *a* "son of Adam," so also the Messiah is *the* "Son of Adam."

37. "The phrase *ben ʾ ādām* can be understood not only as 'a human being' but also as 'son of Adam'" (D. E. Aune, "Son of Man," *ISBE*, 4:578).

38. The origin and meaning of this phrase "Son of Man" goes part and parcel with the contentious debate over Christology in general; see e.g., Ladd, *Theology of the New Testament*, 143–57; and C. Colpe, "ὁ υἱὸς τοῦ ἀνθρώπου," *TDNT* 8:400–77.

39. This resolves the seeming contradiction of usage between Old and New Testaments, as Ladd expressed, "We have already seen that 'son of man' is not an uncommon idiom in the Old Testament, simply designating humanity. This usage has frequently been appealed to, to explain some of the gospel idioms. . . . However, this quite fails to explain the eschatological use of 'Son of Man' in the Gospels" (*Theology of the New Testament*, 145–46).

40. See Leonhard Goppelt, *Typos: The Typological Interpretation of the Old Testament in the New*, trans. D. Madvig (Grand Rapids: Eerdmans, 1982), 90–100, esp. the "typological substratum of the Son of Man sayings," which is rooted in Christ as the "Second Adam" (p. 97).

41. See also Cullmann's discussion on Paul's contrast of Adam and Christ as related to the son of man concept in Judaism (*Christology of the New Testament*, 166–81). For example,

> His whole theology and Christology is so completely embedded in eschatology that he calls the "Second Adam" the "Last Adam" (ὁ ἔσχατος Ἀδὰμ, 1 Cor. 15.45) or the "coming Adam" (ὁ μέλλων, Rom. 5.14). Even if Paul does not directly

refer to Dan. 7 in connection with statements about the "Man," he does share the view that Christ will come on the clouds of heaven. He writes in I Thess. 4.17 that we (together with those who have fallen asleep) "shall be caught up . . . *in the clouds* to meet the Lord in the air." This expectation must go back to Daniel's picture of the Son of Man "coming on the clouds." (p. 166)

See also the little known but useful commentary (though debatable concerning his approach to original sin) of Karl Barth, *Christ and Adam: Man and Humanity in Romans 5*, trans. T. A. Smail (New York: Harper and Brothers, 1956).

42. Conversely, we see in Gen. 3:15 a protological foundation for a theology of the Antichrist, the satanic "seed" and the *huios tēs apōleias*, "son of destruction" (2 Thess. 2:3)—a phrase akin to "son of man," being also applied to historical antichrists (cf. Judas in John 17:12) as well as the eschatological culmination. They are all children of destruction because the devil and his seed are destined to "go to destruction" (Rev. 17:8) on the day of destruction (cf. Isa. 13:9; 2 Thess. 1:9; 2 Peter 3:7)—thus, "It is the last hour, and as you have heard that *antichrist is coming*, so now *many antichrists have come*" (1 John 2:18). Without a protological base of expectation for the "Christ," we have no basic framework for the culmination of sin in "Antichrist," i.e., the "man of sin" (2 Thess. 2:3, NKJV), who typifies the Edenic deception by speaking "like a serpent" (Rev. 13:11, *GOD'S WORD Translation* [Grand Rapids: Baker, 1995]).

43. The rendering of "son of Adam" in light of protological messianic expectation is further reinforced by the functional equation of "son" and "seed" in the OT (e.g., Gen. 4:25; 21:13; 1 Chron. 17:11; Isa. 57:3; Dan. 9:1). Therefore the use of "son of Abraham" (Matt. 1:1) would logically be equated with the promised "seed" of Abraham (cf. Gen. 17:7f.; Rom. 4:13; Gal. 3:29), and the "son of David" (Matt. 1:1; 12:23; par.) would be seen in light of the covenanted "seed" of David (cf. 2 Sam. 7:12; Ps. 89:4; John 7:42; Rom. 1:3). Likewise the "son of Man" would have been understood primarily in the context of the promised "seed" of humanity's parents. The NT genealogies (Matt. 1:1–17; Luke 3:21–38), which are by nature designed *to prove messianic descent*, further confirm this (note the same Greek phrase, *biblos geneseōs*, used in Matt. 1:1, Gen. 2:4, and Gen. 5:1, LXX).

44. Stephen G. Dempster notes,

> In light of the immediate context, the triumph of the woman's seed would suggest a return to the Edenic state, before the serpent had wrought its damage. . . .
>
> Thus should be understood as the first echo of the penalty, in which the woman is given a personal name by Adam. For the first words after the divine judgment are words of hope. Adam names his wife "Eve," "for she is the mother of all the living" (Gen. 3:20). . . . In the context it shows Adam reclaiming dominion in faith through *naming* his wife *the mother*, which cannot help but allude to the more specific role she will have as the one who will provide a seed who will strike the serpent. (*Dominion and Dynasty: A Biblical Theology of the Hebrew Bible* [Downers Grove, IL: InterVarsity, 2003], 68–69)

45. See T. D. Alexander, *From Paradise to the Promised Land: An Introduction to the Pentateuch*, 2nd ed. (Grand Rapids: Baker, 2002), 101–13.

46. Though non-messianic, see the helpful socio-historical, linguistic study by Richard S. Hess, *Studies in the Personal Names of Genesis 1–11* (Winona Lake, IN: Eisenbrauns, 1993).

47. "A central purpose of the eschatological framework of the Pentateuch is to bring the whole of Genesis 1–11 into the realm of Israel's own history and thus prepare the way for an understanding of concepts such as the *Kingdom of God* in terms of the concrete

realities of creation" (John Sailhamer, "Creation, Genesis 1–11, and the Canon," *BBR* 10, no. 1 [2000]: 89).

48. It is assumed that Jude cited an oral tradition derived from the historical Enoch and that this tradition was redacted into the pseudepigraphic books of Enoch (see Gleason L. Archer, *New International Encyclopedia of Bible Difficulties* [Grand Rapids: Zondervan, 1982], 430).

49. Citing *1 Enoch* 1:9: "Behold, he will arrive with ten million of the holy ones in order to execute judgment upon all. He will destroy the wicked ones and censure all flesh on account of everything that they have done, that which the sinners and the wicked ones committed against him" (*OTP*, 1:13–14).

   "The most interesting divergence in Jude's quotation is the insertion of *kyrios* ('Lord'). The term 'Lord' is not in any of the other versions, representing Jude's Christological interpretation of the judgment. In applying a text that referred to God's judgment to Christ, Jude followed the precedent of other New Testament writers (cf. 1 Thess 3:13; 2 Thess 1:7; Rev 19:13,15; 22:12)" (Thomas R. Schreiner, *1, 2 Peter, Jude*, NAC [Nashville: Broadman & Holman, 2003], 471–72).

50. The inclusion of such genealogies must at least be understood as messianically motivated at a canonical level. The general lack of any messianic reference in most commentaries concerning these genealogies is regrettable; see Robert R. Wilson, "Genealogy, Genealogies," *ABD*, 2:929–32; and R. K. Harrison, "Genealogy," *ISBE*, 2:424–28.

51. "This promissory call is the first recorded speech since God's word of judgment at the Tower of Babel, resulting in the creation of the nations (11:5–6,9). This new word to Abram counters the old since it provides for the redemptive plan of 'all peoples' (v. 3). By making his descendants a 'great nation' (v. 2) who will be a 'blessing' (v. 2), the Lord will bring salvation to the scattered nations" (K. A. Mathews, *Genesis 11:27–50:26*, NAC [Nashville: Broadman & Holman, 2005], 105).

52. See the "Excursus on Circumcision" in Gordon J. Wenham, *Genesis 16–50*, WBC (Dallas: Word, 1998), 23–24.

53. Concerning Paul's quotation of these texts in Gal. 3:16, many accuse him of "creative exegesis." However, C. John Collins has made a strong case that Paul is not stretching the text and its messianic orientation, since verb inflections, adjectives, and pronouns are used differently in reference to *zera* ʿ being interpreted as singular versus collective. See "Galatians 3:16: What Kind of an Exegete Was Paul?" *TynBul* 54, no. 1 (2003): 75–86; and Collins, "A Syntactical Note (Genesis 3:15): Is the Woman's Seed Singular or Plural?" *TynBul* 48, no. 1 (1997): 139–48. See also T. D. Alexander, "Further Observations on the Term 'Seed' in Genesis," *TynBul* 48, no. 2 (1997): 363–67.

54. Note the prominent use of the phrase "God of Israel" (ultimately derived from the Abrahamic covenant) in Ex. 5:1; 24:10; 32:27; 34:23; Num. 16:9; Josh. 7:13,19f.; 8:30; 9:18f.; 10:40,42; 13:14,33; 14:14; 22:16,24; 24:2,23; Judg. 4:6; 5:3,5; 6:8; 11:21,23; 21:3; Ruth 2:12; 1 Sam. 1:17; 2:30; 5:7f., 10f.; 6:3,5; 10:18; 14:41; 20:12; 23:10f.; 25:32,34; 2 Sam. 7:27; 12:7; 23:3; 1 Kings 1:30,48; 8:15,17,20,23,25f.; 11:9,31; 14:7,13; 15:30; 16:13,26,33; 17:1,14; 22:53; 2 Kings 9:6; 10:31; 14:25; 18:5; 19:15,20; 21:12; 22:15,18; 1 Chron. 4:10; 5:26; 15:12,14; 16:4,36; 17:24; 22:6; 23:25; 24:19; 28:4; 29:10; 2 Chron. 2:12; 6:4,7,10,14,16f.; 11:16; 13:5; 15:4,13; 20:19; 29:7,10; 30:1,5; 32:17; 33:16,18; 34:23,26; 36:13; Ezra 1:3; 3:2; 4:1,3; 5:1; 6:14,21f.; 7:6,15; 8:35; 9:4,15; Ps. 41:13; 59:5; 68:8,35; 69:6; 72:18; 106:48; Isa. 17:6; 21:10,17; 24:15; 29:23; 37:16,21; 41:17; 45:3,15; 48:1f.; 52:12; Jer. 7:3,21; 9:15; 11:3; 13:12; 16:9; 19:3,15; 21:4; 23:2; 24:5; 25:15,27; 27:4,21; 28:2,14; 29:4,8,21,25; 30:2; 31:23; 32:14f.,36; 33:4; 34:2,13; 35:13,17ff.; 37:7; 38:17; 39:16; 42:9,15,18; 43:10; 44:2,7,11,25; 45:2;

46:25; 48:1; 50:18; 51:33; Ezek. 8:4; 9:3; 10:19f.; 11:22; 43:2; 44:2; Zeph. 2:9; Mal. 2:16; Matt. 15:31; Luke 1:68.

55. The centrality and significance of ethnicity in redemptive history will be discussed further in chapter 6.

56. For commentary on the commonly referenced messianic predictions between Abraham and David—e.g., the "Judaic Prediction" (Gen. 49:8–12), "Balaamic Prediction" (Num. 24:15–19), "Mosaic Prediction" (Deut. 18:15–18), and "Hannaic Prediction" (1 Sam. 2:1–10)—see Hengstenberg, *Christology of the Old Testament*, 1:57–130; Delitzsch, *Messianic Prophecies in Historical Succession*, 47–79; and Kaiser, *Messiah in the Old Testament*, 50–76.

57. Though Moses himself created a prophetic pattern of deliverance, reinforced by prophecy (cf. Deut. 18:15–18), as Klausner describes,

> It was also inevitable that the people should feel compelled to accord the very greatest glory and honor to the exalted and grandiose personality of *the first deliverer*. This was the man Moses, this the great deliverer, who not only ransomed Israel from all its *material* troubles and from *political* servitude, but also redeemed it from its ignorance and its spiritual bondage. He was not only a guide and leader of the Israelite people; he was also a lawgiver and prophet. The exalted picture of Moses necessarily, therefore, impressed itself upon the spirit of the nation and became a symbol of the redeemer in general. (*Messianic Idea in Israel*, 16; italics in the original)

> Note also the prevalent rabbinic tradition of Moses as a messianic prototype (ibid., 17–18).

58. The nature and purpose of these will be discussed further in chapter 6.

59. "Third in importance only to the protoevangelium of Genesis 3:15 and the Abrahamic promise of Genesis 12:2–3 is 2 Samuel 7 (see also 1 Ch 17; Ps. 89), God's promise to David. This chapter sets the tone for the promise-plan of God throughout the rest of the OT" (Kaiser, *Messiah in the Old Testament*, 78).

60. See the apocryphal 2 Esdras 12:32–34:

> This is the Messiah whom the Most High has kept until *the end of days*, who will arise from *the offspring of David*, and will come and speak with them. He will denounce them for their ungodliness and for their wickedness, and will display before them their contemptuous dealings. For first he will bring them alive before *his judgment seat*, and when he has reproved them, then he will destroy them. But in mercy he will set free the remnant of my people, those who have been saved throughout my borders, and he will make them joyful until the end comes, *the day of judgment*, of which I spoke to you at the beginning. (NRSV; italics added)

61. Since the Davidic Covenant is genealogically based, subsequent prophecies often refer to David and his Seed as one—e.g., "*My servant David* shall be king over them, and they shall all have one shepherd. . . . They shall dwell in the land that I gave to my servant Jacob, where your fathers lived. They and their children and their children's children shall dwell there forever, and *David my servant* shall be their prince forever" (Ezek. 37:24–25; cf. Ps. 18:49f.; Isa. 55:3ff.; Jer. 30:9; Hos. 3:5). Though David himself may indeed rule over Israel forever in the resurrection—as Abraham himself will indeed inherit the land of Canaan (cf. Gen. 13:15; 15:8; 17:8)—it will be under the universal governance of the Seed which comes from his own body.

62. Since the context of this passage, both before and after, is the restoring of the Jews "out of all the countries" (Jer. 23:3,8) of their banishment, the governance of the "righteous

Branch" is assumedly over those countries (a common theme throughout the prophets, cf. Joel 3:2ff.; Zeph. 3:8; Zech. 14:2ff., etc.). Thus a universalized translation of Heb. *'ereṣ* (v. 5) as "earth" (KJV, NKJV) instead of "land" (NASB, ESV, NRSV, NIV, NLT) is preferred.

63. The relating of the "righteous Branch" of David (Jer. 33:15) to the establishing of the "day and night" (vv. 20,25; cf. Gen. 1:5) should not be overlooked. Here we have a glimpse into the assumed protologically based worldview of the Scriptures. As such, the Davidic Covenant and the "covenant with day and night and the fixed order of heaven and earth" are inherently tied together under the sovereignty of God. As surely as there will be an eternal new heavens and new earth (their redemption being implied in "covenant"), so also will there surely be a Davidic Branch representing and mediating the divine character, cf. "LORD Our Righteousness" (v. 16, NIV), throughout the earth.

64. "The idea of the messianic Son of God goes back to the promise to David with reference to his descendants who should succeed him on the throne of Israel, and it looks beyond the immediate descendants of David to that greater descendant who should be the messianic Son of God in the fullest sense of the word" (Ladd, *Theology of the New Testament*, 160).

65. Note the correspondence with 4 Ezra, the only intertestamental work that uses "son" in reference to the Messiah (7:28f.; 13:32,37,52; 14:9):

> The days are coming when the Most High will deliver those who are on the earth. And bewilderment of mind shall come over those who inhabit the earth. They shall plan to make war against one another, city against city, place against place, people against people, and kingdom against kingdom. When these things take place and the signs occur that I showed you before, then *my Son* will be revealed. . . .
>
> And Zion shall come and be made manifest to all people, prepared and built, as you saw the mountain carved out without hands. Then he, *my Son*, will reprove the assembled nations for their ungodliness. . . .
>
> Just as no one can explore or know what is in the depths of the sea, so no one on earth can see *my Son* or those who are with him, except in the time of his day. (2 Esdras 13:29–32,36–37,52, NRSV; italics added)

66. See Ladd, "The Son of God," *Theology of the New Testament*, 158–69. Note that in second-temple Judaism the phrase "Son of Man" would have communicated divinity more than "Son of God" (cf. Daniel Boyarin, *The Jewish Gospels: The Story of the Jewish Christ* [New York: New Press, 2012], 25–101).

67. Of the many lines of evidence, there are 1) the self-declaration of Jesus, identifying with the divine name: "Before Abraham was, *I am*" (John 8:58; cf. Ex. 3:14); 2) the declaration of the Jews: "You, a mere man, claim to be God" (John 10:33, NIV), in response to Jesus saying, "I and the Father are one" (10:30; cf. John 14:6–9); 3) the declaration of Thomas directed to Jesus: "My Lord and my God!" (John 20:28); 4) Jesus' common acceptance of worship (cf. Matt. 14:33; 28:9,17; Luke 24:52; John 5:23; 9:38; 20:28); note the radical devotion of the early church as to the divine (e.g., 1 Cor. 1:1–3; 1 Thess. 1:1–3; Titus 1:1–4); so Pliny the Younger wrote to the emperor Trajan that Christians "sang in alternate verses a hymn to Christ, as to a god" (*Letters* 10.96, Loeb ed.); 5) "Who can forgive sins but God alone?" (Mark 2:7; Luke 5:21); 6) "I am the LORD, and besides me there is *no savior*" (Isa. 43:11; cf. Isa. 45:21), cf. "Our citizenship is in heaven, and from it we await *a Savior*, the Lord Jesus Christ" (Phil. 3:20; cf. Luke 2:11; 1 John 4:14); 7) the invocation of the divine name in healings and exorcisms (cf. Matt. 7:22; Acts 3:6; 16:18; 19:13); 8) the Pauline reference to the *shema*: "There is no God but one" (1 Cor. 8:4; cf. Deut. 6:4), followed by "There is one God, the Father, from whom are all things and for whom we exist, and one Lord, Jesus Christ, through whom are all things and

through whom we exist" (v. 6; cf. Isa. 42:5); 9) the Pauline declaration of Jesus being "in the form of God" (Phil. 2:6), followed by "*at the name of Jesus* every knee should bow" (v. 10; cf. Isa. 45:23) and "every tongue confess that *Jesus Christ is Lord*, to the glory of the Father" (v. 11; cf. Isa. 42:8); 10) the identification of "wisdom" as the divine consort (cf. Prov. 3:19; 8:22ff.; Wisdom of Solomon 6:12; 7:25f.; 9:10f.) with Jesus in John 1:1–18; see also the equivalence of "word" and "wisdom" in intertestamental Jewish "Wisdom Tradition," cf. "By the word of the LORD the heavens were made" (Ps. 33:6).

See discussions of divinity and Christology in Richard Bauckham, *God Crucified: Monotheism and Christology in the New Testament* (Grand Rapids: Eerdmans, 1999); Bauckham, *Jesus and the God of Israel: God Crucified and Other Studies on the New Testament's Christology of Divine Identity* (Grand Rapids: Eerdmans, 2008); and Larry W. Hurtado, *How on Earth Did Jesus Become a God? Historical Questions about Earliest Devotion to Jesus* (Grand Rapids: Eerdmans, 2005).

68. Note also those titles which are developed in relation to the "Servant" (Isa. 42:1; 49:6f.) who suffers (Isa. 52:13ff.): i.e., "High Priest" (Heb. 3:1; 4:14f.; etc.; cf. Ps. 110:4; Zech. 6:13), "Mediator" (1 Tim. 2:5; cf. Isa. 59:16; Ezek. 22:30), and "Lamb of God" (John 1:29,36; cf. Isa. 53:7; 1 Peter 1:19; Rev. 5:6).

69. See n. 56 above.

70. Though not entirely unusual (cf. *4 Maccabees* 6:28; 17:21–22), as Joachim Jeremias made clear,

> The oft-repeated assertion that it is inconceivable that Jesus should have ascribed atoning power to his death, that such statements belong rather to the "dogmatic" of the Early Church or of the apostle Paul, is astonishing to anyone who knows the Palestinian sources. Conceptions of the atoning power of death play a large part in the thought of Jesus' contemporaries. Every death has atoning power—even that of a criminal if he dies penitent. An innocent death offered to God has vicarious power of atonement for others. The sources compel the conclusion that *it is inconceivable that Jesus should not have thought of the atoning power of his death. (The Eucharistic Words of Jesus*, trans. Norman Perrin [London: SCM Press, 1966], 231; italics in the original)

71. The various elements of this exposition will be discussed further in chapters 7 and 8.

72. It is the eschatological/apocalyptic glory referenced throughout the prophets (cf. Isa. 11:10; 24:23; 35:2; 40:5; 60:1ff.; 66:18f.; Jer. 33:9; Ezek. 43:5; Dan. 7:14; Hab. 2:14) and reiterated throughout the New Testament (cf. Rom. 5:2; 8:18; 1 Cor. 15:40ff.; 2 Cor. 4:17; Eph. 1:18; Phil. 3:21; Col. 3:4; 2 Thess. 1:10; 2 Tim. 2:10; Titus 2:13; 1 Peter 4:13; 5:1; Jude 24; Rev. 21:11).

73. See Klaus Koch, *The Rediscovery of Apocalyptic,* trans. M. Kohl [London: SCM Press, 1972], 32.

74. Contrary to the common opinion that the "raising up" refers to Jesus' resurrection, and thus the blessing would be ethnically oriented, i.e., to the Jew first and then the Gentile (cf. Acts 13:46). Such an idea had not yet been revealed to the apostles (cf. Acts 10ff.), and therefore Peter's reference to the raising up of Jesus is more likely in reference to the divine sending and to redemptive history as a whole. As David G. Peterson rightly observes,

> Does the expression *"raised up his servant" (anastēsas)* refer to Jesus' first appearance on the stage of history, as the prophet from Nazareth, or to his resurrection from the dead? The verbal link with v. 22 and the quotation from Deuteronomy 18:15 might suggest the former. . . . The use of the word *"first" (prōton)* implies

the sort of sequence portrayed in Isaiah 49:5–6, where the Servant of the Lord is used to "'restore the tribes of Jacob' so that they can be 'a light for the Gentiles' and bring God's salvation 'to the ends of the earth'" (cf. Acts 1:6; 13:46–48; 26:16–18). In other words, that significant "Servant Song," which reveals the way in which God will ultimately fulfill his promise to Abraham, appears to lie behind the final challenge of Peter's sermon. In this sequence of thought, the raising up of Jesus more naturally refers to God sending him as his Servant, to fulfill the divine plan for Israel and the nations. The messianic blessing includes all the benefits of Jesus' saving work outlined in vv. 19–21, together with the gift of repentance *("by turning each of you from your wicked ways")*. (*The Acts of the Apostles*, PNTC [Grand Rapids: Eerdmans, 2009], 184–85)

75. Note the logic of the author in Heb. 9:27–28: Just as there is a two-part "appointment" (Gk. *apokeimai*) for sinful man (death and judgment), so also is there a corresponding two-part "appointment" for the Righteous Man (sacrifice and salvation). Moreover, both appointments are emphasized juxtapositionally, the first appointment being in reference to bearing sin and the second appointment being "without reference to sin" (v. 28, NASB).

76. See n. 5 above.

77. Unfortunately, Christians are often analogous to "Rothschild" descendants, knowing nothing of their financier heritage and often associating their name with street sweepers and the like. The nobility and confidence in our heritage as "Christians" is rooted in our apocalyptic understanding of Jesus as "the Christ" (cf. 1 Peter 4:12–16).

78. George E. Ladd, *The Pattern of New Testament Truth* (Grand Rapids: Eerdmans, 1968) 13–14.

79. The destructive nature of Gnosticism expresses itself in two seemingly contradictory ways: extreme asceticism and extreme indulgence. They are congruent, however, in their *devaluation* of the body and materiality in general; see A. M. Renwick, "Gnosticism," *ISBE*, 2:484–90.

80. *Against Heresies*, 1.26.3 (*ANF*, 1:352).

81. Ibid., 3.11.1 (*ANF*, 1:426). The same testimony is corroborated by Hippolytus, *Refutation of All Heresies*, 7.24 (*ANF*, 5:115), and Eusebius, *Church History*, 3.29 (*NPNF2*, 1:161).

82. "Since in the message to Thyatira the prophetess Jezebel, who teaches within the community (2:20), is accused of teaching the same vices, viz., eating meat offered to idols and practicing fornication, it is generally assumed that she and her friends and followers belong to the same group as the Nicolaitans. But whereas the false apostles, who spread the teaching of the Nicolaitans in Ephesus were migrant missionaries, Jezebel and the adherents to the teaching of Balaam belong to the communities of Thyatira and Pergamum. Thus the Nicolaitans seem to be an integral part of these churches" (E. Schüssler Fiorenza, "Apocalyptic and Gnosis in the Book of Revelation and Paul," *JBL* 92, no. 4 [December 1973]: 568). See also D. F. Watson, "Nicolaitans," *ABD*, 4:1106–7).

83. So Jewish scholar Joseph Klausner commented,

The Stoics and Cynics taught that salvation from the evil in this world is to be sought and found in *salvation from the world itself*, that is, in flight from the storms and passions of this world. Christianity, which was compounded of Judaism and Greek philosophy, has a redeemer of the world, but along with this there are also ascetics who are saved from the evil in the world by flight from the world to desert places and monasteries. Judaism, seeking redemption from the personal evil in this world, found it in *improvement of the world* by a personal Messiah alone. (*Messianic Idea in Israel*, 24; italics in the original)

Apostolic Christianity was *not* "compounded of Judaism and Greek philosophy," but rather retained its simple messianic expectation with the addition of a messianic atonement.

84. *Stromata*, 4.4 (*ANF*, 2:411–12); italics added. See also Origen's "secret martyrdom" in *Exhortation to Martyrdom*, 21.

85. Often the messianic agency is functionally merged so that the ecclesiastical/political leaders become the primary agents, as Eusebius understood Constantine to be head over all (cf. *Oration in Praise of Constantine*, esp. 16–18). For example:

> Not one of those whose words once were heard with awe and wonder, had announced the glorious advent of *the Saviour of mankind*, or that new revelation of divine knowledge which he came to give. Not Pythius himself, nor any of those mighty gods, could apprehend the prospect of their approaching desolation; nor could their oracles point at him who was to be *their conqueror and destroyer*. What prophet or diviner could foretell that their rites would vanish at the presence of a new Deity in the world, and that the knowledge and worship of the Almighty Sovereign should be freely given to all mankind? Which of them foreknew *the august and pious reign of our victorious Emperor, or his triumphant conquests* everywhere over the false demons, or the overthrow of their high places? (*Oration in Praise of Constantine*, 9.4–5 [*NPNF2*, 1:592–93]; italics added)

86. Jürgen Moltmann observes,

> In its christology, Christ was not merely the head of the church. He was also the king of heaven and the pantocrator, thereby legitimating the Christian *imperator* and his empire. As "the anointed of the Lord," the Orthodox emperor had a messianic charge to spread the kingdom of God on earth. *For in the Christian empire God's plan in history was fulfilled. . . .*
>
> In this way, theology aligned both the Christian church and the Christian state towards the kingdom of God; and in this respect it was "an imperial theology," whether it is viewed in its transcendental or its eschatological configuration. Parallel to the church, the emperor was accepted as sacred representative of God's rule over the world. (*The Way of Jesus Christ: Christology in Messianic Dimensions*, trans. M. Kohl [Minneapolis: Fortress, 1993], 54; italics added)

87. As G. F. Chesnut notes in regard to Eusebius,

> As a radical Origenist, he rejected the apocalyptic idea of a future millennial kingdom of Christ on earth in favor of a more Platonic concept of immortal life in some supercosmic realm. But he also believed that this present cosmos would come to a cataclysmic end at some point several generations (or at most several centuries) after his own time. In a kind of "expanded eschatology" the events of the apocalyptic end times were spread out over hundreds of years. The Pax Romana which began under the emperor Augustus was identified by Eusebius with the eschatological kingdom of peace (Isa 2:1–4; Mic 4:1–4), while the emperor Constantine and his descendants were "the saints of the Most High" (Dan 7:18), the eschatological rulers who were to govern Rome, the fourth kingdom (Dan 2:31–45), until the final tribulation, when the world would be destroyed and the last judgment held. ("Eusebius of Caesarea," *ABD*, 2:675)

88. *Life of Constantine*, 2.19 (*NPNF2*, 1:505); italics added. See a similar presentation of Constantine as divine salvific agent in 1.5f.; 1.24; esp. 1.43; 1.46; 2.12 [as Mosaic type]; 2.28; and 2.42. The "Caesars" refer to Constantine's three sons—Constantinus, Constantius, Constans—whom Eusebius goes on to describe: "In the course of this period, his three sons had been admitted at different times as his colleagues in the empire. . . . Having

thus reared a threefold offspring, *a Trinity, as it were*, of pious sons, and having received them severally at each decennial period to a participation in his imperial authority, he judged the festival of his Tricennalia [thirtieth anniversary of his reign] to be a fit occasion for thanksgiving to the Sovereign Lord of all" (4.40 [*NPNF2*, 1:550]; italics added).

89. This point is well demonstrated by Timothy D. Barnes, *Constantine and Eusebius* (Cambridge, MA: Harvard University Press, 1981), 191–207.

90. So Luther chided,

> But one should do to them [papists and monks] as they do to our people and demand that they recant their abominations and prove it by casting off all the abuses that have prevailed against faith and good works in their churches among their people, so that one could know them by their fruits (Matt. 7:16). Otherwise, one cannot believe their mere words and gestures, that is, their sheepskins. Arius, too, should have recanted in the same way, confessed his error, and actually attacked his former doctrine and conduct, as St. Augustine did his Manichaeism, as many people are now doing with their former popery and monkery, among whom, by the grace of God, I can number myself. ("On the Councils and the Church [1539]," *LW*, 41:85)

91. See a rebuttal to the notion of a pretribulational rapture in George E. Ladd, *The Blessed Hope: A Biblical Study of the Second Advent and the Rapture* (Grand Rapids: Eerdmans, 1956); and Robert H. Gundry, *The Church and the Tribulation: A Biblical Examination of Posttribulationism* (Grand Rapids: Zondervan, 1973).

92. *Systematic Theology*, vol. 5 (Grand Rapids: Kregel, 1993), 288.

93. Ibid.; though with qualification: "These events, though not always clearly distinguished in every Scripture, are naturally classified by the character of the conditions and incidents accompanying them" (ibid.). Chafer goes on to awkwardly classify each of the major messianic passages according to their respective plans of salvation (pp. 289–310).

94. Accordingly, the cruciform-messianic function is equally divided. The Messiah comes to make two new covenants, one with the Gentilic church at the cross (which is substantially embodied in the pretribulational rapture—i.e., saving believers from the wrath of God) and the other with the Israelitic kingdom at the second advent; see Chafer, *Systematic Theology*, 4:310–44, esp. 325; John F. Walvoord, "The New Covenant with Israel," *BSac* 103 (1946): 16–27; and Charles C. Ryrie, *The Basis of the Premillennial Faith* (Neptune, NJ: Loizeaux Brothers, 1953), 105–24. See a history of dispensational interpretation of the new covenant in Rodney J. Decker, "The Church's Relationship to the New Covenant," *BSac* 152 (1995): 431–56.

95. Note Cullmann's diagram in *Christ and Time* (trans. Floyd V. Filson [Philadelphia: Westminster, 1950], 188) of concentric circles with the "reign of Christ" equaling the combined circles of the "church" and the "world"—the obvious conclusion (though skillfully evaded) would be that Jesus' mission in this age is to expand the church circle so as to include the world circle, which is likewise the mission of the second advent.

96. *Christology of the New Testament*, 224–26.

97. George E. Ladd demonstrates well the theological train wreck caused by realized eschatology:

> Confession of His Messiahship is at the same time confession of the presence of the Kingdom of God, for it is the mission of the Messiah to bring the Kingdom of God to men. At this point, we must understand that there was for the disciples a problem in the recognition of our Lord's Messiahship even as there was a problem in their recognition of the presence of the Kingdom of God.

We have discovered that the popular expectation of the coming of the Kingdom of God meant that [*sic*] the end of the Age and the manifestation of God's rule in power and glory, when all evil would be purged from the earth. However, Jesus taught that the Kingdom had come but in a new and unexpected form. Although the old Age goes on, the Kingdom of God has invaded the realm of Satan to deliver men from his rule. This was the mystery, the new disclosure of the divine purpose in the mission of our Lord. . . .

His mission, as well as His Messiahship, was a "mystery"; it was not to bring the evil Age to its end and inaugurate The Age to Come. It was rather to bring the powers of the future Age to men in the midst of the present evil Age; and this mission involved His death. Therefore when the crowds tried to make Him king, He withdrew. . . . Even as they rejected His offer of the Kingdom because it was not what they were looking for, so they rejected His Messiahship because He was not the conquering, ruling monarch they desired.

Finally, however, the inner circle of the disciples began to realize that in spite of the fact that the Kingdom was not present in mighty power, in spite of the fact that Jesus was not to be a Davidic King, He was nevertheless the Messiah and the Kingdom was indeed present in His person and mission. . . .

Once they had realized that He was the Messiah, even though in a new and unexpected role, Jesus instructed them as to His further purpose. His purpose was not that of a national restoration of Israel. On the contrary, He would create a new people. . . .

The Greek word, *ekklesia*, is the word most commonly used in the Greek Old Testament to refer to Israel as the people of God. The very use of this word suggests that our Lord purposed to bring into existence a new people who would take the place of the old Israel who rejected both His claim to Messiahship and His offer of the Kingdom of God. (*The Gospel of the Kingdom: Scriptural Studies in the Kingdom of God* [Grand Rapids: Eerdmans, 1959], 109–12)

98. If only Ladd had followed through on "the messianic secret"—"In the future he will be the glorious King (Mt. 25:34), and his Kingdom will then be manifested in great power (Mt. 13:41–43; Lk. 22:29–30). But meanwhile, his messiahship involved not a throne but a cross, not glory but humility, not reigning but dying. His present role is that of the Suffering Servant; only in the future will he be the glorious messianic King. The messianic concept, as entertained by the people, must undergo a radical transformation. . . . For he was the Messiah; but he must suffer before he should enter his glory (Lk. 24:26)" (*Theology of the New Testament*, 180).

99. So Moltmann,

Very early on, renunciation of hope for the parousia was the price paid for Christianity's integration into the Roman empire. In their worship and their persecutions, the first Christian congregations prayed passionately: "Maranatha, come Lord Jesus, come soon" (1 Cor. 16:22; Rev. 22:20). But the Constantinian imperial church began to pray *pro mora finis*—that the end might be delayed—hoping thereby to recommend itself as a religion that supported the state and preserved the world. People who are trying to fit into the world and to gain its recognition are bound to dispense with hope for the messianic kingdom which will change and renew everything. They have to do without the vision of an alternative future in the kingdom of Christ. But for people who embark on a true conversion which takes them out of what they are, present hope for the coming of Christ and his kingdom is important. They need this sustaining staff of hope, in order to free themselves from the present and to confront it freely (1 Cor. 7:31). They no longer love "the nature of this world," which is injustice and violence, but begin to "love the appearance of the Lord." (*Way of Jesus Christ*, 313–14)

100. It is assumed Paul is here referencing those who reject the resurrection of the dead (cf. 1 Cor. 15:12ff., 32ff.), which rests upon an apocalyptic messianic hope (cf. 15:20ff., 45ff.). Thus it is implied that those who do not love the Lord do not cry, *Maranatha!* Akin to the close of the New Testament, i.e., "Come, Lord Jesus" (Rev. 22:20), the Aramaic expression references longing for the age to come. See *Didache* 10.6, "May grace come, and may this world pass away. Hosanna to the God of David. If anyone is holy, let him come; if anyone is not, let him repent. *Maranatha!* Amen" (Michael W. Holmes, ed., *The Apostolic Fathers: Greek Texts and English Translations*, updated ed. [Grand Rapids: Baker, 1999], 263).

101. Anthony Hoekema concludes well:

This same lively expectation of Christ's return should mark the church of Jesus Christ today. If this expectation is no longer present, there is something radically wrong. It is the unfaithful servant in Jesus' parable who says in his heart, "My lord delays his coming" (Luke 12:45). There may be various reasons for the loss of this sense of expectation. . . . Whatever the reasons may be, the loss of a lively, vital anticipation of the Second Coming of Christ is a sign of a most serious spiritual malady in the church. Though there may be differences between us on various aspects of eschatology, all Christians should eagerly look forward to Christ's return, and should live in the light of that expectation every day anew. (*Bible and the Future*, 110–11)

Chapter Six

1. Matthew's "kingdom of heaven" is synonymous with the "kingdom of God," since "heaven" was often a Jewish circumlocution for "God" (see C. C. Caragounis, "Kingdom of God/Kingdom of Heaven," *DJG*, 417).

2. So dispensationalist theologian Eric Sauer articulated, "The 'Kingdom' is the real basic theme of the Bible. It is the surrounding historical frame in which the whole course of revelation is being consummated. All ages and periods of the Divinely revealed ways; all groups and persons addressed, whether Israel, the nations, or the church; all temples, sanctuaries, and redeeming acts; all heavenly and demonic activities, whether in the foreground or background, stand in some way, either positively or negatively, in connexion with the history of the kingdom of God" (*From Eternity to Eternity: An Outline of the Divine Purposes*, trans. G. H. Lang [Grand Rapids: Eerdmans, 1954], 89).

   Sauer could be understood as an early progressive (i.e., inaugurational) dispensationalist, as he continues, "The kingdom itself is the royal saving work of God to the carrying through of His counsels in creation and redemption. Therefore the most correct and inclusive translation of the Greek word *basileia*, used for 'kingdom,' is rather kingly rule than kingly realm. . . . It is the kingship of the Most High working salvation, that is, quite generally, it is the royal authority of the Saviour God, His government as a living and powerful Divine action, revealing itself in ever new forms of self-manifestation, in the course of many dispensations and periods" (ibid.).

3. See Johannes Weiss, *Jesus' Proclamation of the Kingdom of God*, trans. R. H. Hiers and D. L. Holland (Philadelphia: Fortress, 1971; first published in Germany 1892). Weiss's original thesis remains unchallenged: "The Kingdom of God as Jesus thought of it is never something subjective, inward, or spiritual, but is always the objective messianic Kingdom, which usually is pictured as a territory into which one enters, or as a land in which one has a share, or as a treasure which comes down from heaven" (ibid., 133).

4. Contrary to the supposed "complex background" of kingdom language in second-temple Judaism (see D. C. Duling, "Kingdom of God, Kingdom of Heaven," *ABD*, 4:49–56; and Michael Lattke, "On the Jewish Background of the Synoptic Concept, 'Kingdom of God,'" in *The Kingdom of God in the Teaching of Jesus*, ed. Bruce Chilton [London: SPCK, 1984], 72–91). Lattke egregiously presupposes the kingdom as the nonmessianic "royal rule of God" (p. 75), reads that definition back into the Jewish literature, and concludes by separating "the scheme of the two ages, and the coming of the messianic king or judge" (p. 78) from the synoptic definition of the "kingdom of God." See a more realistic survey in G. E. Ladd, "The Kingdom of God in the Jewish Apocryphal Literature: Parts 1–3," *BSac* 109 (January 1952): 55–62; (April 1952): 164–74; (October 1952): 318–31.

5. As George E. Ladd acknowledged,

   The kingdom of heaven must have reference to the kingdom which the Jews in particular expected, the kingdom prophesied in the Old Testament, the earthly Davidic kingdom. Dr. Feinberg affirms: "There is no explanation offered as to the meaning of the 'kingdom' in his (John's) message, for the people knew what was implied by his words. . . . There was no need to describe the conditions and characteristics of the kingdom, for that had been done so repeatedly and minutely. Nor was it necessary to inform them that the kingdom could not and would not be established without the rightful King." "Nor does Christ explain what is meant by these words; His hearers knew full well their import. How unwarranted is the assertion, then, of those who find that Christ's ideas and conceptions of the kingdom involved something far removed from the thought of His hearers." . . .

   It is true that Jesus never defined what he meant by kingdom of God or kingdom of heaven, and we can only assume that the announcement that the kingdom of God was near was full of meaning to his hearers. There is no evidence that they reacted with any measure of surprise to the announcement of either John or Jesus. The Old Testament frequently promised the coming of a time when the kingdom would be restored to Israel; and it is undoubtedly true that this is the meaning which the Jews attributed to Jesus' proclamation. (*Crucial Questions About the Kingdom of God* [Grand Rapids: Eerdmans, 1952], 112; quoting Charles L. Feinberg, *Premillennialism or Amillennialism?* [Grand Rapids: Zondervan, 1936], 87,89)

6. So George N. H. Peters,

> *To comprehend the subject of the kingdom, it is necessary to notice the belief and the expectations of the more pious portion of the Jews.* This is the rule, covering doctrine, laid down by the ablest of writers; it is found in works introductory to the Bible or in defense of the Scriptures . . . as a leading one in the doctrinal interpretation of the Word; its importance and value are urged by various considerations as the only possible way to attain to *a consistent sense* of a doctrine. If the rule applies to doctrine in general, especially ought it to be observed in that of the kingdom.
>
> *Obs.* 1. It is universally admitted by writers of prominence (e.g. Neander, Hagenbach, Schaff, Kurtz, etc.), whatever their respective views concerning the Kingdom itself, that the Jews, including the pious, held to *a personal* coming of the Messiah, *the literal* restoration of the Davidic throne and kingdom, the personal reign of Messiah *on David's throne, the resultant* exaltation of Jerusalem and the Jewish nation, and *the fulfillment* of the Millennial descriptions in that reign. (*The Theocratic Kingdom of Our Lord Jesus, the Christ* [Grand Rapids: Kregel, 1952; first published 1884 by Funk & Wagnalls], 1:183; italics in the original)

. Though dated, the integrity of Peters' argument remains sound.

7. Again Peters well articulated,

> On the face of the opening pages of the New Test. it is taken *for granted* that the Kingdom was something *well known, already the object of faith and hope.* Theologians generally, either unable to reconcile this with their church theories, or deeming it unimportant while acknowledging the fact, pass it by in silence, or give us some apologetics to account for it, which are derogatory to the age, to the believers then living, and to the Word. The destructive critics, seeing here a point of leverage insist upon it that this was evidence of the prevalence of "Jewish forms," and scoff at it as a decided indication of weakness and failure. By us—for we make no apology, needing none—it is regarded as *prerequisite and essential* to the truthfulness and unity of our doctrine. (*Theocratic Kingdom*, 1:181; italics in the original)

8. Those who argue for a realized kingdom generally string together a number of *verses* pulled severely out of context (see the appendix). If the kingdom had finally come, we ought to see paragraph after paragraph, chapter after chapter, of triumphant jubilation in the spirit of Rev. 19:1–9. As Paul condemned a realized resurrection (2 Tim. 2:18) and a realized day of the Lord (2 Thess. 2:2), it would stand to follow that he would condemn a realized kingdom (though 1 Cor. 4:8 would imply as much; see A. C. Thiselton, "Realized Eschatology at Corinth," *NTS* 24 [1978]: 510–26).

9. William V. Crockett uses the same logic (contra annihilationism) concerning eternal conscious torment in Gehenna: "The important thing in interpreting any ancient text is to give proper weight to the meaning of words in the time period in which they are used. . . .

So our task is to determine the everyday perspective concerning the fate of the wicked during the first century" ("The Metaphorical View," in *Four Views of Hell* [Grand Rapids: Zondervan, 1996], 70). It is this "everyday perspective" of a common first-century Jew that ultimately justifies a simple messianic interpretation of the "kingdom of God."

10. George W. Buchanan, *The Consequences of the Covenant* (Leiden: E. J. Brill, 1970), 55.

11. Endless are the warnings of oversimplifying the supposed theological complexity of the kingdom of God; e.g., "The relation of Jesus to the kingdom of God is such that no single formula can do justice to it. We will do well to adopt a fuller vocabulary to represent its nature" (G. R. Beasley-Murray, *Jesus and the Kingdom of God* [Grand Rapids: Eerdmans, 1986], 145). In common fashion Beasley-Murray goes on to base this statement on a poor exegesis of Matt. 11:12; 12:28; Luke 17:21; etc. (see the appendix).

12. "Although the term 'kingdom of God' is rare in Judaism, the idea is almost ubiquitous, either explicitly as the kingdom of the Messiah or implicitly in descriptions of the messianic age" (C. C. Caragounis, "Kingdom of God/Kingdom of Heaven," *DJG*, 418). See also Kaufmann Kohler, "Kingdom of God," *JE*, 7:502–3; and Beasley-Murray, *Jesus and the Kingdom of God*, 46–51.

13. Thus the phraseology of the "kingdom of God" should be treated like other socio-historically relative terminology in the NT—e.g., "cross" (Matt. 27:32; Phil. 2:8), "centurion" (Matt. 8:5; Acts 10:1), "tax collector" (Matt. 5:46; Luke 19:2), "God-fearing" (Acts 10:22; 13:26), "whitewashed" (Matt. 23:27; Acts 23:3), "stadia" (Rev. 14:20; 21:16), etc. Though such terms are not used in the OT, nor are they used today, we understand their historical context and interpret them accordingly.

14. See a summary in G. E. Ladd, "Kingdom of God," *ISBE*, 3:23–29.

15. Though dispensationally motivated, Alva J. McClain articulated well the need for a delineation:

> In a preliminary survey of the very extensive array of Biblical references to the Kingdom of God, especially in the Old Testament, the investigator will be impressed by a series of differences which at first sight may seem to be almost contradictory. Some of the more important of these differences may be stated as follows:
>
> First, certain passages present the Kingdom as something which has *always* existed; yet other places it seems to have a definite historical *beginning* among men. (Compare Ps. 10:16 with Dan. 2:44.)
>
> Second, the Kingdom is set forth in Scripture as *universal* in its scope, outside of which there is no created thing; yet again the Kingdom is revealed as a *local* rule established on earth. (Compare Ps. 103:19 with Isa. 24:23.)
>
> Third, the Kingdom sometimes appears as the rule of God *directly*, with no intermediary standing between God and man; yet it is also pictured as the rule of God through a *mediator* who serves as channel between God and man. (Compare Ps. 59:13 with 2:4–6.)
>
> Fourth, it has been noted that often the Bible describes the Kingdom as something wholly *future*; whereas in other texts the Kingdom is said to be a *present* reality. (Compare Zech. 14:9 with Ps. 29:10.) . . .
>
> Some of the above distinctions, if not all, have been noticed by Biblical scholars and attempts have been made to explain them; sometimes by asserting the existence of one kingdom with two aspects or phases; or by the assumption of two kingdoms. . . .
>
> In one sense it would not be wholly wrong to speak of *two kingdoms* revealed in the Bible. But we must at the same time guard carefully against the notion that

these two kingdoms are absolutely distinct, one from the other. There is value and instruction in thinking of them as *two aspects* or phases of the one rule of our sovereign God. In seeking for terms which might best designate these two things, I can find nothing better than the adjectives "universal" and "mediatorial." These are not exactly commensurate terms, of course, but describe different qualities; the first referring to the *extent* of rule, the latter to the *method* of rule. Nevertheless, in each case the designated quality seems to be the most important for purposes of identification. (*The Greatness of the Kingdom: An Inductive Study of the Kingdom of God* [Winona Lake, IN: BMH Books, 1959], 19–21)

16. As E. R. Craven originally articulated,

The phrases "Kingdom of God," "Kingdom of Heaven," do not indeed occur in exact form in the Old Testament; cognate expressions, however, appear, which may be divided into two classes—(1) Those which refer to the natural Kingdom of God over the universe, Dan. 4:3,34, 6:26; Ps. 145:12,13; (LXX Dan. 3:33, 4:31, 6:27; Ps. 144:12,13). (2) Those in which the then future Basileia of the Messiah was predicted, Dan. 2:44, 7:14,27, (LXX as Heb.); allied to the prophecies from which these citations are made, are Isa. 11, 32, 59:20—66:24; Ps. 2, 72, *etc.* There can be no doubt that *the* Basileia foretold in the latter class was the one contemplated by Jesus, especially in view of the distinct reference to the prophecies of Daniel, and the quotations therefrom, in His great eschatological discourse on the Mount of Olives. ("Excursus on the Basileia," in J. P. Lange, *A Commentary on the Holy Scriptures: Revelation*, trans. E. Moore, ed. E. R. Craven [New York: Scribner's Sons, 1874], 97–98)

17. Unfortunately, this distinction was obfuscated by the early dispensationalists who adopted a dualistic soteriology, delineating between the "kingdom of heaven" and the "kingdom of God" (cf. *Scofield Reference Bible* [New York: Oxford University Press,1909], 996, 1003, 1226; Lewis Chafer, *Systematic Theology*, vol. 7 [Grand Rapids: Kregel, 1993], 223–24; Feinberg, *Premillennialism or Amillennialism*, 194; J. Dwight Pentecost, *Things to Come: A Study in Biblical Eschatology* [Findlay, OH: Dunham Publishing, 1958], 144). Thus the universal kingdom is relegated to the immaterial Gentile plan of salvation, while the messianic kingdom is relegated to the material Jewish plan of salvation. There are not two plans of salvation, but rather two thrones within creation.

18. "The NT combines this emphasis on God's universal kingship with another no less important OT theme, that of the Messiah of the house of David, the Son of Man, the Savior-King who is to come in the eschatological future. God's transcendent supremacy is thereby linked with the prophetic expectation that God's rule will be established in this world under the Messiah-King" (Carl F. H. Henry, "Reflections on the Kingdom of God," *JETS* 35, no. 1 [March 1992]: 40).

19. Though Jesus presently sits enthroned at the right hand of God ruling over all of creation (cf. Matt. 28:18; Eph. 1:20f.; Phil. 2:9; Col. 1:16f.; 1 Peter 3:22), this does not invalidate or nullify the earthly Davidic throne which he will take up upon his return (cf. Luke 1:32; Acts 2:30; Rev. 22:16). The reality of the universal kingdom only reinforces the reality of the messianic kingdom, as is Paul's clear logic in 1 Cor. 15:24–28, esp. v. 27 and its application of Ps. 8:6.

20. So Paul describes the interaction between the divine and messianic thrones in the age to come: "Then comes the end, when *he delivers the kingdom to God the Father* after destroying every rule and every authority and power. . . . When all things are subjected to him, then the Son himself will also be subjected to him who put all things in subjection under him, that *God may be all in all*" (1 Cor. 15:24–28). The phrase "all in all" (Gk. *panta en*

pasin) means "everything in every way" (Eph. 1:23, NIV), referencing the heavens and the earth and all the goings-on therein. Through his Messiah, God will bring the rebellion of Adam to an end, and in this way the disharmony between the throne of God and the thrones of fallen human beings will finally be resolved. Thus God the Father will be honored as the ultimate source of life, sustenance, and salvation from everlasting to everlasting—he will be all in all.

21. So the inaugurational schema proves inadequate by consolidating the two into one semi-Platonic system of "manifestation" or "realization," involving spiritual/abstract vs. physical/concrete divine sovereignty—e.g., George Ladd:

> Although God is now King, other references speak of a day when he shall become King and shall rule over his people (Isa. 24:23; 33:22; 52:7; Zeph. 3:15; Zech. 14:9ff.). This leads to the conclusion that while God is the King, he must also become King, i.e., he must manifest his kingship in the world of human beings and nations. . . . While there is considerable diversity in the description of the Kingdom in the Old Testament, it always involves an inbreaking of God into history when God's redemptive purpose is fully realized. . . .
>
> The coming of the Kingdom for which we pray in the Lord's Prayer means that God's will be done on earth, i.e., that his rule be perfectly realized (Mt. 6:10). The "kingdom" that Jesus appointed for his disciples (Lk. 22:29) is "royal rule."
>
> This is important for the interpretation of Jesus' message, for one of the major problems is that of how the Kingdom of God can be both future and present. If the Kingdom is primarily the eschaton—the eschatological era of salvation—it is difficult to see how this future realm can also be present. However, we have seen that both in the Old Testament and in rabbinic Judaism, God's Kingdom—his reign—can have more than one meaning. God is now the King, but he must also *become* King. This is the key to the solution of the problem in the Gospels. (*A Theology of the New Testament*, 2nd ed., ed. Donald A. Hagner [Grand Rapids: Eerdmans, 1993], 58–61)

The "key to the solution to the problem" of present vs. future sovereignty is not a two-stage inaugurational system. The solution lies in recognizing a twofold governance—a righteous universal kingdom presently ruling over wicked human kingdoms, which will become a righteous messianic kingdom eschatologically, as it was protologically.

22. Note that "installed" (Heb. *nāsak*) refers to the *anointing* of a king (as one poured out into a cast image of a god); see *HALOT*, 703.

23. Isaiah 60 seems to expound upon the covenant God makes with Israel (59:21) in context to "a Redeemer will come to Zion" (59:20). Thus "your" (60:1ff.) would refer to 1) the Redeemer 2) [in] Zion 3) [in] Israel.

24. Note the centrality of the book of Daniel (esp. chap. 7) during NT times in Josephus, *Antiquities*, 10.11.7; see also Daniel Boyarin, *The Jewish Gospels: The Story of the Jewish Christ* (New York: New Press, 2012); and Beasley-Murray, *Jesus and the Kingdom of God*, 26–35.

25. In such a light, Paul takes for granted that Jesus will return "with all his saints" (1 Thess. 3:13) and that in the age to come "the saints will judge the world" (1 Cor. 6:2), though conversely "the unrighteous will not inherit the kingdom of God" (v. 9). For as the Messiah destroys "every rule and every authority and power" (1 Cor. 15:24) and reigns "until he has put all his enemies under his feet" (v. 25), so too will he give to the saints "authority over the nations" (Rev. 2:26)—i.e., "the authority to judge" (Rev. 20:4)—because they have been made "a kingdom and priests to our God, and they shall reign on the earth" (Rev. 5:10).

26. Some mistake this passage as a parable (often referred to as "the parable of the sheep and the goats"). However, "The pericope as a whole is not therefore a 'parable' like those of 24:45–51; 25:1–13 and 25:14–30. Its genre is closer to the majestic visions of divine judgment in the book of Revelation than to synoptic parables" (R. T. France, *The Gospel of Matthew*, NICNT [Grand Rapids: Eerdmans, 2007], 960). It is the simple conclusion of Jesus' chronological presentation of eschatological events in 24:4–31. The Messiah will come on the clouds of heaven (24:30), send out his angels to gather the elect (v. 31), and then "he will sit on his glorious throne" (25:31) and gather all the nations for judgment (vv. 32ff.).

27. Though God reveals himself through different names in the OT—e.g., "Lord-Hosts/Armies" (Heb. *yhvh ṣĕbā 'ôt*; cf. 1 Sam. 1:11; Ps. 24:10; 80:4; Isa. 1:24; 6:5; Jer. 9:15; 48:1; Hos. 12:5; Amos 3:13; Mic. 4:4; Hag. 2:6; Zech. 1:3); "Lord-Shepherd" (Heb. *yhvh rā 'â*; cf. Gen. 49:24; Ps. 23:1; 80:1; Ezek. 34:2); "Lord-Heals" (Heb. *yhvh rāpā '*; cf. Ex. 15:26; Jer. 3:22; Isa. 30:26; Ps. 103:3); "Lord-Jealous" (Heb. *yhvh qannā '*; cf. Ex. 20:5; 34:14; Deut. 4:24; Josh. 24:19); "God-Almighty" (Heb. *'ēl šadday*; cf. Gen. 17:1; 28:3; 35:11; 49:25; Ex. 6:3; Num. 24:4; Ruth 1:20; Job 6:4; Ps. 68:14; 91:1; Isa. 13:6; Ezek. 1:24; 10:5; Joel 1:15); "God-Supreme" (Heb. *'ēl 'elyôn*; cf. Gen. 14:18ff.; Ps. 7:17; 47:2; 57:2; Dan. 7:18ff.); "God-Everlasting" (Heb. *'ēl 'ôlām*; cf. Gen. 21:33; Ps. 90:1ff.; Jer. 10:10; Isa. 26:4); "God-Living" (Heb. *'ēl ḥay*; cf. Deut. 5:26; Josh. 3:10; Ps. 42:2; 84:2; Jer. 10:10); "God-Salvation" (Heb. *'ēl yēša '*; cf. 1 Chron. 16:35; Ps. 65:5; 79:9; 85:4) [as well as some infrequent names, e.g., "Lord-Peace" (Judg. 6:24), "Lord-Provide" (Gen. 22:14), "Lord-Righteousness" (Jer. 23:6; 33:16), etc.]—no name is more prominent and central to the revelation of his nature and character than "Lord/God-Israel" (Ex. 5:1; 24:10; 32:27; 34:23; Num. 16:9; Josh. 7:13,19f.; 8:30; 9:18f.; 10:40,42; 13:14,33; 14:14; 22:16,24; 24:2,23; Judg. 4:6; 5:3,5; 6:8; 11:21,23; 21:3; Ruth 2:12; 1 Sam. 1:17; 2:30; 5:7f.,10f.; 6:3,5; 10:18; 14:41; 20:12; 23:10f.; 25:32,34; 2 Sam. 7:27; 12:7; 23:3; 1 Kings 1:30,48; 8:15,17,20,23,25f.; 11:9,31; 14:7,13; 15:30; 16:13,26,33; 17:1,14; 22:53; 2 Kings 9:6; 10:31; 14:25; 18:5; 19:15,20; 21:12; 22:15,18; 1 Chron. 4:10; 5:26; 15:12,14; 16:4,36; 17:24; 22:6; 23:25; 24:19; 28:4; 29:10; 2 Chron. 2:12; 6:4,7,10,14,16f.; 11:16; 13:5; 15:4,13; 20:19; 29:7,10; 30:1,5; 32:17; 33:16,18; 34:23,26; 36:13; Ezra 1:3; 3:2; 4:1,3; 5:1; 6:14,21f.; 7:6,15; 8:35; 9:4,15; Ps. 41:13; 59:5; 68:8,35; 69:6; 72:18; 106:48; Isa. 17:6; 21:10,17; 24:15; 29:23; 37:16,21; 41:17; 45:3,15; 48:1f.; 52:12; Jer. 7:3,21; 9:15; 11:3; 13:12; 16:9; 19:3,15; 21:4; 23:2; 24:5; 25:15,27; 27:4,21; 28:2,14; 29:4,8,21,25; 30:2; 31:23; 32:14f.,36; 33:4; 34:2,13; 35:13,17ff.; 37:7; 38:17; 39:16; 42:9,15,18; 43:10; 44:2,7,11,25; 45:2; 46:25; 48:1; 50:18; 51:33; Ezek. 8:4; 9:3; 10:19f.; 11:22; 43:2; 44:2; Zeph. 2:9; Mal. 2:16; cf. Matt. 15:31; Luke 1:68). It takes a forehead of flint to reject the ethnical character and commitment of the God of the Bible.

28. A term borrowed from Jürgen Moltmann, *Theology of Hope: On the Ground and the Implications of a Christian Eschatology*, trans. M. Kohl [Minneapolis: Fortress, 1993], 130. See also Moltmann, *The Way of Jesus Christ: Christology in Messianic Dimensions*, trans. Margaret Kohl (Minneapolis: Fortress, 1993), 16; though it seems Moltmann would ultimately reject the role of ethnicity in the eschatological context.

29. As Leslie C. Allen notes,

> It is probably not insignificant that the traditional form of Nathan's oracle to David promises Israel that, as a consequence of his rule, God "will plant them and they will remain where they are, never to be disturbed again." This ideal, sadly frustrated up to now, would be realized in the powerful reign of the coming one, whose renown was to spread throughout the world. Indeed the usage of the phrase "the ends of the earth" in the Judean royal ideology implies a universal empire. A motif of ancient Near Eastern royal claims, it is employed in the royal

psalms to indicate high hopes for the Davidic king. (*The Books of Joel, Obadiah, Jonah and Micah*, NICOT [Grand Rapids: Eerdmans, 1976], 347)

30. See Thomas Cahill, *How the Irish Saved Civilization: The Untold Story of Ireland's Heroic Role from the Fall of Rome to the Rise of Medieval Europe* (New York: Doubleday, 1995).

31. Though generally preterist in assumption and terminally unbelieving (concerning an Israelocentric eschatological kingdom), many historical Jesus scholars share the view that the teaching and mission of Jesus can only be understood in terms of a nationalistic restoration of Israel; see E. P. Sanders, *Jesus and Judaism* (Philadelphia: Fortress, 1985); John P. Meier, *A Marginal Jew: Rethinking the Historical Jesus*, 4 vols. (New York: Doubleday, 1991–2009); and Scot McKnight, *A New Vision for Israel: The Teachings of Jesus in National Context* (Grand Rapids: Eerdmans, 1999).

32. "The same main themes—the redemption of Israel (whether politically or in a new world), a new or renewed temple, repentance, judgment, admission of the Gentiles—crop up in numerous places in Jewish literature and in the New Testament. . . . Thus the existence of 'Jewish restoration eschatology' is supported by the New Testament, and Jesus fits believably into that world-view" (Sanders, *Jesus and Judaism*, 335).

33. C. E. B. Cranfield, *A Critical and Exegetical Commentary on The Epistle to the Romans*, ICC (Edinburgh: T & T Clark, 1979), 581–82. Cranfield is to be commended for his acknowledgement of "the ugly and unscriptural notion that God has cast off His people Israel and simply replaced it by the Christian Church," for "These three chapters [Rom. 9–11] emphatically forbid us to speak of the Church as having once and for all taken the place of the Jewish people" (ibid., 448).

34. J. Christiaan Beker, *Paul the Apostle: The Triumph of God in Life and Thought* (Philadelphia: Fortress, 1980), 90.

35. "Birthright" (Gen. 25:31ff.; 27:36; 43:33; 1 Chron. 5:1f.; Heb. 12:16) is simply "the right of the firstborn" (Deut. 21:17), derived from "firstborn" (Heb. *bĕkôr*, Gk. *prōtotokos*); see John N. Oswalt, "244 רכב (*bākar*)," *TWOT*, 108–10; and "πρωτοτόκια, πρωτότοκος," BDAG, 894.

36. For an overview of the practice of primogeniture in the Bible, see J. M. Wilson and R. K. Harrison, "Birthright," *ISBE*, 1:515–16; and Anne K. Davis, "Israel's Inheritance: Birthright of the Firstborn Son," *Chafer Theological Seminary Journal* 13, no. 1 (2008): 79–94.

37. Though lacking primogeniture language, see the substance of a Jewish birthright theology in R. Kendall Soulen, *The God of Israel and Christian Theology* (Minneapolis: Fortress, 1996), esp. 109–55.

38. "Israel is called the Lord's firstborn (Ex 4:22; cf. Jer 31:9) to show that though it was the youngest of the nations, it occupied the position of leadership and privilege over them" (Oswalt, "*bākar*," *TWOT*, 109). Note the glaring lack of commentary concerning Jewish birthright in most of the major modern commentaries on Ex. 4:22 and Jer. 31:9.

39. The messianic recapitulation of this verse (cf. Matt. 2:15) ought only to *reinforce* Jewish primogeniture, since the Messiah is the king of the Jews (cf. figure 6.4)—contrary to the common supersessionist claim to a "new exodus," realizing the Jewish eschatological hope. Rightly, Barry E. Horner, *Future Israel: Why Christian Anti-Judaism Must Be Challenged* (Nashville: Broadman and Holman, 2007), 197–98.

40. All attempts to reinterpret or mitigate this most basic of Abrahamic promises are baseless. For example, "Christified holy space" (W. D. Davies, *The Gospel and the Land: Early Christianity and Jewish Territorial Doctrine* [Berkeley: University of California Press, 1974], 368); similarly Gary M. Burge, *Jesus and the Land: How the New Testament Transformed "Holy Land" Theology* (Grand Rapids: Baker, 2010).

41. "The purpose of primogeniture then was the systematic and orderly transference of social, legal, and religious authority within the family structure. The firstborn male was made the principal heir and was given a sizeable portion of the estate because it was he who was to perpetuate the family name and lineage and who was to bear the chief burden for the continuance and welfare of the family" (Barry J. Beitzel, "The Right of the Firstborn [*Pi Shnayim*] in the Old Testament [Deut. 21:15–17]," in *A Tribute to Gleason Archer*, ed. W. C. Kaiser Jr. and R. F. Youngblood [Chicago: Moody, 1986], 180; quoted in Davis, "Israel's Inheritance," 85). Thus the "double portion," so often associated with primogeniture (cf. Deut. 21:17; Isa. 61:7), is given to assist the older son in performing his responsibility of leadership for the welfare of the whole. In such a light, Israel will receive "the wealth of the nations" (Isa. 60:5,11; 61:6) in the age to come.

42. Indeed it will be an "economy of mutual blessing" between Jew and Gentile; see Soulen, *The God of Israel and Christian Theology*, esp. 109–40. "God's peace with Israel comes not at the nations' expense, but to their benefit. . . . *God's history with Israel and the nations is ordered from the outset toward a final reign of* shalom *in which the distinction between Israel and the nations is not abrogated and overcome but affirmed within a single economy of mutual blessing. . . . God's historical fidelity toward Israel is the 'narrow gate' that opens on the new creation.* There is no shortcut to the eschaton that bypasses or overrides God's fidelity toward the Jewish flesh and the permanent historical distinction between Jew and Gentile" (ibid., 132–33; italics in the original).

43. In technical terms, this is known as "supersessionism" or "replacement theology" (to be discussed further in chapter 7); see Soulen, *The God of Israel and Christian Theology*; and Ronald E. Diprose, *Israel and the Church: The Origin and Effects of Replacement Theology* (Waynesboro, GA: Authentic, 2004).

44. See G. B. Caird, *Jesus and the Jewish Nation* (London: Athlone Press, 1965).

45. Therefore, "The gospel and the table fellowship it founds *confirms* rather than *annuls* the difference and mutual dependence of Israel and the nations" (Soulen, *The God of Israel and Christian Theology*, 169). Unfortunately, "What began in Jesus' name as Israel's hospitality toward Gentiles as Gentiles, ended as the Gentiles' inhospitality toward Jews as Jews" (ibid).

46. As Caird says,

> Jesus did not intend to found a new religious organization, nor even a new religious community. He intended to bring into existence the restored nation of Israel, promised in the Old Testament prophecies. It was to this end that he accepted baptism at the hands of John, to this end that he appointed the Twelve to be his intimate associates, instructing them that their number was a symbol of their relation to the twelve tribes of Israel. This was why he spoke of his followers as a "little flock"—a word already used in the Old Testament to denote the Israel of the messianic age (Mic. 5.4; Isa. 40.11; Ezek. 34.12–24). (*Jesus and the Jewish Nation*, 16)

47. Indeed, the Gospels are little concerned with the nature of the kingdom, focusing rather on the quality of person who will inherit the kingdom. The driving message of both Jesus and John the Baptist was "*Repent, for the kingdom of heaven is at hand*" (Matt. 3:2; 4:17), echoing the prophets' proclamation that "the day of the LORD is at hand!" (Isa. 13:6, NKJV; cf. Ezek. 30:3; Joel 1:15; 2:1; 3:14; Obad. 15; Zeph. 1:7,14) Such phraseology was tremendously fearful, since the day of the Lord was understood to initiate the kingdom of God (cf. Matt. 10:14f.; Luke 10:11f.). Thus many came out to receive John's "baptism of *repentance* for the forgiveness of sins" (Luke 3:3). The question was never about the nature of the kingdom, but rather about who would be "*considered worthy* to attain to that age and to the resurrection from the dead" (Luke 20:35). Such was the

general tenor of Jesus' preaching (cf. Matt. 5–7; 10:5–40; 11:7–30; 12:25–45; 15:3–20; 16:23–28; 18:3–35; 21:28–44; 23:1–39; 24:4—25:46).

48. The Lukan parallel adds the frightful statement, "Behold, some are last who will be first, and some are first who will be last" (13:30). Those who believed they would be first in the kingdom, i.e., the Pharisees and teachers of the law, would actually be thrown out of Jerusalem into the fiery furnace of Gehenna.

49. "The presence of Abraham, Isaac and Jacob lifts this above any ordinary meal; Jewish tradition not surprisingly gave them a leading role at the messianic banquet (*b. Pesaḥ.* 119b; *Exod. Rab.* 25:8). The imagery of the messianic banquet derives from Isa 25:6 (cf. 65:13–14) and was elaborated in Jewish literature both in the apocalyptic and the rabbinic traditions, but whereas in Isaiah it was a feast 'for all peoples,' Jewish tradition soon made it a blessing specifically for Israel" (R. T. France, *The Gospel of Matthew*, NICNT [Grand Rapids: Eerdmans, 2007], 317).

50. Note esp. "the times of the Gentiles" (Luke 21:24) before the day of the Lord and the Son of Man coming in glory and power (vv. 25–28), which only holds meaning if there are "times of the Jews," so to speak, which follow (cf. v. 31).

51. By contrast, Bruce K. Waltke: "To be sure, prior to Pentecost the unenlightened apostles were still asking when the Lord would restore the national kingdom to Israel (Acts 1:7). The church, however, must not be guided by ignorance. . . . Christ's answer is consistent with the Lukan emphasis that Christ must pass through earthly Jerusalem and its cross on his way to inheriting in heaven David's throne, from which he builds his church through the Spirit while dismantling earthly Jerusalem" ("Kingdom Promises as Spiritual," in *Continuity and Discontinuity: Perspectives on the Relationship Between the Old and New Testaments*, ed. John S. Feinberg [Westchester, IL: Crossway, 1988], 273).

52. See esp. Darrell L. Bock, *Acts*, BECNT (Grand Rapids: Baker, 2007), 62–67. "Jesus's reply in verses 7–8 does not reject the premise of the question, that the kingdom will one day be restored to Israel" (p. 62).

53. The Greek *tithēmi* can also mean "to bring about an arrangement" (BDAG, 1004). In this case it is assumed that the arrangement involves the divine restoration of the Israelitic kingdom (v. 6).

54. Note the concentric parallel between the "witness of mercy" in this age ("in Jerusalem, and in all Judea and Samaria, and to the ends of the earth") and the execution of divine justice through the Israelitic kingdom in the age to come.

55. Contrary to the pragmatic approach of most Gentiles—e.g., Roland Allen, *Missionary Methods: St. Paul's or Ours* (London: R. Scott, 1912); and Donald A. McGavran, *Bridges of God: A Study in the Strategy of Missions* (New York: Friendship Press, 1955).

56. For a cogent introduction, see Daniel C. Juster, *The Irrevocable Calling: Israel's Role as a Light to the Nations*, 2nd ed. (Clarksville, MD: Messianic Jewish Publishers, 2007). See also Horner, *Future Israel*, 253–309.

57. "Irrevocable" (Gk. ἀμεταμέλητος), lit. "feeling no remorse, having no regret" (BDAG, 53). God feels no regret for making covenants with Abraham and his offspring, in spite of their rebellion. This would have seemed obvious to a first-century Jew since Israel already had a long history of waywardness without covenantal abrogation, as Jeremiah made clear: "If I have not established my covenant with day and night and the fixed laws of heaven and earth, then I will *reject* the descendants of Jacob and David my servant and will not choose one of his sons to rule over the descendants of Abraham, Isaac and Jacob. For I will *restore* their fortunes and have compassion on them" (Jer. 33:25–26, NIV; cf. 30:11; 31:37).

58. "As Biblical scholarship makes ever more clear that Jesus and Paul taught a future for national Israel in the eschatological plan of God, the legitimacy of a supersessionist reading of Scripture grows ever more dim to the point of vanishing altogether" (Craig A. Blaising, "The Future of Israel as a Theological Question," *JETS* 44, no. 3 [September 2001]: 439).

59. According to the analogy of tree grafting (vv. 17–24), Gentiles have been "grafted in" (vv. 17,19) to the Jewish olive tree, while unbelieving Jews have been "broken off" (v. 17). However, God is faithful to his promise to the forefathers, and they will one day "be grafted back into their own olive tree" (v. 24). Such unbelieving Jews are who Paul has in mind when he says, "Not all who are descended from Israel belong to Israel" (Rom. 9:6), and similarly, "No one is a Jew who is merely one outwardly" (Rom. 2:28). Paul simply has in mind that God accounts as heirs of salvation those who are Jewish, both according to the flesh *and* according to faith (see figure 6.5). Those who "walk in the footsteps of the faith that our father Abraham had" (Rom. 4:12; cf. John 1:47) are the "Israel of God" (Gal. 6:16). Paul nowhere entertains a nonethnic "spiritual Israel," so commonly held in the church today (see Horner, *Future Israel*, 253–90).

60. Blaising, "Future of Israel," 444.

61. Contrary to the common supersessionist conclusion—e.g., F. F. Bruce: "In all that Paul says about the restoration of Israel to God, he says nothing about the restoration of an earthly Davidic kingdom. Without trying to construct an argument from this silence, we may insist that what Paul envisaged for his people was something far better" (*Romans*, TNTC [Downers Grove, IL: InterVarsity, 1985], 217). Why is an ethnically undifferentiated kingdom "far better" than a differentiated one?

62. *Future Israel*, 68. So Horner concludes concerning Jewish election: "This universal kingdom on a glorified earth will incorporate a blessed unity with diversity, that is, the regenerate nation of Israel will inhabit the fruitful promised land under the reign of Jesus Christ from Jerusalem surrounded by regenerate Gentile nations. In this setting of heaven come to earth, Israel and the Jewish people will be fulfilled (Rom. 11:12), not superseded, and the Gentile nations will happily submit to this divine order as engrafted wild olive branches. To this end was the gospel sent forth (Zech. 14:9; Acts 3:19–21; Rom. 8:18–23)" (ibid., 252).

63. Such a literalistic reading would likewise lead us to conclude that men and women have essentially become androgynous in God's sight. As Ronald Y. K. Fung observes,

> The statement that there is no "male and female" in Christ does not mean, as was believed in later Gnosticism, that in the new era mankind is restored to the pristine androgynous state; nor does it mean that all male-female distinctions have been obliterated in Christ, any more than that there is no racial difference between the Christian Jew and the Christian Gentile. "In Christ Jesus" emphasizes that Paul views the elimination of these antitheses from the standpoint of redemption in Christ, while the context clearly shows that the primary emphasis of the verse is on *unity* in Christ rather than on equality. (*The Epistle to the Galatians*, NICNT [Grand Rapids: Eerdmans, 1988], 175–76)

64. Such unity between Jew and Gentile is also likened to different appendages of "the same body" (Eph. 3:6; cf. 2:16; 4:4), and to siblings with the same father in "the household of God" (Eph. 2:19; cf. 3:15; 4:6), and to different branches grafted into one "olive tree" (Rom. 11:17).

65. So Michael J. Vlach concludes,

> *If one recognizes that there are nations in eternity with specific roles and identities, why would there not be a special role and identity for the nation Israel?* . . .

The concept of nations in eternity does not contradict passages that speak of unity among God's people (see Rev 5:9–10). Nations can coexist in harmony with the equality of salvation and spiritual blessings of which all believers partake. In regard to salvation, there is one people of God, but this concept does not rule out all ethnic, geographical, or gender distinctions. . . .

God appears to have a future plan for nations. One of these nations will be Israel. The final eternal state, thus, will see the final and complete fulfillment of Gen 12:2–3 in which God's plan for Abraham and Israel is to bring blessings to all the families of the earth. (*Has the Church Replaced Israel? A Theological Evaluation* [Nashville: B&H Publishing, 2010], 175–76; italics in the original)

66. This animosity came to a head in the violent enactment (with the aid of the Zealots) of "the restrictive propositions of the Shammaites, known in the Talmud as 'The Eighteen Articles.'" (S. Mendelsohn, "Bet Hillel and Bet Shammai," *JE*, 3:116). These ordinances (c. AD 20) are never listed in the rabbinical sources, but it is assumed they are the basis of the stringent separation between Jews and Gentiles referenced in the NT (cf. Acts 10:28; 11:3; Gal. 2:12).

67. As any Jewish schoolboy knows, Hillel and Shammai (c. 60 BC–AD 20) were the last of the *Zugot* ("pairs" of scholars), the forefathers of the *Tannaim* ("teachers," c. AD 10–220), who produced the Mishnah and much of the Talmudic literature. See an introduction in Mendelsohn, "Bet Hillel and Bet Shammai," *JE*, 3:115–16; and Craig A. Evans, "Hillel, House of," and "Shammai, House of," in *Dictionary of New Testament Background*, ed. Stanley E. Porter and Craig A. Evans (Downers Grove, IL: InterVarsity, 2000), 496–98 and 1106–7. See also Jacob Neusner, *The Rabbinic Traditions About the Pharisees Before 70*, 3 vols. (Leiden, Netherlands: E. J. Brill, 1971); and J. H. Charlesworth and L. L. Johns, eds., *Hillel and Jesus: Comparisons of Two Major Religious Leaders* (Minneapolis: Fortress, 1997).

68. "The rabbis had mixed feelings toward proselytes. Some, like Hillel, were disposed to welcome proselytes and were even inclined to relax the requirements a bit at the outset so that the newcomer could perceive the true spirit of Judaism (Mish *Aboth* i.12; TB *Shabbath* 31a). On the other hand, Shammai viewed proselytes with some suspicion and demanded that they be thoroughly examined before admittance. . . . Indeed, some rabbis argued that proselytes were like a scab that adhered to the Jewish people (TB *Yebamoth* 47b, 109b; *Kiddushin* 70b)" (T. R. Schreiner, "Proselyte," *ISBE*, 3:1008).

69. Jewish theologian Michael Wyschogrod describes how a Gentile becomes a Jew according to the flesh in God's sight:

> We must start with the insight that conversion to Judaism should not be possible. . . . And yet, conversion to Judaism is possible. How? By means of a miracle. A gentile who converts to Judaism miraculously becomes part of the body of Israel. This is far more than merely sharing Jewish beliefs and practices. To become a Jew, a gentile must become seed of the patriarchs and matriarchs and that is what she becomes, quasi-physically, miraculously.
>
> The Talmud speaks of the convert as being born, or reborn, as a Jew. . . . A gentile mother and her son or a brother and a sister who convert to Judaism and then marry each other do not violate the biblical prohibition against incest. This is so because, in the process of conversion, they were reborn and are therefore no longer mother and son or brother and sister. Fortunately, such marriages are rabbinically forbidden. . . . This does not, of course, imply that the biological miracle that accompanies a conversion can be observed under the microscope as changes in the DNA of the convert. It is a theological-biological miracle. . . .

This has to be so because being a Jew requires descent from Abraham and Sarah, and if conversion to Judaism is to be possible, then the convert must become a descendant of Abraham and Sarah. Only a miracle can accomplish this feat. (*The Body of Faith: God and the People Israel*, 2nd ed. [Northvale, NJ: Jason Aronson, 1996], xviii–xix; italics in the original)

70. Though there is much debate concerning the Heb. *gēr* in the OT—i.e., the "sojourner" (Ex. 12:19; 20:10; Lev. 17:15; Deut. 16:11; 29:11; etc.) or "stranger" (Ex. 12:48f.; Lev. 16:29; 19:33f.; Num. 9:14; etc.)—it was generally understood by NT times that they were proselytes, since they were circumcised (Ex. 12:44,48; Josh. 5:5; cf. Gen. 17:12f.), as reflected in the LXX translation of Heb. *gēr* with Gk. *prosēlytos*; see E. G. Hirsch, "proselyte," *JE*, 10:220–24; and K. G. Kuhn, "προσήλυτος," *TDNT*, 6:728–31.

71. K. G. Kuhn notes,

The rite [for the reception of proselytes] consists of three parts: circumcision, baptism, and the offering of a sacrifice in the temple. . . .

As the Israelites in the wilderness had to fulfil three conditions before the conclusion of the covenant, namely, circumcision (cf. Ex. 12:48), sprinkling with water (Ex. 19:10) and an offering (Ex. 24:5), so proselytes must fulfil the same three conditions on entering the covenant. . . .

The non-Jew received thus into Judaism was regarded after conversion "in every respect as a Jew," b. Jeb., 47b. This means in the first instance that like every Jew he is under obligation to keep the whole Jewish Law. In keeping is the saying of Paul in Gl. 5:3. ("προσήλυτος," *TDNT*, 6:738–39)

72. The earliest attestation to such proto-Noahide laws is found in *Jubilees* 7:20–21: "And in the twenty-eighth jubilee Noah began to command his grandsons with ordinances and commandments and all of the judgments which he knew. And he bore witness to his sons so that they might do justice and cover the shame of their flesh and bless the one who created them and honor father and mother, and each one love his neighbor and preserve themselves from fornication and pollution and from all injustice. For on account of these three the Flood came upon the earth" (*OTP*, 2:69–70).

73. Formulated in later rabbinic tradition as seven commandments (derived from Gen. 9:1–7) which are binding on all of humanity (the "children of Noah"): "The prohibitions against (1) idolatry, (2) blasphemy, (3) bloodshed, (4) incest and adultery, and (5) robbery; (6) the injunction to establish courts of law; and (7) the prohibition against eating flesh cut from a living animal" (Nahum M. Sarna, "Excursus 3: The Noachide Commandments," in *Genesis*, JPSTC [Philadelphia: Jewish Publication Society, 1989], 377). See also the definitive study by David Novak, *The Image of the Non-Jew in Judaism: The Idea of Noahide Law*, 2nd ed., ed. Matthew LaGrone (Oxford: Littman Library of Jewish Civilization, 2011).

74. See the relationship between the *prosēlutos* and the *phoboumenoi ton theon* in Kuhn, "προσήλυτος," *TDNT*, 6:741–44. "The attitude of the primitive Palestinian community to σεβόμενοι τὸν θεόν was based on that of Palestinian Judaism. The only non-Jew to have a part in the salvation effected in Jesus was the one who had first become a member of the Jewish people by the acceptance of circumcision and of the obligation to keep the whole Jewish Torah. Otherwise the non-Jew remained a Gentile and as such he would fall victim to God's wrath in the Last Judgment" (p. 743).

75. For an introduction concerning the issues surrounding the apostolic "consultation," see Darrell L. Bock, *Acts*, BECNT (Grand Rapids: Baker, 2007), 486–93.

76. In no way does Gentile faith *fulfill* (Gk. *plēroō*) the hope of the restored Davidic kingdom—contrary to the common Reformed sentiment; e.g., Oswald T. Allis, *Prophecy and*

the Church (Philadelphia: Presbyterian and Reformed, 1945), 145–50; and Anthony A. Hoekema, *The Bible and the Future* (Grand Rapids: Eerdmans, 1979), 209–10.

77. Debate concerning agreement with the prophets seems to stem from the announcement of the *universal destruction* of the Gentiles on the day of the Lord (cf. Isa. 63:1–6; Joel 3:1–3; Zeph. 2). Thus, to be saved from the coming wrath against the nations, it might seem necessary to become a Jew, so as to be found in the company of the righteous (cf. Pss. 1 and 2).

78. Note a similar conclusion in David H. Stern, *Messianic Judaism: A Modern Movement with an Ancient Past* (Clarksville, MD: Messianic Jewish Publishers, 2007), 154–57. See a congruous diagram in Dan Gruber, *The Church and the Jews: The Biblical Relationship* (Hanover, NH: Elijah Publishing, 1997), 131.

79. For example, Kim Riddlebarger finds this passage exemplary of the supposed apostolic "reinterpretation" of the OT: "James saw the prophecy as fulfilled in Christ's resurrection and exaltation and in the reconstitution of his disciples as the new Israel. The presence of both Jew and Gentile in the church was proof that the prophecy of Amos had been fulfilled. David's fallen tent had been rebuilt by Christ" (*A Case for Amillennialism: Understanding the End Times*, 2nd ed. [Grand Rapids: Baker, 2013], 53).

80. As Soulen states,

> This view of the church underlies the decision of the so-called Council of Jerusalem (Acts 15:1–21; Gal. 2:1–10). Those present take it for granted that Jewish followers of Jesus remain obligated to the Torah; at the same time they rule that Gentile followers of Jesus are obligated to observe only the Noachide law. In back of this decision is the belief that what God has done in Jesus engages Jews as Jews and Gentiles as Gentiles. . . .
>
> The church, for its part, should repent of having turned its back upon the original determination of the Council of Jerusalem, where the Jewish obligation to maintain Jewish identity was universally presupposed. (*The God of Israel and Christian Theology*, 170–71)

81. In this regard, see Mark S. Kinzer's balanced work, *Postmissionary Messianic Judaism: Redefining Christian Engagement with the Jewish People* (Grand Rapids: Brazos Press, 2005).

82. See Menachem Elon, *Jewish Law: History, Sources, Principles*, trans. Bernard Auerbach and Melvin J. Sykes, vol. 1 (Philadelphia: Jewish Publication Society, 1994), 190–207.

83. Paul generally seeks unity of faith amidst diversity of election. Consequently he exhorts believers in Rome, both Jew and Gentile: "May the God of endurance and encouragement grant you to live in such *harmony* with one another, in accord with Christ Jesus, that *together* you many with *one voice* glorify the God and Father of our Lord Jesus Christ" (15:5–6; cf. 1:16; 2:9f.; 3:29f.; 4:11f.; 6:15; 9:30f.; 10:12; 11:13f.; 14:5; 15:1). This exhortation is based upon the reality that "Christ became a servant to the *circumcised* to show God's truthfulness, in order *to confirm the promises given to the patriarchs*, and in order that the *Gentiles* might glorify God for his mercy" (vv. 8–9). The distinction between Jew and Gentile (and their respective callings) is here plainly assumed, and Paul goes on to quote Ps. 18:49; Deut. 32:43; Ps. 117:1; and Isa. 11:10, all of which prophesy Jew and Gentile worshiping together under a common messianic Lord in the age to come (cf. Isa. 2:2–4; Dan. 7:14; Rev. 21:24), thus substantiating the present exhortation to unity amidst diversity.

84. Thus Jerusalem is "the center of Old Testament eschatology"; see Donald E. Gowan, *Eschatology in the Old Testament*, 2nd ed. (London: T & T Clark, 2000), esp. 4–20.

85. Note the salvific arrangement and hierarchy that is assumed in Jesus' statement: "Do not take an oath at all, either *by heaven*, for it is the throne of God, or *by the earth*, for it is his footstool, or *by Jerusalem*, for it is the city of the great King" (Matt. 5:35).

86. Though its exact location is disputed and has varied historically; see J. D. Levenson, "Zion Traditions," *ABD*, 6:1098–1102; and Bargil Pixner, *Paths of the Messiah: Messianic Sites in Galilee and Jerusalem*, ed. Rainer Riesner (San Francisco: Ignatius Press, 2010), 320–22.

87. This is in fact the general tenor of the Psalms, as summarized in Psalm 2. "It is worthwhile to re-emphasize that this psalm appears to have been set together with Psalm 1 as an introduction to the entire Psalter. As a result the theme of how Yhwh's *mashiah* will conquer all opposition and rule the world from Zion must be considered as one of the broad, overarching themes of the Psalms, in whose light all the ensuing lyrics, including the royal psalms, should be interpreted" (David C. Mitchell, *The Message of the Psalter: An Eschatological Programme in the Book of Psalms* [Sheffield, England: Sheffield Academic, 1997], 245).

88. So McClain notes the earth's Jerusalocentric geography: "Certainly, if there is ever to be a Kingdom of God on earth, no more appropriate place for its world center could be found than the place hallowed by the sacred memories of the One who there suffered and died for the sins of the world. Furthermore, in this ancient city we have literally the crossroads of the world, joining the three great continents of Africa, Asia, and Europe. Ezekiel speaks appropriately of the location as the 'navel of the earth' (38:12, ASV margin)" (*Greatness of the Kingdom*, 230).

89. On the intertestamental view of the New Jerusalem, see esp. Tobit 13:16–18; 14:5; 4 Ezra 8:52; 10:27–59; *1 Enoch* 90:28–29; *2 Baruch* 4:2–4; 32:2–4.

90. So Gregory Beale comments concerning the "new" heavens and earth, "The allusions to Isaiah . . . in 21:1, 4–5 probably understand Isaiah as prophesying the transformation of the old creation rather than an outright new creation *ex nihilo*. . . . Indeed, καινός ('new'), as we have seen, refers predominantly to a change in quality or essence rather than something new that has never previously been in existence. This usage of καινός is especially found in NT contexts describing eschatological or redemptive-historical transitions" (*The Book of Revelation*, NIGTC [Grand Rapids: Eerdmans, 1999], 1040). The same logic applies to the "new" Jerusalem (though Beale strangely rejects this: "The image of the city is probably figurative, representing the fellowship of God with his people in an actual new creation" [ibid., 1045]).

91. See 1 Maccabees 13:51; 2 Maccabees 10:7; 14:4; see also W. R. Farmer, "The Palm Branches in John 12:13," *JTS* 3 (1952): 62–66.

92. The nature and purpose of biblical typology will be discussed further in chapter 7.

93. Thus the Davidic coronation banquet is also a "proleptic enjoyment of the eschatological banquet in the afterlife," i.e., the messianic banquet: "This tradition is reflected in the description of the victory/coronation banquet of David in 1 Chr 12:38–40, a passage with strong messianic overtones. Here, the warriors gather and celebrate with their new king, the prototype of the Messiah. The nations come bearing gifts in tribute, and 'there was joy in Israel' (v 40). This description reflects the form of the banquet of the end time, which is given a classic description in Isa 25:6–8" (Dennis E. Smith, "Messianic Banquet," *ABD*, 4:789). In like manner, "This suggests that one of the ways in which early Christians interpreted their communal meals (both Eucharist and agape) was as a messianic banquet being celebrated proleptically in the presence of the risen Lord" (ibid., 790).

94. Here it is important to point out that though the Davidic kingdom was of the same substance as the age to come, so to speak (cf. Heb. 2:4; 6:5), it was *not* the age to come, nor was it the messianic kingdom. The equation of the two, so critical to the dispensational schema, sees the church age as an "intercalation" between the OT kingdom of God and

the eschatological kingdom of God. It is believed that the kingdom of God existed substantially in Israel (though the timing of its inauguration is disputed) until the time of the exile and would be restored eschatologically; see Peters, *Theocratic Kingdom*, 1:207–49; Feinberg, *Premillennialism or Amillennialism*, 33–58; and McClain, *Greatness of the Kingdom*, 41–129.

95. For an overview of the complexities of this passage (Rom. 9:1–5), see Douglas J. Moo, *The Epistle to the Romans*, NICNT (Grand Rapids: Eerdmans, 1996), 555–68.

96. The Jewish stewardship of the law (cf. Acts 7:38; Rom. 3:2) seems to be the background of the apostolic "stewardship" of the gospel (1 Cor. 9:17; Col. 1:25), which is entrusted to Jew and Gentile alike, i.e., "servants of Christ and stewards of the mysteries of God" (1 Cor. 4:1), "approved by God to be entrusted with the gospel" (1 Thess. 2:4; cf. 2 Cor. 5:19; 1 Tim. 6:20; Titus 1:3).

97. See Colin Chapman, *Whose Promised Land? The Continuing Crisis over Israel and Palestine* (Grand Rapids: Baker, 2002); Stephen Sizer, *Christian Zionism: Road-map to Armageddon?* (Leicester: InterVarsity, 2004); and Gary M. Burge, *Whose Land? Whose Promise? What Christians Are Not Being Told about Israel and the Palestinians*, 2nd ed. (Cleveland: Pilgrim Press, 2013).

98. See Horner, *Future Israel*; and Vlach, *Has the Church Replaced Israel?*

99. Contrary to Burge's supersessionist conclusions after his vitriolic itemization of Israel's sins in *Whose Land?*, 135–64 (see also Chapman, *Whose Promised Land?*, 141–238).

100. See Dalton Lifsey, *The Controversy of Zion and the Time of Jacob's Trouble: The Final Suffering and Salvation of the Jewish People* (Tauranga, New Zealand: Maskilim Publishing, 2011).

101. 1 Kings 3:1; 6:1,37; 7:12,40,45,48,51; 8:10f.,63f.; 9:1,10,15; 10:5,12; 14:26,28; 15:15,18; 2 Kings 11:3f.,7,10,13,15,18f.; 12:4,9ff.,16,18; 14:14; 15:35; 16:8,14,18; 18:15; 19:1,14; 20:5,8; 21:4f.; 22:3ff.,8f.; 23:2,6f.,11f.,24; 24:13; 25:9,13,16; 1 Chron. 6:31f.; 9:23; 22:1,11,14; 23:4,24,28,32; 24:19; 25:6; 26:12,22,27; 28:12f.,20; 29:8; 2 Chron. 3:1; 4:16; 5:1,13; 7:2,7,11; 8:1,16; 9:4,11; 12:9,11; 15:8; 16:2; 20:5,28; 23:5f.,12,14,18ff.; 24:4,7f.,12,14,18,21; 26:19,21; 27:3; 28:21,24; 29:3,5,15ff.,20,25,31,35; 30:1,15; 31:10f.,16; 33:4f.,15; 34:8,10,14f.,17,30; 35:2; 36:7,10,14,18; Ezra 1:3,5,7; 2:68; 3:8,11; 7:27; 8:29; Neh. 10:35; Ps. 23:6; 27:4; 92:13; 116:19; 118:26; 122:1,9; 134:1; 135:2; Isa. 2:2; 37:1,14; 38:20,22; 66:20; Jer. 17:26; 20:1f.; 26:2,7,9f.; 27:18,21; 28:1,5f.; 29:26; 33:11; 35:2,4; 36:5,10; 52:13,17,20; Lam. 2:7; Ezek. 8:14,16; 10:19; 11:1; Hos. 8:1; 9:4; Joel 1:9,14; 3:18; Mic. 4:1; Hag. 1:2,14; Zech. 7:3; 8:9; 11:13; 14:20f. Note also the Mosaic tabernacle (Ex. 23:19; 34:26; Deut. 23:18; Josh. 6:24; Judg. 19:18; 1 Sam. 1:7,24; 3:15; 2 Sam. 12:20).

102. 1 Chron. 22:2; 23:28; 25:6; 26:20; 28:12,21; 29:7; 2 Chron. 3:3; 4:11,19; 5:1,14; 7:5; 15:18; 22:12; 23:3,9; 24:7,13,27; 25:24; 28:24; 31:13,21; 33:7; 34:9; 35:8; 36:18f.; Ezra 1:4; 2:68; 3:8f.; 4:24; 5:2,13ff.; 6:3,5,7f.,12,16f.,22; 7:24; 8:36; 10:1,6,9; Neh. 6:10; 8:16; 11:11,16,22; 12:40; 13:7,9,11; Ps. 42:4; 52:8; Eccl. 5:1; Dan. 1:2; 5:3; Matt. 12:4; Mark 2:26; Luke 6:4. Likewise in reference to the Mosaic tabernacle (Judg. 18:31; 1 Chron. 6:48; 9:11,13,26f.).

103. Similarly, the apocryphal book of Sirach says, "Have mercy, O Lord, on the people called by your name, on Israel, whom you have named *your firstborn*, Have pity on the city of *your sanctuary*, Jerusalem, the place of *your dwelling*. Fill Zion with your majesty, and *your temple* with your glory. Bear witness to those whom you created in the beginning, and fulfill the prophecies spoken in your name" (36:17–20, NRSV).

And again the apocryphal book of Tobit:

But God will again have mercy on them, and God will bring them back into the land of Israel; and they will *rebuild the temple of God*, but not like the first one until the period when the times of fulfillment shall come. After this they all will return from their exile and will rebuild Jerusalem in splendor; and in it *the temple of God will be rebuilt*, just as the prophets of Israel have said concerning it. Then the nations in the whole world will all be converted and worship God in truth. They will all abandon their idols, which deceitfully have led them into their error; and in righteousness they will praise the eternal God. (14:5–7, NRSV)

104. The eschatological context of this passage is set in the preceding chaps. (54–55) and is confirmed in v. 1, "Maintain justice and do what is right, for my salvation is close at hand and my righteousness will soon be revealed" (NIV).

105. See John W. Schmitt and J. Carl Laney, *Messiah's Coming Temple: Ezekiel's Prophetic Vision of the Future Temple*, 2nd ed. (Grand Rapids: Kregel, 2014).

106. Many complain about the preservation of a Jewish priesthood, especially in the age to come, yet why should such a distinction be offensive? Akin to the delineation between God and humanity, male and female, Jew and Gentile, etc., God ordained Levitical and priestly roles for the shared benefit of all (Num. 6:22–27; Deut. 21:5; 1 Chron. 23:13), in keeping with Soulen's theology of mutual blessing:

> Significantly, the Scriptures consistently portray the Lord's blessing in inextricable connection with relations of difference and mutual dependence among God's creatures. In the primeval sagas (Gen 1–11), God's blessing is connected with difference and mutual dependence within the natural world. This is evident in the relation of the human family and the rest of the created realm, and then again within the human family itself in the relations of male and female, of parents and children, of one generation and the next. In the sphere of covenant history (Gen 12 and forward), God's blessing is connected with the difference and mutual dependence of Abraham and Sarah's chosen children and all the other families, clans, and nations of the earth. *God's work as Consummator, it seems, consistently presupposes and entails economies of mutual blessing between those who are different.* . . .
>
> Difference and mutual dependence are not extrinsic to the supreme good that God appoints for creation but are "intrinsic to the goal itself." The Lord's blessing is available only through the blessing of an other. (*The God of Israel and Christian Theology*, 116–17; italics in the original)

107. The issue of the sacrifices in the age to come (as seen in v. 18, "to burn grain offerings, and to make sacrifices forever") has a long history of contentious debate, with proponents viewing them as a "memorial" (cf. John L. Mitchell, "The Question of Millennial Sacrifices, Part 1," *BSac* 110, no. 439 [July 1953]: 248–67; Mitchell, "The Question of Millennial Sacrifices, Part 2," *BSac* 110, no. 440 [October 1953]: 342–61; and Pentecost, *Things to Come*, 517–31) and critics dismissing them as typologically obsolete (cf. Allis, *Prophecy and the Church*; and Curtis Crenshaw, *Dispensationalism Today, Yesterday, and Tomorrow* [Memphis: Footstool, 1989]). At the heart of the debate is the efficacy of the atonement (cf. Ezek. 45:15,17,20). Those who reject a sacrificial system in the age to come do so based upon a typological interpretation of OT sacrifices, which places them in a difficult hermeneutical position concerning the actual efficacy of OT sacrifices (cf. Lev. 1:4; 4:20; etc.). The answer seems to lie in delineating between the purification of the flesh vs. purification of the conscience (cf. Acts 13:39; Heb. 9:13ff.) in the context of a *transitional messianic age* wherein death and sin still exist (see Jerry M. Hullinger, "The Problem of Animal Sacrifices in Ezekiel 40–48," *BSac* 152, no. 607 [July 1995]: 279–89).

108. G. J. Wenham notes,

> דבע "to serve, till" is a very common verb and is often used of cultivating the soil ([Gen.] 2:5; 3:23; 4:2,12, etc.). The word is commonly used in a religious sense of serving God (e.g., Deut 4:19), and in priestly texts, especially of the tabernacle duties of the Levites (Num 3:7–8; 4:23–24,26, etc.). Similarly, רמש "to guard, to keep" has the simple profane sense of "guard" ([Gen.] 4:9; 30:31), but it is even more commonly used in legal texts of observing religious commands and duties ([Gen.] 17:9; Lev 18:5) and particularly of the Levitical responsibilities for guarding the tabernacle from intruders (Num 1:53; 3:7–8). It is striking that here and in the priestly law these two terms are juxtaposed (Num 3:7–8; 8:26; 18:5–6), another pointer to the interplay of tabernacle and Eden symbolism already noted (cf. *Ber. Rab.* 16:5). (*Genesis 1–15*, WBC [Dallas: Word, 1998], 67)

109. When John "saw no temple [Gk. *naos*] in the city, for its temple [Gk. *naos*] is the Lord God the Almighty and the Lamb" (Rev. 21:22), he was simply referencing the lack of a functional inner sanctuary, echoing Jer. 3:16–17: "In those days, declares the LORD, they shall no more say, 'The ark of the covenant of the LORD.' It shall not come to mind or be remembered or missed; it shall not be made again. At that time Jerusalem shall be called the throne of the LORD, and all nations shall gather to it, to the presence of the LORD in Jerusalem, and they shall no more stubbornly follow their own evil heart." In contrast to the temple complex as a whole (Gk. *hieron*), *naos* was commonly associated with the sanctuary (see "ναός," BDAG, 665–66; and "Temple," *NIDNTT*, 3:781–94).

110. Though ultimately arguing for a realization of "Jewish restoration eschatology," Michael F. Bird summarizes well the Jerusalocentric tenor of Jewish hope during the time of Jesus: "Generally speaking, the basic contours of Jewish restoration eschatology included the re-establishment of the twelve-tribes, the advent of a messianic figure (or figures) to defeat Israel's enemies and reign in righteousness, a new or purified temple, the establishment of pure worship and righteous people, the return of Yahweh to Zion, abundant prosperity, a renewed covenant and the subjugation or admission of the Gentiles" (*Jesus and the Origins of the Gentile Mission* [London: T & T Clark, 2007], 27).

111. See esp. E. P. Sanders, *Judaism: Practice and Belief, 63 BCE–66 CE* (London: SCM Press, 1992), chaps. 5–8; and Oskar Skarsaune, *In the Shadow of the Temple: Jewish Influences on Early Christianity* (Downers Grove, IL: InterVarsity, 2002). As N. T. Wright summarizes,

> The Temple was the focal point of every aspect of Jewish national life. Local synagogues and schools of Torah in other parts of Palestine, and in the Diaspora, in no way replaced it, but gained their significance from their implicit relation to it. . . .
>
> But the Temple was not simply the "religious" centre of Israel. . . . The Temple combined in itself the functions of all three—religion, national figurehead and government—and also included what we think of as the City, the financial and economic world. . . . When we study the city-plan of ancient Jerusalem, the significance of the Temple stands out at once, since it occupies a phenomenally large proportion (about 25%) of the entire city. Jerusalem was not, like Corinth for example, a large city with lots of little temples dotted here and there. It was not so much a city with a temple in it; more like a temple with a small city round it. (*The New Testament and the People of God* [London: SPCK, 1992], 224–25)

112. G. E. Wright, "The Significance of the Temple in the Ancient Near East," *BA* 7, no. 3 (September 1944): 43. G. Schrenk mentions "the general apostolic conception that the new temple is the new community," adding that "the temple is here an image of the

community which through Jesus becomes the temple after the destruction of the earthly sanctuary" ("τὸ ἱερόν," *TDNT*, 3:244, 247). The same basic logic drives Gregory Beale, *The Temple and the Church's Mission*, 169–393; N. T. Wright, *Jesus and the Victory of God* (London: SPCK, 1996), 489–528; Michael Bird, *Jesus and the Origins of the Gentile Mission*, 125–77; T. Desmond Alexander, *From Eden to the New Jerusalem*, 138–92; and T. Desmond Alexander and Simon Gathercole, eds., *Heaven on Earth: The Temple in Biblical Theology* (Carlisle, UK: Paternoster, 2004), chaps. 7ff.

113. Though relegating the temple to a subaltern Jewish plan of salvation, the modified dispensationalists at least preserve a place for a messianic temple in the age to come (see Walvoord, *Millennial Kingdom*, 309–15; Pentecost, *Things to Come*, 512–31; and McClain, *Greatness of the Kingdom*, 247–54).

114. So Sanders argues, "On what conceivable grounds could Jesus have undertaken to attack—and symbolize the destruction of—what was ordained by God? The obvious answer is that destruction, in turn, looks towards restoration. . . . Thus we conclude that Jesus publicly predicted or threatened the destruction of the temple, that the statement was shaped by his expectation of the arrival of the eschaton, that he probably also expected a new temple to be given by God from heaven, and that he made a demonstration which prophetically symbolized the coming event" (Sanders, *Jesus and Judaism*, 71, 75).

  Though criticism of Sanders' approach is manifold (esp. his gratuitous form criticism and his Schweitzerian conclusion that "Jesus was a visionary who was mistaken about the immediately future course of events," p. 327), he does argue convincingly for the centrality of the temple to first-century Judaic life and the common expectation for a messianic temple (cf. pp. 61–90).

115. This rests upon the larger assumption that Israel's calling by God has not been superseded in the NT. In spite of the clear apostolic declaration that "the gifts and the calling of God are irrevocable" (Rom. 11:29), many hold to the idea that one generation's rebellion abrogates the entire covenantal framework of the OT. Take Ladd, for example:

  The rejection of the Kingdom meant judgment for Israel as a nation in history. . . . The temple would be forsaken by God (Matt. 23:38 = Luke 13:35), razed to the ground (Mark 13:2), the city destroyed (Luke 21:20–24). Because Israel rejected the Kingdom, God has rejected the nation and will choose others to be the people of his vineyard (Mark 12:9). In view of the fact that Jesus saw his disciples as the true Israel, the secondary Matthean saying that God will take the Kingdom from Israel and give it to another people (Matt. 21:43) is a correct interpretation. (George E. Ladd, *The Presence of the Future: The Eschatology of Biblical Realism* [Grand Rapids: Eerdmans], 1974, 321–22; italics in the original)

116. Note how in Rom. 11:13–15 Paul ultimately relates his ministry to the Gentiles unto the greater Jewish narrative: "Now I am speaking to you Gentiles. Inasmuch then as I am an apostle to the Gentiles, I magnify my ministry in order somehow *to make my fellow Jews jealous*, and thus save some of them. For if *their rejection* means the reconciliation of the world, what will *their acceptance* mean but life from the dead?" A similar logic of Jewish centricity lies behind Paul's exhortation to the Gentiles in Rome: "Macedonia and Achaia have been pleased to make some contribution for the poor among the saints at Jerusalem. For they were pleased to do it, and indeed *they owe it to them*. For if the Gentiles have come to share in their spiritual blessings, they ought also to be of service to them in material blessings" (Rom. 15:26–27). The Jewish narrative, with the temple at its center, remains true and unchanged throughout the NT.

117. Likewise Peter was not supplanting the temple when he referred to believers being "built up as a spiritual house, to be a holy priesthood, to offer spiritual sacrifices acceptable to

God through Jesus Christ" (1 Peter 2:5). He was simply referencing the ultimate purpose of the temple, i.e., "that you may proclaim the excellencies of him who called you out of darkness into his marvelous light" (v. 9). To read supersessionism into these verses is akin to reading Jesus' rejection of the Decalogue into his command not to hate, lust, covet, etc. (cf. Matt. 5:17–42).

118. It is generally agreed that there is no real pre-Pauline support for the temple-supersession view—e.g., "It is only from the time of Paul that we have certain evidence for the conception" (G. Schrenk, "τὸ ἱερόν," *TDNT*, 3:247).

119. Contrary to Beale's conclusion: "This expectation of a nonliteral temple is, for the most part, a break with Judaism, which consistently affirmed the hope of a final, material temple structure on a scale greater than any before. . . . These Jewish precursors [cf. Qumranic] are parallel to the early Christian hope, which went further and saw God and the Messiah as definitively replacing the temple" (*Revelation*, NIGTC, 1091–92).

120. Contrary to G. E. Ladd: "While the New Testament clearly affirms the salvation of literal Israel, it does not give any details about the day of salvation. . . . As we have already pointed out, New Testament exegesis (Hebrews 8) makes it difficult to believe that the Old Testament prophecies about the 'millennial temple' will be fulfilled literally. They are fulfilled in the New Covenant established in the blood of Jesus. . . . So a nondispensational eschatology simply affirms the future salvation of Israel and remains open to God's future as to the details" ("Historic Premillennialism," in *The Meaning of the Millennium*, ed. Robert Clouse [Downers Grove, IL: InterVarsity, 1977], 28).

Can't a "nondispensational eschatology" (i.e., non-dualistic soteriology) hold to "the salvation of literal Israel" without jettisoning the very heart of Jewish messianic expectation?

121. As N. T. Wright summarizes, "'Day of ʏʜᴡʜ,' 'Kingdom of God,' victory over evil and pagan rulers, rescue of Israel, end of exile, the coming of the Messiah, the new Exodus, and the return of ʏʜᴡʜ himself; and, in and through all of this, the resurrection of the dead. This is the combination of themes which characterizes the first-century Jewish expectation of the future" (*Paul: Fresh Perspectives* [London: SPCK, 2005], 135; cf. Wright, *Jesus and the Victory of God*, 615–31).

Unfortunately, Wright goes on to "rethink," "rework," "redefine," and "reimagine" this eschatology as spiritually fulfilled/realized in the first coming (*Paul*, 135–50; cf. *Jesus and the Victory of God*, 631–53). This is all much akin to Albert Schweitzer's original conclusion: "The Messianic secret of Jesus is the basis of Christianity, since it involves the de-nationalising and the spiritualisation of Jewish eschatology" (*The Quest of the Historical Jesus: A Critical Study of Its Progress from Reimarus to Wrede*, trans. W. Montgomery, 2nd ed. [London: A. & C. Black, 1911], 283).

122. Referencing the "Asiatic theory" concerning the locus of chiliasm in the early church (Asia Minor being a stronghold of chiliasm against the spiritualizing tendencies of the Alexandrian school); see Martin Erdmann, *The Millennial Controversy in the Early Church* (Eugene, OR: Wipf and Stock Publishers, 2005).

123. As discussed in chapter 3, I refrain from using the categories of pre-, post-, and a-millennialism since they lead to more confusion than clarity, as seen in Darrell L. Bock, ed., *Three Views on the Millennium and Beyond* (Grand Rapids: Zondervan, 1999).

124. For a comprehensive analysis of this passage from a chiliastic point of view, see Wilber B. Wallis, "The Problem of an Intermediate Kingdom in I Corinthians 15:20–28," *JETS* 18, no. 4 (Fall 1975): 229–42.

125. See a survey in D. S. Russell, *The Method and Message of Jewish Apocalyptic: 200 BC–AD 100* (Philadelphia: Westminster, 1964), 285–97.

126. See G. E. Ladd, *A Commentary on the Revelation of John* (Grand Rapids: Eerdmans, 1972), 259–74; Ladd, *Crucial Questions about the Kingdom of God*, 133–50; and Jack S. Deere, "Premillennialism in Revelation 20:4–6," *BSac* 135, no. 537 (January 1978): 58–74. The oft-quoted words of Henry Alford deserve repeating: "If, in a passage where two resurrections are mentioned, where certain *psychai ezēsan* ["souls came to life"] at the first, and the rest of the *nekroi ezēsan* ["dead came to life"] only at the end of a specified period after that first,—if in such a passage the first resurrection may be understood to mean *spiritual* rising with Christ, while the second means *literal* rising from the grave;—then there is an end of all significance in language, and Scripture is wiped out as a definite testimony to anything" (*The Greek Testament*, vol. 4 [Boston: Lee and Shepard, 1872], 732).

127. See E. Lohse, "χιλιάς, χίλιοι," *TDNT*, 9:466–71; cf. E. Lohse, "The Cosmic Week and Cosmic Sabbath," *TDNT*, 7:19–20); and Jean Daniélou, *The Theology of Jewish Christianity: The Development of Christian Doctrine before the Council of Nicea* (London: Darton, Longman & Todd, 1964), 396–404.

128. Note also the references to the "millennial banquet" in *Testament of Isaac* 6.13,22; 8.10 (*OTP*, 1:910–11); cf. Matt. 8:11; 22:2; Luke 14:24; Rev. 19:9.

129. So ends *Life of Adam and Eve*: "After this [the death of Eve], all her children buried her with great weeping. Then, when they had mourned for four days, the archangel Michael appeared to them and said to Seth, 'Man of God, do not prolong mourning your dead more than six days, because the seventh day is a sign of the resurrection, the rest of the coming age, and on the seventh day the LORD rested from all his works.' Then Seth made the tablets" (51.1–3 [*OTP*, 2:294]).

130. The pseudepigraphic *2 Enoch* contains short titles for each chapter, and the chapters are sometimes referred to (in the original manuscripts) as a "word":

> After Adam's transgression. God expels him into the earth from which he had been taken. But he does not wish to destroy him in the age to come. Word "28."
>
> "And I said to him, 'You are earth, and into the earth once again you will go, out of which I took you. And I will not destroy you, but I will send you away to what I took you from. Then I can take you once again at my second coming.' And I blessed all my creatures, visible and invisible. And Adam was in paradise for 5 hours and a half. And I blessed the 7th day which is the sabbath in which I rested from all my doings."
>
> God shows Enoch the epoch of this world, the existence of 7000 years, and the eighth thousand is the end, neither years nor months nor weeks nor days. Word "29."
>
> "On the 8th day I likewise appointed, so that the 8th day might be the 1st, the first-created of my week, and that it should revolve in the revolution of 7000; so that the 8000 might be in the beginning of a time not reckoned and unending, neither years, nor months, nor weeks, nor days, nor hours like the first day of the week, so also that the eighth day of the week might return continually."
> (*2 Enoch* 32.1–33.2 [*OTP*, 1:154)

131. *OTP*, 1:426.

132. *OTP*, 2:63–64; italics added.

133. In regard to Adam and his sons returning to the dust, I assume that Moses received the millennial idea by tradition handed down to him (rather than by revelation given directly from God)—and furthermore, that this tradition was based upon real events concerning Adam's death.

134. Whether Peter was quoting this as a timing indicator or just as a generic justification for God's delaying of the day of the Lord is debatable. The early church worked off the

chronology of the LXX (though variations exist between manuscripts), which is approx. 1500 years ahead of the Masoretic Text (MT). Thus the first-century church would have seen Christ's birth c. 5500 AM (Latin *Anno Mundi*, "in the year of the world") based on the LXX, versus c. 4000 AM in the MT (cf. M. Cogan, "Chronology: Hebrew Bible," *ABD*, 1:1002–10; and J. N. Oswalt, "Chronology of the OT," *ISBE*, 673–85). For example, Hippolytus:

> Since, then, in SIX days God made all things, it follows that 6,000 years must be fulfilled. And they are not yet fulfilled, as John [in Revelation] says: "five are fallen; one is," that is, the sixth; "the other is not yet come."
>
> In mentioning the "other," moreover, he specifies the seventh, in which there is rest. But some one may be ready to say, How will you prove to me that the Saviour was born in the year 5500? Learn that easily, O man. . . .
>
> From the birth of Christ, then, we must reckon the 500 years that remain to make up the 6000, and thus the end shall be. (*Commentary on Daniel*, 2.4–6 [*ANF*, 5:179])

Hence "The Christians had believed firmly that Jesus Christ would rise again soon after the world entered the sabbatical millennium. The larger the age of the world, the sooner appeared the New Age. Christian chronographers, therefore, beginning with Clement of Alexandria, Judas, Julius Africanus, Hippolytus, and Eusebius, accepted the Septuagint version as authentic" (Ben Zion Wacholder, "Biblical Chronology in the Hellenistic World Chronicles," *HTR* 61, no. 3 [July 1968]: 453).

By the time the MT was adopted and used in Jerome's translation of the Latin Vulgate (c. 405), chiliasm had been largely abandoned. On second-temple chronography, see Wacholder, "The Calendar of Sabbatical Cycles During the Second Temple and the Early Rabbinic Period," *Hebrew Union College Annual* 44 (1973): 53–196; and Wacholder, "Chronomessianism: The Timing of Messianic Movements and the Calendar of Sabbatical Cycles," *Hebrew Union College Annual* 46 (1975): 201–18. For a general introduction to biblical chronography, see Jack Finegan, *Handbook of Biblical Chronology: Principles of Time Reckoning in the Ancient World and Problems of Chronology in the Bible*, rev. ed. (Peabody, MA: Hendrickson, 1998).

135. "An eschatological understanding of 'my rest' in Ps 95:11 is presupposed in [Heb. 4:1] and is fundamental to the exhortation to diligence to enter God's rest in 4:1–11. It is possible that the hearers were already familiar with this concept through their past association with the hellenistic Jewish synagogue. The principle that unbelief invited exclusion from God's rest (3:19) remains valid in the present and assumes profound significance when rest is understood in this eschatological sense" (William L. Lane, *Hebrews 1–8*, WBC [Dallas: Word, 1998], 98).

136. For an excellent overview of the progression of chiliastic thought in the early church, see Hans Bietenhard, "The Millennial Hope in the Early Church," *Scottish Journal of Theology* 6, no. 1 (1953): 12–30.

137. *The Epistle of Barnabas*, chapter 15:

> The Sabbath is mentioned at the beginning of the creation thus: "And God made in six days the works of His hands, and made an end on the seventh day, and rested on it, and sanctified it." Attend, my children, to the meaning of this expression, "He finished in six days." This implieth that the Lord will finish all things in six thousand years, for a day is with Him a thousand years. And He Himself testifieth, saying, "Behold, to-day will be as a thousand years." Therefore, my children, in six days, that is, in six thousand years, all things will be finished. "And He rested on the seventh day." This meaneth: when His Son, coming again, shall destroy

the time of the wicked man, and judge the ungodly, and change the sun, and the moon, and the stars, then shall He truly rest on the seventh day. (*ANF*, 1:146)

138. Justin Martyr, *Dialogue with Trypho*, chapter 81:

"For Isaiah spake thus concerning this space of a thousand years: 'For there shall be the new heaven and the new earth, and the former shall not be remembered, or come into their heart.' . . . For as Adam was told that in the day he ate of the tree he would die, we know that he did not complete a thousand years. We have perceived, moreover, that the expression, 'The day of the Lord is as a thousand years,' is connected with this subject. And further, there was a certain man with us, whose name was John, one of the apostles of Christ, who prophesied, by a revelation that was made to him, that those who believed in our Christ would dwell a thousand years in Jerusalem; and that thereafter the general, and, in short, the eternal resurrection and judgment of all men would likewise take place." (*ANF*, 1:239–40)

139. Irenaeus, *Against Heresies*, 5.28.3:

For in as many days as this world was made, in so many thousand years shall it be concluded. And for this reason the Scripture says: "Thus the heaven and the earth were finished, and all their adornment. And God brought to a conclusion upon the sixth day the works that He had made; and God rested upon the seventh day from all His works." This is an account of the things formerly created, as also it is a prophecy of what is to come. For the day of the Lord is as a thousand years; and in six days created things were completed: it is evident, therefore, that they will come to an end at the sixth thousand year. (*ANF*, 1:557)

140. Commodianus, *Instructions*, chapter 35:

Adam was the first who fell, and that he might shun the precepts of God, Belial was his tempter by the lust of the palm tree. And he conferred on us also what he did, whether of good or of evil, as being the chief of all that was born from him; and thence we die by his means, as he himself, receding from the divine, became an outcast from the Word. We shall be immortal when six thousand years are accomplished. The tree of the apple being tasted, death has entered into the world. By this tree of death we are born to the life to come. (*ANF*, 4:209)

And Commodianus concludes, "This has pleased Christ, that the dead should rise again, yea, with their bodies; and those, too, whom in this world the fire has burned, when six thousand years are completed, and the world has come to an end" (ch. 80 [*ANF*, 4:218]).

141. Hippolytus, *Commentary on Daniel*, 2.4:

For as the times are noted from the foundation of the world, and reckoned from Adam, they set clearly before us the matter with which our inquiry deals. For the first appearance of our Lord in the flesh took place in Bethlehem, under Augustus, in the year 5500; and He suffered in the thirty-third year. And 6,000 years must needs be accomplished, in order that the Sabbath may come, the rest, the holy day "on which God rested from all His works." For the Sabbath is the type and emblem of the future kingdom of the saints, when they "shall reign with Christ," when He comes from heaven, as John says in his Apocalypse: for "a day with the Lord is as a thousand years." Since, then, in six days God made all things, it follows that 6,000 years must be fulfilled. (*ANF*, 5:179)

142. Methodius, *Extracts from the Work on Things Created*, 9:

But if any one should prefer to differ in these points, let him first say, whether a period of time be not easily reckoned from the creation of the world, according to the Book of Moses, to those who so receive it, the voice of prophecy here proclaiming: "Thou art God from everlasting, and world without end.... For a thousand years in Thy sight are but as yesterday: seeing that is past as a watch in the night." For when a thousand years are reckoned as one day in the sight of God, and from the creation of the world to His rest is six days, so also to our time, six days are defined, as those say who are clever arithmeticians. Therefore, they say that an age of six thousand years extends from Adam to our time. For they say that the judgment will come on the seventh day, that is in the seventh thousand years. (*ANF*, 6:381)

143. Lactantius, *Epitome of the Divine Institutes*, chapter 70:

But since the things which have been spoken concerning the end of the world and the conclusion of the times are innumerable, those very things which are spoken are to be laid down without adornment, since it would be a boundless task to bring forward the testimonies. If any one wishes for them, or does not place full confidence in us, let him approach to the very shrine of the heavenly letters, and being more fully instructed through their trustworthiness, let him perceive that the philosophers have erred, who thought either that this world was eternal, or that there would be numberless thousands of years from the time when it was prepared. For six thousand years have not yet been completed, and when this number shall be made up, then at length all evil will be taken away, that justice alone may reign. (*ANF*, 7:253)

144. Though he "once held this opinion," Augustine argues against the chiliastic position, describing it as such:

Those who, on the strength of this passage [cf. Rev. 20:1–6], have suspected that the first resurrection is future and bodily, have been moved, among other things, specially by the number of a thousand years, as if it were a fit thing that the saints should thus enjoy a kind of Sabbath-rest during that period, a holy leisure after the labors of the six thousand years since man was created, and was on account of his great sin dismissed from the blessedness of paradise into the woes of this mortal life, so that thus, as it is written, "One day is with the Lord as a thousand years, and a thousand years as one day," there should follow on the completion of six thousand years, as of six days, a kind of seventh-day Sabbath in the succeeding thousand years; and that it is for this purpose the saints rise, viz., to celebrate this Sabbath. (*City of God*, 20.7.1 [*NPNF1*, 2:426])

145. For example, Irenaeus: "And there are some, again, who relegate the death of Adam to the thousandth year; for since 'a day of the Lord is as a thousand years,' he did not overstep the thousand years, but died within them, thus bearing out the sentence of his sin" (*Against Heresies*, 5.23.2 [*ANF*, 1:551]). Though uncommon in modern times, the interpretation of Gen. 2:17 as physical death within a millennial-day framework stands, contrary to Hamilton (NICOT), Mathews (NAC), Wenham (WBC), Sarna (JPSTC), and esp. Westermann (CC).

146. *Against Heresies*, 5.30.4 [*ANF*, 1:560]; italics added. See also, "These rewards for the righteous are to take place in the times of the kingdom, that is, upon the seventh day, which has been sanctified, in which God rested from all the works which He created, which is the true Sabbath of the righteous" (ibid., 5.33.2 [*ANF*, 1:562]).

147. It has been increasingly argued that chiliasm was not the dominant view of the early church (e.g., Charles E. Hill, *Regnum Caelorum: Patterns of Future Hope in Early Christianity*, 2nd ed. [Grand Rapids: Zondervan, 2001]). However, the basic thesis that

chiliasm appeared during the second century defies reason in light of so many NT (as well as Jewish intertestamental) references and allusions.

148. Stanley J. Grenz, *The Millennial Maze: Sorting Out Evangelical Opinions* (Downers Grove, IL: InterVarsity, 1992), 44.

149. On the interpretation of Revelation and the millennium during the Middle Ages, see Richard K. Emmerson and Bernard McGinn, eds., *The Apocalypse in the Middle Ages* (New York: Cornell University Press, 1992), 3–158; and Richard K. Emmerson, *Antichrist in the Middle Ages: A Study of Medieval Apocalypticism, Art, and Literature* (Seattle: University of Washington Press, 1981).

150. See Peter Toon, ed., *Puritans, the Millennium and the Future of Israel: Puritan Eschatology, 1600 to 1660* (Cambridge: James Clarke, 1970); see also the insightful overview of Puritan millenarianism by Richard W. Cogley, "The fall of the Ottoman Empire and the restoration of Israel in the 'Judeo-centric' strand of Puritan millenarianism," *Church History* 72, no. 2 (June 2003): 304–32.

151. See a summary in "Millenarianism," *The Oxford Dictionary of the Christian Church*, ed. F. L. Cross and E. A. Livingstone, 3rd rev. ed. (Oxford, New York: Oxford University Press, 2005), 1093–94; see also the fascinating populist account by J. F. C. Harrison, *The Second Coming: Popular Millenarianism 1780–1850* (New Brunswick, NJ: Rutgers University Press, 1979).

152. See Ernest R. Sandeen, *The Roots of Fundamentalism: British and American Millenarianism 1880–1930* (Chicago: University of Chicago, 1970); and T. P. Weber, *Living in the Shadow of the Second Coming: American Premillenialism 1875–1982*, enlarged ed. (Grand Rapids: Zondervan, 1983).

153. So concludes Robert K. Whalen, "Premillennialism," *The Encyclopedia of Millennialism and Millennial Movements*, ed. Richard A. Landes (New York: Routledge, 2000), 588.

154. *Dialogue with Trypho*, 80 (*ANF*, 1:239).

155. *On First Principles*, 2.3.7 (*ANF*, 4:275).

156. Ibid., 2.11.6 (*ANF*, 4:299).

157. Jacob Neusner and Bruce Chilton, *Jewish and Christian Doctrines: The Classics Compared* (New York: Routledge, 2000), 183; italics added.

158. See a historical survey in Craig A. Blaising, "Premillennialism," in *Three Views on the Millennium*, 162–92.

159. See György Heidl, *The Influence of Origen on the Young Augustine: A Chapter of the History of Origenism*, 2nd ed. (Piscataway, NJ: Gorgias Press, 2009). The great historian Norman Cohn summarized,

> The third century saw the first attempt to discredit millenarianism, when Origen, perhaps the most influential of all the theologians of the ancient Church, began to present the Kingdom as an event which would take place not in space or time but only in the souls of believers. For a collective, millenarian eschatology Origen substituted an eschatology of the individual soul. What stirred his profoundly Hellenic imagination was the prospect of spiritual progress begun in this world and continued in the next; and to this theme theologians were henceforth to give increasing attention. Such a shift in interest was indeed admirably suited to what was now an organized Church, enjoying almost uninterrupted peace and an acknowledged position in the world. When in the fourth century Christianity attained a position of supremacy in the Mediterranean world and became the official religion of the Empire, ecclesiastical disapproval

of millenarianism became emphatic. The Catholic Church was now a powerful and prosperous institution, functioning according to a well-established routine; and the men responsible for governing it had no wish to see Christians clinging to out-dated and inappropriate dreams of a new earthly Paradise. Early in the fifth century St Augustine propounded the doctrine which the new conditions demanded. According to *The City of God* the Book of Revelation was to be understood as a spiritual allegory; as for the Millennium, that had begun with the birth of Christianity and was fully realized in the Church. This at once became orthodox doctrine. (*The Pursuit of the Millennium: Revolutionary Millenarians and Mystical Anarchists of the Middle Ages*, 3rd ed. [Oxford: Oxford University Press, 1970], 29)

160. Grenz, *Millennial Maze*, 44.

161. *City of God*, 20.9.1 (*NPNF1*, 2:430).

162. Ibid., 22.11.1 (*NPNF1*, 2:492).

163. See a history of Reformed theology and its strict adherence to Augustinian eschatology in Horner, *Future Israel*, esp. 147–78.

164. For a highly critical yet comprehensive history of ecclesiastical abuse, Karlheinz Deschner, *Kriminalgeschichte des Christentums* [*The Criminal History of Christianity*, no English trans.], 10 vols. (Reinbek, Germany: Rowohlt Verlag, 1986–2013).

165. "It is a fact of history that the Augustinian concept of a Christian theocracy is closely linked with the anti-Semitic attitudes of the medieval church and unbelievably harsh treatment of the Jewish people. Thus it is not surprising that the traditional claim of Christendom to embody the promised messianic kingdom is an embarrassment to Christians involved in dialogue with Jewish people" (Diprose, *Israel and the Church*, 168).

166. For example, dominionist David Chilton concludes by resting the burden of restoration upon the church: "This world has tens of thousands, perhaps hundreds of thousands of years of increasing godliness ahead of it, before the Second Coming of Christ. . . . He has placed us into the great war for world history, with the absolute guarantee that we will win. Even if He has to make the whole universe stand still for us (Josh. 10:12–13), the day will last long enough for us to achieve victory. Time is on our side. The Kingdom has come, and the world has begun again. Now: Get to work" (David Chilton, *Paradise Restored: A Biblical Theology of Dominion* [Tyler, TX: Dominion Press, 1985], 221–22).

167. McClain, *Greatness of the Kingdom*, 438–39.

168. See *Scofield Reference Bible* (1909), 996, 1003, 1226; Chafer, *Systematic Theology*, 7:223–25; and Pentecost, *Things to Come*, 144.

169. See Peters, *Theocratic Kingdom*, 1:207–49; Feinberg, *Premillennialism or Amillennialism*, 33–58; and McClain, *Greatness of the Kingdom*, 41–129.

170. See Peters, *Theocratic Kingdom*, 1:375–91; Chafer, *Systematic Theology*, 4:265–67, 5:333–58; and McClain, *Greatness of the Kingdom*, 304–84.

171. To add to the confusion, between Pentecost and the second advent Christendom is also understood as the "mystery form" of theocracy and dominionistic sovereignty; see Chafer, *Systematic Theology*, 1:45 and 5:352; *Scofield Reference Bible* (1909), 1014; and J. Dwight Pentecost, *Thy Kingdom Come: Tracing God's Kingdom Program and Covenant Promises Throughout History* (Wheaton: Victor, 1990), esp. chaps. 19–20. So Chafer concludes, "The present conditions in Christendom are a mystery form of the kingdom. Since the kingdom of heaven is no other than the rule of God on the earth, He must now be ruling to the extent of full realization of those things which are termed 'the

mysteries' in the New Testament and which really constitute the new message of the New Testament" (*Systematic Theology*, 7:224).

172. George E. Ladd, *The Last Things* (Grand Rapids: Eerdmans, 1978), 47. The scholar Ladd refers to is Oscar Cullmann; see the illustration in *Christ and Time: The Primitive Christian Conception of Time and History*, trans. Floyd V. Filson (Philadelphia: Westminster, 1950), 84 and 145. See an updated presentation of Ladd's kingdom theology in Arthur F. Glasser, et al., *Announcing the Kingdom: The Story of God's Mission in the Bible* (Grand Rapids: Baker, 2003).

173. As Ladd often does. For example: "The Second Coming of Christ will mean nothing less than the disclosure to the world of the sovereignty and lordship which is already his. He is *now* the Lord; he is *now* reigning at the right hand of God. However, his present reign is seen only by the eye of faith. It is unseen and unrecognized by the world" ("Historic Premillennialism," in *The Meaning of the Millennium*, 32). On the contrary, we find throughout the NT that Jesus begins his messianic kingdom at his parousia (cf. Matt. 13:43; Luke 22:29f.; Acts 1:6; 1 Cor. 15:50; Eph. 5:5; 2 Tim. 4:1; 2 Peter 1:11; Rev. 11:15).

174. A point originally made by Johannes Weiss (*Jesus' Proclamation of the Kingdom of God*, 96–97), and recently reiterated by Stanley Toussaint: "If the kingdom began in the ministry of Christ, where is the prophesied judgment in the Gospels? Were the Old Testament prophets and John incorrect in their message? . . . After the prophesied judgment, the kingdom will come" ("Israel and the Church of a Traditional Dispensationalist," in *Three Central Issues in Contemporary Dispensationalism: A Comparison of Traditional and Progressive Views*, ed. Herbert W. Bateman IV [Grand Rapids: Kregel, 1999], 231–32). Unfortunately, Toussaint regresses to the old dispensational conclusions concerning a postponed kingdom and ecclesial parentheses.

175. Craig L. Blomberg, "A Response to G. R. Beasley-Murray on the Kingdom," *JETS* 35, no. 1 (March 1992): 32. Indeed, an even wider array might be included in the academic "consensus," e.g., Cullmann, Ridderbos, Hoekema, Waltke, Poythress, Bock, Fee, Carson, Schreiner, Beker, Dunn, Wright, etc. See also Ladd's baronial list in *Presence of the Future*, 38–39, n. 161.

176. See Elliott Johnson, Stanley Toussaint, Mike Stallard, Michael Vlach, Thomas Ice, Arnold Fruchtenbaum, etc.

177. Clayton Sullivan, *Rethinking Realized Eschatology* (Macon, GA: Mercer University Press, 1988), 65. See Sullivan's list of prominent liberal theologians who "believe the theory that accords best with New Testament evidence is the hypothesis that 'Kingdom of God' was Jesus' distinctive way of referring to this Golden Age for which first-century Jews were expectantly waiting" (ibid., 61).

178. Christopher Rowland, *Christian Origins: An Account of the Setting and Character of the Most Important Messianic Sect of Judaism*, 2nd ed. (London: SPCK, 2002), 133; italics added. See also Dale C. Allison, *Jesus of Nazareth: Millenarian Prophet* (Minneapolis: Fortress, 1998), 152–69.

179. Allison, *Jesus of Nazareth*, 169, n. 279. Sullivan describes it as a theological "bait-and-switch" maneuver between two different definitions of the kingdom:

> Proponents of this theory [inaugurationalism] always use the term *Kingdom* in the singular (not the plural). They do not say, "The Kingdoms were present and future." Rather they assert, "The Kingdom was present and future." This singular usage suggests that *Kingdom* has *one referent*, and that the *same referent* was both present and future. At this point the mediating theologians play a trick upon

themselves and upon others. They are guilty of an unrecognized language error (that is, *a shift in referents*). They fail to perceive that consistent eschatologists and realized eschatologists define the Kingdom of God *differently*. Both use the term *Kingdom* but they use *different referents*. For consistent eschatologists, the referent for Kingdom was the imminent Golden Age of Jewish eschatological hopes; for realized eschatologists its referent was the curative, exorcistic power operative in Jesus. To consistent eschatologists the Kingdom is a place; to realized eschatologists the Kingdom is a power. . . .

Once you and I recognize that Kingdom is assigned two different referents, we are then in a position to perceive that for years the mediating theologians have been allowed to get away with an unjustifiable "bait-and-switch" maneuver. They "bait" us with one conception of the Kingdom, that is, the conception of the Kingdom as a curative power that was present in Jesus. The mediating theologians (appealing to Matthew 12:28, Luke 11:20) look us in the eye and declare, "The Kingdom was present in Jesus' exorcisms." While still looking us in the eye and mesmerizing us with discussions on how *basileia* is to be understood in terms of *malkuth*, the mediating theologians go one step further and affirm, "And by the way, this Kingdom we have told you was present was also future." But in this future claim they abandon their bait's referent to the Kingdom (a curative power) and switch to an entirely different referent (the eschatological interpretation found in Johannes Weiss and Albert Schweitzer). This bait-and-switch maneuver is, I contend, a deceiving manipulation of language. The mediating theologians who use this bait-and-switch maneuver are like crafty Jacob about whom we read in Genesis. Jacob tried to combine his voice and Esau's hands. Yet Jacob's voice and Esau's hands did not belong together. Similarly, the mediating theologians try to combine Dodd's view of the Kingdom with Schweitzer's view of the Kingdom. But, like Jacob's voice and Esau's hands, these two views do not belong together; indeed, they contradict each other and cannot be juxtaposed as mediating theologians attempt to do.

Moreover, having conceded that a futuristic conception of the Kingdom is present in Jesus' teachings, the mediating theologians quietly abandon this awkward conception, allowing it to fade into oblivion. They subsequently switch back to the bait and focus on the conception of the Kingdom as a curative power present in Jesus' ministry. (*Rethinking Realized Eschatology*, 46–48; italics in the original)

180. Ibid., 60; see also chapter 1, n. 77; and Bart D. Ehrman, *Jesus: Apocalyptic Prophet of the New Millennium* (Oxford: Oxford University Press, 1999), 141–62.

181. So McClain declared concerning Schweitzer, who typifies modern liberalism: "It should go without saying that in no Biblical sense can Dr. Schweitzer be called a Christian, and his conclusion regarding our Lord and His Kingdom is an appalling thing" (*Greatness of the Kingdom*, 13).

182. See the discussion in Moltmann, *The Way of Jesus Christ*, 1–37.

183. Martin Buber, *Der Jude und sein Judentum* (*The Jew and His Jewishness*, no English trans.), Cologne, Germany: J. Melzer, 1963), 562; translated and quoted in Moltmann, *The Way of Jesus Christ*, 28–29; italics in the original. Note also the pointed declaration of Jewish scholar Schalom Ben-Chorin:

The Jew is profoundly aware of the unredeemed character of the world, and he perceives and recognizes no enclave of redemption in the midst of its unredeemedness. The concept of the redeemed soul in the midst of an unredeemed world is alien to the Jew, profoundly alien, inaccessible from the primal ground of his existence. This is the innermost reason for Israel's rejection of Jesus, not a merely external, merely national conception of messianism. In Jewish eyes, redemption means redemption from all evil. Evil of body and soul, evil in creation and civilization. So when we say redemption, we mean the whole of redemption. Between creation and redemption we know only one caesura: the revelation of God's will. (Ibid., 29)

184. This is the common claim of many inaugurationalists, who say a declaration concerning the futurity of the kingdom negates the activity of the Spirit in this age.

185. This was previously noted in Ladd's writings (chapter 3, n. 162). See the same general pattern in the writings of Dodd, Cullmann, Caird, Moltmann, Fee, etc.

186. As Chilton describes, "*The center of Christian reconstruction is the Church.* The River of Life does not flow out from the doors of the chambers of Congresses and Parliaments. It flows from the restored Temple of the Holy Spirit, the Church of Jesus Christ. Our goal is world dominion under Christ's lordship, a 'world takeover' if you will; but our strategy begins with the reformation and reconstruction of the Church. From that will flow social and political reconstruction, indeed a flowering of Christian civilization (Hag. 1:1–15; 2:6–9, 18–23)" (*Paradise Restored*, 214; italics in the original).

187. Everett Ferguson, "The Terminology of Kingdom in the Second Century," in *Studia Patristica*, ed. E. A. Livingstone, vol. XVII (Oxford: Pergamon Press, 1982), 670.

188. Ibid.

189. *Presence of the Future*, 243; cf. Benedict T. Viviano, *The Kingdom of God in History* (Wilmington, DE: Michael Glazier, 1988), 32–38.

190. Ibid., 245.

191. Traditionally dated to about 170, the Muratorian Fragment lists the four Gospels, Acts, thirteen epistles of Paul, Jude, two epistles of John, the Wisdom of Solomon, and the Johannine Apocalypse as divinely authoritative, thus revealing the formative nature of the second century to the NT canon. See F. F. Bruce, *The Canon of Scripture* (Downers Grove, IL: InterVarsity, 1988), chap. 12; and Bruce M. Metzger, *The Canon of the New Testament: Its Origin, Significance, and Development* (Oxford: Oxford University Press, 1987), 191–201.

Chapter Seven

1. John R. W. Stott notes,

   Crucifixion seems to have been invented by "barbarians" on the edge of the known world, and taken over from them by both Greeks and Romans. It is probably the most cruel method of execution ever practised, for it deliberately delayed death until maximum torture had been inflicted. The victim could suffer for days before dying. When the Romans adopted it, they reserved it for criminals convicted of murder, rebellion or armed robbery, provided that they were also slaves, foreigners or other non-persons. . . .

   So then, whether their background was Roman or Jewish or both, the early enemies of Christianity lost no opportunity to ridicule the claim that God's anointed and man's Savior ended his life on a cross. The idea was crazy. (*The Cross of Christ* [Downers Grove, IL: InterVarsity, 1986], 23–24)

2. See also the classic survey of crucifixion in the ancient world by Martin Hengel, *Crucifixion in the Ancient World and the Folly of the Message of the Cross*, trans. John Bowden (Philadelphia: Fortress, 1977).

3. So the suffering and glory of the Christ cannot be conflated. "Which texts does Jesus exegete for his companions? We are not told, but the implication with which Luke leaves us is that it does not matter. The pattern exemplified by Moses and the prophets is consummated in a Messiah who suffers. Likewise, all of the Scriptures have their fulfillment in a Messiah who suffers" (Joel B. Green, *The Gospel of Luke*, NICNT [Grand Rapids: Eerdmans, 1997], 848).

4. See Klaus Koch, *The Rediscovery of Apocalyptic*, trans. M. Kohl (London: SCM Press, 1972), 32. Again, such glory would have been understood eschatologically in light of the Prophets (cf. Isa. 11:10; 24:23; 35:2; 40:5; 60:1ff.; 66:18f.; Jer. 33:9; Ezek. 43:5; Dan. 7:14; Hab. 2:14), as reiterated throughout the NT (cf. Rom. 5:2; 8:18; 1 Cor. 15:40ff.; 2 Cor. 4:17; Eph. 1:18; Phil. 3:21; Col. 3:4; 2 Thess. 1:10; 2 Tim. 2:10; Titus 2:13; 1 Peter 4:13; 5:1; Jude 24; Rev. 21:11).

5. Unfortunately, this basic eschatological assumption is generally disregarded—cf. Green, *Luke*, NICNT, 848–49; John Nolland, *Luke 18:35–24:53*, WBC (Dallas: Word, 1998), 1204–5; I. Howard Marshall, *Gospel of Luke*, NIGTC (Exeter, England: Paternoster, 1978), 896–97; Leon Morris, *Luke*, TNTC (Downers Grove, IL: InterVarsity, 1988), 357–58; and François Bovon, *Luke 3: Commentary on 19:28–24:53*, Hermeneia (Minneapolis: Fortress, 2012), 374.

6. "These two sentences in Ps 110 (vss 1 and 4) are among the Jewish scriptural texts most often quoted or alluded to by early Christian writers. Thirty-three quotations and allusions are scattered through the NT, and seven more may be found in other Christian writings produced before the middle of the second century" (David M. Hay, *Glory at the Right Hand: Psalm 110 in Early Christianity* [Nashville: Abingdon, 1973], 15). See esp. the listing in Hay's appendix (pp. 163–66).

7. See a similar analysis of Psalm 110 in the NT by Robert L. Saucy, *The Case for Progressive Dispensationalism* (Grand Rapids: Zondervan, 1993), 69–76.

8. The Messiah's restraint from divine judgment is also related to his priestly ministry in v. 4: "You are a priest forever after the order of Melchizedek." Thus, he is "at the right hand of God . . . interceding for us" (Rom. 8:34), because he "lives to make intercession" (Heb. 7:25) for those who draw near to God.

9. "Ἐκδεχόμενος brings out the meaning of ἕως. It implies, not passive waiting, but eager expectation of the kind which the author recommends to his readers (cf. 11:10;

ἀπεκδέχομαι, 7:28); already the transition from teaching to paraenesis (vv. 19ff.) is anticipated" (Paul Ellingworth, *The Epistle to the Hebrews: A Commentary on the Greek Text*, NIGTC [Grand Rapids: Eerdmans, 1993], 510).

Note also the assumed "remaining time" of τὸ λοιπόν (cf. BDAG, 602), referencing the time until the day of the Lord and the subjection of the enemies of God, as also implied by the many eschatological references to "the Day" (10:25), "the judgment" (9:27), "the promised eternal inheritance" (9:15), and the second coming "to save those who are eagerly waiting for him" (9:28).

10. "Col 3.1–4 stresses the hiddenness of Christ's glory at present; and Mk 14.62 = Mt 26.64; Acts 7.55–56; and Heg [Hegesippus] (EH [Eusebius, *Ecclesiastical History*] 2.23.13) imply that his glory will remain concealed until his return. It is, therefore, a serious mistake to claim that early Christian references to Ps 110.1*b* regularly express convictions about Christ reigning as a royal lord in the present era" (Hay, *Glory at the Right Hand*, 91).

11. Of course this is not a passive waiting, but an active waiting, involving the dynamic pursuit of sinners by the Holy Spirit unto repentance. Indeed, all authority in heaven and on earth has been presently given to Jesus (cf. Matt. 28:18; Eph. 1:21; 1 Peter 3:22), but this authority is being administered in an amnestic manner, so to speak. Thus the delineation between "this age" and the "age to come" is maintained, for we yet await "the day of wrath when God's righteous judgment will be revealed" (Rom. 2:5; cf. Acts 10:42; 1 Cor. 4:5; 2 Tim. 4:1; Rev. 11:18).

12. See Stott, *Cross of Christ*, 145–49; Oscar Cullmann, *The Christology of the New Testament*, trans. S. C. Guthrie and C. A. M. Hall (Philadelphia: Westminster, 1963), 51–82; and Joachim Jeremias, *The Eucharistic Words of Jesus*, trans. Norman Perrin (London: SCM Press, 1966), 226–31.

13. "No other passage from the Old Testament was as important to the Church as Isa. 53, and for this reason no other passage has suffered as much from Jewish polemics" (Jeremias, *Eucharistic Words of Jesus*, 228).

14. On this verse as a summary of salvation history, see Joyce G. Baldwin, *Daniel: An Introduction and Commentary*, TOTC (Downers Grove, IL: InterVarsity, 1978), 168–69; and Stephen R. Miller, *Daniel*, NAC (Nashville: B&H Publishing, 1994), 259–62.

15. See John E. Goldingay, *Daniel*, WBC (Dallas: Word, 1998), 258–59; though in contradiction to Goldingay's presupposition of v. 24: "It does not have a worldwide perspective; it is not speaking of the end of all history, or of the sin of the whole world" (p. 258). So also in contradiction to his conclusion: "There is no reason to refer it exegetically to the first or second coming of Christ" (p. 260). True, "The concern of v 24 is thus Israel and Jerusalem" (p. 258), but the Jewish mind associated God's governance of the whole world (even the whole cosmos) through his dealings with Israel and Jerusalem.

16. Note that all other occurrences of Heb. *qōḏeš haqqoḏāšîm* ("most holy") reference the tabernacle or temple, and things associated with it (cf. Ex. 26:33f.; 29:37; 30:10,29; 40:10; Lev. 2:3,10; 7:1,6; 10:12,17; 14:13; 24:9; Num. 4:4,19; 18:9–10; 1 Kings 7:50; Ezra 2:63; Ezek. 42:13; 43:12; 44:13).

17. Though exegesis of this passage can easily break down into a "Dismal Swamp," as James Montgomery is known for saying (*A Critical and Exegetical Commentary on the Book of Daniel*, ICC [Edinburgh: T & T Clark, 1927], 400), a simple chronological approach culminating in the day of the Lord is assumed in the NT (cf. Matt. 24:4–31 and par.; 2 Thess. 2:1–8) and provides the surest exegetical footing. See also the ten "principle ingredients" of the passage in Kenneth L. Barker, "Premillennialism in the Book of Daniel," *The Master's Seminary Journal* 4, no. 1 (Spring 1993): 35–37.

18. The parallels to Isaiah 53 in these passages are striking and were no doubt derived from there (see Gary V. Smith, *Isaiah 40–66*, NAC [Nashville: B&H Publishing, 2009], 466).

19. Duane A. Garrett, *Hosea, Joel*, NAC (Nashville: B&H Publishing, 1997), 159.

20. So J. E. Alsup defines typology as "that form of biblical interpretation which deals with the correspondence between traditions concerning divinely appointed persons, events, and institutions, within the framework of salvation history" ("Typology," *ABD*, 6:682).

21. See Leonhard Goppelt, *Typos: The Typological Interpretation of the Old Testament in the New*, trans. Donald Madvig (Grand Rapids: Eerdmans, 1982); Richard M. Davidson, *Typology in Scripture: A Study of Hermeneutical Typos Structures* (Berrien Springs, MI: Andrews University Press, 1981). See a liberal discussion in Claus Westermann, ed., *Essays on Old Testament Hermeneutics* (Richmond: John Knox Press, 1963); and a conservative discussion in John S. Feinberg, ed., *Continuity and Discontinuity: Perspectives on the Relationship Between the Old and New Testaments* (Wheaton: Crossway, 1988). See also the Catholic works by A. J. Maas, *Christ in Type and Prophecy*, 2 vols. (New York: Benziger Brothers, 1893–95); and Jean Daniélou, *From Shadows to Reality: Studies in the Biblical Typology of the Fathers*, trans. Dom Wulstan Hibberd (London: Burns & Oates, 1960). For a summary of typology in modern evangelicalism, see W. Edward Glenny, "Typology: A Summary of the Present Evangelical Discussion," *JETS* 40, no. 4 (December 1997): 627–38.

22. So Patrick Fairbairn begins his two-volume classic on the subject: "The Typology of Scripture has been one of the most neglected departments of theological science. It has never altogether escaped from the region of doubt and uncertainty; and some still regard it as a field incapable, from its very nature, of being satisfactorily explored, or cultivated so as to yield any sure and appreciable results. Hence it is not unusual to find those who otherwise are agreed in their views of divine truth, and in the general principles of biblical interpretation, differing materially in the estimate they have formed of the Typology of Scripture" (*The Typology of Scripture: Viewed in Connection with the Whole Series of the Divine Dispensations*, 6th ed., vol. 1 [Edinburgh: T & T Clark, 1876], 17). Of course, we must reject Fairbairn's radically supersessionist and generally Platonic conclusions.

23. Goppelt overstates: "Typology is the method of interpreting Scripture that is predominant in the NT and characteristic of it" (*Typos*, 198). This ignores the multitude of literal references to the messianic suffering and eschatological glory.

24. See "τύπος," BDAG, 1020.

25. G. K. Beale and D. A. Carson, "Introduction," *Commentary on the New Testament Use of the Old Testament*, ed. G. K. Beale and D. A. Carson (Grand Rapids: Baker, 2007), xxvi.

26. Apart from discussions of redemptive history, typology is also used in the NT simply to convey an example or pattern. So Paul is a *tupos* for discipleship throughout the church (cf. Phil. 3:17; 2 Thess. 3:9); the Thessalonians are a *tupos* "to all the believers in Macedonia and in Achaia" (1 Thess. 1:7); and elders are to be a *tupos* "to the flock" (1 Peter 5:3). Similarly, the church has also received a *tupos* of good teaching, which should be universally imitated and replicated (cf. Rom. 6:17; 1 Tim. 4:12; 2 Tim. 1:13; Titus 2:7). Moreover, the earthly tabernacle was a "pattern" (*tupos*) of the heavenly tabernacle (Heb. 8:5, cf. Acts 7:44; 9:24), since the "heavenly archetype" had "its derivative construct on earth" (J. E. Alsup, "Typology," *ABD*, 6:683).

27. Likewise were Adam and Eden understood in second-temple Judaism: "The original paradisiacal condition of creation is used extensively as a pattern for depicting the blessed conditions in the messianic kingdom and the second aeon" (Goppelt, *Typos*, 33).

28. Commonly assumed in the NT, see e.g., Beale and Carson, *Commentary on the New Testament Use of the Old Testament*, 74, 416, 487, 503.

29. Though lacking a clear apocalyptic framework, Osborne's historical approach to typology is to be affirmed: "Events in the past are linked to those in the present, so that God's mighty deeds like the exodus or the return from exile foreshadow the experiences of God's present community, the church. This does not see a direct prophetic link but rather a correspondence in history, in which the current experience relives the past. God is immutable or consistent and acts today just as he did in the past, so typology seeks to identify the theological correspondence between those salvific actions in past and present" (Grant R. Osborne, *The Hermeneutical Spiral: A Comprehensive Introduction to Biblical Interpretation*, 2nd ed. [Downers Grove, IL: InterVarsity, 2006], 328).

30. Likewise, allegorical interpretation is useful, so long as it remains within an apocalyptic framework. The only explicit use of allegory (Gk. *allēgoreō*) in the NT is Gal. 4:24, whereby the two women who bore children to Abraham represent two future covenants, which in turn relate to two future cities—the "present Jerusalem" (v. 25) and the eschatological "Jerusalem above" (v. 26), which will descend giving birth to us (as "our mother") in the resurrection (cf. 4 Ezra 7:26; 9:38–10:59; *2 Enoch* 55:2; *2 Baruch* 4:2–6). Being based upon symbolism and metaphor, allegory is one step removed from redemptive history, whereas typology is based upon similar characteristics of similar entities within redemptive history. Both of these are subject to direct prophecy, which orchestrates redemptive history itself.

31. Cullmann, *Christology of the New Testament*, 56.

32. In this regard, see an excellent commentary by Raymond E. Brown, *The Death of the Messiah, from Gethsemane to the Grave: A Commentary on the Passion Narratives in the Four Gospels*, vol. 2 (New York: Doubleday, 1994), 1453–55.

33. Here we find the unraveling of a multitude of Gentile games revolving around realized eschatology. If the age to come has been realized, then the cross is no longer the standard of this age, and the sufferings of Christ are to be avoided. The logic is straightforward. Yet the apostolic witness cries out against such folly: "Already you have all you want! Already you have become rich! *Quite apart from us* you have become kings! . . . We are fools for the sake of Christ, but you are wise in Christ. We are weak, but you are strong. You are held in honor, but we in disrepute" (1 Cor. 4:8–10, nrsv).

34. See Baruch A. Levine, *Leviticus*, JPSTC (Philadelphia: Jewish Publication Society, 1989), 153–64.

35. By "years" it is assumed Paul is referencing the Sabbath year and Jubilee year. Every seventh year (Sabbath year), Israelite slaves were to be released (Ex. 21:2–6; Deut. 15:12–18), land was to lie fallow (Ex. 23:10–11; Lev. 25:1–7), and the debts of Israelites were to be suspended or cancelled (Deut. 15:1–6). In every fiftieth year (Jubilee year), property was to return to its original owner, Israelite slaves were to be freed, and the land was to lie fallow (Lev. 25:8–17,23–55).

36. On a theology of Sabbath, see esp. Abraham J. Heschel, *The Sabbath: Its Meaning for Modern Man* (New York: Farrar, Straus and Giroux, 1951).

37. Jürgen Moltmann summarizes, "The goal and completion of every Jewish and every Christian doctrine of creation must be the doctrine of the sabbath; for on the sabbath and through the sabbath God 'completed' his creation, and on the sabbath and through it, men and women perceive as God's creation the reality in which they live and which they themselves are. The sabbath opens creation for its true future. On the sabbath the redemption of the world is celebrated in anticipation. The sabbath is itself the presence of eternity in time, and a foretaste of the world to come" (*God in Creation: A New Theology of Creation and the Spirit of God*, trans. Margaret Kohl [Minneapolis: Fortress, 1993], 276).

38. Berndt Schaller, "Sabbath," *The Encyclopedia of Christianity*, ed. E. Fahlbusch and G. W. Bromiley, vol. 4 (Grand Rapids: Eerdmans, 2005), 790.

39. Before the destruction of the temple, these festivals were celebrated by pilgrimage to Jerusalem, and thus are often termed "pilgrimage festivals." Because most people went up to Jerusalem on foot, they also became known as the *Shalosh Regalim* (lit., "three feet"). See Ronald L. Eisenberg, "Pilgrimage Festivals," *The JPS Guide to Jewish Traditions* (Philadelphia: Jewish Publication Society, 2004), 155–57.

40. For a holistic presentation, see Evan Zuesse, "Calendar of Judaism," *The Encyclopedia of Judaism*, ed. J. Neusner, A. J. Avery-Peck, and W. S. Green, vol. 1 (Leiden, Netherlands: Brill, 2000), 32–50.

41. Zuesse describes,

> It thus is possible to see the annual festivals as moving in a three-fold spiral of temporal reference. . . . The third spiral pictures the events of the future and of final things, with the meanings of each festival contributing in logical sequence to the ultimate events: the coming of Elijah (suggested in Passover's cup of Elijah), which spurs a period of unification culminating in a renewal of Jewish faith (Shavuot), a time of apocalyptic woes and confusion (Seventeenth of Tamuz and the Ninth of Av; although Zech. 8:19 assures us that in those days the fast will be transformed into "gladness and cheerful feasts"), the final day of judgment (High Holidays), and the millennial blessings that follow (when all the nations shall come up to Jerusalem to celebrate Tabernacles, Zech. 14:16–19). ("Calendar of Judaism," 40)

42. Likewise the Messiah will fulfill the whole calendar which builds upon the Sabbath, as Moltmann describes (though of course Moltmann inaugurates this Sabbath at the first coming):

> It is only this messianic sabbath that will be "a sabbath without end" (Jub. 2:19–24). The new covenant is everlasting; and this sabbath will be everlasting too. In this sense the messianic sabbath of the world is the End-time correspondence of the original sabbath of God's creation. . . . Sabbath day, sabbath year and Year of Jubilee point in time beyond the time of history, out into the messianic time. It is only the sabbath at the end of history that will be "a feast without end." It is only this sabbath that will fulfil God's creation sabbath and the sabbath feasts of Israel's history in the world. (*God in Creation*, 290)

43. "The preeminent annual festival, called 'the feast of God' (Lev. 23:39; Judg. 21:19) or '*the feast*' (1 Kings 8:2,65; 12:32; Isa. 30:29; Ezek. 45:23,25; Neh. 8:14; 2 Chron. 5:3,7–8; John 7:10; cf. John 7:2), it was the occasion of the dedication of Solomon's Temple (1 Kings 8), the public reading of the Torah (every seven years, Deut. 31:10–11), and the future ingathering of all nations to Jerusalem to worship God (Zech. 14:16)" (Jeremiah Unterman, "Tabernacles, Festival of," *Harper's Bible Dictionary*, ed. P. J. Achtemeier [San Francisco: Harper & Row, 1985], 1014).

44. Daniel K. Falk, "Festivals and Holy Days," *The Eerdmans Dictionary of Early Judaism*, ed. John J. Collins and Daniel C. Harlow (Grand Rapids: Eerdmans, 2010), 640.

45. John Nolland, *Luke 9:21–18:34*, WBC (Dallas: Word, 1998), 491.

46. Contrary to J. Jeremias: "Rather oddly, the Church took over only two of the great feasts in the Jewish calendar, namely, the Passover and Pentecost, but not Tabernacles" ("πάσχα," *TDNT*, 5:901).

47. The concept of "deliverance" (Gk. *rhuomai*) was commonly associated with the Passover, for in the exodus is found the great historical type of eschatological redemption: "It is

the Passover sacrifice of the LORD, who *passed over* the houses of the children of Israel in Egypt when He struck the Egyptians and *delivered* [Gk. *rhuomai*, LXX] our households" (Ex. 12:27, NKJV; cf. 14:30). As Moses was "sent to be their ruler and deliverer" (Acts 7:35, NIV), so also "the Deliverer will come from Zion" (Rom. 11:26; cf. Isa. 59:20). Since the Passover was commonly interpreted eschatologically, it provided gripping imagery for redemptive history as a whole and deliverance from divine wrath, i.e., "Jesus who *delivers* us from the wrath to come" (1 Thess. 1:10; cf. Matt. 6:13; Luke 1:74; Rom. 7:24; 11:26; 2 Cor. 1:10; Col. 1:13; 2 Tim. 4:18; 2 Peter 2:9).

48. Jeremias, *Eucharistic Words of Jesus*, 205–7; italics in the original; quoting Hermann Strack and Paul Billerbeck, *Kommentar zum Neuen Testament aus Talmud und Midrasch* [no English trans.], vol. 1 (Munich: C. H. Beck, 1922), 85. See also ibid., 59, 217f., 251f.

49. The command to "keep watch" (Matt. 24:42) is in contrast to the ungodliness of the world (cf. vv. 37–41), which sets its hopes and desires upon this age, cf. "eating and drinking" (v. 38; cf. Ex. 32:4; Isa. 56:12; Luke 12:19; 1 Cor. 10:7; 15:32). The command is thus unto sobriety concerning messianic expectation, akin to Peter's exhortation, "Therefore, preparing your minds for action, and *being sober-minded, set your hope fully on the grace that will be brought to you at the revelation of Jesus Christ*" (1 Peter 1:13).

50. Though going on to interpret this saying inaugurationally, Jeremias well articulates the assumptions:

> The next meal of Jesus with his disciples will be the Messianic meal on a transformed earth. It will be a fulfillment of the apocalyptic saying: "The Lord of Spirits will abide over them, and with that Son of Man shall they eat, and lie down and rise up for ever and ever" (I Enoch 62.14). Jesus will drink the wine "new," adds Mark (14.25). To be "new" is a mark of the redeemed world and of the time of salvation, of the transformed creation. When Matthew, with equal correctness, adds "with you" (26.29) he is expressing the idea that the passover of the consummation will be a consummation of the fellowship of the community of the redeemed with the redeemer. On a transformed earth, where perfect communion with God will have become a reality through a transformation of the body, Jesus will again, as now at the Lord's Supper, act as *paterfamilias* and break the blessed bread and offer them the cup of thanksgiving—he himself being once more the giver and the server, and his own the recipients, who in eating and drinking receive the salvation gift of God: eternal life. (*Eucharistic Words of Jesus*, 217–18)

51. For a reconstruction of the Passover meal and its adaptation in the Eucharist meal of the early church, see Oskar Skarsaune's chap., "Passover & Eucharist," in *In the Shadow of the Temple: Jewish Influences on Early Christianity* (Downers Grove, IL: InterVarsity, 2002), 399–422.

52. So the *Haggadah* (lit., "the telling," a Jewish guide to the Passover, supposedly first composed c. AD 300, with innumerable editions) also confirms, "Our God and God of our fathers, on this day of the Festival of Matzoth [Unleavened Bread] may there come before You *the remembrance* of us and our fathers, of Jerusalem Your holy city, of the Messiah son of David Your servant, and of all Your people of the house of Israel" (Rabbi Nathan Goldberg, *Passover Haggadah: A New English Translation and Instructions for the Seder* [New York: Ktav Publishing House, 1990], 30; italics added).

Jeremias comments,

> In this very common prayer, which is also used on other festival days, God is petitioned at every passover concerning "the remembrance of the Messiah," i.e. concerning the appearance of the Messiah, which means the bringing about of the *parousia*. We shall see how very strongly this petition that God may "remember"

the Messiah has influenced and even determined the whole passover festival: every passover celebration concluded with the jubilant antiphonal choir which one day would greet the Messiah at his entry into Jerusalem. Consequently the command for repetition may be understood as: "This do, that God may remember me": *God remembers the Messiah in that he causes the kingdom to break in by the parousia. . . .*

This means that the command to repeat the rite is not a summons to the disciples to preserve the memory of Jesus and be vigilant ("repeat the breaking of bread so that you may not forget me"), but it is an eschatologically oriented instruction: "Keep joining yourselves together as the redeemed community by the table rite, that in this way God may be daily implored to bring about the consummation in the *parousia.*" (*Eucharistic Words of Jesus*, 252, 255; italics in the original)

53. Jeremias, "πάσχα," *TDNT*, 5:897. Contrary to that is C. H. Dodd's characterization of the Eucharist as "a sacrament of realized eschatology" (*Parables of the Kingdom*, 3rd rev. ed. [London: Nisbet, 1936], 203). I would rather describe it as "a sacrament of Jewish cruciform-apocalypticism."

54. The *Didache* (also known as *The Teaching of the Twelve Apostles*), generally dated in the late first or early second century, is a Christian handbook of ethical, ecclesiastical, and eschatological admonitions. Note how it relates the Eucharist to the eschatological kingdom in 9.1–4:

Now concerning the Eucharist, give thanks as follows. First, concerning the cup: We give you thanks, our Father, for the holy vine of David your servant, which you have made known to us through Jesus, your servant; to you be the glory forever. And concerning the broken bread: We give you thanks, our Father, for the life and knowledge which you have made known to us through Jesus, your servant; to you be the glory forever. Just as this broken bread was scattered upon the mountains and then was gathered together and became one, so may your church be gathered together from the ends of the earth into your kingdom; for yours is the glory and the power through Jesus Christ forever. (Michael W. Holmes, *The Apostolic Fathers: Greek Texts and English Translations*, updated ed. [Grand Rapids: Baker, 1999], 261)

55. Every parent knows the constant intercession of a child, "Remember, you said . . . " This is precisely the purpose of our gathering—to call upon our Father ("How long, O Lord?" Rev. 6:10, NASB; cf. Ps. 13:1; 35:17; 74:10; 82:2; 94:3) with persistence (cf. Luke 11:1–10; 18:1–8) and "to stir up one another to love and good works . . . all the more as you see the Day drawing near" (Heb. 10:24–25). So Communion epitomizes the life of the church in this age, the community of faith "who have longed for his appearing" (2 Tim. 4:8, NRSV).

56. See Steven R. Swanson, "Hallel," *ABD*, 3:30; cf. Joseph Tabory, *JPS Commentary on the Haggadah: Historical Introduction, Translation, and Commentary* (Philadelphia: Jewish Publication Society, 2008), 111–16.

57. See Jeremias, *Eucharistic Words of Jesus*, 256–62.

58. "The use of Ps. 118:26 is typological in originally depicting the king leading pilgrims to the temple and receiving a greeting of welcome from the priests at the temple, probably on the occasion of some major victory. This greeting/blessing recognized that the king and his entourage came with the Lord's approval. . . . As it was then, so it should be in Jesus' time. He should be welcomed as a leader and agent of God. The association of Ps. 118 with eschatological hope and the Feast of Tabernacles also heightens the sense

of nearness of eschatological fulfillment" (Darrell L. Bock, *Luke 9:51–24:53*, BECNT [Grand Rapids: Baker, 1996], 1558).

Again, Jeremias concludes,

> In the saying concerning the rejected building stone which God makes the key stone (Ps. 118.22) he is said to have seen a prophecy of his own death and exaltation (Mark 8.31 par., cf. 12.10f. par.; Luke 17.25). That Jesus indeed found in Ps. 118 how God would guide his Messiah through suffering to glory, through chastisement to the opened door of salvation, and at the same time the ceaseless praise of God at the time of the consummation, is made probable by the fact that according to Matt. 23.39 (par. Luke 13.35b) he knew the dynamic interpretation given to Ps. 118.24–29 in the Midrash quoted above. (*Eucharistic Words of Jesus*, 259)

59. John 6:53–58 has also traditionally been read according to the Eucharist, and thereby the Passover (cf. v. 4: "Now the Passover, the feast of the Jews, was at hand"), for "neither the Evangelist nor the Christian readers could have written or read the saying without conscious reference to the Eucharist" (G. R. Beasley-Murray, *John*, WBC [Dallas: Word, 2002], 95). If so, then Jesus is declaring in v. 54 the Passover's typological (cf. "real") fulfillment in himself, for "In Johannine parlance, 'real' also carries the connotations of eschatological, typological fulfillment in relation to OT precursors" (Andreas J. Köstenberger, *John*, BECNT [Grand Rapids: Baker, 2004], 216).

60. Thus Jeremias,

> The casual way in which Paul says: τὸ πάσχα ἡμῶν ἐτύθη Χριστός, 1 C. 5:7, suggests that this comparison was already familiar to the Corinthian church. It is indeed common in the NT (1 Pt. 1:19; Jn. 1:29,36; cf. Rev. 5:6,9,12; 12:11) and probably goes back to Jesus Himself, for, since σῶμα/αἷμα == אֲמַר/דְּשַׁב are, like ἐκχύννεσθαι, sacrificial terms, one may conclude that in the sayings at the Lord's Supper (Mk. 14:22–24 and par.) Jesus was comparing Himself with the paschal lamb, and calling His death a sacrifice. This comparison is the core of a rich Passover typology in the primitive Church. ("πάσχα," *TDNT*, 5:900)

61. The common lack of association between v. 5 and v. 7 (thus establishing the eschatological framework for discipleship) is astonishing; cf. Gordon Fee (NICNT), David Garland (BECNT), Anthony Thiselton (NIGTC), Hans Conzelmann (Hermeneia), Craig Blomberg (NIVAC), and Leon Morris (TNTC).

62. As also reflected in the centrality of the temple (see chapter 6, n. 111).

63. See Eisenberg, "High Holy Days," *JPS Guide to Jewish Traditions*, 171–226.

64. Charles L. Feinberg, "Atonement, Day of," *Baker Encyclopedia of the Bible*, ed. Walter A. Elwell and Barry J. Beitzel (Grand Rapids: Baker, 1988), 233.

65. See Reuven Hammer, *Entering the High Holy Days: A Guide to the Origins, Themes, and Prayers* (Philadelphia: Jewish Publication Society, 1998), chaps. 7–9. "Yom Kippur, the Day of Atonement, has long been considered the most sacred day in the Jewish year" (p. 106).

66. See John E. Hartley, *Leviticus*, WBC (Dallas: Word, 1998), 219–20.

67. Bernd Janowski, "Atonement," *Encyclopedia of Christianity*, 1:153.

68. So we have the primary elements of the Jewish calendar tied together by sacrifice: "The cycle of appointed times in the sacred calendar of the Torah includes New Moon feasts, three pilgrimage festivals (Passover/Unleavened Bread, Weeks, and Booths), a festival of trumpet blasts, and the Day of Atonement (Leviticus 23; Numbers 28–29). During the Second Temple period, the Temple celebration of these was lavish" (Falk, "Festivals and Holy Days," 636).

69. Zuesse, "Calendar of Judaism," 45.

70. See Hammer, *Entering the High Holy Days*, 2–6. On pp. 4–5 Hammer quotes Moshe Segal ("The Religion of Israel Before Sinai," *Jewish Quarterly Review* 52 [1963]: 242):

> Three principles, the creation of the world on the New Year, the manifestation of God's kingship over the world on the New Year, and the judgment of the world by God on the New Year . . . are already proclaimed together in a series of liturgical psalms which form a distinct group marked by a close affinity of tone, of language and of thought. These are the joyous and triumphant songs contained in Psalms 95–100, to which belong also Psalm 93 and the first part of Psalm 94. The constantly recurring thoughts in these beautiful songs are God as creator, God as King, God as judge.

71. "It is believed that 'On Rosh Hashanah all the inhabitants of the world pass before God [in judgment] like a flock of sheep' (M. R.H. 1:2). All are judged on Rosh Hashanah, and the verdict is sealed on Yom Kippur [T. Rosh Hashanah 1.13]. The worthy are written into the Book of Life, the unworthy blotted out (cf., Exod. 32:32–33) or entered into a Book of Death" (Zuesse, "Calendar of Judaism," 45).

72. Whether "lamb" here and elsewhere in the NT is in reference to the "Passover lamb" (Mark 14:12; Luke 22:7; 1 Cor. 5:7) or the general sacrifice of lambs in the sacrificial system (cf. Ex. 29:38–42; Lev. 3:7–11; 4:32–35; 5:6f.; Num. 28:3–8) is inconsequential since the calendar was inextricably bound to the sacrificial system, and both related to redemptive history as a whole.

73. See also "his blood" (Rom. 3:25; 5:9; Eph. 1:7; Heb. 9:12; 13:12; 1 Peter 1:2; Rev. 1:5; cf. Col. 1:20; Rev. 5:9).

74. Though an emphasis on typology may seem initially strange, it was by God's set foreknowledge that the first coming of the Messiah would be somewhat "mysterious" (cf. Luke 8:10 and par.; Rom. 16:25f.; Eph. 1:9; 1 Tim. 3:16), so as to confuse the wise and make the haughty stumble (cf. Rom. 9:30–33; 1 Cor. 1:18–25). Those who recognize their own depravity, casting themselves upon the mercy of God, readily receive the veiled prophetic unfolding of divine kindness before the plainly revealed apocalyptic culmination of divine severity. Thus, "slow of heart to believe" (Luke 24:25) is an issue of pride and repentance rather than unenlightenment and gnostic revelation.

75. Goppelt, *Typos*, 3.

76. *Commentary on John*, 10.18; trans. M. F. Wiles, "Origen as Biblical Scholar," in *The Cambridge History of the Bible*, ed. P. R. Ackroyd and C. F. Evans, vol. 1 (Cambridge: Cambridge University Press, 1970), 484; italics added.

77. For an overview of typology in the early church (sympathetic to the Alexandrian school of thought), see Daniélou, *From Shadows to Reality*.

78. "In a passage dealing with Baptism Hippolytus holds it up definitely as the entry into the Paradise of the Church. 'All those who love knowledge must learn how the Paradise, planted in Eden, is a prefiguring of reality. Eden is the name of the Paradise of delights, planted in the East, adorned with two trees, by which we understand the company of the Righteous and the Holy Place where the Church is established.' This interpretation of Paradise, as a figure of the Church, crops up continuously in every tradition" (Daniélou, *From Shadows to Reality*, 26).

79. So Daniélou,

> The Christian life, then, appears as the realization of Paradise. Christ is the tree of life (Ambrose, *de Isaac*, 5, 43) or the fountain of Paradise (Ambrose, *de Paradiso*, 3, 272, 20). But this realization of Paradise is brought about in three different

stages. Baptism is the entry into Paradise (Cyril of Jerusalem, *Procatechesis*; P.G. XXXIII, 357A). Through the mystical life we enter more deeply into Paradise (Ambrose, *de Paradiso*, 1, 1); finally the Martyrs are led into Paradise through their death (*Passio Perpet.* I; P.L. III, 28A). It is rather remarkable that we should find these three stages of Christian life described in terms of Paradise. (Ibid., 25)

Remarkable indeed! The realization of Paradise in this present evil age (Gal. 1:4) is quite incredible.

80. Again, we acknowledge the grace of God at work within the various monastic traditions and ecclesiastical structures (esp. concerning the preservation of the Scriptures and societal order), yet we maintain the fundamental discordance between these and the apostolic witness.

81. For example, Zeno of Verona (fourth-century bishop in northern Italy) exemplifies the reckless use of typology:

As the devil by his plausibility had found a way into the ear of Eve, inflicting a deadly wound, so Christ, entering the ear of Mary, brushes away all the heart's vices and heals the woman by being born of a Virgin. Adam is circumcised on the Lord's cross, and as it was through a woman who had alone touched the deadly tree, that the two sexes had found death, inversely by this man hung on a tree the whole human race is redeemed. Lest the beginning should not appear as completely restored in its former condition, man is first offered on the cross, and during that blessed sleep his side is pierced by a lance, yet it is not a rib which is removed, but by the water and blood, signifying Baptism and martyrdom, the spiritual body of the spiritual woman springs forth in such wise that Adam is renewed in Christ, Eve by the Church. (*Tractatus* 1.13; quoted in Daniélou, *From Shadows to Reality*, 55)

82. Origen makes explicit the inner workings of his allegorical method in his commentary on the Song of Songs:

So, as we said at the beginning, all the things in the visible category can be related to the invisible, the corporeal to the incorporeal, and the manifest to those that are hidden; so that the creation of the world itself, fashioned in this wise as it is, can be understood through the divine wisdom, which from actual things and copies teaches us things unseen by means of those that are seen, and carries us over from earthly things to heavenly.

But this relationship does not obtain only with creatures; the Divine Scripture itself is written with wisdom of a rather similar sort. Because of certain mystical and hidden things the people is [*sic*] visibly led forth from the terrestrial Egypt and journeys through the desert, where there was a biting serpent, and a scorpion, and thirst, and where all the other happenings took place that are recorded. All these events, as we have said, have the aspects and likenesses of certain hidden things. And you will find this correspondence not only in the Old Testament Scriptures, but also in the actions of Our Lord and Savior that are related in the Gospels.

If, therefore, in accordance with the principles that we have now established all things that are in the open stand in some sort of relation to others that are hidden, it undoubtedly follows that the visible hart and roe mentioned in the Song of Songs [cf. 2:7; 3:5; 4:5; 7:4] are related to some patterns of incorporeal realities, in accordance with the character borne by their bodily nature. And this must be in such wise that we ought to be able to furnish a fitting interpretation of what is said about the Lord perfecting the harts, by reference to those harts that are unseen and hidden. (Origen, *The Song of Songs: Commentary and Homilies*, trans. R. P. Lawson, Ancient Christian Writers, vol. 26 [Westminster, MD: Newman Press, 1957], 223)

Commenting on this passage, Daniel Boyarin connects Origen's hermeneutics to his worldview: "Origen's text describes a perfect correspondence between the ontology of the world and that of the text. In both there is an outer shell and an inner meaning. We see accordingly the metaphysical grounding of the allegorical method used by Origen, and indeed by Philo as well. In order for the Scripture to have an 'inner meaning,' there must be an ontological structure that allows for inner meaning. Allegoresis is thus explicitly founded in a Platonic universe" ("The Eye in the Torah: Ocular Desire in Midrashic Hermeneutic," *Critical Inquiry* 16 [1990]: 548). Though few today would so clearly articulate as Origen "the aspects and likenesses of certain hidden things," at a popular level this remains the pervasive hermeneutical approach to the Scriptures.

83. For a sympathetic overview of Origen and his influence, see Jean Daniélou, *Origen*, trans. Walter Mitchell (London: Sheed and Ward, 1955). For a critical assessment, see R. P. C. Hanson, *Allegory and Event* (London: SCM Press, 1959).

84. Some of the most extreme examples are found in Origen's commentaries on the Pentateuch, e.g., concerning the sacrifices:

It will be too much now to describe the diversity of offerings and the ritual and varieties of sacrifices. . . . But in order that we appear to touch briefly in passing on some, indeed almost every offering which is brought has something of the form and image of Christ. . . . Concerning these things, as best we were able, we showed in the preceding how the calf offered by the high priest either in the offering or "for sin" had his form. But the "fatty parts," which were offered in the offering and were "hidden inwardly" and held together with the kidneys, can be understood as that holy soul of he who indeed is "inward." That is, it was covering the secrets of his divinity. But he was held together "with the kidneys," that is, with bodily matter which he had assumed in purity from us. . . . But what of the small kidney yielded to the fire? Does anyone doubt that they indicate there were none of the passions of the generative parts in Christ? But because "the high priest" is reminded "to sprinkle some of the blood of the sacrifice before the Lord seven times," the virtue of the Holy Spirit is evidently designated under the mystery of the seven spirits. The four "horns of the altar," which are anointed "with the blood," point to the passion of Christ as related by the four gospels. The lobe of the liver that is sacrificed—wrath is killed in the liver—in this lobe the swift and provoked power of rage is shown. But I think that the rest of the blood which "is poured out at the base of the altar" represents the form of his grace which "in the last days" after "the fullness of the Gentiles have entered in," all who were the remnant "of Israel" placed in the end, as it were, "at the base of the altar" will also receive the shedding of Christ's blood. (Origen, *Homilies on Leviticus: 1–16*, trans. Gary W. Barkley, Fathers of the Church, vol. 83 [Washington, DC: Catholic University of America Press, 1990], 61–62).

See also Charles J. Scalise, "Allegorical Flights of Fancy: The Problem of Origen's Exegesis," *Greek Orthodox Theological Review* 32, no. 1 (Spring 1987): 69–88.

85. Daniélou, *Origen*, 141.

86. *Typos*, 6.

87. Concerning the distinction between Israel and the church—the *sine qua non* of dispensationalism (Charles C. Ryrie, *Dispensationalism Today* [Chicago: Moody, 1965], 43–47)—their dichotomy is false, since the former refers to *ethnicity* and the latter refers to

righteousness. Thus it is the church vs. the wicked and Israel vs. the nations. Though Jew and Gentile are "fellow citizens" (Eph. 2:19) and "fellow heirs" (Eph. 3:6), their witness is expressed differently in relation to the land, temple, law, etc. This is self-evident in Acts 15:19–21 and 21:20–26. The church is simply the continued *assembly of the righteous,* Old Testament and New, now composed of both Jew and Gentile, stewarding the oracles of God and witnessing to the day of Christ Jesus in their respective manners.

88. Though typology is readily employed to prove the suffering of the Christ (cf. Lewis Chafer, *Systematic Theology,* vol. 5 [Grand Rapids: Kregel, 1993], 42–44, 177–81). Having abandoned their dualistic foundation, progressive dispensationalists have sought to incorporate typology in an inaugurational fashion (cf. Craig A. Blaising and Darrell L. Bock, *Progressive Dispensationalism* [Wheaton: Victor, 1993], 52–53).

89. As Oswald Allis is known for saying: "The primary aim has been to show that Dispensationalism has its source in a faulty and unscriptural literalism which, in the important field of prophecy, ignores the typical and preparatory character of the Old Testament dispensation" (*Prophecy and the Church* [Philadelphia: Presbyterian & Reformed, 1945], 256).

90. See chapter 3, n. 131.

91. Especially if typology were applied to the third divine program concerning the "mystery form" of the kingdom in this age, i.e., Christendom.

92. Bruce K. Waltke, "Kingdom Promises as Spiritual," in *Continuity and Discontinuity: Perspectives on the Relationship Between the Old and New Testaments,* ed. John S. Feinberg (Wheaton: Crossway, 1988), 275.

93. So Darrell Bock comments on Luke 24:26:

> Here the emphasis on glory is a focus on Jesus' position and authority, not just his coming to life. Such glory exists now for Jesus and looks to its manifestation in return (21:27). . . . Jesus is not only alive, he rules. He has entered (εἰσελθεῖν, *eiselthein*; Acts 14:22) into his glory, which means that he has been raised to reign next to God, just as he promised at his trial (Luke 22:69; 23:42–43). As such the background of the remark is Ps. 110 and Dan. 7:14. The great manifestation of that glory is yet to come (Luke 21:27), but Jesus has now emerged from the dark night of his suffering. (*Luke 9:51–24:53,* BECNT, 1917)

94. "Typology as a New Testament hermeneutical endeavor is the study of the Old Testament salvation historical realities or 'types' (persons, events, and institutions) which God has specifically designed to correspond to, and predictively prefigure, their intensified antitypical fulfillment aspects (inaugurated and consummated) in the New Testament salvation history" (Peter J. Gentry and Stephen J. Wellum, *Kingdom through Covenant: A Biblical-Theological Understanding of the Covenants* [Wheaton: Crossway, 2012], 103).

95. The logical inference and application of inaugurationalism is straightforward: "The ultimate objective is the accomplishment of God's Kingdom, *i.e.,* the realization of God's perfect reign in all the universe. This is accomplished by the defeat of his enemies. Christ must reign until He has put all His enemies under His Feet. . . . The Kingdom of God therefore is the reign of God through Christ destroying the enemies of God's reign" (George E. Ladd, *The Gospel of the Kingdom: Scriptural Studies in the Kingdom of God* [Grand Rapids: Eerdmans, 1959], 43).

96. See N. T. Wright, *Paul: Fresh Perspectives* (London: SPCK, 2005), 130–53.

97. So Waltke states,

> On the other hand, the apostles taught that the type of national Israel and its law as a means of governing the nation were done away finally and permanently. The

typological approach of the NT is grounded in an understanding that the new age in Christ fulfills the salvation toward which the old is reaching. . . .

Jesus taught in several places that the true people of God are not to be found in national Israel but in the Christian community that replaced it (cf. Mark 12:1–9; Matt 15:13). His apostles continued his teachings. . . . Although the semi-eschatological nature of the kingdom of God and of "the world to come" entail a more solid form of the kingdom in the new earth (cf. Heb 2:5; 11:10; 13:14), typology in the NT focuses on its comprehensive fulfillment in the Christ and his church. ("Kingdom Promises as Spiritual," 279)

98. As clearly articulated by Barry E. Horner, *Future Israel: Why Christian Anti-Judaism Must Be Challenged* (Nashville: Broadman and Holman, 2007).

99. David S. Ariel, *What Do Jews Believe? The Spiritual Foundations of Judaism* (New York: Schocken Books, 1995), 232.

100. Here we are reminded of Albert Schweitzer, who argued for a Jewish eschatological approach to the Scriptures but yet concluded in a thoroughly Gentilic manner: "This Jesus is far greater than the one conceived in modern terms: he is really a superhuman personality. With his death he destroyed the form of his 'Weltanschauung [worldview],' rendering his own eschatology impossible. Thereby he gives to all peoples and to all times the right to apprehend him in terms of their thoughts and conceptions, in order that his spirit may pervade their 'Weltanschauung' as it quickened and transfigured the Jewish eschatology" (*The Mystery of the Kingdom of God*, trans. W. Lowrie [London: A. & C. Black, 1914], 251).

101. N. T. Wright, *Jesus and the Victory of God* (London: SPCK, 1996), 446.

102. See Ronald E. Diprose, *Israel and the Church: The Origin and Effects of Replacement Theology* (Waynesboro, GA: Authentic, 2004); and Michael J. Vlach, *Has the Church Replaced Israel? A Theological Evaluation* (Nashville: B&H Publishing, 2010).

103. *The God of Israel and Christian Theology* (Minneapolis: Fortress, 1996), 1–2. Soulen continues, "The church, unlike the Jewish people, is a spiritual community in which the carnal distinction between Jew and Gentile is overcome. Accordingly, the church holds that the preservation of Jewish identity within the new Israel is a matter of theological indifference at best, and a mortal sin at worst. Yet the Jews themselves failed to recognize Jesus as the promised Messiah and refused to enter the new spiritual Israel. God therefore rejected the Jews and scattered them over the earth, where God will preserve them until the end of time" (ibid., 2).

Of course, such ideas provided a greenhouse for the Holocaust and other similar events throughout the church's imperialistic history (see James Carroll, *Constantine's Sword: The Church and the Jews, A History* [New York: Houghton Mifflin, 2001]).

104. This becomes almost self-evident when seen in a systematic presentation, e.g., G. K. Beale, *A New Testament Biblical Theology: The Unfolding of the Old Testament in the New* (Grand Rapids: Baker, 2011), 650–773. Though Soulen repeatedly demonstrates in *The God of Israel and Christian Theology* that supersessionist theologians throughout history have found the OT hope fulfilled in the church (see chaps. 2–4), he seems oblivious to the idea of realized eschatology and its causal agency in supersessionism. The same can be said of Horner, *Future Israel*.

105. Here typology is often used to enshroud what is being said—e.g., Gentry and Wellum:

In this important way, then, we view the new covenant as *superseding* the previous covenants. How? By *fulfilling* them, i.e., by bringing to pass what those previous covenants revealed, anticipated, and even predicted through various patterns, types, and instruction. That is why our Lord is presented as the new covenant head, who in his person and work is greater than Adam by undoing what Adam did and thus winning for us the new creation; as the true seed and offspring of Abraham, who brings blessings to the nations by his cross work; as the true Israel, fulfilling all that she failed to be; and as David's greater son, who rules the nations and the entire creation as King of kings and Lord of lords. (*Kingdom through Covenant*, 604; italics in the original)

106. Such belief is also the basis of Islam, which views itself as superseding both Judaism and Christianity. "Judeo-Muslim" is evidently oxymoronic because the two hold fundamentally different views of divine revelation, covenant, and eschatology. Likewise, "Judeo-Christian" becomes oxymoronic with the inclusion of realized eschatology—the God of Israel is universalized, and the future is no longer Judeocentric.

107. Herman Ridderbos, *Paul: An Outline of His Theology*, trans. J. R. De Witt (Grand Rapids: Eerdmans, 1975), 344–45.

108. Waltke, "Kingdom Promises as Spiritual," 274.

109. George Eldon Ladd, *The Presence of the Future: The Eschatology of Biblical Realism* (Grand Rapids: Eerdmans, 1974), 245. Ladd makes this off-handed comment in light of his previous chapter on "The Mystery of the Kingdom" (pp. 218–42), whereby the parables are used as justification that "the Kingdom has come into history in the person and mission of Jesus; and in the same way, the Kingdom will continue to work in the world until the hour of its eschatological manifestation" (p. 242).

110. Bruce K. Waltke, "A Response," in *Dispensationalism, Israel and the Church: The Search for Definition*, ed. Craig A. Blaising and Darrell L. Bock (Grand Rapids: Zondervan, 1992), 359.

111. N. T. Wright, *The New Testament and the People of God* (Minneapolis: Fortress, 1992), 457.

112. N. T. Wright, *The Climax of the Covenant: Christ and the Law in Pauline Theology* (Minneapolis: Fortress, 1992), 147, cf. 240, 243, 261.

113. Being "abandoned because of their sins," the Jews "committed a crime of the most unhallowed kind, in conspiring against the Saviour of the human race in that city where they offered up to God a worship containing the symbols of mighty mysteries. It accordingly behooved that city where Jesus underwent these sufferings to perish utterly, and the Jewish nation to be overthrown, and the invitation to happiness offered them by God to pass to others,—the Christians, I mean, to whom has come the doctrine of a pure and holy worship, and who have obtained new laws, in harmony with the established constitution in all countries" (*Against Celsus*, 4.22 [*ANF*, 4:506]).

114. See esp. Luther's well-known *On the Jews and Their Lies* (1543) in *LW*, 47:121–306. For example, "'Listen, Jew, are you aware that Jerusalem and your sovereignty, together with your temple and priesthood, have been destroyed for over 1,460 years?' . . . For such ruthless wrath of God is sufficient evidence that they assuredly have erred and gone astray. . . . Therefore this work of wrath is proof that the Jews, surely rejected by God, are no longer his people, and neither is he any longer their God" (ibid., 138–39).

115. Colin Chapman, *Whose Promised Land? The Continuing Crisis Over Israel and Palestine* (Grand Rapids: Baker, 2002), 285.

116. R. T. France, *Jesus and the Old Testament: His Application of Old Testament Passages to Himself and His Mission* (Downers Grove, IL: InterVarsity, 1971), 67. France summarizes his typological argument (pp. 38–80) in this manner:

Jesus' types are drawn from a wide range of aspects of Israel seen in the Old Testament; they are not restricted to any one period or any single class. Thus he uses *persons* in the Old Testament as types of himself (David, Solomon, Elijah, Elisha, Isaiah, Jonah) or of John the Baptist (Elijah); he refers to Old Testament *institutions* as types of himself and his work (the priesthood and the covenant); he sees in the *experiences* of Israel foreshadowings of his own; he finds the *hopes* of Israel fulfilled in himself and his disciples and sees his disciples as assuming the *status* of Israel; in Israel's *deliverance* by God he sees a type of the gathering of men into his church, while the *disasters* of Israel are foreshadowings of the imminent punishment of those who reject him, whose *unbelief* is prefigured in that of the wicked in Israel. . . .

In all these aspects of the Old Testament people of God Jesus sees fore-shadowings of himself and his work, with its results in the opposition and consequent rejection of the majority of the Jews, while the true Israel is now to be found in the new Christian community. Thus in his coming the history of Israel has reached its decisive point. The whole of the Old Testament is gathered up in him. He himself embodies in his own person the status and destiny of Israel, and in the community of those who belong to him that status and destiny are to be fulfilled, no longer in the nation as such. (pp. 75–76; italics in the original)

117. "The essence of theological anti-Judaism lies in Christian replacement theology, quite literally Christians' understanding of themselves as replacing Judaism in the affections of God, the Holy One" (Padraic O'Hare, *The Enduring Covenant: The Education of Christians and the End of Antisemitism* [Valley Forge, PA: Trinity Press International, 1997], 6). See also Jules Isaac, *Has Anti-Semitism Roots in Christianity?*, trans. D. and J. Parkes (New York: National Conference of Christians and Jews, 1961).

118. So Waltke concludes his critique of Jewish literalism with the following analogy: "If God promised the fathers $5 and he rewards them with $5,000, is he unfaithful?" ("A Response," 359). Why is an undifferentiated humanity on a new earth so much more valuable than a differentiated one?

119. Dual-covenant theology, beginning in the latter half of twentieth century as a response to the Holocaust, has attempted to assuage the pain of supersessionism which runs rampant in the modern inaugurationalist academy (see a historical overview in *Jews and Christians: Exploring the Past, Present, and Future*, ed. James H. Charlesworth [New York: Crossroad, 1990]). It teaches that God relates equally to Jews and Christians based upon separate covenants (thus no need for Jewish evangelism). However, NT exclusivity, esp. concerning Israel (cf. Acts 4:10ff.; 5:31; 13:38), invalidates dual-covenant pluralism (see David E. Holwerda, *Jesus & Israel: One Covenant or Two?* [Grand Rapids: Eerdmans, 1995]; though of course I must reject Holwerda's supersessionist conclusions).

120. Craig Blaising hits at the root of supersessionism: "To put Israel in the *eschaton* on the basis of a historical-grammatical-literary reading of Scripture is to put the *context* of future Israel there as well. And what that means is a new creation rather than a spiritual-vision eschatology" ("The Future of Israel as a Theological Question," *JETS* 44, no. 3 [September 2001]: 448). Unfortunately, Blaising falls short of providing a truly Israelitic vision for the age to come, involving both framework and mechanism, beyond the general description of being "differentiated in ethnic and communal dimensions" (p. 449). See also Blaising, "Premillennialism," in *Three Views of the Millennium and Beyond*, ed. Darrell L. Bock (Grand Rapids: Zondervan, 1999), 155–227.

Chapter Eight

1. The offense of crucifixion was such that it was madness (Gk. *mania*) to associate it with God, as Justin (c. 100–165 AD) is known for describing: "Our teacher of these things is Jesus Christ, who also was born for this purpose, and was crucified under Pontius Pilate. . . . For they proclaim *our madness* to consist in this, that we give to a crucified man a place second to the unchangeable and eternal God, the Creator of all; for they do not discern the mystery that is herein, to which, as we make it plain to you, we pray you to give heed" (*First Apology*, 13 [*ANF*, 1:166–67]; italics added).

   See a description in Martin Hengel, *Crucifixion in the Ancient World and the Folly of the Message of the Cross*, trans. John Bowden (Philadelphia: Fortress, 1977), 1–10. "A crucified messiah, son of God or God must have seemed a contradiction in terms to anyone, Jew, Greek, Roman or barbarian, asked to believe such a claim, and it will certainly have been thought offensive and foolish" (p. 10).

2. Though theologians in the twentieth century have sought to move the "center" of NT theology toward eschatology, whether "realized" or not (cf. A. Schweitzer, C. H. Dodd, W. G. Kümmel, K. Stendahl, J. D. G. Dunn, N. T. Wright, etc.), the Reformation's anchor in the cross still holds (cf. E. Käsemann, C. E. B. Cranfield, L. Morris, J. I. Packer, etc.). The disputation between Stendahl and Käsemann is well known in the academy and typifies the tension (see Don N. Howell Jr., "The Center of Pauline Theology," *BSac* 151, no. 1 [1994]: 50–70). Of course, there is technically *no center to a timeline*, since the beginning, middle, and end are all of vital necessity (cf. James M. Hamilton Jr., "The Glory of God in Salvation through Judgment: The Centre of Biblical Theology?" *TynBul* 57, no. 1 [2006]: 57–84), though Paul ultimately emphasized the cross and justification by faith in light of creation and eschatological judgment (cf. Rom. 5:9; 1 Cor. 2:2; Gal. 2:20; 1 Tim. 1:15; etc.).

3. So P. T. Forsyth declared, "Christ, I repeat, is to us just what His cross is. You do not understand Christ till you understand His cross. . . . It is only by understanding it that it becomes anything else than a martyrdom, that it becomes the saving act of God. It is only by understanding it that we escape from religion with no mind, and from religion which is all mind, from pietism with its lack of critical judgment, and from rationalism with its lack of everything else" (*The Cruciality of the Cross* [London: Hodder & Stoughton, 1909], 45–46].

4. "It is not easy to see what the laying on of hands means if there is no symbolic transfer to the animal which was to die of the sins being confessed" (Leon Morris, *The Atonement: Its Meaning and Significance* [Downers Grove, IL: InterVarsity, 1983], 47).

5. Thus, "It is clear from Old Testament usage that to 'bear sin' means neither to sympathize with sinners, nor to identify with their pain, nor to express their penitence, nor to be persecuted on account of human sinfulness (as others have argued), nor even to suffer the consequences of sin in personal or social terms, but specifically to endure its penal consequences, to undergo its penalty" (John R. W. Stott, *The Cross of Christ* [Downers Grove, IL: InterVarsity, 1986], 143).

6. In light of this God-ordained, atonemental system, and its centrality within Judaic life, the prophecy of Isaiah 53 concerning a substitutionary messianic sacrifice was readily understood and received (cf. Matt. 8:17; Mark 9:12; Luke 22:37; John 12:38; Acts 8:32–35; Rom. 10:16; 15:21; 1 Peter 2:22–25). Like the sacrificial animal, "He was wounded for our transgressions; he was crushed for our iniquities" (v. 5), for "the LORD has laid on him the iniquity of us all" (v. 6). Indeed, he is "like a lamb that is led to the slaughter" (v. 7), "stricken for the transgression of my people" (v. 8). His life would be "an offering for sin" (v. 10), and hence "he shall bear their iniquities" (v. 11). So the chapter concludes that he

was "numbered with the transgressors" and "bore the sin of many" (v. 12). The sacrificial language of this oracle is unmistakable, and in such light the NT writers interpret the death of the Messiah.

7. Because of selfishness and human depravity, vicarious sin-bearing is relatively uncommon in human relations. However, sometimes debts are paid on behalf of others, penalties are endured in another's stead, and suffering is embraced in lieu of someone else. We consider such examples heroic because they inherently express a measure of love and self-sacrifice. Such sentiment was also common in the ancient world (see Martin Hengel, *The Atonement: The Origin of the Doctrine in the New Testament*, trans. John Bowden [Philadelphia: Fortress, 1981]). No one wants to bear the consequences of their own sin, much less someone else's, yet this is exactly how the death of the Messiah is framed in the NT: "For while we were still weak, at the right time Christ died for the ungodly. For one will scarcely die for a righteous person—though perhaps for a good person one would dare even to die—but God shows his love for us in that while we were still sinners, Christ died for us" (Rom. 5:6–8).

8. Though controversy surrounds the substitutionality of the preposition ἀντί in a few instances, it "characteristically has the meaning 'in the place of,' 'instead of,' whether in the classics or in the χοινή" (Leon Morris, *The Apostolic Preaching of the Cross*, 3rd ed. [London: Tyndale, 1965], 34). See also "ἀντί," BDAG, 87–88; and "ἀντί," *NIDNTT*, 3:1179–80. Likewise, ὑπέρ commonly conveys "a substitutionary thought" (Morris, *Apostolic Preaching*, 62) and is often identical to ἀντί (cf. Mark 10:45; 1 Tim. 2:6).

9. For example: Christ "gave himself *for our sins* to deliver us from the present evil age" (Gal. 1:4). "He himself *bore our sins* in his body on the tree" (1 Peter 2:24). It is Christ Jesus "who died *for us*" (1 Thess. 5:10), "who gave himself *for us*" (Titus 2:14). Indeed, "One has died *for all*" (2 Cor. 5:14), "as a ransom *for all*" (1 Tim. 2:6). "Christ loved us and gave himself up *for us*" (Eph. 5:2). "Christ died *for the ungodly*" (Rom. 5:6), i.e., "Christ died *for us*" (v. 8). He was "delivered up *for our trespasses*" (Rom. 4:25), "becoming a curse *for us*" (Gal. 3:13). "He is the propitiation *for our sins*" (1 John 2:2). God "made Him who knew no sin to be sin *on our behalf*" (2 Cor. 5:21, NASB); as Caiaphas inadvertently prophesied: "It was expedient for one man to die *on behalf of the people*" (John 18:14, NASB; cf. John 11:49). So Paul believed Jesus to be "the Son of God, who loved me and gave himself *for me*" (Gal. 2:20). Indeed, "Christ loved the church and gave himself up *for her*" (Eph. 5:25). So we should not sin against "the brother *for whom* Christ died" (1 Cor. 8:11); cf. "the one *for whom* Christ died" (Rom. 14:15).

10. Similarly, Jesus told his disciples before his death, "The Son of Man came not to be served but to serve, and to give his life as a ransom *for many*" (Matt. 20:28; cf. Mark 10:45). Jesus likened his death to a good shepherd who "lays down his life *for the sheep*" (John 10:11)—prophesying, "I lay down my life *for the sheep*" (v. 15). And, "Greater love has no one than this, that someone lay down his life *for his friends*" (John 15:13).

The atonemental nature of these statements would have been commonly understood: "The idea that the righteous who suffer without being guilty, or who suffer more than their guilt requires, thereby atone for the sins of the people and ward off suffering from others, is very common among the Rabbis [Cf. Str.-B., II, 275ff.]. The sufferings of the patriarchs, Moses, David etc., and the sufferings of more recent figures, especially the martyrs, are evaluated thus" (F. Büchsel, "ἱλάσκομαι, ἱλασμάς," *TDNT*, 3:313).

11. As Joachim Jeremias states,

The oft-repeated assertion that it is inconceivable that Jesus should have ascribed atoning power to his death, that such statements belong rather to the "dogmatic" of the Early Church or of the apostle Paul, is astonishing to anyone who knows the Palestinian sources. Conceptions of the atoning power of death play a large part in the thought of Jesus' contemporaries. Every death has atoning power—even that of a criminal if he dies penitent. An innocent death offered to God has vicarious power of atonement for others. The sources compel the conclusion that *it is inconceivable that Jesus should not have thought of the atoning power of his death.* (*The Eucharistic Words of Jesus,* trans. Norman Perrin [London: SCM Press, 1966], 231; italics in the original)

Note 4 Maccabees 17:21–22: "The tyrant was punished, and the homeland purified—they having become, as it were, a ransom for the sin of our nation. And through the blood of those devout ones and their death as an atoning sacrifice, divine Providence preserved Israel that previously had been mistreated" (NRSV). And 4 Maccabees 6:28: "Be merciful to your people, and let our punishment suffice for them. Make my blood their purification, and take my life in exchange for theirs" (NRSV).

12. This idea has a long history, deriving primarily from C. H. Dodd, *The Apostolic Preaching and Its Developments* (London: Hodder & Stoughton, 1936); and Hans Conzelmann, *The Theology of St. Luke* (London: Faber, 1960). A Lucan vicarious atonement, more in line with Isa. 53 and OT sacrifice, is well articulated by I. Howard Marshall, *Luke: Historian and Theologian* (Grand Rapids: Zondervan, 1970); and Darrell L. Bock, *Proclamation from Prophecy and Pattern: Lucan Old Testament Christology* (Sheffield, England: Sheffield Press, 1987).

13. The assertion that "all sinned" (Rom. 5:12) and "in Adam all die" (1 Cor. 15:22) assumes the passing on of a *sinful disposition* (cf. Gen. 6:5; 8:21) to the progeny of Adam. Otherwise all would not have sinned. So Morris:

> From such passages the idea of original sin is derived. The basic idea in this concept is that the nature that mankind inherits is not the innocent nature of the unfallen Adam, but that stained by sin as the result of the Fall. . . .
>
> Men have always found the pursuit of virtue strenuous. It does not come to us naturally to do good, whereas sin is much easier. We can drift into sin, but we cannot drift into virtue. It is this which points us to the important truth that sin is part of our nature, and not simply the result of our environment. Basically we sin because we are the kind of people we are, and not simply because we see others sinning. The idea of original sin must be retained, for it corresponds both to the teaching of St. Paul, and to the facts of life. (Leon Morris, *The Cross in the New Testament* [Grand Rapids: Eerdmans, 1965], 186–88)

14. So Paul draws from the Psalms (written to the Jews) to emphasize the reality of universal depravity (not only Gentile depravity): "For we have already charged that all, both Jews and Greeks, are under sin, as it is written: 'None is righteous, no, not one; no one understands; no one seeks for God. All have turned aside; together they have become worthless; no one does good, not even one' [Pss. 14:1–3; 53:1–3]. 'Their throat is an open grave; they use their tongues to deceive' [Ps. 5:9]. 'The venom of asps is under their lips' [Ps. 140:3]. 'Their mouth is full of curses and bitterness' [Ps. 10:7, LXX]. 'Their feet are swift to shed blood; in their paths are ruin and misery, and the way of peace they have not known' [Isa. 59:7–8]. 'There is no fear of God before their eyes' [Ps. 36:1]. Now we know that whatever the law says *it speaks to those who are under the law,* so that every mouth may be stopped, and the whole world may be held accountable to God" (Rom. 3:9–19).

15. G. W. Bromiley notes,

> To atone is to bring together in mutual agreement, with the added idea, in theology, of reconciliation through the vicarious suffering of one on behalf of another.

The English word "atonement" traces its origin to the 16th century. The *New Oxford Dictionary* indicates that in the first instance it appeared as two separate words "at onement" (cf. Acts 7:26, AV; Gk *eis eirēnēn*), but it soon became a quasi-technical theological term. Sir Thomas More employed it in 1513, and in 1526 William Tyndale used it to translate Gk *katallagē* in 2 Cor. 5:18. In the Bible the idea of atonement occurs much more widely than the actual use of either *kāpar* or *katallagē* would seem to indicate. ("Atone, Atonement," *ISBE*, 1:352)

16. T. H. Hughes, *The Atonement: Modern Theories of the Doctrine* (London: Allen and Unwin, 1949), 312; quoted in Morris, *Apostolic Preaching*, 214.

17. The NIV and NRSV also pick up the tradition of interpreting the Gk. *hilastērion* word group ("propitiate, propitiation"), used throughout the LXX to translate Heb. *kāphar* ("cover, covering"), as "atone, atonement." Thus, for example, the various translations of Heb. 2:17: "to make propitiation" (ESV, NASB, NKJV), "to make atonement" (NIV, NRSV), "to make reconciliation" (KJV).

18. Stott articulates well the relationship between the holiness of God, the depravity of man, and the messianic atonement:

> All inadequate doctrines of the atonement are due to inadequate doctrines of God and man. If we bring God down to our level and raise ourselves to his, then of course we see no need for a radical salvation, let alone for a radical atonement to secure it. When, on the other hand, we have glimpsed the blinding glory of the holiness of God, and have been so convicted of our sin by the Holy Spirit that we tremble before God and acknowledge what we are, namely "hell-deserving sinners," then and only then does the necessity of the cross appear so obvious that we are astonished we never saw it before. (*Cross of Christ*, 109)

19. For example: "Equally, the favorite notion that sacrifice was 'spiritualized' (Wenschkewitz 1932:6–10) does not really fit the bill. It would be better to speak of its being 'christologized' and 'pneumatized.' Jesus' saving death gives an entirely new meaning to sacrifice as a consequence of his resurrection and the sending of the Holy Spirit. He opened up a new dimension of reality. As a result sacrifice is reduced to its personal core from which ethical consequences can be drawn for Christian faith and life" (Hans-Josef Klauck, "Sacrifice and Sacrificial Offerings: New Testament," *ABD*, 5:891).

20. See Joel B. Green and Mark D. Baker, *Recovering the Scandal of the Cross: Atonement in the New Testament and Contemporary Contexts* (Downers Grove, IL: InterVarsity, 2000), 47–50; Stephen J. Patterson, *Beyond the Passion: Rethinking the Death and Life of Jesus* (Minneapolis: Augsburg Fortress, 2004), 69–101; and J. Denny Weaver, *The Nonviolent Atonement*, 2nd ed. (Grand Rapids: Eerdmans, 2011), 69–82. "The sacrificial system of ancient Israel is another biblical motif frequently assumed to supply the model for satisfaction atonement. This section challenges that assumption and demonstrates that the correlation is more linguistic than substantial" (Weaver, *Nonviolent Atonement*, 69).

21. The attempt by many in the liberal tradition (and some in the conservative) to strip the word "vicarious" of its substitutionary meaning is also unfounded; contrary to, e.g., Weaver, *Nonviolent Atonement*; Vincent Taylor, *The Atonement in New Testament Teaching* (London: Epworth, 1940); and Horace Bushnell, *The Vicarious Sacrifice, Grounded in Principles of Universal Obligation* (New York: Charles Scribner, 1866).

22. Though lacking a clear sacrificial focus, rightly, J. I. Packer and Mark Dever, eds., *In My Place Condemned He Stood: Celebrating the Glory of the Atonement* (Wheaton: Crossway, 2008).

23. Analogous to a bankrupt, homeless man who is promised the good news of receiving a large sum of money. If he has no way of attaining that money, it becomes meaningless. However, if he is introduced to the right people and shown the tasks by which he may receive it, then that mediatorial relationship, in itself, becomes good news.

24. Since the publication of E. P. Sanders' *Paul and Palestinian Judaism: A Comparison of Patterns of Religion* (Philadelphia: Fortress, 1977), the "righteousness of God" (Gk. *dikaiosunē theou*) has been the source of much controversy. Instead of a sacrificial reality with judicial implications (referencing moral standing), many have interpreted the phrase in an abstract relational manner, referencing "covenant faithfulness" (see Sanders, *Paul and Palestinian Judaism*, 523–42; cf. James D. G. Dunn, *Romans 1–8*, WBC [Dallas: Word, 1991], 41–44; N. T. Wright, *What Saint Paul Really Said: Was Paul of Tarsus the Real Founder of Christianity?* [Grand Rapids: Eerdmans, 1997], 118–33; Wright, *Paul: Fresh Perspectives* [London: SPCK, 2005], 25–32).

Thus it is argued that the righteousness of God is primarily "membership language" (Wright, *What Paul Really Says*, 124) relating to ecclesiology in this age, rather than forensic language relating primarily to soteriology and eschatology. However, "covenant faithfulness" is an *implication* of moral righteousness, not the *denotation* of it. Paul often refers to God's "faithfulness" (cf. Rom. 3:3; 1 Cor. 1:9; 10:13; 2 Cor. 1:8), but he rarely associates "righteousness" and "faithfulness" (cf. Rom. 3:3–5) because the former relates to judicial categories while the latter is inherently promissory.

Moreover, Paul speaks relatively little of "covenant" (Gk. *diathēkē*), except in relation to "promise" (cf. Rom. 9:4; Gal. 3:17; Eph. 2:12), and never in association with "righteousness." So Stephen Westerholm concludes, "'Righteousness' itself does not *mean* 'covenant faithfulness.' And—botheration!—when Paul speaks of God's promises he never speaks of God's righteousness, and when he speaks of God's righteousness he never speaks of God's promises" (*Perspectives Old and New on Paul: The "Lutheran" Paul and His Critics* [Grand Rapids: Eerdmans, 2004], 292). Though, of course, "There is no reason to drive a wedge between covenantal and forensic connotations of righteousness" (Michael F. Bird, *The Saving Righteousness of God: Studies on Paul, Justification and the New Perspective* [Eugene, OR: Wipf and Stock Publishers, 2007], 37).

25. This is a straightforward system designed for premodern, illiterate, agrarian peasants. It is only "complex" and "perplexing" to the modern mind, which seeks a deeper meaning beyond the simple transference of sin in the accountancy of God—e.g., "Scholars have long been perplexed over . . . the sacrificial system. On the one hand there is the feeling of responsibility toward the sacrificial material in the Bible—it must be organized, systematized, and understood—yet on the other hand there is the constant uncertainty as to its true religious significance. . . . Sacrificial practice remains a foreign and obtrusive element to the present-day interpreter" (Gary A. Anderson, "Sacrifice and Sacrificial Offerings: Old Testament," *ABD*, 5:871).

26. The phrase περὶ ἁμαρτίας refers to a "sin offering" in forty-four of its fifty-four LXX occurrences, as it does in Heb. 10:6,8; 13:11 (see chap. 11 of N. T. Wright, *The Climax of the Covenant: Christ and the Law in Pauline Theology* [Minneapolis: Fortress, 1992], 220–25). Note also the sacrificial implications on 2 Cor. 5:21, cf. Isa. 53:10 (see Ralph P. Martin, *2 Corinthians*, WBC [Dallas: Word, 1998], 157; and David E. Garland, *2 Corinthians*, NAC [Nashville: B & H Publishers, 1999], 300–302).

27. "Unsurprisingly in both the Jewish Scriptures and in second-temple literature righteousness can be bestowed upon persons as a gift [Pss. 35.27–28; 106.31; Isa. 61.10; Jer. 23.5–6; 33.16; Bar. 5.2,9; Wis. Sol. 12.16; *Ep. Arist.* 280; *Jub.* 1.16; 16.26; 1QH 4.17–23; 14.1–17]" (Bird, *Saving Righteousness of God*, 33).

28. "The righteousness from God" is here clearly contrasted with "their own righteousness" (Rom. 10:3, KJV, NKJV) and "our unrighteousness" (Rom. 3:5), cf. "a righteousness of my own" (Phil. 3:9; cf. Deut. 9:4ff.; Dan. 9:18). This righteousness is simply a *moral uprightness*, in contrast to the immoral transgression of 1) Satan, et al., 2) Adam, and 3) all his progeny (cf. Rom. 3:9ff.; 5:14ff.). OT (Heb. *tsedeq*) and NT (Gk. *dikaiosunē*) "righteousness" is a moral/legal correctness, in contrast to "sin[ners]" (Ps. 1:5; Dan. 9:16; Matt. 9:13, par.; John 16:8; Rom. 3:25; 5:19ff.; 6:13–20; 2 Cor. 5:21; 1 Peter 2:24; 3:18; 1 John 2:1), "iniquity" (Isa. 53:11; 64:6; Lam. 4:13; Ezek. 18:20; Dan. 4:27; 9:16; 2 Tim. 2:19–22), "wickedness" (Deut. 9:4f.; Job. 35:8; Ps. 45:7; Ezek. 18:20; 33:12; Heb. 1:9), "condemnation" (1 Kings 8:32; Job 34:17; Ps. 34:21; Prov. 17:15; Rom. 5:18; 2 Cor. 3:9), etc. See H. G. Stigers, "1879 צָדֵק (*ṣādēq*)," *TWOT*, 752–55; and "δίκαιος-δικαίωσις," BDAG, 246–50.

29. "To be rejected is N. T. Wright, 'Righteousness of God,' 206, who identifies 'we' as the covenant minister, Paul himself" (Paul Barnett, *The Second Epistle to the Corinthians*, NICNT [Grand Rapids: Eerdmans, 1997], 315, n. 69. See N. T. Wright, "On Becoming the Righteousness of God," *Pauline Theology*, ed. David M. Hay (Minneapolis: Fortress, 1993), 200–208. From the early church on, this verse has been understood substitutionally; see Thomas C. Oden, *The Word of Life: Systematic Theology*, vol. 2 (San Francisco: HarperSanFrancisco, 1992), 384. Paul's statement in 2 Cor. 5:21 is somewhat formulaic and "creedal" because he is summarily justifying his plea for reconciliation in vv. 11–20 (see Barnett, *2 Corinthians*, NICNT, 312–15).

30. Despite the rancorous objections of proponents of the so-called "new perspective on Paul" (see the discussion later in this chapter), a genitive of origin ("from God"), rather than a genitive of possession ("of God"), holds true to the context of the passage as a whole (cf. especially Rom. 4:1–5), and coincides with the parallel usage of the genitive of origin in Phil. 3:9 and Rom. 10:3.

31. As Stott says, "My contention is that 'substitution' is not a further 'theory' or 'image' to be set alongside the others, but rather the foundation of them all, without which each lacks cogency. If God in Christ did not die in our place, there could be neither propitiation, nor redemption, nor justification, nor reconciliation" (*Cross of Christ*, 168).

32. Analogous to a car, wherein the engine (cf. sacrifice) enacts the functionality of the transmission, chassis, and suspension (cf. propitiation, justification, and redemption), unto the purpose of transportation (cf. reconciliation). This transportation, of course, finds its apocalyptic destination in the day of the Lord and the age to come.

33. See Morris, *Apostolic Preaching*, 155–74.

34. "Heb *yôm hakkippurîm*—lit 'day of the covering over,' i.e., 'day of appeasement' . . . Yom Kippur was the day above all others on which Israel, as a nation, sought the propitiation of the God against whom they had sinned, together with the consequent blessing of His forgiveness and of reconciliation to Him" (W. Möller and J. B. Payne, "Atonement, Day of," *ISBE*, 1:360).

35. See "ἱλασμός," BDAG, 474; and "ἱλασμός," LSJ, 828.

36. Propitiation is commonly associated with temple and cultic sacrifice, rather than regal office. However, "Though ἱλάσκεσθαι is for the most part a cultic action, it can sometimes be applied to men and . . . can denote the placating of the emperor or his anger" (F. Büchsel, "ἱλάσκομαι," *TDNT*, 3:314). The term is used in both contexts because of the assumption that *the gods rule over creation from temples*. So the Jerusalem temple was understood as God's royal "footstool" (cf. 1 Chron. 28:2; Ps. 99:5; 132:7; Lam. 2:1), and the sacrifices offered there were made to appease the Great King (Ps. 47:2; 95:3; Mal. 1:14).

37. C. H. Dodd is well known for his disdain toward the concept of propitiation, preferring the more impersonal term "expiation." Many modern exegetes have carried on this attitude, caricaturing divine wrath and propitiation as "divine child abuse" in sympathy to feminists (Weaver, *Nonviolent Atonement*, 155–305), laden with images of "sacred violence" (Stephen Finlan, *Problems with Atonement: The Origins of, and Controversy about, the Atonement Doctrine* [Collegeville, MN: Liturgical Press, 2005], 18), which should be taken metaphorically since "wrath is not a divine property or essential attribute of God" (Green and Baker, *Recovering the Scandal*, 54). As Morris said, "Such citations could be multiplied almost indefinitely, for there are many modern writers to whom the concept of the wrath of God is anathema" (*Apostolic Preaching*, 208).

38. See Matt. 5:21–26; Gal. 5:20; Eph. 4:31; Col. 3:8.

39. As Morris notes,

> Among the heathen, propitiation was thought of as an activity whereby the worshiper was able himself to provide that which would induce a change of mind in the deity. In plain language he bribed his god to be favourable to him. When the term was taken over into the Bible these unworthy and crude ideas were abandoned, and only the central truth expressed by the term was retained, namely that propitiation signifies the averting of wrath by the offering of a gift. But in both Testaments the thought is plain that the gift which secures the propitiation is from God Himself. He provides the way whereby men may come to Him. (*Apostolic Preaching*, 210–11)

However, rather than the idea of propitiation being "taken over into the Bible," it seems that the pagan practices were fallen corruptions of the biblical standard, which predated the Mosaic Law (cf. Gen. 4:4f.; 8:20f.).

40. See Stott, *Cross of Christ*, 150.

41. "It is the combination of God's deep love for the sinner with His uncompromising reaction against sin which brings about what the Bible calls propitiation" (Morris, *Apostolic Preaching*, 210).

42. Ibid., 209. Morris goes on to say,

> It may be that wrath is not a perfect word to describe such an attitude, but no better has been suggested, and we must refuse to accept alternatives which do not give expression to the truth in question. Perhaps there is a certain anthropomorphism involved in the use of the term wrath, but it must not be forgotten that, "A false anthropomorphism is to be laid to the charge not of those who maintain that there is in the Biblical sense of the word, such a thing as the wrath of God. It is rather to be laid to the charge of those who encourage the idea that God is like an easy, good-natured, benevolent man." (Ibid., quoting Leighton Pullan, *The Atonement* [London: Longmans, Green, and Co., 1907], 194)

43. Ibid., 174.

44. Here are some examples: "fury" (Ex. 15:7; Lev. 26:28; Deut. 29:28; Ps. 2:5; 7:6; Isa. 10:5,25; 26:20; 30:27; 66:15; Jer. 21:5; Lam. 2:4; Ezek. 5:13,15; 6:12; 19:12; 21:17; 23:25; 24:13; Hab. 3:12); "wrath" (Ex. 32:11; Lev. 10:6; Num. 16:46; Deut. 9:7f.,22; 29:23,28; 1 Sam. 28:18; 2 Kings 22:13,17; 23:26; 2 Chron. 12:7,12; 19:2,10; 24:18; 28:11,13; 29:8; 32:26; 34:21,25; 36:16; Ezra 7:23; 8:22; 10:14; Neh. 13:18; Job 20:28; Ps. 6:1; 21:9; 38:1; 56:7; 59:13; 78:21,59; 89:46; 110:5; Isa. 9:19; 10:6; 13:9,13; 51:17,20,22; Jer. 4:4; 6:11; 7:20,29; 10:10; 21:12; 23:19; 25:15; 30:23; 36:7; 42:18; 50:13,25; Lam. 2:2; 4:11; Ezek. 7:19; 9:8; 13:13; 20:33; 22:22,31; 25:14; 36:6; 38:18; Dan. 9:16; Hos. 11:9; Nah. 1:2; Hab. 3:2,8; Zeph. 1:18; Zech. 8:2,14); "anger/angry"

(Gen. 18:30,32; Ex. 4:14; 34:6; Num. 11:1,10,33; 12:9; 14:18; 22:22; 25:3f.; 32:10,13f.; Deut. 1:37; 3:26; 4:21,25; 6:15; 7:4; 9:8,18ff.; 11:17; 13:17; 29:20,23f.,27f.; 31:17,29; 32:16,21; Josh. 7:1,26; 22:18; 23:16; Judg. 2:12,14,20; 3:8; 6:39; 10:7; 14:19; 2 Sam. 6:7; 24:1; 1 Kings 11:9; 14:9,15; 15:30; 16:7,13,26,33; 22:53; 2 Kings 13:3; 17:11,17f.; 21:6; 22:17; 23:19,26; 24:20; 1 Chron. 13:10; 2 Chron. 25:15; 28:9,25; 29:10; 30:8; 33:6; 34:25; Neh. 9:17; Job 4:9; 9:13; 20:23; 21:17; 42:7; Ps. 6:1; 7:6; 27:9; 38:1; 74:1; 77:9; 78:21,31; 79:5; 80:4; 86:15; 103:8; 106:29,40; 145:8; Prov. 22:14; 24:18; Isa. 5:25; 9:17; 12:1; 13:9,13; 30:27,30; 54:8; 64:9; 66:15; Jer. 3:12; 4:8,26; 7:18,20; 8:19; 10:24; 11:17; 12:13; 18:23; 23:20; 25:6f.,37; 30:24; 32:29f.; 36:7; 42:18; 44:3,8; 49:37; 51:45; 52:3; Lam. 1:12; 2:1,22; 3:66; 4:11; Ezek. 5:13,15; 13:13; 25:14; 35:11; 38:18; Dan. 9:16; Hos. 11:9; Joel 2:13; Jonah 3:9; 4:2; Mic. 7:18; Nah. 1:3; Hab. 3:8; Zeph. 2:2f.; 3:8; Zech. 1:2,12; 7:12; 10:3; Mal. 1:4).

45. Morris, *Cross in the New Testament*, 192. Furthermore, contrary to the impersonal idea of wrath, "It is impossible to think that God is anything other than vigorously active in such a process as that described in Romans 2:5ff. . . . The words describe a positive revulsion. Moreover they speak of God's activity in the day of judgment. That is to say, His personal, vigorous opposition is not exhausted in His present judgments on our sins. It continues to the very end of time and beyond" (ibid., 188–89).

46. "The agony in the garden opens a window on to the greater agony of the cross. If to bear man's sin and God's wrath was so terrible in anticipation, what must the reality have been like?" (Stott, *Cross of Christ*, 77).

47. Morris, *Apostolic Preaching*, 144; italics added.

48. See H. G. Stigers, "1879 קָדַק (*ṣādēq*)," *TWOT*, 752–55; G. Schrenk, "δίκαιος," *TDNT*, 2:182–225; and "δίκαιος-δικαίωσις," BDAG, 246–50.

49. The same word group is translated "So one act of *righteousness* [Gk. *dikaiōma*] leads to *justification* [Gk. *dikaiōsis*] and life for all men" (Rom. 5:18; cf. Rom. 4:5), or "It is not the hearers of the law who are *righteous* [Gk. *dikaios*] before God, but the doers of the law who will be *justified* [Gk. *dikaioō*]" (Rom. 2:13; cf. Gal. 3:11). In other words, "the righteousness of God" inherently speaks of "the justification of God"; and, conversely, to be "justified" can be translated "declared righteous" (Rom. 2:13; 3:20, NIV).

50. "The position is complicated by the fact that, where in English we have two word-groups to express the concepts of 'justice' and 'righteousness' (which seem to us quite different ideas), in Hebrew and in Greek and for that matter in a number of other languages the one word does duty for both concepts" (Morris, *Atonement*, 177).

51. Generally "justify" is used because we do not have an English verb for "make/declare right." Some have suggested the Old English "to rightwise" (Sanders, *Paul and Palestinian Judaism*, 439, 481, 526), or the British "to set to rights" (N. T. Wright, *Surprised by Hope: Rethinking Heaven, the Resurrection, and the Mission of the Church* [New York: Harper-Collins, 2008], 242; Wright, *Justification: God's Plan & Paul's Vision* [Downers Grove, IL: InterVarsity, 2009], 88), but these have not caught on widely.

52. The following examples will serve to illustrate the point: God sits on his throne, executing "righteous judgment" (Ps. 9:4; cf. Isa. 58:2), for "the heavens declare His *righteousness*, for God Himself is *judge*" (Ps. 50:6, NASB). "His work is perfect, for all His ways are *just*; a God of faithfulness and without injustice, *righteous* and upright is He" (Deut. 32:4, NASB). "The LORD of hosts will be exalted in *judgment*, and the holy God will show Himself holy in *righteousness*" (Isa. 5:16, NASB). For he says, "My *righteousness* draws near speedily, my salvation is on the way, and my arm will bring *justice* to the nations" (Isa. 51:5, NIV). For the Lord will "make *justice* the line, and *righteousness* the plumb line" (Isa.

28:17), because "when your *judgments* are in the earth, the inhabitants of the world learn *righteousness*" (Isa. 26:9).

Moreover, the foundation of God's throne is "*righteousness* and *justice*" (Ps. 89:14; 97:2), because the Lord "loves *righteousness* and *justice*" (Ps. 33:5) and "works *righteousness* and *justice*" (Ps. 103:6; cf. Ps. 99:4). The Lord "practices steadfast love, *justice*, and *righteousness* in the earth" (Jer. 9:24). Moreover, he calls people to "*justice* and *righteousness*" (1 Kings 10:9; 2 Chron. 9:8; Eccl. 5:8; cf. Gen. 18:19; Ps. 106:3; 119:121; Prov. 2:9; 8:20; 21:3; Isa. 56:1; Jer. 4:2; 22:3; Ezek. 18:5; 45:9; Amos 5:24), which will culminate in the messianic rule when "a king will reign in *righteousness*, and princes will rule in *justice*" (Isa. 32:1). This messianic king will be "one who *judges* and seeks *justice* and is swift to do *righteousness*" (Isa. 16:5). He will be given the throne of his father David, "to establish it and to uphold it with *justice* and with *righteousness* from this time forth and forevermore" (Isa. 9:7), and "he will fill Zion with *justice* and *righteousness*" (Isa. 33:5). He is the "*righteous* Branch," and he will "execute *judgment* and *righteousness* in the earth" (Jer. 23:5; 33:15, NKJV). For "with *righteousness* he shall *judge* the poor, and decide with equity for the meek of the earth" (Isa. 11:4). Therefore the psalmist prays, "Give the king your *justice*, O God, and your *righteousness* to the royal son!" (Ps. 72:1).

53. Note the Greek term *dikaiokrisia*, "righteous judgment" (Rom. 2:5), which literally combines the two concepts (see G. Schrenk, "δικαιοκρισία," *TDNT*, 2:224–25) and is echoed in the intertestamental literature (cf. 2 Maccabees 12:41; *Sibylline Oracles* 3.704; *Testament of Levi* 3:2; 15:2).

54. The synonym of righteousness is not "faithfulness," per se, as is evident by the relative lack of association in the LXX (cf. Deut. 32:4; 1 Sam. 26:23; Ps. 110:7; Prov. 12:17; Isa. 1:21,26; Jer. 49:5; Hab. 2:4). The NT also reflects this lack of association (a point well made by Mark A. Seifrid, *Christ, Our Righteousness: Paul's Theology of Justification*, NSBT 9, [Downers Grove, IL: InterVarsity, 2000], 38–45); contrary to Richard B. Hays, "Justification," *ABD*, 3:1129–33.

55. One of the problems of interpreting "justification" is the sheer volume of passages that must be addressed, which reflects the centrality of the judicial aspects of the day of the Lord (over the royal and economic aspects). So Morris,

> We have noted that propitiation, although an important conception, is used with reference to the atonement only four times in all in the New Testament. Similarly reconciliation, in which some modern scholars are inclined to see the essential New Testament teaching with regard to the atonement, occurs in only five passages, all of them Pauline. By contrast, he who would expound justification is confronted with eighty-one occurrences of the adjective δίκαιος, ninety-two of the noun δικαιοσύνη, two of the noun δικαίωσις, thirty-nine of the verb δικαιόω, ten of the noun δικαίωμα, and five of the adverb δικαίως. On examination much of this may prove to have little relevance to the atonement, but it remains that the bare enumeration of the number of passages to be considered indicates that we are here dealing with a conception of great importance for the evaluation of the atonement. (*Apostolic Preaching*, 251)

56. Ibid., 253, 293.

57. Morris, *Atonement*, 180.

58. See chapter 7.

59. See G. H. Livingston, "180 אָשָׁם (*āšam*)," *TWOT*, 78–80; and J. C. Moyer, "Guilt," *ISBE*, 2:580–81.

60. So Bird concludes, contrary to the tendencies of those holding to the so-called "new perspective on Paul," "It is wrong to think that the verdict rendered in justification can be reduced to sociological descriptions of group-identity and self-definition. That would evacuate the language of righteousness of its apocalyptic and juridical sense" (*Saving Righteousness of God*, 33).

61. So Paul places his own life in the divine courtroom in anticipation of the day of judgment: "But with me it is a very small thing that I should be judged by you or by any *human court* [Gk. *hupo anthrōpinēs hēmeras*, lit., "by any human day"]. In fact, I do not even judge myself. For I am not aware of anything against myself, but I am not thereby *acquitted* [Gk. *dikaioō*; "justified," KJV, NKJV]. It is the Lord who judges me. Therefore do not pronounce *judgment* before the time, before the Lord comes, who will bring to light the things now hidden in darkness and will disclose the purposes of the heart. Then each one will receive his commendation from God" (1 Cor. 4:3–5).

62. In this passage (Rom. 5:12–21) we see a clear example of the forensic and imputed nature of justification. "The basis of our justification before God is a divine righteousness that comes to us in a way analogous to the way Adam's sin came to us. As we were in him and share in his sin, so we are in Christ and share in his righteousness. In this historic way of understanding the text, the parallel that Paul wants us to see and rejoice in is that just as Adam's sin is imputed to us because we were in him, so Christ's righteousness is imputed to us because we are in him" (John Piper, *Counted Righteous in Christ: Should We Abandon the Imputation of Christ's Righteousness?* [Wheaton: Crossway, 2002], 93–94).

63. Those who hold to the so-called "new perspective on Paul" (see the discussion later in this chapter) claim "the works of the law" are simply the "badges of Jewish membership" (N. T. Wright, *The New Testament and the People of God* [Minneapolis: Fortress; London: SPCK, 1992], 237; cf. 207, 335, 368; Wright, *Justification*, 76, 134, 138, 246)—i.e., observance of circumcision, Sabbath, and kosher dietary laws (cf. James D. G. Dunn, *The New Perspective on Paul*, rev. ed. [Grand Rapids: Eerdmans, 2008], 108–20; Dunn, *Romans 1–8*, lxxi–lxxvii). This has been vigorously refuted; see C. E. B. Cranfield, "The Works of the Law in the Epistle to the Romans," *JSNT* 43 (1991): 89–101; and Moisés Silva, "Faith versus Works of Law in Galatians," in *Justification and Variegated Nomism, Volume 2: The Paradoxes of Paul*, eds. D. A. Carson, Peter T. O'Brien, and Mark A. Seifrid (Grand Rapids: Baker, 2004), 217–48. See a summary of the issues involved in Douglas J. Moo, *The Epistle to the Romans*, NICNT (Grand Rapids: Eerdmans, 1996), 206–17.

64. Concerning James 2:14–26 in particular, Stephen Westerholm states incisively,

> Here we have, in the words of Friedrich Avemarie, "a very old perspective on Paul." It suggests that by the first-century critics, as by Augustine, Luther, and many others, Paul was deemed to have dismissed any role for (good) works in answering the perennial religious question of how a human being can be found acceptable by God. It makes very clear that an insistence that salvation is by faith and grace, not (good) works, was anything but self-evident and uncontroversial in Paul's day. And it underlines the novelty of the new perspective that would limit his concerns to issues deemed more pressing by the modern mind: ethnocentricism, racism, and nationalistic pride. (*Perspectives Old and New*, 407)

65. Of course the so-called "ethnic boundary markers" were included in the consideration of moral righteousness and eschatological judgment. So Seifrid:

> We may think of "works of the law" in general terms as including adherence to the prohibitions against murder, adultery, theft, idolatry and the like, along with circumcision, Sabbath-keeping and food laws (cf. Rom. 2:17–24).

Nevertheless, Paul obviously regards the "works of the law" as bearing an ethnic and national significance. Only a Jew may boast in "the works of the law" or be identified as one who is "of the works of the law." It was by "works" that Israel vainly sought to establish its righteousness before God (Rom. 9:30—10:3). Clearly, then, Paul rejects these works as markers of "religio-national" identity, i.e. as signs of the people who are righteous, and not merely as signs of national privilege. (*Christ, Our Righteousness*, 100–101)

66. The concept of "more good than bad" means nothing on the day of judgment. Our hypothetical 5 percent of bad (i.e., misdeeds in this age) will comprise 100 percent of the trial at the judgment seat of Christ. As a man who loved and served the poor his whole life merits nothing when he stands before the judge for a single murder, so also when humanity stands before its Maker on the last day. In this way "all have sinned and fall short of the glory of God" (Rom. 3:23).

67. Regarding this passage, I am in basic agreement with Moo, *Romans*, NICNT, 218–43; and Thomas R. Schreiner, *Romans*, BECNT (Grand Rapids: Baker, 1998), 178–99; though both seem to lack an adequate emphasis on the day of the Lord and the Jewish apocalyptic framework, which gives ultimate context to the passage.

68. Note the definition of *logizomai*: "1. to determine by mathematical process . . . 2. to give careful thought to a matter . . . 3. to hold a view about something" (BDAG, 597).

69. The popular concept of *imparted* righteousness, common in much of Protestantism, has little to do with the biblical concept of *imputed* righteousness. God imputes (Gk. *logizomai*) righteousness by declaring, accounting, and reckoning the guilty innocent. He does not, as N. T. Wright is known for saying, transfer righteousness as a moral quality like "a substance or a gas which can be passed across the courtroom" (*What Saint Paul Really Said*, 98). So Stott:

> On the one hand, God declined to "impute" our sins to us, or "count" them against us (2 Cor. 5:19), with the implication that he imputed them to Christ instead. On the other, God has imputed Christ's righteousness to us. Many are offended by this concept, considering it both artificial and unjust on God's part to arrange such a transfer. Yet the objection is due to a misunderstanding. . . . What was transferred to Christ was not moral qualities but legal consequences: he voluntarily accepted liability for our sins. That is what the expressions "made sin" and "made a curse" mean. Similarly, "the righteousness of God" which we become when we are "in Christ" is not here righteousness of character and conduct (although that grows within us by the working of the Holy Spirit), but rather a righteous standing before God. (*Cross of Christ*, 148–49)

70. So Emil Brunner rightly highlights the two dominant themes of atonement (though lacking concerning the redemptive theme): the legal one with Christ's death as penalty and the cultic one with Christ as sacrifice (*The Mediator: A Study of the Central Doctrine of the Christian Faith*, trans. O. Wyon [London: Lutterworth Press, 1934], 435–535).

71. This truncated view of redemption is the result of the trickling down of liberally minded scholarship that rejects the objectivity of economic payment and exchange (inherent to the word group) in favor of the generic idea of deliverance. "The original, etymologically grounded sense is thus watered down in biblical usage, and only a very general sense remains. The true rendering, then, is 'redemption' or 'liberation,' not 'ransom.' 'Release' is also possible in Hb. 11:35 and 'remission' in Hb. 9:15. In primitive Christianity the word was used to express a religious content, and it thus took on a special sense which is not found elsewhere" (F. Büchsel, "ἀπολύτρωσις," *TDNT*, 4:355). All of this, of course, is ridiculous, since Paul would never "take a word with a known significance, give it a

new meaning all his own, and use it occasionally in the new sense without explanation" (Morris, *Apostolic Preaching*, 51).

72. See "λύτρον-λύτρωσις," BDAG, 605–6.

73. See Morris, *Apostolic Preaching*, 11–64; and Morris, *Atonement*, 106–31.

74. See L. Morris, "Ransom," *ISBE*, 4:44–45; and W. Mundle and C. Brown, "λύτρον," *NIDNTT*, 3:189–200.

75. As Morris observes,

> The idea of the payment of a price (the "ransom") is basic to all the redemption words. . . . There is always the thought of deliverance at cost. Sometimes it is deliverance from slavery and sometimes from a sentence of death. But both inside and outside the Bible that is the usage. As far as I am able I have searched the literature of antiquity and my conclusion is that redemption, apart from some metaphorical uses which depend on the normal usage, always denotes deliverance from a state of captivity (the prisoner of war), or from slavery, or from a death sentence. And always it is deliverance in a particular way, by the payment of a price. The idea of the payment of a price is fundamental to redemption. (*Atonement*, 118)

76. *Apostolic Preaching*, 26; contrary to, e.g., C. M. Tuckett, "Atonement in the NT," *ABD*, 1:520–21.

77. From Origen there has been debate concerning the recipient of the ransom—esp. God versus Satan (cf. Gustaf Aulén, *Christus Victor: An Historical Study of the Three Main Types of the Idea of Atonement*, trans. A. G. Hebert [New York: Macmillan, 1969], 47–55). It is often charged that for God to receive payment from Himself (in Christ) is an illogical transaction. Why take money out of one pocket and put it in the other? However, was not God the source of the offering in the OT (Lev. 17:11), which he received as a ransom for sin? When everything belongs to God (cf. Ps. 24:1; 50:12; 89:11)—i.e. "from him and through him and to him are all things" (Rom. 11:36)—how else is restitution to be made?

78. On the cost of the messianic sacrifice, see esp. Stott, *Cross of Christ*, 179–82.

79. The association of the *lutrōsis* word group with the *agorazō* word group (cf. 1 Cor. 6:20; 7:23; Gal. 3:13; 4:5; 2 Peter 2:1; Rev. 5:9; 14:4), i.e., "buy in the market" (LSJ, 13), further reinforces the economic ideas inherent to redemption.

80. Here we see the only use of *antilutron* in the Scriptures: "a strong compound meaning 'substitute-ransom'" (L. L. Morris, "Atonement," *NBD*, 103). Combined with *huper pantōn*, "on behalf of all," we have a radical declaration of substitutionality spoken somewhat formulaically (lodged between a petition for peaceful ecclesiology [1 Tim. 2:1–4] and the assertion of apostolic appointment [v. 7]), as though it were common knowledge. Such formulae are indicative of the common hermeneutical culture in the early church (see chapter 7, n. 60).

81. Note *2 Clement* 17:4: "For the Lord said, 'I am coming to gather together all the nations, tribes, and languages.' Now by this he means the day of his appearing, when he will come and redeem us, each according to his deeds" (Michael W. Holmes, *The Apostolic Fathers: Greek Texts and English Translations*, updated ed. [Grand Rapids: Baker, 1999], 125).

82. "Just as the Jews of that day (and of all succeeding ages right down to our own) looked forward to a 'redemption,' so did the Christians. One day their Messiah would return to the earth and thus there would be a great 'redemption' which would be of the greatest concern to them all. The resemblances to the Jewish conception are striking. The wording, the assurance of deliverance, the association of the deliverance with the Messiah, the

earnest looking forward to it, in all these points we have resemblance to the Jewish idea" (Morris, *Apostolic Preaching*, 47).

83. Though the cross was more than just penal, see the excellent survey and defense of substitutionary atonement by Steve Jeffery, Michael Ovey, and Andrew Sach, *Pierced for Our Transgressions: Rediscovering the Glory of Penal Substitution* (Wheaton: Crossway, 2007).

84. Without Jewish apocalypticism and the day of the Lord as a reference point, discussion of the atonement often devolves into a "kaleidoscopic" mélange of different ideas that ultimately speak of nothing; cf. Joel B. Green, "Kaleidoscopic View," in *The Nature of the Atonement: Four Views*, ed. James Beilby and Paul R. Eddy (Downers Grove, IL: InterVarsity, 2006), 157–85.

85. James tenaciously combated this gnostic tendency in the early church (cf. 2:14–26). Some, like Luther (cf. *Preface to the Epistles of St. James and St. Jude*, in *LW*, 35:395–96), pit James and Paul against each other in the struggle over justification by faith. However, Paul never says we are justified by faith *alone*. This phraseology is used only by James (2:24). Though Paul was accused of promoting such antinomian distortions (Rom. 3:8), he clearly fought against them (cf. Rom. 6:1f.,15; Gal. 2:17; 5:13; Titus 1:16). In response to such accusation, Paul preached that Jew and Gentile alike "should repent and turn to God, *performing deeds in keeping with their repentance*" (Acts 26:20), a statement functionally identical to James 2:22 (cf. Rom. 13:9f.; 1 Cor. 13:2; 2 Cor. 9:8; Gal. 5:6; Eph. 2:10; 2 Thess. 1:11).

"For Paul, ultimately the issue is not works versus faith, but law-works (whereby one tries to gain or retain God's approval) versus faith-works (which flow out of an already extant approval in Christ; Gal. 5:6)" (Dan G. McCartney, *James*, BECNT [Grand Rapids: Baker, 2009], 161, n.16). For a comprehensive introduction to the issues involved, see ibid., 161–71 and 272–79.

86. See "πίστις," BDAG, 818–20; and J. B. Scott, "116 אמן ('āman)," *TWOT*, 51–53.

87. See G. W. Bromiley, "Faith," *ISBE*, 2:270–73; and O. Michel, "πίστις," *NIDNTT*, 1:593–605.

88. Thus most theologians reinterpret the literalistic, futurist eschatology of the Scriptures, as typified by Rudolf Bultmann. "It is not easy in the twentieth century to imagine an imminent end of the world at which angels fly down with trumpet blasts from heaven, while the sun is darkened and the stars cease to shine. Consequently many theologians felt it to be a liberation when Bultmann showed the presence of a quite different eschatology in the New Testament—an individual, wholly personal eschatology, bound up with the moment of truth—the eschatology of detachment from the world; and when Bultmann expounded this as being the real eschatology meant by Paul and John and the others" (Klaus Koch, *The Rediscovery of Apocalyptic*, trans. M. Kohl [London: SCM Press, 1972], 67).

89. See Roy Ratcliff, *Dark Journey Deep Grace: Jeffrey Dahmer's Story of Faith* (Abilene, TX: Leafwood Publishers, 2006).

90. For popular rebuttals of the doctrine, see Daniel D. Corner, *The Believer's Conditional Security: Eternal Security Refuted*, 3rd ed. (Washington, PA: Evangelical Outreach, 2000); and David Pawson, *Once Saved, Always Saved? A Study in Perseverance and Inheritance* (London: Hodder & Stoughton, 1996).

91. So Baruch A. Levine in his commentary on Leviticus:

It should be emphasized here, as the workings of the sacrificial system are introduced to the reader, that the laws of the Torah did not permit Israelites to expiate intentional or premeditated offenses by means of sacrifice. There was no vicarious, ritual remedy—substitution of one's property or wealth—for such violations, whether they were perpetrated against other individuals or against God Himself. In those cases, the law dealt directly with the offender, imposing real punishments and acting to prevent recurrences. The entire expiatory system ordained in the Torah must be understood in this light. Ritual expiation was restricted to situations where a reasonable doubt existed as to the willfulness of the offense. Even then, restitution was always required where loss or injury to another person had occurred. The mistaken notion that ritual worship could atone for criminality or intentional religious desecration was persistently attacked by the prophets of Israel, who considered it a major threat to the entire covenantal relationship between Israel and God. (*Leviticus*, JPS Torah Commentary [Philadelphia: Jewish Publication Society, 1989], 2–3)

92. "The nom. (הַגָגָה) occurs 19× and conveys two basic meanings. First, it may signify an inadvertent error or mistake arising from the routine experiences of daily living. . . . Second, the word together with the vb. אָטָ, sin (#2627), functions as a legal and liturgical term in the priestly prescriptions for the guilt offering that atoned for inadvertent sin (Lev 4:2,22,27; 5:15,18; Num 15:24–29)" (A. E. Hill, "שגג גוּ [*šāgag*]," *NIDOTTE*, 4:42).

93. The difference between unintentional and intentional sin is most clearly defined in Num. 15:27–31:

If one person sins *unintentionally*, he shall offer a female goat a year old for a sin offering. And the priest shall make atonement before the LORD for the person who makes a mistake, when he sins unintentionally, to make atonement for him, and he shall be *forgiven*. You shall have one law for him who does anything *unintentionally*, for him who is native among the people of Israel and for the stranger who sojourns among them. But the person who *does anything with a high hand* ["sins defiantly," NIV], whether he is native or a sojourner, reviles the LORD, and that person shall be cut off from among his people. Because he has despised the word of the LORD and has broken his commandment, that person shall be utterly cut off; *his iniquity shall be on him.*

94. The common accusation that forensic justification promotes licentiousness, or that it cannot account for verses such as these, generally fails to account for intentionality in sacrifice and atonement.

95. "παραπίπτω," BDAG, 770.

96. Literal translation of Titus 1:16b by Philip H. Towner, *The Letters to Timothy and Titus*, NICNT (Grand Rapids: Eerdmans, 2006), 711; italics added.

97. The common reference to the circumcision group as "Judaizers" ("Judaizer" being derived from the Greek verb *ioudaizō*, "to live as Jews," found only in Gal. 2:14) seems misleading, since Judaism itself is not an enemy of the cross. It is only the distortion of Judaism that Paul rejected, for "we know that the law is good if one uses it properly" (1 Tim. 1:8, NIV).

98. See a comprehensive history of the debate by Richard N. Longenecker, "The Identity of the Opponents," *Galatians*, WBC (Dallas: Word, 1998), lxxxix–xcvi.

99. "Such 'ecclesiastical statistics' would furnish evidence of the success of their proselytizing mission as well as evidence of their zeal for the law. More important still, this would provide ground for boasting before God, since God would (supposedly) be pleased with their success in winning so many converts to Judaism" (Ronald Y. K. Fung, *The Epistle to the Galatians*, NICNT [Grand Rapids: Eerdmans, 1988], 304–5).

100. The heart of the issue lies in how many members of the church in Jerusalem were considered to be part of the circumcision group. If it was a small portion, as Acts 15:5 might

indicate, then we have a marginal tension affecting a relative few. If it was a large portion, as Galatians 2 and Acts 21 seem to indicate, then we have a greater tension affecting the whole of the early church (of course, the proportions could have changed over time).

101. Concerning the exact nature of this purification, four options are detailed by Darrell L. Bock, *Acts*, BECNT (Grand Rapids: Baker, 2007), 647–48.

102. See esp. Simon J. Gathercole, *Where Is Boasting? Early Jewish Soteriology and Paul's Response in Romans 1–5* (Grand Rapids: Eerdmans, 2002), 197–215.

103. Commenting on Rom. 3:20, Moo states,

> "Works of the law," then, as most interpreters have recognized, refers simply to "things that are done in obedience to the law." Paul uses the phrase "works of the law" instead of the simple "works" because he is particularly concerned in this context to deny to Jews an escape from the general sentence pronounced in v. 19. But, since "works of the law" are simply what we might call "good works" defined in Jewish terms, the principle enunciated here has universal application; nothing a person does, whatever the object of obedience or the motivation of that obedience, can bring him or her into favor with God. (*Romans*, NICNT, 209)

104. See above, n. 63.

105. There has been great dispute over the meaning of Rom. 10:4 (see Moo, *Romans*, NICNT, 636–43), but the context of the argument favors the simple fulfillment of a guiltless moral state in light of eschatological judgment (cf. Thomas R. Schreiner, "Paul's View of the Law in Romans 10:4–5," *WTJ* 55, no. 1 [Spring 1993]: 113–35). "Paul is speaking experientially in this text, so that his point is that Christ is the end of using the law to establish one's own righteousness. . . . Paul is countering here a form of works-righteousness in which the Jews thought that they could attain right standing with God by their works. This is the most natural way of understanding the statement that 'they were seeking to establish their own righteousness'" (ibid., 121–22).

106. There is also great dispute concerning the nature of the "Colossian heresy" addressed in Col. 2 (see Peter O'Brien, *Colossians, Philemon*, WBC [Dallas: Word, 1998], xxx–xxxviii). However, the references to "elemental spirits" (v. 8,20; cf. Gal. 4:3,9), "circumcision made without hands" (v. 11; cf. Eph. 2:11), the passing of judgment "in questions of food and drink" (v. 16; cf. Gal. 2:12) and "with regard to a festival or a new moon or a Sabbath" (v. 16; cf. Gal. 4:10), and "not holding fast to the Head" (v. 19; cf. Gal. 5:4) seem conclusive concerning a reference to the circumcision group.

107. The language of 1 Thess. 2:1–12 seems to indicate that Paul is contrasting the motivations of his ministry with that of the circumcision group (cf. 2 Cor. 5:20; 11:7–21; 12:14–19; Phil. 1:15–18). Of course, his reference to unbelieving Jews (vv. 2 and 14–16; cf. Acts 17:5) would not be unrelated in Paul's mind. Contrary to this is the idea of Greek itinerant "heathen missionaries" (F. F. Bruce, *1 and 2 Thessalonians*, WBC [Dallas: Word, 1998], 26; cf. A. J. Malherbe, "'Gentle as a Nurse': The Cynic Background to 1 Thess. 2," *NovT* 12, no. 2 [1970]: 203–17).

108. Phil. 3:2–21 makes most sense as a single, cohesive argument against the circumcision group. The crude translation of Gk. *koilia* (v. 19) as "belly" (KJV, NKJV, NRSV, ESV) or "stomach" (NIV) makes no sense in context (except maybe as a reference to Jewish food laws). It is the same *koilia* as Rom. 16:18, which is commonly translated "appetites" or "personal interests" (NLT). The offense of the cross ultimately derives from a corrupt "inward life, of feelings and desires" ("κοιλία," BDAG, 550).

109. All such language is reminiscent of the early church fathers' condemnation of the Ebionites. Though there may be a relationship between the two (see Daniel H. King, "Paul

and the Tannaim: A Study in Galatians," *WTJ* 45, no. 2 [Fall 1983]: 340–70), there is no clear evidence (see S. Goranson, "Ebionites," *ABD*, 2:260–61).

110. See Hans-Christoph Hahn, "Boast," *NIDNTT*, 1:226–29.

111. For a survey of the concept of boasting in second-temple Judaism, see Gathercole, *Where Is Boasting*, 37–194.

112. Note that the blindness metaphor is in reference to the cross being a "stumbling stone" (Rom. 9:32), implying that pride causes blindness to the truth. Jesus likewise labeled the Pharisees "blind guides" (Matt. 15:14; 23:16ff.), and said, "For judgment I came into this world, that those who do not see may see, and those who see may become blind" (John 9:39).

113. The "Jew" in Romans 2 only makes sense if he claims to be a believer, for how would an unbeliever cause division *within* the church? In light of the other references to internal ecclesiastical conflict (cf. 3:8; 6:1; 16:17f.), the affiliation is most likely with the circumcision group.

114. Paul explains the purpose of this grace: "so that in the coming ages he might show the immeasurable riches of his grace in kindness toward us in Christ Jesus" (v. 7). Note here the placement of "seated us with him in the heavenly places in Christ Jesus" (v. 6), both followed "by grace you have been saved" (v. 5) and preceded "by grace you have been saved" (v. 8). The idea is that we have been united *with Christ crucified*, and therefore we are confidently "seated . . . with him" (v.6) in anticipation of "the coming ages" (v. 7).

115. The amplifications in the brackets help keep in mind that the attainment of righteousness before God in light of the day of wrath is the overarching theme and purpose of Paul's letter to the Romans. Such an approach should likewise be considered when reading the narrative of Acts. The very outpouring of the Spirit in Acts 2 was upon *only those with faith in Christ crucified*. Thus it was God's sign that only those who believed in him as such (v. 38) would be saved from the great and glorious day (v. 20).

116. The working of miracles by the Spirit (v. 5) is complicated by those of the circumcision group who claimed to have angelic visitations (1:8; cf. Col. 2:18). The Pharisees believed in angels and spirits (Acts 23:8) *for a reason*. Far from today's popular characterizations, the Pharisees commonly drove out demons (cf. Matt. 12:27, par.; Luke 9:49; Acts 19:13) and sought signs, wonders, and miracles (Matt. 12:38, par.; cf. "attested *to you*," Acts 2:22), though for perverse motivations (cf. Matt. 7:15–23).

117. Note Paul's use of "the faith" in the sense of "the body of Christian truth implied in faith" (G. W. Bromiley, "Faith," *ISBE*, 2:270). NT writers had a simple body of theological truth that revolved around a sacrificial understanding of the Messiah's first coming in light of an apocalyptic understanding of his second coming within the overarching framework of Jewish election (cf. Rom. 1:5; Gal. 1:23; 1 Tim. 4:1,6; Jude 3).

118. Morris, *Atonement*, 126.

119. As seen in Plato's characters Thrasymachus (*Republic*, 336–54) and Callicles (*Gorgias*).

120. *The Holy Rule of Our Most Holy Father Benedict: With Declarations and Constitution of the American-Cassinee Congregation*, trans. Boniface F. Verheyen, (Atchison, KS: Abbey Student Press, 1949), chap. 73; italics added; available online at http://www.ccel.org/ccel/benedict/rule.

121. Theological historian Alister E. McGrath observes,

In a passage written toward the end of his career, Luther relates how he tried with all his might to do what was necessary to achieve salvation, but found himself more and more convinced that he could not be saved. *If ever a monk could get to heaven through monastic discipline, Luther remarked, he was that monk.* Yet he kept doubting: "'You didn't do that right. You weren't contrite enough. You left that out of your confession.'" It seemed to Luther that he simply could not meet the precondition for salvation. He did not have the resources needed to be saved. There was no way that God could justly reward him with salvation—only with condemnation. (*Reformation Thought: An Introduction*, 4th ed. [Chichester, UK: Wiley-Blackwell, 2012], 119; italics added)

122. Ibid., 119. Ecclesiastical abuses, as seen in Luther's Ninety-Five Theses, were understood as products of the church's theological abuses; so this question (which drove his theological conclusions) was "*the* central question on his personal agenda" (ibid.).

123. See Alister E. McGrath, *Luther's Theology of the Cross: Martin Luther's Theological Breakthrough*, 2nd ed. (Chichester, UK: Wiley-Blackwell, 2011), esp. 127–60.

124. Ibid., 155; italics in the original.

125. Luther, however, was generally vitriolic in his critique of the pope; e.g., "You see how woefully those err who try to escape eternal damnation by means of their monkeries, cowls, and tonsures. Moreover, such people even offer their supererogatory works for sale and transfer them to others. This, I regret to say, is how we lived in the papacy. You young people, be grateful to God for your better insight, and learn these words well. For death and the devil are in league with the pope and with the Turks' Koran to delude the people into relying on their foul works for salvation" (*LW*, 22:360–61).

126. Especially in light of the common practice of selling indulgences (a major source of papal revenue) for justification and the forgiveness of sins; that is, "The eternal penalties resulting from sinful actions could be reduced, if not eliminated, by payment of an appropriate sum of money to the appropriate ecclesiastical figure" (McGrath, *Reformation Thought*, 123). So, "Luther's doctrine of justification by faith, with its associated doctrine of the 'priesthood of all believers,' thus assumed an importance which far transcended the sphere of academic theology. . . . No payment of any kind was required to receive divine forgiveness" (ibid., 124).

127. Concerning monasticism as a whole, Luther believed it to be antithetical to justification by faith (cf. "The Judgment of Martin Luther on Monastic Vows [1521]," *LW*, 44:243–400; and "Avoiding the Doctrines of Men [1522]," *LW*, 35:125–53)—even saying, "Would to God that all monks and nuns could hear this sermon and properly understand this matter and would all forsake the cloisters, and thus all the cloisters in the world would cease to exist; this is what I would wish" ("Third Sermon, March 11, 1522, Tuesday after Invocavit," *LW*, 51:80).

   Therefore, "In modern history, monasticism suffered a substantial diminution at the time of the Protestant Reformation. Generally, the leaders of the Reformation believed that monastics did not in fact conform to a simple gospel rule of life, that their repetitive prayers, fasts, and ceremonies were meaningless, and that they had no real value to society. In Protestant thought, the pious family tended to replace the monastery as the ideal style of Christian life. Wherever the Reformation was triumphant, the monasteries were disestablished" (C. T. Marshall, "Monasticism," in *Evangelical Dictionary of Theology: Second Edition*, ed. Walter A. Elwell [Grand Rapids: Baker, 2001], 786).

128. As Schweitzer is known for saying, "The doctrine of righteousness by faith is therefore a subsidiary crater, which has formed within the rim of the main crater—the mystical doctrine of redemption through the being-in-Christ" (*The Mysticism of Paul the Apostle*, trans. W. Montgomery [London: A. & C. Black, 1931], 225). Such marginalization of the doctrine of justification has been taken up by many following Schweitzer, including

E. P. Sanders, who prefers "participationist" language instead of mystical union (cf. *Paul and Palestinian Judaism,* 434–42).

129. The phrase "new perspective" in relation to Pauline studies was originally used by N. T. Wright ("The Paul of History and the Apostle of Faith," *TynBul* 29 [1978]: 61–88), but J. D. G. Dunn popularized the well-known phrase ("The New Perspective on Paul," in *Jesus, Paul and the Law* [London: SPCK, 1990; orig. pub. 1983])—both owing to E. P. Sanders and his book *Paul and Palestinian Judaism* (Minneapolis: Fortress, 1977). These make up "the three musketeers of the so-called 'New Perspective'" (Gathercole, *Where Is Boasting,* 16). Though holding many commonalities, Wright describes the internal reality: "There is no such thing as *the* new perspective. . . . There is only a disparate family of perspectives, some with more, some with less family likeness, and with fierce squabbles and sibling rivalries going on inside" (*Justification,* 28).

130. See esp. G. F. Moore, *Judaism in the First Centuries of the Christian Era: The Age of the Tannaim,* 3 vols. (Cambridge, MA: Harvard University Press, 1927–30).

131. See H. J. Schoeps, *Paul: The Theology of the Apostle in the Light of Jewish Religious History* (Philadelphia: Westminster, 1961); cf. Westerholm, *Perspectives Old and New,* 101–200.

132. Originally and most incisively stated by Krister Stendahl, "The Apostle Paul and the Introspective Conscience of the West," *HTR* 56 (1963): 199–215; reprinted in Krister Stendahl, *Paul Among Jews and Gentiles* (Philadelphia: Fortress, 1976), 78–96. All of the major lines of New Perspective thought are found in this article.

133. Stendahl, *Paul Among Jews and Gentiles,* 82.

134. As per Dodd's pupil, W. D. Davies, *Paul and Rabbinic Judaism: Some Rabbinic Elements in Pauline Theology,* 2nd ed. (London: SPCK, 1955).

135. Broadly labeled by E. P. Sanders as "covenantal nomism" (from Gk. *nomos,* i.e., "law"): "Briefly put, covenantal nomism is the view that one's place in God's plan is established on the basis of the covenant and that the covenant requires as the proper response of man his obedience to its commandments, while providing means of atonement for transgression" (*Paul and Palestinian Judaism,* 75). Thus the implication is that "election and ultimately salvation are considered to be by God's mercy rather than human achievement" (ibid., 422). "In short, this is what Paul finds wrong with Judaism: it is not Christianity" (ibid., 552). This assessment ignores Jesus' condemnations of Pharisaical pride (cf. Matt. 23:12; Luke 16:15; 18:9) and Paul's clear characterization of many Jews in the first century as "arrogant" (Rom. 11:18).

136. Stendahl, *Paul Among Jews and Gentiles,* 84.

137. "Paul's discussion [concerning 'righteousness by faith'] cannot be understood unless we know the topic that he and his opponents were debating. The subject matter is not 'how can the individual be righteous in God's sight?', but rather, 'on what grounds can Gentiles participate in the people of God in the last days?'" (E. P. Sanders, *Paul: A Very Short Introduction* [New York: Oxford University Press, 2001], 58).

138. See above, n. 63.

139. "There is not—as we usually think—first a conversion, and then a call to apostleship; there is only the call to the work among the Gentiles" (Stendahl, *Paul Among Jews and Gentiles,* 84–85). See a rebuttal by Seyoon Kim, *Paul and the New Perspective: Second Thoughts on the Origin of Paul's Gospel* (Grand Rapids: Eerdmans, 2002).

140. For example, James D. G. Dunn, *The Theology of Paul the Apostle* (Grand Rapids: Eerdmans, 1998), 334–89; Dunn, *New Perspective on Paul,* 193–212, 367–80; N. T. Wright, *What Saint Paul Really Said,* 118–33; and Wright, *Paul: Fresh Perspectives,* 110–22.

141. See A. Andrew Das, *Paul, the Law, and the Covenant* (Grand Rapids: Baker, 2000); Seifrid, *Christ, Our Righteousness*; Westerholm, *Perspectives Old and New*; and D. A. Carson, Peter T. O'Brien, and Mark A. Seifrid, eds., *Justification and Variegated Nomism*, 2 vols. (Grand Rapids: Baker, 2001, 2004).

142. See John Piper, *The Future of Justification: A Response to N. T. Wright* (Wheaton: Crossway, 2007); cf. Wright's response in *Justification*.

143. Bird, *Saving Righteousness of God*, 89.

144. See G. K. Beale's review of *Justification and Variegated Nomism* in "The Overstated 'New' Perspective?" *BBR* 19, no. 1 (2009): 85–94.

145. Mediating voices between the new and old perspectives include Bird, *Saving Righteousness of God*; Gathercole, *Where Is Boasting*; and Francis Watson, *Paul, Judaism, and the Gentiles: Beyond the New Perspective*, Rev. ed. (Grand Rapids: Eerdmans, 2007).

146. "Sadly, reformed exegetes seem to have ignored the horizontal aspects and those in the NPP over-emphasize to an inordinate degree the horizontal dimensions. A denial of the corporate dimension of God's saving action means that justification is artificially removed from the social context in which Paul rigorously prosecuted justification by faith as a mandate for Gentile inclusion. The status of the individual before God and the status of individuals within a group setting are not mutually exclusive categories… when viewed this way the 'Lutheran' and NPP approach to Paul are hardly contradictory in what they want to affirm," (Bird, *Saving Righteousness of God*, 153).

147. So Moisés Silva:

> It would be folly to deny that (exclusivistic) national and sociological commitments on the part of Paul's Jewish contemporaries were an integral part of the attitudes the apostle was combating. It is no less ill-advised, however, to deduce that first-century Judaism was free from the universal human tendency to rely on one's own resources rather than on God's power. Why should it be thought that ethnic pride and (personal) self-confidence are mutually exclusive factors? The attempt to work for, or at least contribute to, one's own salvation by means of good deeds was hardly absent in the Jewish communities with which Paul interacted. ("Faith versus Works of Law," 246)

148. Wright, being the most articulate and readable of those within the New Perspective, summarizes the concept of covenant, relating it to inaugurationalism:

> The "covenant," in my shorthand, is not something other than God's determination to deal with evil once and for all and so put the whole creation (and humankind with it) right at last. When will it become clear to the geocentrists [condescending reference to traditional Lutheran and Reformed thinkers]? *Dealing with sin, saving humans from it, giving them grace, forgiveness, justification, glorification—all this was the purpose of the single covenant from the beginning, now fulfilled in Jesus Christ.* . . .
>
> Paul's retrieval of this underlying story, and his dialectical engagement with other contemporary Jewish versions of and theories about it, and his rethinking (but not abandoning) of it in the light of Jesus, the Jewish Messiah, the denouement-in-person of the single-plan-through-Israel-for-the-world, the one through whom at last the one God would fulfill the one plan to accomplish the one purpose, to rid the world of sin and establish his new creation—and of the Holy Spirit, the operating power of the single-saving-plan-through-Israel-for-the-world-now-fulfilled-in-the-Messiah, Jesus. (*Justification*, 95–96; italics in the original; information in brackets added))

149. For example, Heikki Räisänen, *Paul and the Law* (Philadelphia: Fortress, 1986); and John G. Gager, *Reinventing Paul* (Oxford: Oxford University Press, 2000).

150. Thus one will notice at a broad level very little eschatological emphasis in Sanders, some in Dunn, and yet more in Wright. However, "Both Wright and Dunn recognize the relationship of justification to the final judgment; the problem is that they minimize this aspect and subordinate it beneath the application of justification to covenantal membership" (Bird, *Saving Righteousness of God*, 101).

151. See Westerholm, *Perspectives Old and New*, 352–407; see also Westerholm's concise (and satiric) article, "Justification by Faith is the Answer: What is the Question?" *Concordia Theological Quarterly* 70 (2006): 197–217.

152. "It is high time that we eschew false dichotomies. The NT does reflect certain sociological concerns not fully appreciated by the Reformers, but it hardly follows from this fact that other elements they saw in the text are false. Again, we may readily agree that Protestantism has often caricatured rabbinic Judaism and that, in the process, it has failed to provide a complete picture of Paul's thought. None of that means, however, that the traditional doctrine of justification by faith is in need of overhauling" (Silva, "Faith Versus Works of the Law," 247).

Chapter Nine

1. Cf. Acts 1:22; 2:32,40; 3:15; 4:33; 5:32; 8:25; 10:39, 41ff.; 13:31; 14:3; 18:5; 20:21–26; 22:15–20; 23:11; 26:16,22; 28:23; Rom. 2:15f.; 3:21; 8:16; 9:1; 1 Cor. 1:6; 2:1; 15:15; 2 Cor. 1:12; Gal. 5:3; Eph. 4:17; 2 Thess. 1:10; 1 Tim. 2:6; 6:13; 2 Tim. 1:8; Heb. 2:4; 3:5; 12:1; 1 Peter 5:1; 1 John 1:2; 4:14; 5:6–11; Rev. 1:2,9; 2:13; 6:9; 11:3, 7; 12:11, 17; 19:10; 20:4; 22:20. See the classic overview by H. Strathmann, "μάρτυς," *TDNT*, 4:474–508.

2. The lack of reference in most modern commentaries to the apocalyptic framework of this passage is astonishing.

3. Concerning the disputed ending of Mark, see chapter 4, n. 21.

4. We could also say the apostles were *monistic* in their worldview of the heavens and the earth and *chiliastic* in their approach to the day of the Lord. However, these must be considered secondary in focus and emphasis. Chiliasm received much greater emphasis in the second century after the Revelation given to John.

5. The inaugurational witness simply mitigates the dominionist approach with a temporal inheritance now unto an eternal, semisupernaturalized inheritance to come. The dispensational witness (classical and revised) complicates things doubly: a heavenly inheritance for Gentiles and an earthly one for Jews. Both witnesses (like their historical predecessors) substantially undermine, in theology and practice, the church's conformity to the cross in this age.

6. See the common usage in Roman courts of law in Allison A. Trites, *The New Testament Concept of Witness* (Cambridge: Cambridge University Press, 1977), 4–15.

7. Though inaugurational in assumption, Lesslie Newbigin articulates well the relationship between God and his witnesses:

> When Israel is told "You are my witnesses" (e.g., Is. 44:8), it is plain that Israel is not being summoned to help God to cope with the otherwise unmanageable powers of the pagan empires, or to organize a movement which will carry out God's purposes in contradistinction to the godless purposes of these empires. They are but a little thing in God's hands. He raises them up and casts them down as he will. Israel's role is to be—precisely—witness of his purpose to these pagan nations to whom it would be otherwise unintelligible. Israel knows what God is doing—or ought to know; the others do not. The revelation of his nature and will which God has given to Israel equips her to understand the meaning of what he is doing.
>
> The New Testament carries the same teaching. Christians are not called upon to organize a movement to counter the powers of paganism. They are called upon to be witnesses to him who is sovereign over history, whose character and will have been revealed and who—in Christ—has done the deed which precipitates the final issue for all mankind. They are called upon to recognize the signs of the times—that is to say the signs of the last days which follow the coming of Jesus and point to his coming again. . . . In him God presents every man, and the whole of mankind, with the possibility of receiving or rejecting the end for which he created all things. The whole of human history, after the coming of Christ until his coming again, is the pressing of this choice to the final issue. And the Church is the body which understands this, which is called to bear witness among the nations to the real meaning of the events amid which we live, and thereby to present to all men and nations the concrete alternatives of acceptance or rejection. (*Trinitarian Faith and Today's Mission* [Richmond: John Knox, 1964], 24–25)

8. Note esp. the language of prophetic witness in John's Gospel:

> The Fourth Gospel, like Isaiah 40–55, is of particular importance for it presents a sustained use of the juridical metaphor. . . .
>
> The Fourth Gospel presents a controversy very similar to the one found in Isaiah 40–55. There the controversy between Yahweh and the false gods turns out to be a lawsuit between God and the world. God is represented by Israel and the world by the pagan nations. Similarly, in the Fourth Gospel God incarnate has a lawsuit with the world. His witnesses include John the Baptist, the scriptures, the words and works of Christ, and later the witness of the apostles and the Holy Spirit. . . .
>
> The idea of witness in John's Gospel is both very prominent and thoroughly juridical, and is to be understood in terms of Old Testament language. (Trites, *New Testament Concept of Witness*, 78–80; see 78–127)

9. See "κρίμα, κρίνω," BDAG, 567–69.

10. "Witness, Testimony," *NIDNTT*, 3:1048.

11. "Witnesses are held accountable for the truthfulness of their testimony. Perjury was, and still is, a serious offense punishable by heavy penalties. This solemn sense of being responsible under God for speaking truthfully appears in Paul, who four times declares, 'God is my witness.' Applied to preachers, this means that they are driven back to the Scriptures as the standard whereby their witness is to be judged" (ibid., 3:1049–50).

12. The same kind of summarization with the same elements is found in 2 Tim. 1:8–11 and Titus 3:3–8. So also Peter summarizes his calling: "I exhort the elders among you, as a fellow elder and a *witness* of the sufferings of Christ, as well as a partaker in the glory that is going to be revealed" (1 Peter 5:1). And John: "That which was from the beginning, which we have heard, which we have seen with our eyes, which we looked upon and have touched with our hands, concerning the word of life—the life was made manifest, and we have seen it, and *testify* to it and proclaim to you the eternal life" (1 John 1:1–2).

13. On the Antichrist, see esp. Joel Richardson, *Mideast Beast* (Washington, DC: WND Books, 2012); and Richardson, *The Islamic Antichrist* (Los Angeles: WND Books, 2009).

14. For example, R. T. France, *The Gospel of Matthew*, NICNT (Grand Rapids: Eerdmans, 2007), 907–10; and Donald A. Hagner, *Matthew 14–28*, WBC (Dallas: Word, 1998), 695–96.

15. Mark places the proclamation of "the gospel" (13:10) in the middle of testifying before governors and kings (v. 9) and being brought to trial (v. 11). Furthermore, the passage is closely paralleled in Matt. 10:16–23, which is similarly incriminatory in tone. Craig Blomberg articulates clearly the negative context of Matt. 24:14 (though strangely concluding with a positive interpretation): "Separated from the previous eight negative signs that do not herald the end is the promise of yet one more preliminary event: (9) the extensive preaching of the gospel (v. 14). Here is the fulfillment of the Great Commission Jesus will give in 28:18–20. Probably it is separated from the other eight items because it is a more positive development" (*Matthew*, NAC [Nashville: B&H Publishing, 1992], 356). This "separation" is imposed (nonexistent in Mark) and does not align with the verses preceding and following.

16. Note the law-court images throughout (cf. Trites, *New Testament Concept of Witness*, 154–74).

17. "How, then, should evangelism be defined? The New Testament answer is very simple. According to the New Testament, evangelism is just preaching the gospel, the evangel. It is a work of communication in which Christians make themselves mouthpieces for God's

message of mercy to sinners. Anyone who faithfully delivers that message, under whatever circumstances, in a large meeting, in a small meeting, from a pulpit, or in a private conversation, is evangelizing" (J. I. Packer, *Evangelism and the Sovereignty of God* [Downers Grove, IL: InterVarsity, 1961], 41).

18. On preaching and teaching in the early church, see esp. Michael Green, *Evangelism in the Early Church*, rev. ed. (Grand Rapids: Eerdmans, 2004), 300–17.

19. See David L. Larsen, *The Evangelism Mandate: Recovering the Centrality of Gospel Preaching* (Grand Rapids: Kregel, 1992), 45–66. See a modern example in Vincent J. Donovan, *Christianity Rediscovered: An Epistle from the Masai* (London: SCM Press, 2001).

20. Like parents who say to their children, "I love you," yet beat them incessantly, so also is the church that speaks a cruciform message of the love of God yet continually abuses and exploits its members for money and power. The words begin to lose their import. Such was the condition of the Corinthian church (cf. 1 Cor. 1–4).

21. A well-known statement made by Sri Lankan missiologist D. T. Niles, cited in Ashish Amos, *The Preaching of Daniel Thambirajah Niles: Homiletical Criticism* (Delhi: ISPCK, 2009), 57.

22. A truth incisively spoken by Arthur Katz and Paul Volk, *The Spirit of Truth* (Charlotte: Morningstar, 1992).

23. See a compilation of early accounts in Herbert Musurillo, *The Acts of the Christian Martyrs* (Oxford: Clarendon Press, 1972).

24. See *The New Encyclopedia of Christian Martyrs*, ed. Mark Water (Alresford, Hampshire, England: John Hunt, 2001), 22–44; cf. Eusebius, *Ecclesiastical History*, 3.1–2 (*NPNF2*, 1:132–33).

25. See *ANF*, 3:36, n. 1. Tertullian thus concludes his *Apology*,

> The oftener we are mown down by you, the more in number we grow; *the blood of Christians is seed.* Many of your writers exhort to the courageous bearing of pain and death . . . and yet their words do not find so many disciples as Christians do, teachers not by words, but by their deeds. That very obstinacy you rail against is the preceptress. For who that contemplates it, is not excited to inquire what is at the bottom of it? Who, after inquiry, does not embrace our doctrines? And when he has embraced them, desires not to suffer that he may become partaker of the fulness of God's grace. . . . As the divine and human are ever opposed to each other, when we are condemned by you, we are acquitted by the Highest. (Ch. 50 [*ANF*, 3:55]; italics in the original)

26. "*Martyrs are the most credible exponents of the value of religion, and this is especially true if there is a voluntary aspect to their martyrdom.* By voluntarily accepting torture and death rather than defecting, a person sets the highest imaginable value upon a religion and communicates that value to others. . . . Christian martyrs typically had the opportunity to display their steadfastness to large numbers of other Christians, and the value of Christianity they thereby communicated often deeply impressed pagan observers as well" (Rodney Stark, *The Rise of Christianity: A Sociologist Reconsiders History* [Princeton, NJ: Princeton University Press, 1996], 174; italics in the original).

27. Or asceticism, as distorted in early monasticism; see Edward E. Malone, *The Monk and the Martyr: The Monk as the Successor of the Martyr* (Washington, DC: Catholic University of America Press, 1950).

28. On the intertestamental background of martyrdom, see W. H. C. Frend, *Martyrdom and Persecution in the Early Church: A Study of a Conflict from the Maccabees to Donatus* (Grand Rapids: Baker, 1981); and Josef Ton, *Suffering, Martyrdom, and Rewards in*

Heaven (Lanham, MD: University Press of America, 1997), 47–61. See esp. 1 Maccabees 2:37f.,50ff.; 2 Maccabees and 4 Maccabees passim; Wisdom of Solomon 2:19f.; 3:1ff.; *1 Enoch* 47.1ff.; *Martyrdom of Isaiah* 5.10ff. (cf. Heb. 11:37); and Josephus, *Wars of the Jews* 2.151ff.

29. Those who spiritualize this passage fail at every level hermeneutically; see Ton, *Suffering, Martyrdom, and Rewards*, 81–83.

30. "One of the repeated emphases of the entire New Testament is that it is the very nature of the church to be a martyr people. When Jesus taught that a man to be his disciple must deny himself and take up his cross (Matt. 10:38; 16:24), he was not speaking of self-denial or the bearing of heavy burdens; he was speaking of willingness to suffer martyrdom. The cross is nothing else than an instrument of death. Every disciple of Jesus is in essence a martyr" (G. E. Ladd, *A Commentary on the Revelation of John* [Grand Rapids: Eerdmans, 1972], 104).

31. As Craig Hovey states,

> The virtues necessary to be a martyr are no different from the virtues necessary to be a faithful Christian. This means that martyrdom is not a special calling for a select few, but the commitment of every Christian and the responsibility of every church. Even though not every individual Christian will be killed, there is no way to distinguish those who will be killed from those who will not. Even though not every Christian will be remembered as a martyr, every church that locates its identity in the cross is obligated to cultivate the virtues necessary to enable all of its members to die for the cause of Christ. Every Christian is a member of a martyr-church. (*To Share in the Body: A Theology of Martyrdom for Today's Church* [Grand Rapids: Brazos Press, 2008], 60)

32. So David Wright observes,

> The making of a Christian preceded the making of a martyr, for the latter needed a strong sense of his or her Christian identity, of the exclusive distinctiveness of the Christian people to which he or she belonged, of the priority of loyalty to Christ over all other calls on his or her fidelity—to parents, for example, or to children—and a strong faith in the resurrection of the body and the life of the world to come. Many a martyr was fired by a vision of heaven ahead. For martyrdom stood for nothing so much as the other-worldly, future-worldly orientation of early Christianity. ("The Testimony of Blood: The Charisma of Martyrdom," *BSac* 160 [2003]: 397)

33. Reflecting on this passage, John Piper writes,

> The most amazing thing about Colossians 1:24 is *how* Paul fills up what is lacking in Christ's afflictions. He says that it is *his own sufferings* that fill up Christ's afflictions. "I rejoice in *my sufferings* for your sake, and *in my flesh* I am filling up what is lacking in Christ's afflictions." This means, then, that Paul exhibits the sufferings of Christ by suffering *himself* for those he is trying to win. In *his* sufferings they see Christ's sufferings. Here is the astounding upshot: *God intends for the afflictions of Christ to be presented to the world through the afflictions of his people.* God really means for the body of Christ, the church, to experience some of the suffering he experienced so that when we proclaim the cross as the way to life, people will see the marks of the cross in us and feel the love of the cross from us. Our calling is to make the afflictions of Christ real for people by the afflictions we experience in bringing them the message of salvation. (*Desiring God: Meditations of a Christian Hedonist*, 3rd ed. [Sisters, OR: Multnomah, 2003], 269–70; italics in the original)

34. "The fact that John saw the souls of the martyrs *under the altar* has nothing to do with the state of the dead or their situation in the intermediate state; it is merely a vivid way of picturing the fact that they had been martyred in the name of their God. In the Old Testament ritual blood of sacrificial victims was poured out at the base of the altar (Lev. 4:7). The souls of martyrs are seen under the altar as though they had been sacrificed upon the altar and their blood poured out at its base" (Ladd, *Revelation*, 103).

35. Note the persecution of the churches (2:9,13; 3:9), the slain souls under the altar (6:9), the great multitude of martyrs from every nation (7:14), the two witnesses (11:7), the judgment of the wicked who destroyed the righteous (11:18), those who "loved not their lives even unto death" (12:11), the dragon making war upon those who hold to the testimony of Jesus (12:17), the beast being "allowed to make war on the saints and to conquer them" (13:7), the patient endurance and blessing of the saints in light of the image and mark of the beast (14:11ff.), the harvesting of the earth's righteous (14:16), those beside the sea of glass "who had conquered the beast and its image" (15:2), the shedding of the blood of the saints causing the bowls of wrath to be poured out (16:6), the Harlot Babylon being drunk with the blood of the saints (17:6), the judgment of Harlot Babylon to avenge the blood of the saints (18:20), the rejoicing of the multitude in heaven for the avenging of the saints (19:2), and the vindication of the martyrs in the millennium (20:4).

36. See Ton, *Suffering, Martyrdom, and Rewards*, 325–78.

37. As German theologian Ethelbert Stauffer noted,

> The early church meditated upon these thoughts further. The first Clemens epistle contains a martyrs' summary in the style of the eleventh chapter of the Epistle to the Hebrews. The *Shepherd of Hermas* looks at martyrdom as the most powerful testimony to the hostility between God and the "world," and for that reason it is the fulfillment of the Christian life. Next, the idea of the "imitation of Christ" [*Mimesis*] becomes dominant in the martyr book of Polycarp (d. 155): the passion of Christ becomes the prototype for the path of suffering of all loyal disciples, even to the smallest detail. And thus teach all those early books of the developing Christianity. The church of the first centuries interpreted the work of Christ by means of the concept of the "Theology of Martyrdom," and vice versa understood the fate of the martyrs through the fate of the Master. ("The Anabaptist Theology of Martyrdom," *Mennonite Quarterly Review* 19, no. 3 [1945]: 181; cf. Stauffer, *New Testament Theology*, trans. John Marsh [London: SCM Press, 1955], 185–88 and 331–34)

38. For example, Craig Hovey: "I have stressed repeatedly that the cross is the height of glory. Rather than dashing hopes for the coming kingdom, the cross is already itself the kingdom to come" (*To Share in the Body*, 99). Hovey also states,

> Those who bear crosses do so in the confidence that a new world has been created in which, despite appearances, the peace of Christ is a more sure reality than the violence of human agonism. The latter is a depleted shadow world that exists solely by reference to the cross. The church, therefore, does not simply witness to facts but displays the new life made possible by life in a new world set in motion by Christ himself. Its offer to the old world is animated only by its promise to persuade without coercion, in which martyrdom signals just how new the new world is since it does not rely on the abortive and evacuated promises of peace enshrined in the strategies of the old world. (p. 62)

39. As seen generally in the Anabaptist tradition (cf. Stauffer, "Anabaptist Theology of Martyrdom").

40. Though etherealizing the future reward and sometimes realizing the new creation through present suffering, this is substantially accomplished by Josef Ton in *Suffering, Martyrdom, and Rewards in Heaven*.

41. Brother Yun describes the practice of believers in China:

> Each Back to Jerusalem missionary receives training in several main subjects. These include:
> 1. How to suffer and die for the Lord. . . .
> 2. How to witness for the Lord. . . .
> 3. How to escape for the Lord. . . .
> If you ever visit one of the places where we are training our Back to Jerusalem missionaries, you will see how serious we are to fulfill our destiny in God. You may see people with their hands handcuffed behind their backs, leaping from second-story windows! (Brother Yun and Paul Hattaway, *The Heavenly Man: The Remarkable True Story of Chinese Christian Brother Yun* [Grand Rapids: Monarch Books, 2002], 276)

42. Ton, *Suffering, Martyrdom, and Rewards*, xii.

43. As William Bramley-Moore wrote in his introduction to *Foxe's Book of Martyrs*, "The history of Christian martyrdom is, in fact, the history of Christianity itself; for it is in the arena, at the stake, and in the dungeon that the religion of Christ has won its most glorious triumphs" (quoted in Water, *New Encyclopedia of Christian Martyrs*, viii–ix).

Appendix

1. See esp. *The Parables of the Kingdom*, 3rd ed. (London: Nisbet, 1936); and *The Apostolic Preaching and Its Developments* (London: Hodder & Stoughton, 1936).

2. See Clayton Sullivan's historical review of the widespread embrace of Dodd's ideas in *Rethinking Realized Eschatology* (Macon, GA: Mercer University Press, 1988), 4–11. For example, Oscar Cullmann, *Christ and Time*, trans. F. V. Filson (Philadelphia: Westminster, 1950); W. G. Kümmel, *Promise and Fulfillment*, trans. D. M. Barton (London: SCM Press, 1957); Herman Ridderbos, *The Coming of the Kingdom*, trans. H. de Jongste (Philadelphia: Presbyterian and Reformed, 1962); G. E. Ladd, *The Presence of the Future: The Eschatology of Biblical Realism* (Grand Rapids: Eerdmans, 1974); Anthony A. Hoekema, *The Bible and the Future* (Grand Rapids: Eerdmans, 1979); Bruce Chilton, ed., *The Kingdom of God in the Teaching of Jesus* (London: SPCK, 1984); Craig A. Blaising and Darrell L. Bock, *Progressive Dispensationalism* (Wheaton: Victor, 1993); N. T. Wright, *The Challenge of Jesus: Rediscovering Who Jesus Was and Is* (Downers Grove, IL: InterVarsity, 1999); Arthur F. Glasser et al., *Announcing the Kingdom: The Story of God's Mission in the Bible* (Grand Rapids: Baker, 2003); and G. K. Beale, *A New Testament Biblical Theology: The Unfolding of the Old Testament in the New* (Grand Rapids: Baker, 2011).

   Some may protest the equation of Dodd's realized eschatology (which was blatantly Platonic) with subsequent inaugurationalism (which is less so). However, the common denominator of both is 1) the material "realization" of divine sovereignty and 2) the present "realization" of OT Jewish eschatology (note again the duplicity of language). Inaugurated eschatology is simply mitigated realized eschatology. If realized eschatology was to be removed from inaugurated eschatology (and somehow its effects reversed), we would be left simply with Jewish apocalypticism.

3. "We conclude that on the historical plane there is no 'eschatology of bliss' in the sayings of Jesus. He gave no promise that the future would bring with it any such perfection of human society as some Jewish thinkers had predicted under the form of a restored kingdom of David. He declared that the Kingdom of God had come. When He spoke of it in terms of the future, His words suggest, not any readjustment of conditions on this earth, but the glories of a world beyond this" (Dodd, *Parables of the Kingdom*, 74).

   Furthermore,

   It appears that while Jesus employed the traditional symbolism of apocalypse to indicate the "otherworldly" or absolute character of the Kingdom of God, He used parables to enforce and illustrate the idea that the Kingdom of God had come upon men there and then. The inconceivable had happened: history had become the vehicle of the eternal; the absolute was clothed with flesh and blood. Admittedly, it was a "mystery," to be understood by those who have eyes to see and ears to hear, by those to whom it is revealed "not by flesh and blood, but by My Father in heaven." (Ibid., 197)

   Going beyond the common stereotypes, we see in Dodd's works (see esp. the conclusion of *Parables of the Kingdom*, pp. 206–10) that his thought would better be understood as a recapitulation of Augustinianism: a manifest kingdom now (cf. church militant) unto a transcendent kingdom after death in the "great beyond" (cf. church triumphant). Dodd assigned the Jewish apocalyptic language to the latter, while justifying the former with the parables and specific verses, such as Mark 1:15; Matt. 12:28; Luke 17:21; etc.

4. For example, "Jesus declares that this ultimate, the Kingdom of God, has come into history, and He takes upon Himself the 'eschatological' role of 'Son of Man.' The absolute,

the 'wholly other,' has entered into time and space. And as the Kingdom of God has come and the Son of Man has come, so also judgment and blessedness have come into human experience. The ancient images of the heavenly feast, of Doomsday, of the Son of Man at the right hand of power, are not only symbols of supra-sensible, supra-histor- ical realities; they have also their corresponding actuality within history" (*Parables of the Kingdom*, 107).

5. See esp. *Parables of the Kingdom*, chap. 5; and *Apostolic Preaching*, chap. 2.

6. Anything that contradicted his theory was generally written off as an interpolation of the early church, which reverted to its Jewish roots because it was under "crisis" for a season but then came to its senses and fell in line with the revolutionary teachings of Jesus: "In the course of time the better minds of the Church, under the guidance of such teachers as Paul and the author of the Fourth Gospel, arrived at an interpretation which did justice to the deeper meaning of the teaching of Jesus. But meanwhile those who took his words literally built up a new Christian eschatology on the lines of the Jewish apocalyptic tradi- tion. It is that which we have in outline in the 'Little Apocalypse' of Mark xiii, elaborated in Matthew, and it is brought to its completion in the Revelation of John" (*Parables of the Kingdom*, 133).

In this way Dodd believed the final book of the Bible to be the ultimate *Anti-Revela- tion* of Jesus Christ(!):

> The God of the Apocalypse can hardly be recognized as the Father of our Lord Jesus Christ, nor has the fierce Messiah, whose warriors ride in blood up to their horses' bridles, many traits that could recall Him of whom the primitive *kerygma* proclaimed that He went about doing good and healing all who were oppressed by the devil, because God was with Him. This line of development led into a blind alley. In the second century its stream of thought ran out into the barren sands of millenarianism, which in the end was disavowed by the Church. . . . The possibility of eschatological fanaticism was no doubt present in the outlook of the primitive Church, but it was restrained by the essential character of the Gospel as apprehended in experience. (*Apostolic Preaching*, 41)

7. Note the irony of Dodd's anti-Jewish rhetoric during the war:

> The hope of Israel had been that the temple should, on "the Day of the Lord" (when the Kingdom of God should be revealed), stand upon its lofty hill as the religious centre of the whole world. Jesus says, on the contrary, that, now that the Kingdom of God has come, the temple has no further place; it will be sunk, hill and all, into the sea. The "faith" by which this comes about is the acknowledgment that the Kingdom of God is here. . . . It is the fig-tree that is to be cast into the sea. The fig-tree, we know, was a symbol of the people of God. Whether it is the temple, or the Jewish community, the meaning is much the same. And here we probably have a clue to the episode of the blasted fig-tree (Mk. xi. 12–14, 20) which introduces the Marcan saying about the mountain. The "fig-tree" is Israel, now doomed to perpetual sterility. (*Parables of the King- dom*, 63, n. 1)

Of course, the assumption behind such casting into the sea and "perpetual sterility" is that the AD 70 destruction of Jerusalem—and all subsequent Jewish calamities—are the fulfillments of realized divine retribution upon "the Jewish community." How can such theology not lead to the justification of Jewish persecution within Christendom? (Cf. James Carroll, *Constantine's Sword: The Church and the Jews, A History* [New York: Houghton Mifflin, 2001].)

8. These verses are repeated, in the most literal sense, *like a mantra*—a sacred utterance quoted *ad infinitum*, seemingly as prayer, that one day it will inspire a movement that will finally establish the longed-for Christian utopia.

9. See Johannes Weiss, *Jesus' Proclamation of the Kingdom of God*, trans. R. H. Hiers and D. L. Holland (German orig. 1892; Philadelphia: Fortress, 1971), 67–74.

10. Though of a different conclusion, I agree with Alva J. McClain's approach:

> In beginning this study it should be held axiomatic that any conception of the Kingdom of God which rests in large part upon a certain interpretation of a single text or passage of the Bible must be regarded with deep suspicion. In this category are the systems built around such passages as, "The kingdom of God is within you" (Luke 17:21), or "I will give unto thee the keys of the kingdom of heaven" (Matt. 16:19), or the parable of the leaven (Matt. 13:33), or the ethical precepts of the Sermon on the Mount (Matt. 5–7), or the 20th chapter of the Book of Revelation. The doctrine of the Kingdom should be determined by an inductive examination of *all* the Biblical material on the subject, and it should not have to stand or fall by the inclusion or exclusion of isolated passages where interpretation may be in serious dispute. (*The Greatness of the Kingdom: An Inductive Study of the Kingdom of God* [Winona Lake, IN: BMH Books, 1959], 16)

11. As Jewish theologian David Flusser put it, "This, then, is the 'realized eschatology' of Jesus. He is the only Jew of ancient times known to us who preached not only that people were on the threshold of the end of time, but that the new age of salvation had already begun" (David Flusser and R. Steven Notley, *Jesus* [Jerusalem: The Hebrew University Magnes Press, 2001], 110). Of course, Flusser justifies this statement by citing Luke 11:20, 16:16, and 17:21.

12. Though the academy commonly chooses the latter, as exemplified by Craig Blomberg: "While an acceptance of the 'whole counsel' of Jesus' teaching in parables demands that one recognize both a present and a future aspect to the kingdom, it was Jesus' teaching about the kingdom's presence which was by far the more distinctive of the two emphases. Jewish thought traditionally looked forward to the kingdom's coming, but had never previously dared to believe that it had arrived" (*Interpreting the Parables* [Downers Grove, IL: InterVarsity, 1990], 302).

13. "Certainly the two principal passages, Matt. 12:28 and Luke 17:21, are spoken in rejoinder to opponents who dismiss its presence" (Weiss, *Jesus' Proclamation of the Kingdom*, 74).

14. See *Parables of the Kingdom*, 43–48.

15. Ibid., 33.

16. Sullivan, *Rethinking Realized Eschatology*.

17. See the initial works by Stanley E. Porter, *Verbal Aspect in the Greek of the New Testament, with Reference to Tense and Mood* (New York: Peter Lang, 1989); Buist M. Fanning, *Verbal Aspect in New Testament Greek* (Oxford: Clarendon Press, 1990); and K. L. McKay, *A New Syntax of the Verb in New Testament Greek* (New York: Peter Lang, 1994); cf. also Stanley E. Porter, *Idioms of the Greek New Testament*, 2nd ed. (Sheffield, England: Sheffield Academic, 1999).

See a summary article by Robert E. Picirilli, "The Meaning of the Tenses in New Testament Greek: Where Are We?" *JETS* 48, no. 3 (September 2005): 533–55. Picirilli's opening statement is indeed true: "The world of scholarship about the Greek verb is in ferment, and the outcome promises to have a significant effect for all of us who interpret the NT."

18. See Porter, *Idioms of the Greek New Testament*, chap. 1. Porter uses the analogy of a parade to demonstrate the *perfective* (traditionally, the aorist tense), the *imperfective* (traditionally, the present and imperfect tenses), and the *stative* (traditionally, the perfect and pluperfect tenses):

> If I am a television correspondent in a helicopter flying over the parade, I view the parade in its immediacy from a vantage outside the action as "perfective"; that is, in its entirety as a single and complete whole. If I am a spectator standing with others along the side of the road watching the parade pass by in front of me, I view the action immersed within it as "imperfective"; that is, as an event in progress. And if I am the parade manager in corporate headquarters considering all of the conditions in existence at this parade, including not only all the arrangements that are coming to fruition but all the accompanying events that allow the parade to operate, I view the process not in its particulars or its immediacy but as "stative"; that is, as a complex condition or state of affairs in existence. (*Idioms of the Greek New Testament*, 24)

19. Picirilli, "Meaning of the Tenses," 535.

20. Scholars across the board, even those who hold to a more traditional view that time is encoded in the tense forms (e.g., Daniel Wallace), are at least in agreement that aspect is primary and that the time element can be suppressed by context: "While those of this persuasion agree that verbal aspect is the primary meaning of the Greek tenses, they hold that there is a secondary meaning in the indicative (and relatively in participles) of time involved" (ibid., 537).

21. See examples in Porter, *Idioms of the Greek New Testament*, 29–39. The "future tense" is grammatically derived from the subjunctive, and as such communicates possibility and expectation. Hence it is often used with future realities, though not exclusively (see ibid., 44–45). "Rather than temporal values, *the future form grammaticalizes the semantic (meaning) feature of expectation*" (ibid., 44; italics in the original).

22. Realized eschatology forces a delineation between the messages of John and Jesus. Though identical terminology is used, it is often claimed that John proclaimed the imminence of the messianic kingdom while Jesus proclaimed its spiritual fulfillment (e.g., Ladd, *Presence of the Future*, 110–11). In light of the multitude of later apocalyptic references, I would contend that this delineation is unjustified. Rather, "Matthew wished to make the words of John in 3:2 and those of Jesus in 4:17 identical: the two heralds preach the same kingdom" (W. D. Davies and Dale C. Allison Jr., *A Critical and Exegetical Commentary on the Gospel according to Saint Matthew*, ICC [London: T & T Clark, 2004], 387–88).

23. Dodd argued that *ēngiken* in Matt. 4:17 was synonymous with *ephthasen* in Matt. 12:28, thus concluding, "Both imply the 'arrival' of the Kingdom. With an eye on the presumed Aramaic original, we should translate both: 'The Kingdom of God has come'" (*Parables of the Kingdom*, 44). This awkward conflation has since been universally dismissed.

24. The wrath of God was associated with the day of the Lord (cf. Ps. 110:5; Isa. 13:9–13; Zeph. 1:15–18), as was the fire of God (Ps. 21:9; Isa. 30:30; 66:15; Zeph. 1:18) and the burning of the wicked like "chaff" (Ps. 1:4; Isa. 40:24; Dan. 2:35; Zeph. 2:2; Mal. 4:1).

25. Contrary to the obnoxious conclusion of N. T. Wright:

> Jesus spent his whole ministry *redefining* what the kingdom meant. He refused to give up the symbolic language of the kingdom, but filled it with such new content that, as we have seen, he powerfully subverted Jewish expectations.
>
> This shift of meaning in the original context, coupled with scholarly misreading of apocalyptic in the modern one, has produced the real problem, which

cannot actually be solved by lexical studies of the Greek word *engiken*. Lexicography is ultimately a branch of history, and bears little fruit if separated from its parent stock. Jesus' redefinition of YHWH's kingdom, as we have studied it so far, indicates that in his view the kingdom was indeed present, but that it was not like Israel had thought it would be. Israel's god was becoming king in and through the work of Jesus; this kingdom would reach its climax in the battle which he was going to Jerusalem to fight; within a generation there would be an event which would show that Jesus was right to claim all this. (*Jesus and the Victory of God* [London: SPCK, 1996], 471–72)

To say the destruction of Jerusalem in AD 70 was the vindication of realized eschatology constitutes the height of Gentile arrogance (cf. Rom. 11:17–25).

26. This, of course, is the liberal conclusion of Schweitzer et al.

27. The scoffers here are assumedly those spoken of throughout chap. 2. They are "false teachers" and "false prophets" who introduce "destructive heresies" (2:1). Though claiming to be Christians, they "turn back from the holy commandment delivered to them" (2:21). Since the tone of both of Peter's letters is so apocalyptic, it would seem these false believers are of a gnostic tendency (note the use of *ginōskontes* in 3:3), akin to those elsewhere described by Paul (cf. 2 Thess. 2:2; 1 Tim. 6:20; 2 Tim. 2:16). As such, realized eschatology has always produced a mocking spirit concerning the apocalyptic.

28. Sullivan, *Rethinking Realized Eschatology*, 67. This passage was C. H. Dodd's "golden nugget," as Krister Stendahl put it (ibid., 75). Yet Sullivan rightly reasons,

An obscure verse should not determine the meaning of unambiguous verses. Matthew 12:28 I Luke 11:20 is an obscure, puzzling statement—Jesus' rejoinder to hostile critics who were accusing him of working in league with Beelzebul. Should problematic Matthew 12:28 I Luke 11:20 be the hermeneutical cornerstone for interpreting the Kingdom? This question becomes acute when one notes that there are more than a hundred statements concerning the Kingdom of God in the Synoptics. The majority of these statements (see "Appendix I") present the Kingdom as a place, not an exorcistic power. The majority of these statements present the Kingdom as future hope, not a present reality. . . .

When this wider interpretive task is undertaken, when all the evidence is considered, hermeneutical weight would have to be assigned to the scores of synoptic statements portraying the Kingdom as a future realm, rather than to Matthew 12:28 I Luke 11:20 (which—according to Dodd—portrays the Kingdom as a curative power). Realized eschatologists reverse this procedure. They assign hermeneutical weight to problematic Matthew 12:28 I Luke 11:20 and ignore the scores of statements portraying the Kingdom as a future realm. (Ibid., 81–82)

29. Ladd asserts, "C. H. Dodd is right in affirming that the most characteristic and distinctive of the gospel sayings are those which speak of a present coming of the Kingdom. . . . Throughout the Synoptic Gospels, Jesus' mission is repeatedly understood as the fulfillment of the Old Testament promises. The sayings about the Kingdom of God as a present reality must be interpreted against this background. The strongest statement is Matthew 12:28: 'But if it is by the Spirit of God that I cast out demons, then the Kingdom of God has come upon you'" (*A Theology of the New Testament*, 2nd ed., ed. Donald A. Hagner [Grand Rapids: Eerdmans, 1993], 63).

30. Usually the argumentation goes something like this: "Jesus himself claims that he exorcises by the power of the Holy Spirit, who descended on him at his baptism, marking the inauguration of God's reign, and who permanently empowers all disciples for ministry

in the messianic age. Verse 28 is arguably the single most important teaching of Jesus on realized eschatology—the present aspect of the kingdom" (Craig Blomberg, *Matthew*, NAC [Nashville: Broadman & Holman, 1992], 202).

Of course, this begs the question, *What about the previous Jewish exorcisms mentioned in verse 27?* Exorcism was a commonly accepted phenomenon among both Jews and Gentiles at that time. Did those exorcisms also mark the realization of the kingdom? And if so, when was the kingdom truly inaugurated? So Sullivan reasons, "If demon exorcism signified that the Kingdom had come, could it be argued that the Kingdom also arrived when Tobias expelled a demon with smoke from the heart and liver of a fish [Tobit 8:1ff.]? In other words, if Jesus' exorcisms 'meant' the Kingdom had arrived, why did not exorcisms by the Jewish exorcists also 'mean' the Kingdom had arrived?" (*Rethinking Realized Eschatology*, 80).

31. Unfortunately, Weiss mistook this statement (as well as Matt. 1:15 and Luke 17:21) to be an overzealous declaration of the imminent arrival of the kingdom: "These are moments of sublime prophetic enthusiasm, when an awareness of victory comes over him" (*Jesus' Proclamation of the Kingdom*, 78). Thus he relates the following analogy:

> Whether he favors the one expression or the other depends on what suits his mood at the time. When storm clouds gather and the lightning flashes on the horizon, one may say: "A thunder storm is coming." But one can also say, pro-leptically: "It is storming." Or, again, when the sun shines warm and brightly for the first time, and the first buds begin to swell, one will usually say: "Spring is near." But who will restrain his feeling of yearning when it joyfully welcomes in these first signs the whole springtime, as if it were already there with all its splendor? (Ibid., 41)

32. See Daniel B. Wallace, *Greek Grammar Beyond the Basics: An Exegetical Syntax of the New Testament* (Grand Rapids: Zondervan, 1996), 564.

33. Thanks to Tim Miller who first suggested this translation. Note also the identification of futuristic aorists in the New Testament and beyond by Chrys C. Caragounis, "Kingdom of God, Son of Man, and Jesus' Self-Understanding, Part I," *TynBul* 40, no. 1 (1989): 20–23.

34. For example, Deut. 28:15,45; 30:1; 31:17,21; Josh. 22:20; Judg. 20:41; 1 Sam. 16:16; 2 Sam. 19:7; 24:13; 2 Chron. 20:9; 32:26; Neh. 9:32; Job 2:11; 3:25; 5:14; 20:22; 21:17; 27:9; Ps. 69:24; 119:143; Prov. 1:26; 3:25; 6:15; 10:14; Eccl. 11:2; Isa. 26:9; 47:9,11; 51:19; Jer. 6:26; 22:23; 44:23; 51:60; Lam. 1:14; Ezek. 7:2,7; 30:4; Dan. 9:13; Hos. 13:7; Amos 4:2; 5:9; 9:10; Jonah 1:7f.,12; Mic. 2:6; 3:11; Zeph. 1:6; 2:2; 3:7.

35. Gordon D. Fee, *The First and Second Epistles to the Thessalonians*, NICNT (Grand Rapids: Eerdmans, 2009), 101.

36. Therefore I agree with the century-old conclusion of James E. Frame:

> In view of the eschatological bearing of ἡ ὀργη, the reference in ἔφθασε (= ἦλθε), not withstanding ἡ ὀργή ἡ ἐρχομέν (1:10), cannot be to a series of pun-ishments in the past . . . nor to a specific event in the past, whether the loss of Jewish independence, or the famine (Acts 11:28), or the banishment from Rome (Acts 18:2; *cf.* Schmidt, 86–90); nor quite to the destruction of Jerusa-lem, even if Paul shared the view that the day of judgment was to be simul-taneous with the destruction of Jerusalem; but must be simply to the day of judgment which is near at hand. ἔφθασε is accordingly proleptic. Instead of speaking of that day as coming upon the sons of disobedience (Eph. 5:6), he speaks of it as at last arrived. Such a proleptic use of the aorist is natural in a

prophetic passage and has its analogy in the Lxx. (*A Critical and Exegetical Commentary on the Epistles of St. Paul to the Thessalonians*, ICC [New York: Scribner's Sons, 1912], 113–14)

37. Contrary to the common convoluted inaugurationalist conclusion. For example, "If this wrath is yet future, why then does Paul speak of it as happening in the past (*ephthasen*, 'has come')? The best explanation of the verb's aorist tense comes from comparing the only other NT combinations of *phthanō epi* ('come upon'; see Mt 12:28; Lk 11:20), where Jesus uses comparable terminology to speak of the kingdom's arrival. The unique force of this verb connotes 'arrival upon the threshold of fulfillment and accessible experience, *not* the entrance into that experience'" (K. W. Clark, "Realized Eschatology," *JBL* 59 [1940]: 379). Just as the kingdom reached the covenant people at Christ's first coming without their enjoying "the experience ensuing upon the initial contact" (ibid.), "so the wrath that will precede that kingdom has come before the Jews' full experience of it" (Robert L. Thomas, "1 Thessalonians," in *The Expositor's Bible Commentary: Ephesians–Philemon*, rev. ed., ed. Tremper Longman III and David E. Garland, vol. 12 [Grand Rapids: Zondervan, 2006], 397).

38. It has long been understood that Hebrew verbs are in the main aspectual. Thus the "prophetic perfect" is commonly used by the prophets (cf. Num. 24:17; Isa. 5:14; 9:2; 42:1; Hos. 10:15; Amos 5:2) to communicate the surety of accomplishment of the oracle being spoken. "The perfect is used to express actions which a lively imagination conceives as completed, but for which the future is more usual in English. . . . It often happens, especially in the higher style, that in the midst of descriptions of the future the imagination suddenly conceives the act as accomplished, and interjects a perfect amidst a number of imperfects. Job 5:20, 23 *hath redeemed* (4:10); Hos. 5:5 Judah *is fallen.* This usage receives an extension among the prophets, whose imagination so vividly projects before them the event or scene which they predict that it appears realised" (A. B. Davidson, *Introductory Hebrew Grammar Hebrew Syntax*, 3rd ed. [Edinburgh: T & T Clark, 1902], 61–62).

39. Note *Gospel of Thomas* 3:

Jesus said, "If those who lead you say to you, 'See, the kingdom is in the sky,' then the birds of the sky will precede you. If they say to you, 'It is in the sea,' then the fish will precede you. Rather, the kingdom is inside of you, and it is outside of you. When you come to know yourselves, then you will become known, and you will realize that it is you who are the sons of the living father. But if you will not know yourselves, you dwell in poverty and it is you who are that poverty." (*NHLE*, 126)

And, *Gospel of Thomas* 113: "His disciples said to him, 'When will the kingdom come?' Jesus said, 'It will not come by waiting for it. It will not be a matter of saying "here it is" or "there it is." Rather, the kingdom of the father is spread out upon the earth, and men do not see it'" (*NHLE*, 138).

And, *Gospel of Mary* 8: "When the blessed one had said this, he greeted them all, saying, 'Peace be with you. Receive my peace to yourselves. Beware that no one lead you astray, saying, "Lo here!" or "Lo there!" For the Son of Man is within you. Follow after him! Those who seek him will find him. Go then and preach the gospel of the kingdom'" (*NHLE*, 525).

40. "That they may get knowledge, the Greeks live abroad and cross the sea, but we have no need to depart from home for the sake of the kingdom of heaven, nor to cross the sea for the sake of virtue. For the Lord aforetime hath said, 'The kingdom of heaven is within you.' Wherefore virtue hath need at our hands of willingness alone, since it is in us and is formed from us" (*Life of Antony* 20; *NPNF2* 4:201).

41. "Moreover, that all men are not without communion with God, is taught in the Gospel thus, by the Saviour's words: 'The kingdom of God cometh not with observation; neither shall they say, Lo here! or, lo there! but the kingdom of God is within you.' But here we must see whether this does not bear the same meaning with the expression in Genesis: 'And He breathed into his face the breath of life, and man became a living soul.' For if this be understood as applying generally to all men, then all men have a share in God" (*On First Principles* 1.3.6; *ANF*, 4.254).

42. None are more thorough in their analysis of this passage, and its various interpretations, than Darrell L. Bock, *Luke 9:51–24:53*, BECNT (Grand Rapids: Baker, 1996), 1408–19.

43. Though we find an interesting comment by Jewish scholar Kaufmann Kohler: "Jesus preached the same Kingdom of God (Matthew has preserved in 'Kingdom of Heaven' the rabbinical expression 'Malkut Shamayim'), and when he said, 'the kingdom of God cometh not by observation [that is, calculation] . . . for, behold, the kingdom of God is among [not within] you' (Luke 17:21, Syriac version), he meant, 'It does not come through rebellion or by force'" ("Kingdom of God," *JE*, 7:503; brackets in the original).

44. Though falsely characterizing the "nationalistic ideal" and failing to carry out his statement, Herman Ridderbos does reference the underlying problem:

> Jesus here refers to the messianic movements and rumors that arose again and again among the Jewish people. They originated in a nationalistic ideal of the Messiah and often made it difficult for its adherents to know what to think with respect to this ideal. This explains the question of the Pharisees about the time "when." When Jesus answers them by saying that the coming of the kingdom and of the Messiah "is not accompanied by observations," he does not mean that we should not "heed" the signs of the times, but he rejects the idea—entertained by the adherents of the nationalistic expectations of the Messiah—that the coming of the kingdom *itself* is something that can only be detected by the well-trained eyes of the "observer." Its appearance will be so (overpowering) that nobody will be in need of any indication nor will have any doubt at all. (*Coming of the Kingdom*, 474)

45. As Josephus described,

> He [Mattathias] also overthrew the idol altar, and cried out, "If," said he, "anyone be zealous for the laws of his country, and for the worship of God, let him follow me;" and when he had said this, he made haste into the desert with his sons, and left all his substance in the village. Many others did the same also, and fled with their children and wives into the desert and dwelt in caves. . . .
>
> Many of those that escaped joined themselves to Mattathias, and appointed him to be their ruler, who taught them to fight even on the Sabbath day. . . . So Mattathias got a great army about him, and overthrew their idol altars, and slew those that broke the laws, even all that he could get under his power; for many of them were dispersed among the nations round about them for fear of him. (*Antiquities* 12.270–78 [trans. William Whiston]; cf. 1 Maccabees 2:27–48)

46. There is, however, some precedent for God coming forth from the wilderness to initiate the day of the Lord (cf. Isa. 35:1; 40:3; 63:1; Zech. 9:14). Moreover, the historical precedent was shaped by Israel coming forth from the wilderness (cf. "the One of Sinai," Ps. 68:8), David gathering his mighty men in the wilderness (1 Sam. 22:2; 23:13), and the prophets receiving the word of the Lord in the wilderness (1 Kings 18:4; 19:9; Heb. 11:38).

47. Josephus also described such movements:

> These were such men as deceived and deluded the people under pretense of divine inspiration, but were for procuring innovations and changes of the government,

and these prevailed with the multitude to act like madmen, and went before them into the wilderness, as pretending that God would there show them the signals of liberty; but Felix thought this procedure was to be the beginning of a revolt; so he sent some horsemen and footmen, both armed, who destroyed a great number of them.

But there was an Egyptian false prophet that did the Jews more mischief than the former; for he was a cheat, and pretended to be a prophet also, and got together thirty thousand men that were deluded by him; these he led round about from the wilderness to the mount which was called the Mount of Olives, and was ready to break into Jerusalem by force from that place. (*Wars* 2.259–62 [trans. William Whiston]; cf. *Wars* 6.351, 7.438; *Antiquities* 20.97–99, 167–72, 188)

48. Bock summarizes the four common interpretations of "signs to be observed" (Gk. *paratērēsis*), yet with no reference to *signs of insurgency* (see *Luke 9:51–24:53*, 1412–14). Ironically, the majority of interpreters argue that Jesus was referring to "general apocalyptic signs" (ibid., 1413), and as such he was supposedly correcting the Pharisees for their overly apocalyptic hope(!). This approach completely misses the point and turns the entire interaction on its head.

49. We would also do well to understand John 3:1–21 in such a light. As "the teacher of Israel" (v. 9), Nicodemus should have understood that flesh and blood cannot inherit the kingdom of God (cf. 1 Cor. 15:50). Therefore one must be "born from above" (John 3:3, NRSV) to inherit/see the kingdom. Being "born of water and the Spirit" (v. 5) is most likely a reference to Ezek. 36, apocalyptically understood (cf. chaps. 37–48); and as the wind "blows where it wishes" (John 3:8), so also human beings do not determine the day of God (cf. Matt. 24:36; Acts 1:7; 1 Tim. 6:15).

In this way, John and Jesus came preaching a radically apocalyptic message. "But *you* [Pharisees sympathetic to zealotry] do not receive our testimony" (John 3:11). Their message inherently undermined the Zealot cause, to which some (most?) of the Pharisees were sympathetic. Thus Jesus rebukes Nicodemus concerning the basic apocalyptic hope of the Law and the Prophets (i.e., "earthly things," v. 12). If Nicodemus was guilty of confidence in the flesh concerning the basics of the day of the Lord, the kingdom, and the resurrection, how then would he understand the "heavenly things" of divine mercy and atonement (cf. Deut. 32:43; Ps. 79:9; Dan. 9:24)? Conversely, the Son of Man "has ascended" (v. 13) to stand in the council of the Lord (cf. Jer. 23:18), and "as Moses lifted up the serpent in the wilderness, so must the Son of Man be lifted up, that whoever believes in him may have eternal life" (vv. 14–15). Hence the whole passage is most sensibly a polemic against confidence in the flesh concerning both the hope to be attained (resurrection) and the means of attaining that hope (atonement).

50. See a defense of this position in John Nolland, *Luke 9:21–18:34*, WBC (Dallas: Word, 1998), 849–54.

The final view to be considered is that of Bultmann (*History*, 121–22) and others that the reference is to a future sudden arrival of the kingdom of God. This view must first accept the possibility of giving ἐντός the sense "in your midst" and then needs to treat this idiomatically as conveying the idea of the kingdom of God being "right there," as having arrived, while all the alert observers have failed to notice anything to base their prognostications upon. This assumes that ἐστιν, "is," should be taken futuristically, but, in the absence of the second negation, this is a natural reading after the obviously futurist force of the present tense ἔρχεται (lit. "comes"). This view is somewhat vulnerable to the frequently leveled criticism that the key notion of a sudden and unheralded arrival of the kingdom of God must be taken as implied, because it is certainly not explicitly present. It is, nevertheless, the view that does best justice to the content of v 21, and the one view that easily makes room for vv 22–37 and does justice as well to Luke's evident concern to link the two sections. (Ibid., 853–54)

51. BDAG, 285.

52. I also find this to be a more natural integration of *entos* (see BDAG, 340–41), used in the NT only here and in Matt. 23:26 ("clean the *inside* of the cup"). Jesus' point concerns salvation coming *into* Israel's midst, rather than coming *out of* it.

53. Rightly, Nolland: "Perhaps best is to see the statement [v. 21] as insisting that when the kingdom of God is due to come it will just be there, right in our midst, with no advance warning and no localized beginning. This understanding fits best with vv 22–37 to come" (*Luke 9:21–18:34*, 854).

Also Ridderbos:

In this connection, therefore, it is improbable that in verses 20 and 21 Jesus should have wanted to divert attention from the eschatological future and direct it to the already "fulfilled" present. This conclusion is also borne out by the future tense in verse 21 ("neither *shall* they say"). That is why in our opinion the words, "For, behold, the kingdom of God is among you," certainly refer to the eschatological coming of the kingdom. As appears from the word "for," they explain why they *shall* not say, "Lo here!, or, lo there!" For when the kingdom comes *it is in your midst*, i.e., it will no longer need any indication, but will fill your whole horizon. (*Coming of the Kingdom*, 475)

54. The "corporate" quality comes from a reference to a plural "you" (Matt. 3:7; 12:28; Luke 17:21). Rather than an individual blessing from God, it is a corporate condemnation of a whole lot cast into the "fiery furnace" (Matt. 13:42).

55. In 2 Thess. it seems that Paul calls realized eschatology "a strong delusion" (v. 11), sent by God to those who "refused to love the truth" (v. 10). The relationship between v. 2 ("a spoken word, a letter seeming to be from us, to the effect that the day of the Lord has come") and v. 15 ("stand firm and hold to the traditions that you were taught by us, either by our spoken word or by our letter") is straightforward. Thus vv. 10–12 are bracketed by statements concerning the corruption of the apostolic witness, identified in v. 2 as the realization of apocalyptic eschatology, i.e., *tō pseudei* ("what is false," or "the lie," NIV). Moreover, the refusal to love "the truth" (vv. 10,12) echoes other Pauline references to Gnosticism and realized eschatology (cf. 1 Tim. 4:3; 6:21; 2 Tim. 2:15–18; 4:4).

56. As argued by Ladd, *Presence of the Future*, 158–64. So the NIV translates: "The kingdom of heaven has been forcefully advancing, and forceful men lay hold of it." Note also the NLT: "The Kingdom of Heaven has been forcefully advancing, and violent people are attacking it." The NIV views "the violent" as those who advance the spiritual kingdom, while the NLT views "the violent" as those who persecute the advancement of the spiritual kingdom. On the latter, see D. A. Carson, "Matthew," in *The Expositor's Bible Commentary: Matthew-Mark*, vol. 9, rev. ed., ed. Tremper Longman III and David E. Garland (Grand Rapids: Zondervan, 2010), 309–10.

57. *Parables of the Kingdom*, 48.

58. Ibid., 49.

59. David L. Turner, *Matthew*, BECNT (Grand Rapids: Baker, 2008), 296.

60. An entire monograph has been written on the four options in v. 12 alone; see Peter S. Cameron, *Violence and the Kingdom: The Interpretation of Matthew 11:12* (Frankfurt: Peter Lang, 1984).

61. Note that this position was the common patristic view; see B. T. Viviano, "The Least in the Kingdom: Matthew 11:11, Its Parallel in Luke 7:28 (Q), and Daniel 4:14," *CBQ* 62 (2000): 41–54.

62. "In agreement with Franz Dibelius and the older Church Fathers, and in grammatical accordance with the text itself, I translate Matt. 11.11: 'He who is least (i.e., Jesus as a disciple of John) is greater than he (i.e., John) in the kingdom of heaven'" (Oscar Cullmann, *The Christology of the New Testament*, trans. S. C. Guthrie and C. A. M. Hall [Philadelphia: Westminster, 1963], 32).

63. Though concerning a different issue (keeping of the law), Matt. 5:19–20 also supports such an approach, since it is based on the two-age apocalyptic framework: "Therefore whoever relaxes one of the *least* of these commandments and teaches others to do the same will be called *least* in the kingdom of heaven, but whoever does them and teaches them will be called *great* in the kingdom of heaven. For I tell you, unless your righteousness exceeds that of the scribes and Pharisees, you will never enter the kingdom of heaven."

64. "Born of women" is a Hebraic idiom (cf. Job 14:1; 15:14; 25:4) and simply refers to the common descendants of Adam. However, Jesus sets himself apart from all other descendants of Adam as "the Son of Adam" (v. 19) who is least in the sight of this world, yet greater than all (even John the Baptist) in the sight of God.

65. "The Jewish background of the question for the great or little one could support this interpretation. The texts distinguish between this and the future world (*Midr. Ruth* 1.17 [128a]; *b. B. Mes.* 85b; *Pesiq. R.* 83 [198b] in Str-B 1.598)" (Ulrich Luz, *Matthew*, Hermeneia [Minneapolis: Fortress, 2001], 139, n. 33).

66. And quite gnostic, cf. *Gospel of Thomas* 46: "Jesus said, 'Among those born of women, from Adam until John the Baptist, there is no one so superior to John the Baptist that his eyes should not be lowered (before him). Yet I have said, whichever one of you comes to be a child will be acquainted with the kingdom and will become superior to John'" (*NHLE*, 131).

67. For example, "In effect, so glorious is the new reality dawning through the ministry of Jesus that the greatest of the era preceding him is yet inferior to the least in the new order of the kingdom" (Donald A. Hagner, *Matthew 1–13*, WBC [Dallas: Word, 1993], 306).

68. Hagner explains:

> Those who take both clauses positively (e.g., Zahn; Ladd, *Presence*) thus find here a statement about the forceful coming of the kingdom in the ministry of Jesus and a coordinate description of the hard way of discipleship. Those who take both clauses negatively (e.g., Hill, Fenton, Green, Schweizer, Patte, Gundry, Gaechter, Maier, France, Mounce, Luz, Davies-Allison) understand the verse to refer to the persecution and difficulty faced by those who represent the kingdom. The violent people who plunder the kingdom are regarded variously as the Pharisees, Zealots, evil spirits, or even Herod Antipas. Among those who divide the clauses, the majority favor understanding the first negatively (the kingdom suffers violence) and the second positively (e.g., Dahl, Schlatter, Schniewind). A few argue for the first to be understood positively (the kingdom comes forcefully) and the second negatively (e.g., Carson, Pamment). (*Matthew 1–13*, 307)

69. "This combination of translations would then lead the verse to be rendered something like 'from the days of John the Baptist until now, the kingdom of heaven suffers violence, and violent people attack it'" (Craig Blomberg, *Matthew*, NAC [Nashville: Broadman & Holman, 1992], 187–88).

70. Cf. the alternate rendering of Luke 16:16: "The Law and the Prophets were until John; since then, the good news of the kingdom of God has been proclaimed, and everyone is

strongly urged to enter it" (HCSB). Thus there is correspondence with the Lukan parallel, though the saying is applied in a different context for different reasons.

71. See an adept handling of this parable in W. D. Davies and Dale C. Allison Jr., *A Critical and Exegetical Commentary on the Gospel According to Saint Matthew*, ICC (London: T & T Clark, 2004), 259–65.

72. "Therefore Jesus' statement here goes back to ch. 10 and refers to the persecution that characterizes the age of mission. John the Baptist is a prime example, imprisoned and soon to be killed at the hands of Herod Antipas. 'From the days of John the Baptist until the present' thus refers to the arrest of John and the opposition Jesus and his disciples have already experienced" (Grant R. Osborne, *Matthew*, ZECNT [Grand Rapids: Zondervan, 2010], 422).

73. Some claim proof of realized eschatology based on the kingdom being the subject of the violence in v. 12. However, the future reality is simply being spoken of as being directly affected by present events. Similarly, Jesus said, "Woe to you, scribes and Pharisees, hypocrites! *For you shut the kingdom of heaven in people's faces.* For you neither enter yourselves nor allow those who would enter to go in" (Matt. 23:13). Jesus clearly had in mind a future reality, as is evidenced by his following references to Gehenna (vv. 15,33). Jesus spoke this way because all present actions will be rehearsed on the day of judgment (i.e., the books are opened). Hence present actions directly affect people's outcomes on the last day, and in this way the future kingdom (composed of saints) suffers violence by present acts of violence against the saints.

74. "To sum up, then: for Jesus and for Matthew, as for the apocalyptic literature in general, the great redemption must be preceded by a conflict between the forces of good and the forces of evil (cf. 1 En. 91:5–6). Further, this conflict has already been joined, from the days of John the Baptist until now" (Davies and Allison, *Matthew*, 256).

75. So Ladd introduced his magnum opus: "The distinctive characteristic about Jesus' teaching is that in some real sense, the Kingdom of God has come in his person and mission (Matt. 12:28). The mystery of the Kingdom (Mark 4:11) is the secret of its unexpected irruption in history" (*Presence of the Future*, xi).

Also, "The very core of his message about the kingdom of God is that the powers of the future eschatological reign have entered into history in advance of their apocalyptic manifestation and are at work now in the world in a hidden form within and among men. This is the 'mystery of the kingdom'" (G. E. Ladd, "Why Not Prophetic-Apocalyptic?" *JBL* 76, no. 3 [1957]: 199).

76. *Parables of the Kingdom*, 79–80.

77. Built on a tense-based translation of the verb "go before" (Gk. *proagō*), this verse is often cited as evidence of realized eschatology (cf. Ladd, *Presence of the Future*, 123, 174, 197–98; and Donald A. Hagner, *Matthew 14–28*, WBC [Dallas: Word, 1995], 614). Osborne summarizes, "προάγουσιν could be a durative present ('are entering,' thus an inaugurated eschatology) or a futuristic present ('are going to enter,' thus a final eschatology)" (*Matthew*, 781, n. 9).

However, the use of *proagō* is not meant to communicate time, but rather *imperfective aspect*, highlighting the dramatic unfolding of the tax collectors and prostitutes entering into eternal life on the last day before the Pharisees and teachers of the law. The context of this saying is clearly eschatological (cf. vv. 9,15,34,40); and in Matthew's other uses, entry into the kingdom is always future (5:20; 7:21; 18:3; 19:23,24). Therefore, "The imagery here would seem to be best taken as of being well along the path that leads into the kingdom rather than of having already entered the kingdom" (John Nolland, *The Gospel of Matthew: A Commentary on the Greek Text*, NIGTC [Grand Rapids: Eerdmans, 2005], 863).

78. Though the Olivet parables (Matt. 24:42—25:30) were spoken privately, they are obviously apocalyptic, and their purpose is to instill the fear of God concerning the coming judgment. In this way, they were spoken to the disciples as would-be apostates (in light of Judas' betrayal). They were in very real danger of becoming the wicked servant (23:48), the foolish virgin (25:3), and the lazy manager (25:18). Thus, they were warned, "Stay awake, for you do not know on what day your Lord is coming" (24:42). Dodd's attempt to marginalize these parables as an invention of the early church is farcical (cf. *Parables of the Kingdom*, 154–74).

79. A similar design is seen in the parables of the two debtors (Luke 7:41–43), the wedding host (Luke 14:7–14), the dutiful servant (Luke 17:7–10), and the Pharisee and tax collector (Luke 18:10–14). All of these were spoken against the prideful, entitlement attitude of the Jewish leaders.

80. Though Jesus speaks to his disciples in Matt. 13:37–52, the parables in these verses are still aimed at the blindness of unbelievers, since they are an explanation (v. 36) of the previous parables.

81. Though Dodd recognized this, he forcefully rejected reason:

> "Leaven" is, in general, a symbol from evil influences carrying infection. In this sense Jesus used it when He spoke of the leaven of the Pharisees (Mk. viii. 15 and parallels). By analogy, it should be used here as a symbol for a wholesome influence, propagating itself similarly by a kind of infection. In that case we should be obliged to suppose that when the Kingdom of God is compared to leaven, the suggestion is that the ministry of Jesus is itself such an influence. . . . The picture, I think, is true to history. The ministry of Jesus was like that. There was in it no element of external coercion, but in it the power of God's Kingdom worked from within, mightily permeating the dead lump of religious Judaism in His time. (*Parables of the Kingdom*, 192–93)

82. Unfortunately the modern academy has largely followed Dodd in his quest to save Jesus from the embarrassment of Jewish apocalypticism: "C. H. Dodd so emphasized the crisis nature of Jesus' own ministry that he interpreted judgment Day to be present whenever people responded to Jesus. Traditional Christianity has often gone to the other extreme and linked judgment exclusively with the Second Coming of Christ. Probably both poles need to be embraced" (Blomberg, *Interpreting the Parables*, 301).

Such sentiment is simply ludicrous. Neither Jesus nor the apostles ever made reference to the judgment of the living and the dead prior to the day of judgment. The statement above expresses the true sentiment of modern scholarship: *that the day of the Lord has already come* (spiritually, of course), which is in clear opposition to the apostolic declaration in 2 Thess. 2:2. "Traditional Christianity" (though often clouded by a Platonic, heavenly destiny) has linked judgment to the second coming of Christ based on a common-sense reading of the Scriptures. Though inaugurationalism mitigates things with a future reality, it still declares that the day of the Lord has already come.

83. J. Christiaan Beker, *Paul the Apostle: The Triumph of God in Life and Thought* (Philadelphia: Fortress, 1980); and Beker, *Paul's Apocalyptic Gospel: The Coming Triumph of God* (Philadelphia: Fortress, 1982).

84. "The primitive Church, while it enjoyed the fellowship of the Holy Spirit, and appealed to the manifest work of the Spirit (somewhat naïvely conceived) as evidence of the dawn of the new Age, did not reflect upon it. Nor did it embody any clear doctrine of the fellowship in its preaching. Such a doctrine first appears in the epistles of Paul" (Dodd, *Apostolic Preaching*, 59).

85. Dodd continues,

> It is noteworthy that as his interest in the speedy advent of Christ declines, as it demonstrably does after the time when he wrote 1 Corinthians, the "futurist eschatology" of his earlier phase is replaced by this "Christ-mysticism." The hope of glory yet to come remains as a background of thought, but the foreground is more and more occupied by the contemplation of all the riches of divine grace enjoyed here and now by those who are in Christ Jesus. . . .
>
> This was the true solution of the problem presented to the Church by the disappointment of its naïve expectation that the Lord would immediately appear; not the restless and impatient straining after signs of His coming which turned faith into fantasy and enthusiasm into fanaticism; but a fuller realization of all the depths and heights of the supernatural life here and now. (Ibid., 63)

86. James D. G. Dunn, *Romans 9–16*, WBC (Dallas: Word, 1998), 822. See Dunn's chart on Jesus' and Paul's use of βασιλεία, δικαιοσύνη, and πνεῦμα (ibid.).

87. Like Jesus and John the Baptist, Paul's omission of any lengthy redefinition of the kingdom strongly supports the idea that Paul took the Jewish eschatology of his day for granted. The attempt by the New Perspective on Paul (see chapter 8) to redefine the sacrificial language of Paul, so as to communicate realized eschatology, is foul.

88. Beyond a broad theological deduction based on the new covenant and the gift of the Holy Spirit, these three verses are quoted almost exclusively as proof of Pauline realized eschatology. Few are bold enough to say Paul interjected realized eschatology into the other eschatological phrases, such as "resurrection," "day of the Lord," "appearing," "wrath of God," etc.

89. *The Gospel of the Kingdom: Scriptural Studies in the Kingdom of God* (Grand Rapids: Eerdmans, 1959), 16–17.

90. The verb (*eimi*) is also aspectually vague, as Porter explains: "A very small number of verbs in Greek (all verbs of the -μι conjugation) never developed a full set of tense-forms, and hence do not participate in the aspectual system. . . . The result is that these verbs offer no meaningful choice between one aspect and another. These verbs, of which εἰμί is the primary example, are called aspectually vague. *Aspectually vague verbs may be used in any verbal context since they do not carry the semantic weight of perfective, imperfective or stative verbal aspect.* Consequently, one must be cautious in giving interpretative significance to use of one of these verbs" (*Idioms of the Greek New Testament*, 24–25; italics in the original).

91. Akin to Jesus' statement, "And this is eternal life [αὕτη δέ ἐστιν ἡ αἰώνιος ζωὴ], that they know you the only true God, and Jesus Christ whom you have sent" (John 17:3). Moreover, Paul's following exhortation in Romans 15:4–13 of harmony between Jew and Gentile assumes a Jewish messianic kingdom—"in order to confirm the promises given to the patriarchs" (v. 8)—culminating in verse 12 with the quotation of Isaiah 11:10.

92. The connection between v. 10 and v. 17 seems universally lacking; cf. Cranfield (ICC), Dunn (WBC), Wright (NIB), Moo (NICNT), Schreiner (BECNT), Fitzmyer (AB), Jewett (Hermeneia), Mounce (NAC), Harrison and Hagner (EBC), Bruce (TNTC), etc. Ben Witherington's translation of βασιλεία τοῦ θεοῦ as "Dominion of God" (reflecting his realized eschatology) seems particularly inappropriate (*Paul's Letter to the Romans: A Socio-Rhetorical Commentary* [Grand Rapids: Eerdmans, 2004], 340).

93. Here William Sanday and Arthur C. Headlam are to be commended for their restraint. "The phrase is used normally in St. Paul of that Messianic kingdom which is to be the reward and goal of the Christian life. . . . The term is, of course, derived through the

words of Christ from the current Jewish conceptions of an actual earthly kingdom; how far exactly such conceptions have been spiritualized in St. Paul it may be difficult to say" (*A Critical and Exegetical Commentary on the Epistle of the Romans*, 3rd ed., ICC [New York: Scribner's, 1897], 391).

94. Heinrich A. W. Meyer is a notable exception to common sentiment:

And so [the kingdom of God] is not here, anything else than the *Messiah's kingdom*, the erection of which begins with the *Parousia*, belonging not to the αἰὼν οὖτος, but to the αἰὼν μέλλων (1 Cor. 6:9,10, 15:24,50; Gal. 5:21; Eph. 5:5; Col. 4:11; 1 Thess. 2:12; 2 Thess. 1:5); not therefore the (invisible) *church*, the *regnum gratiae*, or the earthly *ethical kingdom of God* (Reiche, de Wette, Philippi, Lipsius, following older expositors), *res Christiana* (Baumgarten-Crusius), and the like. *"The Messianic kingdom is not eating and drinking;" i.e.*, the essential characteristic of this kingdom does not consist in the principle that a man, in order to become a member of it, should eat and drink this or that or everything without distinction, but in the principle that one should be upright, etc. (*Critical and Exegetical Handbook to the Epistle to the Romans*, vol. 2, ed. William P. Dickson, trans. John C. Moore and Edwin Johnson [Edinburgh: T & T Clark, 1874], 316; italics in the original)

95. This, of course, was a common apostolic presupposition, as evidenced by Peter: "Since everything will be destroyed in this way, what kind of people ought you to be? You ought to live holy and godly lives as you look forward to the day of God and speed its coming" (2 Peter 3:11–12, NIV; cf. 1 Peter 1:13–16).

96. The verbal similarities between the two verses are also commonly referenced (e.g., Dunn, *Romans 9–16*, 822).

97. Though Gordon Fee strangely comes to the opposite conclusion:

What Paul is concerned about is "the kingdom of God." This is one of the rare occurrences in Paul of this term that dominates the ministry and teaching of Jesus. But the very casual way in which it here appears indicates that it was a regular part of his own understanding of the gospel. In most instances in Paul the term refers to the consummation of the kingdom at the coming of Christ (cf., e.g., 6:9–10; 15:50); but this passage, along with Rom. 14:17, makes it certain that for him the kingdom was "now" as well as "not yet." (*The First Epistle to the Corinthians*, NICNT [Grand Rapids: Eerdmans, 1987], 192)

98. Robert L. Saucy well notes, "The apostle has just chided the Corinthians for their boasting as if they had already attained the kingdom and were reigning as kings (cf. 4:8). He would hardly talk of a present kingdom just a few verses later" (*The Case for Progressive Dispensationalism* [Grand Rapids: Zondervan, 1993], 107).

99. Again, Heinrich A. W. Meyer is notably reasonable in his approach to this passage: "The βασιλεία τοῦ Θεοῦ, again, is not here, as it never is elsewhere (see on Matt. 3:2, 6:10), and in particular never in Paul's writings (neither in this passage nor in Rom. 14:7; Col. 1:13, 4:11; see on these verses), the *church*, or the kingdom of God in the *ethical* sense (Neander: 'the fellowship of the divine life, which is brought about by fellowship with the Redeemer'), but the *Messianic kingdom*, in which, at its expected (speedy) manifestation, those only can become members who are truly believing and truly sanctified (Col. 3:3 f.; Phil. 4:18–21; Eph. 5:5, *al.*)" (*Critical and Exegetical Handbook to the Epistles to the Corinthians*, vol. 1, ed. William P. Dickson, trans. D. Douglas Bannerman [Edinburgh: T & T Clark, 1879], 135).

100. As F. F. Bruce so boldly declared, "In the affirmation that believers have already been brought into the kingdom of God's beloved Son we have an example of truly realized

eschatology" (*The Epistles to the Colossians, to Philemon, and to the Ephesians*, NICNT [Grand Rapids: Eerdmans, 1984], 52).

101. "The aorist tenses point to an eschatology that is truly realized (i.e., God had *already* qualified [ἱκανώσαντι] the Colossians to share in the inheritance, he had *already* delivered [ἐρρύσατο] them from this alien power and had *already* transferred [μετέστησεν] them to his Son's kingdom), while by contrast, the present tense of verse 14, "we have" (ἔχομεν), stresses the continued results of the redemption wrought in the past" (Peter T. O'Brien, *Colossians, Philemon*, WBC [Dallas: Word, 1998], 26).

102. "The aorist forms ἐρρύσατο (delivered) and μετέστησεν (transferred) point to baptism as the event through which the change from one dominion to another has taken place, in that we have been wrested from the power of darkness and placed in the 'kingdom' of the beloved Son of God. . . . There is no mention of an enthusiastic anticipation of the consummation. Rather, just as darkness designates those who are lost, light characterizes the rule of Christ, which here and now shapes the life and conduct of those who are baptized" (Eduard Lohse, *Colossians and Philemon*, Hermeneia [Philadelphia: Fortress, 1971], 38).

Of course, Lohse does not believe Paul wrote Colossians, because "Wherever Paul mentions the 'rule of God' (βασιλεία τοῦ θεοῦ) in his letters, the futuristic meaning of the concept is presupposed, just as throughout primitive Christian proclamation" (ibid., 37–38). "Therefore, Paul cannot be considered to be the direct or indirect author of Colossians" (ibid., 181). If realized eschatology is not present in the letter to the Colossians, then the theological differences are insubstantial, and the differences of expression can be simply attributed to Paul's maturation and "specific circumstances" (ibid., 180).

103. So James Dunn argues against common sense:

The note of realized eschatology becomes even stronger in the next two clauses, for what is described here would elsewhere be thought of as reserved for the end of history/time. . . . More striking still is the fact that elsewhere in the Pauline corpus talk of full sharing in the kingdom of God is always future (1 Thes. 2:12; 2 Thes. 1:5; 2 Tim. 4:1,18; the formulaic phrase "inherit the kingdom of God" in 1 Cor. 6:9–10; 15:50; Gal. 5:21; cf. Eph. 5:5). There is nothing quite like this claim that believers in Christ Jesus have already (aorist tense) been transferred into the kingdom, like a whole people transported from their traditional territory to settle in a new region. (*The Epistles to the Colossians and to Philemon: A Commentary on the Greek Text*, NIGTC [Grand Rapids: Eerdmans, 1996], 77)

104. Assumedly derived from the Prophets (cf. Isa. 9:1–2; 42:6–7,16; 58:8–10; 60:1–3; Amos 5:18–20; cf. *1 Enoch* 92:4–5; 108:11–14; *2 Baruch* 18:1–2). Some seem to give too much weight to the influence of Qumran (cf. Lohse, *Colossians and Philemon*, 36–38) and/or the exodus motif (cf. N. T. Wright, *Colossians and Philemon*, TNTC [Downers Grove, IL: InterVarsity, 1986], 64–66).

105. The translation of *methistēmi* ("transfer, remove, turn away") is also debatable. Occurring only five times in the NT (Luke 16:4; Acts 13:22; 19:26; 1 Cor. 13:2; Col. 1:13), three of those simply mean "remove" (Luke 16:4; Acts 13:22; 1 Cor. 13:2), leaving only Acts 19:26 for comparison: "This Paul has persuaded and turned away [*methistēmi*] a great many people." Justification for "transferred" in Col. 1:13 is extrabiblical—i.e., Josephus (BDAG, 625). Paul's point seems to be akin to Acts 19:26—we have been turned away from the power of darkness toward the kingdom and *parousia* of the Son (cf. 1 Cor. 1:7; Phil. 3:20; 1 Thess. 1:10).

106. Heinrich A. W. Meyer here argued for the proleptic aorist:

The matter is to be conceived *locally* (εἰς ἕτερον τόπον, Plat. *Legg.* vi. p. 762 B), so that the deliverance from the power of darkness appears to be united with the *removing away* into the kingdom . . . that is, *into the kingdom of the Messiah*, Eph. 5:5; 2 Pet. 1:11; for this and nothing else is meant by ἡ βασιλεία Χριστοῦ (τοῦ Θεοῦ, τῶν οὐρανῶν) *in all passages of the N. T.* Comp. 4:11; and see on Rom. 14:17; 1 Cor. 4:20; Matt. 3:2, 6:10. The *aorist* μετέστ. is to be explained by the matter being conceived proleptically (τῇ γὰρ ἐλπίδι ἐσώθημεν, Rom. 8:24), as something already *consummated* (comp. on ἐδόξασε, Rom. 8:30). (*Critical and Exegetical Handbook to the Epistles to the Philippians and Colossians*, ed. William P. Dickson, trans. John C. Moore [Edinburgh: T & T Clark, 1875], 270–71; italics in the original)

BIBLIOGRAPHY

The bibliography is roughly organized according to the progression of the book.

HERMENEUTICS AND WORLDVIEW

Bacote, Vincent E., Laura C. Miguelez, and Dennis L. Okholm, eds. *Evangelicals and Scripture: Tradition, Authority, and Hermeneutics.* Downers Grove, IL: InterVarsity, 2004.

Beale, Gregory K., ed. *The Right Doctrine from the Wrong Texts? Essays on the Use of the Old Testament in the New.* Grand Rapids: Baker, 1994.

Berlinski, David. *The Devil's Delusion: Atheism and Its Scientific Pretensions.* New York: Crown Forum, 2008.

Boman, Thorlief. *Hebrew Thought Compared with Greek.* Translated by Jules L. Moreau. London: SCM Press, 1960.

Boyarin, Daniel. *Border Lines: The Partition of Judaeo-Christianity.* Philadelphia: University of Pennsylvania Press, 2004.

Boyd, Gregory A. *God at War: The Bible and Spiritual Conflict.* Downers Grove, IL: InterVarsity, 1997.

Brown, Walt. *In the Beginning: Compelling Evidence for Creation and the Flood.* 8th ed. Phoenix: Center for Scientific Creation, 2008.

Bultmann, Rudolf. *Jesus Christ and Mythology.* New York: Charles Scribner's Sons, 1958.

——. *New Testament and Mythology and Other Basic Writings.* Edited and translated by Schubert M. Ogden. Philadelphia: Fortress, 1984.

Carson, D. A., and John D. Woodbridge, eds. *Scripture and Truth.* Grand Rapids: Baker, 1992.

Clifford, Richard J. *Creation Accounts in the Near East and in the Bible.* Washington, DC: Catholic Biblical Association, 1994.

Collins, Adela Yarbro. *Cosmology and Eschatology in Jewish and Christian Apocalypticism.* Leiden, Netherlands: Brill Academic, 1996.

Corley, Bruce, Steve W. Lemke, and Grant I. Lovejoy, eds. *Biblical Hermeneutics: A Comprehensive Introduction to Interpreting Scripture.* 2nd ed. Nashville: Broadman and Holman, 2002.

Dembski, William A., ed. *Uncommon Dissent: Intellectuals Who Find Darwinism Unconvincing.* Wilmington, DE: ISI Books, 2004.

Fee, Gordon D., and Douglas Stuart. *How to Read the Bible for All Its Worth.* 3rd ed. Grand Rapids: Zondervan, 2003.

Geisler, Norman L., and William D. Watkins. *Worlds Apart: A Handbook on Worldviews.* 2nd ed. Grand Rapids: Baker, 1989.

Gethin, Rupert. *The Foundations of Buddhism.* OPUS Series. Oxford: Oxford University Press, 1998.

Goldsworthy, Graeme. *Gospel-Centered Hermeneutics: Foundations and Principles of Evangelical Biblical Interpretation.* Downers Grove, IL: InterVarsity, 2006.

Hesselgrave, David J. *Communicating Christ Cross-Culturally.* Grand Rapids: Zondervan, 1978.

Hiebert, Paul G. *Transforming Worldviews: An Anthropological Understanding of How People Change.* Grand Rapids: Baker, 2008.

Himmelfarb, Martha. *Ascent to Heaven in Jewish and Christian Apocalypses.* New York: Oxford University Press, 1993.

———. *Tours of Hell: An Apocalyptic Form in Jewish and Christian Literature.* Minneapolis: Fortress, 1985.

Holding, James P. "Is the *raqiya'* ('firmament') a solid dome? Equivocal language in the cosmology of Genesis 1 and the Old Testament: a response to Paul H. Seely." *Technical Journal* (now *Journal of Creation*) 13, no. 2 (November 1999): 44–51.

Holmes, Arthur F. *Contours of a World View.* Grand Rapids: Eerdmans, 1983.

Horowitz, Wayne. *Mesopotamian Cosmic Geography.* Winona Lake, IN: Eisenbrauns, 1998.

Johnson, Phillip E. *Darwin on Trial.* Downers Grove, IL: InterVarsity, 1991.

Jordan, James B. *Creation in Six Days: A Defense of the Traditional Reading of Genesis One.* Moscow, ID: Canon Press, 1999.

Kaiser, Walter C., Jr., and Moisés Silva, eds. *Introduction to Biblical Hermeneutics: The Search for Meaning.* Grand Rapids: Zondervan, 2007.

Kline, Meredith G. *Kingdom Prologue: Genesis Foundations for a Covenantal Worldview.* Overland Park, KS: Two Age Press, 2000.

———. "Space and Time in the Genesis Cosmogony." *Perspectives on Science and Christian Faith* 48, no. 1 (March 1996): 2–15.

Kraft, Charles H. *Christianity in Culture: A Study in Dynamic Biblical Theologizing in Cross-Cultural Perspective.* Maryknoll, NY: Orbis, 1979.

Kuyper, Abraham. *Calvinism: Six Lectures Delivered in the Theological Seminary at Princeton.* New York: Fleming H. Revell, 1899.

Ladd, George Eldon. *The Pattern of New Testament Truth.* Grand Rapids: Eerdmans, 1968.

Lamont, Corliss. *The Philosophy of Humanism.* 8th ed. Amherst, NY: Humanist Press, 1997.

Lamoureux, Denis O. *Evolutionary Creation: A Christian Approach to Evolution.* Eugene, OR: Wipf & Stock Publishers, 2008.

Marshall, Paul A., Sander Griffioen, and Richard J. Mouw, eds. *Stained Glass: Worldviews and Social Science.* Christian Studies Today. Lanham, MD: University Press of America, 1989.

Moody, D. L. *Heaven: Where It Is, Its Inhabitants, and How to Get There.* Rev. ed. Chicago: Fleming H. Revell, 1884.

Mullen, E. Theodore. *The Assembly of the Gods: The Divine Council in Canaanite and Early Hebrew Literature.* Harvard Semitic Monographs 24. Chico, CA: Scholars Press, 1980.

Nash, Ronald H. *Worldviews in Conflict: Choosing Christianity in a World of Ideas.* Grand Rapids: Zondervan, 1992.

Naugle, David K. *Worldview: The History of a Concept.* Grand Rapids: Eerdmans, 2002.

Newbigin, Lesslie. *Foolishness to the Greeks: The Gospel and Western Culture.* Grand Rapids: Eerdmans, 1986.

——. *The Gospel in a Pluralist Society.* Grand Rapids: Eerdmans, 1989.

Numbers, Ronald L. *The Creationists: The Evolution of Scientific Creationism.* New York: Alfred A. Knopf, 1992.

Orr, James. *The Christian View of God and the World as Centering in the Incarnation.* Edinburgh: Andrew Elliot, 1893.

Osborne, Grant R. *The Hermeneutical Spiral: A Comprehensive Introduction to Biblical Interpretation.* Rev. ed. Downers Grove, IL: InterVarsity, 2006.

Rowland, Christopher. *The Open Heaven: A Study of Apocalyptic in Judaism and Early Christianity.* London: SPCK, 1982.

Schaeffer, Francis A. *The Complete Works of Francis A. Schaeffer: A Christian Worldview.* 5 vols. Wheaton: Crossway, 1982.

Seely, Paul H. "The Firmament and the Water Above, Part 1." *Westminster Theological Journal* 53, no. 2 (Fall 1991): 227–40.

——. "The Firmament and the Water Above, Part 2." *Westminster Theological Journal* 54, no. 1 (Spring 1992): 31–46.

——. "The Geographical Meaning of 'Earth' and 'Seas' in Genesis 1:10." *Westminster Theological Journal* 59, no. 2 (Fall 1997): 240–46.

Sire, James W. *Naming the Elephant: Worldview as a Concept.* Downers Grove, IL: InterVarsity, 2004.

——. *The Universe Next Door: A Basic Worldview Catalog.* 5th ed. Downers Grove, IL: InterVarsity, 2009.

Stadelmann, Luis I. J. *The Hebrew Conception of the World: A Philological and Literary Study.* Rome: Pontifical Biblical Institute, 1970.

Walsh, Brian J., and J. Richard Middleton. *The Transforming Vision: Shaping a Christian World View.* Downers Grove, IL: InterVarsity, 1984.

———. *Truth Is Stranger Than It Used to Be: Biblical Faith in a Postmodern Age.* Downers Grove, IL: InterVarsity, 1995.

Walton, John H. *Ancient Near Eastern Thought and the Old Testament: Introducing the Conceptual World of the Hebrew Bible.* Grand Rapids: Baker, 2006.

———. *Genesis 1 as Ancient Cosmology.* Winona Lake, IN: Eisenbrauns, 2011.

———. *The Lost World of Genesis One: Ancient Cosmology and the Origins Debate.* Downers Grove, IL: InterVarsity, 2009.

Weeks, Noel K. "Cosmology in Historical Context." *Westminster Theological Journal* 68, no. 2 (Fall 2006): 283–93.

Wells, David F., and John D. Woodbridge, eds. *The Evangelicals: What They Believe, Who They Are, Where They Are Changing.* Nashville: Abingdon, 1975.

Whitehead, Alfred North. *Process and Reality: An Essay in Cosmology.* Corrected ed. Edited by David R. Griffin and Donald W. Sherburne. New York: Free Press, 1979.

Wolters, Albert M. *Creation Regained: Biblical Basics for a Reformational Worldview.* 2nd ed. Grand Rapids: Eerdmans, 2005.

Wright, N. T. *The New Testament and the People of God.* Vol. 1 of Christian Origins and the Question of God. Minneapolis: Fortress; London: SPCK, 1992.

Zaehner, R. C. *Hinduism.* 2nd ed. OPUS Series. Oxford: Oxford University Press, 1966.

BIBLICAL THEOLOGY AND THE RESURRECTION

Alcorn, Randy. *Heaven.* Wheaton: Tyndale, 2004.

Alexander, T. Desmond. *From Eden to the New Jerusalem: An Introduction to Biblical Theology.* Grand Rapids: Kregel, 2009.

Allis, Oswald T. *Prophecy and the Church.* Philadelphia: Presbyterian and Reformed, 1945.

Anderson, Kevin L. *"But God Raised Him from the Dead": The Theology of Jesus' Resurrection in Luke-Acts.* Waynesboro, GA: Paternoster, 2006.

Barr, James. *The Garden of Eden and the Hope of Immortality.* Minneapolis: Fortress, 1993.

Beale, Gregory K. *The Temple and the Church's Mission: A Biblical Theology of the Dwelling Place of God.* Vol. 17 of New Studies in Biblical Theology. Downers Grove, IL: InterVarsity, 2004.

———. "Eden, the Temple, and the Church's Mission in the New Creation." *Journal of the Evangelical Theological Society* 48, no. 1 (March 2005): 5–31.

Beker, J. Christiaan. *Paul's Apocalyptic Gospel: The Coming Triumph of God.* Philadelphia: Fortress, 1982.

———. *Suffering and Hope: The Biblical Vision and the Human Predicament.* 2nd ed. Grand Rapids: Eerdmans, 1994.

Brunner, Emil. *Eternal Hope.* Translated by Harold Knight. Philadelphia: Westminster, 1954.

Chafer, Lewis S. *Dispensationalism.* Dallas: Dallas Seminary Press, 1936.

Chilton, David. *Paradise Restored: A Biblical Theology of Dominion.* Tyler, TX: Dominion Press, 1985.

Clifford, Ross, and Philip Johnson. *The Cross Is Not Enough: Living as Witnesses to the Resurrection.* Grand Rapids: Baker, 2012.

Crutchfield, Larry. *The Origins of Dispensationalism: The Darby Factor.* Lanham, MD: University Press of America, 1992.

Cullmann, Oscar. *Christ and Time: The Primitive Christian Conception of Time and History.* Translated by Floyd V. Filson. Philadelphia: Westminster, 1950.

———. *Immortality of the Soul or the Resurrection of the Dead? The Witness of the New Testament.* London: Epworth Press, 1958.

———. *Salvation in History.* Translated by S. G. Sowers. New York: Harper & Row, 1967.

Daley, Brian E. *The Hope of the Early Church: A Handbook of Patristic Eschatology.* New York: Cambridge University Press, 1991.

Davies, Douglas J. *A Brief History of Death.* Oxford: Blackwell, 2005.

Dempster, Stephen G. *Dominion and Dynasty: A Biblical Theology of the Hebrew Bible.* Vol. 15 of New Studies in Biblical Theology. Downers Grove, IL: InterVarsity, 2003.

Dumbrell, William J. *Covenant and Creation: A Theology of the Old Testament Covenants.* Nashville: Nelson, 1984.

Dunn, James D. G. *Baptism in the Holy Spirit: A Re-examination of the New Testament on the Gift of the Spirit.* London: SCM Press, 1970.

———. *Jesus and the Spirit: A Study of the Religious and Charismatic Experience of Jesus and the First Christians as Reflected in the New Testament.* London: SCM Press, 1975.

Fee, Gordon D. *God's Empowering Presence: The Holy Spirit in the Letters of Paul.* Peabody, MA: Hendrickson, 1994.

———. *Paul, the Spirit, and the People of God.* Peabody, MA: Hendrickson, 1996.

Fesko, John V. *Last Things First: Unlocking Genesis 1–3 with the Christ of Eschatology.* Fearn, Scotland: Christian Focus Publications, 2007.

Fudge, Edward W. *The Fire That Consumes: A Biblical and Historical Study of the Doctrine of Final Punishment.* 3rd ed. Eugene, OR: Cascade Books, 2011.

Fuller, Daniel P. *The Unity of the Bible: Unfolding God's Plan for Humanity.* Grand Rapids: Zondervan, 1992.

Gaffin, Richard B., Jr. *Perspectives on Pentecost: Studies in New Testament Teaching on the Gifts of the Holy Spirit.* Grand Rapids: Baker, 1979.

Gage, Warren Austin. *The Gospel of Genesis: Studies in Protology and Eschatology.* Winona Lake, IN: Eisenbrauns, 1984.

Gentry, Kenneth L., Jr. *He Shall Have Dominion: A Postmillennial Eschatology.* Tyler, TX: Institute for Christian Economics, 1992.

Gentry, Peter J., and Stephen J. Wellum. *Kingdom through Covenant: A Biblical-Theological Understanding of the Covenants.* Wheaton: Crossway, 2012.

Glasser, Arthur F., Charles E. Van Engen, Dean S. Gilliland, and Shawn B. Redford. *Announcing the Kingdom: The Story of God's Mission in the Bible.* Grand Rapids: Baker, 2003.

Grabbe, Lester L., and Robert D. Haak, eds. *Knowing the End from the Beginning: The Prophetic, the Apocalyptic, and their Relationships.* New York: T & T Clark, 2003.

Grudem, Wayne A., ed. *Are Miraculous Gifts for Today? Four Views.* Grand Rapids: Zondervan, 1996.

Hamilton, James M., Jr. *God's Glory in Salvation through Judgment: A Biblical Theology.* Wheaton: Crossway, 2010.

Hamilton, Neill Q. *The Holy Spirit and Eschatology in Paul.* Edinburgh: Oliver & Boyd, 1957.

Hanson, Paul D. *The Dawn of Apocalyptic: The Historical and Sociological Roots of Jewish Apocalyptic Eschatology.* Philadelphia: Fortress, 1979.

Hoekema, Anthony A. *The Bible and the Future.* Grand Rapids: Eerdmans, 1979.

———. *What About Tongues Speaking?* Grand Rapids: Eerdmans, 1966.

Kaiser, Walter C., Jr. *The Promise-Plan of God: A Biblical Theology of the Old and New Testaments.* Grand Rapids: Zondervan, 2008.

Kik, Marcellus J. *An Eschatology of Victory.* Philadelphia: Presbyterian and Reformed, 1974.

Koch, Klaus. *The Rediscovery of Apocalyptic.* Translated by Margaret Kohl. London: SCM Press, 1972.

Ladd, George Eldon. *The Last Things: An Eschatology for Laymen.* Grand Rapids: Eerdmans, 1978.

———. *The Presence of the Future: The Eschatology of Biblical Realism.* Rev. version of *Jesus and the Kingdom* (Harper and Row, 1964). Grand Rapids: Eerdmans, 1974.

———. "Why Not Prophetic-Apocalyptic?" *Journal of Biblical Literature* 76, no. 3 (1957): 192–200.

Longenecker, Richard N., ed. *Life in the Face of Death: The Resurrection Message of the New Testament.* Grand Rapids: Eerdmans, 1998.

McGrath, Alister E. *A Brief History of Heaven.* London: Wiley-Blackwell, 2003.

Moltmann, Jürgen. *God in Creation: A New Theology of Creation and the Spirit of God.* Translated by Margaret Kohl. London: SCM Press, 1985.

———. *The Spirit of Life: A Universal Affirmation.* Translated by Margaret Kohl. Minneapolis: Fortress, 2001.

——. *Theology of Hope: On the Ground and the Implications of a Christian Eschatology.* Translated by Margaret Kohl. London: SCM Press, 1967.

Morgan, Christopher, and Robert Peterson, eds. *Hell Under Fire: Modern Scholarship Reinvents Eternal Punishment.* Grand Rapids: Zondervan, 2004.

Morris, Leon. *Apocalyptic.* 2nd ed. London: InterVarsity, 1973.

Nickelsburg, George W. E. *Resurrection, Immortality, and Eternal Life in Intertestamental Judaism.* Cambridge, MA: Harvard University Press, 1972.

Pentecost, J. Dwight. *Things to Come: A Study in Biblical Eschatology.* Findlay, OH: Dunham Publishing, 1958.

Peterson, Robert. *Hell on Trial: The Case for Eternal Punishment.* Phillipsburg, NJ: Presbyterian and Reformed, 1995.

Polkinghorne, John. *The God of Hope and the End of the World.* New Haven: Yale University Press, 2002.

Ridderbos, Herman N. *Redemptive History and the New Testament Scriptures.* Translated by H. de Jongste. Philadelphia: Presbyterian and Reformed, 1968.

Ross, Allen. *Recalling the Hope of Glory: Biblical Worship from the Garden to the New Creation.* Grand Rapids: Kregel, 2006.

Ruthven, Jon M. *On the Cessation of the Charismata: The Protestant Polemic on Post-biblical Miracles.* Rev. ed. Tulsa: Word & Spirit, 2011.

Ryrie, Charles C. *Dispensationalism Today.* Chicago: Moody, 1965.

Saphir, Adolph. *The Divine Unity of Scripture.* London: Hodder & Stoughton, 1892.

Sauer, Erich. *The Dawn of World Redemption: A Survey of Historical Revelation in the Old Testament.* Translated by G. H. Lang. London: Paternoster, 1951.

——. *The Triumph of the Crucified: A Survey of Historical Revelation in the New Testament.* Translated by G. H. Lang. London: Paternoster, 1951.

Schweitzer, Albert. *The Quest of the Historical Jesus: A Critical Study of Its Progress from Reimarus to Wrede.* Translated by W. Montgomery. London: Adam and Charles Black, 1910.

Stanford, Peter. *Heaven: A Guide to the Undiscovered Country.* New York: Palgrave Macmillan, 2004.

VanGemeren, Willem A. *The Progress of Redemption: The Story of Salvation from Creation to the New Jerusalem.* Grand Rapids: Baker, 1988.

Vos, Geerhardus. *The Pauline Eschatology.* Princeton, NJ: Princeton University Press, 1930.

Wagner, C. Peter. *Dominion! How Kingdom Action Can Change the World.* Grand Rapids: Chosen, 2008.

Walvoord, John F., William V. Crockett, Zachary J. Hayes, and Clark H. Pinnock. *Four Views on Hell.* Edited by William V. Crockett. Grand Rapids: Zondervan, 1996.

Wright, Christopher J. H. *The Mission of God: Unlocking the Bible's Grand Narrative.* Downers Grove, IL: InterVarsity, 2006.

Wright, N. T. *The Resurrection of the Son of God.* Vol. 3 of Christian Origins and the Question of God. Minneapolis: Fortress; London: SPCK, 2003.

——. *Surprised by Hope: Rethinking Heaven, the Resurrection, and the Mission of the Church.* New York: HarperCollins Publishers, 2008.

CHRISTOLOGY AND THE KINGDOM OF GOD

Allison, Dale C. *Jesus of Nazareth: Millenarian Prophet.* Minneapolis: Fortress, 1998.

Barker, Kenneth L. "Premillennialism in the Book of Daniel." *The Master's Seminary Journal* 4, no. 1 (Spring 1993): 25–43.

Beasley-Murray, G. R. *Jesus and the Kingdom of God.* Grand Rapids: Eerdmans, 1986.

Becker, Joachim. *Messianic Expectation in the Old Testament.* Translated by D. E. Green. Edinburgh: T & T Clark, 1980.

Beecher, Willis J. *The Prophets and the Promise.* New York: Thomas Y. Crowell, 1905.

Berkhof, Louis. *The Kingdom of God.* Grand Rapids: Eerdmans, 1951.

——. *The Second Coming of Christ.* Grand Rapids: Eerdmans, 1953.

Bietenhard, Hans. "The Millennial Hope in the Early Church." *Scottish Journal of Theology* 6, no. 1 (March 1953): 12–30.

Blaising, Craig A. "The Future of Israel as a Theological Question." *Journal of the Evangelical Theological Society* 44, no. 3 (September 2001): 435–50.

Blaising, Craig A., and Darrell L. Bock. *Progressive Dispensationalism.* Wheaton: Victor, 1993.

Blaising, Craig A., and Darrell L. Bock, eds. *Dispensationalism, Israel and the Church: The Search for Definition.* Grand Rapids: Zondervan, 1992.

Blaising, Craig A., Kenneth L. Gentry Jr., and Robert B. Strimple. *Three Views on the Millennium and Beyond.* Edited by Darrell L. Bock. Grand Rapids: Zondervan, 1999.

Blomberg, Craig L., and Sung Wook Chung, eds. *A Case for Historic Premillennialism: An Alternative to "Left Behind" Eschatology.* Grand Rapids: Baker, 2009.

Boettner, Loraine. *The Millennium.* Phillipsburg, NJ: Presbyterian and Reformed, 1957.

Boyarin, Daniel. *The Jewish Gospels: The Story of the Jewish Christ.* New York: The New Press, 2012.

Burge, Gary M. *Jesus and the Land: How the New Testament Transformed "Holy Land" Theology.* Grand Rapids: Baker, 2010.

——. *Whose Land? Whose Promise? What Christians Are Not Being Told about Israel and the Palestinians.* 2nd ed. Cleveland: Pilgrim Press, 2013.

Caird, G. B. *Jesus and the Jewish Nation.* Ethel M. Wood Lecture, March 9, 1965. London: Athlone Press, 1965.

Carroll, John T. *The Return of Jesus in Early Christianity.* Peabody, MA: Hendrickson, 2000.

Chapman, Colin. *Whose Promised Land? The Continuing Crisis over Israel and Palestine.* Grand Rapids: Baker, 2002.

Charlesworth, J. H., ed. *The Messiah: Developments in Earliest Judaism and Christianity.* Minneapolis: Fortress, 1992.

Chilton, Bruce, ed. *The Kingdom of God in the Teaching of Jesus.* Vol. 5 of Issues in Religion and Theology. London: SPCK, 1984.

Clements, Ronald E. "The Messianic Hope in the Old Testament." *Journal for the Study of the Old Testament* 43 (1989): 3–19.

Clouse, Robert G., ed. *The Meaning of the Millennium: Four Views.* Downers Grove, IL: InterVarsity, 1977.

Cullmann, Oscar. *The Christology of the New Testament.* Rev. ed. Translated by S. C. Guthrie and C. A. M. Hall. Philadelphia: Westminster, 1963.

Davies, W. D. *The Gospel and the Land: Early Christianity and Jewish Territorial Doctrine.* Berkeley: University of California Press, 1974.

Davis, Anne K. "Israel's Inheritance: Birthright of the Firstborn Son." *Chafer Theological Seminary Journal* 13, no. 1 (2008): 79–94.

De Graaf, S. G. *Promise and Deliverance.* 4 vols. Translated by H. E. Runner and E. W. Runner. St. Catharines, ON: Paideia Press, 1977–79.

Deere, Jack S. "Premillennialism in Revelation 20:4–6." *Bibliotheca Sacra* 135, no. 537 (January 1978): 58–74.

Delitzsch, Franz. *Messianic Prophecies in Historical Succession.* Translated by Samuel I. Curtiss. New York: Charles Scribner's Sons, 1891.

Diprose, Ronald E. *Israel and the Church: The Origin and Effects of Replacement Theology.* Waynesboro, GA: Authentic, 2004.

Dodd, C. H. *The Apostolic Preaching and Its Developments.* London: Hodder & Stoughton, 1936.

———. *The Parables of the Kingdom.* 3rd ed. London: Nisbet & Co., 1936.

Edersheim, Alfred. *Prophecy and History in Relation to the Messiah.* London: Longmans, 1885.

Ehrman, Bart D. *Jesus: Apocalyptic Prophet of the New Millennium.* Oxford: Oxford University Press, 1999.

Erdmann, Martin. *The Millennial Controversy in the Early Church.* Eugene, OR: Wipf and Stock Publishers, 2005.

Feinberg, Charles L. *Premillennialism or Amillennialism?* Grand Rapids: Zondervan, 1936.

Froom, Le Roy Edwin. *The Prophetic Faith of Our Fathers: The Historical Development of Prophetic Interpretation.* 4 vols. Washington, DC: Review and Herald, 1946–54.

Frost, Henry W. *The Second Coming of Christ.* Grand Rapids: Eerdmans, 1934.

Gowan, Donald E. *Eschatology in the Old Testament.* 2nd ed. London: T & T Clark, 2000.

Greidanus, Sidney. *Preaching Christ from the Old Testament: A Contemporary Hermeneutical Method.* Grand Rapids: Eerdmans, 1999.

Grenz, Stanley J. *The Millennial Maze: Sorting Out Evangelical Opinions.* Downers Grove, IL: InterVarsity, 1992.

Gruber, Dan. *The Church and the Jews: The Biblical Relationship.* Hanover, NH: Elijah Publishing, 1997.

Gundry, Robert H. *The Church and the Tribulation: A Biblical Examination of Posttribulationism.* Grand Rapids: Zondervan, 1973.

Hamilton, James. "The Skull Crushing Seed of the Woman: Inner-Biblical Interpretation of Genesis 3:15." *The Southern Baptist Journal of Theology* 10, no. 2 (Summer 2006): 30–54.

Hay, David M. *Glory at the Right Hand: Psalm 110 in Early Christianity.* Nashville: Abingdon, 1973.

Hengstenberg, Ernst W. *The Christology of the Old Testament.* 4 vols. Translated by T. Meyer and J. Martin. Edinburgh: T & T Clark, 1854–58.

Henry, Carl F. H. "Reflections on the Kingdom of God." *Journal of the Evangelical Theological Society* 35, no. 1 (March 1992): 39–49.

Horner, Barry E. *Future Israel: Why Christian Anti-Judaism Must Be Challenged.* Nashville: Broadman and Holman, 2007.

Juster, Daniel C. *The Irrevocable Calling: Israel's Role as a Light to the Nations.* 2nd ed. Clarksville, MD: Messianic Jewish Publishers, 2007.

Kaiser, Walter C., Jr. *The Messiah in the Old Testament.* Grand Rapids: Zondervan, 1995.

Klausner, Joseph. *The Messianic Idea in Israel: From Its Beginnings to the Completion of the Mishnah.* Translated by W. F. Stinespring. New York: The Macmillan Company, 1955.

Kromminga, Dietrich H. *The Millennium in the Church: Studies in the History of Christian Chiliasm.* Grand Rapids: Eerdmans, 1945.

Kümmel, Werner Georg. *Promise and Fulfillment: The Eschatological Message of Jesus.* Translated by Dorothea M. Barton. Vol. 23 of Studies in Biblical Theology. London: SCM Press, 1957.

Laato, Antti. *A Star Is Rising: The Historical Development of the Old Testament Royal Ideology and the Rise of the Jewish Messianic Expectations.* Atlanta: Scholars Press, 1997.

Ladd, George Eldon. *The Blessed Hope: A Biblical Study of the Second Advent and the Rapture.* Grand Rapids: Eerdmans, 1956.

——. *Crucial Questions about the Kingdom of God.* Grand Rapids: Eerdmans, 1952.

——. *The Gospel of the Kingdom: Scriptural Studies in the Kingdom of God.* Grand Rapids: Eerdmans, 1959.

Longenecker, Richard N. *The Christology of Early Jewish Christianity.* London: SCM Press, 1970.

Martin, R. A. "The Earliest Messianic Interpretation of Gen 3:15." *Journal of Biblical Literature* 84 (1965): 425–27.

McClain, Alva J. *The Greatness of the Kingdom: An Inductive Study of the Kingdom of God.* Winona Lake, IN: BMH Books, 1959.

McKnight, Scot. *A New Vision for Israel: The Teachings of Jesus in a National Context.* Grand Rapids: Eerdmans, 1999.

Moltmann, Jürgen. *The Coming of God: Christian Eschatology.* Translated by Margaret Kohl. Minneapolis: Fortress, 1996.

——. *The Trinity and the Kingdom: The Doctrine of God.* Translated by Margaret Kohl. Minneapolis: Fortress, 1993.

——. *The Way of Jesus Christ: Christology in Messianic Dimensions.* Translated by Margaret Kohl. Minneapolis: Fortress, 1993.

Moore, Russell D. *The Kingdom of Christ: The New Evangelical Perspective.* Wheaton: Crossway, 2004.

Mowinckel, Sigmund. *He That Cometh: The Messiah Concept in the Old Testament and Later Judaism.* Translated by G. W. Anderson. Nashville: Abingdon, 1954.

Neusner, Jacob, William S. Green, and Ernest Frerichs, eds. *Judaisms and Their Messiahs at the Turn of the Christian Era.* Cambridge: Cambridge University Press, 1987.

Oesterley, W. O. E. *The Evolution of The Messianic Idea: A Study in Comparative Religion.* London: Pitman & Sons, 1908.

Pawson, David. *When Jesus Returns.* London: Hodder & Stoughton, 1995.

Payne, J. Barton. *Encyclopedia of Biblical Prophecy: The Complete Guide to Scriptural Predictions and Their Fulfillment.* Grand Rapids: Baker, 1973.

Pentecost, J. Dwight. *Thy Kingdom Come: Tracing God's Kingdom Program and Covenant Promises Throughout History.* Wheaton: Victor, 1990.

Perrin, Norman. *The Kingdom of God in the Teaching of Jesus.* Philadelphia: Westminster, 1963.

Peters, George N. H. *The Theocratic Kingdom of Our Lord Jesus, the Christ.* 3 vols. Grand Rapids: Kregel, 1952. First published 1884 by Funk & Wagnalls.

Ridderbos, Herman N. *The Coming of the Kingdom.* Translated by H. de Jongste. Philadelphia: Presbyterian and Reformed, 1962.

Riddlebarger, Kim. *A Case for Amillennialism: Understanding the End Times.* 2nd ed. Grand Rapids: Baker, 2013.

Rydelnik, Michael. *The Messianic Hope: Is the Hebrew Bible Really Messianic?* Nashville: B&H Academic, 2010.

Sailhamer, John H. "The Messiah and the Hebrew Bible." *Journal of the Evangelical Theological Society* 44, no. 1 (March 2001): 5–23.

Sanders, E. P. *Jesus and Judaism.* Philadelphia: Fortress, 1985.

Satterthwaite, P. E., R. S. Hess, and G. J. Wenham, eds. *The Lord's Anointed: Interpretation of the Old Testament Messianic Texts.* Grand Rapids: Baker, 1995.

Saucy, Robert L. *The Case for Progressive Dispensationalism: The Interface between Dispensational & Non-Dispensational Theology.* Grand Rapids: Zondervan, 1993.

Sauer, Erich. *From Eternity to Eternity: An Outline of the Divine Purposes.* Translated by G. H. Lang. Grand Rapids: Eerdmans, 1954.

Schmitt, John W., and J. Carl Laney. *Messiah's Coming Temple: Ezekiel's Prophetic Vision of the Future Temple.* 2nd ed. Grand Rapids: Kregel, 2014.

Schweitzer, Albert. *The Mystery of the Kingdom of God: The Secret of Jesus' Messiahship and Passion.* Translated by W. Lowrie. London: Adam and Charles Black, 1914.

Shepherd, M. B. "Targums, the New Testament, and Biblical Theology of the Messiah." *Journal of the Evangelical Theological Society* 51, no. 1 (March 2008): 45–58.

Sizer, Stephen. *Christian Zionism: Road-map to Armageddon?* Leicester: Inter-Varsity, 2004.

Soulen, R. Kendall. *The God of Israel and Christian Theology.* Minneapolis: Fortress, 1996.

Sullivan, Clayton. *Rethinking Realized Eschatology.* Macon, GA: Mercer University Press, 1988.

Van Groningen, Gerard. *Messianic Revelation in the Old Testament.* Grand Rapids: Baker, 1990.

Verbrugge, Verlyn D. "The Heavenly Army on the Fields of Bethlehem (Luke 2:13–14)." *Calvin Theological Journal* 43, no. 2 (November 2008): 301–11.

Viviano, Benedict T. *The Kingdom of God in History.* Wilmington, DE: Michael Glazier, 1988.

Vlach, Michael J. *Has the Church Replaced Israel? A Theological Evaluation.* Nashville: B&H Publishing, 2010.

Wallis, Wilber B. "The Problem of an Intermediate Kingdom in I Corinthians 15:20–28." *Journal of the Evangelical Theological Society* 18, no. 4 (Fall 1975): 229–42.

Walvoord, John F. *The Millennial Kingdom.* Findlay, OH: Dunham Publishing, 1959.

Weiss, Johannes. *Jesus' Proclamation of the Kingdom of God.* First published 1892 in Germany. Translated by R. H. Hiers and D. L. Holland. New York: Charles Scribner's Sons, 1971.

Wright, N. T. *The Challenge of Jesus: Rediscovering Who Jesus Was and Is.* Downers Grove, IL: InterVarsity, 1999.

———. *Jesus and the Victory of God.* Vol. 2 of Christian Origins and the Question of God. London: SPCK, 1996.

THE CROSS AND ATONEMENT

Aulén, Gustaf. *Christus Victor: An Historical Study of the Three Main Types of the Idea of Atonement.* Translated by A. G. Hebert. New York: Macmillan, 1969.

Beale, G. K. "The Overstated 'New' Perspective?" *Bulletin for Biblical Research* 19, no. 1 (2009): 85–94.

Beilby, James, and Paul R. Eddy, eds. *Justification: Five Views.* Downers Grove, IL: InterVarsity, 2011.

——. *The Nature of the Atonement: Four Views*. Downers Grove, IL: InterVarsity, 2006.

Beker, J. Christiaan. *Paul the Apostle: The Triumph of God in Life and Thought*. Philadelphia: Fortress, 1980.

Bird, Michael F. *The Saving Righteousness of God: Studies on Paul, Justification and the New Perspective*. Eugene, OR: Wipf and Stock Publishers, 2007.

Brown, Raymond E. *The Death of the Messiah, from Gethsemane to the Grave: A Commentary on the Passion Narratives in the Four Gospels*. 2 vols. New York: Doubleday, 1994.

Brunner, Emil. *The Mediator: A Study of the Central Doctrine of the Christian Faith*. Translated by Olive Wyon. London: The Lutterworth Press, 1934.

Bushnell, Horace. *The Vicarious Sacrifice, Grounded in Principles of Universal Obligation*. New York: Charles Scribner, 1866.

Carson, D. A., Peter T. O'Brien, and Mark A. Seifrid, eds. *Justification and Variegated Nomism*. 2 vols. Grand Rapids: Baker, 2001, 2004.

Corner, Daniel D. *The Believer's Conditional Security: Eternal Security Refuted*. 3rd ed. Washington, PA: Evangelical Outreach, 2000.

Daniélou, Jean. *From Shadows to Reality: Studies in the Biblical Typology of the Fathers*. Translated by Dom Wulstan Hibberd. London: Burns & Oates, 1960.

Das, A. Andrew. *Paul, the Law, and the Covenant*. Grand Rapids: Baker, 2000.

Davidson, Richard M. *Typology in Scripture: A Study of Hermeneutical Typos Structures*. Berrien Springs, MI: Andrews University Press, 1981.

Davies, W. D. *Paul and Rabbinic Judaism: Some Rabbinic Elements in Pauline Theology*. 2nd ed. London: SPCK, 1955.

Dunn, James D. G. *Jesus, Paul, and the Law: Studies in Mark and Galatians*. London: SPCK, 1990.

——. *The New Perspective on Paul*. Rev. ed. Grand Rapids: Eerdmans, 2008.

——. *The Theology of the Apostle Paul*. Edinburgh: T & T Clark, 1998.

Fairbairn, Patrick. *The Typology of Scripture: Viewed in Connection with the Whole Series of the Divine Dispensations*. 6th ed. 2 vols. Edinburgh: T & T Clark, 1876.

Forde, Gerhard O. *On Being a Theologian of the Cross: Reflections on Luther's Heidelberg Disputation, 1518*. Grand Rapids: Eerdmans, 1995.

Forsyth, P. T. *The Cruciality of the Cross*. London: Hodder & Stoughton, 1909.

——. *The Work of Christ*. London: Hodder & Stoughton, 1910.

Gager, John G. *Reinventing Paul*. Oxford: Oxford University Press, 2000.

Gathercole, Simon J. *Where Is Boasting? Early Jewish Soteriology and Paul's Response in Romans 1–5*. Grand Rapids: Eerdmans, 2002.

Glenny, W. Edward. "Typology: A Summary of the Present Evangelical Discussion." *Journal of the Evangelical Theological Society* 40, no. 4 (December 1997): 627–38.

Goppelt, Leonhard. *Typos: The Typological Interpretation of the Old Testament in the New*. Translated by Donald Madvig. Grand Rapids: Eerdmans, 1982.

Gorman, Michael J. *Cruciformity: Paul's Narrative Spirituality of the Cross.* Grand Rapids: Eerdmans, 2001.

——. *Inhabiting the Cruciform God: Kenosis, Justification, and Theosis in Paul's Narrative Soteriology.* Grand Rapids: Eerdmans, 2009.

Green, Joel B., and Mark D. Baker. *Recovering the Scandal of the Cross: Atonement in the New Testament and Contemporary Contexts.* Downers Grove, IL: InterVarsity, 2000.

Hanson, R. P. C. *Allegory and Event.* London: SCM Press, 1959.

Hengel, Martin. *The Atonement: The Origin of the Doctrine in the New Testament.* Translated by John Bowden. Philadelphia: Fortress, 1981.

——. *Crucifixion in the Ancient World and the Folly of the Message of the Cross.* Translated by John Bowden. Philadelphia: Fortress, 1977.

Hill, Charles E., and Frank A. James III, eds. *The Glory of the Atonement: Biblical, Historical & Practical Perspectives.* Downers Grove, IL: InterVarsity, 2004.

Hughes, T. H. *The Atonement: Modern Theories of the Doctrine.* London: Allen and Unwin, 1949.

Jeffery, Steve, Michael Ovey, and Andrew Sach. *Pierced for Our Transgressions: Rediscovering the Glory of Penal Substitution.* Wheaton: Crossway, 2007.

Jeremias, Joachim. *The Eucharistic Words of Jesus.* Translated from the 3rd German ed. by Norman Perrin. London: SCM Press, 1966.

Kim, Seyoon. *Paul and the New Perspective: Second Thoughts on the Origin of Paul's Gospel.* Grand Rapids: Eerdmans, 2002.

King, Daniel H. "Paul and the Tannaim: A Study in Galatians." *Westminster Theological Journal* 45, no. 2 (Fall 1983): 340–70.

Klausner, Joseph. *From Jesus to Paul.* Translated by W. F. Stinespring. New York: Macmillan, 1943.

Maas, A. J. *Christ in Type and Prophecy.* 2 vols. New York: Benziger Brothers, 1893–95.

McGrath, Alister E. *Iustitia Dei: A History of the Christian Doctrine of Justification.* 3rd ed. Cambridge: Cambridge University Press, 2005.

——. *Luther's Theology of the Cross: Martin Luther's Theological Breakthrough.* 2nd ed. Chichester, UK: Wiley-Blackwell, 2011.

——. *Reformation Thought: An Introduction.* 4th edition. Chichester, UK: Wiley-Blackwell, 2012.

Moltmann, Jürgen. *The Crucified God: The Cross of Christ as the Foundation and Criticism of Christian Theology.* Translated by R. A. Wilson and John Bowden. London: SCM Press, 1974.

Morris, Leon. *The Apostolic Preaching of the Cross.* 3rd ed. London: Tyndale, 1965.

——. *The Atonement: Its Meaning and Significance.* Downers Grove, IL: InterVarsity, 1983.

——. *The Cross in the New Testament.* Grand Rapids: Eerdmans, 1965.

Packer, James I. "What Did the Cross Achieve: The Logic of Penal Substitution." *Tyndale Bulletin* 25 (1974): 3–45.

Packer, James I., and Mark Dever, eds. *In My Place Condemned He Stood: Celebrating the Glory of the Atonement.* Wheaton: Crossway, 2008.

Patterson, Stephen J. *Beyond the Passion: Rethinking the Death and Life of Jesus.* Minneapolis: Augsburg Fortress, 2004.

Pawson, David. *Once Saved, Always Saved? A Study in Perseverance and Inheritance.* London: Hodder & Stoughton, 1996.

Piper, John. *Counted Righteous in Christ: Should We Abandon the Imputation of Christ's Righteousness?* Wheaton: Crossway, 2002.

———. *The Future of Justification: A Response to N. T. Wright.* Wheaton: Crossway, 2007.

———. *The Justification of God: An Exegetical and Theological Study of Romans 9:1–23.* 2nd ed. Grand Rapids: Baker, 1993.

Plantinga, Cornelius, Jr. *Not the Way It's Supposed to Be: A Breviary of Sin.* Grand Rapids: Eerdmans, 1995.

Pullan, Leighton. *The Atonement.* London: Longmans, Green, and Co., 1907.

Räisänen, Heikki. *Paul and the Law.* Philadelphia: Fortress, 1986.

Ridderbos, Herman N. *Paul: An Outline of His Theology.* Translated by J. R. De Witt. Grand Rapids: Eerdmans, 1975.

Sanders, E. P. *Paul: A Very Short Introduction.* New York: Oxford University Press, 2001.

———. *Paul and Palestinian Judaism: A Comparison of Patterns of Religion.* Philadelphia: Fortress, 1977.

———. *Paul, the Law, and the Jewish People.* Philadelphia: Fortress, 1983.

Saphir, Adolph. *Christ Crucified: Lectures on 1 Corinthians 2.* London: James Nisbet, 1873.

Schoeps, H. J. *Paul: The Theology of the Apostle in the Light of Jewish Religious History.* Philadelphia: Westminster, 1961.

Schweitzer, Albert. *The Mysticism of Paul the Apostle.* Translated by W. Montgomery. London: Adam and Charles Black, 1931.

———. *Paul and His Interpreters: A Critical History.* Translated by W. Montgomery. London: Adam and Charles Black, 1912.

Seifrid, Mark A. *Christ, Our Righteousness: Paul's Theology of Justification.* Vol. 9 of New Studies in Biblical Theology. Downers Grove, IL: InterVarsity, 2000.

Stendahl, Krister. "The Apostle Paul and the Introspective Conscience of the West." *Harvard Theological Review* 56, no. 3 (1963): 199–215.

———. *Paul Among Jews and Gentiles and Other Essays.* Philadelphia: Fortress, 1976.

Stott, John R. W. *The Cross of Christ.* Downers Grove, IL: InterVarsity, 1986.

Taylor, Vincent. *The Atonement in New Testament Teaching.* London: Epworth, 1940.

Watson, Francis. *Paul, Judaism, and the Gentiles: Beyond the New Perspective.* Rev. ed. Grand Rapids: Eerdmans, 2007.

Weaver, J. Denny. *The Nonviolent Atonement*. 2nd ed. Grand Rapids: Eerdmans, 2011.

Wenham, David. *Paul: Follower of Jesus or Founder of Christianity?* Grand Rapids: Eerdmans, 1995.

Westerholm, Stephen. *Israel's Law and the Church's Faith: Paul and His Recent Interpreters*. Grand Rapids: Eerdmans, 1988.

——. "Justification by Faith Is the Answer: What Is the Question?" *Concordia Theological Quarterly* 70 (2006): 197–217.

——. *Perspectives Old and New on Paul: The "Lutheran" Paul and His Critics*. Grand Rapids: Eerdmans, 2004.

Witherington, Ben, III. *The Paul Quest: The Renewed Search for the Jew of Tarsus*. Downers Grove, IL: InterVarsity, 1998.

Wrede, William. *Paul*. Translated by Edward Lummis. London: Philip Green, 1907.

Wright, N. T. *The Climax of the Covenant: Christ and the Law in Pauline Theology*. Minneapolis: Fortress, 1992.

——. *Justification: God's Plan & Paul's Vision*. Downers Grove, IL: InterVarsity, 2009.

——. *Paul and the Faithfulness of God*. Vol. 4 of Christian Origins and the Question of God. Minneapolis: Fortress; London: SPCK, 2013.

——. *Paul: Fresh Perspectives*. London: SPCK, 2005.

——. "The Paul of History and the Apostle of Faith." *Tyndale Bulletin* 29 (1978): 61–88.

——. *What Saint Paul Really Said: Was Paul of Tarsus the Real Founder of Christianity?* Grand Rapids: Eerdmans, 1997.

Zwemer, Samuel M. *The Glory of the Cross*. London: Marshall, Morgan & Scott, 1928.

WITNESS AND MARTYRDOM

Allen, Roland. *Missionary Methods: St. Paul's or Ours?* London: R. Scott, 1912.

——. *The Spontaneous Expansion of the Church: And the Causes which Hinder It*. London: World Dominion Press, 1927.

Bonhoeffer, Dietrich. *The Cost of Discipleship*. Rev. ed. Translated by R. H. Fuller. London: SCM Press, 1959.

Donovan, Vincent J. *Christianity Rediscovered: An Epistle from the Masai*. London: SCM Press, 2001.

Frend, W. H. C. *Martyrdom and Persecution in the Early Church: A Study of a Conflict from the Maccabees to Donatus*. Grand Rapids: Baker, 1981.

Green, Michael. *Evangelism in the Early Church*. Rev. ed. Grand Rapids: Eerdmans, 2004.

Hovey, Craig. *To Share in the Body: A Theology of Martyrdom for Today's Church*. Grand Rapids: Brazos Press, 2008.

Katz, Arthur, and Paul Volk. *The Spirit of Truth*. Charlotte: Morningstar, 1992.

Larsen, David L. *The Evangelism Mandate: Recovering the Centrality of Gospel Preaching*. Grand Rapids: Kregel, 1992.

Malone, Edward E. *The Monk and the Martyr: The Monk as the Successor of the Martyr.* Washington, DC: Catholic University of America Press, 1950.

McGavran, Donald A. *Bridges of God: A Study in the Strategy of Missions.* New York: Friendship Press, 1955.

Miller, Timothy. *Poised for Harvest, Braced for Backlash: Birthing New Testament Movements When Jesus Disrupts the Systems.* Maitland, FL: Xulon Press, 2009.

Moltmann, Jürgen. *The Church in the Power of the Spirit: A Contribution to Messianic Ecclesiology.* Translated by Margaret Kohl. London: SCM Press, 1977.

Musurillo, Herbert. *The Acts of the Christian Martyrs.* Oxford: Clarendon Press, 1972.

Newbigin, Lesslie. *Trinitarian Faith and Today's Mission.* Richmond: John Knox, 1964.

Packer, J. I. *Evangelism and the Sovereignty of God.* Downers Grove, IL: InterVarsity, 1961.

Piper, John. *Desiring God: Meditations of a Christian Hedonist.* 3rd ed. Sisters, OR: Multnomah, 2003.

Stauffer, Ethelbert. "The Anabaptist Theology of Martyrdom." *Mennonite Quarterly Review* 19, no. 3 (1945): 179–214.

Ton, Josef. *Suffering, Martyrdom, and Rewards in Heaven.* Lanham, MD: University Press of America, 1997.

Trites, Allison A. *The New Testament Concept of Witness.* Cambridge: Cambridge University Press, 1977.

——. *New Testament Witness in Today's World.* Valley Forge, PA: Judson Press, 1983.

Wright, David. "The Testimony of Blood: The Charisma of Martyrdom." *Bibliotheca Sacra* 160, no. 640 (October 2003): 387–97.

Yun, Brother, and Paul Hattaway. *The Heavenly Man: The Remarkable True Story of Chinese Christian Brother Yun.* Grand Rapids: Monarch Books, 2002.

GENERAL STUDIES AND COMMENTARIES

Alexander, T. Desmond. *From Paradise to the Promised Land: An Introduction to the Pentateuch.* 2nd ed. Grand Rapids: Baker, 2002.

Alexander, T. Desmond, and Simon Gathercole, eds. *Heaven on Earth: The Temple in Biblical Theology.* Carlisle, UK: Paternoster, 2004.

Allison, Dale C. *Resurrecting Jesus: The Earliest Christian Tradition and Its Interpreters.* New York: T & T Clark, 2005.

Ariel, David S. *What Do Jews Believe? The Spiritual Foundations of Judaism.* New York: Schocken Books, 1995.

Bailey, Kenneth E., *Jesus Through Middle Eastern Eyes: Cultural Studies in the Gospels.* Downers Grove, IL: InterVarsity, 2008.

Barker, Margaret. *The Gate of Heaven: History and Symbolism of the Temple in Jerusalem.* London: SPCK Publishing, 1991.

Barnes, Timothy D. *Constantine and Eusebius.* Cambridge, MA: Harvard University Press, 1981.

Barron, Bruce. *Heaven on Earth? The Social and Political Agendas of Dominion Theology.* Grand Rapids: Zondervan, 1992.

Barth, Karl. *Christ and Adam: Man and Humanity in Romans 5.* Translated by T. A. Smail. New York: Harper and Brothers, 1956.

Bateman, Herbert W., IV, ed. *Three Central Issues in Contemporary Dispensationalism: A Comparison of Traditional and Progressive Views.* Grand Rapids: Kregel, 1999.

Bauckham, Richard. *God Crucified: Monotheism and Christology in the New Testament.* Grand Rapids: Eerdmans, 1999.

——. *Jesus and the God of Israel: God Crucified and Other Studies on the New Testament's Christology of Divine Identity.* Grand Rapids: Eerdmans, 2008.

Beale, Gregory K. *A New Testament Biblical Theology: The Unfolding of the Old Testament in the New.* Grand Rapids: Baker, 2011.

Beale, G. K., and D. A. Carson, eds. *Commentary on the New Testament Use of the Old Testament.* Grand Rapids: Baker, 2007.

Bell, Richard. *The Origin of Islam in Its Christian Environment.* London: Macmillan, 1926.

Biggs, Charles. *The Christian Platonists of Alexandria: Eight Lectures.* Oxford: Clarendon Press, 1886.

Bird, Michael F. *Jesus and the Origins of the Gentile Mission.* London: T & T Clark, 2007.

Blomberg, Craig L. *Interpreting the Parables.* Downers Grove, IL: InterVarsity, 1990.

Bock, Darrell L. *Proclamation from Prophecy and Pattern: Lucan Old Testament Christology.* Sheffield, England: Sheffield Press, 1987.

Brown, Colin. *Christianity and Western Thought: A History of Philosophers, Ideas and Movements.* Downers Grove, IL: InterVarsity, 1990.

Bruce, F. F. *The Canon of Scripture.* Downers Grove, IL: InterVarsity, 1988.

Buchanan, George W. *The Consequences of the Covenant.* Leiden, Netherlands: E. J. Brill, 1970.

Cahill, Thomas. *How the Irish Saved Civilization: The Untold Story of Ireland's Heroic Role from the Fall of Rome to the Rise of Medieval Europe.* New York: Doubleday, 1995.

Cameron, Peter S. *Violence and the Kingdom: The Interpretation of Matthew 11:12.* Frankfurt: Peter Lang, 1984.

Carroll, James. *Constantine's Sword: The Church and the Jews, A History.* New York: Houghton Mifflin, 2001.

Carson, D. A. *Exegetical Fallacies.* 2nd ed. Grand Rapids: Baker, 1996.

Charlesworth, J. H. *Jews and Christians: Exploring the Past, Present, and Future.* New York: Crossroad, 1990.

Charlesworth, J. H., and L. L. Johns, eds. *Hillel and Jesus: Comparisons of Two Major Religious Leaders*. Minneapolis: Fortress, 1997.

Cohn, Norman. *The Pursuit of the Millennium: Revolutionary Millenarians and Mystical Anarchists of the Middle Ages*. 3rd ed. Oxford: Oxford University Press, 1970.

Coleman, Simon. *The Globalisation of Charismatic Christianity: Spreading the Gospel of Prosperity*. Cambridge: Cambridge University Press, 2000.

Collins, John J. *The Apocalyptic Imagination: An Introduction to Jewish Apocalyptic Literature*. 2nd ed. Grand Rapids: Eerdmans, 1998.

Collins, John J., ed. *Apocalypse: The Morphology of a Genre*. Semeia 14. Missoula, MT: Scholars Press, 1979.

Cook, David. *Studies in Muslim Apocalyptic*. Princeton, NJ: Darwin Press, 2002.

Couch, Mal, ed. *Dictionary of Premillennial Theology: A Practical Guide to the People, Viewpoints, and History of Prophetic Studies*. Grand Rapids: Kregel, 1996.

Crenshaw, Curtis. *Dispensationalism Today, Yesterday, and Tomorrow*. Memphis: Footstool, 1989.

Cross, Frank M. *Canaanite Myth and Hebrew Epic*. Cambridge, MA: Harvard University Press, 1973.

Crossan, John Dominic. *The Historical Jesus: The Life of a Mediterranean Jewish Peasant*. San Francisco: HarperSanFrancisco, 1991.

Dalman, Gustaf. *The Words of Jesus*. Translated by D. M. Kay. Edinburgh: T & T Clark, 1902.

Daniélou, Jean. *Origen*. Translated by Walter Mitchell. London: Sheed and Ward, 1955.

———. *The Theology of Jewish Christianity: The Development of Christian Doctrine before the Council of Nicea*. London: Darton, Longman & Todd, 1964.

DeSilva, David A. *Introducing the Apocrypha: Message, Context, and Significance*. Grand Rapids: Baker, 2002.

De Vaux, Roland. *Ancient Israel: Its Life and Institutions*. New York: McGraw-Hill, 1961.

Dodd, C. H. *The Founder of Christianity*. London: Macmillan, 1971.

Doner, Colonel V. *Christian Jihad: Neo-Fundamentalists and the Polarization of America*. Littleton, CO: Samizdat Creative, 2012.

Eisenberg, Ronald L. *The JPS Guide to Jewish Traditions*. Philadelphia: Jewish Publication Society, 2004.

Elon, Menachem. *Jewish Law: History, Sources, Principles*. 4 vols. Translated by Bernard Auerbach and Melvin J. Sykes. Philadelphia: Jewish Publication Society, 1994.

Emmerson, Richard K. *Antichrist in the Middle Ages: A Study of Medieval Apocalypticism, Art, and Literature*. Seattle: University of Washington Press, 1981.

Emmerson, Richard K., and Bernard McGinn, eds. *The Apocalypse in the Middle Ages*. New York: Cornell University Press, 1992.

Fanning, Buist M. *Verbal Aspect in New Testament Greek.* Oxford: Clarendon Press, 1990.

Fee, Gordon D. *The Disease of the Health and Wealth Gospels.* Vancouver: Regent College Publishing, 1985.

Feinberg, John S., ed. *Continuity and Discontinuity: Perspectives on the Relationship Between the Old and New Testaments.* Westchester, IL: Crossway, 1988.

Finegan, Jack. *Handbook of Biblical Chronology: Principles of Time Reckoning in the Ancient World and Problems of Chronology in the Bible.* Rev. ed. Peabody, MA: Hendrickson, 1998.

Fiorenza, E. Schüssler. "Apocalyptic and Gnosis in the Book of Revelation and Paul." *Journal of Biblical Literature* 92, no. 4 (December 1973): 565–81.

Flusser, David. *Jewish Sources in Early Christianity.* Tel Aviv: MOD Books, 1989.

Flusser, David, and R. Steven Notley. *Jesus.* Jerusalem: The Hebrew University Magnes Press, 2001.

France, R. T. *Jesus and the Old Testament: His Application of Old Testament Passages to Himself and His Mission.* Downers Grove, IL: InterVarsity, 1971.

Grudem, Wayne. *Systematic Theology: An Introduction to Biblical Doctrine.* Grand Rapids: Zondervan, 1994.

Hagner, Donald A. *The Jewish Reclamation of Jesus: An Analysis and Critique of the Modern Jewish Study of Jesus.* Grand Rapids: Zondervan, 1984.

Hammer, Reuven. *Entering the High Holy Days: A Guide to the Origins, Themes, and Prayers.* Philadelphia: Jewish Publication Society, 1998.

Harrison, J. F. C. *The Second Coming: Popular Millenarianism 1780–1850.* New Brunswick, NJ: Rutgers University Press, 1979.

Hatch, Edwin. *The Influence of Greek Ideas and Usages upon the Christian Church.* 6th ed. London: Williams and Norgate, 1897.

Hayward, C. T. R. *The Jewish Temple: A Non-Biblical Sourcebook.* London: Routledge, 1996.

Heidl, György. *The Influence of Origen on the Young Augustine: A Chapter of the History of Origenism.* 2nd ed. Piscataway, NJ: Gorgias Press, 2009.

Hellholm, David, ed. *Apocalypticism in the Mediterranean World and the Near East.* Tübingen, Germany: Mohr-Siebeck, 1983.

Hengel, Martin. *Judaism and Hellenism: Studies in Their Encounter in Palestine during the Early Hellenistic Period.* 2 vols. Translated by J. Bowden. Philadelphia: Fortress, 1974.

Heschel, Abraham. *The Prophets.* New York: Harper & Row, 1962.

——. *The Sabbath: Its Meaning for Modern Man.* New York: Farrar, Straus and Giroux, 1951.

Hess, Richard S. *Studies in the Personal Names of Genesis 1–11.* Winona Lake, IN: Eisenbrauns, 1993.

Hill, Charles E. *Regnum Caelorum: Patterns of Future Hope in Early Christianity.* 2nd ed. Grand Rapids: Zondervan, 2001.

Holwerda, David E. *Jesus and Israel: One Covenant or Two?* Grand Rapids: Eerdmans, 1995.

Hullinger, Jerry M. "The Problem of Animal Sacrifices in Ezekiel 40–48." *Bibliotheca Sacra* 152, no. 607 (July 1995): 279–89.

Hurtado, Larry W. *How on Earth Did Jesus Become a God? Historical Questions about Earliest Devotion to Jesus.* Grand Rapids: Eerdmans, 2005.

——. *Lord Jesus Christ: Devotion to Jesus in Earliest Christianity.* Grand Rapids: Eerdmans, 2003.

Isaac, Jules. *Has Anti-Semitism Roots in Christianity?* Translated by D. and J. Parkes. New York: National Conference of Christians and Jews, 1961.

Jeremias, Joachim. *Jerusalem in the Time of Jesus.* Translated from the 3rd German ed. by F. H. and C. H. Cave. London: SCM Press, 1969.

——. *New Testament Theology: The Proclamation of Jesus.* Translated by J. Bowden. New York: Charles Scribner's Sons, 1971.

——. *The Parables of Jesus.* Translated by S. H. Hooke. Rev. ed. New York: Charles Scribner's Sons, 1963.

Jones, David W., and Russell S. Woodbridge. *Health, Wealth & Happiness: Has the Prosperity Gospel Overshadowed the Gospel of Christ?* Grand Rapids: Kregel, 2011.

Kaiser, Walter C., Jr. *Recovering the Unity of the Bible: One Continuous Story, Plan, and Purpose.* Grand Rapids: Zondervan, 2009.

——. *Toward an Old Testament Theology.* Grand Rapids: Eerdmans, 1978.

Käsemann, Ernst. *New Testament Questions of Today.* Translated by W. J. Montague. London: SCM Press, 1969.

Keener, Craig. *Miracles: The Credibility of the New Testament Accounts.* 2 vols. Grand Rapids: Baker, 2011.

Kinzer, Mark S. *Postmissionary Messianic Judaism: Redefining Christian Engagement with the Jewish People.* Grand Rapids: Brazos Press, 2005.

Ladd, George Eldon. *A Commentary on the Revelation of John.* Grand Rapids: Eerdmans, 1972.

——. *A Theology of the New Testament.* 2nd ed. Edited by Donald A. Hagner. Grand Rapids: Eerdmans, 1993. First published 1974 by Eerdmans.

——. "Why Not Prophetic-Apocalyptic?" *Journal of Biblical Literature* 76, no. 3 (September 1957): 192–200.

Lifsey, Dalton. *The Controversy of Zion and the Time of Jacob's Trouble: The Final Suffering and Salvation of the Jewish People.* Tauranga, New Zealand: Maskilim Publishing, 2011.

MacArthur, John. *Charismatic Chaos.* Grand Rapids: Zondervan, 1992.

Marshall, I. Howard. *Luke: Historian and Theologian.* Grand Rapids: Zondervan, 1970.

McGinn, Bernard. *The Presence of God: A History of Western Christian Mysticism*. 5 vols. New York: Crossroad, 1991–2012.

McKay, K. L. *A New Syntax of the Verb in New Testament Greek*. New York: Peter Lang, 1994.

Meier, John P. *A Marginal Jew: Rethinking the Historical Jesus*. 4 vols. New York: Doubleday, 1991–2009.

Menzies, William W., and Stanley M. Horton. *Bible Doctrines: A Pentecostal Perspective*. Springfield, MO: Gospel Publishing House, 1971.

Metzger, Bruce M. *The Canon of the New Testament: Its Origin, Significance, and Development*. Oxford: Oxford University Press, 1987.

Meyers, Carol L. *The Tabernacle Menorah: A Synthetic Study of a Symbol from the Biblical Cult*, Piscataway, NJ: Gorgias Press, 2003.

Mitchell, David C. *The Message of the Psalter: An Eschatological Programme in the Book of Psalms*. Sheffield, England: Sheffield Academic, 1997.

Mitchell, John L. "The Question of Millennial Sacrifices, Part 1." *Bibliotheca Sacra* 110, no. 439 (July 1953): 248–67.

——. "The Question of Millennial Sacrifices, Part 2." *Bibliotheca Sacra* 110, no. 440 (October 1953): 342–61.

Moore, G. F. *Judaism in the First Centuries of the Christian Era: The Age of the Tannaim*. 3 vols. Cambridge, MA: Harvard University Press, 1927–30.

Neusner, Jacob. *The Rabbinic Traditions About the Pharisees Before 70*. 3 vols. Leiden, Netherlands: E. J. Brill, 1971.

Neusner, Jacob, and Bruce Chilton. *Jewish and Christian Doctrines: The Classics Compared*. New York: Routledge, 2000.

Novak, David. *The Image of the Non-Jew in Judaism: The Idea of Noahide Law*. 2nd ed. Edited by Matthew LaGrone. Oxford: Littman Library of Jewish Civilization, 2011.

Numbers, Ronald L. *The Creationists: The Evolution of Scientific Creationism*. New York: Alfred A. Knopf, 1992.

Oden, Thomas C. *How Africa Shaped the Christian Mind: Rediscovering the African Seedbed of Western Christianity*. Downers Grove, IL: InterVarsity, 2007.

O'Hare, Padraic. *The Enduring Covenant: The Education of Christians and the End of Antisemitism*. Valley Forge, PA: Trinity Press International, 1997.

Pannenberg, Wolfhart. *Systematic Theology*. Translated by G. W. Bromiley. 3 vols. Grand Rapids: Eerdmans, 1991–98.

Picirilli, Robert E. "The Meaning of the Tenses in New Testament Greek: Where Are We?" *Journal of the Evangelical Theological Society* 48, no. 3 (September 2005): 533–55.

Porter, Stanley E. *Idioms of the Greek New Testament*. 2nd ed. Sheffield, England: Sheffield Academic, 1999.

——. *Verbal Aspect in the Greek of the New Testament, with Reference to Tense and Mood.* New York: Peter Lang, 1989.

Pritchard, James B., ed. *The Ancient Near East: An Anthology of Texts and Pictures.* 3rd ed. with supplement. Princeton, NJ: Princeton University Press, 1969.

Richardson, Joel. *The Islamic Antichrist: The Shocking Truth about the Real Nature of the Beast.* Los Angeles: WND Books, 2009.

——. *Mideast Beast: The Scriptural Case for an Islamic Antichrist.* Washington, DC: WND Books, 2012.

Rowland, Christopher. *Christian Origins: The Setting and Character of the Most Important Messianic Sect of Judaism.* 2nd ed. London: SPCK, 2002.

Rowley, H. H. *The Relevance of Apocalyptic: A Study of Jewish and Christian Apocalypses from Daniel to the Revelation.* Rev. ed. New York: Harper & Brothers, 1946.

Russell, D. S. *The Method and Message of Jewish Apocalyptic: 200 BC–AD 100.* Philadelphia: Westminster, 1964.

Ryrie, Charles C. *The Basis of the Premillennial Faith.* Neptune, NJ: Loizeaux Brothers, 1953.

Sailhamer, John H. *Genesis Unbound: A Provocative New Look at the Creation Account.* Sisters, OR: Multnomah, 1996.

——. *The Pentateuch as Narrative: A Biblical-Theological Commentary.* Grand Rapids: Zondervan, 1992.

Sandeen, Ernest R. *The Roots of Fundamentalism: British and American Millenarianism 1880–1930.* Chicago: University of Chicago, 1970.

Sanders, E. P. *Judaism: Practice and Belief, 63 BCE–66 CE.* London: SCM Press, 1992.

Scalise, Charles J. "Allegorical Flights of Fancy: The Problem of Origen's Exegesis." *Greek Orthodox Theological Review* 32, no. 1 (Spring 1987): 69–88.

Schreiner, Thomas R. *New Testament Theology: Magnifying God in Christ.* Grand Rapids: Baker, 2008.

Skarsaune, Oskar. *In the Shadow of the Temple: Jewish Influences on Early Christianity.* Downers Grove, IL: InterVarsity, 2002.

Stark, Rodney. *The Rise of Christianity: A Sociologist Reconsiders History.* Princeton, NJ: Princeton University Press, 1996.

Stauffer, Ethelbert. *New Testament Theology.* Translated by John Marsh. London: SCM Press, 1955.

Stern, David H. *Messianic Judaism: A Modern Movement with an Ancient Past.* Clarksville, MD: Messianic Jewish Publishers, 2007.

Tabory, Joseph. *JPS Commentary on the Haggadah: Historical Introduction, Translation, and Commentary.* Philadelphia: Jewish Publication Society, 2008.

Thiselton, A. C. "Realized Eschatology at Corinth." *New Testament Studies* 24 (1978): 510–26.

Toon, Peter, ed. *Puritans, the Millennium and the Future of Israel: Puritan Eschatology, 1600 to 1660.* Cambridge: James Clarke, 1970.

Vermes, Geza. *Jesus in His Jewish Context*. Rev. version of *Jesus and the World of Judaism* (SCM Press, 1983). Minneapolis: Fortress, 2003.

———. *Jesus the Jew: A Historian's Reading of the Gospels*. London: William Collins Sons, 1973.

Viviano, B. T. "The Least in the Kingdom: Matthew 11:11, Its Parallel in Luke 7:28 (Q), and Daniel 4:14." *Catholic Biblical Quarterly* 62 (2000): 41–54.

Von Harnack, Adolf. *Marcion: The Gospel of the Alien God*. First published 1924 in Germany. Translated by John E. Steely and Lyle D. Bierma. Jamestown, NY: Labyrinth Press, 1990.

Vos, Geerhardus. *Biblical Theology: Old and New Testaments*. Grand Rapids: Eerdmans, 1948.

Wacholder, Ben Zion. "Biblical Chronology in the Hellenistic World Chronicles." *Harvard Theological Review* 61, no. 3 (July 1968): 451–81.

———. "The Calendar of Sabbatical Cycles During the Second Temple and the Early Rabbinic Period." *Hebrew Union College Annual* 44 (1973): 53–196.

———. "Chronomessianism: The Timing of Messianic Movements and the Calendar of Sabbatical Cycles." *Hebrew Union College Annual* 46 (1975): 201–18.

Weber, T. P. *Living in the Shadow of the Second Coming: American Premillenialism 1875–1982*. Enlarged ed. Grand Rapids: Zondervan, 1983.

Westermann, Claus, ed. *Essays on Old Testament Hermeneutics*. Richmond: John Knox, 1963.

Williams, J. Rodman. *Renewal Theology: Systematic Theology from a Charismatic Perspective*. 3 vols. Grand Rapids: Zondervan, 1988–92.

Wilson, Marvin R. *Our Father Abraham: Jewish Roots of the Christian Faith*. Grand Rapids: Eerdmans, 1989.

Witherington, Ben, III. *The Jesus Quest: The Third Search for the Jew of Nazareth*. Downers Grove, IL: InterVarsity, 1997.

Wyschogrod, Michael. *The Body of Faith: God and the People Israel*. 2nd ed. Northvale, NJ: Jason Aronson, 1996.

SUBJECT INDEX

SCRIPTURE INDEX